The Victorious Counterrevolution

D1528635

THE

VICTORIOUS

COUNTERREVOLUTION

The Nationalist Effort in the Spanish Civil War

Michael Seidman

THE UNIVERSITY OF WISCONSIN PRESS

Publication of this volume has been made possible, in part, through support from the Program for Cultural Cooperation between Spain's Ministry of Culture and United States Universities.

The University of Wisconsin Press
1930 Monroe Street, 3rd Floor
Madison, Wisconsin 53711-2059
uwpress.wisc.edu

3 Henrietta Street
London WC2E 8LU, England
eurospanbookstore.com

Published in Spain as *La Contrarevolución Victoriosa: La Zona Nacional*, copyright © 2011 by Michael Seidman

5 4 3 2 1

Printed in the United States of America

Maps are reprinted by permission from *The Franco Regime, 1936–1975* by Stanley G. Payne, copyright © 1987 by the Board of Regents of the University of Wisconsin System.

Library of Congress Cataloging-in-Publication Data
Seidman, Michael (Michael M.)
[Contrarevolución victoriosa. English]
The victorious counterrevolution: the nationalist effort in
the Spanish Civil War / Michael Seidman.
p. cm.
Includes bibliographical references and index.
ISBN 978-0-299-24964-9 (pbk.: alk. paper)—ISBN 978-0-299-24963-2 (e-book)
1. Spain—History—Civil War, 1936–1939—Economic aspects. 2. Spain—
History—Civil War, 1936–1939—Social aspects. I. Title.
DP269.8.E2S4513 2011
946.081'41—dc22
2010014291

To Gladys for her support and wisdom.

Half dozen communists, half dozen fascists, three thousand men and women of Santa Eulalia who wanted the extremists and traitors to let be.
Elliot Paul, *The Life and Death of a Spanish Town* (1937)

Contents

Illustrations

Acknowledgments

This social and economic history of the Nationalist zone during the Spanish civil war attempts to explain the Insurgents' success not only in defeating their Republican enemy but also in comparison to the failed efforts of their counterrevolutionary counterparts in Russia and China in the twentieth century.

The University of North Carolina Wilmington has aided this project in many ways. A research reassignment (what most mortals outside of the UNC system call a sabbatical), summer grants, Moseley Awards, and an outstanding interlibrary loan service helped the book come to completion.

Individuals helped as much as my home institution. Stanley Payne inspires on many different levels. Anthony Oberschall brought a global perspective. Sasha Pack offered an intelligent and thoughtful critique. William Christian assisted me with the Carlist poster. Luis Linde, Nigel Townson, Carlos Márquez, and Jim Amelang provided emotional and intellectual solace in Madrid.

Abbreviations

AS   Auxilio Social, Nationalist aid organization
CEDA   Confederación Española de Derechas Autónomas, political party
          that was closely linked to the Catholic Church
CCP   Chinese Communist Party
CNT   Confederación Nacional del Trabajo, anarchosyndicalist trade
          union federation
CTV   Corpo Truppe Volontarie, Italian expeditionary force in Spain
FAI   Federación Anarquista Ibérica, militants who attempted to keep
          the CNT anarchosyndicalist
FET   Falange Española Tradicionalista de las Juntas de Ofensiva
          Nacional Sindicalista, Spanish fascist party
FNTT   Federación Nacional de Trabajadores de la Tierra, UGT's
          agricultural workers' union
GMD   Guomindang, Chinese Nationalist Party that fought CCP during
          civil war
PLA   People's Liberation Army, Communist military during Chinese
          Civil War
POUM   Partido Obrero de Unificación Marxista, anti-Stalinist
          Communist political party
SF   Sección Feminina, Falangist women's organization
SNAT   Servicio Nacional de Abastecimiento y Transportes, Nationalist
          management board for food and transportation
SNT   Servicio Nacional del Trigo, Nationalist wheat control
          bureaucracy
UGT   Unión General de Trabajadores, Socialist trade union federation

The Victorious Counterrevolution

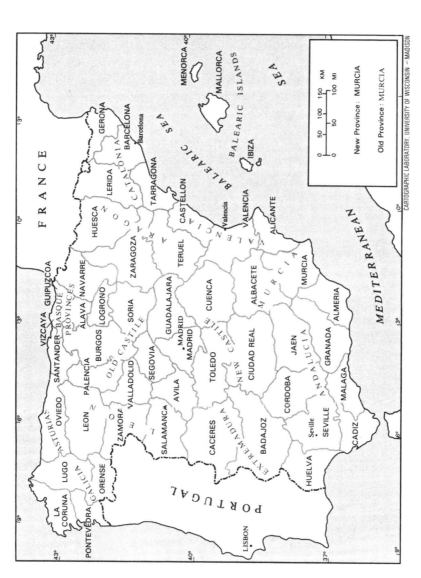

Provincial divisions of modern Spain

Introduction

Despite the estimated 20,000 books on the Spanish civil war, the literature still lacks a comparative perspective that breaks through the Pyrenees-like border that has isolated it from the rest of Europe and the world. Reflections on other major revolutions, counterrevolutions, and civil wars in global history can yield valuable insights into the Spanish conflict. Comparisons with the British civil war in the seventeenth century, French Revolution in the eighteenth, the revolutions of 1848, the Paris Commune of the nineteenth century, and, most importantly, the Russian and Chinese revolutions and civil wars of the twentieth century can place the Spanish conflict in perspective and throw new light on its outcome.

Comparisons are inescapable in any history. Even when historians focus on one case, they inevitably compare. By avoiding comparisons, the implication is that the object studied is unique. Of course, every civil war is unique, but comparative history will help define what exactly is exceptional, which can only be known when similarities among cases are explored. Analysts of the Spanish civil war have employed comparative history, but they have often done so on political and, more recently, cultural grounds. They have compared the Spanish Second Republic (1931–36) to Weimar Germany (1919–33) and to the postwar period of liberal Italy (1918–22). The Spanish, German, and Italian left and right—especially their fascists—have frequently been equated and contrasted. While it is true that the extreme right helped destroy the Spanish, German, and Italian democratic experiments, these all succumbed for very different reasons. Neither Italy nor Germany suffered the full-scale civil war that introduced the new regime in Spain.

All comparisons imply an agenda, but some will yield more fruitful results than others. The Russian and Chinese civil wars remain the most appropriate comparisons since each of these conflicts occurred during the twentieth century in agrarian nations that lacked a dynamic bourgeoisie, engaged foreign powers, and endured approximately three years. They confirm the twentieth-century pattern or "general causes" that social or "proletarian" revolutions erupt in underdeveloped or "backward" nations. Like Russia and China, 1930s

Spain remained a poor country, with per capita income similar to the level Britain had reached in 1860. More than half its population was tied to the farming sector, which contributed 60 percent of the country's total production. Of course, many agrarian countries have undergone civil wars in the twentieth century. The Greek civil war (1941–49) is a possible foil to its Spanish counterpart, but it lasted nearly three times longer and did not possess the revolutionary or counterrevolutionary dimensions of the Iberian war, during which a radical social revolution challenged both property rights and traditional religion. A similar rationale explains why the Mexican Revolution (1910–20) will not be analyzed here. Although ethnic divisions in the Basque country and Catalonia contributed to the outbreak and the development of the Spanish civil war, they did not constitute its raison d'être, as in many contemporary wars in Africa and the Middle East. Spain should be analyzed not as a full-fledged member of twentieth-century bourgeois Europe, such as Italy and Germany after World War I. More than the fascist model, which in these two nations saw the domination of the party over the military, the Spanish counterrevolution repeated patterns found in nineteenth-century France, where the military repressed the revolutionaries of 1848 and the Paris Commune.[1]

As in 1848, the Second Republic of 1931 had to confront a host of problems that other European nations with much stronger economies than Spain's had taken many decades to resolve. Issues of land reform for peasants, social welfare for proletarians, separation of church and state, subordination of military to civilian government, and the definition of the nation with regard to regional nationalisms were all on the overloaded agenda of the Second Republic. To complicate matters further, the Spanish Republic was unable to reestablish order after the revolutionary Asturias Revolt in 1934 as effectively as the French Third Republic had after the Paris Commune. The Spanish Second Republic could not attract the rural smallholders who proved to be —along with urban workers—the base of the French Third Republic. In fact, the victory in February 1936 of the coalition of the Spanish left, the Popular Front, once again unleashed radical forces. Ultimately, though, in twentieth-century Spain as well as in nineteenth-century France, antidemocratic and rural counterrevolutionary forces triumphed over urban revolutionary ones. Nationalist and fascist (Falangist) hyperbole about "revolution" really masked an effective counterrevolution. The Spanish counterrevolution echoed the reaction of French local elites against the Revolution of 1848 and the Paris Commune. Both Spanish and French movements found long-term religious precedents in the Counter Reformation and a neotraditionalist Catholic revival. The Spanish Republic and civil war produced a twentieth-century cultural counterrevolution without precedent in any other Western nation. These cultural and material counterrevolutions found their base in the countryside, not the city.[2]

A number of Marxist historians have argued that Bonapartism might be a useful concept to understand the early Franco regime. Like the French bourgeoisie, which fought the urban National Workshops and rural social democrats in 1848 and then turned to Louis-Napoléon, the Spanish middle classes confronted a combination of rural and urban revolutionaries. Thus, it was not surprising that, like their nineteenth-century French counterparts, they would resort to military rule. Yet Bonapartism inherited and promoted a revolutionary legacy that Francoism did not. Napoleon had been a product of the French Revolution, and he accepted and even spread its doctrines and practices of equality and tolerance. The Nationalist zone was not so much Bonapartist but a product of rural reaction. In fact, Nationalists often were called and sometimes called themselves "Whites." Consequently, the Soviet Union served as a countermodel for the entire right. In that country, "working-class" leaders had taken control and eliminated the aristocracy and the bourgeoisie, a fate that the Nationalists of all stripes united to avoid. Their support came from industrial capitalists and agrarian elites, but it also included many medium and even poor peasants. The neglect of the role of the peasantry in the Nationalist zone is a reflection of historiographical emphasis on political and diplomatic history and therefore on Spanish and foreign elites.[3] The same historiographical orientation has omitted an examination of minorities that played key symbolic and real roles in the conflict—Gypsies, Protestants, and Jews.

Considering many of the most significant revolutions and multiyear civil wars, the Spanish case is exceptional. It is the only one in which counterrevolutionaries defeated revolutionaries: in the English civil war, Parliament won major victories; the French revolutionaries proved able to overcome their domestic (and foreign) enemies; the revolutionary American North conquered the counterrevolutionary South; and, most relevantly, the Bolsheviks and Chinese Communists won in the twentieth century. Unlike all the preceding revolutionary forces, the Spanish Republic was unable to capitalize on its very considerable assets, which included initial control of the overwhelming majority of population, the capital city, treasury, and most of the state apparatus. Thus, in comparative perspective the victory of the Spanish counterrevolution is surprising. Yet while the comparative study of revolution remains a hot topic, counterrevolution in general and the peculiarities of the Spanish case are largely unexamined.[4]

An exception of considerable stature is the comparative framework established by Arno Mayer.[5] Although his work makes an attempt to situate the Spanish and Russian conflicts into what it calls "the international civil war of the twentieth century," its disregard of social history and its advocacy of a return to a traditional political economic approach limit its usefulness. The most unfortunate consequence of this rejection of social history is the omission of any examination of the experience of ordinary men and women on each side of the conflicts. Thus, although his ideal types of counter-revolution ("pre-emptive, posterior, accessory, disguised, anticipatory, externally licensed, and externally imposed") are undoubtedly useful, they predictably ignore much of the internal workings of the opposing forces. The following examination of the Spanish counterrevolution offers an alternative comparison that might cast new light on prevailing interpretations of civil wars. The comparative method can help to reexamine assumptions and challenge notions of inevitability of outcome. Outcome cannot with any certainty be predicted, since if it could, the wars themselves would not have taken place. This lack of inevitability demonstrates the originality and uniqueness of analogous subjects and situations.

Most historians agree that the quantity of foreign aid was a major, if not the most important, factor that determined the outcome of the conflict. The Republican loss has often been attributed either to fascist support for its enemy or to the "betrayal" of the democracies during this period of appeasement of the European dictators. Liberal and leftist historians largely blame the defeat of the Spanish Popular Front on an imbalance of foreign intervention that favored the Nationalists.[6] This argument is somewhat plausible, and a reasonable consensus is that the Nationalists had a distinct quantitative and qualitative advantage in guns and aircraft over their Republican opponents. However, by focusing attention too exclusively on diplomatic and political events, the emphasis on foreign aid has the disadvantage of overlooking social and economic history. The focus on politics and foreign intervention has neglected more prosaic issues of food and animals or has simplistically assumed that geography—in other words, the Nationalist control of major agrarian regions—is sufficient to explain the relatively abundant food supplies in their zone.[7]

To understand the Republic's defeat, it is also necessary to evaluate how much citizens in the Republican zone struggled to overcome foreign "betrayal" and to sacrifice for victory. Just as pertinently and often overlooked was how each side used its foreign aid. Foreign aid was a necessary but not sufficient factor for victory. Proficient employment of assistance from abroad was as important as the quantity and quality of aid received. To assess effectiveness, comparative history comes in handy. It is clear that Nationalists used their support from Germany and Italy much more efficiently than their counter-revolutionary counterparts, the Russian Whites and the Chinese Nationalists, employed Allied support. Spanish Nationalists may have also utilized foreign help better than their Republican enemies. British, French, and Americans were reluctant to back a Republican government that, they believed, would not employ their support wisely. For example, high-ranking French military and civilian officials—Marshal Philippe Pétain, Chief of Staff Maurice Gamelin,

Admiral François Darlan, and Air Minister Guy La Chambre—all doubted in March 1938 the Republic's ability to manage military aid judiciously.[8]

The comparative approach raises doubts about a direct relationship between the amount of foreign aid and victory. The Russian counterrevolutionaries received immeasurably more than their Red enemies but still lost their civil war. White misuse of their aid frustrated the Allies, who gradually reduced their generosity. The corrupt Whites squandered so much foreign support that massive Allied assistance ultimately succored the Bolsheviks since much of it fell into their hands. Bolshevik success was, in large part, a consequence of White corruption. Furthermore, foreign governments' support for the Whites helped the youthful Soviet leadership portray itself as directing a national liberation struggle against foreign imperialists. The Chinese Nationalists were similarly improvident. They misused vast quantities of U.S. aid, which fell into the hands of the Communists, who could credibly portray themselves as the creators of a strengthened New China. The Chinese comparison is especially useful for several reasons. It not only offers a lens on the demographically largest civil war but also permits a more global assessment of the Spanish conflict that breaks with the reigning Eurocentrism of analysts of both right and left.[9]

Evaluations of the Russian and Chinese counterrevolutionaries show the exceptional performance of the Spanish right in warfare. Its victory was by no means as predetermined as diplomatic and political historians have indicated. Its triumph was immeasurably assisted by the fact that, unlike its Russian and Chinese counterparts, the Spanish army did not suffer through a world war and was able to combat vigorously the revolutionary foe. The neutrality of Spain during World War I, which was one of the most astute policies ever undertaken by Spain's governing elites, may have prevented that nation from following the Soviet example. Even though Spanish counterrevolutionaries never suffered from the same scale of numerical disadvantage as their Russian White counterparts, they nonetheless defeated a larger army. Spanish reactionaries could rely on a competent officer class that, in contrast to its Russian and Chinese counterparts, had not been decimated and destroyed by a world war and then corroded by many months of revolution.[10]

Like the officer corps, neither propertied nor clerical leaders of Spain had suffered the disruptions of the Great War. In 1936, army, church, state, and industry were largely intact. Spanish counterrevolutionaries began their struggle in a far stronger position than their Russian counterparts after World War I. Unlike Russian Orthodoxy, Spanish Catholicism founded mass political movements that were prepared to battle the anticlerical left. Rightists were fond of quoting the nineteenth-century clerical philosopher Jaime Balmes and endorsed his belief that the Catholic religion was the glue that held Spain together. They rejected John Milton's Protestantism but applied to their own struggle his depiction of the English civil war as a war of God against the devil. Nationalists adamantly refused to separate national and religious identity.

Their Republican enemy began the conflict with some formidable advantages. Republicans controlled 14 million persons (60 percent of the population), 80 percent of industry, and areas that contributed 70 percent of the state budget. Until the end of the struggle, the Republic possessed Barcelona and Madrid, Spain's two major cities. Yet it still lost the war. On the other hand, the Nationalists were gradually able to overcome their initial disadvantages. After thirteen months of warfare, *franquistas* dominated 14 million of Spain's 24 million inhabitants and 64 percent of its territory. In contrast, the Russian Whites could not take the vital center nor could the Chinese Nationalists hold it. Without the Spanish counterrevolutionaries' efficient use of available resources, their initially failed *pronunciamiento* (military rebellion) would not have emerged triumphantly.[11]

The model of pronunciamiento had no precise equivalent in Russia. With the exception of the failed Decembrist Uprising of 1825, Russian soldiers had no tradition of military coup d'états. Russian officers' political inexperience and naiveté contrasted sharply with the Spanish generals' ability to form a coalition of the entire right around Generalísimo Francisco Franco. Furthermore, at least some of the counterrevolutionaries in Spain were aware of the mistakes of their White analogues. Several hundred White veterans of the Russian civil war fought in Nationalist ranks, and they may well have served as educators or at least reminders of fatal errors.[12] A counterrevolutionary victory required that Russian Whites and Chinese Nationalists use their limited resources as effectively as possible. Instead, both engaged in an orgy of shortsighted self-gratification that prevented them from creating a viable economy and securing their rear.

Although the Spanish Nationalists quickly annulled popular Republican land reform projects, many medium- and smallholders—who remembered the violations of property rights and the low worker productivity that had punctuated the Republican years—appreciated their protection of property and soundness of currency. Nationalist propaganda constantly contrasted their protection of smallholdings with the inability of the "reds" to prevent thefts of crops and other commodities. In fear of their lives and land, small farmers and renters abandoned their plots, which usually did not exceed ten or fifteen hectares, and fled Republican-occupied parts of Andalusia. They were more than happy to support the Franco dictatorship, and it is doubtful that reactionaries were able to facilely manipulate them. Many of these small producers and their family members served in the Nationalist Army, which proved capable of feeding and, to a lesser extent, clothing them.[13]

While historians have produced a large number of books and articles concerning the Republican zone, they have left the Nationalist zone in relative neglect. For whatever reason, the Republic has left a richer documentary legacy than its opponents. The possibility that Nationalist officials manipulated archives by removing compromising documents cannot be excluded.[14] Even those who presumably had privileged access to archives during the Franco regime have noted the relative scarcity of Nationalist data.[15] An exception to the focus on the Republican zone—Rafael Abella, *La vida cotidiana durante la Guerra civil: La España nacional*—addressed many issues that other historians had abandoned. A Nationalist sympathizer and an admirer of the fascist leader, José Antonio Primo de Rivera, Abella nonetheless had a fine sense of everyday political, material, and cultural existence in both zones. He argued convincingly that if the Republicans had possessed military organization and discipline that equaled the artistic achievement of their painting and poetry they might have won the war. Although pioneering, Abella's work was marred by recourse to concepts of Spanish or Hispanic character that supposedly explained anarchism, pitiless repression, and battlefield behavior. The few examples of his unsustainable generalizations will suffice: "The immensely Hispanic virtues of bravery and boldness" were common to both sides in the conflict. "The best infantry in the world was Nationalist and the second best was Red." Abella may have been correct that Iberians had a special devotion to a "cult of death," but he neglected to analyze it. He assumed that Nationalist economic regulation was effective and ignored the resistances it provoked. Even if Abella did not entirely neglect the indifferent or uncommitted, he remained a firm believer in the "two Spains" of left and right. An amateur historian, Abella shunned references and neglected dates, making it impossible to check sources or, ultimately, to periodize. Abella had many virtues, among which was a great descriptive ability and recounting fascinating anecdotes, but he neglected coherent historical analysis.

Like Abella, I have also consulted newspapers. They are an indispensable source for a history of the Nationalist zone, even though diffusing government propaganda was their central purpose. The franquista state removed publishers and editors at will, freed them from "democratic licentiousness," and relieved them of their role as the Fourth Estate. The press immediately became submissive and groveling toward the Franco regime, which placed it under the control of the Propaganda Service of the Interior Ministry. It ordered journalism to act "in defense of the interests of the nation" and to become an "instrument" of the New Spain. The interior minister—Franco's brother-in-law, Ramón Serrano Súñer—was praised in a *Caudillo*-like manner as the "spiritual father of all the journalists of the Empire." Newspapers that attempted to fulfill their watchdog function—for instance, by seemingly innocuous reporting on poor service by a local bus company or obliquely criticizing actions taken by the authorities—were fined hundreds of pesetas and forced to offer profuse public apologies to the authorities. Like priests, reporters were placed on the state payroll.[16]

Despite its role as the vulgarizer of the regime's propaganda, newspaper coverage is useful. Given the second-rate quality of most books and magazines circulating in the Nationalist zone, newspapers took on added importance for the literate. Papers were not always mendacious since they had to be relevant and sporadically credible to attract a readership. Constant falsehoods about events and people familiar to readers would have promoted a complete and counterproductive skepticism. Newspapers' local coverage—auto accidents, dog bites, horse kicks, mule bucks, wife beatings, abortions, homicides, suicides, rapes, and especially petty crime reports—can be particularly useful. In addition, the papers were rooted in provincial capitals, which provided a municipal and regional perspective that is often missing from a historiography dominated by national studies. To offset and challenge the official journalistic perspective, I have used available primary sources from the Archivo General de Administración. The confidential nature of these documents provides a check on the triumphalism of Nationalist public discourse.

The first chapter of this book, "The Destruction of the Second Republic," examines the legacy of the Republic, the pronunciamiento against it, and the repression that complemented the revolt of the officers and their civilian supporters. The partial failure of the coup led to the civil war in which Moorish troops played a key role. Their participation propelled the war of movement, which lasted from the beginning of the uprising in July 1936 to November 1936, when a stalemate developed at the gates of Madrid. Henceforth the Spanish civil war, like its Russian and Chinese counterparts, became a war of attrition in which the side that secured its rear and marshaled its resources most efficiently would win.

The second chapter, "Authoritarian Political Economy," examines the economic measures that permitted the Nationalists to triumph. Price supports for wheat gratified the rural base of their zone, whose heartland was the cereal-growing areas of the peninsula. Nationalists encouraged healthy policies of animal husbandry, which enabled them to supply both meat and pack animals for their troops and civilian population. These practices rather than their endowment in natural resources were the explanation of Nationalist superiority in this crucial endeavor. In 1930s Spain, few commodities were more important than animals, which were indispensable for both food and transportation, but Spanish civil war historiography has always neglected natural creatures (mules, cows, etc.) in favor of the man-made varieties (fascists, Communists, etc.). Franquistas provided generous incentives to the fishing industry, which was able to furnish massive amounts of canned sardines and other tinned seafood to soldiers. Monetary incentives for fishermen and farmers would have been ineffective without a solid currency, and amongst twentieth-century counterrevolutionaries, the franquistas were exceptional in their ability to establish monetary stability and to collect taxes. The latter—not expropriations of leftists—provided the bulk of the funds that financed the war effort. The financial sacrifices of the propertied once again distinguished the Spanish reactionaries from their Russian and Chinese foils. The industrial sector functioned efficiently, as did public health and particularly the postal service.

The third chapter, "Catholic Neotraditionalism," explores the revival of religious tradition. The counterrevolution was not merely a desire to return to a mythical past but was also an energetic reaction to the revolutionary challenge. Women were ordered to be paragons of Catholic virtue and, at the same time, work for the good of the military. Chaplains and priests, who led the cultural counterrevolution, found a groundswell of support among rank-and-file believers who either continued or returned to the faith of their mothers. In birth and death, Catholic ritual and spiritual practices prevailed among elites and masses. Nationalist art was self-consciously clerical and militaristic, its music patriotic and traditionalist. Its enemies remained those of the church—leftists, Masons, Jews, and Protestants.

Although neotraditionalism lent coherence to the cultural counterrevolution, it cannot explain the Nationalist victory. Franco's forces did not win because they manipulated national symbols better than their enemies.[17] The recent emphasis on cultural history has substituted cultural determinism for a supposedly discredited social one, but histories that replace social and materialistic analysis with a cultural and linguistic perspective cannot explain the causes, course, and outcome of the civil war. In short, calories were as meaningful as culture. Moreover, investigations that center on collective symbols and discourses overemphasize accommodation to group identities and ignore individual resistances to them. Like social history, cultural history must expand to encompass a variety of egotisms, which conflict with both revolutionary and counterrevolutionary movements.

These individualisms are analyzed in chapter 4, "Defiance of the State." Violations of price controls, denunciations, hoarding, stealing, looting, begging, deserting, and whoring have—with few exceptions—been ignored in the literature. Probably the overwhelming majority of persons inhabiting the Nationalist zone engaged in some form of prohibited or illegal activity during the civil war. The actions of these countless individuals revealed a profound distrust of the state and an understandable struggle for survival under a regime that liked to see itself as fashioning a "totalitarian" New Spain. This social and economic disobedience would eventually push the Francoist state to transform the authoritarian political economy that it had mandated during the civil war and to introduce a more market- and consumer-oriented one.

The conclusion, "Flawed Victory," chronicles the difficulties of the immediate postwar economic authoritarianism. I have tried to avoid the fallacy of
reversibility—in other words, if the outcome had been reversed, the same
factors that explained the Nationalist victory could be cited to explicate the
Republican victory.[18] Nationalist superiority in avoiding inflation, collecting
taxes, providing food, encouraging healthy animal husbandry, and offering efficient government services elucidate their triumph as much as foreign aid or a
supposedly greater cultural coherence. Their material successes distinguished
Spanish counterrevolutionaries from their Russian and Chinese colleagues.

My history of the Nationalist zone—like all histories—is admittedly in-
complete. It deliberately has tried to avoid topics that have received excellent
coverage from other historians. Thus, it does not analyze at any great length
the Nationalist repression of tens of thousands of its enemies. Nor does it
examine in any detail theater, novels, or poems. The recent and fascinating
emphasis on memory and postwar representations of the conflict has been
neglected in favor of what might be called history, that is, unearthing new
evidence that challenges old interpretations and helps to destroy myths.

1

The Destruction of the Second Republic

The Second Republic (1931–39) modeled itself on the ideals of the French Revolution and the French Third Republic. It intended to go beyond liberty and fraternity and introduce some sort of social equality or redistribution of wealth. Yet it faced special problems to achieve its project in backward Spain, which on the basis of civic culture, literacy rates, and economic development was at the level of England or France in the second half of the nineteenth century.[1] The Third French Republic (1870–1940) had begun after significant spurts of industrialization and modernization during the Orleanist monarchy (1830–48) and the Second Empire (1852–70). It had also proved capable of maintaining bourgeois order by crushing ruthlessly the last major working-class revolt, the Paris Commune of 1871. Furthermore, the Third Republic took decades to secure itself politically. Only in 1905 was the church separated from the state and the military subordinated to civilian control. The Second Spanish Republic inherited graver social and political problems than the French Third Republic. In 1931, Spaniards had to confront a tangled bundle of thorny issues—the conflict between church and state, the relationship between the military and civilian government, regional nationalisms, and educational reform. The Second Republic tried to solve them more quickly than its French counterpart. Most importantly, it faced unresolved agrarian issues that placed Spain in the ranks of underdeveloped nations. At the same time, the Iberian nation had a more powerful and better-organized working-class movement, which, unlike the French Third Republic at its origin, it could not or would not eliminate militarily.

The Second Republic heralded an age of mass politics and of higher expectations but was unable to generate the economic growth during the decade of global depression to satisfy them. The first years of its existence were characterized by a coalition of the enlightened urban middle classes—grouped in various Republican parties—with the working classes of the Socialist party

13

and its trade unions. This alliance attempted to imitate the progressive Western model of nonrevolutionary change. However, its program of moderate land reform, reduction of military spending, and anticlericalism alienated the still powerful forces of landowners, church, and many military officers. Anticlerical sentiments in the governing coalition were influential enough that authorities first refused to intervene when mobs began burning churches in Madrid. The inability of local police to engage in competent crowd control spurred the government to create an urban, more modern national police force, the Assault Guards. They were eventually to number 30,000, approximately the same size as the Civil Guard, the traditional rural police force.

As the Republic failed to resolve the profound problems it had inherited, the right gathered strength. In 1931 the dominance of anti-Republican components of the clerical right was uncertain, and some Catholics were willing to give the new regime a chance. Others, known as traditionalists, who identified as Spanish and Catholic, resisted any attempt at secularization. The strength of reactionary Catholicism grew as the Republic offered religious freedom to non-Catholics and instituted other measures—such as divorce, civil marriage, lay education, and dissolution of the Society of Jesus—which ended the confessional state that had marked Spain since the Middle Ages. The prospect of eradicating Catholic education was particularly galling to the faithful. These fairly conventional steps separating church from state were needlessly complemented by gratuitous attacks on religious practices that estranged believers who were potential supporters of the Republic. In 1932 new legislation that secularized burials and banned Holy Week processions offended many of the faithful.

The attempt to reduce the power of the military was nearly as infelicitous as the efforts to decrease the influence of the church. Manuel Azaña, prime minister of the Republican-Socialist government, was highly influenced by the post-Dreyfus French model of civilian control of the military and tried to adapt it to Spanish conditions. Yet it was much more difficult to impose civilian dominance in a nation whose elites had frequently depended on direct military control of the state to ensure order and protection of property. Azaña's reforms (1931–32) drastically reduced the size of the bloated and caste-bound armed services. Despite the needed downsizing and the generosity of retirement benefits, the reforms estranged a large number of officers. The unpopularity of the reforms encouraged a pronunciamiento against the Republic. Known as the *sanjurjada*, after one of the coup's prime movers, General José Sanjurjo, it failed to rally sufficient military or civilian backing, and Civil Guards and Assault Guards easily crushed it in August 1932. The Republic showed itself strong enough to overcome the plotting of its enemies. The shattering of the pronunciamiento lent the regime new prestige, and the parliament, the Cortes, proceeded to approve a Catalan autonomy statute in September 1932. The measure satisfied moderate Catalan nationalists by granting considerable powers to the Catalan regional government, the *Generalitat*, but allowed the Spanish state to maintain control over the armed forces, foreign policy, and tariffs. The attempt by Basques to gain their own autonomy was less successful during the early years of the Republic.

In 1931–32 the Socialist labor minister, Francisco Largo Caballero, introduced wide-ranging labor legislation. The least controversial were bills that expanded accident, maternity, and retirement insurance to hundreds of thousands, if not millions, of new workers. An array of other measures—which regulated disputes, promoted trade unions (especially Largo's own, the UGT or Unión General de Trabajadores), limited working hours, and restricted labor mobility with the aim of reducing unemployment—aroused more opposition. Public works projects, especially a massive hydraulics program, were undertaken, but the jobs created were never enough to offset growing unemployment of the 1930s. The solution of the Spanish governments of the late 1950s and 1960s—to export people and import foreign capital to modernize the economy—was, of course, unavailable during the Great Depression. Although the Spanish revolution and civil war were not direct results of a classic scissors crisis, they were—at least to some degree—products of the worldwide economic downturn.

Perhaps the most difficult problem that the Second Republic had to confront was that of land reform. Especially in the south, landless laborers—who were often anticlerical and hostile to their bosses—worked the large estates or *latifundia*. Even in the north, where an important number of relatively prosperous (and often Catholic) peasants farmed their own fields, uneconomical dwarf plots, or *minifundia*, dominated. The overwhelmingly majority of farms—possibly 42 million out of a national total of 54 million—possessed less than an acre, even though some families held more than one miniplot. Tiny farms of under 20 acres amounted to 99.1 percent of all holdings. More than 50,000 larger holdings of over 200 acres and more than 1,000 latifundia occupied 35 percent of all cultivated land. Inefficient and absentee ownership on large estates compounded this problem of unequal distribution of land. Until the late 1950s, the backwardness of Spanish industry stubbornly restricted the opportunities of the underemployed or landless to find work in cities. This essentially captive labor force gave larger owners little incentive to mechanize production.

The Second Republic confronted the land problem but became a victim of its own reforming zeal. Its agrarian reforms alienated many small producers throughout the peninsula, whose numbers had increased during the first third of the twentieth century. These smallholders frequently cultivated the villages' marginal or recently privatized communal lands. Their high-intensity agriculture, especially olive and wine growing, made them particularly sensitive to labor costs, which constituted a large share of their business expenses. In fact, their need for day labor increased the bargaining power of the rural proletariat, whose misery nevertheless remained among the worst in Europe. The laudable Republican-Socialist attempt during the 1931–33 period to increase wages and improve working conditions sharpened the class struggle in the countryside and estranged medium and smallholders who used hired labor. The ill-advised Law of Municipal Boundaries (Términos Municipales) of April 1931 prohibited the hiring of workers from districts outside the locality of the owners' holdings. However, not all localities had a sufficient number of wage laborers to execute the tasks required. In eastern Andalusia the law often shut out peasants and renters, who needed extra income as pickers for the olive and grain harvests, from the labor market. Some smallholders and renters had the custom of adding to their income by gathering the harvest in different localities, a traditional practice that the law prohibited. The legislation was so misguided that even anarchists and anarchosyndicalists in certain districts opposed it.[2]

Modest landowners were also hostile to the labor arbitration boards (Jurados Mixtos), established in May 1931. These boards usually regulated labor contracts, salaries, and working hours to favor wage laborers not owners, whether large or small, who labeled them "the cancer of agriculture." A decree of 1 July 1931 increased overtime pay for wage laborers. The Law of Compulsory Farm Labor (Laboreo Forzoso) of September 1931 obligated both renters and owners to give employment to workers living in their districts and thus reduced their freedom to contract the laborers they wished to hire. The Law of Workers' Placement (Ley de Colocación Obrera) of November 1931 further restricted the owners' right to employ wage earners of their choice by opening Bolsas de Trabajo where employers were required to hire their laborers. The legislation again harmed both big landowners and medium farmers. Both had their own loyal clientele of workers, some of whom voted for and even joined right-wing organizations.[3]

Powerful rural Socialist or anarchist unions enrolled 70 percent of the active population in Seville province. These organizations restricted use of machinery, rejected piecework, organized day laborers, and attempted to monopolize the labor market. To fight against them, family farmers turned to counterrevolutionary organizations, often led by *latifundistas* and local oligarchs. After World War I, similar class struggles in the countryside had pushed Italian farmers to support the Fascist movement, which promised to reduce the power of organized wage laborers in northern Italy. As in Italy, leftist workers' unions sometimes achieved a de facto monopoly on hiring, thereby exasperating both big and small owners. Higher labor costs moved landowners to raise rents on their tenants. In 1932–33 the latter delayed payments or took liberties with landlord property, including that of smallholders who leased tiny parcels to sharecroppers. The Law of Agrarian Reform (Ley de Bases de Reforma Agraria) of September 1932 undermined the security of long-term medium and small renters in certain provinces, such as Granada, by threatening expropriation of their parcels if they belonged to large landowners. By the end of 1932 many small farmers were hostile to the Republic's agrarian reforms, which they believed had betrayed their interests.[4]

Higher costs for labor, deflated prices for their produce, and reduced possibilities of export threatened to ruin renters and small owners. Socialist mayors frequently issued decrees banning the use of machinery, once again alienating landowners. Socialists also attempted to limit the employment of female workers to preserve a monopoly for their own members. Socialist and anarchist unions led strikes where workers attacked "scabs," bosses, and their machinery. Assaults on markets, food shops, and bakeries, including the smashing of merchant's shop windows during strikes, were frequent. In the fields the pilferers expropriated small quantities of wheat and olives along with a chicken or two. Robberies, assaults, and arson attacks often went unpunished. Major insurance companies offered property owners policies against "robbery and popular uprisings" and compensated holders for their losses. The state often seemed powerless to control lawbreakers. One of the most troubled provinces, Seville, experienced a turnover of seventeen civil governors, greater than any other during the Second Republic.[5]

In retrospect, it is evident that the reforms of the first two years of the Republic alienated as many as they pleased. The progressive legislation aroused as much distrust and alienation among property owners, military officers, and Catholics as devotion and gratitude among wage earners and enlightened bourgeois. In other words, if the Republic's reforms created a social base of support that would be committed to its defense, it also provoked a counterforce that became dedicated to its destruction. Angry small farmers, fearful large landowners, and devout Catholics formed the electorate of the clerical and well-financed CEDA (Confederación Española de Derechas Autónomas) formed in 1933. It had the distinction of being the first mass Catholic political party in Spanish history. Controversy over the "fascist" nature of CEDA was common during the Second Republic and persists today among historians of contemporary Spain. CEDA was certainly not a Christian democratic party, such as the Populari in Italy. Christian democracy was much weaker in Spain during the 1920s and 1930s than in Italy, France, or Belgium. Nor was CEDA, despite the style of its youth wing, a fascist movement. Its links to the church and the old elites were too strong. In Spain, unlike Italy and Germany, the radical right had a very small popular base. It lacked the masses of war veterans, students with dim career prospects, and ruined petty bourgeois so prominent in the rise of fascism. Only a small number of fanatical advocates of *hispanidad* convinced themselves that Spanish imperialism had a glorious future. Thus, the influence of Spanish fascism was quite reduced prior to the outbreak of the civil war. Fascism as a mass movement was the creation of a pronunciamiento. In Spain, the counterrevolution dominated fascism, not vice versa.[6]

On the radical left, the anarchosyndicalists of the CNT (Confederación Nacional del Trabajo) gave no respite to the new regime and provoked periodic revolts. In January 1932 the FAI (Federación Anarquista Ibérica), which largely controlled the CNT at this time, prepared to incite a social revolution and proclaimed libertarian communism in the Catalan mining district of the Alto Llobregat and Cardoner. In Sallent (Barcelona) syndicalists seized the powder kegs and dynamite of the potash factory and raised the red flag on the town hall. The governor of the province called in police, who easily put down the rebellion. A year later another wave of libertarian revolts erupted throughout the country. In Barcelona on 8 January, CNT bands attacked military barracks, and in several Catalan villages and towns libertarian communism was proclaimed. Money, private property, and "exploitation" were abolished—until government troops arrived to suppress the revolt. Whereas in Catalonia and in northern Spain, the Republic's Assault Guards and Civil Guards acted with some restraint, in the south they repressed the leftist rebels brutally. When an anarchist-inspired rebellion broke out in Casas Viejas (Cádiz) in January 1933, Assault Guards ruthlessly killed twenty-two townspeople, twelve in cold blood. Although the Socialists supported the government, the massacre undermined the Socialist-Republican coalition that had dominated the new republic. The scandal of Casas Viejas, the repression of the revolutionary left, and disappointment with land reform radicalized a large number of workers and peasants. Prior to the 1933 elections the CNT enthusiastically propagated its antipolitical ideology and advocated abstention.[7]

During the elections of November 1933, the divisions among the left prevented the Socialists from forming an alliance with the left Republicans. The right, especially the CEDA, profited from middle-class and Catholic fears about the collectivist and anticlerical direction of the new Republic. The misnamed Radicals—actually a centrist grouping—emerged with 104 deputies, CEDA with 115. The Socialist total dropped to 60 because of the split with the left Republicans, but the former retained their percentage of the popular vote. Alejandro Lerroux of the Radical Party formed his government in December 1933.

In 1933 the victory of the right, which was backed by many small peasants and renters, led to the revenge of the employers. They violated the reformist legislation, boycotted the Jurados Mixtos, reintroduced piecework, and reduced wages to "salaries of hunger." The bosses were no longer restrained from firing leftist workers, smashing their organizations, and imprisoning trade union and Socialist militants. Rising unemployment disciplined other wage earners. In June 1934 the sharpening of class struggle culminated with the violent general strike of the Socialist agrarian union, Federación Nacional de Trabajadores de la Tierra (FNTT). Strikers attacked "scabs," assaulted big and small employers, and sabotaged farm machinery. The right had the political upper hand and jailed strike leaders and their local supporters. In the countryside work depended on the fear and the favors of landlords and local bosses, or caciques. The latter were loosely defined and often indistinguishable from medium or even small owners.[8]

By October 1934 the Radicals concluded that they could govern only with the support of CEDA. Many on the left feared that the right-wing Catholic party would acquiesce in a "fascist" coup d'état in Spain. Even the moderate—and Catholic—president of the Republic, Niceto Alcalá Zamora, doubted that the CEDA leader, José María Gil Robles, would be loyal to the Republic and was reluctant to call him to form a government. Nevertheless, on 4 October Alcalá Zamora permitted the creation of a cabinet that included three ministers from CEDA. The following day in Asturias, militant coal miners, increasingly politicized by what they viewed as the failure of the "social" Republic and radicalized by deteriorating working conditions, began their Asturias insurrection, the prelude to the civil war that was to erupt two years later. Approximately 20,000 to 30,000 Asturian miners rebelled against what they perceived to be the "fascist" orientation of the new right-wing government in Madrid. In several weeks of intense action, General Francisco Franco and his African troops brutally suppressed them. Like many Third World armies today, the Spanish military proved more effective against the internal enemy than foreign foes. The Americans had defeated it in 1898, and the Moroccan insurgents nearly did so in 1921. One of the lessons that many leftist militants drew from the Asturias repression was a vow to eliminate the officer corps (and their civilian and clerical supporters) before it could exterminate them.

In Catalonia at the same time as the Asturias Revolt, Lluís Companys, the leader of the Catalan nationalists grouped in the moderately leftist Esquerra, declared the "Catalan state within the Federal Spanish Republic." This attempt at Catalan independence failed miserably. It clearly demonstrated the limits of Catalan nationalism, whose social base was too narrow to form an independent nation. The Catalan bourgeoisie had long made its peace with Madrid and the traditionalist elements of central and southern Spain. It lacked the strength to overcome their influence and the dynamism to dominate the entire nation economically and politically. Thus, radical Catalan nationalism could not count on the support of a large part of the big bourgeoisie that depended on Madrid for protection and favors. Without the backing of the upper class and much of the organized working class, radical Catalan nationalism in the 1930s was the province of the petty bourgeoisie—technicians, shopkeepers, *funcionarios*, clerks, artisans, and sharecroppers. Their nationalism was cultural as well as political and involved a renaissance of Catalan as a spoken and written language in urban areas. The economic possibilities of a nationalism that called for a separate Catalan state were severely restricted because the feeble Catalan industries depended upon tariffs granted by Madrid and on the impoverished markets in the rest of the peninsula. Catalan nationalism might mean a desirable political and cultural independence from a bureaucratic and overly centralized Spanish state, but many Catalans of varying social origins realized that, given the condition of regional industries, a separate nation might well lead to their economic destruction.

The failed insurrections in Catalonia and Asturias generated severe repression of the left by the right-wing government. Various estimates placed the number of political prisoners in Spanish jails between 20,000 and 30,000 individuals. Throughout 1935 the left correctly feared a continued government crackdown. In southern rural areas numerous workers were fired, wages lowered, and working conditions changed arbitrarily. The CEDA chief, Gil Robles, minister of war from May to December 1935, appointed extreme rightists to very sensitive and key positions in the military. The government's intention was to create—as the French had done after the Paris Commune of 1871—a republic of order that could protect private property and the church. The effort was, of course, ultimately unsuccessful. Furthermore, the ruling coalition was weakened by scandals that discredited the Radical Party.

The left drew together to end the right's repression. In January 1936 the Socialists, Republicans, UGT, Catalan nationalists, Communists, and the *trotskysant* POUM (Partido Obrero de Unificación Marxista) formed the electoral coalition known as the Popular Front. Its program was extremely restrained since the representatives of the Republican parties made it clear that they rejected the three most significant proposals of the Socialists—nationalization and redistribution of land, nationalization of banks, and a vaguely defined "workers' control." Although some conservatives were favorably impressed by the moderation of the Popular Front's program, the failure of the left to agree on some of the most important social and economic issues anticipated the ruptures that would occur during the civil war and revolution.

Although the CNT was not formally a partner in the Popular Front, it had its own reasons to dread continuation of the *bienio negro*, or the government of the right. Many of its militants had been jailed, and some were facing the death penalty, which the right had restored in 1934. In April of that year in Zaragoza, the Confederation had embarked on a two-month general strike, one goal of which was the liberation of jailed militants. The Popular Front promised amnesty for prisoners; in return, the CNT toned down its campaign for abstention, which affected only its most devoted militants. Although some unions and leaders reiterated the official position against political participation, others deviated from the classic anarchist position. This policy of the "negation of the negation," gave the green light to the rank and file to vote for the Popular Front. Even famous FAI member Buenaventura Durruti openly advocated that CNT members go to the polls.

As might be expected, the electoral campaign polarized voters. The right was divided, and its more moderate components, including the very few Christian democrats, enfeebled. In February 1936 the Popular Front won an important victory. Nationwide, it captured 47 to 51.9 percent of the votes, compared with 43 to 45.6 percent for the right. The right did well in Catholic strongholds of the north and north center, the left in impoverished agrarian regions of the south and the southwest. The abstention rate of 28 percent—in comparison with 32.6 in 1933—indicated persistent apathy and only a marginal depoliticization.[9] The fascist Falange won merely 46,466 votes, conceivably the lowest voting percentage of a fascist party in all of Europe. The left's victory heightened rightist fears that the Popular Front would violently secure the separation of church from state, reduce the power of the military, encourage regional nationalisms, and promote land reform. In addition, the weight of the radical left in the Socialist Party and the influence of the CNT raised the specter that it would not be the moderate Republicans, such as Manuel Azaña, who would secure features of the unfinished bourgeois-liberal revolution but, rather, as in Russia in 1917, working-class revolutionaries who had no respect for private property.

Reports of the victory of the Popular Front in the elections of February 1936 led to riots, church arsons, and prison revolts. When unidentified "masses" in certain regions burned churches and convents and destroyed the offices of right-wing newspapers and political parties, many large and small property owners blamed the Popular Front. Public order became a major problem for the left Republican-Socialist government. Its leader, Azaña, was hesitant to use the army to jail or shoot protesters and rioters, many of whom supported the government. On the other hand, Azaña was also reluctant to disarm the military since it might be needed to stop insurrections organized by the extreme left. The Republic became symbolic of unrest and disorder to many Spaniards. Parents commonly labeled squabbling among children "a republic." A Republican officer admitted, "It was idiotic to argue that Spain was a paradise. . . . Hundreds of churches were burned, hundreds were killed, many more injured, innumerable strikes. . . . Rational people knew that we were living on a volcano." The poorest sectors of the population, which had probably suffered the most from the depression, exerted strong pressures for change. Tenant farmers knew that the Popular Front government would be reluctant to move against them. Day laborers in large parts of Andalusia, with or without union encouragement, began to occupy private farms and demand higher wages and less work from their owners. Certain leftist municipalities threatened direct expropriation of private farms for landless peasants. More formally and lawfully after February, the Institute of Agrarian Reform redistributed hundreds of thousands of acres to tens of thousands of peasants. In late March in the province of Badajoz, more than 60,000 peasants, under the direction of the FNTT, took over 3,000 farms. Shouting "Long Live the Republic," they set to work on their new land.[10]

Of course, many on the right could not share this enthusiasm. For conservatives, the Popular Front endangered private property. In rural areas Andalusian proletarians' wishes to expropriate the land in the spring of 1936 alarmed both large and small property owners. In Jaén province, leftist Casas del Pueblo were able to completely monopolize the labor market. Strikes of Andalusian peasants and day laborers increased sharply in the spring of 1936. Strikers harassed and even imprisoned bosses who refused their conditions. In Jimena (Cádiz) employers were forced to accept a salary pegged at 5 pesetas daily for a workday that was five hours or less. In other localities productivity diminished even as workers demanded the equivalent of eight hours of wages for six hours of work. In many cases rural wages doubled. Those fired during the bienio negro—even for violent offenses—were often rehired. Other, more productive, workers could not find jobs. Immediately before the outbreak of war, Gallegan laborers, who were accustomed to working the harvest in Castile, were warned that they would no longer be hired.[11]

The challenges to property rights and the perceived breakdown of public order in the countryside—the majority of violent deaths between February and July 1936 occurred in rural areas—further diminished support for the Republic among a significant number of smallholders. In the countryside, roadblocks were established to demand contributions in favor of Socorro Rojo Internacional, a kind of "red" Red Cross. Alcalá Zamora, the president of the Republic, who was traveling without an escort near his Priego (Córdoba) estate, was forced to pay 1,000 pesetas when his car was detained. Both big and small property owners identified the rule of the left—whether during the first or last years of the Republic—with theft of trees, olives, grapes, and other produce. The inability of elected authorities to rein in the violators outraged them. Even in the north, in parts of the Basque country and Navarre, local rightists feared—often for good reason—for their property. The Republican government was perceived as being unable to establish order, a very grave fault for much of rural Spain of the 1930s.[12]

At the same time, urban workers demanded rehiring of, and back pay for, wage earners sanctioned and fired during the bienio negro. In Barcelona "endemic" strikes erupted for less work and higher salaries. Domestic and foreign capitalists reacted negatively. The Catalan capitalist elite repeated its hoary, but partly credible, warning that "the reigning anarchy" might destroy its firms. For example, in early July the director of General Motors

Nationalist poster showing Civil Guards as the guarantors of order and progress.

in Spain advised the Sindicato de Obreros Metalúrgicos that it was considering shutting down its Barcelona assembly factory because, in large part, of increased labor costs. "Continual workers' demands for salary increases" made the company ponder firing its 400 employees. To make matters worse, "workers are not working with the same efficiency they once had. We need more cooperation from them." In provincial towns, such as Granada, attacks on shops, factories, and even the tennis club frightened both big and small bourgeois, who rushed to join the Falange. In May 1936 Madrid workers ate in hotels, restaurants, and cafés and then walked out without paying. Their wives, accompanied by armed militants, went "proletarian shopping" in grocery stores and refused to pay the bill. A similar wave of "social crimes" occurred in Tenerife. A good number in Andalusia pilfered from shops and neglected to pay rent. The fall in rent receipts led urban landlords in Seville and throughout Spain to neglect meeting their fiscal obligations. In Melilla, Communists and Socialists insulted officers in public and traded clandestinely with the French zone to acquire arms.[13]

In addition to threats to property, the right feared persecution by the increasingly politicized police forces of the Republic. State-sponsored police actions would culminate in the assassination on 13 July 1936 of an extreme-right leader, José Calvo Sotelo, when for the first time in the history of parliamentary regimes a detachment of state police murdered a leader of the parliamentary opposition.[14] Political and social violence in Spain was probably more severe than in other European countries—Italy, Austria, and even Germany—that experienced the breakdown of democracy in the interwar period. The extent of bloodshed reflected the underdeveloped and polarized nature of Spanish society and the inability of its weak state to control either supporters or opponents. The absence of what they considered to be a neutral and property-protecting government encouraged important sectors of the right to rebel.

PRONUNCIAMIENTO

The demands and disorders following the victory of the Popular Front promoted plotting against the Republic by a broad coalition of anti-Republican forces. The Spanish armed forces had a tradition throughout the nineteenth and twentieth centuries of intervening to guarantee internal order against "anarchy" and assaults on property. Many officers were determined to smash the Popular Front, which they associated with the "anti-Spain" of Marxism, Catalan and Basque separatisms, Freemasonry, and even Judaism. They were joined by Falangists, ultraconservative monarchists known as Carlists, and more "liberal" advocates of Alfonso XIII, the Alphonsines. The most important rebellious officers were *africanistas*, who had often experienced fierce combat in North African colonial wars. The Insurgents' individual reputations for valor, courage, and efficiency—Emilio Mola, José Millán Astray, Gonzalo Queipo de Llano, José Enrique Varela, Luis Orgaz, Sanjurjo, and ultimately Franco—provided a model and a mystique for their troops that their Republican enemies completely lacked. Franco possessed what the Moroccans called *Baraka*, or good fortune, a belief that quickly spread among Spaniards. The africanistas who led the rebellion intended to conquer the peninsula as they had domesticated Morocco and, more recently, Asturias. Their anti-Republican coalition would call itself Nationalist. Whatever the accuracy of the label, it became a very powerful symbolic weapon in the hands of the right. The call of "nationalism" may have been more mobilizing than that of "Republic." The latter was a much more ephemeral entity than the "Spain" to which the Nationalists referred when they shouted their slogan, "Viva España."

Republicans contested the Insurgent attempt to monopolize nationalism by commonly labeling their adversaries "Fascist," thereby linking them to Germany and Italy. Other hostile, but possibly more accurate, terms for the Nationalists were "Insurgents" and "rebels." These labels stressed that the Nationalists had rebelled against the legally constituted democratic Republic. Those who sided with the Insurgent officers called their adversaries "reds" or, more formally and less frequently, "Marxists." The Republic was ambivalent about its own collectivist revolution and usually did not employ the term in its sloganeering. Unlike the Bolsheviks, it never adopted the red flag. Most of those who supported the Republic preferred to be known simply as Republicans. Some favored "Loyalist" since they were loyal to the legally established Spanish state that the military rebellion was trying to destroy. Generally, I shall adhere to each side's terminological preferences for itself. In other words, "Nationalist" and "Republican" will appear frequently in the following pages. "Loyalists," "Insurgents," and "rebels" and will be used more sparingly. "Fascist" and "red" will remain between quotation marks.

Communist, Socialist, and anarchist activists and militiamen prevented the successful execution of a relatively peaceful pronunciamiento in the tradition of the nineteenth or early twentieth century. Unlike the previous coup by Miguel Primo de Rivera in 1923, the rebellious officers had to confront the armed activists of the various parties and unions that claimed to represent the Spanish people or, more specifically, the working class. Hundreds of leftist militants formed defensive and offensive militias. Without these male and female fighters of the CNT, UGT, FAI, PSOE (Partido Socialista Obrero Español), PCE (Partido Comunista de España), and POUM, the military rebellion would have easily succeeded. *Milicianos'* guerrilla warfare stopped it with enthusiasm and bravery. They defeated rebellious officers in Madrid, Barcelona, and in parts of the north, thus keeping the most urbanized and advanced parts of the peninsula in loyal hands. The local climate of hostility or acceptance often determined the success of the military rebellion. In addition to the commitment of leftist organizations, the loyalty of police and Civil Guards was a decisive factor. In the major urban centers, professional Republican forces of order often joined amateur militiamen. Sensing the political leanings of their fellow urban residents, soldiers and police in the principal cities were often wary of supporting the military rebellion. For example, fifteen companies, or 3,000 Security and Assault Guards, stationed in Barcelona declared themselves unconditionally loyal to the Generalitat. In Almería the military rebels would have been successful but for the intervention of soldiers and sailors faithful to the Republic.[15]

Many of the most accomplished officers revolted. Although only four of eighteen top generals "rose up," eighteen of thirty-two generals who commanded a brigade, forty-four of the fifty-three most important garrisons, and a clear majority of officers joined the rebellion. So did approximately half the forces of public order. The Insurgents controlled 53 percent of the army, including 60 percent of the artillery, 49 percent of the Civil Guard, 35 percent of the navy and air force, and 32 percent of the Carabineros (border police) and Assault Guards. Their commitments ensured control of towns and villages throughout Spain by those favorable to the pronunciamiento. Most importantly, the Nationalists led the 40,000 professional soldiers of the Army of Africa. The Army of Africa had helped to suppress the sanjurjada of 1932 and, of course, the Asturias Revolt of 1934. It proved absolutely essential for Franco's victory. In addition, the Nationalists had 50,000 poorly trained men from the peninsular army. In contrast, the Republicans could count on 50,000 soldiers, 7,000 officers, and 33,000 men from the security forces.[16]

Immediately after the outbreak of civil war, recruiters on both sides appealed to a minority with political commitment. The willingness to volunteer varied greatly, even within the same province. Generally, volunteering was rare on both sides, and propaganda to encourage enlistment was consequently voluminous. Few of the common folk had any ideological commitment and just wanted to be left alone. In Nationalist-controlled Andalusia and Extremadura only 9,400, or 1 to 3 percent, of the eligible male population aged twenty to forty years old volunteered. In Castile and León 1 to 7 percent signed up. In Galicia the percentage did not reach even 1 percent. In Rioja, Aragon, and especially Navarre, where Carlism was popular, the proportion was higher—from 15 to 30 percent—but even in these provinces the vast majority of eligible men attempted to avoid volunteering and fighting. Although a devoted centralizer who was violently opposed to all "separatisms," Franco expressed his gratitude to the exceptional sacrifices of Navarre by allowing it the fiscal privileges and provincial autonomies that he denied to Guipúzcoa and Vizcaya. Once the initial stage of war passed, the pool of Carlist volunteers rapidly dried up, even in Navarre. By February 1939 the Falange militias possessed 72,608 men, and despite their efforts to recruit throughout the Nationalist zone, the Carlist *requetés* had only 23,768. In other words, for every Carlist fighter there were three Falangists. The Primera de Navarra remained one of the outstanding shock units of the Nationalist Army only because North Africans and legionnaires took the place of dead or wounded Navarrese. Nationalists seemed more determined to make the militiamen effective fighters by requiring them as early as 23 September 1936 to serve outside their home regions if they wished to receive their pay. Rightist militias were formally subordinated to the military hierarchy by the end of 1936. The more fissiparous Republicans took a much longer time to professionalize their Popular Army.[17]

Although only a relatively small minority of Spaniards volunteered, it was significant in comparative perspective. In contrast to the very low level of volunteering in the Chinese or Russian civil wars, the Spanish counterrevolutionary response was impressive. Perhaps only in Finland and the Baltic area during the civil wars of 1917–18 was there a similarly enthusiastic participation of the more conservative population in opposition to the left. The Spanish aristocracy, a privileged and sometimes corrupt class, set an example, and their proportion of volunteers matched other strata of society. Rightist volunteers (militiamen) numbered 35,000 in July 1936 and 70,000 by October. The number of volunteers eventually reached 90,000 to 100,000. However, an unknown but significant number of leftists trapped in the Nationalist zone signed up to avoid punishment or execution as "reds," one of the reasons for the dramatic growth of Falangist militias. Opportunists are numerous in civil wars, where fence sitters and free riders constantly show their desire to avoid risks.[18]

The Foreign Legion, the Nationalists' most elite professional force, demonstrated the ambivalence of commitment. In the first week of August, nearly 3,000 volunteers had enrolled in Seville's Tercio under the direction of Colonel Juan Yagüe. Some Legion volunteers were committed reactionaries, but others were adventurers or opportunists. As the war endured, the Legion was inundated with Spanish conscripts who had little desire to fight. Volunteer legionnaires, whose salary was tied to the length of their contract of two to ten years, always received more compensation than regular army draftees. Their family members were ineligible for a combatant subsidy, but they were promised fine clothing and received "excellent" and copious meals. Like other Nationalist troops, legionnaires usually had coffee for breakfast, lunch, and dinner. Staples were bacon, bread, and sausage. Their women and children were able to follow them, and the former acted as washerwomen for the troops. To enroll more soldiers, recruiters of the Tercio dropped standard requirements and permitted all males between seventeen and thirty-six to enroll without a height minimum or proof of age.[19]

The Legion was a secular and, in many respects, a heathen outfit with a good number of men sporting "lascivious" tattoos. In 1938 the Legion enrolled 1,238 foreigners, two-thirds of whom were Portuguese. In addition, there were 72 Frenchmen, 42 Germans, 59 Argentines, and 46 Cubans, along with a handful of other nationalities. Yet most Cubans, Argentines, and other Latin Americans of Spanish origin were—like most of their countrymen—pro-Republican. They made sure to register with their consulates so that they would not be drafted into the Nationalist army. This perfectly legal act outraged the civil governor of Las Palmas, who regarded their lack of commitment as equivalent to draft dodging. He complained that Spanish emigrants to Cuba and other Latin American republics remembered that their sons were foreign only when conscription affected them. They then rushed to register their children as foreigners at the appropriate consulates "without any other motive than to evade the sacred duty of defending the Fatherland."[20]

Already by the end of the first weeks of the pronunciamiento, the Nationalists dominated rural Spain while the Republic held the major urban areas. The Republic had an initial advantage because it had taken control of relatively developed regions with modernized transportation and communication networks. It controlled 56 percent of the northern railroad lines and 81 percent of the Madrid-Zaragoza-Alicante line. After six months of conflict, the Nationalists controlled only 33 percent of total kilometers and did not increase that percentage substantially until the end of the war. Their only major railroad repair and maintenance facility was located in Valladolid, which suffered from lack of materials and skilled labor. Two-thirds of motor vehicles and an even greater percentage of gasoline and oil stocks remained in Republican hands. The Republic also had a clear superiority in gasoline storage and transportation facilities.[21]

Initially, the Republic controlled 60 percent of Spanish territory and 70 percent of the tax base. However, it had only 30 percent of agricultural products, but this included 90 percent of citrus, 50 percent of oils, and 80 percent of rice. The Republicans possessed an overwhelming initial advantage of weapons, textiles, and manufactured goods. However, it should be remembered that Spanish industry had survived because of high tariffs and that Spanish manufactures were not competitive on the world market. To gain foreign currency to buy raw and finished materials, both bands would have to export agricultural products, whose revenues would be insufficient to finance the war. The battle to earn foreign currencies was a standoff. Republicans held the citrus-growing regions and thus the most profitable and largest food exports of the early 1930s. During the war, Loyalists would trade them for other food products—flower, eggs, milk, potatoes, and sugar—that their zone lacked. Loyalists controlled 57 percent of Spanish vineyards. The adversaries evenly divided Spain's olives, nuts, and tobacco. Even in March 1937—after the Republic had lost large parts of Andalusia, Extremadura, and Castile—the Comisión Nacional de Ordenación de Cultivos concluded that the Republican zone was self-sufficient and would be able to export oil, rice, vegetables, and fruits. It should have won the war of attrition if it had organized its agriculture effectively.[22]

The exports of Andalusia (wines, oils, and ores) and the Canaries (fruits and vegetables) quickly fell into Insurgent hands. The Nationalists, possessing the Castilian plains, had more than twice the wheat of their adversaries. They were also much better supplied with beef and pork. A key to their victory was their ability to maintain their geographical advantage and to employ it to good effect. The Nationalists would import much less food from abroad than their enemies and export their iron ore, pyrites, cocoa, raw wool, and coal. They managed to feed their army and their rear, an accomplishment never matched by the Republic or the Russian and Chinese counterrevolutionaries. During the Russian civil war, a worker in the Ukrainian city of Kharkov summed up the ideological mobility of many in various kinds of conflicts: "That power is good which gives us bread." The lack of food sparked workers' opposition and the famous Kronstadt rebellion in Communist Russia. Support for the Bolshevik regime—and for the Russian Whites—was connected to availability of food rations as much as to purely political considerations.[23]

As in the British civil war, in the Spanish conflict the cities sided with the "progressive forces," but contrary to the winning sides in the British, French, American, and Russian civil wars, the Republic's control of urban centers and their revenues did not provide the margin of victory. Nevertheless, it would retain urban bases in Madrid and Barcelona until the end. At the close of July 1936, Catalonia, Basque country, Asturias, Cantabria, and the Levante remained in Republican hands. Militia columns sent from urban Catalonia conquered eastern and lower Aragon, approximately half of that region. In the Valencia region the CNT and UGT dominated the rebels in several weeks. Although this gave the Republic a definite numerical superiority, it was not nearly as great as the four to one or five to one advantage that the Bolsheviks possessed over the Whites during the Russian civil war. Yet numbers do not guarantee victory. A huge host may in fact be counterproductive, as in the Spanish Republican case where its soldiers suffered from a poor diet.[24]

REPRESSION

Seldom has the issue of Francoist repression and terror been placed in a comparative context of civil wars. The ability of the Spanish Nationalists to control their rear was decisive in their victory. In contrast, the Russian Whites never managed to accomplish this fundamental task. They had to struggle with popular (but anti-Bolshevik or Green) peasant uprisings in their rear. The more territory the Whites' Volunteer Army conquered, the more conspicuous was its inability to ensure elementary order for the population. Contemporary British observers concluded that if the Whites had reestablished law and order, they would have won over the peasants. The disorganization of White General Anton Denikin's rear in southern Russia caused his defeat. The British mission suggested that its intervention would have been most effective if its soldiers would have been stationed not on the front but in Denikin's rear to act as a police force to stabilize his communications, especially the railroads.[25]

In Siberia the Whites were equally inept. Admiral Alexander Kolchak, the leader of the counterrevolutionary forces in Siberia, could not count on the security of his rear or on the vital communications link along the Trans-Siberian Railway. That vast territory should have been a reservoir of critical support for his government. Instead, the presence of the *atamans* (warlords) made it a no-man's-land, where Kolchak's authority remained merely nominal. His armies received no recruits from Eastern Siberia, and supplies along the Trans-Siberian were subject to constant raids by renegade bands practicing a vicious form of plunder. The situation in Siberia reflected the Whites' inability to rein in what was called *atamanshchina* (warlordism). In contrast, the Bolsheviks were able to use the vital train links to achieve their goals.[26]

The Chinese Communists were also able to secure their rear. A British observer reported that the marches of opposing armies had left the peasantry without food. To avoid starvation, peasants had to rob and turn bandit. Banditry was a venerable phenomenon in China, and "the real interest lies in whether the Communists will be able, by better administration, to remove the causes of banditry. While banditry in itself is not a menace to a Chinese regime, its prevalence or otherwise is a reliable indication of a regime's efficiency." By this standard, the Communists created an efficient regime. They claimed to have eliminated 78,000 bandits in Honan during the first half of 1949 and 100,000 in central China between May and September 1949. By the end of 1949 the Communists had effectively crushed local or "bandit" revolts.[27]

Like the Chinese and Russian Communists, the Nationalists were able to impose a puritanically terrorist order on the population. Spanish Insurgents never seriously suffered from partisan activity behind the lines. Franquistas did not have to confront the decentralized Green rebellions that confounded both Whites and Reds during the Russian conflict. The disruptive potential of a *guerrilla* by "bandits" or others in mountainous Spain was enormous, and the fact that it did not develop significantly during the conflict demands explanation. Certainly, even the most brutal occupations by modern armies have not eliminated partisan actions. Furthermore, in civil wars, the side with inferior weapons usually adopts guerrilla fighting. Terror plus adequate food supplies help to explain the quiet and lack of guerrilla warfare in the Nationalist rear. Falangists, Civil Guards, and regular soldiers usually eliminated quickly any concrete threats by preventing theft and raiding from dissidents. *Guerrilleros* received at best limited support from peasants and the country people among whom they operated. Once again, rural society sided from fear and self-interest with the Nationalists. Nationalist authority was easier to impose because the old elites who supported Franco had not undergone the degree of disruption that their Russian and Chinese counterparts had suffered during the world wars of the twentieth century.

In much of Spain there was no civil war. Instead, in the Republican zone the revolution terrorized and eliminated priests and the wealthy; in the Nationalist zone, a bloodier terror against leftists accompanied the counterrevolution. In Republican Spain the repression killed approximately 50,000; in the Nationalist zone, 100,000. In parts of rural Spain, those who questioned the policies of the caciques and large landowners were often put to death. For example, in Sartaguda (Navarre), 84 men were killed in this village of approximately 1,000 residents. The military ultimately controlled civilian right-wing forces of the Falange and was complicit in their violence. In fact, the massacres of "reds" served to bind the executioners together and to carry out "a social and political prophylaxis." The massive bloodletting not only eliminated the left but intimidated the moderate right.[28]

Queipo de Llano exemplified Insurgent violence. The general began by using several thousand men to take control of Seville's center, its electrical and gas stations, and its major routes of access. His soldiers skillfully intimidated the large but disorganized urban working-class militias. They made sure that the workers' neighborhoods were cut off from the city's downtown, which the rebels dominated. Wage earners defended their *barrios* in Seville and other southern cities with snipers and ineffective barricades—as in Paris during the June Days and the Commune. In one of the first acts of his regional dictatorship, Queipo threatened with execution all workers who went on strike or abandoned their jobs, whether municipal or private. He vowed to provide the same treatment to union leaders. On 22 July, Queipo announced to his audience that two union leaders had been shot and a number of municipal workers fired. They were replaced by "scabs," perhaps drawn from Seville's large unemployed population.[29]

Foreshadowing the entire conflict was the rebels' concern for the bread supply of Seville, the largest city (population 300,000) under their control. Two neighboring towns—Dos Hermanos and Alcalá de Guadaira—furnished the bulk of Seville's *pan*. During the Republic, Alcalá de Guadaira—also known significantly as Alcalá de los Panaderos—had participated in strikes that had left Seville breadless. In response to Queipo's coup, the unions again called for a general strike and restricted bread provisioning to the provincial capital. The Insurgents were more determined to break the strike than to kill their enemies, although unfortunately these two goals were, to a large degree, compatible. By 23 July, bread from Alcalá de Guadaira was available for purchase at Seville's town hall. The counterrevolutionary commune had consolidated itself.

The General, as he was known in Seville, implemented terror "without precedents" in southern Spain. On 23 July, Queipo claimed that most workers, "convinced that we never joke," were laboring normally. At the same time, "given the sparse adherence to my orders," he again threatened to shoot without trial "any person who resists or disobeys." The following day, he reported, only the bricklayers, masons, and other construction laborers continued their work stoppage. By 24 July, the Encarnación, the most important market in the city, had resumed functioning and by mid-August had returned to normal. On the same day, work patterns were "normal" in Seville. Butchers, some of whom had been fired at the beginning of the movement, were chopping; taxi drivers, chauffeuring; dockers, unloading. The murderous threats had broken the strike of cemetery workers who were now burying the hundreds of corpses of "reds" rotting in the summer heat. On 25 July, public transportation and even the famous tobacco factory were functioning. In the following days, construction and ceramic workers returned to work, but, Queipo menaced, their leaders would be shot as had been the president of the Grocery Employees' Union, who had been "guilty" of fomenting strikes. Queipo urged workers to murder union officials who prevented them from working. Unions—such as those of the firemen, tobacco, and electrical workers—were encouraged or compelled to dissolve and "donate" their funds to the army. By 28 July the general strike had been broken.[30]

Salaries in both the city and the countryside were immediately lowered to pre–Popular Front levels. The municipality demonstrated counterrevolutionary continuity by dismissing employees who had been fired during the bienio negro. Employers and landowners rehired reliable proletarians. Workers were sacked if they "lacked respect for the employer, his family, or his agents."[31] In practice, however, dismissals became difficult since the regime usually guaranteed job security in return for political quiescence and the acceptance of low salaries and miserable working conditions.

Queipo broke the strike at the Pirotecnia de Sevilla, the only arms factory in Nationalist hands, and, working three shifts at reduced pay, its daily production rapidly and dramatically increased from 40,000 cartridges to 1 million. Most of its workers were female, some of whom had volunteered. By July 1937 the factory overflowed with applications from 800 women whom it could not hire. Early in the conflict, the Pirotecnia sent through friendly Portugal millions of cartridges to General Mola, the key organizer of the rebellion, whose troops in the Sierra of Madrid and in the Basque country desperately needed ammunition. Queipo's ability to quickly employ the resources under his control gave the lie to the Socialist Indalecio Prieto's own radio address in early August that the insurrection was finished because the government controlled "all financial . . . and industrial resources."[32]

Both sides were pitiless and prolific in creating martyrs. Resisters were shot, usually without trial, often against the walls of cemeteries. In Seville, Moroccan *Regulares* (indigenous troops) and recently incorporated Falangists wanting to earn the confidence of their leaders were assigned to firing squads that executed their victims. Spain had hundreds of local Mur des Fédérés, the killing grounds of the Père Lachaise cemetery that finished off the Paris Commune. In Seville alone during Queipo's reign, 6,000 workers and peasants were assassinated. In southeastern Spain (Seville, Cádiz, Huelva, Badajoz, and Córdoba) leftists killed 800, including prominent priests and rightists, whereas rightists eliminated 25,000. In Granada, between 26 July 1936 and 1 March 1939, 2,102 were interred by "order of the Military Tribunal" and by "gunfire." In Granada province 5,000 "disappeared."[33]

To avoid such a fate, leftists fled from their native villages and towns into the Republican zone or hid in the countryside. Neighbors—including priests—denounced many victims, and strangers—often Falangists—executed them outside their villages. The dead were used to intimidate the living. Almost all of these deaths were not only brutal but also humiliating. The bullet-ridden body of an FNTT leader and Socialist deputy, Felipe Granado Valdivia, was hung from the Alconétar bridge (Cáceres). At the beginning of the conflict, the unnamed bodies of the assassinated were left rotting in the summer heat. They quickly decomposed and emitted a dreadful stench. Eventually the remains were buried in ditches that served as mass graves. The victims were stripped of all individuality, remained nameless and never recorded by the state. The atmosphere of terror prevented family members from identifying their deceased. The practice of interring assassinated leftists in the same common ditch as the dozen or so fetuses from impoverished mothers who had naturally aborted reinforced the victims' anonymity and indignity. A similar disrespect for the dead was also common on the Republican side, where the recently massacred were identified only as "fascists." In Huesca province these included 226 priests (including 1 bishop) and 3 nuns. Leftists disinterred and publicly mutilated the skeletons and corpses of buried monks, nuns, and aristocrats. These multiple degradations contrasted with the fate of the corpses of one's own heroes or martyrs. Nationalists guaranteed their volunteers a free and dignified burial. As a sign of respect for the military, they even offered the last rites and an identifiable burial spot to Republican soldiers who were executed by military firing squads drawn by lot.[34]

The devout Catholic Antonio Bahamonde turned against the Nationalists because of their blood-thirsty methods. He claimed credibly that Queipo "documented" the crimes of the "reds" with photographs of those shot by his own troops. Bahamonde accurately predicted that the assassinations and *paseos* would be remembered: "How are children going to forget and live in harmony with those who assassinated their parents?" Nationalist brutality repulsed Bahamonde and another Catholic, Antonio Ruiz Vilaplana, and both initiated the focus on Francoist repression that would continue into the twenty-first century. Neither author was complacent with his own church, which consented—often enthusiastically—to the killings of those who had never committed acts of violence. Rarely did clergymen plead for mercy or a pardon for the sentenced. In fact, they sanctioned killing in the name of a crusade that would explicitly defend both Catholic lives and property against threats of injury, expropriation, and death.[35]

The first military officer to use the radio, Queipo employed it to promote fear among his enemies and to embolden his allies. Mola claimed that he was ready to admit the failure of the pronunciamiento and go into French exile when on 19 July he heard the broadcast of his fellow conspirator and decided to remain and "resist." Queipo's vulgar and often mendacious showmanship attracted a large national audience, even though the poverty of purchasing power had restricted the number of radios in Seville and much of the rest of Spain. Only the comfortable classes possessed their own receivers, which were taxed and had to be registered with authorities. Public and private establishments that owned radios with loudspeakers were obligated to air official news coverage to their customers. Nevertheless, many cafés and bars apparently ignored the law. If discreet, radio owners could listen to the news broadcasts from the other side. Cinemas in the Nationalist zone suspended their films to broadcast the general's nightly talk. For nonlisteners, newspapers throughout the Nationalist zone published his speeches.[36]

Interpretations of Queipo that stress his mental imbalance, sadism, and individual resentment are certainly plausible. Nonetheless, he created an efficacious counterrevolutionary model in Andalusia. The relative success of Sevillian mobilization encouraged Queipo's supporters to argue convincingly that his capture of Seville was essential for Nationalist victory. His men quickly secured the military airport of Tablada, making possible the first major airlift in history. Spanish air crews received indispensable help from Germans and Italians, who provided the necessary planes that landed thousands of legionnaires from Africa. For almost all the Regulares, it was the first time they had flown. By August 1936 the airlift had transported more than 10,000 soldiers from Morocco to the peninsula. At the close of September, with the help of German flight crews, the number had risen to 14,000 soldiers along with hundreds of tons of equipment and arms.[37]

Military officers and civilian administrators throughout the Nationalist zone copied the violent union busting of Queipo's model. They dissolved

Huelva's Bolsa de Trabajo (Labor Exchange) and fired its 136 workers. The mayor attributed "the ruin of the municipality" to "the growth of wages" but pledged to rehire "honorable workers who did their jobs." In Vigo, too, unions were dissolved, contracts rendered void, and dock workers rehired individually by employers. The military governor guaranteed the "right to work" without the interference of working-class organizations. As in Seville, in Santiago de Compostela public transportation workers were militarized.[38]

In fact, in some ways Queipo became a victim of his own success. The *ABC* published in Seville became the most widely read and circulated newspaper of the Nationalist zone. It promoted Queipo's own cult of personality, a precedent that Franco would develop and deepen once his fellow conspirators had named him "the supreme leader" on 21 September 1936. In February 1938, when the first official national government was constituted and Madrid still remained under Republican control, ministries were decentralized and divided among Bilbao, Valladolid, Vitoria, Santander, and Burgos. Seville was left out of the pickings. This reflected not only its geographical distance from Castile and the north but also the Generalísimo's distrust of Queipo's independent power base. One of the first measures taken by the new government was to suspend his nightly radio speeches, which had endured thirty months.[39]

In sharp contrast to the Republican zone, where rents went unpaid and evictions were banned, Queipo ordered the end of both urban and rural rent strikes, which had lasted for several months. Once again, the general threatened energetic and merciless measures. The only exceptions were the unemployed, who were commanded to negotiate agreements with their landlords to pay their debts. He praised owners "as willing to sacrifice" but urged them to be patient with the "worthy" unemployed, a category that did not include "vagrants" or leftists. "We believe that the land should belong to those who work it, but the owner must also be fairly paid because we are not thieves." With Queipo's backing, wealthy landowners, attired in traditional Andalusian seigniorial garb, formed with their servants two cavalry squadrons on horseback. These aristocrats directed the militia columns in Andalusia, whose goal was to recuperate the large tracts that day laborers had occupied after the victory of the Popular Front. Thus, in Spain the countryside dominated the city. As during the June Days of 1848 or the Paris Commune of 1871, counterrevolutionaries could call upon rural constituents—whether in Morocco or the peninsula itself—to smash revolutionaries.[40]

Despite the Falange's repeated claims that it was making a national or national-syndicalist revolution, the Franco zone was counterrevolutionary par excellence. Those who wanted a return to a period of order and authority emerged dominant. In fact, in the early days of the insurgency, some—calling themselves "republicans of order"—joined the Nationalist cause.

Throughout the Nationalist zone, property titles were reconstituted wherever revolutionaries had destroyed them. In Galicia those who refused to pay rent, invoking "Marxist norms," were supposedly shot. In that region, the so-called caciques exhibited remarkable flexibility. A number had nicely accommodated themselves to the Republic but rapidly switched sides when it was clear that the pronunciamiento would prevail. They were adept at replacing Republican Phyrgian caps with either Carlist red berets or Falangist blue shirts. Indeed, during the civil war, "cacique" became another name for a rural egotist and profiteer with some means. The supposedly "ignorant and backward" countryside facilitated their continuing influence. Caciques and their dependents in local government were willing to back any regime that assured them a continuation of their power in rural areas.

The "venerable cacique"—with the tacit support of the "masses"—always managed to outmaneuver the committed Falangist. Despite Falangist revolutionary rhetoric, the new regime had no intention of eliminating *caciquismo* and was willing to accommodate its interests. Caciques recognized that most peasants—and many workers—were, like themselves, concerned with their individual interests. At their best, caciques could sometimes cushion the unreasonable demands of a distant state. In other words, caciques sustained their traditional role as a buffer between a centralized state and their individual clients, whose interests—as long as they did not conflict with their own—caciques attempted to protect. Perhaps this explains why repression in regions of Gallegan caciquismo was less bloody than in rural areas of southern Spain and more politicized urban zones throughout the Nationalist zone. In Galicia Nationalists imitated the Italian Fascist model of exiling bourgeois political opponents and banished some doctors from their hometowns. For instance, a physician from Mellid (La Coruña) was fined 10,000 pesetas and exiled to Vimianzo. A national or international reputation and a willingness to work for those in power spared other medical authorities known for their leftist affiliations.[41]

Many from various social classes were apolitical, and, for example, in the city and province of Seville over 32 percent of the population had abstained from voting during the Second Republic. Large numbers who did vote, approximately 80 percent for the left, were hardly committed partisans. The Falange was overwhelmed by the influx of former members of the traditional right and of left-wing movements. Many of them "should have never joined." Even after the forced unification in April 1937 of the Falange with the Carlists, the new official state party—the awkwardly named Falange Española Tradicionalista de las Juntas de Ofensiva Nacional Sindicalista (FET)—had few sympathizers and little presence in the countryside or on the coasts. Thus, the old elites, not a novel "agrarian Fascism," dominated the Nationalist zone. At the beginning of the war, some put on a blue shirt to fake Falange membership. Others wore the red beret without authorization. One activist recognized that "the indifferent" were "very important numerically." Falangist violence repulsed many newcomers who had no love for any political formation. Most joined the FET for opportunistic reasons—to save their own skins or to eliminate their enemies. In Burgos, of 233 veterans who were members of the Falange, only 49, or 21 percent, had been members before 19 July 1936. In Santa Cruz de Tenerife the Falange had no presence until the military rebellion and then grew rapidly afterward. According to the civil governor, most who joined it were "profiteering egotists." Even its leader, Juan Cañizares, was "perfectly undesirable, ignorant, greedy, hateful, and vengeful." The Falange proved to be a weak mobilizer of the masses. Although certain practices were ostensibly banned—such as influential persons writing letters endorsing their clients and friends for jobs and other state benefits—venerable powerbrokers continued to dominate Nationalist Spain.[42]

Many Falange members often neglected to pay their dues or only paid them under duress, such as threat of a two-week arrest. The Seville branch menaced the expulsion of members who were consistently late payers, a problem that had also plagued leftist unions and parties in the Republican zone. The Teis (Pontevedra) chapter actually expelled seven Falangist cadets and twenty adolescent *Flechas* "for indiscipline and indifference." Six other cadets and twenty more Flechas were warned of imminent exclusion if they skipped another meeting. Members were advised that attendance was mandatory. The failure to pay dues led to the dismissal of four. Dozens of members of youth and women's organizations were threatened with discharge or even arrest if they did not appear for either mass meetings or, in the case of young women, collection duties for party charities. Apathetic individuals who were reluctant to meet their financial and labor obligations constituted a permanent feature of the Falange both during and after the war. Members were warned against spreading rumors and gossip.[43]

MOORS

The North African mercenaries airlifted by Germans and Italians to Queipo's Seville proved crucial for the Nationalist victory. Moroccans and other African troops saved the Nationalist war effort, just as soldiers and resources from their empires rescued the British and French during World War I. Franco and his generals appreciated African troops more than any other group of soldiers. Nationalists pushed ideological interpretations of the Moroccan sacrifice, which, they argued, was against atheism or for the love of Spain. Queipo and others claimed that Moroccans had devotedly kept the keys to the homes of their ancestors who had been expelled from Granada.[44]

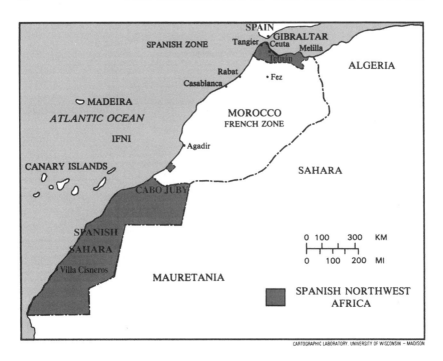

Spanish possessions in northwest Africa

Yet material rewards were much more convincing to these mercenaries than spiritual ones. Moroccan enrollment had little to do with ideological appeals against "godless Republicans" or Marxism, which were concepts that were unfamiliar to most recruits from rural Morocco. However, Nationalist propaganda of the fable of a "Jewish-Masonic-Communist" conspiracy against the traditional order did raise interest among North Africans. The Moroccan forces, 99 percent of whom were illiterate, may not have known much about Masons and Communists, but they were certainly aware of Jews. They had a tradition of pillaging local Jews, and many believed they were going to Spain to fight Christians and loot Jewish stores and homes. As early as 1860, as the Spanish troops approached Tetuán, Muslims sacked the homes of the 6,000 Jewish inhabitants whom they viewed as Spanish allies. In July 1907, *moros* had again engaged in looting in the Jewish quarter and committed atrocities against its inhabitants.[45]

Rank-and-file Moroccan troops and their Spanish officers shared a common and occasionally murderous anti-Semitism. At the outbreak of the civil war, young Sevillian girls decorated the arriving Moroccans with Sacred Heart talismans believed to stop bullets and found that they were delighted to combat in Spain since "we have not been able to fight Jews for some time." "The Moors have a powerful African loathing for the reds. They call them bad Spaniards and nothing more than Jews, the greatest insult that a Moor can utter." Like their Spanish Nationalist officers, including Franco, Moroccans deliberately confused Jews with "reds." According to a Jesuit chaplain in the Legion, the Moors were happy to fight a holy war against atheists and "international Jewish scheming." Their local military and spiritual leaders continually harped upon the latter theme.[46]

The constant propaganda seems to have convinced many rank-and-file Moroccan soldiers to identify Judaism with atheism and Communism. In a demonstration in Larache, Arabs celebrated the Nationalist conquest of Málaga in February 1937 by chanting "death to the Jews." In August 1937 twenty-three Jews—the majority women and children—were injured during a riot of Moorish soldiers in El Ksar. Nationalist authorities responded by fining the Jewish community. Like other Arab nationalists, Moroccan nationalists opposed British and French imperialism, admired the Nazis, and despised Jews. The Spanish Nationalist press was pro-Nazi and unrelentingly pro-Arab, prefiguring the pro-Axis and anti-Zionist position that Spain would take during World War II.[47]

To solidify their alliance with the Islamic mercenaries, Nationalists fomented myths concerning the Moorish presence in the peninsula. The "two peoples" (Spaniards and Moors) were "racial twins" and "have the same mentality and character as a result of eight centuries of cohabitation." The Falangist intellectual Ernesto Giménez Caballero maintained that both groups shared the same blood, a unique position for a European fascist in the late 1930s. Arab culture supposedly resembled its Spanish counterpart, and Moorish songs reflected a popular vision that Franco was "a good knight fighting Evil."[48]

Moorish notables were regularly honored when they visited Spanish cities, including Córdoba and its spectacular mosque (*mezquita*). In a visit to Seville, the Grand Visir of eastern Morocco, Abd-el-Kadar, praised Franco as a defender of "God's cause." Accompanied by 600 Moorish notables and 1,000 pilgrims who were soon to embark on a journey to Mecca, the Grand Visir heard the Caudillo announce "Spain and Islam are two peoples who have always understood each other." The Generalísimo urged "the faithful" to combat the "faithless" and promised to establish a chair of Arabic studies in Córdoba. His press referred patronizingly but affectionately to the Moroccans as "moritos." Censors diplomatically eliminated disparaging and racist comments about Moroccans, which could be found in Franco's own account of his North African service, *Diario de una Bandera* (1922). Adoring crowds genuinely offered ovations and *vivas* during the dress parades of Moorish troops, adulation that bolstered their esprit de corps. The regime was partly successful in creating a kind of monotheistic unity—which purposely ex-cluded the Jews—against the "atheist" enemy. In Zaragoza not only Spanish and Italian soldiers but also German Protestant and Islamic Moroccan troops visited and venerated the Virgin of Pilar.[49]

Much of the historiography on Moroccan troops in Spain revolves around the supposed failure of the Republic to adopt enlightened policies that would have given Morocco its independence and therefore, it is assumed, induced the moros to support the Loyalists. Yet even if the Republic had backed Moroc-can nationalists, they were too weak and divided to impede Spanish Nation-alist recruitment of soldiers. In fact, Moroccan nationalists, including their leader Abdeljalak Torres, cooperated closely with the Insurgents in many ar-eas. The Fityanes, the youth group of Torres's Partido Reformista Nacional, adopted some fascist practices. Its members paraded in Tetuán wearing green shirts, giving the Roman salute, and shouting "Allah Akbar!" In the 1930s, Moroccan nationalism was urban and bourgeois, and Spanish recruitment occurred among rural elites and proletarians. Spanish Nationalists permitted Moroccan nationalist propaganda and activities in the cities but prohibited them in rural areas where the *caídes* (tribal leaders) cooperated fully with the imperialists. In Morocco as in Spain itself, counterrevolutionaries drew their strength from the countryside. Throughout the early twentieth century, Span-ish authorities had won the cooperation of caídes by bribing them with seeds, barley, and cash. Spanish officials also gave their moros license to loot (espe-cially livestock and grains), pillage, and rape other Moroccans. The North African peasants, especially the *rifeños*, had a tradition of engaging as mer-cenaries. Some had fought for the French as early as the Franco-Prussian War of 1870–71. Their descendants signed up in large numbers for World War I. Opportunities were rare for peasants in impoverished North African rural regions, particularly during periods of poor harvests.[50]

The fundamental motive for the successful recruitment of tens of thou-sands of Moroccans was economic. During the drought of 1936, the Moroc-can peasants who joined Franco's forces—many of whom came from the French zone—received dramatically increased conscription bonuses, cloth-ing, four kilos of sugar, a can of oil, bread proportional to the number of their children, and two months' pay in advance. Families that did not offer volunteers were sometimes punished by denial of food supplies. Spanish en-ticements and repression diminished much resistance to the Nationalist war effort. More than a dozen caídes throughout the Spanish Protectorate who opposed the recruitment were executed. In the first weeks of war, "hundreds" of natives enlisted with the unwritten understanding that they would be per-mitted to engage in their traditional practices of looting. As in Morocco, the volunteers felt that pillaging was their right. Indeed, many had signed up because of the opportunities for robbing and raping that were tolerated by their officers. One unit, the Tiradores de Ifni, numbering approximately 1,000 troops, at times received more in booty than in regular pay. Their right to loot could be circumscribed, and when they robbed respectable (i.e., non-"red") citizens, they might be sentenced to death. The motivation to loot made them less effective soldiers in situations when pillaging was unlikely, such as capturing barren territory or strategic hills.[51]

Franco was aware of the attraction of material incentives both in the Protectorate and in the peninsula itself. On 19 July he immediately raised wages of *legionarios* 1 peseta per day. Regulares (Africans) became well-paid elite troops, whose salary jumped from 3 pesetas at the start of the war to 5 pesetas in 1937 and more in 1938. Habitual remuneration, decent uniforms (at least initially), and good fare attracted natives. Warm meals offered meat with beans or rice. Cold rations consisted of cans of sardines or tuna, dates, figs, chocolate, and bread—in sum, a diet much superior to their Republican enemy. Almost all Moroccan soldiers interviewed by historians fondly remembered the abundance of food, which contrasted with the reigning hunger both in Morocco and in large parts of the Republican zone. Republican authorities tried counterbribes to prominent Moroccans who were more than willing to take the kickbacks but reluctant to switch from their comfortable relationship with the camp they correctly expected to win.[52]

On the eve of the civil war, the Spanish Protectorate lodged a total number of 34,000 troops, 18,000 European (almost all Spanish), and 16,000 Moroccan. Immediately after the civil war erupted, each *caíd* was required to recruit 500 soldiers from his respective tribe (*cabila*). Poor harvests of the mid-1930s and close cooperation between Spanish officers and tribal chiefs facilitated enlistments. Approximately 70,000 enrolled, primarily for economic reasons. The number of persons who depended upon their wages and benefits may have reached 500,000. Applying the successful Moroccan precedent to the peninsula, in December 1936 Franco told Manuel Hedilla, the provisional chief of the Falange, to recruit 10,000 soldiers "among Gallegan peasants, poor but conservative and Catholic, who have many problems because of a bad harvest."[53]

By the beginning of 1937, 31,440 colonial troops were fighting in Spain. In February 1937, 50,000 North Africans were combating the Republicans. By the end of the war, 60,000 to 80,000 African troops—primarily from Morocco but a few from Spanish Guinea, Senegal, and Mali—had been deployed in the peninsula. Of these, 11,500 were killed and 55,500 were wounded, a tremendous casualty rate. Over 50 percent of the severely wounded who were permitted to return home became military instructors of new recruits. By the end of the war, Moroccan veterans had earned dozens of medals. Of the 9,000 combatants from the Ifni-Sahara region, 1,200 died in the conflict, including 110 officers. Nationalists enrolled 14 percent of the Ifni's population and drained the territory of nearly all able-bodied men. North African military achievements were remarkable and were matched only by the International Brigades in the Spanish civil war. Like the International Brigaders, their morale declined at the end of the war, but they maintained their commitment to the Nationalist side. Also similar to International Brigaders, Moorish units were diluted with the entrance of Spanish recruits throughout 1937 and especially 1938. Many of the new conscripts had less training and desire to combat than volunteers, and some of them—at least before a second examination in mid-1937—had successfully attempted to exploit a limp, small stature, bad eyesight, poor hearing, or mental instability to avoid military service.[54]

Moroccans participated in all the major Nationalist offensives throughout the war. Few of the africanistas or *africanomilitaristas* who directed them spoke any Arabic or Moroccan dialect, but they understood the North African culture of warfare. Their soldiers' robbing, raping, and killing of prisoners quickly gained a fearsome reputation among the enemy. Moors often shot and shamelessly pillaged refugees and deserters to the Nationalist zone, and those who wanted to abandon the Republican side attempted to surrender only to their countrymen. The Africans became renowned for their ability to attack the enemy silently and to pursue him in retreat. Commanders, aware of their reputation, would place them in the most dangerous positions. Republican militiamen responded by shooting Moroccans on sight. The latter replied with "unrestrained hatred of reds." The aggressive assaults and the war cries of the moros were enough to scatter Republican militias. In fact, the reputation of Moroccans was so terrifying that during the Battle of Brunete in the summer of 1937, Gallegan fighters, who were not known for their pugnacity, were ordered to dress up like Moors to scare their Republican enemy.[55]

The knife and the machete were among their preferred weapons. Ears, noses, and especially testicles were prize trophies of the moros. Since the Asturias Revolt, Moors had won the deserved reputation of silently slitting the throats and beheading sentries and other soldiers. Decapitations were apparently a Moorish custom, practiced by Moroccan sultans and other leaders on their conquered foes. These fierce warriors would severe fingers to acquire rings or pull teeth to extract gold. Spanish troops were also capable of mutilating their enemies. During the Asturias campaign in September 1937, Republicans resisted ferociously and hacked to death over a dozen requetés. The tendency of Nationalists and others to attribute the worst atrocities to the moros exonerated their own responsibilities for murders and rapes. Like the Regulares, European legionarios also became known for their thieving, raping, and mutilations of the bodies of their dead enemies. However, torture and mutilation, it seems, occurred less frequently among Spanish soldiers.[56]

Less publicized but equally important, the Moroccans fed themselves and the Spanish during the first months of war when their territory was severed from the peninsula, which had regularly supplied it with wheat, rice, and sugar before the war. Basic training was conducted by fellow Moors, usually sergeants, who—unlike their European counterparts—were refused the status of noncommissioned officers. They were also in charge of imposing severe discipline on wayward soldiers. Not Spaniards but fellow Moroccans performed beatings and whippings. Their Spanish commanders were expected to expose themselves to equal if not greater danger in battle. Appropriate authorities thoroughly investigated complaints of brutality and mistreatment of Moroccans at the hands of Spanish officers, a few of whom were killed by their own Moorish troops. Death sentences were issued for the few cases of collective African insubordination and revolt. Perhaps the Nationalist army might have been able to make their Moorish mercenaries even better soldiers if they had been more willing to promote the meritorious. Although several academies were established to train young Moroccans from influential families committed to the Nationalists, only one Moroccan—Mohammed ben Mizziam ben Kasem, usually known as El Mizzian, rose to colonel and only a very few others became officers of any rank. More became corporals and sergeants, but they resented their inability to rise further.[57]

Republicans accused Moors of looting churches, but they were more interested in pillaging commodities that soldiers and civilians would purchase. Throughout the war, Nationalist officials showed less hostility to markets than the Popular Army and permitted Moorish vendors to sell food, wine, tobacco, and other commodities. In fact, the most important cause of Moroccan desertion was their entrepreneurial desire to become street merchants. Even though everyone suspected vendors of desertion, their commercial activities were often tolerated because they offered an invaluable morale-raising service for the Insurgent forces. Moroccan sutlers sold clothes, shoes, food, watches, radios, cutlery, jewelry, rings, pens, shaving equipment, and gold teeth. They improvised numerous flea markets or, despite the constant danger, peddled commodities directly to soldiers on the fronts. Frontline sutlers earned increased profits to support their large families (which may have included several wives) at home. The price of cigarettes and cognac sold on an active front was nearly ten times higher than in the rear. Successful sutlers risked death from the enemy and even from fellow North Africans and Spaniards who were tempted to kill and rob them. Tobacco and hard liquor—two commodities that helped to relieve stress in an uncertain environment—were the most popular items for both Spaniards and Moors. Despite the Moroccans' own reputation for small-scale war profiteering, authorities tried to protect them from Spanish merchants who overcharged.[58]

The North African population solicited noncombatant positions—translators, butchers, cooks, waiters, nurses (usually male), and (female) prostitutes. Hundreds of sex professionals accompanied elite troops, and women with little fear of the front served other units. During rest and recreation, Moroccans could purchase pleasure from North African professionals. In a macho culture where *maricón* and *marica* were among the worst insults, Franco's officers were told to tolerate the practice of sodomy among Moroccans. In another example of multiculturalism *avant la lettre*, Seville radio broadcasted an Arab-language program of news and music.[59]

Municipalities authorized cafés that resembled the establishments of Tangiers in which North African waiters offered cigarettes, sugared tea, Moorish coffee, and even kif and hashish. These commodities were very popular among groups of Moroccan fighters who would freely indulge at the front. Certain Moorish units, such as Franco's own equestrian honor guard, did not depend on quartermaster for their meals but were paid in cash and allowed to prepare food and beverages themselves. Moroccan martial tradition and "tribal" sociability reinforced small-group loyalty. Supplying beverages, food, and sex may have been more important to the continued Moorish participation on the Nationalist side than—as so many historians have argued— promising Morocco independence. The reward of basic material goods for their service meant more to the mercenaries than ideological or political promises. After the war ended, many deserted to stay in Spain—prefiguring the large North African immigration in the late twentieth-century—and continued their profit-making and wage-laboring activities. They sold food to hungry Barcelonans following the capture of that city. Nonetheless, most were eventually deported, but a few did manage to remain as street vendors, especially of carpets.[60]

As the war endured, like their Spanish allies and enemies, North African enthusiasm to enlist diminished. Desertions increased as the casualties of these shock troops mounted, and pay seemed retarded or insufficient in the face of growing inflation. Moroccans looked for excuses to avoid the front, claiming, for example, that they had terrible toothaches. Health officials countered by extracting teeth without anesthesia, a medical procedure that convinced potential shirkers to perform their duties without delay. Reflecting shortages in the Nationalist zone, their shoes and clothing became unsuitable for winter conditions.[61]

The granting of leave caused intense friction. Moroccans demanded *permisos*, but especially during the first months of the war, officials were reluctant to authorize visits to the Protectorate since many overstayed their leave. Furthermore, soldiers on leave discouraged enlistment by providing a truer and harsher view of the dangers of war than official propaganda was willing to admit. In February 1937 *El Sol* reported a riot in Espinosa de los Monteros (Burgos) among *rifeños* who protested late pay. In December 1937 insufficient food supplies provoked violent demonstrations against Nationalist authorities in Larache, Xauen, and the Melilla region. In March 1938 a Carlist unit suppressed a riot by Regulares stationed in Cella (Teruel). The massive mobilization of moros threatened to create severe labor and food shortages in the countryside, a situation that Colonel Juan Beigbeder, the high commissioner of Morocco and future foreign minister, worked hard to avoid in 1937. In the Protectorate wives of soldiers denied leave claimed that their husbands had abandoned them and sued for divorce under Islamic law. In the streets of Ceuta, after drinking bouts, "numerous Moors, soldiers, and civilians" engaged in brawling. In response, the high commissioner prohibited sales of alcoholic beverages to Muslims. In September 1938, peasants protested against the general mobilization decreed by franquista officials. Many of Franco's African soldiers came to increasingly resent the privileges of the caídes.[62]

Despite limitations on leave and strict censorship (no letters—even those hand-carried—could be sent sealed, and censors worked full time eliminating discouraging news from missives), rumors of proselytizing, conversions, deaths, and injuries reached the Protectorate and provoked the kind of discontent that Nationalist authorities wanted to avoid at all costs.[63] The growing disgruntlement among Africans casts doubt on the argument of many historians that the Caudillo himself wanted to lengthen the war to secure his own political power. Franco's supposed plan to delay winning the war would have been very risky, if not foolhardy, particularly for an individual whom biographers have painted as cautious. Just as importantly, this "great man" view of history repeats a conventional perspective, which the franquistas themselves shared, that only leaders make history. A more global view of the conflict, which incorporates growing Moroccan discontent, demonstrates the inadequacy of a focus on one "great" man, and "history from below" provides a perspective that shows that the Caudillo was far from omnipotent.

Some Moroccan prisoners and deserters vowed to their Republican captors that they had been tricked into coming to Spain by promises from military authorities that they would be compensated with plots of land in Andalusia, Murcia, and Valencia. Others claimed that the Nationalists had promised to return the Córdoba mezquita to Morocco after granting it independence. Even though perhaps 1,700 Moroccans abandoned Nationalist ranks during the conflict, desertions to the Popular Army were rare. Instead of fleeing to the enemy, dissatisfied Africans transferred to other Nationalist units, remained in the peninsula as vendors, or returned to Morocco to join family members. In other words, Moroccan flights occurred for personal—not ideological—reasons. Of thirty-two deserters in the 10th Tabor of Ceuta, only one defected to Republican ranks. Their officers concluded that "these desertions are a result of individual choice." At the end of the war, authorities threatened four presumed Moroccan deserters with severe punishment if they did not immediately return to their Regulares unit in Palencia.[64]

To maintain the loyalty of wavering Moroccans, the regime mixed sticks and carrots. In Alcazarquivir in April 1937, it inaugurated an old-age home, public housing, a library, and a radio station. In February 1938, to win back shifting public opinion, franquistas donated 10,000 lambs to the poor, distributed seeds to the population, and, once again, bribed important caídes. These lambs demonstrated the ability of sheep farmers in Badajoz and Cáceres to supply an essential sector of the Nationalist zone with *halal* meat. Serrano Súñer arranged for Muslim children to visit cities in mainland Spain, where some met the Caudillo. Auxilio Social (AS) established a Muslim children's dining hall in a Ceuta neighborhood and offered free meals to needy children. During the civil war in the Protectorate, the regime built twelve mosques, two of which were inaugurated by the interior minister. It also constructed water treatment plants, public washing establishments, roads, and schools. The education budget of the Protectorate increased fivefold during the war. The Caudillo organized on his own initiative pilgrimage cruises to Mecca from 1937 through 1939 at subsidized prices that included a much reduced fare or even free passage for children. The cruises received wide publicity throughout the Protectorate and in the Nationalist zone.[65]

Franco's Spain established at least sixteen hospitals for Moroccans, where North Africans were well treated and amply fed. Nationalist authorities hoped physical separation would avoid friction between Moslems and Christians, particularly the Spanish draftees of 1938 in whom the Nationalist leadership had little confidence. Inevitable tensions between missionary Catholics devoted to their *Cruzada* and devout Moslems involved in a supposed *Jihad* increased as the war endured. The former were accused—often accurately—of trying to convert the latter, especially the wounded recovering in hospitals. Franco did whatever possible to prevent offense to Islamic religious sensibilities throughout the conflict and intervened to prohibit all attempts by priests, nuns, and charity women to proselytize in Christian and Moslem facilities. His order banning conversions was posted in large print inside the hospitals of the Nationalist zone.[66]

Authorities rewarded the wounded with significant cash bonuses. Spanish personnel made efforts to learn some Arabic since their patients often spoke little Spanish. In health facilities—which were often remodeled Catholic edifices—Nationalists provided services for Moorish bathing, prayers, and other rituals, over which imams presided. Muslim patients could be certain that they were not consuming pork, that their meat was butchered according to Islamic norms, and that the customs of Ramadan and other religious holidays were being observed. A mosque was established on the grounds of the Hospital Militar de Bella Vista in Vigo and another at the Hospital de La Barzola in Seville. At the inauguration of the latter, thousands of pesetas were directly distributed to the Moroccan patients. In the former establishment during Ramadan, Vigo sent its municipal band to entertain patients, who were offered treats during the festivities. The walls of the Granada hospital, one of the largest, were covered with lofty Coranic maxims in Arabic. Moorish dignitaries regularly visited their countrymen in military hospitals. In 1938 a few hospitals in northern Spain began employing a handful of female Moroccan nurses. Officials of the Moroccan desk (Asuntos Marroquíes) made sure that the families of the deceased soldiers received their money orders.[67]

WAR OF MOVEMENT

In August and September the Army of Africa, composed of indigenous troops and crack Spanish or European legionarios, advanced north from their base in Seville to Mérida and Badajoz, then continued up the Tagus (Tajo) valley toward Toledo and Madrid. In their retreats throughout the war, Republican militiamen often abandoned to the enemy valuable equipment, including weapons, radios, clothes, and cognac. The Nationalists continued to use terror to discourage their real and potential enemies. One of the most infamous massacres occurred at Badajoz, near the Portuguese border. The city of 40,000 was fiercely defended by 4,000 militiamen—who, although outmanned and outgunned by the enemy—offered formidable resistance to the African columns. After losing well over 100 legionarios, the nationalists captured the town on 14 August. More shockingly, according to foreign journalists, Yagüe's troops executed at least several thousand men who were suspected of fighting for the Republic. The bullring was notoriously drenched in the blood of the victims. Their corpses were heaped on piles and then burned, providing yet another example of the humiliation of the enemy and disdain for his individuality. Africanistas also permitted their men to loot shops and stores, even those owned by rightists. Portuguese travelers imported the many jewels and timepieces that the Moors had plundered. Throughout the conflict, moros were fond of stealing watches, and they often demanded at gunpoint that civilians remove them from their wrists. Timepieces were a particularly prized commodity among soldiers since they allowed the division of a monotonous day and accurately anticipated mealtimes. Sewing machines, usually the Singer brand, were also popular since women—whether European or African—especially appreciated them. A military proclamation that stolen property be returned immediately to its owners was ignored. Moros gained a reputation as incorrigible thieves, even among committed Nationalists. Nurses who attended them in hospitals constantly had to take precautionary measures to prevent their pilfering.[68]

In nearby Mérida, legionarios, Falangists, and Regulares reportedly assassinated at least 1,000 Republicans. Africanistas secured their rear in the bloodiest manner. Near Mérida, Republican women were purportedly raped before being executed. Some Spanish officers allotted one or two hours to

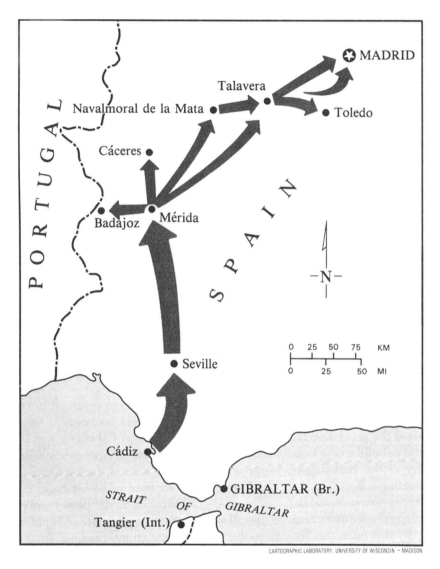

Route of the Army of Africa

their Moroccans to scour a town for booty and women, whereas others executed Africans who raped Spaniards. El Mizzian—the highest-ranking Moroccan officer in Franco's forces who rose to general and eventually became a
marshal of Morocco after it gained its independence in 1956—did not deny
that forty of his men collectively ravaged and killed two young "red" women.

In the rest of the Nationalist-conquered province, repression and terror were equally barbaric. The Nationalist subjugation of Mérida and Badajoz achieved their objective of severing rail and road communications between Portugal and the Republic.[69]

The number of victims in Badajoz province surpassed those of Badajoz city. Perhaps the degree and intensity of violence can be partly explained by the fact that in this province land reform had been an extremely contentious issue. In Extremadura an estimated 10,000 wealthier peasants joined the great landowners to fight for Franco. Badajoz province counted 6,610 victims, whereas the quieter Segovia had "only" 357. For example, Almendralejo (Badajoz) was a relatively prosperous town of nearly 18,000 residents, the majority of whom voted monarchist. When Nationalists took the town in August, over 1,000 people were executed. As in Queipo's Andalusia, the Nationalist bloodletting in Extremadura decapitated the workers' movement and terrorized its surviving sympathizers. If some of them took to the hills and plotted attacks against the franquistas, others chose to desert or to surrender without resisting.[70]

At the end of September the loss of Toledo, where the Loyalist effort had begun auspiciously, capped a series of Republican defeats. In July those supporting the military rebellion had been forced to retreat into the Alcázar, the fortress-castle of the medieval capital and seat of the Infantry Academy. Under the leadership of Colonel José Moscardó, more than 1,000 Civil and Assault Guards, Falangists, and a few military cadets took the women and children of known leftists as hostages and withstood a two-month Republican siege. The string of victories by the advancing Army of Africa bolstered their morale. Franco decided that relieving the Alcázar was a top priority, even though it might cost him a quick victory in Madrid. He believed that the propaganda benefit of a rescue of the Alcázar defenders justified a delay in capturing the Spanish capital. On 26 September as Colonel Varela and the Army of Africa approached the fortress, a few hundred *milicianos* offered only token resistance and retreated toward Madrid. Militias abandoned the entire contents of the Toledo arms factory to the Nationalists. They also left tons of wheat and thousands of heads of livestock in enemy hands. The capture of the Alcázar on 27 September ended the ten-week siege, and the Nationalist zone predictably rejoiced.

Moscardó subsequently became another symbol of resistance and courage for the Insurgents, and the defense of the Alcázar became a mythical example of Nationalist resistance. The rank-and-file soldiers enthusiastically cheered the capture of Toledo, and it became perhaps the most moving legend of Nationalist victories. It undoubtedly inspired the tenacity of resistance of small groups of Nationalist soldiers at the beginning of key battles throughout the war—Oviedo, Brunete, Belchite, and Teruel—who knew that their high command would spare no effort to relieve them. Franco's rescue of the Alcázar also showed that he preferred to secure his rear before undertaking new operations.[71]

In the north early in the conflict, well-equipped, well-armed, and highly motivated Carlist Navarrese conquered much of the Basque country and significant parts of Aragon for the Nationalists. Most of these requetés, who were usually Navarrese *labradores* in civilian life, were well provisioned throughout the conflict under all but the most exceptional circumstances. Melding urban with rural interests, the Junta Central de Guerra Navarra organized the supply of troops and administered the rear. Navarrese villages felt responsible for the material welfare of their volunteers. In the early months of the war, the parishioners of Vitoria initiated a collection in the name of the Virgin and of the Fatherland. Nurses and musicians used these funds to transport food and provide entertainment for the front. Requetés assured their loved ones in their letters to home that they were eating well. The same could be said of Catalan and especially Andalusian volunteer units who possessed, at least at the beginning of their campaign, "everything [they] needed." Even after the Battle of Madrid in November 1936, Sevillian and Zamoran troops received from home food, tobacco, clothes, and even good wine. The latter was so plentiful at times that German cooks bartered their sausages for it. Early in the war, Carlist medical services functioned efficiently.[72]

Carlists wanted to close the French border at Hendaye and eliminate the Basque Republican threat to their rear. After the bloody triumph at Badajoz, General Franco ordered 700 legionarios to reinforce the troops of the Carlist commander, Colonel Alfonso Beorleguí, who was directing the campaign to take the border town of Irún. Between 26 August and 4 September, the 2,000-man force of attackers—including Carlists, legionarios, Falangists, and Civil Guards—opposed an equal number of defenders. These Irún defenders —anarchists, Basque Nationalists, Catalan nationalists, and committed Republicans—were as politically heterogeneous as Nationalist forces. Superior organization and armament gave the victory to Colonel Beorleguí, who was mortally wounded in action. Complementing Yagüe's successful scission of Portugal in the south, Beorleguí succeeded in cutting off the Republic from the French border at the western end of the Pyrenees. The progressive capture of Basque towns and villages allowed the Nationalists to gain significant quantities of arms and rich stocks of food accumulated by the Basque Nationalist government. On 13 September the Insurgents took San Sebastián (Guipúzcoa) without a fight from militias demoralized by the Irún defeat. The ferocity that marked warfare in southern Spain was largely absent in the Basque campaign. Neither side made a policy of shooting prisoners, although early in the war the military infamously executed sixteen Basque priests involved in "separatist" politics. A shared Catholicism, a less acute agrarian

Women and girls of San Sebastián give an enthusiastic welcome to the anti-Republican forces marching to occupy the city. September 1936, Associated Press of Great Britain. Southworth Spanish Civil War Collection, Mandeville Special Collections Library, University of California, San Diego.

problem, and a culture of local cordiality acted to restrain political assassinations and the most brutal aspects of war.[73]

In Aragon the front quickly became stable and quiet. Aragon tranquility benefited Nationalists more than Republicans, since the latter initially outnumbered the former ten to one. By January 1937 the Republican prevalence had dropped to four to one, but—as in other peaceful sectors—Republicans did not take advantage of their numerical superiority to conquer enemy territory. Republican Prime Minister Largo Caballero concluded that "discipline, morale, and leadership can multiply military effectiveness by four." Despite considerable gaps and unguarded areas of a very irregular line, militiamen— as George Orwell and others have pointed out—became unaggressive. In three weeks Orwell fired only three shots. Even in the early months of the war, each side agreed "not to plug one another" and conducted conversations with the enemy. Desertions of dozens of soldiers (not officers) occurred monthly on both sides. Nearly half defected without firearms, indicating a significant shortage even among Nationalist troops. Individual and small-group flights lengthened the conflict and helped to turn it into a war of attrition.[74]

On the Aragon front the Catalan Carlists, all of whom had escaped from the "red" zone, were well fed but not well equipped and possessed only a few rifles. This was apparently sufficient to maintain their positions on the quiet front of Mediana. Although the Carlist command created a mobile column that would sporadically attack the enemy, foreign volunteers who yearned for

Nationalist troops who participated in the capture of Irún and San Sebastián receive a rous-
ing welcome from the people of Burgos when they return to the town for a rest. July 1937,
Keystone View Co. Southworth Spanish Civil War Collection, Mandeville Special Collections
Library, University of California, San Diego.

action—White Russians and French volunteers from the right-wing Croix-de-
Feu—left Aragon to join the Legion. Some of them were killed in battles surrounding Madrid. The reigning peace frustrated a few warriors who remained.
In the Legion a British volunteer, Frank Thomas, became disgusted at the lack
of fighting spirit among Spanish soldiers in the spring of 1937 and deserted.
His experience was similar to that of committed International Brigaders, who
were dismayed at the failure of their Spanish comrades to advance in battle.
Thomas's choice was ironic since certain requetés abandoned their own units
that were stationed on quiet fronts to join the Legion. The Nationalist high
command was aware of the pernicious effects of mixing elite units, such as
the Carlist Tercio de Lácar, with draftees and attempted with limited success
to regroup the most committed volunteers in new formations.[75]

In the small town of Codo, forty kilometers south of Zaragoza, the Carlist
Tercio de Montserrat was comfortably installed with the willing aid of inhabitants: "Each requeté had a home where he could spend some time, get his
clothes washed, and eat if he wished." The town, which lacked drinking water
and other necessities, not untypical in 1930s Spain, nevertheless welcomed the

approximately 200 Catalans with whom they maintained a solid and even affectionate relationship founded on reciprocity between soldiers and villagers. Peasants paid the requetés to harvest fields of wheat or fruit trees located in no-man's-land. Soldiers also recovered herds of sheep wandering near "red" lines. Despite the primitive conditions, requetés ate well. Their diet improved as they consumed many grilled chickens and lamb chops accompanied by Aragon wines.[76]

At the beginning of October, the Republic was still enduring an unbroken chain of defeats and had yet to achieve its Valmy. The Insurgents sustained their assaults on several fronts. On the sea, with Benito Mussolini's aid and assistance, the Nationalists began to dominate the Mediterranean. On land, on 16 October after weeks of hard fighting, the Insurgent garrison in Oviedo, which was being besieged by militant Asturian miners, was finally relieved. As in 1934, professional Moroccan forces played an indispensable role in the capture of Asturian territory. The rescue of Oviedo repeated Nationalist success in relieving beleaguered garrisons, such as Moscardó's at the Alcázar of Toledo. Republican aviation had alienated potential supporters by indiscriminately bombing the provincial capital. The Nationalist capture of Oviedo was a real and symbolic blow to the Republic and some of its most stalwart defenders, the Asturian miners who had volunteered to fight in relatively large numbers and had a history of tough—even legendary—resistance.[77]

In late October 20,000 to 25,000 Nationalist troops—mainly Moroccans and legionarios—under the command of General Varela, approached Madrid. The arrival of a shipment of Soviet supplies and arms, especially first-rate tanks and planes (for which the Republic would pay dearly) bolstered the defenders. Tanks were insufficiently numerous and sophisticated to play a major role in the conflict, but the November shipment of Russian aircraft gave Republicans air superiority, possibly for the first time, and Nationalist troops sometimes proved as panicky under air attack as leftist militiamen. On occasion, Moorish Regulares fled and abandoned their equipment as quickly as Republican militiamen. The traditional tactics and motivation of the Army of Africa—mobility, stealth, and looting—proved ineffective. Moors had been excellent in the field, especially when attacking in small teams or at night. However, they became disconcerted when they encountered fierce opposition, as they did from Spanish and international troops at the gates of the city. The Battle of Madrid in November 1936 demonstrated their inexperience in urban warfare. Stiff Republican resistance created logistic difficulties and lowered morale. The Moroccans lacked healthy food and water and subsisted on a canned sardine diet. The Republican enemy fired on cooks bringing hot food from the rear. Moorish soldiers engaged in self-mutilation to avoid a worse fate. The failure to capture the capital resulted in the splitting up of colonial troops and their redistribution as shock troops on different fronts.[78]

The successful defense of Madrid, summarized by the well-known slogan recycled from World War I, "No Pasarán" (they shall not pass), was the greatest military achievement of the Republic. Loyalist forces met the challenge of the Army of Africa and stymied its attempt to capture Madrid. In the history of modern civil wars, no side has won without conquering the capital. London remained in the hands of Parliament; Paris was controlled by revolutionaries during the Great Revolution, by conservatives in 1848, and captured by counterrevolutionaries in 1871; Washington was held by the federal government; Moscow (and Petrograd) controlled by the Soviets; and the Chinese Communist Party (CCP) conquest of Beijing meant the end of the Chinese conflict. Franco could not expect to win quickly without Madrid. Likewise, in the great international conflicts of the twentieth century, capitals have proven decisive. The Battle of Madrid was similar to the Battle of the Marne in World War I or the Battle of Moscow in World War II. The failure to capture the capital—whether Paris, Moscow, or Madrid—stopped rapid advances and turned all three wars into slogging matches, where the side with superior logistics would triumph.

Franco's priority continued to be the capital, but as the next important Nationalist offensive against Madrid began, the franquistas easily captured Málaga, a poorly defended coastal city. To conquer it, the Nationalists employed ten thousand Moors, 5,000 requetés, and fourteen battalions (over 11,000 men) of Italian volunteers under the command of Mussolini's trusted supporter, the Italian General Mario Roatta. So that the glory of their victories in Spain would reflect favorably upon his Fascist regime, the Duce insisted upon an autonomous Italian organization for his nearly 50,000 combatants. The Italians' luxury of all kinds of equipment mightily impressed the Nationalists. The Fascists had plentiful supplies of trucks and artillery, possessed small numbers of tanks and planes, and naval artillery that could bombard Málaga during battle. Certainly, in the early stages of the war, aid from Germany and Italy far outweighed that of the Republic's allies. However, the quality of Italian troops varied. Most Italian volunteers were recruited from the ranks of Fascist squads of Black Shirts. Some came from the regular armed forces and had experienced combat in Ethiopia; whereas, others had been pressured or deceived into going to Spain. Like many Spaniards in the armed forces, a large number were opportunists. They had come to Spain more eager to advance their careers than to fight "reds."[79]

On 6 February tens of thousands began a mass exodus along the coastal road from Málaga to Almería, where Nationalist aircraft heartlessly harassed and strafed them. Some died from exhaustion, whereas others committed suicide. According to an official Republican inquiry, the retreat was "mad." Even less fortunate than fleeing refugees were militants of the left who remained trapped in the city. Approximately 5,000 of them were put to death. Málaga won the unenviable reputation for undergoing the worst repression that franquistas had to offer, with the possible exception of the Badajoz massacre. The victors took 10,000 prisoners, but those soldiers who survived purges were eventually recycled into Franco's army.[80]

The Battle of the Jarama at the beginning of February 1937 coincided with the capture of Málaga. The goal of the Nationalist offensive at the Jarama was to consolidate the siege of Madrid by cutting the Madrid-Valencia road and therefore to intensify an already acute food shortage. General Orgaz, the Nationalist tactical commander, had some 40,000 troops at his command, many of them African. To maintain discipline and morale, Nationalist officers mixed uncommitted and potentially unreliable conscripts with combat veterans and political militants. Prisoners with leftist sympathies whom the Insurgents had conscripted found themselves fighting on the same side as dedicated Falangists and requetés. Rains forced the Nationalists to wait until 6 February to launch their assault. At first, it appeared that the Insurgents would attain their objectives. Air strikes of the German Condor Legion supported Orgaz's heterogeneous forces. Nazi aid to the Nationalists was largely devoted to supporting this aviation force, which proved to be the most ruthless and effective in the war. The Nationalist intelligence service functioned well and enabled them to attack the weakest and least experienced units, which offered little resistance and fled.[81]

Nevertheless, the Popular Army recovered and achieved a degree of coordination and combativeness that it seldom equaled. Certain Republican units fought bravely, notwithstanding the depletion of munitions supplies and the failure of the quartermaster to provide food and drink for two days. Forty new Russian planes helped them to achieve air supremacy over the Condor Legion. The Republic's aerial success stimulated its troops, and the intervention of the International Brigades blunted the offensive. They were more militarily experienced and probably more motivated than many Spanish Republicans. By 16 February Orgaz had clearly failed to achieve his goal of cutting the highway. A week later the exhausted fighters on both sides could no longer carry on the battle. The Jarama showed that both camps needed foreigners to supplement insufficient native militancy. Nearly 3,000 Internationals were killed or wounded, including many of the best volunteers. The Internationals' courage was equaled by the Regulares of Ceuta and of Alhucemas, who also suffered extremely heavy casualties. Nationalists endured over 6,000 killed or wounded, Republicans over 7,000. The sacrifices of the Army of the Center arrested the despair caused by the Republican defeat at Málaga. Notwithstanding, a Nationalist general believed that the Republic never recovered from this deprivation of its bravest and most aggressive infantrymen.[82]

The Battle of Guadalajara was yet another attempt by Nationalists to rupture the post-Jarama stalemate around Madrid. After the Jarama, troops adopted defensive strategies. The franquistas knew that Republican defensive lines in the Guadalajara sector were weak and without fortifications, since 10,000 men guarded a front of eighty kilometers. Republican soldiers lived peacefully, disregarded discipline, and communicated infrequently with high-ranking officers. Franco decided to relieve pressure on Orgaz's tired and discouraged forces near the Jarama. In early March the Generalísimo concentrated approximately 50,000 soldiers around Sigüenza (Guadalajara). Twenty thousand of them were legionarios, Moroccans, and some Carlists—led by Moscardó, the hero of Toledo's Alcázar. Nationalists lacked sufficient numbers and depended on Italian forces—30,000 Italian volunteers of the Corpo Truppe Volontarie (CTV)—to seize the initiative. The Italians were well clothed and equipped, and the Fascist expeditionary force possessed such an abundance of foodstuffs that they refused to eat Spanish dishes such as chickpeas. In contrast, their Spanish allies possessed only requisitioned cars, sandals, and knives to save on ammunition. A member of a family that the Falange dispossessed in the province of Burgos reported that the well-furnished Italian soldiers tended to loot less than Civil Guards.[83]

The Italian Fascists' easy success at Málaga encouraged overconfidence. The Duce expected a spectacular victory since the Republican troops facing them had earned a lackadaisical reputation. On 8 March the Italians broke through the front and quickly dominated the heights, but bad weather slowed the Nationalist advance and limited the use of the Condor Legion. The poor Spanish roads delayed Italian convoys. Once the offensive was under way, the Insurgents and their Italian allies had to face some of the toughest Republican forces, which had been hastily assembled to halt the threat of the encirclement of Madrid. Enrique Líster's 11th Division, which was composed of the German XI International Brigade, a Basque Brigade, and the ex-Communist First Brigade, was stationed between Trijueque and Torija. The competent anarchist commander, Cipriano Mera, headed a division that included the XII International Brigade led by the anti-Fascist Garibaldi battalion. For five days, from 12 to 17 March, the CTV contained with difficulty counterattacks from a Republican elite immeasurably aided by a revitalized air force. Republican airfields at Alcalá and Guadalajara were close to the battle zone, and their hard surfaces made them less dependent on inclement weather.

Nationalist support services broke down. Treatment of the Insurgent wounded was deficient. Reports criticized the inability of the Nationalist quartermaster to provide hot meals, warm drinks, and alcoholic beverages. Disheartened and demoralized Italians, who were inadequately clothed for a winter battle, abandoned their equipment, brutalized local villagers, and fled in small groups of two or three. Nationalist observers criticized the faint-heartedness of both Italian officers and men. Fascist generals and their staff refused to leave their vehicles to stop their troops from breaking and running. For his part, General Roatta was angry that his Spanish allies never launched even a minor counteroffensive that would have tied down Republican reserves and prevented them from massing against him.[84]

The Italian retreat, which was sudden enough to be termed a rout, stopped a few miles short of the bases from which their advance had started. Roatta complained that a good number of men were "older married men who are not very aggressive."[85] Many lacked the most elementary military training. In other words, elements of the Italian expeditionary force suffered the same lack of motivation as their allies and enemies. The ill-named Battle of Guadalajara (which was untouched by the fight) once again confirmed the stalemate around Madrid. Both sides suffered important casualties. About 2,000 Republicans were killed and 4,000 wounded. Four hundred Italians died, 1,800 were injured, and 500 were captured or missing. The Popular Army snared hundreds of prisoners and large quantities of weapons and supplies during the battle.

International contributions to Guadalajara were even more significant than at the Jarama. The presence of tens of thousands of foreign activists and mercenaries once again bolstered the militancy of both sides. Without their heroism and sacrifice, the Spanish war would have ended much more quickly and with less bloodshed. The defensive victory at Guadalajara, which the Republican chief of staff, Vicente Rojo, called "the most rapid and orderly concentration of forces ever carried out by the Republic," sparked elation among anti-Fascists all over the world. Even for a good number of Insurgents, the Italian defeat represented a triumph of Spanish bravery over Italian arrogance and pretensions. At Franco's headquarters, the Italian defeat created an "absurd sense of satisfaction." Spanish Nationalists gloated over the failure of Mussolini, who had made little secret of the contempt he felt for Franco and his Spaniards (who, according to the Duce, "had a weak desire to fight and lacked personal bravery").[86]

As at the Jarama, the Nationalists had once again failed to encircle the capital. Franco was forced to abandon his plans for a quick end to the war through the conquest of Madrid, and the struggle for the capital would not resume on a large scale until the end of the war. The battles for Madrid demonstrated that the victory of rural elements over urban Spain would occur only in a war of attrition. The Nationalist failure to take the capital should not mask the fact that they were able to alter their strategy from a quick victory in a colonial-style war to fight a protracted struggle, where a mobilized political economy would prove the deciding factor. It is significant that the study of what is today called political economy emerged during the English civil war, when Parliament ultimately achieved logistical superiority and victory over the Royalists.[87]

WAR OF ATTRITION

Stymied by resistance around Madrid, Franco's decision to conquer the north was probably his wisest. He adopted a gradualist strategy and confronted the enemy region by region. The Generalísimo would modify his plan only to respond immediately to each and every Republican counteroffensive. Nationalist divisions became increasingly effective in combined-arms coordination of infantry and artillery and "liberated" the north. The conquest of the north gave the demographic and, just as importantly, the industrial advantage to the Nationalists. Tens of thousands of young men either volunteered or were drafted and, if captured, recycled into Nationalist forces. Exceptions were made for Republican officers and snipers, who were executed. Requetés risked the same treatment if they fell into "red" hands. The north's skilled labor, factories, and workshops would help turn the tide in a long war. The Nationalist command was able to build a potent force of maneuver that would be quickly transported to halt the Republican attacks at Teruel and on the Ebro and launch effective counteroffensives.[88]

Following the stalemates around Madrid, attention once again turned to the war in northern Spain. After the fall of San Sebastián, Basque Republicans maintained 30,000 to 40,000 militiamen of their own, along with several thousand anarchist and UGT volunteers. Compared to their enemies, the Basques were poorly armed. Their weapons, especially small arms, were so varied that it was difficult to supply them with appropriate ammunition. The services of the Republican Army of the North functioned poorly, and soldiers and sappers possessed only sandals and summer clothing in the winter of 1936–37. Many men became ill. Jealous of their autonomy, they were reluctant to cooperate with the national government. For its part, Madrid was hesitant to aid the region. In addition, there was considerable friction and distrust between the Basque Nationalists and the Popular Fronts of Asturias and Santander. The Basque leadership was bourgeois and Catholic, the Asturian and Santanderian were proletarian and anticlerical.[89]

As had occurred in the Russian and Chinese civil wars, in the north many rank-and-file soldiers on both sides were unclear about what they were fighting for (or against). They calculated the risk of being sent to prison or a concentration camp and abandoned the front when it was opportune. Mola's forces experienced "continuous" desertions, which—like their adversary—generally affected common soldiers, not officers. The frequency of desertions limited psychiatric casualties on both sides. Some mentally disturbed soldiers simply went home. Others were admitted into hospitals, where they constituted 2 to 3 percent of patients. The onset of bad weather in the fall of 1936 tested the commitment of Franco's troops. More deserted as the climate became colder and wetter. Most deserters were from specific regions—such as Galicia—where "great and secret leftist propaganda" was spread in the rear. Nationalists were more fortunate than Republicans since their deserters were often limited to Galicians and Catalans. Officers, including Moscardó, were frustrated that the extensive and sparsely covered front prevented competent surveillance and enabled the Catalans to defect. Their treason disheartened remaining soldiers. In the Basque country, Nationalist officials recommended ceaseless vigilance and the establishment of a system of informers to stop enemy propaganda. Nationalists threatened to deport family members of any known deserters or "red" sympathizers. Peasants became resigned to serving on the Nationalist side, especially when they believed that Franco would win. Many also feared that the "reds" who attacked the church would also deprive them of their plots and livestock.[90]

After the Battle of the Jarama, the Nationalist leadership temporarily accepted the deadlock around Madrid and began to concentrate 40,000 to 50,000 troops under the command of Mola for an offensive in the north. They included Carlists, Moroccans, and Italians. Just as importantly, the Condor Legion again provided air support and operated virtually unopposed, since its Basque adversaries had no antiaircraft artillery and few planes. German aviation was able to terrorize at will civilian populations and untrained troops. The latter, lacking experience and weaponry to counter aircraft, deserted from even fortified positions. Observers agreed that the dominance of fascist aviation was crucial for the Nationalist victory in the north, but it was by no means the only factor. The lack of confidence and cooperation between the Basques and their Asturian and Santanderian allies hindered the defense of Vizcaya. Each regional authority printed its own money and several types of currencies circulated. The lack of a single currency discouraged commerce and promoted urban vouchers that could not be exchanged beyond municipal limits. Peasants refused to accept local currencies and wanted only Bank of Spain script.[91]

The Basques planned to defend the provincial border of Vizcaya, while constructing a defensive "Iron Ring" around the city of Bilbao, their industrial base. The ring had been conceived in October 1936 as a way to utilize Basque industrial expertise and manpower. They might have better used their energies feeding their own soldiers, who ate badly, and the civilian population, which starved. In late April as the Nationalists approached Bilbao, the Condor Legion destroyed Guernica (Vizcaya), foreshadowing the mass aerial destruction initiated by the Third Reich during World War II and then intensified by the Western Allies. The center of the town was reduced to rubble;

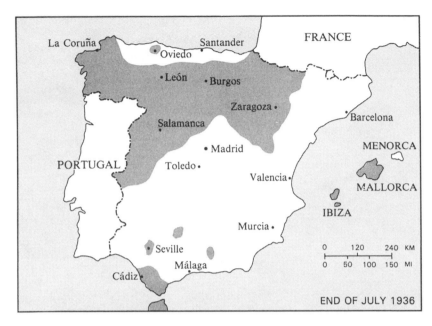

END OF JULY 1936

MARCH 1937

Expansion of the Nationalist zone, 1936–39

La Coruña
• Oviedo
Santander
• León • Burgos
Zaragoza •
Salamanca
• Madrid
PORTUGAL
Toledo •
Valencia •
Murcia •
• Seville
Málaga
Cádiz •
FRANCE
• Barcelona
MENORCA
MALLORCA
IBIZA

0   120   240 KM
0   50   100   150 MI

OCTOBER 1937

La Coruña
• Oviedo
Santander
• León • Burgos
Zaragoza •
Salamanca
• Madrid
PORTUGAL
Toledo •
Valencia •
Murcia •
• Seville
Málaga
Cádiz •
FRANCE
• Barcelona
MENORCA
MALLORCA
IBIZA

0   120   240 KM
0   50   100   150 MI

JULY 1938

several hundred were killed and many more wounded. Conceivably the goal of the bombing was to intimidate the population of the industrial towns of the Ría de Bilbao so that they would offer minimal opposition. The Madrid/ Valencian government was able to send the Basques a few planes, but they still proved incapable of seriously challenging Nationalist air superiority. Many Basques felt that the Republic had abandoned them, and their resistance did not impress their enemies. Throughout the Vizcaya campaign, Basques continued to leave behind the dead and wounded. During their soldiers' "shameful" and panicked flight, they even abandoned "their divine and marvelous chefs who had prepared a sumptuous and exquisite menu." These cooks were not shot but instead integrated into the unit. Their skills provided welcome relief from the staples of canned tuna, sardines, and marmalade that the Carlist Tercios habitually carried in their backpacks.[92]

The material and moral deficiencies of Republican forces in the north resembled those responsible for the earlier defeat in Málaga. The Nationalist advantage in artillery and aviation, the ineffectiveness of the Republican plan of defense, and the demoralization of Republican troops permitted the penetration of Iron Ring on 12 June. Bilbao was ordered to put up a stiff defense but did not do so. In fact, behind the backs of their Republican partners, the Basque Nationalists undertook secret negotiations to surrender to their Italian Fascist foes. Two hundred thousand fled before the Nationalists entered the city on 19 June. Both officers and men deserted massively. The flights of the former are usually blamed on the distrust and pessimism of the latter, but the reverse could also be true. At any rate, Bilbao would not be Madrid, and its capture more than compensated for the Nationalist setback at Guadalajara in March.

When the franquistas entered Bilbao, they put into practice their policy of "practical generosity" and fed a city that was starved for food. The Carlists of the Tercio de Lácar shared their rations with the hungry of Bilbao. Like Allied soldiers on the Western Front during World War I, Nationalist troops were overweighed with supplies. During the Bilbao campaign, they carried fifteen or twenty kilos of provisions and equipment. The Navarre quartermaster claimed that it was also able to feed the rear, spending millions of pesetas in the month of June alone. Supplying hungry towns was of incalculable political importance. The Falangist women of the AS often undertook the job, which reflected the traditional female role as nurturer. They had the task to put into practice the Francoist slogan "No Spaniard without bread." Under strict discipline that forbade them from loitering at the front, the Falangist women's organization (Sección Feminina, or SF) distributed clothes to the troops. The female Hilfsarbeit and Winterhilfswerks in Nazi Germany had inspired Pilar Primo de Rivera, the leader of the SF, to initiate similar welfare programs in Spain. Well after the war, the protofeminist Pilar, the sister of

Postcard image of the games of the Sección Feminina, which contains a quote from Franco: "If we desire a greater Spain, we should not try to straighten old trees; we must look toward youth." Southworth Spanish Civil War Collection, Mandeville Special Collections Library, University of California, San Diego.

the founder of the Falange, José Antonio, retained her loyalty not only to her brother but also to the Nazi model and to the Führer himself.[93]

Republican price controls and rationing had not prevented hunger in its northern zone, whose population had allegedly assaulted trains carrying food supplies. Basque and other children from the north who were sent into exile to the Soviet Union expressed grateful astonishment that their meals were so abundant in their new country. One of the great weaknesses of the Basque defense was its inability to nourish not only its civilian population but also its troops. They depended nearly totally on foreign, especially British, shipments of victuals. Basque dependence inspired the witticism that Bilbao would never fall to the fascists because the Basques would give it first to Great Britain. The Nationalist blockade was far from complete, but nonetheless it discouraged normal trade and regular fishing activity.[94]

The victories in the north tipped the scales and reinforced the Insurgent advantage in resources. By October 1937, Nationalists controlled 70 percent of Spanish territory, 60 percent of population, 61 percent of olive oil, 65 percent of Spanish wheat, 67 percent of fish, 68 percent of potatoes, 59 percent of poultry, 67 percent of goats, 70 percent of pork, 70 percent of sheep, 75 percent of beef, 80 percent of steel, and 66 percent of explosives. By the end of 1937 rice production was the only major food product in which

Republicans retained superiority. Nationalists dominated 68 percent of the merchant marine and held the modern gasoline supply facilities of Bilbao and San Sebastián.[95]

Republicans prepared an attack to counter Nationalist victories in the north. After considerable discussion and disagreement, Loyalist leadership decided that the battle would take place near Brunete, fifteen miles west of Madrid and a quiet front since the January struggle at the Coruña highway. In early July about 50,000 of the best troops of the nearly 600,000-strong Popular Army concentrated to launch an attack that was supposed to envelop the besieging army from behind and thus lift the Nationalist grip on the capital. Republican troops had sufficient weapons, including Russian aircraft and tanks that were usually superior to Italian and German models. The Popular Army made an initial breakthrough on 6 July, but, as in other consequential confrontations, a small force of Nationalists mobilized quickly to check the attack. The Nationalist defense of the village of Boadilla was so firm that Republican officers, armed with loaded revolvers, had to stand behind their men and compel them to attack. The enemy's bravery and skill in defending positions around Majadahonda earned the admiration of Republican forces and their commissars. One Republican commander at Brunete, Gustavo Durán, reluctantly concluded that Nationalist forces generally showed more discipline and more capacity for maneuver than his side. By 13 July, Nationalist reinforcements had stemmed the offensive. The franquistas' rapid mobility recalled, oddly enough, the unusually nimble armies of the French Revolution.[96]

The fortitude and tenacity of small garrisons of Moors and Falangists who were stationed in small towns and villages surrounding Brunete allowed Nationalist officers enough time to call up several hundred trucks full of reinforcements, who were able to check Republican assaults. Franco's decision to relieve the Alcázar strengthened small-group resistance, provided an example of timely relief, which repeated itself in major battles throughout the civil war, and reinforced trust between frontline garrisons and a high command that spared no effort to support its besieged.[97] Casualties were extremely high, and medical personnel remembered the Battle of Brunete as among the bloodiest of the entire struggle. The Nationalists lost approximately 10,000 men, the Republicans 25,000, many of whom were among the most able and militant troops. The Battle of Brunete may have retarded the fall of Santander, but it failed to break the siege of Madrid. In the end, the Republic lost more than it gained.

On 23 August, the Popular Army initiated a series of actions that aimed— as had the Battle of Brunete—to divert Nationalist efforts in the north. The goal was to capture Zaragoza, an important regional center of almost 200,000 inhabitants. It had been a former anarchist stronghold whose quick seizure by Nationalists at the beginning of the conflict had embarrassed libertarians. Like Seville, Zaragoza was one of the few urban capitals of an essentially rural Nationalist Spain. Both sides had tolerated the quiet and frequently unguarded front near the city for almost a year. Significant desertions from the Nationalists seemed to have encouraged the Republican assault.[98]

Codo-Quinto-Mediana-Belchite on the Aragon front was not a continuous line but a system of strategically located and colonial-style blockhouses. They reflected the general nature of the Spanish conflict, where hundreds of thousands of men covered 1,750 kilometers of front. In contrast, on the Western front during World War I, millions of soldiers held only 650 kilometers of front. The quantity of soldiers per mile was six times less than on the Western front in 1914, and the density of artillery was even smaller.[99] The Spanish conflict has often been seen as a continuation of World War I, both militarily and politically. In other words, it is often assumed that Spain extended the struggle between democracy and dictatorship in a modern trench war much like the Great War. However, the Spanish civil war more closely resembled what we would call today a Third World conflict, where logistic failures of provisions and transport often immobilized troops.

The Republicans paid a high price for any territory they captured. Between 24 August and 6 September the Zaragoza offensive transformed itself into a battle for the much less significant town of Belchite (3,000 inhabitants). Thousands of Republican troops attacked on 24 August, and, as on other fronts, a small number of dedicated Nationalist troops halted the advance. The requetés were told that their job was to resist any enemy attack for at least six hours so that reinforcements from Zaragoza could arrive. The Carlists had limited ammunition and targeted the charging horses of their enemies. Their excellent fortifications permitted them to hold out for many hours against overwhelming numbers. Most died fighting, even though they were supported by Nationalist aviation that bombarded Republican forces while airdropping supplies. Short of food and water, Belchite's defenders finally surrendered to the Popular Army on 6 September. The Republicans took a few requetés prisoner and apparently treated them well. Local resistance around Belchite had slowed down, if not stopped, the offensive. Nationalist commanders transferred reinforcements from Castile—many of whom were veterans of Brunete—who blocked the Republican offensive's main objective of capturing Zaragoza. Their engagement showed the combat effectiveness of what has been called "primary group cohesion," that is, where buddies in a unit take priority over other collective and individual loyalties, including family ties. It is this melding of the individual into a small community of comrades that is the essential building block of the military. Nationalist small-group cohesion was reinforced by the confidence that their command would spare no effort to rescue besieged units. Republican efforts in Aragon did not succeed in diverting sufficient Nationalist troops from the north to alter the outcome there. Despite the capture of Belchite, Prieto, now minister of defense, was understandably depressed that approximately 10,000 Republican troops who fought 7,000 defenders had hardly advanced.[100]

The campaign for Santander began on 14 August. Republicans controlled the heights of the Cantabrian range, but Nationalists possessed the advantage in weaponry, especially in artillery and aviation. Quickly, on 16 August the Nationalists captured the armaments factory at Reinosa. Next, the Italian and Spanish Black Arrows broke through the front by the sea. On 26 August the Nationalist Army of the North walked into Santander and captured Castile's only port. Resistance collapsed quickly, and as thousands of men fled, they discarded all kinds of weapons and materials. The loss of Santander constituted another major defeat for the Republic. The conquering Italian CTV fed the hungry civilian population of the Castilian port.

The final chapter of combat in the north began in Asturias on 1 September. Progress was slow given the mountainous terrain and the toughness of certain Asturian units who bravely battled a clearly superior enemy. The heroism of Asturian troops surpassed the Basques or Santanderians. Courage, though, could not compensate for the failure of the distribution system in the north. The lack of communication with the center reinforced the Nationalist advantage in supplies and weapons. In the end, the region fell to the Insurgents in seven weeks. They had planned well for the mountain war that Asturian geography imposed. Their columns could not use the roads that Republican forces had "carefully destroyed," but Insurgent mule trains, composed of herds of hundreds, overcame this obstacle, even if soldiers were reduced to consuming the native products of apples (and its derivative, cider), cabbage soup, and occasionally fresh milk. In contrast, Republican forces lacked both mules and horses to supply their mountain forces. Nationalist aviation, composed almost entirely of German planes and personnel, went unchallenged. On 15 October Insurgent forces linked up in the mountain town of Infiesto, and panic spread among Asturian defenders. The Condor Legion returned from the Aragon front and carpet bombed the trenches of the Asturian miners. On 21 October the Insurgents entered the port city of Gijón, which they sacked and looted. As in Santander, they found large stores of unused supplies.[101]

The Nationalist victory in the north meant the conquest of the wealthiest and most densely populated region. The Republican northern army surrendered en masse. Two hundred thirty thousand combatants were lost or quickly recycled as Nationalist soldiers. The captured north would provide Insurgents with sufficient reserves to counter Republican attacks and offensives elsewhere. Nationalists were able to exploit the Asturian coalfields and the industries of the Basque country. Very quickly, the franquistas mobilized the northern war industries, which had remained stagnant and unproductive under Republican control. Since the whole northern coast fell to the Nationalists, they could henceforth concentrate their naval efforts in the Mediterranean. At the same time, their entire army could move south. Many historians have commented that the loss of the north was the severest blow to the Republic, which forfeited approximately 25 percent of its manpower, much of its aviation and pilots, and more than 50 percent of its industrial potential.[102]

Nationalists celebrated the conquest with feasts. The Navarrese were as proud of their culinary achievements as they were of their purely military ones. For example, after the capture of Durango, requetés were able to eat "rice pudding for dessert," always a favorite, which was taken from "the enormous warehouse of the Basque government's quartermaster." They also consumed "succulent paellas." Special banquets fêted a collective medal awarded to a brave company, patron saint's days, individual promotions, or significant victories—for example, the fall of Bilbao in June 1937. In July 1937, Carlists celebrated the Festival of Saint Ignatius, "Spanish Captain of the Armies of Christ," with an "extraordinary meal" in the presence of their commander, Colonel Rafael García Valiño. Other less formal victory celebrations—such as one in Bárcena de Pie de Concha (Cantabria) in August 1937—were accompanied by intense and loud chanting encouraged by the availability of large quantities of wine. During these festivities, a truck loaded with peaches, plums, pears, and various sorts of melons arrived from Navarre. After the conquest of the entire north in October 1937, García Valiño invited his soldiers to dine at a fine hotel, where they were deliciously fed and luxuriously lodged. After digestives, cigars circulated among the conquerors. Whether smoked in a fancy restaurant or after cold rations on an active front, cigars bolstered self-esteem and made the men feel like "enriched plutocrats." The ritual of a special meal together—often in a superior urban hotel—was a way of thanking soldiers for their success and of solidifying group unity. The ability of the quartermaster to provide, even sporadically, hot meals provided welcome relief from tinned food. Cooks and mule drivers prided themselves on their ability to deliver warm multicourse meals under dangerous conditions to frontline soldiers. The Carlists considered repasts "sacred" and believed that they had resisted their liberal enemies in the nineteenth century because they were better fed.[103]

After the fall of Gijón in late October, Republican intelligence information revealed that Franco was again planning to attack Madrid. The Republican high command proceeded to launch a new offensive, which it expected would throw the Nationalists off balance. Republicans chose the Aragon town of Teruel, a minor provincial capital with 17,000 inhabitants and an unenviable reputation for the harshest climate in Spain. The struggle over its possession announced the centrality of the Aragon theater in 1938. The fight to control this region would decide the outcome of the war. The Republican high command gathered 77,000 troops, 3,000 motor vehicles, and 2,000 horses, impressive logistical achievements. The battle did not initially involve the International Brigades, and it was hoped that it would remain a purely Spanish affair. Republicans inaugurated the top-secret Teruel offensive on 15 December. Like the previous surprise attack at Brunete, it achieved immediate success. Soon, however, the Popular Army met stiff resistance from a small (approximately 4,000 men) Nationalist garrison stationed in the town of Teruel.[104]

Although Republicans were able to achieve their initial objective, the ferocity of a much smaller number of Nationalist defenders again stymied their strategy. Insurgent troops who held Teruel, however, had not sufficiently fortified their position, and the Republican vanguard managed to enter the city on 19–20 December. Despite the reversal of roles—the Nationalists were defenders and the Republicans attackers—the hand-to-hand fighting resembled that of Madrid's University City in November 1936. The Condor Legion supported the defenders from the air. What had previously occurred so often on the Republican side befell the Nationalists at Teruel, and scarce supplies of food and drink led to the latter's demoralization. After four days without supplies, the "reds" lured Nationalist soldiers away from their positions with the bait of bread and water. Republican offers of sustenance and peace dissolved commitment and induced Insurgent fighters to capitulate. On 8 January after a valiant effort recalling the Alcázar defense, the Nationalist garrison finally surrendered.[105]

Opinion in the Nationalist zone was profoundly shocked and upset by Republican success, the first time the Popular Army had been able to capture an enemy provincial capital. The Generalísimo felt compelled either to respond to the Republican challenge or lose both national and international prestige. He decided to forgo his plan for a Madrid offensive and concentrated his efforts on recapturing Teruel. In contrast to the situation at Brunete, Franco no longer had many of his finest troops tied down by the campaign in the north. The Nationalist counterattack became increasingly effective. Certain Republican brigades defending Teruel bravely withstood some of the most violent Insurgent aviation, artillery, and tank assaults of the war, while others abandoned their lines. The massive draft in the Republican zone remedied the manpower loss of the Army of the North but had filled the ranks with replacements who had little training or will to fight.

Teruel was the great winter battle of the war, and neither side was ready to confront the cold. Dozens froze to death because of insufficient clothing, boots, or blankets while temperatures descended to -12°C. Frostbite took a toll on countless fingers and toes. Some Nationalist soldiers tried to stay awake by drinking large quantities of coffee but died frozen in their sleep. Inexhaustible requetés chanted all the way to the front and even during the battle itself until the "cruel cold" froze their spirits. Fires, which revealed their position to the enemy, were not permitted. On New Year's Day 1938 the quartermaster managed to provide the first (cold) meal for the men at three o'clock in the afternoon. Mules carrying needed provisions lost their way in the blizzard or fell into unseen pits. Their drivers, usually Andalusians, were sometimes helpless to revive them. One *mulero* had to relieve his beast of the 150 kilos he was carrying and affectionately coax the poor animal to stand up. By 3 January the temperature had fallen to -18°C, and—prefiguring the Battle of Stalingrad—meals arrived frozen. The soldiers managed to re-heat them, but the food and wine had lost all taste. Requetés found large tins—probably from the Soviet Union, which sent massive food aid to the Re-public in 1937—of corned beef in the "red" trenches, but the cold prevented thawing and eating them. Their own cans of tuna had to be sawed into frozen pieces. Sickness—rare in December—began to multiply in January. Evacu-ation of the wounded was difficult, if not impossible. Hundreds of deser-tions from each side demonstrated that both camps had difficulty feeding and clothing their troops in winter battle. On New Year's Day, the combination of the cold and the intense machine-gun fire panicked North African stretcher bearers, who dropped a wounded officer on the ground in order to flee more quickly. In response, fellow Regulares clubbed them to death. On 22 January the Tercio was relieved and counted 200 dead or wounded who had been sent to hospitals in the rear. By 4 February when the unit had returned to the fray, the enemy offered much less resistance. At the end of the first week of Febru-ary, the food and weather improved.[106]

By the third week of February, Nationalist counterattacks and the supe-riority of their artillery and aviation forced the Popular Army to abandon Teruel itself. Many hungry Republican soldiers surrendered en masse with-out offering significant resistance. One of the principal motivations for ad-vancing rapidly was the possibility of capturing tobacco, food, clothing, and drink from the enemy. Conversely, a key stimulus for surrender was to eat the enemies' ample rations. Requetés captured tinned meat, cognac, wine, and tobacco. The Nationalists took 14,500 prisoners and found 10,000 Repub-lican corpses. Hundreds and perhaps thousands of others abandoned their arms as they escaped the provincial capital. Although the Nationalists suf-fered losses of nearly 44,000 during the Battle of Teruel, Prieto—the minister of defense, whom French journalists incorrectly labeled "the only great man of the Republic"—became not a Spanish Clemenceau but rather a convinced defeatist.[107]

The prevailing calm in the south and center permitted Nationalists to transfer the bulk of their forces eastward and to prepare a major post-Teruel offensive toward the Levante and Catalonia. Between Zaragoza and Teruel, Franco concentrated 100,000 men, hundreds of Italian and German planes, and dozens of tanks. The knowledge that Republican troops and civilians were weakened by material shortages, especially the lack of food, bolstered Nationalist morale. On 9 March a devastating artillery and aerial barrage began the offensive. The dominance of Insurgent aviation, estimated at four to one, demoralized even the best Republican troops. Aviation attacks alarmed the men but, according to senior officials, were never sufficiently intense to justify a massive disengagement. A desperate Republican political commissar preferred to take his own life rather than fall into the hands of enemy crusaders.[108]

Belchite, which Republicans had conquered at such great cost eight months earlier, and Quinto (Zaragoza) fell quickly. Tank formations using German panzer tactics encircled entrenched Loyalist troops while aircraft bombed them when they retreated. In their romp through a number of conquered Aragon villages, some Nationalist troops engaged in looting of household goods. The Moors, in particular, strengthened their already widespread reputation for sacking, massacre, and raping civilians. In early April Franco's forces captured Tremp and Lérida, whose Popular Front could raise only a few dozen men for a last-ditch defense. The lack of truck transportation prevented the arrival of sufficient reinforcements. The capitulation of both towns was a severe blow to the Republican effort. Lérida's fate showed that the Loyalists had lost yet another provincial capital. In addition, the fall of Tremp, which supplied Barcelona with much of its electricity, forced Spain's greatest industrial city to depend upon outdated steam-generating plants. Industrial production was adversely affected, and its collapse endangered the entire region. Hydroelectric power in Catalonia was the equivalent of coal during the Russian and Chinese civil wars. The side that controlled the power sources would be victorious.[109]

Militia units integrated into a greater mass of maneuver composed an essential element in the Nationalist drive to the sea. The Popular Army proved unable to counter the Nationalist offensive with its own reserves, which the Insurgents had demonstrated were absolutely necessary in a trench war with extensive fronts. The Nationalists and their Italian allies, equipped with excellent means of transport and regular food supplies (coffee, bread, wine, and an inexhaustible stock of almonds), marched to the sea, overcoming various levels of Republican resistance, and arriving at Vinaroz on 15 April 1938. Thousands of Popular Army troops surrendered, and Nationalist forces were repeatedly ordered to respect their lives. The victors took advantage of their conquest to bathe in the Mediterranean and to rid themselves of their lice. With difficulty, they washed in salt water with the harsh Quartermaster's soap and gorged themselves on local oranges. After the fall of Vinaroz, the division of the Republic resembled the crucial separation of the Confederacy that General Ulysses S. Grant had executed during the U.S. Civil War.[110]

The success of the Nationalist spring offensive raised the prospect of immediate Loyalist defeat. Franco believed that he could quickly capture Valencia and the rest of Catalonia. The Republic seemed doomed but was able to survive for several reasons. The persistent fear of French intervention, which aimed to prevent a German ally on its southern border, may have convinced Franco to slow the offensive. The Generalísimo became alarmed that the conquest of Catalonia might provoke direct French assistance to the Republic and switched his objective to Valencia. From 17 March until 13 June, the French Republic allowed a new flow of arms and supplies, not all of Soviet origin (Czech shipments were significant), to its Spanish counterpart. The border opening was particularly important since Nationalist and Italian control of the Mediterranean made it very perilous for the USSR to ship its aid by sea. Plentiful equipment (including 300 Soviet airplanes and 25,000 tons of material) and fresh troops enabled Republicans to defend the Valencia region and thus halt the Nationalist advance. Despite the reclosing of the French border on 13 June, Russian supplies, purchased in part on credit, continued to flow to the Republic.[111]

The solid defenses of Valencia redeemed the Republican reputation damaged by the easy conquest of the Bilbao belt (*cinturón*). In addition, geography and climate helped the Loyalists. The mountainous terrain created numerous obstacles to the Nationalist advance. The solid bulk of the Maestrazgo constituted "a geographic maze well suited for defense." Republicans were also assisted by bad weather, which made offensive movements much more difficult. The abundant and profound fortifications around Valencia itself rendered Nationalist attacks futile. Republican aviation may have equaled Nationalist air power. Between 18 and 23 July, Franco's forces suffered thousands of casualties. General García Valiño fretted about several companies of Republican commandos engaging in sabotage missions behind his lines. Nevertheless, his elite forces maintained their morale. Requetés celebrated peaceful interludes during the drive through the treacherous Maestrazgo with "paella, veal, dessert, wine, and cognac" followed by customary chanting. Navarrese *Margaritas*, who took their name from the daisy flower and had been assigned to care for the considerable number of wounded, welcomed the beginning of summer with alcohol-fueled partying.[112]

Prime Minister Juan Negrín and his closest advisors decided that only a spectacular military action could alter the declining fortunes of the Republic. They especially wanted to relieve pressure on the Valencia and Extremadura fronts, where Nationalists were making some progress. As the site of a new offensive, they chose a bend of the Ebro River, between Fayón (Zaragoza) and Benifallet (Tarragona). The Battle of the Ebro, as it became known, would develop into the longest and bloodiest struggle of the entire conflict. After July, it may have been the Ebro offensive—not Republican fortifications—that was ultimately responsible for Loyalist control of Valencia. The Republican goal was to confuse communications between the Nationalists in the Levante and Catalonia and to restore, if possible, direct links between Catalonia and the rest of Republican Spain. The Popular Army concentrated 80,000 men and 100 heavy guns. Recent recruits, who were not the optimum fighting age, formed the overwhelming majority of many divisions.[113]

The Battle of the Ebro, which many have termed the "decisive" battle of the war, showed the ability of elite, often Communist, units of the Republic to launch a complicated and technically demanding attack, which the enemy did not suspect. The Ebro had been a quiet front, where both sides traded without any thought of firing on each other. As on many tranquil fronts throughout Spain, Nationalists exchanged food (cognac, sardine cans, jam, bananas, and tobacco) for manufactured goods (rolling paper, sandals, and clothes) produced in the Republican zone. They also swapped newspapers, although only the most convinced militants believed much contained in their pages. Nationalist soldiers were initially overwhelmed and did not resist, as they had at Brunete, Belchite, Teruel, and other battles. According to a requeté chaplain, the Battle of the Ebro "emboldened" the enemy, who initiated "a powerful counter-offensive."[114]

But soon the familiar pattern asserted itself: the Nationalists were able to quickly call up reserves. With great difficulty, they slowly advanced against a foe who resisted ferociously but showed little ability to maneuver or to infiltrate Nationalist positions. The lack of Republican aggressiveness in Extremadura and on other fronts allowed Nationalists to move the 74th Division from Villanueva de la Serena (Cáceres) to reinforce the Ebro line. Reorganized and reinvigorated elite units were transferred to the Ebro front. From the first day Nationalist domination of the air restricted Loyalist mobility. The entire Condor Legion and heavy artillery that were thrown into battle devastated Republican troops. Units of the Popular Army hoarded trucks and food supplies, and it proved especially difficult to transfer heavy artillery across the river. These deficiencies and the shortage of trains led to the suspension of planned offensives.[115]

It should be noted that the Republican attack on the Ebro coincided with the Nationalist conquest of the Serena pocket in Extremadura, leaving this very fertile region in Franco's hands. One of the reasons for the Nationalist victory in La Serena was that their forces on this front were better supplied than their Republican counterparts. Strategically, the loss of the Serena pocket meant the end of any Republican hope of separating the Nationalist armies in the north from those in the south. The defeat was also significant since only the lush lowland areas of Valencia matched the Serena Valley in agricultural wealth.[116]

The eventual failure of the Ebro offensive showed that Popular Army soldiers did not lack bravery but rather food and matériel. Like the German

Army on the Western Front during their offensives of the spring and summer of 1918, hungry and thirsty Republican soldiers slowed their advance to take advantage of the alcoholic beverages, tobacco, shoes, and clothing that their better-supplied enemy had abandoned. The first and perhaps only priority of the hungry is to satiate their appetite. Famished and thirsty soldiers are, of course, more likely to surrender. The search for basic commodities reflected the shortages of the Republican zone, where, for instance, tobacco became so valuable that it sometimes replaced inflated Republican currency as a medium of exchange. On the black market, six packs of Lucky Strikes purchased a horse steak.[117]

The shortage of shoes explained the difference in popularity among front-line troops between the poets Miguel Hernández and Rafael Alberti. Soldiers appreciated Hernández, a former goat herd who wore sandals, and were offended by the gleaming high boots of Alberti. Republican workers transporting heavy boxes of munitions over many miles had little to cover their feet. Their barely clod colleagues, only a few of whom could swim, crossed the river on rickety, improvised bridges or unstable small boats and then had to carry heavy combat equipment over twenty kilometers. They became completely exhausted. Their uniforms were often a bunch of rags. The bulk of soldiers had the same type of sandals and even guns as their fathers possessed in the North African and Cuban wars, and even as their grandfathers in the Carlist wars. These hempen sandals were unable to protect feet from pebbles, brambles, cold, or wetness. They "soak[ed] up moisture like blotting paper." Their enemies—Spanish and Moroccan—were relatively well-clothed and shod. So were certain Republican units behind the lines, a situation that led Rojo to complain directly to Negrín.[118]

Republican rations and water were sparse, especially in the mountains during July and August. The major source of liquid remained the Ebro, and provisioning depended on mule trains. Republican troops initially quenched their thirst by drinking strong wine that they found in local villages. Satiation of this sort led to indisposition and alcohol poisoning. Canned sardines, an occasional tin of Russian meat, and a bit of bread nourished the men but also aggravated their thirst. When soldiers ventured out of their protected positions to scour the countryside for food and drink, they became vulnerable to enemy aircraft and artillery. At the end of July, as a hungry Jim Lardner—the son of the writer, Ring, and the last American International Brigader to die in the war—left his parapet to pick apples, an enemy plane struck him, and he expired one month later. When Internationals were withdrawn from the battlefield at the end of September 1938, they were replaced by draft dodgers, prisoners, and deserters, who, compared to their foreign predecessors, had little desire to fight. The category of the self-injured multiplied on both sides during the Battle of the Ebro. Franco ordered that soldiers who wounded themselves be assigned the most dangerous tasks available. Like his leftist enemies, the Caudillo believed in "rehabilitation by work."[119]

Insurgent forces had fewer and less severe problems of logistics and transport. Nationalist soldiers shouted to the hungry enemy across the trenches the details of their daily diet. Their conditions of hygiene, clothing, shoes, and tobacco were consistently superior to that of their Republican foe. In general, medics rapidly evacuated the injured. In the most intense September days of fighting, stretcher bearers, working only at night, died trying to transport the wounded. The injured claimed to be well treated in Zaragozan hospitals, staffed by nurses "from all social classes who had abandoned their studies or their jobs when the fatherland was in danger." Their roads were open and immune to Republican aviation or artillery until very near the front. When necessary, trucks easily transported reserves and rushed in reinforcements and heavy guns. Nationalist elite forces outnumbered their adversaries, and Insurgent manpower reserves were much greater by the summer of 1938. Insurgent infantry was composed of 30 percent volunteers, a remarkably high percentage. Of these, two-thirds were Spanish and one-third foreigners, usually from North Africa.[120]

As in previous battles, volunteer units—legionarios, Regulares, *mehallas* (the sultan's force), Falangists, and requetés—remained the most valuable troops, whose training and performance were superior to other combatants. For instance, they were made aware—unlike their Republican counterparts— of the great costs of wasting munitions. Franco's elite forces, not conscripts, had borne the brunt of the fighting in the first two years of the conflict. This reliance on a limited number of relatively well-trained and motivated shock troops, not Franco's own personal desire to monopolize power, lengthened the war.[121] Not until mid-1938 did the Generalísimo begin to use his new mass army of over 1 million men, but choice troops still did much of the fighting in every major battle, including the Ebro. Chaplains may have sacrificed themselves as much as the elite forces. During the Battle of the Ebro, more than forty of them were killed or wounded in action. As in the Republican Army, young draftees were often militarily unreliable and ideologically unmotivated. However, the Insurgents blended these draftees with volunteers. The result of this mixture was a fighting force that was able to maneuver more effectively than its Republican enemy. Officers' amalgamation of volunteers and conscripts was an important factor in their triumph. The politically reliable were able to watch and control the uncommitted. For example, one corporal and two soldiers were routinely assigned to watch sixty conscripts who were subjected to "severe discipline." The Civil Guards were ready to assist them if insubordination occurred in the rear. The movements of recently drafted young men—usually eighteen- to nineteen-year-olds—were closely scrutinized.[122]

Nationalist infantry outnumbered Republicans by two to one and artillery by twenty-five to one. Their aviation—which some have labeled the "decisive" factor of the battles of 1938—was far superior. Franco calculated correctly that he could defeat the enemy in a war of attrition on the Ebro. His artillerymen, who in this war generally inflicted the most injuries but suffered the fewest casualties, were highly experienced. Their weapons were newer, in better condition, and malfunctioned less, thereby inflicting fewer accidental injuries on their operators than similar Republican arms. In the closing months of 1938, Nationalists received dramatically increased aid from the Germans. In the middle of November, Germany and Nationalist Spain signed a new agreement in which Franco's continuing need for arms induced him to make major concessions to his Nazi ally, which gained favorable mining rights and a Spanish promise to pay the entire expenses of the Condor Legion. In greater quantities than ever before, German weapons and matériel flowed rapidly to Nationalist forces. On the other side, despite bureaucratic obstacles and the exhaustion of the gold deposited in Moscow, the Soviets continued to ship supplies to the Republic; nevertheless, the badly needed material did not reach Catalonia until February 1939, when it was nearly too late to help Popular Army forces.[123]

Like their enemies, troops facing Republican attacks, especially those battling in the hills and mountains, sometimes lacked water and were compelled to drink wine, the only beverage available in large quantities. In fact, they even served it to their mules. Parched troops of both sides agreed to permit unhindered access to a well in no-man's-land until their officers put a stop to this reasonable arrangement. Nationalists overcame their shortage of tanker trucks by transporting in regular trucks large bars of ice insulated by bags to prevent spillage. Usually they had water, bread, sardines, jam, meat, milk, and even chocolate and coffee. The latter became increasingly valuable and harder to find as the war endured. Illegal trafficking of coffee—like clothes and shoes—grew intensively at the end of the conflict. The quartermaster could provision brand-name anis, cognac, and wafers. *Madrinas de guerra* (pen pals) sent their correspondents canned clams and crayfish. In fact, their good meals and clothes during the Ebro battle attracted both recruits and deserters. The Republican enemy thought Insurgents had "everything that they wanted." In August and at other times during the battle, Margaritas distributed sweets, liquors, and tobacco, and, in return, the young men recounted sanitized versions of their war stories. In September hot meals and mail from home were brought from the rear. They demanded—and usually got—well-flavored food. Spices, such as garlic, remained abundant and inexpensive.[124]

The Nationalists could fulfill their unwritten contract with their military and civilian populations. Their logistic strengths enabled them to sustain seven counteroffensives on the Ebro. The Republicans had concentrated their first-rate forces and much of their resources on the Ebro or in the defense of

Distribution of bread to the starving inhabitants of Barcelona after Insurgent troops had
entered the town. Thousands of hungry Barcelona inhabitants jammed the streets whenever
one of the distribution carts appeared. February 1939, Associated Press of Great Britain.
Southworth Spanish Civil War Collection, Mandeville Special Collections Library, University
of California, San Diego.

Valencia. Their corresponding weaknesses in quality and quantity of troops
and supplies in the center, Levante, Extremadura, and Andalusia made them
unable to launch more than one offensive simultaneously. Conversely, Nationalists were able to transfer troops from fronts where enemy forces were,
at best, second-rate and, at worse, famished. General Rojo seemed powerless
to make his various armies reinitiate hostilities in their own sectors to support the Ebro offensives. His recruiters were forced to round up both younger
(eighteen- to nineteen-year-old) and older (over thirty-year-old) men who
had already accumulated records as draft dodgers. Their commitment to the
Republican cause was mixed. Some became reliable fighters, but others attempted to desert.[125]

As casualties mounted on the Ebro, Popular Army soldiers began to
abandon the lines. Even well-armed Republican troops would surrender to
a lightly armed enemy. Provisioned franquistas offered deserters goat cheese,
tuna, jam, bread, and packages of cigarettes. Catalans serving in the Republican army who had the good fortune to be captured by their countrymen in
the Tercio de Montserrat were given chocolate, a treat they had not tasted for

a long time. In Andalusia and Extremadura where the Tercio de Montserrat was transferred to halt the Popular Army's diversionary offensive of January 1939, Republican soldiers—many very young who were nourished mainly by acorns—surrendered without resistance to the Catalan requetés.[126]

During the Battle of the Ebro, Nationalists suffered comparably few desertions. Many potential turncoats—leftist militants who had saved their skins by joining Franco's forces—had already abandoned Nationalist lines by 1938. In January, once the roads were cleared of the enemy, the Insurgent troops received copious meals, drink, tobacco, and draftees to relieve them. By mid-November Nationalists claimed to have buried 13,275 Republican soldiers, a disagreeable task usually carried out by prisoners. Franco called the Ebro "the greatest, hardest, and ugliest battle of the whole war." The clash generated enormous casualties, but many of them were caused by poor food, thirst, and exhaustion. Thus, it was fitting that the victory celebration of the Tercio de Montserrat was an enormous banquet, a half dozen courses and a dozen wines and liquors. As Franco's troops advanced into Catalonia, some shared their cold rations with hungry Catalan families. Their offers of sardines and other staples helped ease communication with young women who spoke little Castilian.[127]

On 26 January 1939 Yagüe's troops entered Barcelona and encountered virtually no resistance. The Catalan capital, which doubled as the capital of the Basque country in exile, did not repeat the heroic defenses of Madrid and Valencia. It should be recalled that the defense of Madrid occurred before the conflict turned into a war of attrition, during which large urban populations persistently suffered from acute hunger. The fall of Barcelona spurred severe infighting among Republicans. The sharpening internal struggles in the larger context of continuing logistical failures led to the collapse of the Republican effort. At the end of March 1939, Nationalist forces entered Madrid and easily completed the conquest of the Republican zone.

2

Authoritarian Political Economy

AGRICULTURE

When a British anti-Communist, Frank Thomas, arrived on a train from Lisbon to Salamanca in October 1936 to volunteer to fight for Franco, his fellow third-class passengers offered him an abundant and free breakfast of meat, cheese, and wine. When he reached Burgos, which would soon become the official capital of the movement, he noticed no shortages but rather provincial normality. As has been noted, both sides had to feed hundreds of thousands of soldiers, but the Nationalists accomplished this more ably. The Insurgent ability to provide sufficient food to maintain the morale of their troops was critical to their victory. It was especially important in preventing the kind of demoralization that afflicted the Popular Army. The men of the latter felt that authorities had broken their contract by not furnishing them with enough calories or clothes. The Republic should have copied the Bolsheviks, who had learned during the Russian civil war that supplying soldiers and their families with sufficient rations was the key to keeping desertion under control. To encourage a return to the ranks, Russian Communists awarded economic concessions to troops and their families, including an amnesty for peasant rebels and tax dodgers.[1]

The explanation for the adequate food supplies in Nationalist Spain and the lack of provisions in the Republican zone is usually geographical: The Nationalists controlled the great wheat-producing regions and much of the coasts and thus could better supply their forces. On the other hand, the Republicans were forced to feed large cities—Madrid, Barcelona, and Valencia. As in the case of foreign aid, it is assumed that recipients of either foreign or natural largesse will use them correctly and efficiently. This type of analysis is overly deterministic and Eurocentric. It ignores the cases of Chinese and Russian counterrevolutionaries, who also had foreign aid much greater than their enemies and held control of vast areas that could have been productive. Nor can this static analysis explain why the Republicans did not attack the food-rich areas of the enemy nor why the Nationalists were successful in conserving and expanding their zone.

78

The availability of food at a reasonable price has been attributed to a severe and continuous vigilance of hoarding and profiteering, but repression
played only a small part. Even though in August 1936 Nationalists permitted expropriations to finance the war, the regime—unlike the Soviets—never
developed a vast confiscatory apparatus to expropriate growers. The Franco
state was also much more restrained in its confiscations than its Republican enemy. Incentives for producers were largely sufficient. Indeed, the recent
historiographical concentration on repression, which is quite understandable after government policies that obscured terrible Nationalist violence for
forty years, has hidden the ability of the franquistas to supply their military and civilian populations during wartime. The focus on repression also
continues the political orientation of Spanish civil war historiography and
fosters the consequent neglect of social and economic issues. In the context
of twentieth-century counterrevolutions, the Nationalist ability was unique.
During the Russian civil war, Allied foreign observers depressingly concluded
that White officers had learned nothing from World War I, when nearly 2 million soldiers deserted, and continued to disregard the well-being of their men.
As in the Great War, the White command failed to supply its own troops in
Siberia and in South Russia.[2]

The franquista victory throws doubt on an analysis that attributes the loss
of Russian Whites to their political ineptitude and their lack of a credible
program of land reform.[3] Like the Russian Bolsheviks, although less radically, the Spanish Republicans pushed agrarian reform and even revolution
but nonetheless failed to win. The victory of reactionary Spaniards suggests
that progressive ideology and social radicalism may be less significant than
other factors, especially the ability to feed and clothe—however rudimenta-
rily—military and civilian populations. Lenin correctly predicted that Russian peasants would not fight for the Whites, but the Bolshevik leader did not
attribute this lack of peasant enthusiasm to the Whites' reluctance to engage
in land redistribution but rather to their inability to provide the essentials of
food, clothing, and other necessities that keep armies content.

Despite its ultrarevolutionary reputation, the Chinese Communist Party
(CCP) was willing to retreat from its program of revolution and even reform
in order to increase agricultural production. Whenever leftist enthusiasm for
overthrowing the old social order attained temporary ascendancy, the insis-
tent need for grain, fodder, and other agricultural commodities helped pull
the Communist leadership back toward a more moderate policy. The Chinese
Communists could not fight a war and radically change land ownership at the
same time. They realized that massive disruption and the dislocation of rich
and middle peasants would create a steep decline of production. Their policy
of reducing rents and interest payments, which was established during the war
against the Japanese, allowed peasants more surplus to feed the troops. The

expansion of Communist forces during World War II was based largely upon the "extent of disposable food surpluses." Some CCP cadres complained that land reform made army recruiting more difficult, since peasants wanted to stay at home and profit from their new holdings. On 4 May 1946 the Communist leader, Liu Shaoqui, urged efforts to win over "middle peasants": "If the rich peasants are hit too hard, the middle peasants will waver, and production in the liberated areas will be adversely affected."[4]

In early spring 1947 the CCP concluded that its attack on the more prosperous strata of the rural economy, in other words, on the renters and owners, had adversely affected production in Manchuria by reducing the supply of agricultural credit, seeds, draft animals, and fodder. The beneficiaries of its land reform program lacked the skills, experience, and labor power to produce a surplus for the market. In late 1947 the policy of "land to the tillers" was halted or delayed. At that time, Mao Zedong was concerned that the confiscation of land had cost the party too many potential allies. In 1948, a year of intensified fighting, the CCP stressed "the primacy of production in support of the war effort over that of deepening the revolution." In January 1948 CCP leaders attempted to embark on radical land reform to break the landlords' power at the local level, but "having learned from past experience, the party was careful not to let the land reform program get out of control. It tried to prevent excessive actions of the overzealous 'left.'" High-ranking cadres opposed radical land policy as "leftist opportunism" that would harm agricultural output. In April 1948 party agencies ordered the halt of land redistribution from the rich to the poor. On 25 May 1948 the CCP directed that land reform should not be carried out unless certain conditions were met. First, the area in question was "militarily secure"; second, the "masses" favored land reform; and third, cadres were ready to prevent the "spontaneous activity of the[se same] masses." Furthermore, no land reform should occur until the "GMD [Guomindang, Chinese Nationalist Party] reactionary forces" were eliminated. Thus, the "newly liberated areas" and party agencies abandoned land reform in favor of a return to the more moderate policy of rent and interest rate reduction that had been in effect during the Anti-Japanese War.[5]

The movements of Communist forces were usually "dictated by the necessity to avoid government troops and the desire to obtain the rice of the new harvest." The top priority of the Communist high command was "to acquire the cereal harvest." The party's ability to supply both "beans and bullets" astonished high-ranking American intelligence officials. To carry out the transport of the necessary victuals, the CCP conscripted with coercive methods similar to the GMD hundreds of thousands, if not millions, of peasants. The Communists imposed quotas on each village and threatened severe punishments for lack of fulfillment. In June 1948 a party organ reported that of the

30 million people under Communist control, only 4 million (13 percent) had undergone land reform. Chinese Communists once again showed their flexibility and adaptability.[6] They executed policies that restrained the revolution much more effectively than their brother party in Spain.

The Spanish Nationalists were conspicuous among all belligerents because they avoided the shortages that stymied their Republican adversaries, not to mention both Russian Whites and Chinese Nationalists. As has been seen, the more ample Nationalist supply of food encouraged wavering Republican troops to desert. Hungry deserters—who were often recycled into the Nationalist army—were especially noticeable in 1938, the last full year of the war. The franquistas captured 300,000 prisoners among Republican troops, 40,000 of whom were reprocessed as soldiers. Nationalist propaganda directed to Republican soldiers emphasized Insurgents' full stomachs more than any other theme, even though the Republic's "worthless" currency ran a close second. Nationalists boasted of the unadulterated "white bread of Franco," the most popular type until the rise of the ecological movement in the late twentieth century. Increasingly, though, Spaniards in Franco's zone consumed "whole meal bread," which came to be regarded as a partial solution to deepening wheat shortages. By the end of 1938, corn and other grains were regularly mixed into wheat bread in several provinces.[7]

Foreign observers confirmed the riches of Nationalist Spain in foodstuffs and its lack of inflation. A pro-Nazi German reported that from the very beginning of the war, the Insurgents were aware of the need for an increase in agricultural production to feed their army. The continuity and the normalcy of economic existence, the low cost of living, and the considerable buying power of the average wage also impressed foreigners in the Nationalist zone. A British consul reported that "in spite of the fact that Spain has for nearly a year been waging a civil war of the most bitter description, life in those parts of this consular district [Seville] dominated by Franco's forces still runs a relatively normal course. The principal activities of the district are agriculture and mining, and for the products of both the demand is greatest at the moment." From July 1936 to the first months of 1938, food prices remained very stable even as the costs of shoes and clothing soared.[8]

In Andalusia and Castile, Nationalists overturned agricultural "experiments," in other words, proletarian land occupations, and eventually returned the expropriated land to its original owners, whose titles were confirmed in September 1936. The formal return of property confiscated during the Republican and revolutionary periods was general throughout the Nationalist zone. As a counterpart, authorities—civil governors, Policía Rural, and local mayors—ordered owners of lands in recently "liberated" villages to begin to farm without delay. The Cámera Agrícola auctioned harvests of abandoned farms and leased their fields to willing labradores or other peasants. In the spring of 1937 the Policía Rural compelled farmers to plow their land and prune their fruit trees.[9]

The concern for agricultural production restrained the counterrevolution. Nationalists adhered to a pragmatic productivism rather than the putative variety of their Republican enemies, whom—Insurgents claimed with a good deal of validity—often left the fields in disarray. The needs of the armed forces took precedence over all else. When new owners were producing effectively, Nationalist authorities were reluctant to intervene to immediately return the land to its original proprietors. The priority given to the "Battle of Wheat" delayed property owners' repossession. Rather than immediately expelling the radical *yunteros* of Extremadura who had "illegally" occupied farms, agricultural authorities offered them incentives to produce grains and meat. Officials were pressured not to disrupt existing communities and to increase output by putting fallow lands under plow. The Junta de Defensa Nacional was willing to lend resources for planting and harvesting of land that the hated Republican agrarian reforms had awarded to peasants. Provincial juntas, which were active during the entire war, followed the lead of the Junta de Defensa Nacional, which decreed in August 1936 that production needs of a war economy must be upheld even at the short-term expense of property rights. In Andalusia and Extremadura the yunteros and others were permitted to remain and work until the end of the harvest season, 30 September 1937. Those who had participated in the land occupations of the spring of 1936 were gradually replaced by others whom landowners considered more reliable.[10]

Sharecroppers and renters were encouraged to obey their contract with landlords and pay them in kind, usually grain. The latter custom, which was still widespread throughout rural Spain in the 1930s, benefited landlords in a period of inflation. They could select (or reject) the sheaths of grain offered by their renters and speculate with the stored commodity. Owners were certainly delighted that Nationalists' steady territorial gains increased the demand for their wheat. Authorities tried to make available sufficient labor to harvest crops, if necessary by suspending local public works projects. One of the first decrees of the Junta de Defensa Nacional allowed for forced labor, a phenomenon common to all sides in many civil wars. Municipalities organized a revived *corvée* (medieval labor service) to take in the harvest and could fine those villagers who refused to help. Raimundo Fernández Cuesta, the minister of agriculture in Franco's first government in 1938, appointed the agronomist Ángel Zorrilla Dorronsora as head of the Servicio Nacional de Reforma Económica y Social de la Tierra (SNREST, later integrated with the SRA or Servicio de Recuperación Agrícola). His organization was willing to tolerate farming by "peasant communities" as long as they produced adequately. With victory, the SRA encouraged the return of all land to its original titleholders, but the process was, on occasion, painstakingly slow, at least in the eyes of owners. The SNREST eventually dispossessed 800,000 farmers, or 20 percent of the agricultural population, of some amount of property that they had received from the Republic. Following the war, the landholding pattern of the 1940s came to resemble that of the 1920s.[11]

WHEAT AND BREAD

Before the war, the overwhelming majority of Spanish cereal growers—approximately 1 million farmers—were unable to make a living wage. The relatively small minority who possessed animals that could plow their own fields and who could rent their beasts to others usually succeeded in making ends meet, but even they were totally dependent on the fluctuating price of wheat. An even tinier percentage of farmers made "adequate profit" during normal harvests. Thirty percent of the Spanish wheat harvest was produced by small owners, and this proportion rose to 40 percent in the most intense wheat-growing areas. Even in regions of large holdings, small producers and tenants continued to produce a significant percentage of the harvest.[12]

An early Christian democrat, Severino Aznar, qualified the family farmers of northern Spain as living in "a horrible human slaughterhouse," where infant mortality was among the highest in Spain. This was a shocking statement, since infant mortality rates in Seville in 1900 ranked third in the world, after Bombay and Madras. Northern Spain was a region of economically unhealthy *minifundios*. Zamora province contained nearly 100,000 proprietors, and almost all of them possessed at least one parcel in the countryside. To supplement their income, Ávila peasants had to work as part-time day laborers. In Álava, where microfundios also dominated, the average farm was ten to twelve hectares, frequently dispersed throughout the village. No large farmer existed in the entire province of Segovia. "On average each family with a team of animals" had only fourteen hectares. Many farmed half that number. As in the old regime, approximately 50 percent of the arable land was left fallow. The farming family itself consumed much of its wheat harvest. Plots were not only tiny but also scattered all over the village, making the use of most machinery uneconomical. An official provincial report in 1938 declared of Segovian peasants that "in general even when they work their own land they cannot make ends meet." They remained dependent on the village commons for grazing their animals. In Galicia massive conscription had weakened the ability of remaining family members to manage their tiny and dispersed plots. They needed workers and could not afford to hire day laborers. The poverty of the Castilian villages, such as Villar de Cobeta (Guadalajara), appalled Catalan requetés. Exposure to the misery of Andalusia led even devout Catholics to feel that the church had abandoned its mission of helping the poor.[13]

Despite this stubborn structural poverty, Spanish Nationalists were able to feed their civilian and military populations by providing incentives for wheat growers. As early as August 1936 the Comisión de Agricultura y Trabajo Agrícola attempted to use state power and financial resources to insure the continuity of wheat production. On 1 September, in the midst of the harvest season, the Junta de Defensa Nacional in Burgos decreed that the price of a metric quintal (100 kilograms) of wheat could not fall below 45 or 46 pesetas. This was undoubtedly welcome in provinces like Segovia, Ávila, Valladolid, Burgos, and Salamanca, where often more than half the cultivated land was devoted to wheat production. In Salamanca the wheat harvest brought in 75 million pesetas in a normal year, compared to the next most valuable product, barley, which was worth 21 million. The price guarantee was undoubtedly much greater incentive than the many pages of rules and regulations on wheat production issued by regional authorities, such as Queipo de Llano. In Córdoba province the price support was raised to 50 pesetas for 100 kilos in early 1937. This stimulated wheat growing in a province that was usually identified with olives but also produced 1.5 million metric quintals of wheat annually. From the beginning of the war, the Nationalists controlled La Vega, the richest agricultural district of Granada, and it retained its high output throughout the conflict.[14]

On 30 September 1936 the Junta de Defensa Nacional initiated an ambitious 60 million peseta program for loans to wheat farmers. On 28 October the Generalísimo decreed 40 million pesetas of tax-free loans for wheat growers, excluding absentee owners, in Nationalist-controlled areas in Andalusia and Castile. The loans would cover about 20 percent of the wheat grown in the Nationalist zone. In Andalusia, Queipo limited all loans to a maximum of 5 percent interest, and authorities in other provinces tried to eliminate usury from the countryside. The general made seeds (both wheat and corn) available to 9,000 agriculturists, setting a precedent for the Nationalist regime and the Federación Católica Agraria's program in La Coruña.[15]

In August 1937 Burgos issued a decree law that created Servicio Nacional del Trigo (SNT). The SNT formalized ideas concerning agrarian production that had been circulating in the Nationalist zone. The Falange and other rightist movements were antiliberal economically as well as politically, and they wanted to guarantee a reasonable profit to wheat growers and affordable bread to consumers. Likewise, the SNT refused "liberal capitalism," which gave the city an "advantage" over the countryside. The minister of agriculture, Fernández Cuesta, remarked that "in a way this war is a struggle of the Marxist industrial urban proletariat of the large northern cities against the noble peasantry of the center of Spain." Eduardo Aunós—Primo's labor minister, Franco's special economic emissary to Mussolini, and future justice minister—implied that the Caudillo's program to liberate peasants from "the ruthless tyranny" of the laws of supply and demand was inspired by what Aunós thought were successful Nazi agrarian policies.[16]

Antiurban discourse found a receptive hearing among wheat producers. Before the civil war, Castilian cereal farmers became alienated from a Republic that had always, they believed, favored the cities over the countryside and in which industrial goods seemed overpriced in relation to agricultural commodities. Because of several decent harvests in 1935 and 1936 and adequate storage facilities, prices fell significantly. In June 1935 the value of Castilian wheat (1929 = 100) was 93, and in June of 1936 it was 77. In response, the SNT "was determined to resolve the peasant problem in a totalitarian manner by assuring their [growers'] profits." To frighten already suspicious peasants, Nationalists circulated horror stories about the Republican collectivization of the harvest.[17]

In a radio address, Franco called the "battle of wheat the first battle of the rear as important as or even more so than those on the front." Introduced by the Generalísimo himself, the SNT's most important task was to increase the price of wheat to incentivize wheat growers who had suffered from low prices throughout the Great Depression. The augmentation reflected the demand from Castilian and other rural areas for an immediate response to the sharp rise in costs of industrial goods, especially chemical fertilizers, in the Nationalist zone. Falangist ideologues realized that price supports for wheat were the best way to "overcome the centuries-old apathy of the peasant masses." They advocated a price of 60 pesetas per metric quintal. Reports circulated that peasants would refuse to plant because of low or nonexistent profit margins.[18]

The SNT depended on a large and well-paid bureaucracy (provincial inspectors earned 8,000 pesetas annually, accountants 5,000, secretaries 3,250), which would last well into the 1950s. Falangists and others used all the influence at their disposal to obtain these posts. The SNT gave provincial offices flexibility to raise prices in their districts, and initially the agency restricted the amount of land devoted to wheat planting. It urged farmers not to sell their wheat until the new—and higher—prices went into effect. The state guaranteed payment of the *tasa* (price control) and thus provided some predictable security for the labradores. The regime self-consciously favored rural interests, including those of small producers and, to a certain degree, rural proletarians. Small producers and agricultural workers who were paid in kind—usually with wheat—were exempted from the milling tax that the SNT imposed on others. Thus, the SNT allowed them to profit from a moderately inflationary environment. The wartime presence and postwar extension of the black market would also favor those, including landlords, who were paid in kind.[19]

Private banks participated in financing wheat production and offered credits, which, including the state's contribution, totaled 300 million pesetas. Each producer could borrow a maximum of 25,000 pesetas at 4 percent interest, a rate that became standard for Bank of Spain commercial loans on 1 December 1938. This considerable investment found no counterpart in the Republican zone. The state guaranteed purchase of the harvest and offered several moratoriums on the payment of loans and debts. According to Fernández Cuesta, there were 650,000 wheat farmers in Spain, 450,000 of them in the Nationalist zone, and 250,000 of them would take advantage of the loans. In 1938 the loan program was extended to provide seed to farmers. The easy money conciliated peasants, farmers, and even many provincial savings bankers. The latter argued: "Today a farming village is more valuable than an industrial one. The reason is clear—man needs, above all, food." In 1930s Spain, agriculture (8.5 to 10 billion pesetas annually) outclassed industry (7 billion), and bankers urged the government to continue to make the primary sector supreme by increasing prices for food products. "Usury" nevertheless persisted, especially in more isolated parts of the Nationalist zone, for example, among the *minifundistas* of the hills of Sanabria (Zamora). These peasants were unable to pay their rent and therefore borrowed money using their rye harvest as collateral.[20]

The SNT controlled not only the price paid to growers but also the price of flour that millers and bakers purchased. The SNT allowed millers to reject farmers' wheat if it contained more than 3 percent impurities, a clause that millers employed frequently. By the end of 1937 in Zamora province and in the beginning of 1938 in others, the agency urged an increase in production by planting wheat on all available land, a recommendation that a number of farmers followed. It also encouraged labradores to plant seeds of a higher quality, usually from Arévalo and Toledo. Supplying peasants with improved seed was extremely costly to the state. The SNT realized that a large number of peasants asked for more seed than was necessary, hoarded them, or illegally tried to resell them for a higher price. Administrators sometimes threatened offenders with fines. Nevertheless, SNT officials concluded that it would be better to tolerate "abuses," continue to provide labradores with fertile seed, and then tax their profits. SNT authorities usually rejected what they believed were counterproductive attempts to punish farmers who failed to declare in advance the amount of their wheat harvest and instead argued for compensation at the normal tasa. They knew that stiff penalties for failure to declare—which had been levied in 1937—would discourage large amounts of wheat from entering the regulated marketplace and would encourage the sale of undeclared quantities as animal feed. Officials also were aware that hostility to peasant interests would push both labradores and landowners onto the black market or the unofficial economy. Administrators were therefore flexible and often ignored regulations on mandatory travel authorizations in order to ensure that mills had wheat to grind. The unofficial economy bolstered individual incomes and relieved hostility against the state.[21]

Throughout much of the war, SNT officials were much more aggressive with inaccurate statements from middlemen, for example, millers and warehousemen. In December 1937 in Cádiz province, an SNT inspector confiscated thirty-two wagons of hoarded wheat and fined the guilty miller 20,000 pesetas. In smaller towns and villages, millers were warned that milling wheat to use as animal feed (*pienso*) would result in the closing of their businesses. Officials followed through on their threats, shutting and confiscating the product of five Teruel mills that had ground wheat destined for humans into feed. The offending *molineros* had displayed a lamentable "rebellious nature" and their *ayuntamientos* an "indifference" toward regulations. Given fears that even low-cost bread would be used as feed, bakers were warned not to allow families to acquire more bread than was necessary for human consumption. Millers' and bakers' interests were subordinated to those of both peasants and consumers.[22]

SNT policies usually favored growers and raised compensation for wheat purchases from producers, while keeping the price of bread relatively stable. In Zaragoza during the Battle of the Ebro, military authorities paid millers 90 percent of the value of flour sold but seldom made good on the remaining 10 percent. Millers whose material interests and machinery had suffered during the "red" domination pleaded with the state—often unsuccessfully—for financial assistance. Thus, sacrifices and taxes fell mostly on the urban groups—especially bakers—who were continually urged to contribute "voluntarily" and not to raise prices. Warehousemen grumbled about the low rents that the SNT paid for use of their facilities. In cities they complained about their poor profit margins and high transportation costs. Nevertheless, those businesses with good military contracts could prosper. Under the management of Gabriel Artiach, Bilbao's major biscuit factory furnished Nationalist soldiers with this highly nutritious, transportable, and long-lasting hardtack.[23]

Producers initially responded enthusiastically to the Servicio's offer to purchase their crop. The beginning price in August 1937 was set at 46 to 48 pesetas per metric quintal and had risen to 53.4 to 56.4 pesetas by June 1938. By the end of 1937 the official price in certain provinces might not have been high enough to encourage sales, since larger wheat growers were compelled to sell directly to the SNT. Rural interests—the Federación Católica Agraria de Burgos and the Federación de Sindicatos Agrícolas Católicos de Zamora—continued to demand further augmentations. Castilian *campesinos* became dissatisfied with the official wheat price in 1938. Although they were grateful for the rise in compensation since the outbreak of war, labradores of Sahagún (León) claimed that the cost of their tools and supplies—such as twine, rope, belts, and collars for draught animals—increased much faster than the wheat price. They feared labor shortages and wanted to switch to growing wine, barley, or oats. Regional officers believed that peasant complaints were justified. SNT officials realized that a price that was too low would encourage peasants to hoard their grain, feed it to their animals, or sell it privately. As the market price rose for pienso—rye, barley, corn, and oats—more peasants were tempted to disobey regulations and use wheat as animal feed. The Civil Guard of Mondoñedo (Lugo) became skeptical when only 9 of 469 *agricultores* and labradores declared that they had sufficient wheat to sell on the marketplace.[24]

Dozens of villages in Navarre and dozens of labradores and laborers in Palencia respectfully requested that the small producers be able to keep a greater percentage of their wheat harvest in order, they claimed, to feed their families. The smallest landowners—those in most need—felt victimized by a system that, they asserted, would not allow them to retain enough grain to maintain self-sufficiency. They refused to declare their harvest or to deliver it to the mills. SNT authorities in Burgos rejected their request to keep a larger percentage of the yield but continued to excuse their failure to declare their stocks. In certain provinces officials instituted progressive quotas: holders of more than fifty hectares had to deliver 90 percent of their harvest; more than fifteen hectares, 80 percent; and less than fifteen hectares, 60 percent. Authorities were reluctant to impose forced deliveries since they were aware they would encounter resistance and that disgruntled labradores would respond by planting only the minimum the following year. Instead, they offered increased monetary incentives to get small producers to turn over their crop.[25]

In contrast to its Republican enemies and to its own postwar record, the Servicio's policies and wartime conditions encouraged the production of the main staple of the Spanish diet in the Nationalist zone. Output of wheat increased dramatically from 15,527,100 metric quintals in 1936 to 21,175,600 in 1937 and then leveled off to 19,308,200 in 1938. At a June 1937 meeting in Valladolid, the Asamblea Cerealista, which included representatives from all the major wheat-growing provinces in the Nationalist zone, agreed to export 300,000 tons of wheat to a "friendly nation." In 1937 Spain sold modest amounts of wheat and wheat bran to Portugal. In 1938 Germany received at least 300,000 metric quintals. At the beginning of that year, official statistics claimed that 800,000 tons of wheat—along with 160,000 tons of sugar, 200,000 calves, and 41,000 pigs—were available for export to foreign nations and to recently conquered "red" zones. In 1938 the Valladolid cereals market, one of the most important in Spain, reported excellent conditions for spring planting.[26]

The SNT success was qualified. Despite the promise of higher prices, local shortages appeared toward the termination of the war. In Cádiz province at the end of 1938, "villages without flour and bread" multiplied despite the efforts of mayors, Junta de Abastos, and the governor. The usual fifty wagons of flour shipments per month from Castile had been halted, and for many residents their only sustenance was an average of 360 grams of bread per day or considerably less than one pound. Authorities feared queues, conflicts, and revolts. Labradores responded by hoarding their small quantities of grain, acts of "cheating" that the local SNT was powerless to stop. Officials realized that it would create a "vast upheaval" to confiscate the stashes. Labradores became cynical about the future of the wheat crop. They correctly believed that the Servicio lacked sufficient number of sacks for their product. Without containers, machines, transport, and fertilizers, growers became reluctant to plant at the end of 1938. Despite (or perhaps because of) imposed maximum prices, fertilizers became extremely scarce and expensive during the conflict, and at its end, a female merchant was fined 25,000 pesetas for overcharging and hoarding them. A fertilizer scarcity of over 10,000 tons rendered farmers in Granada province desperate. An American firm exchanged 12,000 tons of fertilizer valued at 3 million pesetas for mountains of almonds, olive oil, and potassium. Catholic agrarian organizations knew that they would gain adherents if they could sell fertilizer at affordable prices. The fertilizer and other scarcities revealed that Nationalists had failed to find replacements for essential industrial goods produced in the Republican zone. Potential labor shortages during the 1938 summer harvest discouraged many labradores, and the SNT responded by attempting to organize the use of mechanical harvesters.[27]

In reaction to various pressures, including the expectation of "liberating" the entire peninsula, the minister of agriculture raised the tasa 10 percent from July 1938 to July 1939. To encourage small farmers to deliver their wheat, the SNT guaranteed them the highest price and menaced them with future confiscation at a lower price if they did not cooperate. SNT provincial officials in León encouraged a greater 1939 harvest by promising an increase of 5 pesetas for each metric quintal of wheat grown on land left unplanted in 1938. The incentive seems to have had only a marginal effect. In certain provinces—for example, Valladolid and Zamora—the price increases were even greater in response to a poor harvest caused by drought. The SNT quickly extended the higher prices to the entire country. SNT functionaries believed that the hikes were needed to encourage wheat production to feed the rapidly growing population of the expanding Nationalist zone and that—in contrast to the Soviet model—forced deliveries of wheat would be counterproductive. A higher price might encourage previously self-sufficient campesinos to grow more and sell some of their crop in the market. Labradores supposedly welcomed the increase enthusiastically, but many SNT officials worried that peasants were delaying the sale of their reserves until higher tasas took effect.[28]

In many ways the SNT was similar to older Republican programs designed to enhance various rural constituencies. A 20 January 1934 decree encouraged cotton growing by providing stable prices and subsidized seed.

The government-subsidized cotton project continued during the war in the Nationalist zone, but the limited amount of irrigated land in Andalusia and other Insurgent areas circumscribed this initiative. Nevertheless, it gave the Nationalists another opportunity to promote rural property owners. So did sugar beet price supports. Like wheat farmers, beet growers could be unappreciative, and some violated their contracts with sugar producers by selling their crop to others to acquire animal food. Cotton agriculturalists were also ungrateful, since they would ask for more cotton seed than they could sow and use the excess to feed their animals, as peasants did in the Soviet Union. Burgos also decreed minimum prices for grapes during the harvest. It attempted to enforce a regulation established in January 1936 that required the obligatory distribution of a quarter liter of table wine to all clients who purchased a meal costing between 3 and 10 pesetas. Wine unused and untouched by customers was recycled to soup kitchens. Establishments that did not follow the rules were fined from 100 to 1,000 pesetas. The price of olive oil was increased by fiat, and some reports claim that it doubled from 1936 to 1937. A good 1938 olive harvest may have lowered the price.[29] A decree promoting corn production imitated the SNT's "success" in stimulating wheat growing and regulated the price and distribution of *maíz*. It offered advances of 100 to 200 pesetas to peasants willing to plant corn on their dry or irrigated land.[30]

Although during the last year of war, the authorized price of wheat and other commodities was no longer high enough to prevent the birth of an extensive unofficial economy, rural interests were generally satisfied, and soldiers and civilians commonly had enough to eat. Segovia reported stable bread prices and abundant food, despite the need to supply troops who were stationed only eighteen miles from its capital. The province possessed more than enough wheat, barley, and flour. León enjoyed stable supplies of cereals and only a 20 percent rise in the price of commodities, but the requisitioning of trucks sometimes created obstacles. Nevertheless, beans, potatoes, and beef were plentiful. Álava lacked eggs, meat, and flour because the quartermaster monopolized the latter. Huesca remained largely self-sufficient in most foodstuffs but experienced shortages of meat, eggs, and milk. In Zamora province wine prices were allowed to rise to market value. The contracts with the military ensured decent profits. In Huelva "government policy," which tended to "increase the value of agricultural commodities," benefited both farmers and livestock ranchers, who appreciated the 65 percent increase in food prices.[31]

The Nationalists were proud of their economic normality, that is, the availability of many (but certainly not all) agricultural commodities at reasonable prices. Their radio broadcasted restaurant menus of popular establishments to listeners in the Republican zone. After the Battle of the Ebro, Insurgent authorities issued a ministerial order that restricted the number of courses that hotel restaurants could serve. In order to build a food reserve to feed soon-to-fall Barcelona, lunches were to be limited to hors d'oeuvres, two dishes, and dessert; dinners offered soup, two dishes, and dessert. "Not bad," one historian-participant commented, "during the third winter of war."[32]

ANIMAL FEED

Despite their centralist ideology, the Nationalist zone developed distinct regional economies. The civil governors, who were usually military officers, and the Intendencia Militar (quartermaster) had enormous power to set prices and limit exports in each province. This gave them a certain flexibility but made coordination difficult at the national level where their pricing policies sometimes conflicted with those of the SNT, various ministries, and Falangist unions. The production and consumption of animal feed demonstrated the localisms of the Nationalist zone. For example, corn growers in Zaragoza province were outraged that they had to sell at the official price of 48 to 52 pesetas per metric quintal, whereas their Navarrese neighbors received 76 to 80 pesetas on the free market. In contrast to wheat, the relative reluctance to establish price supports and monetary incentives for animal feed—corn, barley, oats, and straw—favored the military quartermaster and *ganaderos*, who preferred cheap sustenance for their flocks. Barley and other grains were easier to grow than wheat since they did not need the same kind of intensive preparation or expensive inputs.[33]

The quartermaster purchased large amounts of animal feed through its open bidding process. Open bidding was the preferred way of awarding military contracts and avoided the thorny issue of adherence to unreasonable price controls, which would discourage peasants and farmers from feeding both animals and humans. In Ávila army buyers bought directly from peasants at the prices that the latter demanded. This was a very effective way of supplying both beasts and soldiers, but it raised protests from provincial officials who noted that the purchases "greatly disturbed food provisioning, especially in the capital (Ávila), because farmers prefer to wait in the countryside where the Quartermaster buys their produce at a high price rather than traveling to the capital or other places where they must not only pay the cost of transportation but also obey price controls." In Valladolid the military monopolized the purchase of barley, rye, oats, and other grains for its animals. Although it raised prices for nonmilitary consumers, the army's siphoning at the point of production relieved rural producers of the burden of transporting their commodities to markets.[34]

In Galicia, which grew half of Spain's corn, maíz was considered "the main agricultural product." In the spring of 1938, governors forbade corn and barley supplies to leave Pontevedra province and gave the military quartermaster a monopoly on their purchase. In Andalusia, corn became scant by

early 1937, a situation that Queipo blamed on hoarding. He therefore confiscated it at the maximum price of 41 pesetas per 100 kilos. Farmers were
urged to purchase the impounded corn at provincial distribution centers. In
southern Spain the demand of the Intendencia Militar was so great that inexpensive corn was lacking for the pack animals of farmers. In Granada the
price of some types of animal feed rose 74 percent after the outbreak of war.
Provincial authorities had to exert pressure on middlemen to supply the mules
of the Patronato de Queipo de Llano and ship grain to Morocco. However,
by late 1938 the army quartermaster decided to end forced requisitioning of
40 percent of barley and 25 percent of oats in eleven provinces of the Nationalist zone. In other words, the quartermaster generally had enough voluntary
offers to dispense with mandatory delivery of animal feed from farmers.[35]

Whatever its drawbacks and contradictions, the Spanish Nationalist solution of open bidding punctuated by compensated confiscations was preferable to looting, which had occurred in so many civil wars, including in the
Republican zone. The Nationalist policy repeated one of the few successful
procurement efforts of the Russian Whites. Only during the Ice March of
early 1918, which had saved the embryonic White movement, did the Russian counterrevolutionaries generously compensate the peasantry for the food
they took. General Lavr Kornilov insisted that his forces pay for supplies even
at "inflated" prices that "amounted to extortion" by the Kuban peasants. As
shall be seen, the White Russian procurement policies—essentially looting—
that followed the successful Ice March destroyed the counterrevolutionary
movement.[36]

The Chinese Communists had more than twenty years of experience in
governing rural areas, which had allowed them to experiment, test, and correct
their policies before the civil war of 1946–49. Mao's Red Army (PLA) avoided
pillaging the peasantry by raising its own animals, growing its own food, and
becoming largely self-sufficient in grain and vegetables. The Chinese Communists' tolerance of the free market and their enlightened revenue-raising
techniques were essential in winning over the "semipeasants" and traders of
North China. In that region the Guomindang's unwisely heavy taxation alienated these small buyers and sellers. In response, the CCP sought to impose a
more progressive system, which exempted the poorest families. The traders
responded by assisting and fighting for the Communists during both the anti-
Japanese and civil wars. Market-oriented peasants collected grain, stored it,
and shipped it to the front lines of the PLA. Not land reform, but flexible
taxation policies and willingness to tolerate a market economy induced the
peasantry to cooperate with the Communists.[37]

The CCP defended rural interests better than the Guomindang. Chinese
Nationalist General Pai Chung-hsi concluded that his forces incurred the bitter hatred of the masses by purchasing provisions at a low rate. Several of-

ficials attributed the increasing popularity of the "bandits" (Communists) to heavy GMD food taxation and urged an immediate 50 percent reduction. Provincial governors worried that GMD requisitioning would lead to rebellion at the front and in the rear. The obligations placed on the peasantry proved self-defeating, since the compulsory contributions were so onerous that many farmers chose to leave their land uncultivated. A GMD publication attributed famine in Shantung to counterproductive policies of heavy military taxation by its own armies. In this province "the unbearable military burden imposed on the farmers" caused starvation. The peasants' duties included not only supplying the troops with massive amounts of food and fuel but also countless hours of forced labor. In response to this severe exploitation, able-bodied men in "pacified" (Nationalist) villages had fled, and their flight had fomented food scarcities. General Li Yu-tang admitted that "the Communist bandits have used the slogans of 'no military service' and 'protection for the refugees'" to win over those who had fled from famine to their zone. A GMD journalist recommended that the government adopt the "stratagem" of the "bandit troops," which he defined as "the system of soldier-farmer cooperation, making military operation and production go hand in hand." He also advised heavier taxation on the urban wealthy and less on farmers.[38]

ANIMAL HUSBANDRY

The availability of meat in many markets can be attributed not only to Nationalist control of cattle-rich provinces, such as Galicia and Rioja, but also to an authoritarian political economy that allowed the army and other provinces to substitute for the missing demand of large urban areas under Republican control. The Nationalist military was given first priority to purchase meat supplies and replaced Madrid, Barcelona, and Valencia as markets for canned food and other commodities made in Asturias, Galicia, Rioja, and Navarre. In contrast to the Republican zone, where "red" money was regarded skeptically, livestock producers in the Nationalist zone were willing to accept its currency for their cattle and other animals. In January 1937 the Federaciones Agrarias Católicas and the quartermaster signed an accord that lasted until the end of the conflict allowing the Federaciones to establish a monopoly on supplying meat to the northern front. Gallegan and Meridian firms furnished canned meat products to Franco's troops. During the Battle of Belchite in August 1937, besieged Carlist forces demanded the immediate delivery of "10,000 tins of meat."[39]

Beef and dairy products followed a course similar to wheat. Gallegan Falangists knew that only high prices for their animals would win over to the "new regime" peasants, who were overwhelmingly apolitical and non-ideological: "The peasant masses will decide to support our movement on the basis of the price of cattle."[40] Politically uncommitted groups in Galicia, such as peasants in the north and center and many women throughout the province, would sustain the franquista state if it could deliver materially. Galicia was divided between less economically developed areas in the southern part of the province where *foros*, which provided insecure tenure over small plots, were common and more affluent regions in the north where more modern forms of capitalist ownership dominated. Since the end of the nineteenth century, the small and medium landowners of the most prosperous parts of the province had exported their meat to the rest of Spain. Comfortable rural proprietors supported rightist political parties and associations and sided with the Nationalists.

Gallegan producers demanded a revalorization of meat prices. It seems that this occurred at least in part by early 1937. However, by the summer of 1937 the Catholic Agrarian Federation complained that prices at the livestock fairs were "bankrupting farmers." La Coruña's civil governor responded by promising to root out "corruption" at the fair and weighing all animals on scales attended by municipal officials. Lugo's civil governor ordered mayors to give preference to livestock sales to the military quartermaster. Although profitable, doing business with the army required effective quality control. One industrialist, several salesmen, and a veterinarian were subjected to court martial proceedings for selling rotten meat to the quartermaster. The Asociación General de Ganaderos de España, successor of the Mesta, established its office in Burgos and arranged a meeting with the Caudillo, always sensitive to rural interests. In August 1937, a few days after the Nationalists had captured Santander, he responded to pressure from Federación Católica Agraria and raised the price of milk 40 percent.[41]

Gallegan campesinos reacted rapidly to market conditions and were stimulated by the rise of prices to produce more pork, which was often the base of their own diet. Lugo authorities declared that provincial and municipal tax revenues had increased substantially because of "higher prices of agricultural commodities," particularly "the increased price of livestock." Almost every family in the countryside possessed "a head of livestock, either fully or 50 percent owned." Yet the peasants' ability to generate more meat was limited by the small scale and the scattered placement of their tiny holdings, which often provoked disputes over pasture and water rights. Their farming remained "archaic" and dependent on the use of the primitive "Roman plow." Although the province was devoted to animal husbandry—especially cattle—little milk, cheese, or butter was produced. Nor was there an industrial slaughterhouse; thus, cows were shipped live to other regions.[42]

In January 1938, national authorities established in each provincial capital a Junta Provincial Reguladora de Abastos de Carne, whose task was to control meat production and price. The Junta was usually composed of the civil governor as president, a representative from the military quartermaster, an agrarian technician, the head of the provincial veterinary organization, and two livestock farmers (*ganaderos*), one from the livestock chamber and the other from the Falange. The Falange played only a minor role in this and many other *juntas* and committees, including those of its own unions where it was outmanned by representatives from the military and various employers' organizations. The local Juntas de Economía y Abastos of Oviedo limited Falange representation to one "consumer named by the FET" in a four-person committee. The Junta Provincial de Abastecimientos y Transportes of Huelva mandated only one Falange delegate on a seven-man committee.[43]

Juntas and committees became forums where interest-group politics were debated and often decided. In the summer and fall of 1938 they raised meat prices—including those paid to ranchers by the army quartermaster—in certain provinces. The Junta de Abastos in livestock-rich Asturias gave priority of purchase to the military quartermaster and attempted to regulate all animal sales. The Asturian Junta prided itself on flexible price controls, which took into account the region's dependence on highway transport—made more costly by the destruction of bridges and vehicles during the first year of the war—and the necessity for producers to make profits. Given the shortage of motor vehicles, sellers and buyers needed to use draught animals, which made transport slower and more expensive. The Andalusian provincial juntas were forced to raise beef prices in Seville, which had been stable from July 1936 to March 1938, because of the decline of Galician exports to Andalusia. Although Burgos began to run short of meat, Salamanca province had a sufficient quantity to supply its military and civilian population. Its authorities reported significant increases in cows, sheep, goats, and pigs from 1932 to 1937. Segovia noted a "surplus" of livestock and a drop in the price of veal from 1936 to 1938.[44]

In Galicia and other provinces, eggs became a top priority. The concern for *huevos* showed their real and symbolic power in Spanish cuisine and culture. Closely connected to the human reproductive organs—both male and female—the egg symbolized life and (re)birth. They were an excellent meat substitute and easy to digest. International statistics revealed that Spain produced only 20 percent of its own production in peacetime. The egg shortage became so severe that the governors of La Coruña, Álava, and Valladolid wanted to reserve them exclusively for hospital patients. Like other coveted commodities, eggs encouraged profiteering. One Gallegan merchant was only too happy to sell to hospitals in other provinces where his eggs fetched a much higher price and was fined 10,000 pesetas for overcharging. In Zamora, "bad Spaniards" purchased eggs at the tasa and trucked them to recently liberated Bilbao, where they drew twice as much. In Asturias, egg dealers were also fined 10,000 pesetas for hoarding their supplies. The same was true for León, where one trucker was sanctioned 1,000 pesetas for attempting to transport them without the proper license. The León civil governor ordered that all egg sales be limited to the official marketplace. Tens of thousands of overpriced eggs were confiscated throughout La Coruña. Both big and small sellers had to pay fines, including the Unión de Exportadores de Porriño, a major poultry and egg producer, which was penalized 10,000 pesetas for exporting thousands of eggs from the province without permission. Price controls on eggs seemed especially ineffective in the countryside. Nevertheless, by February 1938 the egg crisis had subsided in Galicia, although other shortages ensued. At the end of 1938, in preparation for the capture of Barcelona and Madrid, Serrano Súñer limited the consumption of eggs in restaurants and bars to one per customer.[45]

Mules played perhaps the least celebrated but most critical role in the Spanish civil war. Mules and their handlers (*acemileros*) were essential for supplying troops in the mountainous and unpaved paths throughout the Spanish peninsula. The animals served as Franco's jeeps, and their drivers became rural proletarian heroes in the Nationalist zone. In lines worthy of Soviet or Republican Socialist realism: "Fighting against the elements and the enemy, persevering under all kinds of danger, and struggling against the rebelliousness of his assistant—the mule—the handler's continual and silent triumphs contribute to the celebrated military victories." The ignorant had the misimpression that being a handler was a cushy job, and some volunteered for the position, but acemileros had one of the most difficult tasks in the military. Most were of rural origin, had managed pack animals in their youth, and had never attended school. They were notoriously independent, and earned a reputation among chaplains for their earthy, if not foul, language. An acemilero had to be constantly at the disposition of his charges, who could be neither over- nor underfed. Watching their flock gave them little time to relax.[46]

The handlers had a special pride in their ability to deliver hot food in heavy metal pots to hungry soldiers on the march. During many campaigns throughout the war, mule trains, although exposed to enemy fire, permitted the delivery over long distances of both warm and cold meals. Unfortunate animals sometimes fell into ravines while descending steep and slippery paths in the mountains. Nor was the headlong tumble of mules over cliffs unusual. Many other beasts succumbed to illness. Mules were famously stubborn, and in many languages they have set the standard of obstinacy. They sometimes dumped their heavy loads of food and munitions and refused to traverse rivers or other natural obstacles. When they bucked the cargo off their backs, the acemilero was forced to reload them and entice them forward at all hours of the day and night. One handler became so frustrated by the refusal of his mule that he got down on his knees with his arms extended in front of the beast and pleaded: "After we die, I would like you to be reborn a handler and I the mule." A tired and recalcitrant beast forced another acemilero, Valentín Hernández Bateo, to load on his own back the boxes of desperately needed medications. One of the most elite units in the Nationalist Army, la Primera de Navarra, had as many as 700 mules supporting its operations, and its convoys impressed even soldiers with deep rural roots. Artillery units also used large numbers of mules to transport heavy weapons. Machine gunners employed their own *mulos*, who had the added advantage of remaining relatively calm during bombardments. During the Basque campaign at the end of September 1936, the arrival of a mule with four boxes of ammunition, manufactured in Seville earlier that month, allowed the Tercio de Lácar to continue its struggle in the Calamúa Mountains. The creatures were essential around the Jarama, where they played a central role in establishing Nationalist control of the right bank. Mulos served as the ambulances or even hearses that transported sick, injured, and dead soldiers on both sides. The seriously wounded had difficulty staying on their backs, but the Nationalists devised a system whereby the mule carried two injured men who were balanced on stretchers on each side of the beast. Chaplains commuted to the cemetery and the church on their backs.[47] Many historians have reasonably concluded that foreign aid or Moroccan mercenaries were the "decisive" factors that ultimately gave victory to the Nationalists. Yet pack animals were as "decisive" as fascist weapons or Regulares.

Insurgents in Andalusia were able to attract horsemen, trainers, and stable boys into their well-equipped mounted police and army units, whose mobility captured "red" villages and restored "order" in the countryside. Officer training classes often included horseback riding lessons. The Spanish army had an important cavalry division, the Cría Caballar, many of whose officers joined the Nationalists. The division, which also contained a battalion of bicyclists, remained Franco's most rapid reserve unit. The cavalry earned a reputation for bravery and effectiveness during the Battle of Teruel and again during the final battles in Catalonia in January 1939. In February 1938 during the fight for Teruel, the Montejurra unit—which, like other Carlist units, were among the most valuable Nationalist troops—managed to capture four horses and a large supply depot from the Republican quartermaster. Throughout the conflict, the capture of steeds was an important prize for both sides. Carlists admired their *caballos* and the horsemen who drove them into artillery fire at the end of the Battle of Teruel. Soldiers stationed on extensive fronts used mounts—and, when possible, motorcycles—to communicate among themselves. An officer on a horse in the mountains became nearly as common as one in a car in the cities. In fact, high-ranking officers in the field had their own steeds.[48]

On the symbolic plane, one photograph taken at the beginning of the conflict showed Nationalist supporters giving a fascist salute to a passing horse, surely an honor that the latter could not fully appreciate. The equestrian portrait of the Caudillo, emphasizing the continuity of his leadership with Spanish monarchs, was displayed throughout the Nationalist zone. So were pictures of his personal Moorish guards and their Arabian steeds, both associated with the Spanish imperial success. The Guardia Mora, formed in February 1937 by a squadron of Regulares, delighted onlookers at parades and other occasions—whether festive or solemn. The Caudillo gave to the Jalifa of Morocco four beautiful horses valued at least 35,000 pesetas, "of the Spanish-Arab breed," a blending of the races that would have pleased Giménez Caballero and other lesser known franquista ideologues. Franco himself loved horseback riding both as a young officer and an aging Caudillo.[49]

Horses, mules, and donkeys were perhaps more exposed to death than their masters. As pack animals, they carried munitions and became bombs themselves when hit by enemy fire. Mules were easier targets than men and, furthermore, did not seek cover. Instead, even during battle, frightened ones usually hovered around their handler. To be a beast in battle could be extremely dangerous. Gunners facilely shot them, since trenches were not usually large enough to provide cover even for modest-sized four-legged creatures. In engagements on the Guadiana in Extremadura in August 1936, twenty men and forty horses perished. In early May 1937 during the Bilbao campaign near Mount Vizcargui, a Republican sniper caught sight of a group of mules and shot nine before their handlers could move the remaining animals to safety. In this case, the handlers' carelessness "permitted their four-legged traveling companions and excellent servants to ascend to a better place." On 27 August 1937 during the Battle of Brunete, four soldiers and twenty-five mules and horses died in a Republican artillery bombardment. During the Maestrazgo campaign in July 1938 an enemy artillery shell fell on a mule carrying grenades that detonated, killing eleven and injuring fifty-two requetés. When lost at night, the movements of creatures attracted trigger-happy sentinels. Thus, an ample supply was even more necessary than in peacetime.[50]

The chaplain of a Carlist Tercio expressed the unsentimentality of a rural society toward its working beasts. At the end of April 1937 near Durango, an artillery shell blew up a mule carrying a hot meal from the rear. The chaplain regretted that the warm food was adulterated with animal blood more than the violent death of the mule. One requeté morbidly joked that his mates "should come and eat the exquisite paella." During the Asturias campaign, the plunge of two mules over a precipice was reported matter-of-factly and without regret. During the Battle of Teruel, a good number—like the men they served—froze to death and became "harder than a rock." The detailed descriptions of dead, deformed, and mutilated animals may have substituted for a reluctance to depict disfigured human bodies, a common sight on the battlefield. Other, more fortunate mules brought Fundador cognac, which

Postcard image depicting soldiers and their animals in the north. Southworth Spanish Civil War Collection, Mandeville Special Collections Library, University of California, San Diego.

had the virtue of not freezing, to men in the frigid mountains. The cold had the sole merit of preventing dead animals, men, and excrement from smelling. It preserved corpses that—given the black humor of warring soldiers—were called "cold cuts," whose food and clothing were quickly recycled. Sleeping near mules and horses could provide some warmth, even at the cost of foul odors, noise, and kicks. In May and June 1938 a shortage of mules, in part the result of their high mortality in the Battle of Teruel, severely handicapped the Nationalist campaign in the Maestrazgo and its drive to capture Valencia. During this campaign through mountain villages with bad roads, troops tired of their constant cold rations, sometimes alleviated by a rabbit caught and grilled on the spot or, more rarely, by a hot meal that mules "miraculously" delivered from the rear.[51]

Many men developed an affectionate relationship with the beasts. The Tercio de Lácar awarded them nicknames, which signaled both friendship and individual identity. Requetés called the oldest of the herd the Catalán. They spoiled and loved him for his many contributions and services, and his death, caused by an artillery shell during the Battle of Ebro, saddened the entire unit. The Navarrese usually treated their animals with affection. They named one whom they requisitioned (as they had confiscated automobiles in the city) "el Durruti." "Durruti" was joined by the requisitioned "el burro Ascaso," who was sporadically appreciated for "his magnificent services" in carrying heavy loads up steep mountain paths. The pair was ironically named after the famous (or infamous in requeté eyes) anarchist duo. "Ascaso" proved to be worthy of his namesake. He was a stereotypically stubborn creature with an "anarchist" temperament that bit his handlers and bucked his load to the ground, usually during the most dangerous moments of battle. During one fight, "Ascaso" refused to budge, and his handler had to light a match under the animal's belly to get him out of the line of fire. On the other hand, Carlists praised "Durruti" for his fortitude and stamina during long marches of the Asturian campaign. The unit eventually exchanged "Durruti" for a truck, but his former masters—and, even more so, the mule himself—were disheartened to see his new boss burden the beast with much more cargo than he had previously carried. The wounding of three mules during the reconquest of Teruel was a heavy material and spiritual loss for the Carlist Tercio.[52]

Although predominantly rural Spanish society did not yet treat its pack animals as pets, soldiers nevertheless felt a strong sentimental attachment to their charges. So did civilian *muleros*, who demanded that they be photographed holding sardine cans on top of their *mulicos*. A good number of units had mascots. During the Battle of the Ebro in July 1938, a requeté from Manilva (Málaga) was ordered to furnish ammunition to a battery of the First Division of Navarre. During the operation his mule was wounded in the front leg, and the soldier was ordered to stay with the animal until it healed. Even though the mule recuperated in two weeks, the *malagueño* remained in the village of Lucena del Cid with a local prostitute for six weeks, thereby missing the bloodiest action of the Battle of the Ebro. Authorities prosecuted him for desertion, but perhaps because of his spotless war record and his successful care of the mule (good handlers were usually without rank but always invaluable), he was acquitted.[53]

During the Battle of the Ebro, mules were essential for both sides. Swimming, they accompanied boats as the Popular Army crossed the river and then brought supplies to frontline soldiers on hilly outposts. Nationalists requisitioned from surrounding villages 270 mules and donkeys, which transported 60,000 hand grenades and tens of thousands of bullets and shells. Lanterns guided the animals up the steep mountain paths. Their light and braying attracted Republican fire, which killed a large number of the working creatures, but most made it up the hill and delivered their potentially deadly cargo. The fact that Nationalists could requisition so many beasts of burden on short notice indicated that their zone retained healthy practices of animal husbandry. Veterinary organizations rushed to their aid. These associations often had a right-wing orientation and had lost members during the Republican purges at the beginning of the civil war. For example, the Asturian veterinary association reported that four of its associates had been "vilely assassinated by Marxists." Colleagues mourned the death of a twenty-two-year-old who had died "defending the fatherland" at Navalperal on 4 August 1936. Queipo praised the courageous action of a military veterinarian who took over the town hall of Jerez de la Frontera at the beginning of the rebellion. Nationalist veterinary groups eliminated their left-wing colleagues and served either the military or the municipality. In Málaga the latter earned at least 5,500 pesetas per year, compared with a metallurgical engineer's salary of 10,000 pesetas or a country physician's of 12,000.[54]

Very early in the conflict, veterinarians were ordered to verify the ownership of every animal butchered in municipal slaughterhouses. They kept elaborate statistics on numbers and species of beasts in each province. These figures were absolutely essential for supplying transport, meat, and indispensable by-products such as skins. Vets were also expected to report on farmers who were reluctant to butcher their beasts because of a low tasa. A "concentration camp" for unclaimed animals was established to avoid unauthorized sales of livestock whose ownership was unknown or contested. This established a precedent throughout the Nationalist zone whereby local officials returned animals taken by "reds" to their rightful owners. If no one claimed the beasts, they were sold at public auction. In Córdoba province by the end of December 1936, 5,000 head, including a large number of mules, had been returned to their original owners. Unclaimed beasts were used for the harvest and eventually sold. The military received 207,076 pesetas as a result of these auctions.[55]

Echoing the prohibition on butchering issued in the fall of 1936 by the Comisión de Agricultura de Junta de Técnica del Estado, the civil governors of Córdoba and Zamora ordered local veterinarians to prohibit the slaughter of female livestock and to make stud services available to all ranchers and cattle farmers. Throughout the conflict, vets ensured the safety and survival of all types of farm animals but especially females of reproductive age. They attempted to closely control breeding. In the provinces of Zamora and Burgos, policies of preservation were effective, and the numbers of cows, sheep, pigs, and goats increased substantially from 1935 to 1938. The Intendencia Militar was able to requisition large numbers of mules and horses, a prerequisite of a successful war effort. The army gave high priority to the supervision of horse breeding throughout its zone. Livestock were registered and counted. This was a difficult task, since in some provinces—such as Pontevedra and Granada—impoverished peasants followed the custom of slaughtering young calves when they lacked the resources to raise them to maturity or bring them to market. The Burgos government advertised throughout Spain to encourage breeders to sell their horses and mules to the government. After Nationalists captured parts of the provinces of Toledo and Madrid at the end of 1936, they claimed to have rounded up 400 teams of mules to sow wheat.[56]

Throughout the war, provincial veterinarians issued bulletins on contagious diseases affecting livestock (such as foot-and-mouth) and procedures for
quarantining and destroying infected animals. Vets were aware that diseases—
such as *viruela ovina*, *carbunco bacteridiano*, and *perineumonía*—that had
been eliminated from more advanced European nations still periodically decimated herds in Spain. With the cooperation of the Civil Guard, they effectively
stopped the sale and circulation of beasts—including those destined for the
quartermaster—from zones suspected of transmitting contagious diseases.
Violators of quarantine prohibitions merited fines of hundreds of pesetas.
The Servicio Nacional de Ganadería established a Salamanca center—the
Colegio Oficial Veterinario—which tested the effectiveness of vaccines and
serums. It promised livestock farmers compensation for any damages caused
by its medications. It should be noted that instruments that tortured animals
and destroyed their hides—*aguijón* and *pincho*—were banned in much of the
Nationalist zone as they had been under the Republic. However, it proved difficult to root out the use of the *aguijón*, and the Comité Sindical del Curtido
sponsored a contest, with awards totaling 5,000 pesetas, for the best essays on
how to eliminate this "barbaric" custom from the Spanish countryside.[57]

The all-male bodies of health officials were also charged with policing milk
vendors, most of whom were females who were frequently tempted to use
milk from diseased cows or adulterate healthy milk with water. Vets fined
dozens who tried to sell their animals without the proper health certificates.
In León four butchers were sanctioned 10,000 pesetas and another sixteen,
5,000 pesetas "for falsifying veterinary certificates." Vets also threatened to
close down sausage-making factories and workshops that had avoided inspection. Fearing outbreaks of trichinosis, they even attempted to halt the
Christmas-season practice of familial slaughter of pigs. Veterinarians usually
cooperated with the municipality and the state, but at the end of the war,
when meat shortages were critical and potential profits enormous, one issued
safe-conduct passes without justification and was fined 500 pesetas. Less successfully, authorities tried to limit "middlemen" and encouraged peasants to
sell their beasts directly to agricultural unions and state organizations. Immediately after the war's end, working animals and tractors that had been
requisitioned by the military were returned to their owners, who needed them
for the upcoming harvest. This restoration contrasted with the animals expropriated in the Republican zone, whose owners never saw them again.[58]

In the Nationalist zone, animals remained plentiful throughout the conflict. In June 1937 the Nationalist slaughterhouses reported the deaths of
12.2 million sheep, 3.5 million pigs, 2.8 million cows, and 2.7 million goats.
One year later, the census estimated that 14.7 million sheep, 4.2 million pigs,
3.4 million cows, and 3.2 million goats had been slaughtered. If accurate,
these figures show nearly a 20 percent increase of livestock during the war,

undoubtedly a major factor in the Nationalists' victory. Official statistics in Zamora, which prided itself on being one of the richest livestock provinces, revealed growth in three of four categories of animals normally consumed for meat. The number of cows had increased 6 percent (from 88,175 in 1935 to 93,493 in 1938); sheep, 62 percent (from 426,830 to 693,148); and goats, 44 percent (from 76,399 to 108,521). Only pigs declined 15 percent (from 73,813 to 63,001). The augmentations were partially attributed to adherence to the prohibition of the slaughter of females of reproductive age and to the relative lack of consumption of mutton and goat meat. Cows were by far the most valuable animals and beef the most prized meat. One hundred thousand cows were worth nearly twice as much (42 million pesetas) as 700,000 sheep (28 million pesetas). The average price of a cow was 450 pesetas and a sheep, 40. In fact, the province reported that it had an excess of some 20,000 sheep. It should also be remembered that in addition to cheese and hides, animals furnished tallow for soap and other crucial products.[59]

Animal fairs—which required significant organizational efforts to provide food, water, measuring instruments, space, adequate sanitation, and disease prevention for thousands of beasts—occurred regularly throughout Nationalist Spain. At fairs in Jerez de la Frontera, 533 mules, 531 horses, 239 donkeys, and 110 cows went on sale on the opening day. When another fair opened four months later in May 1937, the numbers had increased to 767 mules, 885 horses, 683 donkeys, and 649 cows. The animals most in demand at this fair were working mules, which fetched the price of nearly 1,000 pesetas each, an increase of 25 percent from before the war. The Córdoba fair, where the military was an active buyer, saw the heaviest trading in mules, which were selling for 1,500 and 1,750 pesetas. Mules were so essential in rural Spain that property owners were defined by the number that they possessed—"the owner of a pair of mules or two pairs of mules" or, more generally, "un yuntero."[60]

Gypsies, who dominated the spring 1938 Seville fair, sold and bought 6,260 mules, 4,195 horses, 2,130 donkeys, 1,530 pigs, 885 sheep, and 655 cows, all at prices substantially higher than in 1937. Gypsy traders often profited from the steep rise in prices for pack animals. Mules in particular remained hot items. At the Seville fair in the fall of 1938, 4,225 head—of which 1,525 were mules—were sold. The most important buyer was Queipo's Southern Army, which paid 1,000 to 2,000 pesetas for mules, and 700 to 1,400 for horses. The opening of the Seville fair of April 1939 saw the entrance of 1,775 mules, 1,507 horses, and 790 donkeys, totaling 4,072. On the second day, the total number of beasts was 4,380. The decline in numbers from 1938 was explained by the contagion of foot-and-mouth disease among the absent species.[61]

Three thousand animals were displayed at a busy 1938 Burgos fair that was honored by the presence of the minister of agriculture, who awarded prizes to the best livestock farmers. One of his goals was to improve the stock and especially to increase butter and milk production in the province. Authorities in Zaragoza sponsored awards for improved animal breeding totaling 5,000 pesetas. With a similar goal, juries of experts granted awards amounting to tens of thousands of pesetas to cattle raisers and other livestock farmers at contests held throughout Asturias. Local officials tried to encourage participation at their fairs by making them tax free.[62]

Asturias was proud of the rapid recovery of its livestock, its ability to supply the quartermaster with thousands of cattle, and its export of meat to other regions. At the Oviedo fair, with nearly 1,400 animals, mules appeared in numbers and at prices—2,000 to 3,000 pesetas—similar to prewar years. A team of oxen cost approximately 2,000 pesetas and a horse 300 to 600 pesetas. As in Seville, Gypsies played an important role as traders at the Oviedo fair. One claimed that he had spent time in the "leftist zone" where the "reds" had tried unsuccessfully to make him work "like a black." He much preferred the greater Nationalist tolerance of free trade to what he considered Republican forced labor. By 1939 military necessities had diminished the supply of mules for sale, and mining companies snapped up the best ones available on the market. The price of a good mule rose 40 percent to approximately 5,000 pesetas, the cost of a used car. Cows sold for less than half that price. At other times and places, mules and horses—animals that were not regularly eaten in the Nationalist zone—were valued, respectively, at 500 and 300 pesetas per head. In March 1939 at the "Botijero" (Zamora) fair, individual mules were selling for 2,750 pesetas, pairs for 5,000, donkeys for 170 to 300, and horses for 1,500. As a point of comparison, a new passenger car seems to have been worth 7,500 pesetas and a truck 10,000 to 15,000.[63]

In Galicia and León fairs were highly regulated. At a fair at La Coruña, nearly a dozen fines—ranging from 100 to 1,000 pesetas—were issued. However, both buyers and sellers often eluded controls, selling animals outside the official weigh station with the complicity of the local mayor. To overcome restrictions, some falsely posed as army buyers, thereby enabling them to offer higher prices to sellers who assumed that the quartermaster could and would pay a higher price for beasts. The commerce of live animals was generally—but not always—free of price controls, but in almost every province the price of meat was regulated. As the war endured, meat prices rose, indicating the existence of a de facto free market. The official price of butchered animals climbed 15 percent from September to December 1938. Market prices for living beasts remained high, meat was rationed, and Zamora prohibited livestock export at the end of the war. By March 1939 distribution was limited to 125 grams per Zamoran. High prices encouraged illegal export of possibly diseased animals.[64]

Nationalist journalists boasted that their supplies greatly surpassed those of their enemy, who, they claimed, ate their working animals, including mules.

Although repeated ad nauseam, the charge was quite plausible. Like the Nationalists, the Republican army confiscated large numbers of pack animals, but in the Republican zone peasants often preferred to consume their own beasts rather than have them "purchased" by the "red" militias or the Popular Army in exchange for useless vouchers. Furthermore, as the conflict dragged on, Republican money became increasingly worthless and less than able to entice farmers to give up their prized possessions. In fact, Nationalists claimed—with much validity—that the "Marxists" had slaughtered "thousands and thousands of head of livestock" in the first few months of the war. Toledo's loss of two-thirds of its livestock compelled Nationalist authorities to introduce teams of draught animals that labored where most needed. The Junta Provincial Reguladora de Abastecimientos de Carne of Vizcaya reported that the number of cattle had fallen during Republican rule from 100,334 in July 1936 to 36,304 in July 1937. Under Nationalist control, it recovered to 89,306 head. The number of sheep declined from 97,150 before the war to 10,509 under Republican control and then rose to 97,159 under the Nationalists. Only pigs did not recover their former count.[65]

When they conquered Castellón, Nationalist authorities declared that the deficiency of pack animals and other means of transport constrained the harvest to remain in the *pueblos*. Therefore, wheat and other surpluses were fed to the surviving animals, not to residents of towns and cities. The situation of Teruel province was similar. In the autumn of 1937 the slaughter of horses was authorized in the Republican zone, and some butchers took advantage of the situation to manufacture donkey sausage. The number of sheep and goats dropped from 908,000 before the war to 521,200 at its end. Cows fell from 11,400 to 4,200. The "immense majority" of poultry vanished. Perhaps the most damaging for agriculture was the disappearance of working mules, which declined from 33,907 to 18,907. After the war, military authorities sent 370 mules to the region as an emergency relief measure for pueblos, which had lost 75 percent of their pack animals. At the end of 1939 the Ministry of Agriculture allotted 2.5 million pesetas to acquire draught animals for Teruel. In Tarragona "the dramatic decline of livestock," including pack animals that the "Marxists" had consumed, prevented proper farming. The lack of beasts, which were often the only form of transportation in the hill country, further isolated mountain towns. In the Pyrenees mules frequently served as the main means of transportation. By the end of the conflict, 300 horses of the Barcelona municipality, employed by its sanitation department, had been consumed for meat; only 50 remained. Likewise, thousands of cows had been eaten, and less than a thousand emaciated ones remained alive, leaving Barcelona without milk. The dearth of animal food led to the slow deaths of pets in urban households.[66]

The civil war was responsible for the demise of approximately one-half of Spanish livestock, including rabbits, ducks, turkeys, doves, and chickens. Draught animals—donkeys, mules, and horses—survived somewhat better. Franco's decree on restocking had little short-term effect, and postwar Spain experienced a significant deficit of beasts of burden. Thousands of mules had to be imported from France, Portugal, and the United States and hundreds of horses from the Netherlands. After the war, Tarragona, a province of Catalonia known for its big and hard-working mules, needed to bring in 16,000 mules. Las Palmas initiated a campaign to export its surplus animals, especially females, to recently liberated "red" provinces that required both working and breeding stock.[67]

HUNTING

Franquista authorities insisted on keeping close tabs on the possession of firearms. As in the Republican zone, many ignored authorities' threats to subject those without licenses to the severest penalties and illegally retained their weapons. The tendency of certain members of the Falange to arrogantly display their pistols disgusted officials. Tight controls were placed on hunting, an extremely popular occupation throughout much of rural Spain. Nationalist authorities banned hunting in certain areas, such as parts of Asturias and Galicia, where *guerrilleros*, or deserters, were hiding. Orense and Lugo saw continual "cleansing operations" against deserters from "red" Asturias who would raid and rob isolated villages. In response, Lugo authorities also outlawed hunting with firearms. In Huesca, which bordered France and normally issued 6,000 licenses annually, hunting was largely prohibited. The ban had the ecological benefit of allowing endangered species to reproduce.[68]

Hunting licenses were awarded only to the politically reliable or to soldiers on leave. Some, such as the Asociación Cazadores Coruña, suggested banning all hunting until the troops returned home so that the "heroic comrades" would be able to "enjoy this sport." In Seville successful applicants for licenses had to meet two requirements. They could not be delinquent on taxes and had to contribute to the combatant subsidy an amount equal to the cost of the hunting permit. In Burgos 6,000 hunting licenses that allowed the use of firearms raised 60,000 pesetas for provincial coffers. In Palencia the number of permits jumped from 516 in 1936 to 1,896 in 1937. Perhaps to alleviate meat shortages, local governments promoted hunting by trying to keep ammunition prices at levels that existed before the war. They also encouraged the return of lost hunting dogs. Furthermore, they wished to stop continual and frequent poaching, which sometimes involved the pursuit of endangered animals and fish. Like hunting, fishing formed a part of rural culture in many provinces, and Burgos provincial authorities issued 3,000 fishing licenses annually, the highest number in Spain. Using explosives to catch fish

was common, although officially banned but nonetheless tolerated if violators were soldiers.[69]

FISHING

Like mules, sardines were among the uncelebrated heroes (or antiheroes) of
the Nationalist zone. Canned sardines provided several times more caloric
value than equal amounts of beef. Sardine oil had the added advantage of
being flammable, which allowed soldiers to read as it burned. The customary cold ration of the Nationalist troops on the march—canned sardines
and stale bread accompanied by wine and the occasional sweet—was ample
enough that soldiers generously shared it with captured Republicans—sometimes before they shot them.[70]

The Gallegan fishing industry quickly adjusted to Nationalist rule. Like
other food producers during the Depression, both ship owners and sailors
complained about the low price of sardines prior to the war (one kilo was
worth only 5 céntimos) and, like wheat farmers, demanded a government-
imposed minimum price. The low price had deactivated 1,000 Gallegan fishing boats. Before the war, strikes and labor agitation, aggravated by the low
profit margins of the canneries, were widespread in areas dependent on fishing. After 18 July 1936, protest was violently suppressed. Agitators or even
absent workers were shot.[71]

During the conflict, the canning industry in Vigo, the center of Spanish
fishing, generally functioned normally, especially compared to the Republican
zone, whose fleet and canning factories were comparatively unproductive.
The Vigo industry was able to satisfy greatly increased demand from both
the military and civilians. Nevertheless, at the end of August 1936 a shortage of oil and tin, whose value was several times greater than the sardines
themselves, created a bottleneck that caused the stoppage of canneries and
the temporary grounding of much of the fleet. Scarcities of necessary materials and the desire to control the market forced the "all-powerful" employers'
organization, the Unión de Fabricantes de Conservas de Galicia, to regulate
fishing catches. The Union charged what it wished in army and government
contracts. The same sort of commanding industrial monopoly, known as the
Consorcio, also existed on the Huelva fishing coast. Both organizations effectively dominated the trade, despite Falangist desires to break their power.[72]

In close cooperation with the industrialists, the state played a large role
in regulating the industry. Authorities limited the size and days of catches
and banned illicit fishing, which threatened to exterminate local salmon. Sea-
sonal prohibitions on fishing were common in the industry, and heavy fines
were threatened against violators. The minister of industry, Juan Antonio Su-
ances—a Gallegan himself—declared that the Caudillo took a special interest

in the fishing and canning industries of his native region. Officials' first priority was to supply the military quartermaster, whose demand substituted for
that of Madrid and sustained the industry during the war. The military controlled exports of fish and other commodities from the province. Fleet owners
in Huelva automatically set aside 3 percent of their catch for the army. Spain
was the third-largest European fish processor, and canned fish may have been
the second-largest Spanish export after oranges. Industry leaders, such as Pascual Díez de Rivera, the head of the franquista Servicio Nacional de Pescado,
claimed that fishing and related industries were "the second Spanish source of
wealth," employing hundreds of thousands. In Galicia perhaps 100,000 were
dependent on the industry; in the Mediterranean, 28,000.[73]

Galicia was by far the wealthiest fishing region, supplying 66 percent of
sardines and 30 percent of fish. Even during the conflict, the Gallegan industry was dependent on exports, and in 1937 shipped 12.5 million kilograms
to Germany. Canneries employed some 40,000 persons. Pontevedra province
alone had 15,000 fishermen, sixty-two canning factories, and twenty-nine
salting companies. Vigo (population 66,000) was also the most important
city of the region, and its population was more than double and its wealth
nearly six times that of its titular capital, Pontevedra (population 30,600).
Vigo was by far the greatest fishing port in Spain, and its catches were approximately four to five times the size of its closest competitors—Huelva,
Pasajes, Cádiz, La Coruña, and the Canary Islands. In Vigo, fishing crews
totaled nearly 9,000 men, and cannery factories numbered 42, employing 664
men and 6,217 women. Vigo furnished nearly 70 percent of Gallegan seafood
conserves. The city saw a significant expansion of ship building for the fishing
fleet and related industries.[74]

Despite periodic shortages of oil, sardine supplies were especially ample
during 1937 and 1938, when they increased by at least 16 percent in comparison with the good catches of 1934 and 1935. One report placed the increase of the overall fishing catch from a turbulent 1936, when "work was
constantly disrupted," to 1937 at 28 percent, or from 47,188,101 to 60,620,871
kilograms. By way of comparison, in 1937 the Cádiz port received approximately 10 million kilos of fish. In Vigo during the first nine months of 1938,
41,247,156 kilos were caught. The average price of seafood in 1936 was 0.46 pesetas per kilogram and in 1937, 0.43, which was the same price per kilo as
in 1935. In 1938 the price rose to 0.76 per kilo, which helps to explain the
relative quiescence of fisherman during the civil war. During the year 1937
the catch once again was approximately equal to that of 1935. Vigo billed
itself as the "world's preeminent sardine port" and claimed to have caught
more sardines in 1937 than in any previous year. The natural wealth of the
region was evident when "an enormous influx of fish, eels, turbot, and other
types of seafood" periodically invaded the Ría de Pontevedra. Sardines were

so abundant in Gallegan port cities that bars offered them without charge to their clients.[75]

The price per kilo of sardines in 1936 and 1937 was 0.19 pesetas. Since the disruptions of the war had reduced the size of the national fishing fleet by 35 percent, profits and wages accrued to fewer owners and fishermen. Despite a shortage of qualified marine personnel, many of whom had been drafted, Nationalists were able to deliver considerable quantities of sardines and other commodities. Fishing industry representatives regarded the stability of the sardine price as positive, since the 1937 catch was 13 million kilograms higher than in 1936. Authorities satisfied the industry by establishing a minimum price for sardines, which composed approximately half the Gallegan seafood catch. The platform price was maintained even in summer, when supplies were more abundant and prices seasonally lower. The franquista ship owners liked to contrast the production of their own fleet with the inefficiency of the "reds," who had controlled the northern Atlantic coast during the first year of the conflict when the smaller Asturias fishing fleet was out of action. In 1938 the owners became confident enough of market conditions to demand the end of any minimum or maximum price controls.[76]

In fact, sardines were perhaps too plentiful, and one Moroccan deserter complained to the Communist newspaper, *Mundo Obrero*, that the steady diet of canned fish made him "nauseous." A dedicated requeté grumbled plaintively "always sardines." Profits from sales during the war were ample enough to allow industrialists, such as Gaspar Massó, who was president of the Unión de Fabricantes de Conservas de Galicia during the war, to modernize his factories. The Massó brothers' plants, which extended 10,000 square meters, processed not only a large variety of seafood—sardines, tuna, clams, anchovies, mussels, and squid—but also ten tons of meat daily. In addition, they used the by-products to produce animal feed for the region's livestock. The industrialists possessed their own docks and a fleet of five fishing boats. The scale of their enterprise was said to be "American" and ranked among the largest in the world. Grateful that the movement had eliminated their class enemy, the Massó brothers, like other fishing fleet owners and industrialists, provided strong support for the Falange. The future deputy, Remigio Hevia Mariñas (1946–49), owned a factory employing 60 workers of both sexes, which produced 10,000 cans of sardines per day. Gallegan sawmills, one of which engaged 400 workers, provided the canneries with wooden crates.[77]

After wheat, fish may have been the most important foodstuff in the Nationalist zone. Certainly, the Generalísimo and his civil governors were eager to enforce labor peace between owners and fishermen, who had to be legally registered and whose ranks were purged of leftists. Only 18,000 of 50,000 fishermen in Pontevedra province joined the state-sponsored union, and most of these members either rejected or ignored the Falangist rhetoric it offered.

The principles of the movement were unpopular among workers and peasants in the province, where even Nationalist authorities acknowledged the continuing influence of caciques. This indifference also characterized the modest classes of Huelva. The perennial problems of illiteracy and alcoholism persisted among fishermen. Their wages sustained a dense network of taverns in all port towns. One of the latter counted 1,150 fishermen, 57 taverns, and 69 bars. In the fishing, mining, and industrial region of Asturias, alcoholism also became a major issue. Habitual drunkenness on the breadwinners' paydays led to poverty among family members, who were forced to find sustenance at public charity organizations. The civil governor blamed, in part, bar and tavern owners who served drunken workers, and he threatened to shut down their establishments if they continued to profit from workers' vices. Fortunately, though, few took seriously the advice of the Falangist leader, Manuel Hedilla, to exterminate the lazy.[78]

CURRENCY

Fishing, animal husbandry, and agriculture in the Nationalist zone would have failed without a solid currency. Domestic and foreign markets had faith in a Nationalist victory as well as fervently desiring it. Fears of Communist influence and practices in the Republican zone pushed sectors of the international bourgeoisie to help the Insurgents. The assassinations and expropriations of Spanish colleagues in the Republican zone and relatively fresh memories of the Soviet precedent of confiscation, elimination, and exile during the previous decade led international financiers to distrust the Republic. Banks in the Nationalist zone had closer relations with foreign financial institutions than those in the Republican zone. Bank managers and directors shared a world view that endorsed the Nationalist protection of property. Wealthy conservatives—such as Francisco Cambó, Juan Ventosa y Calvell, and especially Juan March—secured international financial support amounting to millions of dollars.[79]

The Republic's failure to convince owners that it could protect property rights plagued it internationally and domestically. Although the Republic sporadically attempted to protect foreign interests, owners of all nationalities stayed skeptical about its ability or desire to preserve private property. Unlike its Nationalist enemy, it could not float bonds attractive to domestic or foreign lenders. English and American banks sabotaged its efforts to transfer funds to purchase desperately needed supplies, forcing it to turn to the Soviet banking system and its branches in America and Europe in order to overcome Western financial hostility. Conservatives used Russian intervention in the war—in the form of an irregular flow of supplies and approximately 3,000 military personnel—to argue against aid to the Republic.[80]

The British, French, and Americans refused to advance substantial credits to the Republic, whereas the Germans, Italians, Portuguese, and the Texas Oil Company generously offered them to the Insurgents. Nationalists purchased 75 percent of their petroleum products, often on credit, from U.S. companies. Credit was indispensable to Franco's victory and his construction of a national state, the "political correlate of a developed money economy." Credit compensated for the Nationalist lack of gold and precious metals. The Insurgent triumph—like those of Parliament in the English civil war or of the North in the U.S. Civil War—rested on healthier and more fortunate finances. Unlike the Republic, Franco's forces did not have to pay their main suppliers in precious metals or foreign currencies.[81]

From the beginning, Burgos—the official seat of government from October 1936 to the end of the war—forbade the export of foreign currency and fixed the peseta at its prewar level. This helped stabilize prices in the Nationalist zone at least until 1938–39. Republican attempts to freeze prices by decree were much less successful. Republican soldiers, who had been initially among the best paid in the world, became disappointed when inflation quickly devalued their 10-peseta daily salary. They also were frustrated when the official daily rations—630 grams of bread, 250 of meat, 200 of vegetables, 20 of coffee, 50 of sugar, and a quarter liter of wine—could not be furnished. In contrast, Franco's rank-and-file soldiers received 3 to 4 pesetas per day. Although their pay was initially lower than their Republican enemy, as the conflict endured the standard of living of the Nationalist soldiers quickly surpassed that of their foes. Higher salaries in solid currency incentivized soldiers to move up in rank. Bravery and tenacity were rewarded with substantial bonuses.[82]

In contrast to their Russian and Chinese counterparts during their civil wars, the Spanish counterrevolutionaries managed to earn international confidence in their currency, an achievement that general histories of the conflict have neglected to analyze sufficiently. In the Nationalist zone in November 1936, authorities made sure to record the amount of money by stamping circulating banknotes. The director of stamping operation, the banker Epifanio Ridruejo, had escaped from Madrid to Burgos, demonstrating the preference that most capitalists and technocrats had for the Nationalist side. The stamping and the lifting of restrictions on withdrawals, which had been imposed on 12 September 1936, or even earlier in certain provinces, forced savers to brave "enormous queues" and "great difficulties" and redeposit their holdings into bank accounts by the established deadlines. However, these measures also restrained inflation through limitation on the issue of any new currency. Likewise, financial authorities outlawed the use of Republican currency in their zone. In the spring of 1937, old script was withdrawn from circulation and replaced by a newly designed issue. Nationalist ability to tax consumption and profits also restricted inflation.[83]

The lack of hyperinflation in the Spanish Nationalist zone stands in stark contrast to the counterrevolutionary experiences in Russia and China and to the Republican zone. In the latter, the emission of all kinds of banknotes by local and municipal authorities made any accounting impossible. Further- more the Republican peseta was not accepted throughout its own zone, and the trader or traveler had to show his safe-conduct pass to exchange money at banks or other institutions. The Republican zone resembled Southern Rus- sia under White control in 1918–19 when the Volunteer Army was not able to introduce a common currency in the districts it controlled. White areas experienced a shortage of paper money, especially notes of small face value. Their absence very much complicated everyday life. Everyone from merchants to bootblacks printed their own small change, a situation that bred "much quarrel and discontent." The monetary disunion reflected Russian Whites' "fragmentation" and the "inability to act in cohesion" that cost them victory in the war. In North Russia (Murmansk) barter dominated exchanges since no viable currency existed. Admiral Kolchak's control of the Imperial trea- sury and most of its gold did not prevent his Siberia from undergoing hyper- inflation. Peasants in White-controlled Russia refused to sell their produce for paper money. They rejected White banknotes and withdrew their foodstuffs from the market. Inflation in the White zones contributed to rampant corrup- tion since authorities were unable to live on official salaries.[84]

Inflation contributed more than any other single issue to the decline of the GMD's ability to rule and was a basic reason for their defeat. Between Decem- ber 1945 and December 1946, total currency issued increased from 1 trillion to 3 trillion dollars, marking an increase of 300 percent. Between December 1946 and April 1947, total currency increased to 6 trillion dollars, or a 100 percent increase in the short period of four months. It was officially announced that on 31 March 1948, currency issue stood at 70 trillion dollars. Two months later it increased to 135 trillion, showing nearly another 100 percent increase in the even shorter period of two months. In the first two years of the Chinese civil war, the issuance of banknotes and the requisitioning of foodstuffs formed the two main sources of income of the GMD government. In Chinhsien (Jiangxi) in early 1946, seven kinds of currency circulated: puppet Manchurian notes, money issued by the Soviets, (Chinese) Communist notes, national currency, national currency with the seal of the official Northeast department, Cen- tral (GMD) government notes, and Japanese yen. The uncertainty of accep- tance fueled inflation, and the lack of small change halted market activity or eating in restaurants. People waited in lines stretching four city blocks to exchange their bank drafts into cash. At the end of 1947 when Communist military forces pressured Chengtu (Szechuan), the city suffered from a scar- city of paper money. It became impossible to withdraw money from a bank account or to cash a check. The military monopolized all available cash.[85]

Neither peasants nor businessmen, who exported much of their capital to Hong Kong, wanted government paper money. Shanghai's rice shortage was entirely man-made since the Yangtse delta produced bumper crops in 1948. However, farmers were reluctant to part with their produce for government script, and rice merchants were intimidated from purchasing because they feared rice riots and popular expropriation. Only barter and the use of government reserves of gold and silver could overcome peasant reluctance to trade. Deaths occurred from "the stampede of crowds queuing up for gold purchases."[86]

In sharp contrast, like Spanish Nationalists, Chinese Communists tapped the resources of their zones without creating economic chaos and runaway inflation. In south Hopei taxes were considerably lower than in GMD territory, and prices of foodstuffs and daily necessities were, with the exception of fuel, much cheaper than in most GMD areas. In south Hopei Communist currency did not suffer from depreciation, "being based as it is on a more stable agrarian economy" than Nationalist money. Paradoxically, the Chinese Communists managed money better than their "capitalist" class enemies.[87]

Likewise in Republican Spain, many refused to accept Republican currencies for real goods and consequently relied on barter. For example, Spanish smugglers of fugitives into France demanded either silver or franquista currency in return for their services. In contrast, the Nationalist peseta was universally accepted in its area of circulation. In this sense, the Nationalists created a nation, at least monetarily. Currency evasion was less important in the Nationalist zone than in Republican areas. The *Times* of London attributed the strength of their peseta to "the intelligent finances of the Nationalists that count among their supporters some of the best business and financial minds." Many historians have argued that it was the militarization of the Nationalist zone that led to its victory; however, advice and cooperation of civilian experts also contributed greatly to the Nationalist triumph. Their monetary conservatism continued the orthodox practices of the prewar Republic. At the end of 1936 the Republican peseta had depreciated 19 percent and the Nationalist, 7 percent; at the end of 1937 the Republican peseta had fallen 75 percent and the Nationalist, 17 percent; and at the end of 1938 the Republican peseta had lost almost all value and the Nationalist, only 27 percent. The steep currency devaluation prevented Republicans from purchasing abroad desperately needed supplies—such as foodstuffs—that the Non-Intervention Committee had not prohibited. The Non-Intervention Agreement, brokered by Britain and France in the summer of 1936 to halt direct foreign involvement in the conflict, banned only military equipment and personnel, not what we would today call humanitarian aid. As in the counterrevolutionary zones during the Russian and Chinese civil wars, inflation contributed to rampant corruption in the Republican zone because functionaries—such as postal workers—were not able to live on their official salaries and felt compelled to supplement their inadequate income with illicit gains.[88]

Of course, the expectation that the Nationalists would win increased the value of their currency and reduced that of the "reds." Initially, many savers in the Insurgent zone were reluctant to put stamped or new money into banks and instead hoarded it at home. Soon, however, in Andalusia money that had been withdrawn in the first days of the conflict was redeposited into banks. Burgos savings banks claimed that deposits rose rapidly in comparison to the wave of withdrawals that occurred after the electoral triumph of the Popular Front. In Pontevedra the Caja Provincial de Ahorros saw a 64 percent increase in deposits from 1936 to 1939. Álava officials asserted that merchants' bank accounts grew rapidly. With the major stock markets of Madrid and Barcelona closed during the war and that of Bilbao opened only in 1938, investors left their savings in banks. Financial institutions paid relatively low rates of interest (1.25 to 3.5 percent) but paid them regularly. Although private banks experienced intrusive state intervention, bankers made considerable profits. Banks in the Nationalist zone absorbed a wealth of savings, and their deposits jumped from 1 billion pesetas before July 1936 to 3 billion two years later. Andrés Amado, the minister of finances, assured a foreign reporter that Franco's zone accumulated "enormous available funds"—often from war profits—which could be used to advance credit. The confidence of savers, whose accumulated resources the state could tap, sustained franquistas.[89]

Savers bought farm animals or, more frequently, real estate, whose prices became inflated. The inflation of both urban and rural real estate values was yet another reason for landowners' support for Franco. In this context, it should be recalled that labradores and tenant farmers often paid their *propietarios* in kind after the wheat harvest. Thus landlords (and black marketers) were securely protected from the relatively mild inflation in the Nationalist zone. Rural landowners directly benefited from policies of higher agricultural prices, which increased their earnings 25 percent, especially compared to urban landlords and bondholders whose rent and interest payments remained the same. SNT officials in León argued for the end of rent payments in kind in order to reduce owners' profits. To compete with real estate investments, municipalities eventually offered thirty-year bonds at 6 percent. In May 1938 the Burgos government reestablished interest payments to holders of state bonds, a measure that reaffirmed domestic and foreign confidence in the Nationalist peseta. Many large private companies that had floated loans prior to the war made good on their obligations.[90]

Queipo authored a financial model that spread throughout the Nationalist zone. At the very beginning of the war, he worked closely with private banks, especially the Banca Díez Vergara in Jerez de la Frontera, to control currency exchange. Queipo urged all who had foreign bank accounts to exchange their currencies for pesetas, anticipating the establishment in November 1936 by the Junta de Defensa Nacional of a Foreign Money Commission (Comité de Moneda Extranjera) that would regulate foreign currencies. His actions were in line with the Junta's 14 August prohibition of the export of gold. In March 1937 the Foreign Money Commission decreed that all Spanish citizens had one month to declare the amount of their foreign currencies, stocks, bonds, and gold to the Nationalist government, which compensated them at below (foreign) market exchange rates and reaped a harvest of millions of pounds, dollars, and other currencies. The Insurgent regime effectively controlled all foreign currency transactions, much to the dismay of importers and exporters throughout its zone. Queipo dictated the "skillful" devaluation of the peseta to attract British pounds from Gibraltar. Manufactured goods from the Rock—especially textiles—continued to be smuggled into the peninsula and traded on the black market throughout the war. The "viceroy of Andalusia" established a Junta reguladora de importaciones y exportaciones de la Zona Sur de España, which the military quartermaster chaired. His policies helped to ensure the continuation of exports of citrus fruits, sherry wines, olives, and especially olive oil to northern European nations. The influx of foreign currencies and tax on exports bolstered the Nationalist treasury. All Spanish exports had to be paid in foreign currencies, preferably dollars and pounds, which were turned over to the Delegación Militar de la Hacienda Pública within three days. Only offices of the Bank of Spain were authorized to purchase foreign currencies. In early 1938, Nationalists claimed to have a healthy trade surplus.[91]

Whereas Republican exports declined drastically, exports from the Nationalist zone probably remained stable during the conflict. Early in the war the Republican government temporarily prohibited food and chemical exports to reserve their use for its own needs. In contrast, Nationalist exports greatly helped finance the war effort. In 1938 the Comité de Moneda Extranjera received 48 percent of its foreign currencies from Spanish exports. The percentage would have been higher if the Nationalist peseta had not been overvalued on foreign exchange markets. In the spring of 1937 the Nationalist peseta was worth nearly three times more than its Republican counterpart on the international market. By the fall of 1938 it was worth six times. Exports of sherry wines from Andalusia and bananas from the Canary Islands increased from 1936 to 1937 but declined in 1938. Other Nationalist food exports—meat, fish, wheat, vegetables, fruits, olive oil—to the friendly nations of Germany, Portugal, and Italy increased from 1936 to 1937 but fell considerably in 1938. In addition to earning needed foreign currencies, exports were another way to provide an additional incentive to producers. Great Britain, Germany, and Italy were most interested in ores and pyrites.[92]

Spanish farmers generally welcomed Nationalist currency as much as they rejected the Republican militias' promissory notes. Peasants who insisted on selling their produce for the same sum in Nationalist currency that Republicans had paid were considered outrageous price gougers. In November 1938 at the end of the Battle of the Ebro, a woman in Benisanet (Tarragona) demanded the Republican price of 200 pesetas for a pair of chickens from a requeté lieutenant. He offered her the going rate of 15 pesetas in Nationalist currency. She refused and found her chickens confiscated as "prisoners of war." Peasants learned to make their own quick calculations concerning the value of various currencies circulating during the conflict. After the conquest of major towns and cities, personnel of the Bank of Spain facilitated in marketplaces and later in banks the exchange of Republican currency for legal Nationalist script. When Barcelona was conquered, twenty trucks delivered 100 million pesetas of Bank of Spain bills. The exchange rate reflected the disdain for Republican money, whose holders were essentially expropriated.[93]

In contrast to the disarray of Russian and Chinese businessmen, whom world wars had impoverished and demoralized, wealthy members of the Spanish bourgeoisie worked hard to help the Nationalists and bring down the Republic. They even reexported their capital, which they had invested abroad during the Republican years, to help the Nationalist cause. The Burgos government provided them with loans and easy credit to reconstruct their enterprises, and hundreds reestablished their businesses and lent their talents and capital to the franquistas. Francisco Luis Rivière refused to be discouraged by revolutionary control of his factory in the Republican zone and quickly restarted his Trefilerías Rivière in Pamplona. Monarchists, who had considerable influence in the army, were also helpful in raising money. Navarrese bankers and businessmen, such as José Fernández Rodríguez, donated hundreds of thousands of pesetas to the war effort in Navarre, the Basque country, and elsewhere. The Navarre regional government, Carlists, Falange, and various charities all benefited from businesses' largesse. The Spanish aristocracy was equally, if not more, supportive. Their financial holdings, jewels, and precious metals served as collateral for the loans that the London bank Kleinworts offered Juan March and the Nationalists. Ten of the 250 *grandes* of Spain, the elite of the Castilian aristocracy, died fighting for Franco, and forty were assassinated by the "reds." Thirty members of the monarchist and entrepreneurial Ybarra family, including a marquis and a count, were either assassinated or died in combat for the Nationalists. Other great families—the Domecqs and the Medinas—had almost all their sons of military age in service.[94]

DONATIONS

Donations and taxes helped to finance the war effort not just in Andalusia but eventually throughout Nationalist Spain. In the first months of the war the Nationalist war effort was often dependent on gifts. Queipo—who liked to repeat Napoleon's maxim that in war three things were necessary: money, money, and money—placed the highest priority on raising funds for his soldiers. Interpretations that emphasize Queipo's rebelliousness and his mental instability may neglect his leadership of a bourgeois social movement that was willing to make significant material sacrifices to defeat the left. His and other fund-raising efforts should be contrasted with the degenerate atmosphere in the Russian counterrevolutionary zone, where cocaine and vodka were consumed in enormous quantities. Kolchak's headquarters in Siberia was "filled with moral decadence and seedy corruption." Russian Whites had difficulty taxing the wealthy, who usually lacked any spirit of sacrifice. A similar destructive self-indulgence occurred during the Chinese civil war. American intelligence officials discreetly criticized their Chinese Nationalist allies for "the corruption on a vast scale" that accompanied the procurement of men and supplies for the GMD military. In July 1947, British observers contrasted the one-third of China controlled by totally "corrupt" Nationalist officials with the highly centralized and obedient third that was under the domination of Communist authorities. Well-informed Chinese concluded that GMD corruption was "the mother of the CCP." In early 1948, liberal Chinese intellectuals declared that GMD officials used the war for private gain but Communists used it to build support in the countryside.[95]

Queipo's radio speeches may have devoted more time soliciting funds than intimidating workers. He and other commentators continually reminded the wealthy that the pronunciamiento had saved their possessions. As early as 22 July, women began donating their precious metals and jewels to the movement. The Burgos government made an analogous appeal for donations in early August. A wealthy widow gave a large part of her jewelry collection in honor of "the army that fights for the salvation of Spain." The vouchers and receipts for the deposited gold and jewels did not show off donors' wealth but instead revealed their obligation to aid the cause. In November 1936, officials established a mint (Casa de la Moneda de Burgos), which created gold bars from thousands of kilos of jewelry and registered precious stones. At the end of 1937 General Fidel Dávila, the president of the Junta Técnica del Estado, assumed control of the mint. The Laboratorio de Oro Nacional in Burgos appraised the content of the precious stones and metals of the more than two million donated rings, earrings, bracelets, and watches. Collectors of the stones and metals were often volunteers whose work was generally free of corruption. Nevertheless, a few generous gifts ended up on the fingers or necks of the wives of influential Falangists. The precious metals campaign reflected the severe shortage of gold in the Nationalist treasury, especially compared with their enemies, who controlled the fourth-largest gold deposit in the world.[96]

By 22 July 1936 Queipo claimed that almost 1 million pesetas had been donated in only three days. Food importers offered to feed troops without charge. Another company tendered 3 million pesetas worth of fuel. Five banks opened accounts to accept donations for the troops. The village of Alameda (Málaga) became a model because it "donated" thousands of pesetas, precious metals, large amounts of olive oil, wheat, barley, and chickpeas. Residents of Cádiz were praised for giving their jewels, rare coins, and precious metals. Businessmen, landowners, and other well-off persons who wrote large checks for the military were proclaimed examples of a patriotic abnegation that was copied throughout the Nationalist zone. Ecclesiastical valuables (including the gold crown of the Virgin of Macarena) and charity bullfights filled Queipo's coffers. Municipal bondholders, many of whom were women, patriotically donated their principal and interest to the town treasury. By mid-September 1936, 300,000 pesetas worth of bonds had been donated, mostly from the middle classes who had purchased this kind of secure investment.[97]

Queipo's subordinates recruited aristocrats with close ties to wealthy bourgeois to raise funds. The Duke of Medinaceli collected 2 million pesetas from olive exporters. Large aristocratic owners, who were influential with authorities, felt obligated to contribute thousands of pesetas and the output of hundreds of hectares to the "Movement which was saving Spain" in order to prove their bona fides to Nationalist authorities. A prominent stockbreeder donated his bulls. Voluntary and coerced donations and regular taxation quickly created a considerable economic reserve by 1937. According to Queipo's granddaughter, Seville collected thirteen tons of supplies from 23 July 1936 to 31 May 1939.[98]

Long lists of donations filled the pages of newspapers, and each province competed with others to collect the funds needed to purchase an ambulance, airplane, and other war material. Gold holders in Córdoba were urged to donate their precious metal and jewels since the province was considerably below others in donations. In Ávila, gifts were large at the war's beginning and continued to be impressive through 1938. However, the numerous authorized charities employed increasingly coercive tactics to raise funds. This tendency to use force and sanctions was sometimes counterproductive since it discouraged potential givers. In Segovia province, donations in cash, wheat, gold, and silver amounted to over 4.5 million pesetas by August 1938. León doubled Segovia by contributing 8.5 million pesetas to various Nationalist causes and charities. In Orense province donations amounted to 8 million pesetas during roughly the same period. The most generous givers came from the middle classes, not from the wealthiest groups, who attempted to avoid giving according to their means. Officials praised the generosity of Asturians, especially those of the middle classes, who were never "stingy." Huesca provincial authorities reported 2 million pesetas collected. They established a

Junta Recaudatoria Civil, which acted as a kind of taxing authority that certified charities and assigned individual contributions on the basis of wealth. Álava province collected donations valued at nearly 4 million for fifteen different militaristic charities. The number of charities and fund-raisers expanded so rapidly that local authorities were compelled to limit their number and authorize their functioning.[99]

The proliferation of charities and giving was remarkable. For example, the Midwives' College started its own fund for the army. The most significant, the Suscripción Nacional—first encouraged by Queipo—added donations both in cash or kind to Nationalist coffers. The Suscripción raised approximately 400 million pesetas, a considerable sum equivalent to three to six months of Nationalist revenues during the civil war. Suscripción Nacional funds collected in Zaragoza and Teruel were devoted to the purchase of nine fully equipped Heinkels priced at a total of 765,000 German marks. Gifts to the armed forces were often personal items with private and affectionate meaning. For example, people gave a shirt, necklace, or earrings to soldiers' funds. Of course, much giving was not disinterested, and donors, especially those with leftist and anticlerical backgrounds, sought to ingratiate themselves to the new authorities. For instance, "a Communist who renounced his Marxism" gave fifteen packages of tobacco to the "Savior Army."[100]

Associations of landowners and capitalists had a tradition of subsidizing directly the forces of "order," who returned the favor by serving as strikebreakers. In Galicia and La Mancha, chambers of commerce had honored and materially rewarded the Civil Guard and the military after the October 1934 revolt. During harvest times, when the potential power of workers' organizations dramatically increased, rural landowners were more than willing to offer room, board, and salaries to the security forces. Several months before the coup, during a general strike in Lugo, teams from the military quartermaster made bread to supply the population. Wealthy individuals throughout rural Spain personally financed preparations for the revolt. Thus, it is hardly surprising that employers' organizations "constituted the principal economic support of the Uprising" by paying the salaries of various police forces. Bosses, their wives, and daughters also provided rightist militias with provisions and meals. In Huelva the Cámara de la Propiedad Urbana showed its "gratitude" to the soldiers "that had saved them" by initiating a fund for those in uniform. Even though the state eventually reimbursed bosses, they were ordered to pay the salaries of their employees who had joined the Falange, Carlist, and other militias. In Andalusia Queipo threatened employers with "the most severe punishment" if they did not remunerate their workers on time.[101]

Exiled Catalan businessmen, such as Francisco Cambó and his colleagues of the Lliga Catalana, were more than willing to make major contributions to the Nationalists despite their misgivings concerning their anti-Catalanist attitudes. Cambó, who made much of his fortune as a representative for foreign companies, devoted considerable amounts of his own money to promote the franquista cause through bankrolling the creation and distribution of propaganda at home and abroad, particularly in France, Italy, and Great Britain. His wealth and international connections helped facilitate purchases of arms and supplies for the rebels. In November 1936 Cambó complained about having to pay substantial sums—at least 25,000 pesetas per person—to the FAI and the POUM to liberate kidnapped friends, associates, their wives, and their children from the hands of revolutionaries.[102]

Like Cambó, Juan March used his money and influence to promote the Insurgents. He spent perhaps 5 million lire to buy three hydroplanes to help secure Nationalist control over his native Mallorca. Wealthy Catalans in exile contributed a large part of the 410 million pesetas raised abroad for the Nationalists. The Carlist Joaquim Bau i Nolla became president of the commission of Industria, Comercio y Abastos de la Junta Técnica del Estado and the highest-ranking Catalan in the Nationalist zone. His commission nominally oversaw the provisioning of the army. Bau was a kind of closet (economic) liberal who was dedicated to limiting state intervention, which he believed to be economically counterproductive. Bankers and industrialists associated with the Lliga—Josep M. Tallada i Paulí, Fèlix Escalas i Chamení, and Pere Madí i Russinyol—also became important financial advisors of the Nationalists. In the eyes of these individuals, the revolution meant the control of their businesses and other assets by criminal elements. They resisted revolutionary nationalizations not only in the Republican zone but also—and much more successfully—in the Nationalist one. They probably made price controls, which had officially prohibited increases superior to those in effect in July 1936, more flexible than they otherwise might have been.[103]

Those who refused to donate "voluntarily" were labeled "Jews" and subjected to small and large fines tailored to their means. Sanctions for failing to contribute to official charities and social works surpassed those imposed for violation of price controls. In La Coruña two citizens of Mellid were fined 5,000 pesetas and another 1,000 for "their mediocre contributions to national charities and their cacique scheming." Another was fined 2,000 for similar reasons. Many others—perhaps thousands—were also forced to pay according to their means. The wealthy—industrialists and merchants—were obligated to contribute the largest amounts, both in absolute and percentage terms, to Nationalist charities. The oxymoronic military commander of the Canaries ordered that "the capitalist and agrarian bosses contribute monthly to the voluntary charity for the unemployed." Exports of tomatoes and potatoes were also taxed for the unemployment fund. In Las Palmas all citizens were required to donate at least 0.6 pesetas every month to Auxilio Social.

Compulsion may explain why, "throughout the war, the donations in money and in kind to Falangist charities by representatives of the privileged classes were constant." Gifts from the humbler sectors complemented those of the comfortable classes.[104]

Individuals who withdrew money from banks or hid it became counter-models. Politician and former liberal cacique the Count of las Torres de Sánchez-Dalp was forced to pay a fine of 500,000 pesetas because Queipo thought his donation to the army of 25,000 pesetas was insufficient. The general humiliated the oligarch by forcing him to shave his beard. Immediately after the war's end, Sánchez-Dalp was again fined 10,000 pesetas for his "failure to donate patriotically." Further fines showed that he had become the exemplary whipping boy of local Nationalist authorities. Another rich landlord of Jerez, Sr. García Salto, was suspected of hoarding. His house was searched, 500,000 pesetas were found, and he was jailed. In mid-August 1936 Queipo informed those who had recently purchased gold that he would assume that it came from looting and that they would also suffer "maximum" punishment. On the following and successive days, the general reported that large quantities of gold and jewels were being donated to the cause. Queipo requested that banks provide him with names of those who had made large withdrawals and threatened to confiscate their wealth and punish them severely. The Auxilio Social later copied his example of establishing a system of informers to seek information on those who refused to donate to the cause. As a social incentive, Andalusian and Falangist charities publicized the names of donors.[105]

Pressure for contributions steadily increased as the war endured. A Las Palmas resident was fined 5,000 pesetas for his failure to donate. In San Roque the local leader of the Falange accosted a woman returning from church and accused her of not donating sufficiently to the Nationalist cause. In imitation of the Italian Fascist campaign, which had urged citizens to donate their rings during the Abyssinian War, Nationalist newspapers called on their readers "not to shake the hand of a man or woman who, after ten months of war, still wears a gold wedding ring that the Fatherland needs." Governors threatened to publish the names of the comfortable who held onto their cash.[106]

Both sides opened the contents of safe deposit boxes, but Nationalist authorities left them in the hands of private banks, whereas Republican officials confiscated them. Nationalist officials legalized this process and controlled it more tightly, in contrast to the Republican zone, where the opening and expropriation of personal and familial possessions traumatized many in the middle classes. Once again, franquistas displayed their unprincipled but pragmatic respect for private property, an attitude that ultimately helped them win the war. The state was envisioned as undertaking direct economic initiatives only when private enterprise failed or national interests required it.[107]

REVENUES

Whether collected by the state, private charities, or the Falange, the collections of donations and taxes showed an ability to sacrifice that was rare in twentieth-century counterrevolutions. The Nationalist treasury took several significant measures to finance the war. It created five major new taxes while maintaining previous obligations, and it delayed interest payments on the state's debt to its own citizens (decree of 11 August 1936). Although we lack the plethora of statistics that more advanced nations generate, it is estimated that taxes allowed the treasury to finance at least 30 percent of its expenses. The remaining 70 percent came from loans offered by the Bank of Spain (9,000–10,000 million pesetas) plus Italian aid and a smaller amount of German assistance. During the conflict the Nationalist treasury received revenues of 3,700 million pesetas and spent 12,000 million pesetas, leaving a deficit of 8,300 million. The Bank of Spain financed the deficit through loans and credits.[108]

The considerable financial support of Germany and especially Italy can be seen as a variety of "matching grants," common in American philanthropy, whereby large donors match the sums of small donors who demonstrate to the former that the more modest contributors are dedicated to the cause both emotionally and financially. The fascist powers, foreign banks in Lisbon and London, and American multinationals believed the Nationalists to be good risks because they were able to finance a substantial part of their purchases by themselves. For example, at the end of December 1936 General Dávila ordered the state petroleum company CAMPSA to pay 200,000 dollars to the Texas Oil Company. The latter firm had supplied gasoline to CAMPSA prior to the conflict and continued to fuel Franco's needs during the civil war, even if local shortages occurred. In other words, the initial impulse of international capitalists and financiers to aid the Insurgents was confirmed by the latter's ability to sacrifice their money and blood. In sum, Burgos was able to amass in credits from foreign states and banks roughly 700 million dollars, which was approximately equivalent to the sale of the gold of the Bank of Spain by Republican authorities. Yet if the numbers are similar, the effort was not. Generally, Nationalists either had to export or to appear to be winning to receive credits; the Republicans, the official government of Spain, were fortunate to inherit a treasure of precious metals and currencies. The Francoist state was able to pay off both the German and Italian loans on very favorable terms. The Germans spent 500,000,000 marks in Spain, 33 to 50 percent of which was devoted to equipping the Condor Legion.[109]

The Spanish war demonstrated once again that foreign aid was not an independent variable and usually remained contingent on the performance of the recipient. The British Cabinet halted funding for its allies, the Russian

Whites, in 1919, even though the latter had received vast quantities of British munitions and money. During a war cabinet meeting of July 1919, the prime minister, David Lloyd George, demonstrated total disillusionment with his Russian allies. Lloyd George asked why 2 million pounds were required to encourage trade in South Russia, "one of the richest [territories] in Europe." The secretary of state for war, Winston Churchill, replied that the peasants would only exchange their produce for imported commodities. Many cabinet members agreed with their prime minister that the Whites would "squander" further supplies and that Britain might be saddled with the responsibility of feeding the population in White-controlled areas of southern Russia. The ministers doubted that they had the financial and maritime resources to accomplish this task and concluded that Britain could not prevent the collapse of Denikin's zone. Even General Alfred Knox, a hard-core supporter of the Whites, "was disgusted at the Reds wearing British uniforms" and said that the British would supply nothing more to Kolchak because everything they furnished reached the Bolsheviks. The United States also refused to provision the urban population in Odessa until the stocks of hoarded foodstuffs were made available to "the masses," who suffered while a few Whites made enormous profits, "a combination which inevitably breeds Bolshevism."[110]

In the Chinese civil war, the United States was tempted to halt its assistance to the GMD, which was wasting extensive American aid and uncontested air superiority. President Harry Truman remarked to his cabinet in March 1947: "Chiang Kai-Shek will not fight it out. [The] Communists will fight it out—they are fanatical. It would be pouring sand into a rat hole [to give aid] under present conditions." Secretary of State George Marshall noted sardonically that Chiang "is faced with a unique problem of logistics. He is losing about 40 percent of his supplies to the enemy. If the percentage should reach 50 percent he will have to decide whether it is wise to supply his own troops." The Communists were masters at buying and stealing American and Japanese weapons from GMD units. Nevertheless, the United States eventually provided more than 1.4 billion dollars to the GMD from the end of World War II to 1949. On the other hand, Maoists seemed to employ much more limited Soviet assistance effectively, especially for crucial supplies of key industrial commodities that they could not obtain elsewhere. They produced a food surplus, which they exported to the Soviet Union through the Russian-controlled port of Dairen in return for arms. These weapons helped secure the PLA's survival in the face of GMD offensives in late 1946 and early 1947. They also set up spy and clandestine supply networks in Nationalist cities to obtain medications, radios, and other industrial supplies that were absolutely essential for their isolated rural base areas. Agents could easily obtain Chinese Nationalist currencies and use them to purchase essential commodities.[111]

CCP control of the countryside and transportation allowed them to feed their own forces and cut off grain shipments to GMD-controlled cities and towns. Indeed, after the Japanese surrender the Communists agreed "that they would not resist the Central Government troops in the occupation of the major cities of North China provided that the troops were kept in the cities." In other words, control of the source of the food supply was the essence of CCP strategy, which starved GMD-controlled cities. In Changchun (Jilin) "a few hundred persons daily die from hunger." "The situation at Changchun, of course, forms one of the most tragic episodes of the age. The Communists quite some time ago launched the movement to uproot the sprouts of all [agricultural] growth in the suburbs, and for the area within a 40 *li* perimeter of the city, all farm produce was entirely wiped out. The inhabitants inside the city are even worse off than animals, for to them such things as distillers [*sic*] grains, leaves of trees, stalks of melons, wild herbs and dried grass have become delicacies of the greatest value. The tragedy of man eating man is reported to have happened in the no-man's-land around the city." Despite the GMD commitment of holding "fast to Changchun, which is the symbol of our [Chinese] territorial sovereignty in the area," it fell at the end of October 1948. As in Spain, the resources of the north allowed the insurgents of both countries to conquer the south.[112]

The CCP control of food supplies rendered Chinese Nationalists dependent on American and Australian food imports. Foreign provisions were desperately needed to feed the major cities of Beijing and Tientsin in Hebei province. American officials revealed that distribution was nearly a complete failure "with less than ten percent of food received actually distributed in areas of direst need." The balance was sold in cities or areas where need was not as acute. Authorities recommended the continuation of food shipments to China only if distribution bottlenecks were corrected and allocations made on the basis of actual need, not political interests. Urban food shortages— often caused by speculation and personal hoarding—contributed to hunger and inflation that eroded confidence in the GMD and increased support for the Communists.[113]

Many historians have argued that the Western democracies "betrayed" the Spanish Republic by refusing to assist it sufficiently. We can never know with any certainty if Western aid would have turned the tide against the Nationalists. Yet it might have had negative consequences for the democracies themselves. Aid to the Republic would have deeply divided public opinion in both Britain and the United States, as it had in France. The hypothetical question can be raised whether, even with significant Allied help on the scale of aid to the Russian Whites and Chinese Nationalists during their civil wars, the Spanish Republicans would have emerged victoriously. In response to Western aid, Germany and Italy might have increased their assistance to Franco. Perhaps— like Russian and Chinese counterrevolutionaries—Republicans would have wasted the assistance of the Western allies and lost the war. In the Spanish case, such an outcome and divided domestic opinion might have discouraged the democracies from resisting the fascist powers and further increased Western inclination toward appeasement. Great Britain or even the United States could have concluded—like Stalin's Soviet Union in the summer of 1939— that it would be wiser to come to an agreement with Adolf Hitler's Germany, the uncontested winner of the proxy war in Spain, than to fight it. Failure in Spain could have increased the influence of the pro-German "peace" faction in Great Britain and the isolationists in the United States.

Unlike the Popular Front governments both before and after the outbreak of civil war, Nationalists collected taxes, especially from urban residents. Franquistas rejected what they considered to be the "Marxist" refusal to pay debts. This willingness and ability to tax counterbalanced their enemies' advantage in gold reserves. In Andalusia Queipo enforced the orderliness and regularity of revenue collection and distribution. He imposed special taxes on olive oil, soap, and stamps to raise money for Granada province, which the war had divided nearly equally between Insurgents and Loyalists. In Seville officials extended the hours of treasury offices and warned taxpayers not to be delinquent. Collections raised enough to meet obligations to both civilian and military employees. Queipo imposed a tax on workers with stable jobs, a 2 to 3 percent tax on municipal employees, and a surcharge on purchases in department stores to provide for the unemployed. He established soup kitchens, which became a model for the AS, to feed thousands of the poor, including— perversely enough—the widows and children of the breadwinners whom his forces had eliminated. By early September Queipo's office claimed that the municipality was nourishing 12,000 people per day.[114]

The general introduced a new tax on urban employers by ordering that they pay the salaries (3 pesetas daily, 2.25 of which were designated for meals, 0.75 to take home, and an extra bread ration) of legionnaires and all militiamen from right-wing organizations. The latifundista Mariano Pérez de Ayala was appointed to administer these revenues. Queipo knew that regular pay was essential for troops' morale, and Nationalists became aware of their competitive advantage since the Republican enemy did not always meet the payroll of its soldiers. At the end of July, business and consumer taxes, which fell disproportionately on the urban poor, were increased substantially. Similar levies—especially on alcoholic beverages and coffee substitutes such as chicory and roasted barley—brought in large amounts in other provinces. In Galicia new taxes of 1 to 2 percent were imposed in 1937 on fish, beef, quarry, and wood sales.[115]

Throughout Andalusia and Extremadura—Granada, Cádiz, Cáceres, Seville, and elsewhere—lotteries, whose proceeds flowed to the army, were established. Queipo led another forced donation campaign to raise funds for one of his most prized charities—the construction of low-cost public housing for workers, employees, and injured war veterans. The construction of affordable working-class housing was part of his drive against "liberal capitalism" and for what he called "patriarchal capitalism." The general became particularly well known for his policies of providing homes for injured war veterans and for families with many children. He decreed a partial holiday for back rents on nonluxury housing, but enforced the collection of current rents. By March 1937, 5,186 petitions for rent relief had been decided and 490,517 pesetas of back rents pardoned. Soldiers and their families particularly benefited from the general's leniency. Landlords were ordered to pay their certificate of occupancy, without which they could not rent legally.[116]

Throughout the war the municipality of Seville waged a campaign to force delinquent urban residents (shopkeepers, merchants, artisans, landlords, and high-end renters) to pay their back taxes for the legal limit of five years. Both the provincial and municipal Hacienda repeatedly warned those in arrears that they must pay immediately. The warnings may have had some effect, since the treasury was inundated with a flood of "patriotic" revenue. The military and civil governor of Huelva province declared that its revenues had more than doubled when compared with October 1935. The city reported a 6 percent (10,600 pesetas) increase in food tax revenues in October 1936 compared with October 1935.

The Falange managed to impose its own progressive and monthly tax, called the Ficha Azul, throughout the Nationalist zone. Eventually a March 1938 law formalized this obligation to finance the charities of the Auxilio Social. Germany and, to a lesser extent, Italy contributed both cash and goods to the AS. In Andalusia, Sección Femenina (SF) members aggressively solicited Auxilio donations every Sunday. Pedestrians were obligated to give at least 30 céntimos. Those who could not afford this sum were advised to stay indoors. In Segovia province in 1938, the Ficha Azul raised 34,000 pesetas, collections 162,000, and donations 19,000, or approximately 18,000 pesetas per month. In León the monthly sum collected averaged 20,000 pesetas, most of which was from the more urbanized areas of the province. On 13 November 1938 in San Sebastián, 214 young women belonging to AS accumulated 16,185 pesetas and distributed 5,828 badges. In Huelva the *señoritas* and their organization were particularly successful and amassed 80,000 per month. The numbers demonstrate that methodical collection became much more significant than donations as the war endured.[117]

The purchase of badges commemorating the first anniversary of the rising was compulsory in Andalusia in July 1937. In a burst of renewed and pragmatic megalomania, Queipo demanded total participation. His representative in Badajoz was ordered to make sure that no inhabitant shirked the obligation. All residents of the territories controlled by the general were required to donate "voluntarily" either 3 or 5 pesetas, according to their means. Married and single females staffed tables and booths that sold badges indicating the contribution had been met. The female fund-raisers made sure that all passersby displayed the appropriate emblem. Shop owners and industrialists were compelled to purchase them for all their employees. The administration effectively obligated the wealthiest to purchase any unsold badges. Nonparticipants were reported to the Civil Guard. Such tactics became extremely unpopular among nearly all citizens but achieved 100 percent participation and raised more than 3 million pesetas.[118]

Members of the AS and the SF, accompanied by their male comrades, forced shopkeepers and homeowners to purchase tickets for bullfights, whose proceeds benefited Falange charities. Señoritas roamed the streets soliciting cigarettes, cigars, and candies for hospitalized soldiers. The Falange collected mandatory donations from patrons in bars, restaurants, and theaters during the war. The strong-arm tactics of fascist collectors reminded many of the Popular Front when youthful solicitors of the Communist Red Cross (Socorro Rojo Internacional) had extorted money from large and small business owners. The latter, however, felt the Falange fund-raisers were much more belligerent and demanding than the "reds" that preceded them. Falangists insisted on large sums and threatened those who did not pay with imprisonment. Other charities, such as the Nationalist Red Cross, used similar strong-arm tactics.[119]

Nevertheless, evasion was not eliminated. The leader of the AS, Mercedes Sanz Bachiller, insisted on penalizing those who refused to pay. Some resisted and treated the young female collectors "disrespectfully." Fourteen citizens of La Coruña were fined 100 to 250 pesetas for their lack of courtesy. Dozens of fines for the same reason or for failure to contribute were imposed in large and small towns throughout Galicia. In Cáceres, authorities were disappointed at the response to the Ficha Azul and other charities and felt compelled to sanction the least generous. In Las Palmas, authorities levied a 5,000-peseta fine on a wealthy individual who refused to give and had insulted collectors. Immediately after the end of the war, twelve citizens of several Sevillian villages were sanctioned from 50 to 500 pesetas for evading the Ficha Azul. For the same reasons, another dozen were fined from 100 to 10,000 pesetas.[120]

As had occurred in the nineteenth century and throughout most of the twentieth, rural property owners continued to avoid paying their proportional share of taxes. The Cámara Agrícola de Sevilla and the Federación Económica de Andalucía called on all their members to display their patriotism by meeting their assessments. The Cámera was financed by a tax, established in April 1933, paid by relatively wealthy proprietors. Apparently, a number of property owners in various provinces used the excuse of the "anarchic" conditions during the Popular Front to refuse or delay payment of their obligations. Many failed to contribute the social security tax for their employees. This reluctance to make social security payments for maternity and retirement funds continued during the war. The SNT sometimes refused to cooperate with treasury officials who wanted to impound or withhold wheat subsidies or bank deposits of growers who owed taxes. Once again, rural abuses were tolerated and rural interests favored.[121]

Urban residents were therefore forced to sacrifice more than others. In provincial centers like Burgos, Salamanca, and Valladolid, which saw a dramatic increase in government and military staff, the upper classes were compelled to share their living space. Although the military could not expel occupants, it was allowed to requisition homes, with the important exception of those of single women. Vacant apartments were reported to authorities, who made sure their superiors and colleagues had places to live. Burgos' population jumped from 40,000 to 115,000 because of the war. Its municipal taxes increased despite the protests of merchants, shopkeepers, and ordinary citizens. In Vigo the Cámara Oficial de la Propiedad Urbana urged its members to fulfill their previous pledges destined for the military and promised to send its collectors into the homes of the recalcitrant.[122]

Taxes were more easily collected in the city than in the countryside. The Seville Cámara de la Propiedad Urbana urged the quick payment of all back taxes in accordance with the decree of the Junta de Defensa Nacional and for the "salvation of Spain." Seville's revenue commissioner emphasized that taxes had not been raised and that his office was asking only for payments that had existed under previous "anti-National" and "antipatriotic" governments. He threatened to prosecute evaders for rebellion. Urban landlords and businesses were menaced with fines on unpaid assessments, and slackers were sometimes listed by name in newspapers. Small businesses— cafés, bars, restaurants, taverns—were in jeopardy of losing their licenses if tax payments, based both on license fees and the volume of their sales, were not current. In Galicia, a region that had resisted the Popular Front's suggestion of a tax surcharge on property, Nationalist authorities insisted on prompt payment of all local levies. Pontevedra and Cáceres officials complained of the inability of Popular Front municipal governments to tax their residents and compelled modest and wealthy delinquents who had skipped taxes during the Second Republic to contribute. In the Canary Islands the military decree of 17 November 1936, which established an employer contribution based on the number of mobilized personnel, imposed quotas under the threat of heavy sanctions on urban employers.[123]

In the Canaries, shipping costs were subsidized by the state to encourage export to foreign countries of sugar, bananas, and other commodities. In return, the state took 30 percent of foreign currencies gained in these transactions, but localities obviously benefited. The Cabildo Insular de La Palma declared an increasing budget surplus every year of the war. The Las Palmas treasury, which collected a large percentage of its revenues from import and export taxes, was able to provide funds for both military and civilian populations. Santa Cruz de Tenerife reported considerable success in collecting back taxes from *ayuntamientos* that had not paid them after the electoral victory of the Popular Front. Its treasury was "in good shape." Whereas in 1936 it had a deficit of over 700,000 pesetas, in 1937 it reported a surplus. Its assets rose steadily and quickly from 733,000 pesetas in 1936 to nearly 1 million in 1938.[124]

The relative prosperity of Vigo's maritime economy was reflected by the increase of the collection of customs duties, which jumped significantly in the second half of 1937 and in the first few months of 1938. Pontevedra province reported a "flourishing economy," which augmented tax revenues in 1937 even though 11 percent of taxpayers remained in arrears. In Vigo, national tax collections rose more than 2.5 million pesetas in the first half of 1938 compared with the same period in 1937. Customs duties were by far the main component of municipal revenues, which increased by 1 million to 6,513,759. Vigo experienced the doubling of revenues from 1936 to 1937 and a slight increase from 1937 to 1938. In the first trimester of 1939, Vigo's revenues augmented 322,276 pesetas, or 23 percent more than the first trimester of 1938. In Orense in 1938, tax revenues rose 1,352,145 pesetas to total 10,317,193. In Pontevedra a 4 percent increase was reported. In León, municipal revenues climbed 14 percent from 1936 to 1937, and the city earned a budget surplus of nearly 80,000 pesetas even though its expenses increased over 292,000 pesetas, or 10 percent. The city of Segovia reported a budget surplus of 300,000 pesetas. Municipalities often heavily taxed alcoholic beverages, making temperance campaigns fiscally unfeasible and unwise. Oviedo and other cities attempted—often unsuccessfully—to tax animals, meat, and wine entering their jurisdictions.[125]

In August 1936, Nationalist functionaries, typically urban dwellers who earned less than 4,000 pesetas annually, were forced to donate one day's pay per month, and for those making more than that sum, two days per month. On 17 August 1936 the Municipal Employees' Association gave its first check to Queipo for over 8,000 pesetas, which had been collected from this initial payday. In September, functionaries contributed another 4,800 pesetas. In Spanish Morocco, residents were asked to give 5 percent of their salaries, and both foreign and domestic companies were approached for gifts. The revenue was turned over to the Suscripción Nacional.[126]

Inland provinces also increased their revenues. Álava noted that suppliers of the Diputación refused to cooperate until they were paid for services provided during the Popular Front period. The new civil governor cracked down on tax evaders and managed to increase collections dramatically. Segovia province collected taxes "very normally," and its municipalities—administrative units that were often in arrears in other provinces—met their obligations. Ávila reported that taxpayers were unusually prompt. In Zaragoza, province tax revenues remained stable and even increased from 1936 to 1937. Seville reported similarly positive revenues, especially in contrast to the years of the Second Republic, when evasion was frequent. In 1936, 36,688,000 was collected; in 1939, 49,422,000. In 1937 Navarre established an exceptional—and lucrative—progressive income tax to finance the war.[127]

In Palencia province, collections of national taxes were generally prompt and regular. The Nationalists used the 20 December 1932 law, passed during the leftist bienio and modified on 14 November 1935, to levy income and luxury taxes on those with revenues superior to 80,000 pesetas annually. The wealthy who complained about heavy taxation were told to consider the British model, which assessed the rich at a much higher rate. The Junta Técnica del Estado threatened professionals, who had gained the reputation of presenting "laughable declarations," with "maximum sanctions." In January 1939, authorities promulgated a special war profits tax—applicable to both individuals and companies—which progressively assessed profits more than 7 percent of capitalization. Given its late implementation, it became more of a peacetime than wartime tax. In Vigo, twenty-one owners failed to file the correct forms to pay the tax, and many other industrialists and merchants followed their example. Capitalists contested the new tax in the Jurado de Utilidades. Nevertheless, under the category of "liquidation of war profits," the firm of Hijos de Simeón Ga. y Cía. paid 354,124 pesetas in 1937, and other industrialists in Lugo contributed 60,000 or 33,000 pesetas. In contrast, the total of fines for violation of price controls during the entire war period in the province of Lugo was fewer than 30,000 pesetas. Accounting and legal firms offered professional help to capitalists to pay dozens of national, provincial, and local assessments. The regime may have represented the interests of the big bourgeois, but—unlike many other counterrevolutionary regimes—it was able to fine and tax them to finance its war effort. In this context of fiscal pressure, the return of tax-exempt status to church property at the end of the war showed clearly the privileges of that venerable institution.[128]

Employers were forced to verify that their employees had paid their *cédula personal*—a highly unpopular head tax necessary to acquire an identity card and a passport. The latter had to be approved by the Civil Guard and military authorities. In many provinces, such as Pontevedra, cédulas were the largest producer of revenue. During the Second Republic, some provinces claimed that few paid the proper amount. Even during the war in the Nationalist zone, many underreported their revenues, their rent, and their tax payments to purchase a less costly cédula. Several villages in Asturias completely evaded head-tax payment. To increase collections, authorities undertook investigations to verify personal data submitted. In Pontevedra the efforts increased cédula revenues by 15 percent from 1936 to 1939. Provincial authorities in Huelva claimed greater revenues from the cédula in 1937 than in any previous year.[129]

Vehicles and their proprietors were also taxed. Trucking and bus companies were assessed according to a Republican law of 11 March 1932. Small businessmen and workers who rented cars and trucks were relieved of their back license fees but had to pay their current registration (*patente*), usually levied biannually. An additional registration certificate was imposed for all vehicles, including official cars and trucks, in May 1937. In Asturias, owners of luxury automobiles and motorcycles, which had been requisitioned by the army, were nevertheless forced to pay their patente. To raise revenue, the city of Oviedo imposed a ten-peseta tax on bicycles.[130] The latter became especially important as vehicles and fuel became scarcer and more expensive.

Inspired by the Third Reich, Queipo initiated the "one-course meal," which was adopted throughout the Nationalist zone on 31 October 1936. Once again, the levy fell mainly on urban consumers. The tax on the one-dish meal (*día del plato único*) was decreed for two days per month and, after 16 July 1937, one meal per week. Provincial authorities had a good deal of autonomy and collected revenue from the día del plato único every Friday and *día sin postre* (the day without dessert) every Monday. In the hotels and restaurants of Seville and later in the rest of the Nationalist zone the customer was billed for a three-course meal, and the difference in price was collected by the provincial government. Hotels contributed 50 percent of the meal price, hostels 40 percent. A standard reduced menu was established, along with fines for those who violated the law.[131]

The plato único became an important source of revenue. Its proceeds provided resources for social services, for instance, kindergartens, day-care centers, orphanages, and similar establishments. In 1938 in Segovia province, 1,773,000 pesetas were expected to be collected, or approximately 150,000 per month. In contrast, fines produced only 64,000 pesetas per year. León province amassed a monthly average of 126,000 pesetas. In Lugo province, monthly revenues from the plato único averaged 69,000 pesetas. Fines for nonpayment amounted to only 3 percent of overall revenues. Huelva collected 69,000 per month, but its fines rose to 16 percent of revenue. In Orense the plato único produced 1.5 million pesetas during one year. In Huesca the 25,000 pesetas collected monthly were the principal source of provincial revenue for welfare and social needs. Falangist and Catholic youth solicited funds from public establishments and from private homes. In Seville all who earned more than 6 pesetas per day were expected to contribute a small portion (usually less than 0.1 percent) of their wages. Catholics regretted that the original idea had originated in Nazi Germany and was not a Spanish or religious initiative. Nevertheless, many saw the plato único as a Catholic gesture, an attitude endorsed by the regime itself.[132]

Even though many did participate, resistance to the tax remained strong throughout the war. One governor threatened to send the police to the doors of "recalcitrant and bad patriots" who refused to give. Authorities invented elaborate control techniques to stop constant attempts at fraud. The minister of interior and civil governors threatened to levy heavy sanctions, jail violators, or even confiscate the violating hotel or restaurant. Not all hotel and restaurant owners were cowed into submission, and some reduced the quantity and quality of their servings while retaining their prices, thereby increasing their profits. Alternatively, other establishments overcharged and offered sumptuous suppers composed of black market ingredients. Authorities fined the Hotel Condestable in Burgos 10,000 pesetas and nationally publicized the sanction.[133]

Tax policy was oriented to support the military. Like successful revolutionaries, the franquistas seem to have depended on regular collection of taxes, thereby providing soldiers with steady pay rather than unpredictable plunder. It is often forgotten that pay is a powerful incentive not only for mercenaries but also for the most ideologically committed soldiers. In January 1937 the regime introduced the "combatant subsidy" of between 2 and 8 pesetas—tied to income, number of dependents, and residence—which was designated for the family members of rank-and-file, frontline soldiers who had been the principal breadwinners of their households. Juntas Provinciales and ayuntamientos initially administered it. They financed it by a 10 percent luxury tax on tobacco products, alcoholic beverages in public establishments, perfumes, jewelry, and cinema and theater tickets, including those that benefited charities. In May 1938 the combatant subsidy expanded to jewels, furs, antiques, and art objects. Provincial civil governors were given authority to lengthen the list of taxable commodities. The governors took advantage of this new power to levy the tax on regional delicacies, beauty salon services, and fine wines. In many provinces—Segovia, León, Huesca, and Huelva—50 percent of the funds collected for the plato único financed the combatant subsidy. This transfer again represented a shift of urban resources to rural interests. Rural provinces that had fewer large cafés, bars, theaters, and cinemas collected less than provinces with a significant urban population.[134]

In April 1938 the distribution of the subsidy was reformed to take into account household income and living costs. In the immediate postwar period, the subsidy was tightly restricted to impoverished veterans incapable of working and to their immediate family members. In addition to the subsidy, other benefits to veterans included exemption of low-income families of soldiers and militiamen from rent and energy payments. As an added incentive to his soldiers, Franco reserved half of available jobs in national, provincial, and municipal governments to his veterans. Soldiers' widows also received employment preference.[135]

Essentially an urban sales tax, the combatant subsidy—like other sales taxes in civil wars—proved difficult to collect. Authorities complained that "Spaniards are unaware of the importance of the combatant subsidy." Even though threatened with 500-peseta fines, Spanish shop owners frequently neglected the necessary paperwork and delayed payments. In principle, the consumers were presented with the official stamp of the subsidy when they purchased their merchandise at a store or received their food and beverage from the waiter. Many clients—with the cooperation of the waiting staff—were also reluctant to pay the tax, which raised their bill. Córdoba merchants and shop and bar owners were fined 500 to 5,000 pesetas for evading the tax. One Córdoba bar owner and a baker were sanctioned 1,000 pesetas and another café proprietor 2,000 for keeping the collected funds. Eight establishments in Cádiz province were fined 100 pesetas each for not collecting it. Even so, throughout Cádiz, resistance to the tax continued. In Huelva the civil governor walked into a shop and purchased a chocolate bar. The merchant did not provide him with the required receipt and was penalized 500 pesetas. In Asturias dozens of merchants also resisted levying the combatant tax and were collectively fined thousands of pesetas. Refusals were marked throughout León, where the Falange termed local evaders "enemies of the fatherland" who did not merit living in "National Spain." In Las Palmas, where violations were "constant," twenty-five were fined 100 pesetas each and seven others 50 pesetas for avoiding the tax. Fines of much larger amounts were imposed on at least a dozen others.[136]

Sevillan authorities warned "numerous employers" and their employees that they were aware of the widespread refusal to collect the tax. The Seville chamber of commerce grumbled that "some firms" had not contributed their fair share of the subsidy. At the end of the war, several dozen owners throughout Seville province were fined from 25 to 1,000 pesetas for their "lack of patriotism" in collecting revenue for the combatant subsidy. Over 100 businessmen in towns and villages throughout the province continued to resist collecting the tax and were sanctioned, on the average, several hundred pesetas each. In response to the refusals, which were considered "hostile to the Glorious National Movement," the Seville Junta had to issue rules dictating that all tickets to any sort of event (cinema, theater, bullfight, pool, cabaret, dance hall, etc.) had to be stamped as proof that the 10 percent surcharge had been paid. After payment, to prevent reuse, the stamped ticket had to be immediately rendered invalid by the client, a procedure that consumers easily and frequently ignored, despite widespread publicity campaigns. Seven towns and villages in the province neglected to turn in municipal registers necessary to levy the tax and were threatened with fines. Furthermore, businesses—especially many small shops—avoided payment or manipulated receipts so that they could be reused. Resistance may have strengthened when the province raised the surcharge on many items and services from 10 to 20 percent on 1 March 1938. Indeed, provincial authorities threatened to fine members of Comisiones Locales if they did not reveal refusals to pay. A simple excuse of sellers from every region of Nationalist Spain was that they had exhausted their supply of tickets and were unable to acquire more since the issuing office was closed. At the end of the war, nearly a hundred Seville bar owners and shop owners were fined from 85 to 3,000 pesetas for evading the sales tax. The levy proved nearly impossible to collect from unregistered street merchants.[137]

The civil governor of Pontevedra criticized mayors of the major cities and towns of his province for neglecting its "tax collection," resulting in "a huge deficit." He fined five owners from 100 to 500 pesetas for evading the tax. In Lalín (Pontevedra) eighteen street merchants were penalized 25 pesetas each for irregularities when collecting the levy. The governor continued to complain that the collection was insufficient. The La Coruña governor called for mayors to make certain that merchants and others met their obligations. Hundreds—if not thousands—of established business owners in Galicia, Zamora, and Oviedo were subjected to a wide range of fines for failure to follow proper procedures.[138] So were a few consumers who failed to authenticate the stamps that accompanied their order.

Collections for the subsidy may have been particularly resented since proceeds went to poorer families who had acquired a reputation as welfare cheats. In León province, able-bodied workers avoided agricultural labor, especially during harvest season, if their families received the subsidy. In Ávila a few from the smallest and most impoverished villages found that the subsidy was greater than their wages and refused to work the fields. In Granada, inspectors investigated recipients and excluded "plenty" who did not qualify. All physically able male family members were compelled to take the first available job offered. In Ceuta, local committees kept a close watch on shirkers since many preferred not to work in order to receive the full subsidy. Decrees modifying the application of the subsidy specified that local authorities corroborate "the true situation of the interested parties; in other words, if they work regularly." Nineteen family members of combatants were fined from 50 to 500 pesetas for violating the regulations. Recidivists earned penalties of thousands of pesetas.[139]

Regardless of means, almost all soldiers (except legionarios who were specifically excluded) believed that they had a right to the subsidy, and a good number who did not meet the qualifications attempted to deceive authorities. Furthermore, neighbors refused to inform authorities about these "abuses." One town councilor in Vedra (Coruña) who had amassed a small fortune but nevertheless tried to receive assistance was fined 5,000 pesetas. Seville officials warned all those who had enrolled by falsifying or omitting information to remove their families from the list immediately. Inspectors required family members to appear before them. The governor of Las Palmas estimated that 25 to 30 percent of recipients engaged in some kind of fraud. In Galicia one man and seven women who had hidden their sources of income were fined from 100 to 250 pesetas and ordered to return all subsidies received. Another man who held a regular position as a municipal tax collector was fined 25 pesetas for receiving a combatant subsidy and had his rent subsidy eliminated. The Pontevedra and Las Palmas civil governors called for removing all the ineligible.[140]

Efforts to obtain the subsidy both unified and split families. On the one hand, Santa Cruz de Tenerife authorities reported that unmarried couples with adult children were exchanging religious wedding vows for the first time in order to qualify for the subsidy. Wives who had married their soldier husbands after 18 July 1936 were generally declared ineligible. On the other hand, spouses of soldiers and their children separated themselves from large and comfortable households that sheltered several generations in order to reduce their household size and income and thereby receive government support. Provincial authorities were aware of the female maneuvering but were frequently powerless to stop it. Nationalist authorities wanted to avoid situations where those assisted by the regime lived more comfortably than employed proletarians. If this occurred, the latter would lose "the incentive to work." The state rightly distrusted its own citizens.[141]

The combatant subsidy proved too popular. In León the number of families receiving aid jumped from 1,174 in May 1937 to 9,012 one year later, and the amount of assistance rose from 177,000 to 528,000 pesetas. In Huelva by August 1938, 10,000 families were receiving subsidies, which amounted to the enormous sum of 900,000 pesetas per month. In Granada the amounts paid were similar and, given the fiscal situation of the divided province, the Ministry of the Interior had to provide 50 percent funding for the program. The national government made a similar commitment to Cáceres, which spent over 13 million on subsidies. In Ávila, payments quickly expanded and began to outpace contributions. The numbers of assisted soldiers rose from 2,905 in July 1937 to 4,414 in June 1938. Unsurprisingly, given the need to enlist tens of thousands of Moroccans, the costliest commitment seemed to have occurred in the Protectorate. In Ceuta the number of families covered from May to December 1937 nearly doubled, from 7,000 to 13,300, and to support them the government collected a monthly average of 1.4 million pesetas. Neither International Brigaders nor their families expected similar subsidies, a political and fiscal reality that demoralized foreigners in Republican ranks.[142]

In late 1938 the Nationalists introduced another subsidy, Subsidio Familiar, designed to assist large rural families. The program added extra pesetas for each conscript's child, independent of income. It targeted the agrarian proletariat of provinces, such as Palencia, where families averaged six children, in contrast to Barcelona with only three. Thousands of employers and tens of thousands of families participated. The family subsidy, combatant subsidy, full employment in the countryside, and the price increases of both commodities and agricultural labor constituted transfers of wealth from the urban to the rural population. During the war in the Castilian heartland, many "modest families" experienced an improved standard of living. It is not surprising that their members offered either passive or active support to the Nationalists.[143]

At the end of the war the minister of finances, Andrés Amado, earned a "gran cruz de la orden de Isabel la Católica," one of Spain's most prestigious honors, because of his success in increasing tax revenues. Amado had been a close collaborator of Calvo Sotelo and a creator of the CAMPSA energy monopoly. His Hacienda claimed that its collections jumped 410 million pesetas from 1937 to 1938; 118 million in extra revenue was obtained from newly "liberated" territories, and 292 million more from increased collections. The only type of taxation that declined was that from customs, which the autarkic policies of the regime reduced. As many have noted, the conquest of the north gave the Nationalists the wide variety of financial, industrial, and demographic resources they needed to win a war of attrition. For example, in newly liberated Oviedo, local authorities insisted that all unpaid taxes be paid. Evaders were subject to late fees as well as to the accusation of being disloyal to the regime. Oviedo tax revenues recovered rather quickly in 1938. Mine owners were publicly urged to pay their contribution or face the loss of their concessions.[144]

The stability of private property in the Nationalist zone provided a tax base that its enemies lacked. Fiscal policies and practices sharply separated the Nationalist zone from its Republican counterpart, since the latter found it impossible to collect direct taxes. In effect, in Loyalist Spain, property owners—whose ranks were greatly diminished by collectivization, confiscation, and flight—no longer paid taxes on their belongings or earnings. Government revenue agents were reluctant to levy charges on salaries for fear of being labeled exploiters. By the end of 1937 the Republican treasury had lost nearly all capacity of collection. The Generalitat performed fiscally somewhat better, but the Republican attempt to sell bonds in 1938 to finance the war effort was an unmitigated failure. This was hardly surprising since not only did the Republic appear to be losing the war but also its cities had reneged on their obligations to bondholders.[145] As in White Russia and Nationalist China, tax collections fell dramatically in the Republican zone as inflation soared. In contrast, in the Nationalist zone relatively heavy taxation helped to prevent an inflationary spiral.

EXPROPRIATIONS

At the beginning of the uprising, Falangists and the military often looted or destroyed the homes and property of those with progressive politics, frequently a prelude to the termination of their lives. Falangists and Civil Guards would take whatever they coveted and mockingly tell the leftist owners "Spain will pay" or "Give Azaña the bill." The Falange sacked and confiscated the offices of the moderate left newspaper, *El Liberal*, and Queipo fined its owners 10,000 pesetas. *El Pueblo Gallego*, founded and owned by the center-left politician Manuel Portela Valladares, was turned over to the Nationalist government and eventually to the Falange. Many proceeds from expropriations undoubtedly found their way into private—and corrupt—hands. For instance, whereas honest officials would turn over the confiscated property to the various fund-raising campaigns for the army, prison employees embezzled monies and possessions abandoned by their executed charges. In early September 1936, high-ranking Falange officials in Seville attempted to limit spontaneous expropriations and forbade any confiscation without official authorization. So did the military authorities and the Civil Guard, who in certain parts of Galicia tried to limit the violent and corrupt behavior of local Falangists who had acquired enemies among the old elites. The *benemérita* may have been successful in stopping a few crimes, but prosecutions of Falangist criminals were, as a rule, unsuccessful.[146]

A decree of 13 September 1936 allowed the Junta de Defensa Nacional to confiscate the possessions of all parties and organizations of the Popular Front. In January 1937 the Junta Técnica del Estado—originally established in October 1936 under the direction of Generals Fidel Dávila and Francisco Gómez Jordana to coordinate the rear with military needs—created an administrative and judicial office to manage the sequestered properties. Because of the recent emphasis on Nationalists' political repression, historians have exaggerated the revenue obtained from these expropriations and have consequently underestimated the financial contribution of regular tax collection. Although in a few regions the confiscation of trade-union property may have represented a substantial gain for the military and its Falangist allies, in most of the Nationalist zone its contribution was marginal to war financing. Queipo was said to have ordered that the repair of all destroyed bridges and sewers be financed through the expropriations of the property of revolutionaries, but it is highly doubtful that these confiscations provided sufficient revenue.[147]

Civil governors took charge of a broad range of public services and constituted the main link between national authorities and provincial elites. They were allowed considerable discretion in their many functions and often determined the fate of confiscated property in their province. In rural Spain—the base of the Nationalist movement—the land of leftists was turned over to provincial authorities, who had to manage or maintain the confiscated farms and businesses, which proved to be a tricky task. Many investors were reluctant to bid on or purchase expropriated property. Authorities rented leftists' property to the willing, who were not always its most productive caretakers. Nationalists wanted to punish their political enemies but soon realized that the wives and children of the sanctioned would remain destitute wards of the state or of Catholic charities unless given the opportunity to work. They concluded that if family members of the original owners paid rent to the government, they could remain on the expropriated property. Many, though, had already chosen to flee to the "red zone."[148]

Expropriations of leftists in Las Palmas (Canarias) and Andalusia provided only a diminutive amount of wealth. A few donkeys and other animals contributed merely marginally to the war effort. In Granada province fewer than 2,000 cases were initiated and over 1,000 *fincas* confiscated, most of which were without much worth. The total revenue derived from confiscations was approximately 600,000 pesetas, considerably less than Granada's donations to the army and equivalent to the minister of interior's one-month contribution to the province's combatant subsidy. In Burgos 1,082 cases of expropriations were initiated; however, most had only modest worth. Eighty percent of the estates were assessed under 20,000 pesetas, mostly small rural plots whose value did not reach 10,000 pesetas. The income from the expropriated Segovian properties was also low—only 163,000 pesetas in a budget of millions. In Huelva the figures were very similar. In Asturias the state pursued nearly 7,000 expropriation cases, amounting to the relatively large sum of 1.5 million pesetas and involving hundreds of individuals. Public auctions were held to sell the machinery and even the socks, stockings, and knitwear that had been the property of leftist organizations. Some of these belongings were awarded to those in the same industry or trade whose property had been damaged by "reds."[149]

INDUSTRY

The Francoist state and, more precisely, the quartermaster gave priority to equipping the army. In its major city, Seville, during the crucial first few months of the war, munitions factories were increasingly able to furnish the southern and northern armies with millions of desperately needed cartridges, tens of thousands of hand grenades, and thousands of artillery weapons and shells. At the same time, the southern zone under Queipo led an effort to create industrial zones in Andalusia. His efforts were part of the explanation for relatively rapid industrial mobilization in Franco's zone. Catalans fleeing the Republican zone were encouraged to regenerate the industries they had abandoned and whose products were sorely needed. Entrepreneurs—such as

Ignacio Coll, founder of the Sociedad Anónima Damm, and Luis Alfonso Sedó, director of Manufacturas Sedó—reestablished their firms in Seville. With the assistance of Sedó, Joaquim Bau, and other Catalan refugees, workshops fashioned 5,000 army jackets and pairs of pants by the end of 1936. Three thousand looms spun 1,250,000 meters of fabric. By mid-1938, 10,000 workers in 41 factories produced, monthly, 60,000 army jackets, 70,000 pairs of pants, 79,000 shirts, 66,000 pairs of socks, 62,000 towels, and other articles, including flannel shirts and canvas. The Intendencia del Ejército del Sur claimed to have distributed millions of garments to its soldiers and those of the Legion. Textile industries in Granada also contributed hundreds of thousands of meters of cotton cloth.[150]

Textile production multiplied threefold in franquista Andalusia from 1935 to 1939. Despite some opposition from Catalan industrialists, Queipo encouraged the foundation of Hilaturas y Tejidos Andaluzas, S.A. (Hytasa), in Seville in 1937. The new company amalgamated a number of smaller local companies and received an exemption from stiff customs duties to import Swiss machinery. Seville firms manufactured a variety of industrial products—beer, ice cream, paper pulp, medications, and linseed oil—during the conflict. In 1937, Seville province experienced the greatest expansion of corporations in all of Spain, besting Salamanca, the headquarters of the Generalísimo. The Andalusian city became the Spanish headquarters of many foreign firms. Branches of IG Farben and other German firms, whose directors had escaped from "red" Barcelona, sold drugs (analgesics, vaccines, serums, and other medications), dyes for textiles, and explosives for Franco's military. Some Italian firms also set up shop in Seville, where Hispano-Suiza repaired the various aircraft that Fiat had sold to the rebels. Despite its putative nationalism, the Insurgent leadership pragmatically permitted the continuation of the dependence of Spanish capitalists on their foreign partners, who made "spectacular" profits during the war. In 1938 the Spanish branch of Bayer won a company trophy (the Bayer *Pokal*) for its sales volume. Most basic medications were available in the Nationalist zone and underwent only a moderate price inflation of 10 to 20 percent. There were plans—unfulfilled during the war—to produce tractors in the Andalusian capital, a market that American manufacturers, such as Caterpillar, dominated.[151]

The Baleares, especially Mallorca, supplied shoes and ranked third in the creation of new enterprises in the Nationalist zone. A total of 57 Mallorcan firms, which produced a record of 10,000 pairs of boots per day, were placed into the service of the Nationalist army. The number of workers in Mallorcan factories nearly doubled during the conflict. The Mallorcan textile sector furnished clothes for Nationalist soldiers as did the industries of Salamanca province. During the conflict, Zaragoza's population increased from 180,000 to 350,000 inhabitants, and it also became a center of textile and shoe production, fabricating 2,000 pairs of boots per day. In Redondela (Ponte-vedra) factories were able to produce, daily, 5,000 shirts and 3,000 uniforms, making the town one of the largest centers of the Spanish garment industry. All shoe factories in the province of Orense worked for the military, and peas-ants who made several pairs of calfskin shoes and tried to sell them to civil-ians at county fairs found their stocks confiscated by authorities. All calves were reserved for the exclusive use of the military, which tried to entice shoe-makers into its ranks. Footwear quickly became scarce in Santiago, Oviedo, and other cities. Rubber soles were even dearer, and Serrano Súñer fined two wholesalers of imported rubber 100,000 pesetas and another 75,000. As a warning to others, the Nationalist media publicized the sanctions nationally. Local authorities followed the minister's lead and penalized their own shoe sellers thousands of pesetas. Given the shortage, no wonder Spaniards were greatly impressed by the Germans' and Italians' "magnificent boots."[152]

Despite public and private efforts, serious shortages of clothes existed in the Nationalist zone. New uniforms could not be furnished for all victory parades, and the requetés who marched in Pamplona at the end of October 1937 to celebrate the fall of the north appeared in their makeshift uniforms, with muddy helmets and faded red berets. Moroccan troops wore captured Republican clothing. In Palencia, supplies ran out during the summer of 1937, most stores having nothing to sell. Buttons, needles, and shoelaces had to be imported from "friendly nations"—Germany, Italy, and Portugal.[153]

The inability to supply their soldiers with proper uniforms was particu-larly galling to Nationalists, who associated vestimentary informality with the laxity of the Popular Front. Disgusted by the informal dress, which reminded him of the "disastrous times of the democratic Popular Front," the civil gov-ernor of Las Palmas ordered all those who attended official ceremonies to wear proper uniforms. Generally, the Nationalist troops seemed to have en-gaged in more rituals—whether religious or military—than their Republican counterparts, who adhered to relative casualness and invention. Republican ceremonies and uniforms were less standardized than those of their enemies, who were known for their vestimentary militarization. For the formal victory ceremony and homecoming parade in Pamplona on 30 November 1937, the requetés were reequipped with new uniforms to replace their tattered ones. Sartorially correct, they received a Collective Military Medal from General Dávila. As the Nazi Nuremburg rallies demonstrated, the appearance of mar-tial efficiency could convince ordinary citizens and fence-sitters of the power and probable victory of the militaristically clad party.[154]

Segovia reported that while food prices remained stable, the costs of cloth-ing and shoes had doubled. Merchants took advantage of the hike to make "huge profits." The civil governor responded by levying twenty-one fines from February to August 1938, amounting to 75,795 pesetas. These were considerable amounts for a rural province and showed the governor's desire to make examples of violators. In Granada, Cáceres, Ávila, and Huesca, the situation was similar. In Huesca, clothing and footwear costs rose 50 percent, and "greedy" shopkeepers often took advantage of the situation. One shoe vendor who attempted to make a 100 percent profit was fined 4,000 pesetas. Many smaller merchants received 25-peseta sanctions, even though municipal police were frequently unwilling or incapable of enforcing price controls. Serrano Súñer subjected the guild of Palma de Mallorca textile firms to a fine of 1 million pesetas for hoarding, speculation, and excessive profiteering. His motivation was "to defend the general interest and the modest classes." This spectacular fine of urban capitalists—which was once again given wide publicity in the Nationalist press—intended to show to urban sectors, such as workers and public functionaries who were contributing new taxes—that the Francoist state was vigilant in defending their interests as consumers. In April and May 1939, fines of tens and even hundreds of thousands of pesetas were levied on Mallorcan, Castilian, and Andalusian firms. In the latter region, González Byass—a brand-name company that throughout the war had sponsored hundreds of advertisements praising Nationalist forces and their Caudillo—was sanctioned 10,000 pesetas for violating the tasa. Burgos fined Malagan industrialists and merchants nearly 570,000 pesetas, including 439,000 levied against tanneries and their outlets and 75,000 against a cod importer. Immediately after the war's end, the national Comisaría general de Abastecimientos persisted in imposing hundreds of thousands of pesetas in *multas* on dozens of "shopkeepers without conscience" throughout the peninsula who sold at high prices or trafficked clandestinely at the expense "of the working classes."[155]

Women continued the tradition, practiced during the African campaigns, of collecting or making clothes for soldiers. As wage laborers they were expected to sacrifice more than men, who retained the best jobs and benefits. According to the Fuero del Trabajo of 1938, the state had the sexist obligation to provide only male Spaniards with employment. The Hytasa factory, a textile firm founded in 1937 in Seville, exclusively employed men. In other important firms and in branches of the administration, only veterans were eligible for employment and were preferred for day-laboring jobs.[156]

Male authorities tried to persuade women to volunteer to make garments for soldiers by inducing sentiments of culpability: "Your soldiers . . . protect you while you sleep calmly in the city. . . . Canary woman, you have all the comforts of the rear. Stop going to the movies, taking a walk, and gossiping. Instead, lessen the burden of the Canary soldiers fighting on the front." In Vigo the war supposedly transformed women's behavior: "Women do not dress up so frequently. They are modest and work harmoniously like sisters in Christ to make garments for those on the front." Females were urged to volunteer to knit wool attire for troops who needed jerseys, jackets, gloves, and socks during winter. Female Andalusian, Extremaduran, Navarrese, and Basque volunteers responded by making wool sweaters, capes, and vests for the troops. In Álava the Servicio Social de la Mujer had several hundred women laboring in twenty-four workshops in Vitoria and throughout the province. The quartermaster awarded the Basque señoritas its Medalla de Intendencia. Mobilization of women and war mobilization in general may have been more extensive in the Nationalist zone than in the Republican, just as in the U.S. Civil War the semifeudal South mobilized more fundamentally than the capitalist North. In any case, in this area and so many others, we lack the statistics and other information to make definitive comparisons.[157]

After food, wool was the largest budget item of the female-dominated Delegación Nacional de Asistencia a Frentes y Hospitales in Navarre. Blankets and raincoats were in special demand during the winter, and donors—many of whom were women—contributed hundreds. In the fall of 1937, Queipo confiscated all wool in his zone and asked women to produce winter garments for the troops. He and governors of other provinces also denounced trading of military blankets—often captured from the Republicans and trafficked by Nationalist soldiers on leave—and insisted that civilians return any in their possession to the quartermaster. Owners of army blankets were warned that if they did not return the items by 10 November, they would be considered thieves and subject to military justice. Apparently, a sector of the public ignored the general since the following winter he had to make the same brutal threats.[158]

Nationalists were much more successful producing beverages than clothes. Alcoholic drinks have always been important for Western armies, and Spanish troops were no exception. Opinion in the Insurgent trenches said that the best preparation for offensives was González Byass, a cognac made by an Andalusian grower who, like other major producers, was extremely supportive of the counterrevolutionary movement and its fascist allies. Soldiers of both armies did not doubt "that a good ration of alcohol stimulated going over the top." Indeed, troops renamed cognac "over the top" (*saltaparapetos*). During cold nights a *pelotón* (sixteen to twenty men) of legionarios customarily received a bottle of brandy. One requeté commented that "we volunteers loved wine and liquor. The wineskin passed around before, during, and after an attack brought us all together." Partaking of what is aptly called spirits often bolsters morale. Soldiers in many wars have recognized that drinking—and more recently in Vietnam, taking drugs together—initiates and reinforces the group. In the nineteenth and twentieth centuries, the French army was happy to provide brandy to its warriors; likewise, the British army offered rum. Alcohol and caffeine have helped many men go over the top.[159]

Breweries, whose workforce was militarized, augmented beer output by

80 percent from the middle of 1936 to the end of 1937. Beer production was assessed with a tax of 15 pesetas for each hectoliter, which constituted yet another urban levy. The production of Asturian cider doubled from 1937 to 1938. For certain Nationalist soldiers, alcohol was only too available. Despite their continual labors, puritanical chaplains were unable to stop the frequent drunken binges of their men. A few soldiers became so intoxicated that they shouted "long live the Republic" and insulted Franco himself. The result was their imprisonment or even execution. Republican forces found access to wines and liquors more limited.[160]

The Nationalists' controlled capitalism proved more effective than their enemy's collectivist experiments. The Insurgents considerably outperformed the Republicans in the industrial sphere, despite the fact the latter benefited initially from overwhelming superiority. To put it another way, if the Republicans had overcome their agricultural disadvantage as the Nationalists had surmounted their industrial weakness, the Republicans might have won the war.

PRODUCTIVITY

The working-class militants who were trapped by the Nationalists were either eliminated or terrorized into laboring for their class enemies. Throughout the peninsula and in the Canary Islands before the war, a union card—from CNT or UGT—had often been necessary to get or retain a job during the Popular Front. Entire regions, such as Asturias, were thus considered to be deeply "red." It was not in the Nationalists' interest or within the realm of possibility to execute or imprison all members of left unions and parties. It was inevitable that many card-carrying leftists would—through luck or misfortune—end up in Franco's army, fields, and factories.[161]

Nevertheless, labor productivity was generally greater in the Nationalist than in the Republican zone. Output probably improved more in rural areas where the Falange and the church often established an effective system of everyday espionage. Burgos authorities adopted and propagated the slogan "the harvest is sacred." In Córdoba, where the White terror had eliminated thousands of leftists, workers' production increased after the plunge produced during the Popular Front, and harvest collection returned to "normal." Queipo quickly suspended the Jurados Mixtos, which had often rendered judgments favorable to workers. Nationalists were pleased to overturn the ban on the use of agricultural machinery or employment of female laborers that had been in effect during certain years of the Second Republic. Queipo's act prefigured the abolition of the Jurados in May 1938. Zamora's civil governor, Lieutenant-Colonel Raimundo Hernández, attempted to roll back the gains of the Popular Front, for example, regular employment, or *el turno*, by permitting agricultural employers to hire only productive workers, not "the lazy or misfits."[162]

Yet by early 1937, growing labor shortages led to a decline of productivity, especially among newly employed and inexperienced agricultural workers, who ignored piecework regulations and demanded to be paid at the same rates as more industrious laborers. Manpower shortages raised wages for harvesters, 400 of whom and their accompanying draught animals were transported by train to Córdoba province to pick olives in early 1937. By late spring 1937 a black market had developed for Córdoba workers. Farmers and construction companies were paying wage earners' salaries above the regulated norms. The Córdoba civil governor issued a stiff warning to both laborers and employers to stop this practice. During the excellent harvest of 1937 the governor established productivity guidelines for workers and promised employers that he would try to recall mechanics, who were performing their military duties, to manage harvest machinery. The "egotist" bidding war among employers for harvesters continued. The latter were paid double for working during the customary June holidays. By August, official wages for male olive harvesters had increased 40 percent. During the "splendid" harvest of mid-October, another 10 percent increase was decreed for nonpiecework laborers, and other increases for different categories of workers followed. In November the Córdoba governor lamented the acute labor shortage that recent heavy rains had aggravated. Córdoba advertised to entice Gallegan workers to its farms, but only a few of the long-term unemployed were dispatched.[163]

Unpredictable meteorological conditions fostered higher pay. Bad weather delayed the planting of cereals, and sowers' contracts with cereal farmers expired. The olive season then arrived, and olive farmers offered the same workers new contracts to harvest their crop. An "illicit" bidding war over wage workers between cereal and olive farmers ensued, a struggle the governor attempted to halt by decree. He recognized that "the lack of hands" had encouraged "the professional vagrants, who live almost exclusively in the capital, who prefer leisure to productive labor, and who survive on the wages of the weaker sex." He told the Civil Guard to register the names of those who refused wage labor, whom he would provide with employment.[164]

Obviously, these Córdoba workers hardly agreed with the Falange's Fuero del Trabajo, which called work "heroic." The Fuero, signed by Franco on 9 March 1938, was generally hostile to individual incentives, and it repeated the mistakes of other failed counterrevolutionary movements by calling on peasants and workers to sacrifice fully for the *patria*, Spain, and other high-minded abstractions. Instead of solid monetary incentives, it offered a fascistic ideology that lauded the peasant as a paragon of racial purity and national identity. The Fuero's effect was limited, and the Nationalists triumphed not because of the Fuero but rather despite it.[165]

In Galicia and Castile, some proposed hiring Portuguese laborers, others enlisting Falange youth (the *Flechas* between fifteen and eighteen years old) to work the fields. In the fall of 1937, provincial authorities in La Coruña reported a weekly drop of unemployment by 600 persons, but the wage-labor scarcity persisted. In "liberated" Toledo, Nationalist authorities brought in teams of *segadores* from Galicia and Extremadura. Zamora province reported a shortage of 1,485 skilled and semiskilled harvesters and an excess of 268 female and child laborers. The latter—legally and illegally—were common throughout urban and especially rural Spain. Available wheat harvesters— at least in Pinilla de Toro (Zamora)—were sometimes compelled to labor twenty hours per day instead of the legal limit of twelve hours during harvest season. The import of Gallegan workers and the maximum use of the 1,760 mechanical harvesters were supposed to alleviate the Zamoran labor shortage. However, the scarcity nevertheless persisted and repeated itself during succeeding harvests. In the late spring of 1938, Castilian farmers launched a campaign to recruit 400 Gallegan wheat harvesters. In León, women took over the agricultural work of conscripted males. Unemployment had effectively disappeared in that province, in Huelva, and in Lugo, and the result was lower productivity among many agricultural workers. The replacement of experienced workers by novices resulted in the fall of output in Huesca. The dominant political perspective on the civil war, which has focused nearly exclusively on repression of left-wing parties and unions, has ignored full employment and the consequent rise in the cost of wage labor. These two factors greatly contributed to relative labor passivity in the Nationalist zone.[166]

The labor shortage hindered agrarian output. In Palencia, tenant farmers blamed the failure to pay their rent in kind on the lack of hands. The elderly had to be mobilized for the sowing season. The 1938 harvest in Zamora and throughout much of the peninsula was "one of the worst of the century." Rising wages quickly surpassed the established norms and placed small producers, who could not afford the higher costs, at a disadvantage. Employers put their laborers to work illegally on Sundays even though they were obligated to attend Mass. Growers learned to be self-sufficient and were forced to follow the biblical injunction to plant only what they could sow. In 1939, Zamorans were permitted to plant as much wheat as they wished, but the most important Zamora newspaper asserted that the 1939 harvest would also be insufficient, in part due to the "lack of labor" in the Nationalist zone.[167]

As in Córdoba, farmers were allowed some but not complete flexibility in increasing wages for harvesters and permanent workers. In Huelva at the end of 1937, agricultural wages were raised 20 percent. Given the increase in the price of olive oil, Seville authorities again augmented wages in early 1938. Unauthorized salary hikes and illicit hiring, which probably benefited many female workers, continued throughout the spring of 1938. Productivity did not recover, and the civil governor warned that "low output will be punished." Employers had a duty to maintain a decent output and to dismiss those who produced below generally accepted standards. Five Córdoba truck farmers were fined 5,000 pesetas each for paying workers wages exceeding legal limits. These fines were publicized throughout Spain to caution employers not to increase wages unduly. During the excellent olive harvest of the fall of 1938, olive harvesters were promised 8.5 pesetas per day, an increase from the previous year.[168]

Franco's creation of the Juntas Agrícolas on 20 October 1938 was a response to the labor shortage, especially during periods of planting and harvesting. Directed by mayors with the assistance of local Falange leaders, the Juntas aimed to supply the necessary labor to farmers despite the growing needs of the military. The Juntas also provided incentives for laborers, facilitated overtime, and encouraged the sharing of machinery and draught animals. Juntas were ordered to give priority treatment to families with members at the front or whose animals had been requisitioned by the army. The head of the SNT hoped that with the cooperation of local authorities, the statistical gathering procedures of the Juntas would reduce the hoarding of wheat, a difficult task given that 50,000 wheat growers existed in the province of León alone. The Juntas had a limited impact since farmers often ignored the requirement to hire workers through placement offices (oficinas de colocación).[169]

In the countryside those who suffered the most economic distress in the Franco zone were not the laboring proletariat per se—except for those labeled as "reds" who had been killed, jailed, or exiled—but rather nonproducers, such as invalids, children, and the elderly who were without subsidies or pensions and thus depended on charity. The Nationalists did provide pensions to widows and family members of their soldiers who were killed in action. Of course, Republican children and widows were not as fortunate, and a good number of the latter had to prostitute themselves to survive. Franquistas put into effect, in their own nasty way, the Pauline paraphrase, "Those who don't work, don't eat."[170]

Industrial production jumped in the "liberated" regions where Insurgents militarized the workforce, taxed its overtime hours, and forced it to deliver fixed quotas. The production of steel, used to make cannons and other weapons for the franquistas, recuperated "tremendously." Asturian iron and steel production at least doubled under Nationalist control. In the Mieres factory, output increased dramatically. This metallurgical plant had employed 580 workers who manufactured 2,596 tons during the "leftist period," but by July 1938, 1,082 workers produced 7,870 tons. Output of steel and other types of metal increased tenfold. In mid-1938 each worker produced on average 3.7 times more than during "red domination." Wages remained stable; therefore, workers were much more productive but not fully compensated for their gains. The Fábrica de Metales de Lugones experienced similar increases of output and productivity. Copper and brass production climbed, respectively, five- and sevenfold during 1938 compared with the year of Republican control. The Moreda factory saw an eightfold augmentation of tonnage, with a workforce reduced from 837 to 779. Its wire production—including the barbed variety used on the extensive fronts—jumped almost four times. Some of the increased production in the north went to Nazi Germany as payment for the Luftwaffe's expenses for its destruction not only of the Republican military but also of parts of the north itself.[171]

Nationalist newspapers widely publicized the remarkable increase in coal and iron production and productivity. In Asturias coal production had fallen from 1,780,394 tons in 1936 to 245,368 in 1937, and then under Nationalist control climbed to 3,537,859 tons in 1938. The Insurgents ended regulations that had limited working hours during holidays and had permitted vacations: "Employers, employees, and workers are reminded that any failure to fulfill an obligation is a crime." Deliveries of Asturian coal to the port of Bilbao rose from 35,400 tons in January 1938 to 99,700 in May. The Peñarroya mines (Córdoba) supplied some coal, but given supply problems in 1937, Germany became the principal provider of coal in the final months of that year. In Vizcaya 1.4 million tons of ore were produced in 1936, only 0.7 in 1937 when the mines were mostly under "red" control, and 1.8 million in 1938 under Nationalist rule. The production of the copper mines of Huelva, whose output was badly needed to earn foreign currencies, quadrupled during the war. The jump in productivity was also true for miners and workers who labored in areas—such as León and Córdoba—that had never been conquered by the "reds." An official inspection by experts of the provincial government in the quarries of Valdeasores of the S.A. Asland (Córdoba) demonstrated that after the election of the Popular Front in February 1936, daily output had dropped 47 percent. "The [Nationalist] government cannot tolerate these abuses" and "will not hesitate to establish production quotas if necessary." Production gains should not be attributed exclusively to terror, since in no other industry in this period was the correlation between labor productivity and calorific input more direct than in mining.[172]

As in agriculture, in industry, too, wages generally increased. In northern metallurgical factories, workers' salaries were augmented 7 percent for the unskilled and 12 percent for the skilled at the end of 1938. The wages of adjusters, tinsmiths, mechanics, electricians, millers, and lathe operators rose even more. In Seville, because of the labor shortages already mentioned, the increases were much greater: 32 percent for skilled workers and 38 percent for unskilled. The highest authority in the Canaries—the military commander Carlos Guerra Zagala—admitted that workers were undoubtedly reluctant to accept Nationalist ideology but were happy to receive higher wages.[173]

The capture of the Río Tinto (Huelva) mines provided the Insurgents with men, animals, and vehicles of all types. At the end of August 1936, Queipo announced that workers and employers of Río Tinto had reached an agreement "under the presence of military authorities." However, so many miners had been killed, jailed, or fired that the company had to initiate a provincewide advertising campaign to find new ones. Furthermore, it had to offer relatively high wages to thousands of remaining skilled (and nonleftist) miners who received a minimum salary of 8.5 pesetas, which with piecework incentives could rise to 10 to 12 pesetas per day. In addition, the company offered housing and employment for miners' wives. The combination of fringe benefits, high salaries, and repression, which included militarization of the workforce, contributed to the relative labor tranquility in the Andalusian mines during the war.[174]

In Asturias and León the Falange required all applicants requesting reemployment in the mines to answer a questionnaire that demanded information concerning their political/union affiliation and the activities they undertook during the "red period." The new regulations were quickly used in the hiring practices of many branches of Asturian industry and commerce. Approximately 200 of 480 miners who had been laboring in the El Peñón mines reapplied for their former positions. In the Baltasara mines of Mieres, the number of miners reapplying for positions was "considerably reduced" compared with the prewar personnel. The low rate of reapplication indicated a high degree of political commitment among workers. If police officials readmitted a miner, he automatically became subject to the military code of justice and could not seek employment in another mining company. The latter provision limited turnover and open bidding wars among firms. At least initially, the military was the main customer of coal production. Both the draconian rules and the militarization of workers, who were compelled to salute their superiors, undoubtedly increased labor discipline, but the shortage of personnel and accompanying higher wages also helps explain the enhanced level of production and productivity in the mines. As a further incentive, mining companies offered workers credits worth 5 to 6 pesetas daily in local cooperatives.[175]

In many other branches productivity improved notably. Even though the Nationalist zone suffered shortages, the paper plants of Guipúzcoa and Vizcaya were more productive under Insurgent than Loyalist control. In 1937, paper production increased 29 percent in Franco's zone. During 1937 the increase of glass manufacture, which was scattered throughout the Nationalist zone, was even more spectacular and saw a tenfold jump in output and productivity. Nevertheless, by the fall of 1938 there was an acute shortage of bottles, and Falangist youth groups undertook recycling campaigns. Soap production declined in 1937 but recuperated in 1938. Like most other commodities, it became scarce following the war. In contrast, the Republic, which held the heavy industry of the Basque country for the first year of the war and Catalonia for the entire conflict, never managed to equal the Nationalist arms industry of Seville, Plasencia, Oviedo, and La Coruña and the Basque industry during the final year of the conflict. Respect for private property, a stable currency, and sufficient nutrition encouraged this sector in the Nationalist zone to return quickly to normal operation.[176]

Officially, labor inspection was not completely forgotten, and employers were reminded to respect the laws restricting working hours and setting standards that had been passed during the first third of the twentieth century, including the early years of the Second Republic. The Servicio de Inspección del Trabajo levied 70,000 to 160,000 pesetas in fines per month in 1938. It claimed to have inspected workplaces more frequently than its Republican predecessor. Dozens of employers were fined hundreds of pesetas for violations of labor laws. For example, inspectors sanctioned a sawmill owner 10,000 pesetas for employing thirteen-year-olds for eleven-hour days at very low wages and another *patrono* 10,000 pesetas "for usury and condemning the Fuero de Trabajo." Large insurance companies—including La Providence, La Preservatrice, Mutua General de Seguros, Mutualidad Naviera de Vigo, and MAPFRE—were fined tens of thousands of pesetas for violations of work accident legislation.[177]

A by-product of the Fuero del Trabajo, the Magistratura del Trabajo, was created in May 1938 and was the Nationalist heir of the Jurados Mixtos. The Magistratura has been seen to have generally favored employers' interests. Nevertheless, some of its decisions seemed to have reflected continuity with the social reforms of the Second Republic. The Magistratura ordered the mining firm Hullera Española to pay compensation to a worker who had lost both his hands in an accident that had occurred during "red rule." It also decided that other firms should disburse injured employees their annual wage or a portion of it for life. The court granted some compensation to the family of a dead miner, fined several employers for dismissing workers improperly, and demanded their rehiring. The court justified its decision by citing as precedent the labor legislation passed by the Republic in 1932. Other companies were sanctioned dozens of pesetas "for denying workers time to fulfill religious duties." The Magistratura decided many cases involving workers' claims of underpayment by their employers.[178]

TRANSPORTATION

Like the Bolsheviks during the Russian civil war, the Nationalists gave the highest priority to railroad lines for the transport of troops and material. The quartermaster controlled the allocation of wagons, another example of its privileged status. Under the authority of the Junta de Defensa Nacional,

Nationalists militarized railroad personnel for the entire war and threatened recalcitrant workers with execution. Railroad administrators overcame a lack of skilled labor and technicians and a deficiency of machinery through foreign assistance and clever improvisation. They consistently managed the system more efficiently than their Republican enemies and, until the end of the conflict, avoided the corruption that afflicted railroad networks during other civil wars, especially the Russian conflict. Whereas Republicans attempted organizational innovations, Nationalists maintained the prewar enterprises that were able to accommodate, at least partially, their military and civilian needs. Before the war Gallegans had complained that the poor train connections to Madrid and Barcelona lowered the sales of their meat and fish in the major markets. Nevertheless, railroads moved four to five times more fish from Vigo than did trucks. Rail and sea—by far the least expensive transport—were able to supply the Seville market sporadically with fresh seafood.[179]

Nevertheless, trains were often excruciatingly slow and could take several days to move only a few hundred miles. Their tardiness increased as the civil war endured. Although troop trains had priority over civilian ones, in February 1939, soldiers needed "four interminable days" to get from Catalonia to Ávila. One train full of requetés left Pamplona at 11:00 p.m. and arrived at Cizur, seven kilometers away, at 9:00 a.m. Overwhelmed railroads aggravated supply shortages, especially that of wheat, whether foreign (Argentine) or domestic. Storage facilities were often inadequate, and consignees were ordered to unload their merchandise from arriving trains within twenty-four hours or face severe penalties and fines. Police patrolled railroad yards and trains, which remained tempting targets for burglars. They caught several railroad thieves—one of whom had posed as an injured war veteran in order to gain the confidence of victims—in possession of stolen luggage.[180]

Regular bus lines, where they existed, were much prompter than railroads and alleviated some of the pressure on passenger trains. Their relative efficiency, rapidity, and flexibility transformed them into the unnoticed organizational achievers of the Nationalist zone. Soldiers frequently found hitchhiking preferable to trains and had little difficulty obtaining rides from passing drivers. Trucks were usually the most efficient way to move troops and supplies. Unlike railroads, which were overwhelmed by the volume of traffic, trucks could deliver packages on time. They complemented the railroad network by picking up soldiers and supplies at train stations and moving them expeditiously to the front, even though maximum speeds on poor Spanish roads were forty to fifty kilometers per hour. Trucks also supplemented animal transport. They delivered mules and other pack animals to fronts, where the beasts could then move supplies to the troops. As has been seen, mules were indispensable in transporting basics in a country with an inadequate road network. The movement of large numbers of trucks meant that an offensive was being prepared. On countless occasions throughout the entire war, they transported large numbers of Nationalist—and Republican—forces. At the end of the conflict, 1,500 trucks supplied a "liberated" Madrid. Without reliable vehicles, the Nationalists would have lost the war.[181]

Despite their hostility to the U.S. democracy, Nationalists preferred American vehicles to German and Italian ones. Acquisition of trucks from U.S. manufacturers was vital to Nationalist victory and oddly prefigured the role of American vehicles on the eastern front during World War II and the postwar influx of American capital into Spain. Although the military could delay payments to Spanish citizens, it had to immediately pay foreigners—especially Americans—for its purchases of heavy vehicles. Franco used his foreign exchange earnings to buy at regular intervals 12,000 Ford (its Federal was particularly prized), Studebaker, and General Motors trucks. In comparison, the Nationalists procured only 1,800 German and 1,200 Italian lorries. As they did for their mules and horses, elite units cherished their vehicles and gave them nicknames. When a bomb fell on a Ford Federal, they called the damaged vehicle a "wounded veteran" and had it completely repaired. Buses were also acquired from American firms. Before the war, American automobile and tire companies, such as Firestone, Ford, and General Motors, had established networks of dealerships and service centers throughout Spain and dominated the Spanish market, which needed heavy-duty vehicles that could withstand imperfect roads and move in muddy conditions. When the war terminated, American dealerships in Barcelona recuperated and repaired large numbers of vehicles. In contrast, at the beginning of the war, the Republicans purchased a large number of trucks from the Soviet Union and continued to rely on Russian vehicles.[182]

Throughout much of the twentieth century, Spain was divided between "the Spaniard with a car and those with only sandals." During the Second Republic, military and civilian strikebreakers defending landowners and businessmen had employed the automobiles of the comfortable classes to combat work stoppages. To tackle the Asturias Revolt of October 1934, the military confiscated the trucks and cars of the bourgeoisie. The Junta de Defensa Nacional decreed a similar expropriation on 28 July 1936. One of Queipo's initial measures, adopted on 30 July 1936, was the "militarization" of all vehicles and their drivers. As usual, he threatened saboteurs of the edict with execution. He dissolved the taxi union and turned its funds over to the military, a precedent to be copied by Nationalist authorities throughout Spain. In Vigo, too, the military commander, Felipe Sánchez, requisitioned all vehicles. Although owners were very reluctant to surrender their cars and trucks, a good number—realizing confiscation was inevitable—preferred to donate their vehicle to the army. Some Navarrese bequeathed their automobiles willingly.[183]

Monopolization of vehicles, which were always considered a great prize when captured in battle, meant effective domination of highways and roads, a top priority of the Insurgents. At the beginning of the conflict, vehicles were put to use to move troops—especially African mercenaries, Carlists, and Falangists—through Andalusia and Extremadura. In southern Andalusia, small groups of Nationalist volunteers under military command moved in light trucks and cars and conducted a vigorous war to occupy and control towns and villages. Vehicles were also employed for the gruesome task of transporting the bodies of assassinated leftists. The capture of a fleet of motorized vehicles from the "Red-Separatists" during the Vizcaya campaign in early April 1937 made requetés extremely proud.[184]

In the Nationalist zone the military obtained control over vehicles, demonstrating once more its unquestioned authority. The possession of vehicles reflected the new hierarchy. High-ranking officers and great clergymen reserved the best passenger cars, driven by a chauffeur, for their own personal use. The military offered promotions to chauffeurs by creating a corps of *sargentos provisionales de automóviles*. The air force offered experienced truck drivers 13.5 pesetas daily, a very decent salary. Tractor drivers, the tractors themselves, and their parts were drafted or requisitioned. So were other agricultural machines.[185]

Unwise expropriations created transportation bottlenecks. As the war endured and even after it ended, authorities organized regular sharing and requisitioning of vehicles with compensation for owners and drivers. They restricted expropriations to military authorities and, by implication, excluded the Falange in certain provinces. Following the conquest of Asturias and complaints of Oviedo merchants, the military governor forbade the confiscation of vehicles supplying the city. This province experienced a severe shortage owing to the destruction of 1,000 of its 1,500 trucks during the first year of fighting. Oviedo businessmen and the military developed a system in which owners alternated sharing their vehicles with the army. In November, proprietors of light passenger cars were compelled to share their vehicles with authorities for one week per month. General Latorre, the military governor of Asturias, assured Gijón employers that he would permit them to use a number of vehicles sufficient to allow normal commercial and industrial activities. In return, the industrialists agreed to tolerate some featherbedding to absorb the unemployed. Nevertheless, problems persisted, and military chauffeurs— or civilians posing as uniformed soldiers—trafficked goods illegally throughout the province. Asturias and León continued to lack a sufficient number of trucks to restore normal commerce. Provincial authorities requested from the national government the immediate delivery of 500 trucks.[186]

As in the Russian civil war, food was available, but the means to transport it to urban consumers were lacking. During the Aragon offensive in 1938, military needs so dominated animal and mechanical transport that Zaragoza mills could no longer supply the civilian population, and provincial authorities requested permission to requisition 30 percent of the grain of local peasants to alleviate the shortage. By the end of 1938, Granada millers asked military authorities to return their trucks so that they could transport flour. In Rute (Córdoba) millers whose trucks had been confiscated had difficulty acquiring grain. The constant demand for skilled truck drivers subverted the traditional gendered division of labor. When an owner of a tiny trucking firm was drafted, his wife became the chauffeur of the firm's vehicle.[187]

Unwise military requisitions could reduce villages to self-sufficiency. In Huesca province fewer than 1,500 vehicles were in service in July 1936. Most of them were trucks (420), buses (287), and taxis (129). Only 640 were passenger cars. Huesca province had only 110 vehicles for civilian use, and its government declared that the lack of transportation was its "most serious problem." Mules and other beasts could not fill the gap. Lack of truck transportation caused the isolation of coastal Lugo. In Orense the military requisitioned 150 of the best trucks from a provincial total of 350. Military requisitions left Ávila with only 27 trucks for civilian purposes, and some of them were awaiting costly spare parts. Taxis were virtually absent from its streets. Cáceres reverted to using animal transport "quite intensively."[188]

Like Barcelona anarchists and Moscow Red Guards, counterrevolutionaries of various sorts employed cars for joy riding and other frivolities. Accidents were common, and reckless driving injured significant numbers of Falangists and others. Cruising imprudently demonstrated a crass *macho* bravery. Inexperienced or exhausted truck drivers fell asleep at the wheel, resulting in injuries to more than a half dozen requetés. A nineteen-year-old Falangist perished riding on the mudguards of an automobile overloaded with his comrades. The military commander of La Coruña had to call all drivers of requisitioned vehicles to order and compel them to obey normal traffic laws, including speed limits. El Ferrol authorities issued similar warnings. Segovia province convicted twice as many in 1936 for "negligence," often associated with reckless driving, than in 1935. The mayor of Las Palmas complained that the disregard of traffic laws showed "backwardness and ignorance" and would no longer be tolerated. The fascination with the power and prestige of the passenger car crossed political lines and pointed to the consumerist future of Spain. In 1930s Iberia the automobile—like firearms, which also provoked many accidents among the inexperienced—symbolized power, success, and domination. Asocial driving continued throughout the war.[189]

Nationalists were impressed by the design and affordability of the "people's car"—the Volkswagen—whose production line was inaugurated by the Fürher himself. Franquistas were confident that the Fallersleben factory would become the greatest in the world, surpassing the Ford plants in Detroit. Nationalist newspapers were also enthusiastic about the highway construction projects of the new Reich. The CTV was admired because it possessed the best automobiles and trucks in Spain. Many Spaniards—regardless of their politics—yearned to put behind them the era of horses and mules, which were still heavily used even in urban areas.[190]

In contrast to the Republican zone, where cars were infrequently returned to their owners, the military insisted that the vehicles be restored to their original proprietors. In the middle of August 1936 the Seville commandant of transports called on owners to pick up several dozen trucks and sedans, which the military had confiscated, from storage at the Plaza de Toros. Return of unneeded vehicles continued throughout the war. Proprietors were encouraged to claim their requisitioned cars, and newspapers published the make, model, and license plate numbers of vehicles the military no longer needed. Owners whose cars or trucks were their main means of livelihood were requested to reclaim them. At the end of the war in Seville alone, hundreds of vehicles were returned to their proprietors.[191]

The Nationalist war budget included funding for vehicle acquisition and maintenance, although owners were seldom fully compensated for use and consequent (and considerable) deterioration. The military adopted a similar policy concerning requisitioned animals, which were also returned to their owners after the completion of proper paperwork. In Galicia, owners whose vehicles were indispensable for their work were compensated with a subsidy of 6 pesetas per day (plus 1 peseta for each child in the owner's family) during the period of requisition. An Álava commission elaborated another reimbursement scale based on type and weight of vehicle. At the end of 1937 a special tax was imposed on all vehicles to recompense owners whose requisitioned trucks had suffered damages. In León 159 truck owners whose vehicles the military had requisitioned were compensated a total of 73,000 pesetas.[192]

POSTAL SERVICE

The post office was especially important in 1930s Spain since telephones—common only in large urban areas—served only 8 percent of Spanish households. During the conflict telecommunications became less useful, as both bombs and beasts destroyed telephone wire. Like the CCP courier service, which became the swiftest and most reliable in China during its civil war, the Nationalist postal service operated much more effectively than its Republican counterpart. The latter earned a "public and notorious reputation for disorder." Nationalist transportation experienced approximately 20 to 40 percent increases in cost compared with the hyperinflation in the Republican zone. Corruption was often a rational response to insufficient pay. As in areas controlled by the GMD during the Chinese conflict, Republican functionaries' salaries were so inadequate that they had to steal in order to live.

In the Russian, Chinese, and Spanish civil wars, transportation presented the most opportunities for pilfering, and Spanish Republican drivers became reputed for their selfishness. The "dirty business" of chauffeurs and their agents created "scandals worthy of fascists."[193]

Soldiers needed mail, which provided both economic and emotional relief. One low-ranking Catalan in the Nationalist army commented that the mail service never failed to bring "to the combatants the invaluable letters from family members, friends, and pen pals, which gave us strength to carry on at the worst times." Those who were separated from their families in the Republican zone depended on the mail sent through third parties abroad for news of their relatives. Several months after the outbreak of hostilities, a chaplain on the Madrid front was able to send successfully a letter to his family in Republican-occupied Mallorca, and his relations responded with a telegram. The mail would dependably arrive no matter where the unit was stationed. The distribution of correspondence was often the most exciting part of the day for the rank-and-file soldier. A chaplain gained popularity among his troops for his willingness to deliver letters to his men who were dispersed throughout the long Madrid front.[194]

Efficient transportation by trucks, automobiles, and if necessary, mules, led to the easy availability of care packages, which bolstered spirits and helped to prevent looting of local inhabitants. Soldiers' families, girlfriends, and *madrinas* (female pen pals) trusted the honesty and reliability of the Nationalist postal services. Mothers, wives, and girlfriends sent jewelry and good-luck charms to their soldiers via the post. Unpilfered care packages—the ultimate demonstration of food surplus—arrived regularly, satisfying the recipient and solidifying the unit with whom he shared the contents of the parcel. Checks, which could be easily cashed, were greatly appreciated. Soldiers regularly used mail order to furnish themselves with sweets, cognac, and fine sausage from large and small companies throughout the Nationalist zone. During the 1937 Christmas season, a Las Palmas (Canarias) firm offered to send any frontline soldier 15 packs of cigarettes and 25 cigars in exchange for a postal order of 10 pesetas. In the fall of 1938 the Cuban branch of the Falange donated 150,000 packs of cigarettes, 100,000 cigars, and 6,000 pounds of pipe tobacco, whose first destination was the Ebro front. The postal service was especially important for Moroccan troops, who not only communicated with their families by mail but also sent them checks and the booty they had collected on the peninsula. Relatively costly local and national stamps funded the service.[195]

PUBLIC HEALTH

Public cleanliness was not a high priority in Spanish popular culture in the 1930s, and campaigns against littering and spitting in the streets and bars of

Seville produced scanty results. The urban initiatives against stray dogs and cats that carried rabies and a noise reduction initiative were equally ineffective. Nationalist authorities attempted to promote hygiene in rented apartments and homes by requiring a health inspection before occupancy, but they met considerable resistance among landlords and tenants. Both would conspire against the provincial housing authority (Fiscalía de la Vivienda) that mandated sanitary improvements and sometimes fined transgressors. Landlords resisted to avoid increased expenses, whereas tenants feared that the improvements would lead to a rent hike. Furthermore, physicians who doubled as municipal health inspectors worried that if they fined or recommended changes in housing owned by the wealthy they would lose their best-paying patients and become proletarianized. In Huelva province, "rural physicians" received insufficient remuneration from municipalities and were aware that condemning the housing of "powerful landlords" would mean personal poverty, if not hunger. Thus, 80 percent of housing remained "unhealthy." Queipo's officials embarked on a noisy—but probably unsuccessful—campaign to sanitize apartments and homes throughout Seville province. The campaign encountered opposition from landlords, who found many ways to block official initiatives.[196]

The Fiscalía de Vivienda's struggle against unhealthy housing may have affected landlords less than the poor, who constructed makeshift homes on the outskirts of towns and cities. The Fiscalía tried to limit the options of the impoverished by prohibiting "the construction of huts, shacks, housing, or industries inside the protective perimeter that must exist around cemeteries and urban developments." Nevertheless, in Huelva over 6,000 persons inhabited caves and shacks unworthy of a "civilized country." Even for the most convinced Nationalists, Las Hurdes (Cáceres) continued to be a shameful example of Spanish backwardness. They admitted that 15 percent of its population did not have sufficient revenues to survive. As had their ancestors, rural people and animals cohabited promiscuously and unhealthily in homes with dirt floors and makeshift thatched roofs. In Tenerife a good number of the "lowly classes" inhabited "numerous caves" that lacked basic sanitation. In Lugo province, "sanitation is simply awful." Tuberculosis—along with venereal diseases, the great scourge of the period—affected a high percentage of residents, making a number of young men ineligible for the military, but Lugo province lacked its own sanitarium. Only 25 percent of the housing in the province met hygienic standards. Ávila rural housing was "nasty, without ventilation or light. People and animals are crammed together. . . . Anopheline mosquitos breed in puddles" and caused malaria, rural Ávila's most widespread endemic disease. Both soldiers and civilians all over Spain and the Canary Islands suffered from malaria, but quinine was available only for the military. Ávila villages, whose taxes depended upon lightly assessed municipal lands, could not provide proper sanitation or education for their residents. In Palencia and Las Palmas, multiple families shared a single toilet. Animal waste often contaminated the water supply of Segovian peasants, who lacked a sewage system. Parts of Galicia and Huesca shared similar conditions. In the latter province only 20 percent of pueblos had a reliable supply of clean water, which was also scarce in Extremadura. Seville (population 300,000) lacked potable water for many, if not most, of its inhabitants. Dirty water could lead to the spread of typhoid fever, especially in rural areas where sanitary practices were often unknown. Álava reported 134 cases in 1937. The governor of Las Palmas testified that typhoid fever was endemic in the province.[197]

Nationalist soldiers suffered from lice-borne diseases—trench fever and a lethal variety of typhus—but considerably less than Republicans, not to speak of Russian Whites, nearly half of whose troops may have caught the disease. For several reasons, franquistas avoided the epidemics of typhus that apparently cost the lives of thousands of Republican soldiers, including members of the International Brigades. First, soap and basic medications were generally obtainable in their zone, helping to limit the spread of illness. Second, standard conscription procedures in the Nationalist zone required vaccination of recruits against typhus. Soldiers also received antityphus pills. Before the Battle of the Ebro, a large number of fighters had been immunized against the disease. A pharmaceutical company in Santiago de Compostela, which employed 150 female production workers, manufactured—among other items—tens of thousands of antityphus vaccines. This firm, one in Burgos, and another in Granada also fabricated an array of over-the-counter drugs consumed by troops on the northern front. Tens of thousands of doses of antityphus and antismallpox vaccines were distributed to civilians throughout the Nationalist zone. Seville and Las Palmas residents were required to receive the smallpox inoculation. So were Gallegans before and during the war. Public sanitation officials initiated a mandatory immunization program when typhus erupted in several small towns in Seville province.[198]

In certain provinces, numbers of suicides and infanticides remained stable. Nationalists publicly regarded infant mortality rates in their zone as satisfactory. Their complacency is questionable, since, for example, infant mortality rose significantly in the Canaries, Huesca, and Álava. Yet the increase was probably much less significant than in the Republican zone or during the other major civil wars of the twentieth century. In the city of Vitoria, mortality per 1,000 nearly doubled from 1936 to 1937. This suggests that although the countryside remained unhealthier than the city, urban areas of the Insurgent zone also suffered during the conflict. Part of the explanation for the increase of urban and provincial mortality was that more women were engaged in wage labor and could not regularly breastfeed their infants, who had to rely on inadequate formula. Even though the Nestlé Company operated freely in the Nationalist zone, unadulterated condensed milk became rare and costly. Furthermore, abortions and infanticides often increase in wartime. In Nationalist Spain the Catholic revival intensified the stigma of illegitimacy so powerfully that some mothers may have abandoned their natural infants. After the civil war the regime made a successful effort to improve infant and pediatric care, and infant mortality rates dropped significantly.[199]

Hospitals, which were installed in converted church buildings that had been expropriated during *desamortización*, acquired a positive reputation in the Nationalist zone. Although complaints were not unknown and shortages of sheets and bandages bothersome, hospitals became identified as institutions where soldiers could eat a hot meal and "forget field huts, clean off mud, and flee miserable conditions." One injured requeté praised the creativity of cooks who offered delicious "bread with bacon or pork fat." Twelve military hospitals existed in Guipúzcoa, six of which were in San Sebastián alone. They offered such a welcome break—including the presence of "respectable" women—from military life that wounded soldiers and officers often wished to remain in a health facility even after their injuries had healed.[200]

The relative efficiency of Nationalist services, their ability to supply men and beasts, their solid currency, and their revenue-raising capabilities provided the foundation for the victory of both counterrevolutionary arms and culture.

3

Catholic Neotraditionalism

The venerable Spanish antagonism to secularization reinforced a distrust of modernity, which was identified with cosmopolitan females, "anti-Spanish" leftists, Jews, and Protestants. The trauma of collective attacks on property and religion pushed much of the middle class to reembrace a traditional religion. Persons recently "liberated" from Republican control gave thanks to God and to various local saints and virgins. The religious persecutions carried out by the "reds" in Catalonia led many bourgeois, who had been sympathetic to Catalan nationalism, to support the Nationalists. In contrast, in the Basque country, which experienced fewer priest killings and attacks on property, the Catholic middle classes generally supported the Republic.

A former Republican, Queipo recalled on 9 August 1936 that Azaña may have been correct when he stated that Spain was no longer Catholic, but the general tapped into the anxieties of property owners when he declared "all men" must now entrust themselves to God "if they wish to live." In contrast to their enemies, whose anticlericalism was often a factor of division and alienated both Basque Nationalists and foreign powers, the Catholicism of the Nationalists was a common denominator that rallied many small and medium landowners in rural Spain who were disgusted with Republican attacks against the church.[1]

Attitudes toward women in the Nationalist zone were self-consciously traditionalist. In male-dominated organizations, they usually served only as secretaries and typists. Republican women had more varied tasks and were able, unlike their Nationalist counterparts, to work in the post office and in the quartermaster's office. Males had priority for salaried employment. Nationalist officials discouraged two female members of the same family from working for the government. Women were expected to be faithful wives, devout mothers, and conscientious caregivers. They also had to make extra efforts to support the troops as workers, fund-raisers, and pen pals. The ex-Republican Queipo crudely expressed the traditionalism of the Nationalists. The general ridiculed the "red" employment of women as soldiers, which, he

ESPAÑA FUÉ, ES Y SERÁ INMORTAL

Falangist poster linking its fascist present to Spanish Catholicism's missionary past.

derided, revealed the enemy's lack of "real men." The theme was repeated in the Nationalist press, which argued that its zone had "enough virile males" to allow women to remain at home unmolested. Franquistas especially detested *milicianas*, whom chaplains claimed were even more aggressive and violent than their male counterparts. Early in the war, police were on the lookout for *rojas*, and in the La Coruña neighborhood of Santa Lucia, they detained a woman who was accused of supplying "rebels" with food and explosives.[2]

As has been seen, Falangist women specialized in the customary female activity of caregiving. The Falange woman's organization, Sección Feminina, encroached on the terrain of social services traditionally held even in "liberal" Spain by the Catholic Church. Feeding the civilian population complemented the terrorist, but effective, policing operations that prevented a guerrilla from developing behind Nationalist lines. In October 1936 the leader of Nazi-inspired Auxilio de Invierno, Mercedes Sanz Bachiller, inaugurated a collective dining room for children in Valladolid. The soup kitchens again showed the Nationalist authorities' abilities to efficiently organize the rear. Auxilo de Invierno, which became Auxilio Social in May 1937, diligently performed its tasks and in 1938 became a state-funded charity. After October 1937 all women between the ages of seventeen and thirty-five who wanted government jobs or professional titles were compelled to participate in the AS for at least six months during a three-year period. Institutions that employed undocumented women would be fined. Females who were absent or tardy during the six- to eight-hour workday were to be punished to the fullest extent allowed by the regulations. Only women working in the lowest-paid jobs received exemptions. Nonetheless, many females were able to avoid serving in the AS because their employers and the authorities ignored the requirement. Despite massive repression in conquered Asturias, some continued to resist the labor and other demands of their Falangist "sisters." A close collaborator of Queipo reported that the Falange in Andalusia was unable to win over most women. The abolition of divorce and the suspension of coeducation may have contributed to the unpopularity or indifference of many females to the new regime.[3]

With the full cooperation of the military, the AS excelled in feeding hungry cities that had fallen to the Nationalists. After the capture of Bilbao and Vizcaya, it collaborated with transport managers to deliver 1,319 tons of provisions, including tens of thousands of loaves of bread and 30,000 cans of condensed milk. A "liberated" Santander received similar help. At the end of 1937 its communal kitchens provided lunches and dinners for 63,000 children in the peninsula. Many of their charges were sons, daughters, and widows of assassinated "reds," who suffered from discrimination and humiliation. To eat in the collective dining room, they were forced to stomach an opening prayer, wear a blue shirt, or give the fascist salute. However perverse the rituals, the communal kitchens of the Nationalist zone contrasted with the scarcity of food in large parts of the Republic. Only good connections—often to the parties, unions, and Popular Army—could provide urban residents with sufficient calories.[4]

Germans and Italians assisted the efforts of the Spanish fascist females. The German pharmaceutical firm Bayer supplied the Falangist women with vitamin supplements, necessary in regions of the peninsula, such as León, where avitaminosis was common. Foreign and domestic fascists understood that provisions were the best propaganda in the "red" zone. The AS fed the residents of recaptured Teruel, where Nationalist forces had surrendered in large part because of the lack of food, in the harsh winter of 1938. By June it had established nineteen collective kitchens in Teruel province and had planned the transport of victuals throughout Spain, whose entire territory, it was thought, might be quickly "liberated." The AS also nourished hospital patients and offered special diets to diabetics. One franquista resident remembered fondly the entrance of the Nationalists into Madrid: "How beautiful it was when Franco entered Madrid with all those Moors in full dress. . . . They [Insurgents] distributed chocolate, condensed milk, and bread. I ate more that day than any other day of the war."[5]

The nongovernmental organizations of the period, including the Quakers whose sympathy for the Nationalists was quite circumscribed, nonetheless recognized the efficiency of the collaborators of Sanz Bachiller. In return, the AS particularly appreciated the Quakers' donation of vehicles, which were used as ambulances or to transport food and medicines. The AS was effective in feeding areas served by major transportation routes but neglected isolated towns and villages. Given the textile shortages in the Insurgent areas, clothing poor children proved difficult.[6]

Another traditional caregiving function of women was as wet nurses, who remained common throughout 1930s Spain. The persistence of wet nursing revealed a predominantly rural society where relatively well-to-do urban families recruited poorer women from the countryside to breast-feed their infants. In contrast to more developed economies, which provided a greater range of job opportunities, the Spanish economy of the 1930s offered few job possibilities for rural women. More urbanized societies provide easily available and healthy artificial alternatives to breastfeeding, such as the marketing of cows' milk and bottle-feeding. Although food-processing firms had a presence in northern Spain, baby formula was either unavailable or unpopular. Spanish dairy farming was less specialized and less sanitary than in more advanced European nations. During the civil war, mayors of provincial capitals in the Nationalist zone were constantly fining milk vendors for unhealthy practices. Mothers could not trust the commercial milk supply and continued to rely on the customary methods to nourish their infants.[7]

In larger numbers women were encouraged to become *madrinas de guerra*. The program proved so popular among soldiers that newspapers could not devote sufficient space to print the names of all the men who requested pen pals or godmothers. Despite the response of "dozens of thousands" of females, demand outpaced supply, and a large number of soldiers paid for classified ads to attract a madrina. Even young Japanese women were solicited as pen pals for sailors and legionarios. It was claimed that the enthusiastic response from Japanese females overwhelmed the translating capacity of the Spanish embassy. Some soldiers initiated an experimental program with the somewhat original title "Temporary Fiancés" (*Novias Provisionales*) to acquire female pen pals.[8]

Grocery and other stores developed services to facilitate the mailing of madrinas' packages to their men at the fronts. The care packages sent by "godmothers" to their "godsons" contained tobacco, canned food, sausage, chocolate, and—to nurse the soul—scapularies of the Sacred Heart. Pen pals sent not only luxury items but also winter coats, socks, and shoes. The gifts reinforced the solidarity between men and women, the war and home fronts. Several stories illustrate the good fortune female pen pals imparted. Card games, accompanied by intense smoking, were a common pastime of soldiers, who frequently wagered their future paychecks. One godmother was so generous with her godson, sending him a penknife, flute, cans of milk, writing paper, and envelopes, that when faced with large gambling losses he bet her name. He lost, and the winner wrote to her politely asking to accept him as her new godson. At the beginning of the Maestrazgo campaign, mule trains brought the Tercio de Lácar their meals and mail, "which they received with more joy than food." Among the letters was one from a señorita who was president of the *Margaritas* of Anzuloa (Guipúzcoa) and who offered a madrina de guerra to every requeté in the company. The men quickly accepted the offer. One godson was especially fortunate, since his madrina had earned the reputation as one of the best chefs in Bergara region of the Basque country.[9]

The madrina program reinforced soldiers' self-image as defenders of helpless females and provided welcome relief from their all-male environment. Godmothers, some of whom were women whose families remained in the Republican zone, were often assigned to soldiers without girlfriends. Many participants, who were attracted by the photographs their pen pals had sent them, harbored the hope that madrinas would become *novias*. In more than a few cases, pen pals became not only girlfriends but ultimately wives. Soldiers often used their leave to make the acquaintance of their madrinas, and the latter sometimes visited their godsons near the front, where they washed and cooked for them. Some correspondents maintained amicable relations with their madrinas for many years following the war. The epistolary exchange was particularly important for Nationalist soldiers who were cut off from their families in the Republican zone. They found a substitute solace in the literary network of female pen pals who rooted them deeper into the Insurgent zone and made them less likely to desert.[10]

On quiet fronts, correspondents—who were mostly university-trained officers in a sea of semi-illiterate or illiterate conscripts—possessed the time and inclination to express their emotions and affections to their female pen pals. Although respectable love was on their minds, the madrina could also serve more platonically as a substitute for the Virgin on the part of war-hardened veterans. The officers and sailors of the *Almirante Cervera* defied the popular image of fun-loving men in uniform to request high-mindedly that the city of Seville be declared their madrina de guerra "that upholds its sublime mission . . . to provide female spirituality to warriors." At the end of the war, Colonel Arias, the head of the 74th Division, praised "the Spanish woman: silent, intense, firm . . . resigned but staunchly patriotic."[11]

The Republic briefly experimented with a godmothers' program but discontinued it because authorities feared that information about the parlous state of the rear might demoralize frontline troops. The Republican zone had no official campaign that promoted correspondence between masses of female civilians and male soldiers. Furthermore, as mentioned, the reliability of its postal service and the availability of paper proved inferior to those of its enemy. During the last year of the war, a severe paper shortage in the Republican zone would have made exchanges between pen pals problematic.[12]

Women also organized essential charities for the troops. The custom of providing a large meal and ample drink for soldiers at the front and in the rear during Nochebuena was quickly established. The official Christmas charity, the Aguinaldo para el combatiente, was administered by the Carlist Delegación Nacional de Asistencia a Frentes y Hospitales. Its "female warmth" raised over 9 million pesetas for the 1937–38 season, allowing—it was claimed—every soldier to receive a gift. These presents especially heartened men whose families could not send them packages. In 1937–38 the increasingly centralized state was able to collect much more for the *Navidades* than during the first wartime Christmas. Healthy rank-and-file soldiers received a present of food (cookies, candy, sausage, cheese), drink (a bottle of cognac), and tobacco; officers were given wines and cigars; hospitalized soldiers received 5 pesetas in cash. Seven hundred trucks moved the packages to the troops. The provinces of Vizcaya, Guipúzcoa, and Seville were, respectively, the largest donors. In Burgos the Aguinaldo gathered 350,000 pesetas, or 10 percent of the ordinary municipal budget. Likewise, the 1938–39 Aguinaldo was equally impressive, collecting 1,215,732 pesetas in Seville alone and 14,496,611 nationally.[13]

Yet refusals to give were not unknown. The civil governor of Las Palmas was disappointed with the amount of contributions and warned the wealthy under his jurisdiction that those who had not yet contributed sufficiently to the Aguinaldo had better do so immediately. In Zamora, authorities fined many who declined to donate to the Christmas charity. In León the chief provincial policeman complained that "elements hostile to the Glorious Movement . . . circulate repugnant advice to give as little as possible to patriotic charities. Even worse, they laugh at those who donated generously and call them fools."[14]

Señoritas of Frentes y Hospitales collected cigarettes and redistributed them to injured soldiers. Tabaco del Soldado distributed hundreds of thousands of cigarettes to men in uniform. In the daily lives of soldiers, including that of their chaplains, perhaps no substance was more important than tobacco. Tobacco, especially its blond varieties—whether Russian, English, or American—was always highly prized. Although Spain produced only 7 or 8 million kilos, 28 million were consumed annually in the peninsula. The substance served as a stimulant, appetite suppressor, and a medium of social exchange, including trade with the enemy. Chaplains knew that the distribution of cigars and cigarettes bolstered morale. Nonsmoking chaplains won popularity among their legionarios by sharing their own rations of tobacco and their stash of alcoholic beverages. Others would organize collections to purchase cigarettes for their men. In the Legion, cooks served a similar function by offering tobacco and brandy to their comrades. Early in the conflict the Nationalist air force demonstrated the leaf's importance by making a special effort to drop into the besieged Alcázar of Toledo both food and tobacco. The lack of the latter rendered the besieged more desperate than the dearth of the former. When tobacco was unavailable, the men experienced severe withdrawal symptoms. Addicted soldiers smoked corn leaves extracted from mattresses.[15]

In the last Christmas of the war, seventy trucks departed from Seville alone to transport 40,000 packages to the troops. The Caudillo declared the Aguinaldo of the 1938–39 Christmas and New Year's season a great success. As the Catalonia campaign raged, Pamplona sent its Carlists generous quantities of tobacco (usually cigars) and alcoholic beverages, transported to the front on mules. Soldiers greatly appreciated these and other goodies—candy, chocolate, cookies, and rolling paper. Nationalists claimed that as a Christian gesture of goodwill, their soldiers on the Madrid front shared their gifts with enemy troops stationed in the opposing trenches. Troops' generosity was an extension of the frequent exchanges between the two adversaries. Republicans traded rolling paper for Nationalist tobacco, and each side allowed the other to read its newspapers. Both camps arranged unwritten agreements that permitted the free use of no-man's-land to gather crops or water. When fighting erupted on one of the many quiet fronts, as in World War I, officers on both sides imposed short truces to collect the bodies of their dead and injured.[16]

Food for the troops was the largest item of the budget of Navarre Margaritas of the Asistencia a Frentes y Hospitales. The Carlist women purchased over 200,000 cans of jam and condensed milk and several hundred thousand kilos of chocolate and sweets (turrón, guirlache, mazapán). Wool for sweaters ranked a distant second. Alcoholic beverages (40,000 bottles of cognac) and tobacco (4,600,000 cigarettes and 60,000 cigars) were ranked third and fourth. In the summer Margaritas even succeeded in providing ice cream to troops in the field. The town of Pamplona was the major financial backer of their efforts. The capture of northern cities and countryside continued to provide not only staples but all sorts of gourmet products, such as cans of pickled partridge.[17]

Margaritas also acted as mail clerks, seamstresses, washerwomen, nurses, and teachers. At the war's outbreak, they began a daily mail service for combatants in the fronts of Somosierra and Guipúzcoa. As the conflict expanded, the automobiles of their postal service followed Carlist troops to various fronts. Sometimes, vehicles returned with the "martyred" bodies of dead requetés. During the conflict they delivered 40,000 letters to the mayors of the towns and villages of the requetés. Margaritas dispatched to the fronts thousands of crucifixes, rosaries, and medals—worth a total of 21,600 pesetas. They sewed their slogans ("Detente bala") and symbols (Burgundy crosses) into the garments. They often sent clean clothes and brought back the requetés' laundry to be washed, disinfected, and mended within a week. By the end of the conflict, 216,000 parcels had been delivered, and 116,000 packages of laundry had been returned. In the hospitals they cared for the injured and offered literacy classes. They were in charge of informing the mayor and the family, especially the mother, of the condition of a wounded requeté. They also collected personal objects of the dead and delivered them to his family, "providing his relatives with comfort." These tasks of feeding, nurturing, and remembering—typically female roles—reinforced the already close links between the home and war fronts. A requeté fondly remembered their "marvelous" efforts.[18]

One Margarita, Agustina Simón, transcended these typically female vocations, and during the Republican assault on Belchite in August 1937, she was captured pistol in hand after battling the enemy, who, in turn, executed her along with her Carlist companions. She became known as "the Belchite heroine," and a play based on her life was performed as a benefit in Pamplona on 8 November 1938. The theatrical piece showed how she learned "to love Spain and its conceptions of God, Fatherland, and King" and described "brilliantly the life of this martyred Margarita." Other Margaritas were ready to volunteer for dangerous posts if men were lacking. They possessed a particularly strong organizational loyalty and were reluctant to join the less aristocratic and more plebian SF, however "unified." The material and spiritual ties between Carlist units and their hometowns may help to explain why the Nationalist officers, who were officially responsible for feeding, clothing, and paying militiamen, continued to group the men according to region.[19]

Unlike men, enemy women were usually—but, as we have seen, not always—exempt from assassination. However, they were subject to rape and, even more frequently, to a humiliating buzz cut. Falangists and Moroccans were reputed rapists. In different incidents from April 1938 to April 1939, the latter raped thirty-four Catalan women, usually murdering them to eliminate potential witnesses. During this period, moros assassinated a total of sixty-four persons, of whom twenty-one were female. Nationalist officers shot a few of the perpetrators, especially if guilty of crimes against rightists. A number of moros "savaged the young daughter of a legionnaire. They will be severely disciplined as a lesson to others." Marriage between Moroccans and Spaniards was discouraged, if not forbidden. However, certain africanista commanders brought their Moroccan mistresses surreptitiously to Spain. Behind the lines, both sides generally respected marriage vows, and women who became pregnant during their husbands' absences were objects of opprobrium. However, males were given more license, and a number took advantage of the nonrecognition of civil marriage—nullified by the decree of 12 March 1938—"to make a new life with women they knew during the war." Lawyers—almost all male—suffered from the Nationalist abolition of divorce, which reduced their case load and fees.[20]

Female flesh had to be covered. Catholic organizations considered coeducational dancing a particularly perilous and un-Spanish activity. The mayor of Marín (Galicia) banned all public dances in his town to compel young women (señoritas) to make garments for soldiers in their spare time. Returning to an earlier prudery, which would endure through the 1950s, the civil governor of Pontevedra demanded that female beachgoers wear a "complete bathing suit and skirt." Marxists and Communists had supposedly promoted "a worship of nature," which was designed to "dechristianize and demoralize the traditional purity of youth." Even in the guise of physical education and sporting activities, "nudism" would be severely punished. Those who did not follow instructions were fined. Fear of flesh extended even to children, who were denounced and ridiculed if they swam in the nude. The pleasures of the urban night raised special concerns, and children were banned from entering movie theaters and variety shows after dark.[21]

Female refugees from Madrid and Barcelona provided models of urban sophistication and style for their provincial counterparts. Male authorities reacted by synthesizing puritanism and anti-Communism. They warned young women not to use red lipstick or fingernail polish. Fashionable señoritas were accused of being "red because they put on rouge. . . . When Spain mourns, women must follow, and red on lips, face, and fingernails is offensive." Official

disapproval of provocative dress, smoking, and makeup alienated many females, but these puritanical measures may have inspired sacrifice in others.[22]

CHAPLAINS

Nationalist chaplains were a particularly dedicated group who reflected the
neotraditionalist commitment to what the church had labeled a "crusade."
Chaplains possessed a special hatred of the Second Republic, which had dissolved their corps and "expelled" the Jesuits in 1932. The role of chaplains
in many armies has been multifaceted. They were unique in their ability to
transcend rank and often served as ombudsmen who could cut through red
tape by mediating between officers and men. In the Spanish conflict they also
functioned as literacy instructors. Assigned to a battalion, Tabor, or Bandera, each chaplain ministered to the spiritual needs of approximately 500
to 1,000 men.[23]

Chaplains played an indispensable role among the many believers enrolled
in Nationalist ranks. Devout Catholics—for instance, seminary students—
volunteered to fight, and they died in proportionally large numbers. Soldiers'
confessions cleared consciences of moral doubt and increased their fighting
ability. Indalecio Prieto asserted that the enemy whom he most feared was
"the requeté who has just received communion." Republican newspapers reported that priests themselves were ferocious in battle. Policarpo Cía Navascués and Savador Nonell Bru, chaplains, respectively, of the Tercio de Montejurra and of the Tercio de Montserrat, emphasized their requetés' crusading
spirit, religious devotion, and military tradition. Even if the middle and upper
classes dominated, the requetés included members of various social groups
who rallied to defend the faith. Many had been members of Acción Católica
or the Federació de Jóves Cristians. These militants frequently died or were
wounded in battle. All found comfort in daily rituals and prayers. "Never
during three years of warfare did we stop praying the rosary together." The
rosary remained the most popular prayer among Nationalist troops.[24]

The political and ideological orientation of much of the literature of the
Cruzada has sometimes exaggerated the weight given to religion in the Nationalist army. The *Boletín de Estado* declared the official creation of the
chaplain's corps on the tardy date of 12 May 1937, although—as in many
other domains—Queipo de Llano was in the vanguard by requesting the enlistment of volunteer chaplains in the first month of the war, well before the
official decree. Carlist units had as many and sometimes more physicians than
chaplains. Despite the fact that they were often exposed to the dangers of the
front, chaplains were paid considerably less than doctors and even veterinarians, a difference that lessened their prestige. Chaplains of the requetés and
Falangists were the most privileged, but they—unlike physicians—were often

Nationalist poster depicting Spain as crusader and defender of the faith.

from modest or even poor rural families, who viewed the vocation as a social promotion. A minoritarian current of unofficial anticlericalism identified
chaplains as gluttons.[25]

Chaplains—and some Margaritas—offered literacy classes to soldiers.
Instruction was sorely needed. Although Nationalist comic strips written for
children ridiculed Republican soldiers as illiterate yokels, the Insurgents—
given their greater rootedness in rural Spain—suffered higher illiteracy rates
than Loyalists. Álava had the lowest at 27 percent, Segovia 32 percent, Vizcaya
33 percent, Navarre 34 percent, Ávila 50 percent, Granada 62 percent, Huelva
65 percent, and Murcia a startling 70 percent. Zaragoza province had a rate
of 40 percent, 35 percent among males and 44 percent among females. Lugo
estimated 60 percent illiteracy (260,000 of a total population of 480,000, adjusted for underage children) and attributed the high percentage to several
causes. First, impoverished municipalities had difficulty funding schools. Second, dispersed populations often lived far from educational establishments.
To improve rates the provincial government recommended doubling or tri-
pling the number of primary schools.[26]

Rural areas had roughly double the percentage of illiterates in major cities. In Ciudad Real, campesinos who applied for loans would sign documents
with their thumb print. In the countryside only a small number of wealthy
families could afford to educate their children and not compel them to abandon school to work the fields. Even when rural children could attend, they
often demurred since schools had terrible reputations. Thus, chaplains' and
Margaritas' classes benefited rural residents much more than urban ones.
Like Republican instructors, they enjoyed teaching the quick learners and,
at the same time, indoctrinating unbelievers, whom they termed "little pa-
gans." One Jesuit chaplain, who ministered to a Seville *tercio*, complained
that over half his unit was either "total or partially illiterate," statistics that,
he admitted frankly, were "a shameful stigma of the Spanish past." In the
Counter-Reformation tradition, a Jesuit chaplain organized various sections
to teach his men letters and the catechism. Students had to contribute 3 pesetas per month for books and other educational material. These conscripts
may have been illiterate and ignorant, but they were neither stupid nor illogi-
cal. When their Jesuit instructor asked them "who is more powerful—Christ
or the Jews who crucified him," they responded with the religiously incorrect
but logical, "then, the Jews, because if they weren't, they couldn't have killed
him." Although the *padre* insisted that they were wrong, they nevertheless
remained unconvinced.[27]

With female assistance, the clergy attempted to re-Christianize large parts
of Andalusia, Asturias, and the Canaries that had become indifferent or hostile to the church during the late nineteenth and early twentieth centuries.
Chaplains who accompanied troops "liberating" villages would baptize chil-

dren born during "red" rule. The SF sponsored the forced baptisms of ten children—some of whom were teenagers—in the "liberated" mining town of Río Tinto. In Zamora four girls—eighteen, fifteen, eight, and six years old— and one twelve-year-old boy, "victims of error" and the "sick ideas" of their parents, were baptized. So were one family's five children, whose ages ranged from five to eighteen, in the pueblo of La Hiniesta (Zamora). These compulsory ceremonies continued the practice of the Catholic right, which had sponsored baptisms at mass meetings during the Second Republic. Hospital employees of Villagarcía celebrated the baptism of a wounded soldier with a festive meal. After the war ended, mass baptisms, which had been delayed "during the perverse period," took place in Valencia, where fifty children in the parish of Santo Tomás received the sacrament. In Madrid and Barcelona hundreds, if not thousands, of children underwent the ritual. Couples who had married in a civil ceremony retook their marriage vows in church. The Oviedo bishop reported that he had legalized 1,000 marriages and had baptized, in clusters, several thousand children.[28]

As had their nineteenth-century predecessors, chaplains offered religious medallions (*detentes*) to their men to ward off death and injury. The detentes proved extremely popular with Spanish and even Moorish soldiers, who called them "bullet stoppers." Troops requested Catholic devotional objects—crucifixes, rosary beads, medals of saints, scapulars, and assorted icons, which were believed to bring good luck—as much as they demanded other objects such as pen and paper, watches, and cameras. Mothers, wives, and girlfriends gave their soldiers scapulars and crucifixes for protection. In contrast to the "pornographic postcards" possessed by soldiers in the Republican zone, religious postcards were distributed and sent to family members, especially mothers who appreciated images of Christ, the Virgin, and other female saints. A dying soldier requested that his medal of the Virgin be returned to his mother and his Sacred Heart to his father. The wearing of religious icons facilitated connection of a more skeptical male population to their more devout female relatives and friends. Nuns mailed icons to their favorite officers. Carlist soldiers often displayed so many medals that they resembled pilgrims marching to a holy site. Certain units of legionnaires ritually kissed their chaplain's cross before entering battle or after being wounded.[29]

Faced with the intensely irrational and violent environment of war, many soldiers came to believe in the miraculous powers of religious medals and images. In war even Protestant and Jewish soldiers, whose religions manifest powerful currents of iconoclasm, have adopted talismanic behavior and attached special value to amulets and other pious trinkets. As the Americans say, "there are no atheists in foxholes." Out of fear of discovery and consequent punishment, religious Republican soldiers and civilians hid their amulets. If captured, the trinkets could serve as a safe conduct pass to an enemy who

A Carlist poster celebrating the Sacred Heart monument at El Cerro de Los Angeles
(left), Santa Teresa de Ávila (center), and the Basilica de Pilar in Zaragoza (right).

might be more lenient with Catholic prisoners of war. Priests in particular
recounted countless stories of medals and other amulets stopping otherwise
lethal bullets and bomb fragments. Chaplains had the unenviable task of
mailing the many medals that had failed to perform miracles to family members of the deceased.[30]

DEATH

The Spanish war caused 300,000 to 500,000 deaths, 300,000 exiles, and 300,000
political prisoners in a population of 25,000,000. The Spanish civil war may
have been the only contemporary conflict where the number of victims of
political terror almost matched the number of battlefield deaths. "Political
justice" on both sides produced between 150,000 and 200,000 victims. Republicans assassinated 50,000 right-wingers and the Nationalists, 120,000 to
130,000 leftists. Insurgents eliminated 50,000 to 100,000 political opponents
during the war and 50,000 in the decade following the conflict. As they gained
territory, the Nationalists had an unprecedented opportunity to exact revenge
on their enemies, even if it cannot be ruled out that the Republicans might
have engaged in a slaughter of a similar order of magnitude had they won. Yet
some of their most prominent politicians—for example, Prieto and Azaña—

publicly opposed the political assassinations. No equally important Nationalist supporter adopted a similarly humane attitude. The Republican air force lacked some of the lethal efficiency of its fascist-trained enemy. Republican airplanes caused the deaths of 4,000 in the Nationalist zone, whereas Nationalist planes killed 11,000 noncombatants in the Republican zone.[31]

The chaplains' ministry inevitably revolved around death, funerals, and burial. The Republican enemy had no comparable specialist of death, whose job was to sanctify and dignify deceased warriors. The priest was often responsible for identifying the dead, a difficult task even during small battles, where mutilation of distinguishing characteristics was frequent. He also informed family members of the loss of their son and played a privileged role in consoling mothers. The latter were often more devout than fathers, and dying sons insisted that their last confessor convey their final words to their mothers. Parents were grateful to receive any possessions of their dead son. Chaplains had the unwelcome duty of authoring letters to explain soldiers' deaths to their relatives. The latter insisted on learning whether their sons had received the last rites and what they had said immediately before their expiration. Chaplains often had to deceive parents of soldiers who were victims of accidents or friendly fire. Priests served as protectors of the dead, and one, for instance, was outraged that a dead soldier's boots had been stolen from his cadaver at the morgue. They informed the family of the location of the grave and helped to arrange visits of grieving relatives who would transport the corpse to their village.[32]

Priests presided over "Christian" executions to satisfy official public opinion. Nationalist newspapers and chaplains stressed that before being put to death, deserters and "rebels" (i.e., Loyalists or Republicans) confessed and took communion "fervently." The Republican mayor of Barco de Valdeorras (Orense) was said to have kissed the cross several times before his execution. A Nationalist chaplain who was present at twelve wartime executions stated that all but one person made confession. His task was not an easy one. After a prisoner was shot, "I approached him to offer extreme unction, but his head, which had been the target, was almost completely destroyed." According to the Spanish bishops' collective letter of 1 July 1937, "At their legal executions, the great majority of our communists reconciled with the God of their parents. In Mallorca only 2 percent died unrepentant, in the south no more than 20 percent, and in the north no more than 10 percent." Even though some victims might have erroneously hoped that confession might possibly save them from the ultimate sentence, proximity to death unleashed desires to pray and a return to ritual. Even in relatively anticlerical Madrid in 1935, the enormous number of religious burials (9,656) massively outweighed the very few civil burials (145). In Nationalist concentration camps a majority of prisoners seemed to have conformed—at least outwardly—to mandatory religious rituals.[33]

Despite a Republican culture that saw extreme unction as an unhealthy practice both physically and mentally, mortally wounded Republican soldiers requested the last rites. Some pleaded that their corpse be given a decent burial, and Insurgents granted their wish. The devout believed that those interred without Christian rites were buried "like dogs." Frequently, soldiers—Nationalist deserters and those wounded Republicans who fell into franquista hands—asked the chaplain to tell their mothers that they had received the last rites and to comfort their bereaved relatives. It is hardly surprising that the specialist in death would provide a link to those who gave birth. Priests were happy to communicate with mothers since the clergy attributed to them the persistence of the Catholic tradition during the lay Republican years. A Carlist chaplain from Pamplona claimed that the only reason the *madres* in his province encouraged their sons to volunteer was to defend religion. No more than a minority of soldiers publicly proclaimed their faith in the Republic ("Viva la República") as the firing squad executed them. On the other side, Civil Guards and Falangists sometimes objected to dying enemy soldiers receiving confession since "reds have no right to go to heaven."[34]

Falangists and others denied their enemies a dignified burial and would refuse to place a cross on the grave of their "red" enemy. Conversely, during the Battle of the Ebro, one Republican soldier from Badajoz, where Nationalist repression had been most murderous, defied his orders by refusing proper burial to dead Moroccans and legionnaires. He preferred to leave them rot in the open. Of course, Regulares and legionarios were known to shoot their prisoners, and Republicans retaliated by torturing them if captured. During the period of *paseos* and *sacados*, families of victims were never informed—at least officially—of the fates of their loved ones. Nor were family members permitted access to the corpses of their deceased. Even if they knew the location of the corpse, relatives justifiably feared reprisals and frequently refused to identify the dead. Later, when more regular courts-martial were institutionalized, a firing squad—often composed of moros since Spaniards were reluctant to volunteer—executed the victims. In reconquered Oviedo province, military tribunals condemned approximately 3,400 to death, executed 2,100, and pardoned 556. Six hundred ninety-one prisoners remained on death row, expecting the confirmation of their sentence. The executed were buried in a common ditch in the local cemetery but nevertheless identified individually. A few of the most egregious offenders were killed by the *garrote vil*, an instrument of torture that strangled the condemned. The property of the dead was distributed according to their wishes, usually among their cellmates or family members. The Falangist newspaper of León reported that a woman, Luzdivina Bayón Gutiérrez, was arrested on 18 July 1937, "the anniversary of the Glorious National Movement." Bayón "put flowers on the graves of those shot for being hostile to the cause. She placed flowers forming a Republican flag on that of Lorenzo Martínez Baca." Widows and orphans of leftists were shunned by entire villages, including former friends.[35]

Nationalist soldiers were continually astonished at the failure of the Popular Army to bury its dead. During the Irún and San Sebastián campaign the "reds" abandoned not only their weapons and equipment, a regular practice according to Nationalist soldiers, but also their deceased. Insurgents made sure that their own buddies received proper burial. However, in the midst of battles both sides were forced to abandon their dead or burn their bodies by throwing gasoline on a collective pyre. Their comrades sometimes offered them only a primitive grave in a natural cavity topped with a light cover of dirt and a few surrounding stones. During the fight, desperate Carlists and Falangists would use the cadavers of their dead comrades as parapets. Proper burial was often difficult in the hard and dry ground of hilly Spain. Dead bodies were stripped of clothes and shoes and then left to blacken, rot, and be consumed by starving dogs, rats, and other creatures. Both bands would cooperate in killing the animal scavengers but might shoot the human ones. The odors could become so putrid that unofficial truces encouraged soldiers on both sides to find and bury the corpses. During the Battle of the Jarama or again around Madrid in the first half of 1937, ceasefires allowed the two bands to inter the hundreds of bodies piled up in the Casa de Campo and other sites. In the Aragon campaign of March 1938, the requetés found a makeshift but dignified grave of an International Brigader who had been recognized as a martyr of the "international proletariat" by his comrades. A buddy might leave a personal object of the deceased—a letter, book, identity card—in the makeshift tomb.[36]

The sacrifice of sons for the army was an enormous emotional and economic burden. Male family members would spend large sums of money and days on the road to recover the corpses of their loved ones. They correctly feared that their relative's mutilated body might be easily confused with that of his fallen comrades. Requirements to wear an identification bracelet were regularly ignored, and uniforms and other marks of identity were often torn apart in battle or discarded in the operating room. Both sides sometimes claimed unknown corpses. In one case the CNT and the Legion left competing inscriptions that affirmed the long-dead cadaver as their own. Thus it is understandable that a lieutenant serving near his brother on the Madrid front took great risks to retrieve his corpse.[37]

Reburial could create conflict between the deceased's family and officialdom. Relatives would illegally rebury their dead sons with the complicity of chaplains and captains. However, when the *capitán general* of Zaragoza refused an aggrieved father permission to reinter the body of his son, the outraged father "grabbed the captain-general by his lapels and said: 'I gave my son to the fatherland, and now you don't allow me to take him home.

Funeral in the village of Simancas of a Nationalist soldier who was killed on the northern front. His flower-decked coffin lies at the roadside, while his comrades-in-arms march past in a last salute, watched by women and children. Simancas (Valladolid) was famous as a repository of the national archives of Spain. August 1936, Keystone View Co. Southworth Spanish Civil War Collection, Mandeville Special Collections Library, University of California, San Diego.

I am taking him anyway.' He went to the cemetery with two men, dug up the casket, tied it to a taxi, and took it to Luena" (Santander).[30]

Nationalists knew the importance of a proper and dignified burial for morale. Franco himself had written the Foreign Legion's code, which required that legionarios retrieve the cadavers of their comrades even at the risk of their own lives. The Navarrese and Carlists in general were known to follow the tradition of accompanying the corpse and casket to its native village, despite the consequent reduction of military manpower. Carlist units had a tradition of providing suitable burials for their dead—furnishing caskets, washing the body, praying, and offering pensions to widows. During the Battle of the Ebro in the bloody August of 1938, the Carlist dead were interred in a small cemetery and their graves marked with makeshift crosses. After its recapture by the Nationalists, the Tercio de Montserrat returned to Codo—the scene of their great battle of the summer of 1937—to recover, identify, and rebury "in a Christian manner" the bodies of their fallen comrades. The painstaking process of identification of the approximately sixty bodies prefigured the present-day efforts made by descendents of unidentified Republicans who are equally determined to dignify those executed by the Nationalists.[39]

The voyage to the village of the deceased and the ensuing funeral reinforced the closeness of the section, a primary focus of group loyalty. The rites also solidified the village right. The dead or even those on extended leave would be substituted by another male member of the family who often desired to avenge the death of their relative. Family and village solidarity had an ugly side, in which threats and even murder were used to increase the numbers of volunteers. Worse, a good number of funerals were followed by reprisals and executions of neighbors who were classified as disloyal to the movement. On 15 November 1936 the bishop of Pamplona, Marcelino Olaechea, a fervent supporter of the Nationalists, publicly condemned these murders. On 23 August 1936 Olaechea had been among the first to use the term "crusade" and had pleaded for the faithful to give "great alms" to the Junta de Defensa Nacional. However, in November he urged his male and especially his female parishioners to exert their greatest efforts to stop the executions. Perhaps the most honored of the many Jesuit chaplains, Fernando Huidobro, wrote directly to Franco to condemn the assassination of prisoners and Republican soldiers who had surrendered.[40]

Executions had a popular sadistic side that only a painter with the talent of Goya could have captured. In September 1936 in Valladolid, large numbers of persons—including women, boys, and girls—attended the public executions by firing squads of the condemned. "An unusual number of people have been seen congregating in the place where the executions take place. Among them are children, young girls and even some ladies. These [executions] are public, it is true; but their enormous gravity . . . is more than sufficient reason for people, whose religious convictions are in many cases openly displayed, not to attend, even less take their wives and children." The crowd not only enjoyed watching the executions but lightheartedly indulged in coffee and *churros* purchased from the stands established for the occasion. In Salamanca the presence of "fanatical" older unmarried women (*solteronas*) at the deadly ceremonies infuriated Miguel de Unamuno. Executions as public spectacles were not limited to Castile but also occurred in Queipo's Andalusia. In Badajoz, youngsters were encouraged to attend the executions of a Socialist deputy and the former mayor, a scene that attracted a crowd of 200 persons. An "extremist" and "revolutionary" corporal was publicly shot in Sanlúcar de Barrameda (Cádiz). These displays showed an *ancien régime* desire to intimidate (and entertain) all sectors of the population with the spectacle of death.[41]

The practice of the Catholic cult of the dead increased the cohesion of various components of the Nationalist zone. It linked the rich to the poor, who in an impecunious province such as Segovia remained "essentially Catholic." In Cebreros (Ávila) a brotherhood (*cofradía*) established the ritual of dining after a funeral in order to solidify their friendship. Based on the violent death of its founder, Christianity has a particular affinity and closeness to death, and the priest "was a crucial intermediary between the world of the living and the dead." Catholic doctrines of personal immortality and resurrection were reflected in the cries of a community of mourners that the deceased soldiers—like José Antonio and other famous "martyrs"—remained "*presente*" after their deaths. They were never absent spiritually. A Jesuit chaplain interpreted the Legion's slogan, "Long Live Death" ("Viva la muerte"), not as heathen, fatalistic, or militaristic but as a Christian "answer to the mystery of the afterlife." Belief in an afterlife allowed sincerely devout Catholics to sacrifice their lives for the crusade. Christ, it was claimed, had resolved the greatest problem: "Christ, divine physician who knows how to heal and can resolve the problem of death."[42]

Representatives of the Carlists, Falange, youth groups, and the branches of the military and police found themselves united in mourning around the flag-draped casket of the deceased—whether Falangist or requeté. Comrades transported the deceased's coffin on their shoulders. Music—both religious and secular—brought the mourners to their feet. The band of the Irish Brigade, which was formally attached to the Legion, played at funerals of those killed in action, perhaps its greatest contribution to the Nationalist war effort in an otherwise notoriously undistinguished performance. The flag and the religious processions recaptured the public spaces lost during the Republic and reminded mourners of the past sacrifices of other heroes fallen for God and country. Family members, however distraught, appreciated the gesture of solidarity and the participation of comrades during the ceremony. Decorated officers were buried with a special place of honor in the cemetery. Surviving officers celebrated their dead soldiers by placing crosses and inscriptions on their graves. The most prestigious heroes received an elaborate tombstone. Eventually, the most grandiose of all tombs paid homage to José Antonio and Franco at the Valley of the Fallen.[43]

Nationalist funerals sharply contrasted with the rituals of the civil burials of the Republican enemy, where mourners raised clenched fists and chanted the *Internationale*. Nationalists considered Christian burial as an ecumenical gesture of great generosity and humanity, but it could also be seen as part of a religious crusade that asserted clerical control over the Republican dead and denied their individual right to remain agnostics, anticlericals, or atheists. Sometimes, chaplains would cover enemy bodies with a coat of dirt and pray for their souls. Catholics were especially outraged by Republican desecration of the Teruel cemetery, where crosses were mutilated and gravestones overturned.[44]

The cemetery was regarded as "sacred grounds," as holy as the church, where no eating, drinking, shouting, or playing was permitted to disturb the "eternal sleep of souls." In December 1938 the Council of Ministers abrogated the 30 January 1932 law that had secularized cemeteries. Catholics asserted that secularization denied proper respect for the dead. The repeal also ordered the destruction of "all inscriptions and symbols of Masonry or any others that are hostile to the Catholic religion or to Christian morality." In Asturias, families were given a week "to remove gravestones and inscriptions that are an affront to the Glorious National Movement." Officials repressed All Saints' Day celebrations in cemeteries, which were supposedly tasteless, populist, and commercial. They imposed price controls on rituals and fined a funeral home 500 pesetas "for overcharging to move a combatant's corpse." On anniversaries of deaths, prosperous families of fallen soldiers placed notices in newspapers, asking friends to remember them in their prayers.[45]

Funeral rituals showed both the respect and the distance that Catholics offered to their Islamic allies. Military authorities initially ignored the correct procedures for burying Moslems and interred some in Christian cemeteries. Quickly, protests of Moroccans led them to rectify their mistakes. *Adules*, notaries familiar with Islamic law who could earn 300 pesetas per month, washed the bodies of deceased moros and, when possible, buried them in Islamic cemeteries. After one battle during the Asturian campaign, forty to fifty moros chanted over the body of a dead comrade. Covered by a *chilaba*, or a white sheet, the corpse was interred with its face toward Mecca, and a tin half-moon marked the grave. Islamic cemeteries were established in Griñon, Burgos, and Zaragoza. In contrast, Jews were not as fortunate and had no special burial ground. Some of them joked that they were denied the right to die in Spain. Because of objections from Moslems and Catholics, both of whom opposed burial alongside "infidels," Islamic corpses were put to rest in civil cemeteries, ironically enough, alongside the "reds" that the Moroccans had come to fight. As with the Christian dead, Nationalist authorities made sure that the possessions of the deceased were transmitted to their families. Spanish officials were careful not to offend the dignity of Islamic soldiers in life and in death. Even the most fervent Christians usually respected their dietary rules and religious customs. In fact, Spanish chaplains came to admire and perhaps envy the religious devotion of Muslim troops, who prayed and fasted even under the most dangerous conditions. Yet Moslem deaths were not given the same publicity as those of their Christian counterparts, and few campaigns were launched to preserve their memory.[46]

ART

Nationalist art reflected traditional religious values more than fascist modernity. A clerical rather than fascist aesthetic dominated their zone. *ABC* (Seville), the most circulated and elaborate newspaper in the Nationalist zone, offered photographers 10 pesetas for each published photograph, and the result of the competition was more religious than secular or fascist. The experimentation of the great urban centers of Spain was usually distrusted in the Nationalist zone. To many franquistas, both Catholicism and art evoked beauty. As shall be seen, avant-garde urban art and fashion was often considered anti-Spanish and attributed to nefarious Jewish influence. The famous writer Pío Baroja propagated an anti-Semitism based on his own Nietzschean view that Jews harbored a deep resentment against Europeans. The supposed Semitic desire to "discredit our continent" resulted in the tastelessness of contemporary theater, novels, erotic movies, and cubism. Jewish *ressentiment* explained "the legitimation of homosexuality by Freud and his followers."[47]

If sophisticated visual creativity won wars, the Republic would have achieved an easy victory. Instead of originality, the Insurgent regime promoted neotraditionalist sacred and religious art and ardently defended it against revolutionary and Republican iconoclasm. Sacrilege offended national as well as religious sentiment, since most Catholics believed that their religion was the exclusive Spanish faith. The youth branch of Acción Católica pleaded for "Eucharistic acts of redress" for the monument of the Sagrado Corazón de Jesús, "shot by twentieth-century Jews in the heart of Spain." Other outraged Catholics blamed the anticlerical destruction of the monument, which had been inaugurated in 1919 by King Alfonso XIII at the Cerro de los Ángeles (Madrid), on a Masonic conspiracy. The eternal enemies of Spain had attacked an icon that represented the unity of monarchy, nation, and religion.[48]

The decree of 22 April 1938 established a Junta de Cultura Histórica y del Tesoro Artístico (the *junta* appellation suggested Spanish resistance to a foreign invader), presided over by the civil governor in each "liberated" province to inventory and restore damaged art. The Asturian Junta de Cultura asked all who had photographed artistic monuments or works "destroyed by red hordes" to send their pictures to the civil governor to help officials in their reconstruction campaign. Frontline troops lent a hand to the rebuilding of destroyed churches. The Academia Nacional de Bellas Artes met in San Sebastián and celebrated the Generalísimo for his "restitution to Spain of paintings, statues, and tapestry stolen by Marxists." In October 1937 the Falange of Santander established a "provisional museum" in Santillana del Mar of 190 mutilated objects from churches and chapels, and the Seville Junta de Cultura organized an exhibition of "art objects destroyed by Marxists." These displays were, in their own bizarre ways, tributes to the visual power of iconoclasm. Another exhibition in Vigo featured mutilated art, particularly the Santo Cristo de Ochandiano, and other images damaged by the "international savagery" of the "reds." Tens of thousands of persons in towns throughout the Nationalist zone, including large groups of soldiers and school children, saw this traveling exhibition of "Christian and Western civilization." The reactions of most viewers probably resembled the repulsion that many Christians, Hindus, and Buddhists felt toward the iconoclasm of the Chinese Cultural Revolution or the Afghani Taliban. However, the traveling exhibition ignored the relative lack of funding for art restoration and recuperation in the Nationalist zone. Catholic internationalism led to the founding of the Obra de los Altares y Cruces de España, for which Belgian Catholics raised money for chasubles, chalices, and other religious objects to replace those that anticlericals had destroyed. Argentine sympathizers contributed twenty-seven crates of religious objects to the Cruzada, a transnational example of bringing coals to Newcastle.[49]

Academies undertook the defense of traditional art and culture. The Academia Sevillana de Buenas Letras honored the Córdoba sculptor of religious images, Juan de Mesa (1583–1627), with a commemorative stone plaque on the façade of the Church of San Martín. It also featured lectures on fourteenth-century Seville painting. Queipo opened the exhibition at Seville's Círculo de Bellas Artes on Juan Martínez Montañés (1658–1749), a well-known sculptor of religious icons during Spain's Golden Age. Falangist circles in Santiago greatly appreciated Emanuel López Garabal's image of a suffering Christ. They also exhibited conventional and uncontroversial nineteenth- and early-twentieth-century *costumbrista* paintings by Felipe Gil Gallango. The Gallegan landscape painter Felipe Bello Pineiro found admirers among Falangists. Paintings and poetry of local scenery—both Spanish and Moroccan—were enthusiastically endorsed.[50]

The folk art of the *patria chica*, especially the hometown of the Generalísimo, was esteemed. Pilar Primo de Rivera sometimes attended exhibitions, which featured artisanal products such as the lace and pottery representative of each region. Zamora established a regional costume museum. The traveling variety show Teatro Ambulante de Campaña presented acrobats, jugglers, plays, and a "folkloric" concert titled Costumbres Aragoneses accompanied by a large orchestra. The 1938 Good Friday procession in Zaragoza synthesized the resurrection of images disfigured by "reds" with the martyrdom of soldiers and the suffering of their mothers: "[One hundred] soldiers wounded in Aragon carried a sacred Christ, mutilated by Communists. [One hundred] mothers who had lost their sons on the battlefield accompanied an image of our Lady of Sorrows." Frentes y Hospitales organized a show in Bilbao of "military liturgical art" that displayed portable altars and various religious objects.[51]

At the International Exposition in Paris in 1937, Nationalist Spain's exhibit contrasted sharply with those of its Republican enemies and fascist allies. Instead of the modernist building designed by Josep Luis Sert containing Pablo Picasso's *Guernica* or the German pavilion's hardworking Aryan workers, the franquistas erected a chapel in the Vatican pavilion that they opened on the feast day of Santa Teresa. Teresa was also the patron saint of the SF and of the military quartermaster, which regularly celebrated her 15 October holiday throughout Spain, often with big banquets. Fittingly, José María Sert's altarpiece *Intercession of Saint Teresa in the Spanish War* was proudly displayed under the Vatican flag.[52]

At the Twenty-First Biennial of Venice of 1938, the Spanish entry was Quintín de Torre's sculptures made for Bilbao's Holy Week. "Spain's glorious tradition . . . that General Franco defends" inspired both Ignacio Zuloaga and the figurative painter Pedro Pruno, who contributed *Angels in the death of Franco's soldier* to this prestigious international exhibition held in Fascist Italy. Another sculptor—Enrique Pérez Comendador—and a handful of other well-known painters (Álvarez de Sotomayor, Gustavo de Maeztu, José Aguiar, José de Togores, and Mariano Fortuny) also displayed their works. One of the most appreciated artists, Carlos Sáenz de Tejada, won the endorsement of many Nationalist aesthetes for his El Greco–like portraits of requetés, Falangists, and women committed to the Nationalist cause. Other painters—Domingo Viladomat and José Caballero—subordinated Surrealist influence to neotraditionalism, just as poster artists in the Republican zone used cubism to convey Socialist realism.[53]

With great publicity, an International Exhibition of Sacred Art celebrated the end of the conflict during its inauguration on Easter Day (10 April) 1939 in Vitoria. A number of Spain's highest political and religious authorities—Gómez Jordana, Pedro Sainz Rodríguez, Conde de Rodezno, and Cardinal Isidro Gomá—sponsored the show, which the academician Eugenio d'Ors had conceived. Contemporary artists and artisans who were inspired by church doctrine and liturgy contributed images that were "austere" with "a religious tone." Attempting to avoid "exaggerated modernist tendencies" and "individualist ramblings," the exhibition displayed traditional works of goldsmithing, ornaments, books, photographs, and architectural projects by artists from at least a dozen countries. The Spanish items served as an "example for other nations." Portraits of the victorious Caudillo framed by Toledo's Alcázar also won official praise.[54]

The aesthetics of the press were usually religious, and their advertisements conventional, but sometimes photographers were attracted by more fascistic rituals. Nationalist films, such as *España Heroica* (1938), combined numerous scenes of "red" iconoclasm with a fascist and militaristic aesthetic. Glorious military feats and rebuilding by the Servicio de Trabajo de la Falange checked unrelenting Republican destruction.[55] With its phalanxes of shovel-carrying uniformed laborers marching in formation, the Servicio de Trabajo copied on a smaller scale the style of the Nazi Labor Service depicted in the *Triumph of the Will*. Heroic soldiers and workers defeated dynamiting miners and leftist arsonists who had, the film mendaciously asserted, destroyed Guernica.

Poster celebrating—with a hint of Surrealist modernism—Falangists, Carlists, and other Nationalist forces.

The victors generously reconverted Republican prisoners into productive laborers who reclaimed profaned but sacred monuments, such as the church at Covadonga, the site of one of the first Christian victories against the Moors in 722.

Many old religious fiestas—Fiesta of the Blessed Virgin, Maundy Thursday, Good Friday, and Corpus Cristi—were maintained. In 1937 the regime revived the national holiday—which the Republic had suppressed—that celebrated the apostle Santiago, "Spain's patron saint" and, according to Serrano Súñer, no longer the warrior "Santiago the Moorkiller" but somehow a victim of "Jewish perfidy." In 1938, Cardinal Gomá, the primate of Spain, militarized the Virgin's holiday, Immaculate Conception (8 December), by declaring it also the Day of the Crusader that celebrated soldiers who were defending Spain from atheistic Communism. New work-free holidays were also decreed. For example, 18 July was doubly celebrated as "the birth of the National Movement" or the "Glorious National Uprising" and, as a sop to Falangists, the "Festival of the Celebration of Work" since the leftist 1 May holiday was abolished. The day of the forced unification of the Falangists and Carlists, 19 April, became the Festival of Unity. The work-free National Festival of the Caudillo was fêted on 1 October, the date of his elevation to Generalísimo. The Commemoration of the Death of José Antonio (21 November) and the Day of the Fallen (28 or 29 October) were normal workdays in the peninsula. Apparently neither one dead *jefe* nor tens of thousands of the fallen were equivalent to one living Caudillo. Provincial authorities invented holidays that commemorated their integration into the Movimiento Nacional. Not all acknowledged the new political fiestas. In 1939 approximately a dozen small-town residents in Zamora, including the mayors of the villages of Valparaiso, Granja de Moreruela, and San Marcial, were fined because they worked the fields on "Victory Day."[56]

Popular artistic expression centered on Catholic holidays and processions, whose spectacle continued to delight large crowds, especially in Andalusia. Seville's Holy Week remained a great tourist attraction. Religious displays—for example, parades with floats of giants—which had been periodically halted during the Second Republic, returned for the supposed delight of children and adults alike. Pilgrimages to Santiago, Covadonga, and other holy sites also attracted a following of thousands of Spaniards—mostly women motivated as much by nationalism as Catholicism. During one pilgrimage to Covadonga, a local bishop addressed a crowd of 3,000, including regional military and political leaders, on the theme of the Sacred Crusade needed to save Spain and urged his listeners to offer prayers to General Franco and his army. A crowd of 400 persons from Oviedo visited the tomb of the Apostle at Santiago and other shrines in the north. Most traveled to pilgrimage sites by bus or train, but some of the extremely dedicated did so on foot.

Periodically, several hundred foreigners, especially French Catholics, joined them during their trips to Santiago. The "prosperity and abundance" of Nationalist Spain astonished the head of the French center, Casa de Velázquez (Madrid), and noted historian of Spain, Maurice Legendre. During a 1938 pilgrimage, he expressed his wish to see the emergence of a General Franco in France.[57]

Devout Nationalist combatants promised themselves and their God to visit Santiago after the war terminated. The mother of one Asturian soldier sewed a *detente* into his army jacket and pledged that if he returned safely "she would travel shoeless and silent from Cangas to Covadonga during nine days and climb the stairs to the sanctuary on her knees. She scrupulously fulfilled her promise." Franco's wife, Carmen Polo, led an excursion to the Virgin of Pilar in Zaragoza, a popular pilgrimage site, which was allegedly the location of a miracle when Republican bombs dropped from a plane perforated the roof of the Cathedral but failed to explode. Lectures on the Spain of the Catholic kings were offered to the pilgrimage crowds. Military ceremonies—graduation of the *alfereces* and *sargentos provisionales*—nearly always included not only a festive banquet but also religious elements, including a Catholic Mass, even if held in Morocco. Soldiers on leave frequently attended church, sometimes with the less spiritual mission of seeing and perhaps meeting the young women of the village.[58]

As in the Republican zone, but less consistently, attempts were made to edify the masses. Certain towns offered traveling theaters, which performed plays from Spain's Golden Age. Dionisio Ridruejo, propaganda chief of the regime, explored the possibility of establishing Misiones Populares de Cultura to provide theater for frontline troops. Yet popular amusements—flamenco dance, band concerts, bullfights, Carmen costume contests (judged by an Argentine actress who played her in a movie)—attracted far greater audiences. Despite objections by chaplains and other moralists, gambling on cockfights, dog races, Basque *pelota*, card games, and various lotteries aroused enormous participation. Although regulations prohibited games of chance, gaming soldiers bet and frequently lost their entire pay. As the notoriously anti-intellectual but verbally agile Millán Astray stated, "What is gambling? The art of losing everything except hope of winning." In fact, the Las Palmas police banned unauthorized gambling—lotteries, card games, etc.—which the state was unable to tax. Nevertheless, the regime promoted superstition—a facile belief in the "predictions" of the sixteenth-century "cabalistic prophet" Nostradamus, who forecast the victory of Franco in the imagination of his supporters.[59]

The neotraditionalist culture repressed a variety of behaviors it labeled "immoral." It respected the Roman Index and banned authors who opposed the movement. "We condemn to flame books that are separatist, Marxist, supporting the Black Legend, anti-Catholic, those of a morbid romanticism, those that are pessimistic." Recalling Torquemada's biblioclasm, the Caudillo's hometown and other cities throughout the Nationalist zone publicly burned "pornographic" and "extremist" literature. Neotraditionalists constantly linked pornography with leftist politics as expressions of anticlericalism. Religious authorities presented a very broad definition of "pornography," which included "Socialist, Communist, and libertarian" literature. A chaplain reported that in conquered enemy trenches, his men found an anthology of Karl Marx, pamphlets by André Marty and Léon Blum, and "pornographic novels" by Pancho Villa, Alexandre Dumas, and Victor Hugo. The traditionalist orientation led to book burnings of anticlerical authors—José Nakens, A. Martín de Lucenay, Joaquín Belda, and Peter Kropotkin. Fear of arrest for possessing "subversive" literature pressured many individuals and families to destroy their private libraries.[60]

Nationalists demonstrated yet again the veracity of Heinrich Heine's famous dictum, "Where they burn books, they will also ultimately burn people." Throughout Nationalist Spain, Republican schoolteachers were signaled out for death. A Gallegan newspaper quoted the talkative Millán Astray: "There is not enough earth to bury those teachers who educate children with the raised clenched fist." Most Republican instructors were purged, but a large number, especially females, eventually returned to service, given the manpower needs of the education system. Rationalist schools and foundations were abolished, and religious instruction and crucifixes reimposed in primary and secondary schools. The crucifix also returned to the courtroom, where judges and magistrates had to swear unconditional loyalty to the Caudillo. A resurrected sexism expressed itself by abolishing coeducation, female participation in night schools, and limitations on female employment opportunities. Lay schools and their libraries were turned over to the Catholic teaching orders.[61]

Textbooks were revised according to the principles of the movement. A long list of books banned from schools—including seemingly inoffensive basic mathematics texts—was issued. Public libraries and those of working-class organizations were purged of "dangerous," "Marxist," and "anti-Catholic" books and magazines. Only "patriotic" and "orderly" elements, who received military approval, could consult the banned texts. This "evil" literature was replaced by a teaching manual titled the *Libro de España*, which emphasized that Catholic Spain had saved Europe from Islam, the Reformation, and Marxism. Literate soldiers publicly requested—and received—only edifying textbooks and respectable novels. The extremely limited selection of reading material in most Spanish towns reminded one anti-Communist correspondent of his boyhood in Ireland where only religious books and "cheap . . . generally tenth-rate" fiction were available. Inadequate illumination for reading in the rooms of Spanish hotels and boarding houses reflected the country's low level of literacy. The dearth of the quantity and quality of books bolstered the importance of newspapers in the Nationalist zone.[62]

MUSIC

Musical expression was more diverse than visual arts. War reinforced and intensified group musical identities within a neotraditionalist framework. Popular songs became what Ramón Menéndez Pidal called "autor-legión," in other words, communal works that were altered according to the changing needs and desires of the collectivity. "There was much work . . . but also much singing, and 'Oriamendi' for the requetés, the Falangist hymn, and the 'Novio de la Muerte' for the Spanish Legion, could be heard over the tramp of feet and the roar of the motor traffic on every road and in every town square of Nationalist Spain." The Nationalists' more conservative culture echoed a society in which the omnipresence of commercialized mass communications had not yet eliminated rural traditions of participatory folk music. Soldiers requested instruments—guitars, lutes, violins, bugles, mandolins, clarinets, flutes, tambourines, saxophones, accordions, drums—more than gramophones or radios.[63]

The high group morale of the requetés, who were often employed as shock troops, was echoed in their constant singing—sometimes stimulated by significant consumption of wine or cognac—of religious, local, regional, and national favorites. "We sing and drink as during the San Fermín Festival [of the Running of the Bulls]." The chanting—which constantly bolstered collective confidence—reflected the religious and political traditions of Carlism with its emphasis on religion and king. The classic songs of the crusade—the "Oriamendi" (the Carlist anthem), "National March," and the triumphant hymn of Montejurra were treasured. The Carlists insisted so fervently on promoting their "Oriamendi" that in 1938 authorities sought to ban the leaflet titled *Patriotic Hymns of the Army and the Armed Forces* that had failed to include it. Requetés celebrated victories—and even defeats—with enthusiastic singing, and many of their *tercios* and other units had their own bands and orchestras, composed of dozens of members, whose instruments accompanied the merry Navarrese songs and lifted the spirits of both soldiers and civilians. They mixed sacred and profane music. During the Bilbao campaign in June 1937, after one primitive but hot meal—meat, potatoes, and homemade jam—they sang about their "happy" village Berbinzana and the "flowers and cream" of Navarre. Their songs sometimes contained lyrics poking fun at their commanders, and their bands attracted thousands of civilians at free concerts in cities and hospitals throughout the Nationalist zone. Likewise, small amateur orchestras entertained troops with music, song, and even magic acts. One requeté commented, "Songs whether of war or love were always sharply nostalgic and unified us." A demoralized enemy declared, "We cannot fight those guys who can even sing together."[64]

The Tercio de Montserrat had its own Catalan tunes ("El Virolai," "l'emigrant," and "l'Ampudà"). On the Guadalajara front, which had been quiet since the famous failure of the CTV, Catalan requetés competed vocally by singing their Carlist hymns to drown out the enemy's "Internationale" and "A las barricadas." During festivities, requeté pianists and violinists offered their comrades after-dinner performances of the classics. Some Catalan sentimentalists in Republican ranks were tempted to desert when they heard enemy Carlists intone "El Virolai." The chanting of religious songs and prayers demoralized believers enrolled in the Republican Army and even enticed a few of them to abandon their lines. Of course, a shared knowledge of Catholic hymns and Christmas carols was common to all Spaniards.[65]

The bands of the Legion and other units also provided free concerts. The Legion chanted its "Sweetheart of Death," "Marching Hymn," and ribald Spanish ballads. It had its own organ-grinders who accompanied advancing troops. Radio Castilla popularized the "Legion's Hymn." The Falange sang its "Cara al Sol" and, with unification, was forced to accept the "Oriamendi." In February 1937 Franco signed a decree making the "Marcha Real" ("Marcha Granadero") the national anthem, a fitting tribute by militarists to a song that the king of Prussia had gifted to the Spanish in the eighteenth century. The Caudillo declared the "Cara al Sol," "Oriamendi," and the "Legionnaire's Song" "national hymns," whose performances required listeners to stand. Resistance to the law was not unknown and took the form of remaining seated, which was considered a grave offense. Each Moroccan unit had its own band, known as *nuba*. North African legionnaires and Regulares chanted continuously and responsively, often accompanied by the rhythmic clapping of palms, cans, stones, and other objects. Some musically inclined requetés did not appreciate their "droning" and "atrocious racket," but others went native and joined their fellow soldiers.[66]

Of course, all Republicans could sing the "Riego Hymn." Socialists and Communists had the "Internationale," which International Brigaders chanted in many languages, and anarchists intoned the less well known "A las barricadas." A battalion of the Aragon FAI, whom one requeté considered a courageous foe, chanted a song of its own creation during the Battle of Teruel. The Basques were devotees of "Euzko gudariak" ("Basque Warriors"); the Catalans, "Els Segadors." During the Battle of the Ebro, Republican soldiers sang "Aunque me tires el puente" and "Si me quieres escribir." The latter song was unusual, since its verses could be chanted by both sides. The various nationalities of International Brigaders intoned their own ditties—"La Carmagnole" of the French, the "Valley of the Jarama" for the Americans,

"Bandiera rossa" of the Italians, and "Spaniens Himmel breitet seine Sterne" for the Germans. Condor legionnaires had their own band, which played for Spanish audiences, and their own anthem, the Condor "Fliegermarsch."[67] Bertolt Brecht responded to the presence of German pilots in Spain with the only poem he wrote about the Spanish conflict:

> My brother was a pilot,
> He received a card one day,
> He packed his belongings in a box
> And southward took his way.
>
> My brother is a conqueror,
> Our people are short of space
> And to gain more territory is
> An ancient dream of the race.
>
> The space that my brother conquered
> Lies in the Guadarrama massif,
> Its length is six feet, two inches,
> Its depth four feet.[68]

Praying and singing together provided the unit with links to what they considered a glorious past of social and political struggles and religious wars. Singing also helped to pass the commonly eventless and boring time on the front. On quiet fronts, soldiers engaged in vocal competitions with the enemy. Some ditties stressed the benefits of martyrdom; others expressed a macho and humorous defiance of death:

> Si la Guerra dura mucho
> Y son fuertes los combates,
> Han de valer las mujeres
> Al precio de los tomates.[69]

MOVIES

Affordability and accessibility transformed the cinema into the most popular public spectacle. Nevertheless, material and political conditions for both spectators and theater owners rendered movie going more difficult during the war than it had been previously. Defective prints of the several thousand films authorized in the Nationalist zone and the unkempt theaters in which they were shown discouraged potential customers. So did intrusive censorship. The decrease in the number of Hollywood films, which were forced to share the Spanish market with German and Italian movies, reduced audience size and revenues. In fact, faced with the parlous financial situation of the

theaters, authorities permitted films that had entered Spain before 18 July
1936 to circulate even if their stars were pro-Republican.[70]

Both Catholics and Falangists objected to many American productions.
Hollywood's "studios . . . betray[ed] their Jewishness" by supporting the
"red" government of Barcelona. John Dos Passos's *Tierra de Libertad* and William Dieterle's *Blockade* were dismissed as Communist propaganda. Dieterle
had also directed "the famous film," *The Life of Emile Zola*, "on the forgotten Dreyfus Affair that displayed a Jewish and pacifist cunning." One journalist, Federico Casas, argued for placing both Clark Gable and Norma Shearer
on a cinematographic "Index" of banned actors. Both had played starring
roles in the "Jew" Samuel Goldwyn's *Idiot's Delight*, which Casas deemed
antifascist. Instead of watching productions by the "evil Jewish serpent,"
Spanish spectators should view German and Italian films. In that manner,
"the battles won by men" would not be lost by "women and children whom
the big screen perverts."[71]

The ultra-Catholic Confederación Nacional de Padres de Familia engaged
in a campaign against "wicked" and "perverse" films. The Catholic press condemned films that portrayed adultery as "completely immoral. They should
not be seen." The movies of the American studios "are devoted to lowering
morality to weaken and enslave other peoples," a critique that contemporary
Islamists would endorse. During and immediately after the war, Catholic
and other Nationalist publications and organizations, including the Padres
de Familia, fumed that Spaniards had short memories and enthusiastically
attended American films produced by the "Jews and Masons" of Paramount
and Metro-Goldwyn-Mayer. The Catholic critics were correct that even the
Falangist newspapers—perhaps reflecting their greater acceptance of urban
modernity—were frequently enthusiastic about Paramount and MGM productions. The Falangist press promoted Hollywood films, which were usually dubbed in Spanish. Yet the Falange's attitude toward Jews in the cinema
was hardly tolerant and repeated that of Nazi propaganda minister Joseph
Goebbels: "Lummiere [*sic*] made the first films, but today the cinema is the
classic Jewish tool."[72]

Yet despite the censorship of their love scenes, strikes, and anything hint-
ing of political protest, Hollywood films remained extremely popular in the
Nationalist zone, as they were in the Republican zone. Audiences enthusiastically received Warner Bros. productions—such as *Bordertown*, starring
Paul Muni, and *Parachute Jumpers*, with Douglas Fairbanks, Jr. MGM was
praised as the "prestigious brand Metro-Goldwyn-Mayer," which produced
marvelous spectacles: "It's a Metro film and that is enough to guarantee its
lushness." Benefit performances of MGM films raised funds for Frentes and
Hospitales. A massive audience viewed its *China Seas*, starring Clark Gable
and Jean Harlow, following the patriotic address of the military commander

Catholic Neotraditionalism

of Vigo. MGM comedies with Jack Benny, Constance Bennet, or Gable were "very fine looking" and "extremely entertaining." The studio's production of *Riffraff* (1936), "a beautiful film," showed that Harlow and Spencer Tracy remained great performers. *Sequoia* with Jean Parker showed the "tremendous success of a Metro blockbuster." MGM's *Small Town Girl* with Janet Gaynor and Robert Taylor came highly recommended. The "very famous" Eddie Cantor made "wonderful," "grand," and "very entertaining" films. His *Strike Me Pink* was a "tremendous success" in both zones. Al Jolson's *Casino de Paris* was simply "marvelous." MGM's *Camille*, directed by George Cukor and starring Greto Garbo and Robert Taylor, presented a rural and traditionalist idyll in line with the ideology of the Nationalist zone. Falangists praised *The Dark Angel*, produced by Samuel Goldwyn and written by Lillian Hellman, as "beautiful," "extraordinary," and "a masterpiece."[73]

Although theaters screened many German and Italian films, American films still dominated. The fondness for U.S. cinema contrasted with Vichy France, where it was largely banned. *Tarzan and his Mate* (1934), dubbed in Spanish, with Johnny Weissmuller and Maureen O'Sullivan, was "the greatest of adventure movies" and an "MGM blockbuster." Paul Lukas's and Rosalind Russell's *The Casino Murder Case* was "sensational." Westerns, however mediocre, were enthusiastically received. The films of the singing cowboy, Ken Maynard, whose horse "Tarzan" also became a star, were critically and popularly acclaimed. At the same time, the German propaganda film *Triumph of the Will* was admired for showing "the impressive German organization, both military and civilian." *Der Herrscher* (1937), which promoted the *Führerprinzip* and starred Emil Jannings, the most famous Nazi actor, was "the major cinematographic event of 1937–38." Theaters showed many other German productions, including a number in the original language for troops of the Condor Legion and other German speakers. The ecumenical approach led to odd combinations. In one Seville theater the presentation of *Liberation of Bilbao* by the Fascist Instituto Italiano Luce was followed by a science fiction/ horror film, *The Invisible Ray*, starring Boris Karloff and Bela Lugosi.[74]

German and Italian filmmakers had difficulty competing with the American star system in a country whose moviegoers were fully acquainted with U.S. actors and actresses, especially those from the MGM studio. Gable was one of MGM's "great stars," Loretta Young "the most likeable star," Boris Karloff "the ace of horror actors," Peter Lorre "a great star," Norma Shearer "the sweetest actress," and the ever popular Laurel and Hardy the "kings of laughter." Even though the comic duo did not impress movie critics, they admitted that "the public laughed its head off" during their films. Laurel and Hardy attracted 40,000 children into their fan clubs. The accolades to Shirley Temple—"brilliant," "an infant prodigy," and "the perfectly accomplished artist"—were baffling since she had vociferously declared her support for the

Republic and accused Franco's air force of killing children. A surfeit of other stars—Douglas Fairbanks, Helen Hayes, George Raft, Paul Muni, Fred Astaire, Lon Chaney, Lionel Barrymore, Ginger Rogers, Claudette Colbert, Joan Crawford, Greta Garbo, Myrna Loy, Robert Montgomery, Francis Lederer, Frederick March, Edward G. Robinson, George Raft, Fred MacMurray, Katherine Hepburn, Charlie Chan, Joe E. Brown—attracted paying viewers.[75]

Franquistas ignored their profound anti-Semitism when it suited them. As has been seen, the Jewish origins of stars and filmmakers did not adversely affect their popularity in the peninsula. The press ignored the Jewish ancestry and youthful leftism of the Hungarian-born British director Alexander Korda, "one of Europe's greatest cinematic geniuses." His production of the *Scarlet Pimpernel* (1934) "was extremely relevant" because it showed "the horrors of the French Revolution." In their own movie making, the Insurgents employed the services of the German-Jewish refugee Enrique Guerner (né Heinrich Gärtner Kolb). Familiar with all aspects of the cinema, Guerner was a first-rate cameraman and director of photography. His technical knowledge became so indispensable to the Nationalist film industry that the Caudillo facilitated Guerner's adoption of Spanish nationality so that the German government could not demand his extradition. He not only worked on Nationalist documentaries during the conflict, some of whose scenes Frédéric Rossif later used in his antifascist *Mourir à Madrid* (1963), but he also served as the lead technician in Franco's own production of *Raza* (1941). At the beginning of the war, the arrival in the port city of Vigo of exiled German-Jewish biographer Emil Ludwig (né Emil Cohn), "one of Europe's outstanding intellectuals," was celebrated. However, by the spring of 1938, Ludwig had become a persona non grata in Francoist Spain and was compared to the likes of the failed Russian Socialist Alexander Kerensky and the Communist author Henri Barbusse.[76]

ANTI-SEMITISM

Anti-Semitism in the Nationalist zone served a variety of functions. First, it expressed the distrust of the equal rights, religious tolerance, and economic freedom that the Enlightenment had introduced. Nationalist anti-Semitism denied the equality of all citizens before the law. The New Spain did not welcome nor would it provide equal treatment to Jews. Nationalists rejected a secular republic and economic liberalism, both supposedly results of Jewish influence. Second, as has been seen, anti-Semitism appealed to Muslims and allied them with neotraditionalist Catholics and to fascists in Italy and Germany. Third, hatred of Jews confirmed a conspiratorial view of history that connected Jews to Masons and to Communists, as the power brokers of a distrusted modernity. Finally, and least wellknown, Nationalist anti-Semitism represented a glorification of rural values and a revulsion for cosmopolitan urban life.[77] Insurgent neotraditionalism rejected many post-Enlightenment aspects of European modernity in a manner similar to the contemporary radical Islamist refusal of Western dominance.

The Jewish question came to symbolize loathing for the Second Republic, which, like its French model, had attempted to create a secular and tolerant state. The Falange and reactionary Catholics—especially the Jesuits smarting from the limitations imposed by the Republic—made clear that they detested the nineteenth century as "liberal, decadent, materialist, and Frenchified." Spanish greatness was identified with Imperial Spain of the Counter Reformation. Liberals in the nineteenth century and Marxists in the twentieth, the new *marranos* (secret Jews) continued their hatred of Catholic Spain and dedicated their lives to its destruction. Franco stated that "critical distance is liberal and is foreign to our movement." Spanish anti-Semites considered the Jews not the creators of monotheism but rather the coauthors of a godless Republic. "Jewish gold" controlled the Republic's press. Albert Einstein's support for the Republic revealed him to be merely "the Jew A. Einstein."[78]

Jews—both real and imagined—were the enemy. In the former category were French Prime Minister Léon Blum, Soviet Ambassador Marcel Rosenberg, and the Socialist/Communist politician Margarita Nelken. The latter was representative of "her hungry tribe of peddlers," and "as a good Jewess is a born vulgarian." Among imagined Jews were liberals, such as Salvador de Madariaga, "a deserter of both Spains, a hybrid like a mule"; the Catalan nationalist Luis Companys, "descendent of converted Jews"; and the Socialists Indalecio Prieto and Fernando de los Ríos. The far right especially detested De los Ríos and regarded him as a dangerous foe of the Inquisition who had called the expulsion of the Jews the beginning of Spain's decline. They mocked him as Fernando Ríos "the Jew," "the great Sephardi," and "the rabbi" who had betrayed his country by addressing the "anti-España" Sephardic Synagogue of New York. Furthermore, this professor had great influence "in Zionist circles." The Institución Libre de Enseñanza, closely associated with De los Ríos, denigrated Spain by spreading the Jewish-authored Black Legend. The leaders of the Institución Libre were "sages" in the tradition of the sages of Zion. A Jesuit chaplain termed the Republican cultural center Fundación del Amo the "Synagogue" of De los Ríos. Fellow Jesuits were pleased that the Insurgents destroyed the lay culture of the Ciudad Universitaria, which had "ruined Spain," and replaced it with pure Christian faith. Some Jesuits concluded that extreme right-wing youth movements, including the Hitler Youth, had healthily revitalized Europe.[79]

A Nationalist "expert" on Jews, the Baron de Santa Clara, added the moderate Republicans Niceto Alcalá Zamora and Miguel Maura to the list of those with "Jewish blood." He brazenly declared that "the clenched fist is a Jewish ritual." "The synagogue" fought "against Spain." The Republican foe was "Jews" supported by Jews. The Republic had permitted "the invasion of Spain by the Jewish race." Although the Baron's figure of more than 10,000 Jews fighting in Republican ranks may have been roughly accurate, he tendentiously fantasized that "more than 50,000 Jews" made their home in Republican Spain and that in the Republican zone "numerous premises have been converted into synagogues where Semites meet to read the Talmud." Jewish International Brigaders led the fight against Nationalist Spain with the goal of defending the Jewish "race." When Nationalists finally defeated the Republic, they rejoiced in the common fate and flight of both Republican and German-Jewish refugees to Mexico.[80]

The oldest ideology revived the traditional religious hatred of Jews and meshed it into a conspiratorial view of history. José María Pemán was among the most famous of franquista intellectuals. A propagandist, poet, director of the Real Academia Española, and head of the Comisión Depuradora del Magisterio Nacional, Pemán proclaimed that "evil intellectuals must die." His *Poem of the Beast and Angel* blamed Spain's ills on the synagogue and the Masonic lodge, the sources of wickedness in his Manichean vision. This imagery was not restricted to elite franquista intellectuals but permeated Nationalist Spain. "The synagogue" became a metaphor for the entire left, whose leaders were, like their supposed Jewish allies, "plutocrats." Pemán's analysis was shared by many Catholics, who condemned the "anti-Spain constituted by the Jewish bank and its assistants—secret Masonic societies and Marxist groups directed by Moscow." The well-known Jesuit author Constantino Bayle demanded the "uprooting of the poisoned Jewish-Masonic seed." The Falangist press agreed: "The Jew invented Masonic lodges and created the Soviet hell. He is the enemy of Western civilization." "Today Spain not only fights for its own interests but also to deliver the world from Marxist and Jewish rabble."[81]

Juan Pujol was another right-wing "expert" on Jews. Pujol, who had been a CEDA deputy from 1933 to 1936, became a highly placed official in Franco's propaganda bureaucracy and received subsidies from the Nazis. He contributed front-page articles on Jewish influence. France was in the power of a "Jewish-Masonic organization" and was undergoing the same anarchy that Spain had experienced during its Republic. Jews controlled the French press, parliament, and its finances, but the French obsession with recuperating two small provinces (Alsace and Lorraine) had blinded them to their domination by "the foulest and toughest of all invaders." The Nationalist press obligingly repeated the theme of French xenophobes who called the influx into Paris of foreign physicians and medical students a "Jewish invasion." A cartoon taken from the extreme-right publication *Je suis partout* that depicted three French ministers with stereotyped Jewish noses all named "Señor Levy" reinforced the analysis. In the French city of Perpignon a "bank monopolized by Jews" financially assisted the "reds" with the help of the Soviets. The visit of Charles Maurras to Burgos—the Francoist Nuremburg—received great publicity. The highest Nationalist officials, including Serrano Súñer and the Caudillo, welcomed Maurras, the leader of the pioneering anti-Semitic Action Française. The latter's neotraditionalism had greatly influenced Renovación Española and other rightist groups in Spain. The Nationalist presses often reiterated Action Française's opinions on the French situation. Maurras's traveling companion, the sculptor Maxime Real de la Sarte, remarked that "the only common base of Latin culture is Roman Catholicism and the rejection of revolutionary, Masonic, and Jewish thinking."[82]

Léon Blum was singled out for special abuse ("Jew Blum," "Semite Blum," and the "Hebrew Blum") in the Nationalist press and became the object of the wildest charges. Blum and the Mason Jean Longuet plotted the "revolutionary strike in Málaga, Granada, and Córdoba" in 1930. Blum, the Marxist Jew and millionaire, desired to prolong the civil war. "This Jew" was the president of a firm that made great profits supplying the Spanish Republic. Jesús Pabón, a former member of CEDA and an honored franquista intellectual, regurgitated the same charge. Blum was an important representative of "the Jewish internationals," whose protest against the *Anschluss* with Austria was "supremely insidious and poisonous."[83]

Blum's book on marriage was described as being among the most "cynical" and "repugnant" in the history of literature. *Du Mariage* (1907) was "perversely immoral" and destructive of the family. The work deserved "the first prize of pornography," a genre that many Nationalists attributed to Jews. In fact, Blum's assault on tradition equaled Stalin's terrorism. His revolutionary desire to eliminate tradition was attributed to his "Jewish" commitment to the modern trilogy of Judaism, Masonry, and Marxism. "The work of the Jew is one of the most powerful battering rams that the skeptical and satanic imagination has ever invented to destroy the Christian family." Blum's influence had led a recent change of the French Civil Code, which suppressed the clause that the wife ought to obey her husband. The alteration constituted "a new Storming of the Bastille in the current revolution against the family." Legislation that permitted civil marriage and divorce were "the work of Masonry and Judaism." "Jewish clutches" had de-Christianized French women and had propagated a model for the remaining European democracies.[84]

At the outbreak of war, *ABC* (Seville) called for "death to the Jewish international rabble." The alliance of Jews and Masons, who were constantly linked as enemies of Spain, provided an easy explanation of the decline of traditional belief and authority. Masonry was founded on Jewish principles and served Jewish interests. Both groups exhibited a mysterious and threatening "inscrutability," whose "secrets" members vowed never to reveal to the uninitiated. Masonry cooperated with "shady Jewish scheming" to destroy "Spanish Catholic civilization." Cardinal Gomá declared in November 1936 that "the war is punishment for secularism and corruption. . . . Jews and Masons poisoned the national spirit with absurd doctrines, with Mongolian and Tartar tales transformed into a political and social system by groups manipulated in the shadows of Semitic internationalism." A Carlist chaplain attributed the profanation of churches throughout Andalusia at the outbreak of civil war to "the Jewish-Masonic command." According to the German consul in Seville, both Spain and Germany had the same enemies: "Masonry, Marxism, and Judaism." Serrano Súñer fully agreed. Forty percent of Jews were Masons. Both groups worked together to disseminate the "Black Legend." Immediately after the war a "new Jewish-democratic offensive" attacked Spain.[85]

According to Pujol's article "Jewish-Masonic Intrigue," which appeared in the Catholic press, Jews used Masons in the League of Nations, British parliament, City of London, Blum government, and Soviet Union to dominate Spain. Woodrow Wilson, "the founder of the League of Nations," "surrounded himself with Hebrews": Henry Morganthau, U.S. Ambassador to Turkey and treasurer of the Democratic Party; Louis Brandeis, the Supreme Court justice; Bernard Baruch, director of war industries; and Jacob Schiff, the banker. Other articles in the press articulated similar fictions. "The ultra-Mason," Woodrow Wilson, was the instrument of the Jewish fraternal organization B'nai B'rith, which "had always and still participates in the revolutionary movement." B'nai B'rith was the force behind the establishment of the League of Nations and the Russian Revolution. The former was controlled by "hysterical and alcoholic American-Jewish jurors whose mission is to declare the criminal democracies not guilty and bribe them with Jewish gold." American Jewish bankers had decided that the United States should go to war against Germany and funded the Russian Revolution. Jews dominated the proceedings at the Versailles conference, where all or nearly all the delegates demanded kosher menus. Furthermore, the "sinister" League had hired a large number of Jewish functionaries, who were undoubtedly collaborating with "the remaining occult forces—Communism, Masonry, and plutocracy—of the Jewish international."[86]

The Nationalists identified "reds" and Jews just as they had equated Masons and Jews. "Jewish Communism" was a frequent theme in the Nationalist press. The "red" zone was equated with "Jewish rule." The Jewish Diaspora supported the "reds." Queipo charged that "Jewish paid press in the U.S." and the "Jewish bank" fought against the Nationalists. Only Sephardic Jews opposed Communism. Nevertheless, "Judaism is . . . one of Spain's most powerful wartime enemies." He identified the URSS as "Unión Rabínica de los Sabios de Sión." General Mola was convinced that Jews continued to despise Catholic Spain because it had expelled them. "Universal Jewry" was already "boss of Russia and tries to take over our own country." Although Georgian, Joseph Stalin was "unconditionally submissive to Judaism." According to Eduardo Aunós, a key ideologue during the civil war who was invited to address graduation ceremonies of newly minted *alfereces provisionales*, Marx's *Das Kapital* was the "New Talmud of a tormented and destructive Judaism, full of hateful aggression against Christian society." Since all Jews were antifascists, to fight against anti-Semitism was to advocate Communism. Pío Baroja agreed with Aunós that Marxism was an expression of Jewish ethnicity and its insatiable desire to level European civilization. "Jewish Communism" was also responsible for the legalization of abortions and divorce in the Republican zone.[87]

In this climate traditional Catholic anti-Semitism attempted with difficulty to distinguish itself from the newer racist variety. The Baron de Santa Clara refused "anti-Jewish propaganda . . . which was very racist and anti-Christian," while arguing that Jews controlled the world. They were responsible for Socialism, Communism, Internationals, Masonry, and revolutions. The Jews, backed by the Masons, had provoked the defensive war of the Japanese against Chiang Kai-Shek, the principal Jewish-Masonic-Bolshevik agent in the East. Thus, Japan was engaged in "a vanguard combat" "against the Jewish international." Catholic ideologues of the Falange, such as the priest and publisher Fermín Yzurdiaga, attempted to reject racism and the efforts of enemies to identify Falangists with Nazism and Italian Fascism. In fact, it was precisely its antiracism and its anti-Semitism based on the supposed alliance between Jews, Communists, and Masons that distinguished the Falange from its fascist counterparts. Yzurdiaga claimed that the Falange remained in the tradition of the Catholic monarchs Ferdinand and Isabel: "The essence of Catholicism is anti-racist." "We must open a channel for the well-intentioned Jew and attract him to Catholic civilization instead of Jewish greed and power." According to José Antonio, "For Spain the Jewish problem will never be one of race but rather faith." Less theoretically, in Zaragoza during the civil war, the few Jews present were given the choice between conversion and death. They chose the former in a widely publicized ceremony in the city's cathedral.[88]

Racially oriented anti-Semites described Jews as "international microbes" and the Jewish people as a "poisonous snake." According to F. Bonmati de Codecido, a well-known monarchist novelist and historian, Jews were "racial enemies," who had sabotaged and undermined Spain since the era of Ferdinand and Isabel. The journalist Jesús Huarte argued that Jews were a "racial element" that destroyed the peoples with whom they inhabited. Aunós charged that "the survival of Jewish traits can explain much of Spanish decadence." Speculative capitalism, significant among certain sectors of the Spanish population, was "an inherent tendency of the Jewish race." The AS traced the prevalence of diabetes in Córdoba province to "the Jewish presence during a prolonged period." The ubiquitous military psychiatrist Antonio Vallejo Nájera blamed "the revolutionary labor of Judaizers" for Spanish decline. Jews were wealthy capitalists who exploited the poor. The Talmud justified Jewish robbing and seducing Gentiles. Nationalist newspapers gloatingly reported that the "reds" had fined a Jew who "earned fabulous profits from the hunger of the people." Pío Baroja proudly displayed his Basque racism at the expense of the Jews, whose own racism, he claimed, trumped their own interests.[89]

The Inquisition was a "sublime" institution, badly maligned by "sectarians." Isabel was perhaps the monarch that Nationalists most admired because she expelled Jews from Spain "forever." The Catholic monarchs provided a wise model for the fascist nations. Indeed, German and Italian racial laws—which the Nationalist press welcomed—merely copied the Catholic monarchs who had made Spain great. Jews' cooperation with Islam had permitted the latter to take possession of most of the peninsula during the early medieval period. Likewise, Jewish collaboration with the British and the Dutch in the sixteenth and seventeenth centuries was the cause of Spanish decadence. The Falange of Santa Cruz de la Palma demanded, "The Russians should leave! Those who feel Jewish should do the same!" In 1938 the governor of Las Palmas noted that some Jews had come to the island after 1933, and he urged their eventual expulsion.[90]

Nazi propagandists in Spain with the cooperation of the Spanish Nationalist press promoted the theme of an "invasion" by unassimilated Jews into France, other Western democracies, Italy, Poland, and the USSR. Jews who tried to assimilate—for instance by changing their names—were to be rejected out of hand. César González Ruano, a prominent author who also received German subsidies, related that the Jesuit publication La Civiltá Cattolica declared in 1890 that Jews—whose Talmud had promoted their inflated superiority complex—always pursued their interests at the expense of all nations in which they settled. In an article praising the "rebirth" of Germany under the Nazis, ABC (Seville) argued, "Jews are not only a danger for Germany but for the entire world." The "Jewish" and "Semitic" mayor of New York, Fiorello LaGuardia, who had called Hitler a "fanatic who endangered the European peace," defamed him. Instead, the Führer was "the savior of Germany," whose birthday was rightly celebrated.[91]

Nationalists supported official discrimination against Jews in every European nation. According to Arriba España, "Poland had the worst misfortune that could ever happen to a country: three million Jews live in its territory. If one Jew is abominable, this number must produce foul-smelling miasmas in the military and Catholic atmosphere of Poland." The press congratulated Poland for adopting measures "against Communists, Masons, and Jews." Rumania was praised for revoking post-1922 naturalizations, prohibiting Jews from collaborating on Rumanian newspapers, establishing rural businesses, and selling alcohol, tobacco, and other commodities. When French Jews protested these acts of official discrimination, they were accused of "scheming." Great Britain's objection to Rumanian anti-Semitic legislation was the result of "fear of the powerful Jewish economic organization."[92]

The Night of the Broken Glass, or *Reichspogrom*, of 9–10 November 1938 was blamed on a "Jewish provocation," launched by foreign Jews who had prepared a campaign of "anti-German defamation." The "political champions of the Jewish cause" used this campaign to deny Germany the return of its African colonies and to maintain the oppressive Versailles Treaty. "The Jewish attack against the Munich Agreement" desired to provoke a war between the democracies and "totalitarian states." "Jewish agitation" threatened world peace. Fortunately, the "anti-German propaganda" of "international Judaism" had failed, since Czechoslovakia and the Western democracies improved their relations with Germany in November 1938. Despite its "enormous resources," "the Jewish International" was unsuccessful in stopping Germany and Italy from their campaigns against "the Christ killers." "All men of good will . . . are finally uniting their efforts to eradicate" the Jews. Semites were plotting against Germany in Africa, a continent over which they exercised economic domination, and opposed the just colonial demands of Germany.[93]

The Nationalists invented their own victimist and Nazi-inspired response to *Kristallnacht*. Franklin Roosevelt—with his "Hebrew scruples" and his State Department full of Semites—sympathized with persecuted Jews but was oblivious to the suffering of murdered Catholics and other rightists. According to the grossly inflated statistic furnished by the Falangist and diplomat Merry del Val, the Spanish Republic had assassinated 400,000 persons. Foreign politicians, such as John Simon, chancellor of the exchequer in Neville Chamberlain's cabinet, who protested the plight of Jews during the Night of the Broken Glass, were unwise. The Reich and other nations that enacted anti-Jewish measures were merely defending themselves against a dangerous and alien race. It was the Jews, not the Germans, who were violent. Indeed, the Falangist press reiterated Goebbels's flight of fantasy that the assassination of German diplomat Ernst vom Rath was an attempt by "international Judaism" to provoke a new war against Germany since the Munich Agreement had frustrated the Jews' attempt to "exterminate" the Germans. The Night of the Broken Glass was merely a spontaneous reaction of self-defense on the part of the German masses. "The North American press" lied about the honest efforts of the German government to restrain the natural anti-Semitic reaction of the German people. According to the author and journalist Luis Moure Mariño, protests against German actions showed the control that the Jews exercised over the media, banks, and Marxist organizations. Jewish protests were superfluous, since, despite their "crimes," Jews had prospered under the first years of the Third Reich. Recycling Judeophobic myths, the Nationalist press asserted that Jews controlled 70 percent of Berlin real estate and 550 of the 850 German textile factories.[94]

Anti-Semitism was not merely imposed from above but also found considerable popular resonance. In Nationalist Spain, "Jew" was always an insult. As has been seen, those who refused to donate their wealth to the Nationalist cause were labeled "Jews." The laws of political economy were merely excuses for "Jewish exploitation." A junior officer, on hearing about the battlefield tours organized by the official tourist agency, threatened to kill "like a Jewish dog" anyone who promoted the excursion. "Jewish dog" was frequently employed as a derogatory expression. When a merchant in Oviedo was caught trading illegally, the civil governor fined him 2,000 pesetas and confiscated his 146 hams. The local newspaper accused him and other middlemen of engaging in "Jewish dealing." The Nationalist press employed such pejorative terms as "judiada," associated in Castilian with bad intentions and injustice. The Republic itself was a "Sanhedrin of disgusting murderers." Popular opinion associated Jews with crafty but implacable Shylockian moneylending, obsessive bargain hunting, heartless evictions, and fraud. Journalists, such as González Ruano, stereotypically asserted that for Jews "money is first. Jews are crazy for gold." To be suspected of Jewish origins was extremely hazardous. A Vigo industrialist, Jorge Grimberghs, placed a large advertisement in *El Pueblo Gallego* denying the "calumny" that he was Jewish or a Mason. Instead, he was a "good Catholic" and claimed to have official documents to prove it.[95]

Attempts by Jews to immigrate to other European nations and even to South Africa were opposed on the basis that Jews and their Yiddish language were not European. Bulgaria and Mexico were correct in their policies of rejecting the Jews' attempts to find refuge in their countries. The Nationalists argued that Jews should be persecuted and expelled and that no nation should accept them. In effect, the argument amounted to an appeal for their disappearance and destruction. The lack of sympathy for any sort of Jewish homeland is not surprising since the Spanish Catholic press had opposed Zionism during the Second Republic and continued to propagate anti-Zionist positions during the civil war.[96] The position of British conservatives differed sharply from those of their Spanish counterparts. During World War I and afterward, Arthur Balfour and Winston Churchill championed the formation of a Jewish homeland to provide oppressed Jews in Eastern Europe with an alternative to Communism. The Zionism of British conservatives was designed to separate Jews from Bolshevism.

In contrast, Spanish neotraditionalists blithely identified the two movements of Zionism and Communism. Zionism, or "Jewish nationalism," repulsed "healthy European opinion" because it favored "Masonic and Bolshevik manoeuvres." Although Bolshevist, the Zionist project somehow gained "the approval of the potent international bank" and, of course, the Jewish-controlled foreign press. Moure Mariño insisted that "the solution to the Jewish problem would never occur in Palestine," an opinion of many franquista intellectuals. The Arabs, the rightful owners of all Palestine, were merely victims of the "crimes" and "terrorism" of the Jews. "International Zionism was one of the enemies that Spain was battling." The "International Zionist Organization" had taken the side of the "anti-España." The Nationalist journalist Joaquín Pérez Madrigal, who became one of the most prominent radio broadcasters in the Nationalist zone, held the traditional anti-Semitic view of Jews as "a race that killed the Lord." Like Giménez Caballero and Franco himself, Pérez Madrigal argued that Jews lacked any military virtues. He held the pre-1948 view "that Jews are reds, everyone knows. That Jews are courageous, that Jews are soldiers, no one believes."[97]

The preeminent Catholic newspaper, *El Debate*, had sustained since the 1920s the "authenticity" of the *Protocols of the Elders of Zion*, "amply proven by the awful experiences of many nations." The program of the *Protocols*—"the spiritual, economic, and political conquest of the world by the Jews"—was "adopted by the first Zionist congress in 1897 in Basil." A recent international symposium at Erfurt (Germany) had irrefutably proven the *Protocols* to be genuine. The *Protocols* showed the vicious nature of the Jewish people, "leeches who sold the blood of Jesus." According to Baroja, the *Protocols* confirmed Jewish plans to conquer the world. The real enemy of "Spain" was "the Secret Jewish Committee that governs the Jewish Diaspora throughout the planet, which it is more than ever determined to dominate." Henry Ford's *The International Jew* was translated and widely distributed so that the public could be informed of "its most potent foe."[98]

Franquistas seconded the Nazi line that Jewish machinations explained the reluctance of the democracies to fully support the nationalist cause. The figment of the Judeophobe imagination that "Jews had vast sums invested in Bilbao industries and insurance companies," interests that would be threatened if Mola took the city, motivated British insistence that its war ships, the HMS *Hood* and the *Drake*, accompany merchant vessels into the port of Bilbao in April 1937. Other Nationalist newspapers reiterated the charge of collusion between the Basque Nationalists and the "Jewish-English Bank." The minister of foreign affairs, Anthony Eden, had engineered an agreement with "the London Masonic lodge whose mission was to manage Jewish-Masonic efforts against National Spain."[99]

Christian democrats were automatically deemed "Jewish" since Christian democracy—like Basque nationalism—profoundly challenged the neotraditionalist claim that the Nationalists represented the true and only Catholicism. French Christian democrats were influential in parts of Latin

America, where Insurgents hoped to gain support among the faithful. The liberal French Catholic Jacques Maritain opposed the Carlist concept of a militarized Christ the King and interpreted Jesus as a charitable and generous teacher. Maritain, who was critical of the Nationalist effort, was dismissed as "a Jew [who] is the boss of the infamous campaign against authentically Catholic and traditional Spain" and "a supposedly converted Jew" who represented the "Jewish democrats." Serrano Súñer likened Maritain's knowledge to that of the Elders of Zion. The Catholic philosopher "received homages from lodges and synagogues." Maritain's defender, François Mauriac, was equally "shady." Apparently, Mauriac had turned against the rightists after a Nationalist officer told him, "Medicine is in short supply and costly. . . . We have got to kill them ["the reds"] in the end, so there is no point in curing them." The future Nobel Prize winner in literature wrote to Serrano Súñer, "For millions of Spaniards, Christianity and fascism have become intermingled, and they cannot hate one without hating the other." Another French Catholic, Georges Bernanos, an anti-Semite who had originally supported the Nationalists, became repulsed by their violence, which he had witnessed on Mallorca, and joined the ranks of liberal Catholics. His switch provoked the charge that he was a propagandist for an international Masonry.[100]

Jews were identified with hostile metropoles. Since the Middle Ages, European Jews had been an urban people. By the 1930s they controlled "the press, radio, theater, cinema, and big banks." Leftist iconoclasts who mutilated statues of Christ obeyed the dictates of the Levys in New York, Paris, and London. Big-city Jewish-owned newspapers—"the Jewish media"—subtly and overtly supported the "reds." *El Pueblo Gallego* spoke of a plot by "Jewish newspapers" to slander the Nationalists. "The Jewish and Masonic media" fabricated the "myth" that the Nationalists were responsible for the destruction of Guernica. In Paris during the Popular Front, "the Jews climbed into the highest journalistic positions," an opinion seconded by Maurras. "This Jewish and antifascist journalism is responsible for all the lies printed against Spanish Nationalists." It halted and censored the publication of William Foss and Cecil Gerahty's *Spanish Arena* (with a foreword by the Nationalist diplomat the Duke of Alba), which affirmed the Communist-Masonic-Jewish plot against Spain. A reporter from the Fascist *Corriere della Sera* repeated the accusation that "Jewish antifascism" was pro-Bolshevik and congratulated Foss and Gehraty for revealing links between Jews, Masons, and Communists. The Jewish editor of the Left Book Club, Victor Gollancz, "is making millions off leftist literary works of all stripes."[101]

Fellow journalists described Juan Pujol as a "great reporter" and "the leader of journalists." Serrano Súñer appreciated Pujol and received him at the end of the war. Pujol linked traditional forms of Spanish anti-Semitism based on religion to a new hatred of the Jewish people based not only on

race but also on their urban machinations. According to Pujol, in Catalonia
Jews who had converted during the Inquisition lived in urban centers and had
infected Christian Catalans with the virus of separatism. Like Pujol, large
elements of the Spanish right were suspicious of "the cities of the so-called
great democracies," which produced "strikes, subversion, loss of spiritual
values, meaninglessness, and absence of military virtues." The movement's
first desire was to annihilate "this filthy conglomeration of all the dregs of
European society that crowd around the great Spanish cities." According to
the imagination of one of General Mola's informers, Jews were plotting with
Masons, including Prieto, to detonate deposits of explosives located in the
subway systems of major cities. For some, the Spanish civil war was a struggle
of two civilizations—the urban and the rural. The former was proletarian,
collectivist, materialist, and promiscuous; the latter was peasant, individualist, disciplined, and spiritual. Rural civilization was amenable to dictatorship;
urban to parliamentarianism. Fortunately for Spain, ruralism triumphed in
the civil war. "The victory of our arms against Judaism, Masonry, and Marxism also means the triumph of a profound rural consciousness and the Spanish economy against a decadent and foreign urban domination."[102]

ABC (Seville) deftly elaborated antiurban mythologies by reporting that
a certain Rabbi Leifer and his spouse trafficked large quantities of illegal
drugs in Paris, New York, and Jerusalem by hiding them in his Talmuds.
Stories on Jewish criminals and conmen were widespread. Jews "live outside
of all laws and morality. Just look at the police files of all major cities, and
you will see that a Jew is behind every fraud." As one headline had it, "Not
all Jews are gangsters, but all gangsters are Jews." The story claimed that
a Jewish mafia dominated New York. In Europe, Jews engaged in fraud by
selling in Austrian small towns fake religious relics—medallions, statues, and
church garments—purportedly made in Spain. While the relics in Austria
were inauthentic, Jews had purchased objects that "reds" stole from the great
cathedrals of Spain—for example, in Jaén—exported them, and sold them at
"exorbitant prices." Paris also had its "cinematographic" Jewish mafia, led by
Bernard Nathan, "the king of film" who bilked millions from investors with
the complicity of the French Popular Front. According to Enrique de Angulo,
a prewar reporter in Barcelona for *El Debate*, in "red" Barcelona "Sephardic
rule tyrannized the entire city. . . . Jews conceived and executed the tortures
of the red S.I.M. [the Republican intelligence service] and broke all world records in cruelty." Pío Baroja shared this Judeophobic vision and blamed "this
Jewish ferment" for "extremist utopias."[103]

Loose Jewish women became the urban countermodels for their supposedly austere Catholic counterparts: "Your jewelry and other frills cannot copy
the foul fashions of Jewish and treasonous France." "Jews centralized in Paris
dictate" the latest styles and "colonize" European women. They imposed an

"immoral," "anarchic and grotesque" mode on Spanish females. The women of Spain's most cosmopolitan cities must stop following "tastes decreed by the disgusting but gilded Parisian Jews" and adopt styles in line with a "holy nationalism." "Our women . . . forget that New Spain's totalitarian nationalism demands that they liberate themselves from all foreign and especially Jewish hegemony." Jews could easily manipulate "the inexperienced minds" of women and children through their popular but "poisonous" cinema. Although the Juventud Femenina de Acción Católica did not mention Jews directly, it fretted about foreign influences and explained the war as God's vengeance against immorality.[104]

The civil governor of León believed the civil war was an attempt to save Spain from "Jewish-Masonic barbarism." Men did this by fighting, women by renouncing the latest fashions. They must dress modestly, wear stockings (which were often hard to find in the Nationalist zone), not apply makeup, obey unflinchingly, and stop smoking (a habit of "red" militiawomen). Smoking should become a purely masculine habit. Females who overused red cosmetics and frequented movie theaters were suspiciously subversive. Burgos officials insulted females without stockings, and the Civil Guard threatened to punish women who entered churches without them. A frontline soldier wrote "we reject modernity and frivolity in the New Spain. We demand the end of all foreign and Masonic fashions." Recalling themes of various prewar Catholic "crusades" and contemporary Islamism, women were constantly told to be modest and moral. A soldier stationed in Logroño reported "women attend church suitably attired, dressed in black with a black veil covering their head." Anti-Christian liberals and Jewesses created feminism. Highly paid Jewish feminists dominated the despised League of Nations.[105]

Yet it must be pointed out that—unlike their National Socialist allies during their war—Nationalists did not execute significant numbers of Jews as Jews or Gypsies as Gypsies. The latter were found all over Spain, while the former were concentrated in Spanish Morocco. Nationalist officials did not systematically persecute the two "nomadic" nations. In North Africa they attempted to keep the relations between the three monotheistic religions peaceful. In Ceuta, where 300 to 350 well-integrated Jews lived, 22 Jews were executed, not as Jews but rather as leftists or Masons. However, in contrast to Muslim Masons, whose religion spared them from capital punishment, Jewish Masons were put to death. Movements of Jews in the Protectorate were severely restricted, and they could not freely move between cities. In Melilla, where 3,400 Jews were residents, only a few were executed, again because of their politics, not their religion. They seem to have had excellent prewar relations with the Spanish troops quartered in their city. However, young Jews drafted into the Nationalist army were subject to humiliation and beatings. Furthermore, the Jewish community was forced to make very significant "voluntary" contributions to the Nationalists and to the Falange, which extorted at least 500,000 pesetas from them. Occasionally, Falangists informally expropriated their property. Queipo practiced the same coercive policies on the small Jewish community in Seville, which handed over 138,000 pesetas to the general. Other Jews dispersed throughout the peninsula, including 3,000 who had arrived after the Nazis came to power, were usually not subject to physical violence. Nevertheless, they were placed under police surveillance, their synagogues closed, their religion banned.[106]

PROTESTANTS

Spanish neotraditionalists came to resent Protestants almost as much as Jews. The simultaneous rejections of Protestantism and Judaism, which had pioneered the path to advanced capitalism and socialisms, reflected not only traditional Spanish Catholic intolerance but also an insular fear of modernity. The presence of Protestantism—like Masonry, Socialism, and Communism—was part of the hated heritage of the modern. In the 1920s, Spanish bishops had disapproved of the influx of Protestant (and Rotary Club) "propaganda" and urged the government to ban it. Wenceslao González Oliveros, who held a chair of legal philosophy at the University of Salamanca, synthesized the abhorrence that neotraditionalist Catholics felt toward the two faiths. The erudite professor agreed with both Max Weber, who argued that Protestantism founded contemporary capitalism, and Werner Sombart, who attributed its origins to "sordid Judaism." The latter required usury, which led to plutocracy, but the intrinsically capitalist Reformation fostered Puritanism, or what this franquista intellectual labeled "English Hebrewism." Both Jews and Protestants subordinated everything to moneymaking, and both were "eternal enemies of our fatherland." González Oliveros, who was appointed the civil governor of Barcelona immediately after the war, attributed what he saw as the logical consequence of capitalism—Communism—to the influence of both religions.[107]

More tentatively and with less polemical power, Protestantism—like Judaism—was linked to Communism. According to Serrano Súñer and many others, Spain "served the Christ's Church by fighting against Protestant heresy," anticipating the Nationalist struggle against Communism. Spain nobly fought "the dangerous political heterodoxy of the Reformation" and "the vile egotism of Protestant England," as it combated during the civil war "the great modern heresy, . . . dehumanized and atheist Marxism." The Nationalist counterrevolution saw itself as embodying the defense of Western civilization, but it was much more anti-Protestant than anti-Islam. Its press championed heroes of the Counter Reformation—Philip II and Charles II. It also praised the Council of Trent for defeating "anti-Catholic and destructive

Protestantism." Women (and men) were reminded that Saint Teresa supposedly fought against the Lutheran threat.[108]

Cardinal Gomá, the primate of Spain, linked Protestantism to the Enlightenment and the French Revolution. Others agreed that the Enlightenment's *Encyclopédie* injected "the venom of impiety" throughout Europe and fomented the French Revolution. According to a well-connected British volunteer in the Legion, his fellow officers assumed that all Protestants were Masons. Unlike Catholics, Protestants did not have a "creed" and did not know "the Truth." Instead, each individual had to find her truth in the Bible. The variety of Protestant denominations in the United States, "the classic land of Protestants," resulted in "an anthill. . . . It's a madhouse."[109]

In the early modern period, reactionary Catholics had associated Protestants with the historical decline of Spain and the creation of the Black Legend; in the late modern era, neotraditionalists identified Protestants with economic superiority and industrial clout. Like the current Islamist antagonism toward the contemporary West, the seeming superiority of a rival religion created violent resentment and absurd conspiracy theories. However, as in the Islamic world, the power of Protestant nations—Great Britain, the United States, and the German ally—restricted the expression of Nationalist hostility. However "barbaric," the United States was nonetheless a force that could not be facilely dismissed.[110] Unlike the Jews, whom Western democracies would defend only timidly and sporadically, the United States, Great Britain, and perhaps even Germany could be counted on to protest public persecution of Protestants.

Nevertheless, Protestants were attacked and censored in Nationalist Spain. Authorities persecuted—and sometimes physically eliminated—Protestant clergy and closed or destroyed their churches. Perhaps twenty pastors were shot, but given their unwillingness to alienate gratuitously the great powers, Nationalists constantly denied their repression of Protestant clergy. The Nationalist harassment of a half dozen Protestant communities in the Sierra de Gredos (Ávila) showed the neotraditionalist dedication to the perpetuation of the Inquisition. In Piedralaves and El Barraco (Ávila), Protestants were executed as casually as leftists. Local authorities refused the dead proper burial and converted their churches into a prison.

These killings inspired Professor Miguel de Unamuno to alter his analysis of the uprising. The world-renowned intellectual had initially supported the Insurgency as a defense of Christianity and public order. However, he soon learned that his friend Atilano Coco, a Protestant pastor and Mason, had been arrested and was in danger of execution. Unamuno unsuccessfully tried to help Coco and became disillusioned with the Nationalists. Their war on critical thinking, militaristic sloganeering ("Long Live Death!"), and resentment against Catalans and Basques led to his famous public outburst at the

University of Salamanca on 12 October 1936 during a ceremony marking the Day of the Race (Columbus Day). In front of cocked weapons and fascist war cries ("Death to Intellectuals"), he made the most courageous defense of academic freedom in the twentieth century by telling the Insurgents that their words and actions profaned the temple of the intellect. His liberal defiance and "Erasmusian" sympathies led to his house arrest and complete ostracism from neotraditionalist circles. Several months later, immediately before his death, he classified the new state as "an imperialist-pagan African-type militarization" that had instituted a "stupid regime of terror."[111]

The distributors of Protestant Bibles in Zamora were not merely "mercantilist" but also agents of "discord" in the service of enemy "democratic" powers. "We cannot tolerate any diffusion of heresy." Spanish Protestants in the Nationalist zone were pressured to convert to Catholicism. Children of Protestant families were watched to see if they attended Catholic church. Authorities and townspeople ostracized Vigo's small Protestant colony. In February 1937 Franco declared to British visitors that religious tolerance and "complete freedom of worship for Protestants" were guaranteed in the Nationalist zone, but this was simply false. A "Protestant and Marxist" merchant was fined 3,000 pesetas for hoarding and overcharging. Under a pseudonym, the Caudillo himself resumed the anti-Protestant and anti-Jewish offensive after the birth of the state of Israel.[112]

Since the Nationalists were reluctant to alienate public opinion in the United States and Great Britain, they often employed "Masonry" and "Mason" as code words for Protestantism and Protestants (and those who tolerated Jews). In private correspondence to the Ministry of the Interior, the civil governor of Las Palmas stated that the British colony, the biggest numerically on the island, represented the "Masonic interest." Both Franco and Queipo de Llano believed that England and France were "our eternal enemies and agents of our decadence." The poet Pemán proposed that even British Tories were "Jew-Masons" and that British and American multinationals—Royal Dutch Shell and Standard Oil—resulted from the merger of the synagogue and the lodge. Pemán's poetry repeated the malicious cocktail invented by the Russian Whites during their civil war—a mixture of Jews and Protestants ("the American octopus" and "the English leopard") equaled Bolshevism. The popular editor and confidant of the Franco family, Father Juan Tusquets, agreed entirely.[113]

The neotraditionalist program of religious revival and hostility, if not hatred, toward Protestants, Jews, Masons, and Marxists bolstered believers' faith but could not overcome the wide variety of resistances to the authoritarian state.

4

Defiance of the State

Probably the majority of residents of the Nationalist zone defied some aspect of its authoritarian moral and political economy. The most respectable citizens engaged in illegal economic practices, the least reputable in their traditional calling of crime. All shared a distrust of the state and a commitment to their own personal interests and survival. Very few conformed as either buyers or sellers to the price controls established by the regime. The desire of individuals to defy the state qualifies analyses by historians and social scientists who often stress that the twentieth century is the age of the politicized and nationalized "masses." Instead, the latter fought for their personal interests and challenged the politics and policies of both revolutionaries and counterrevolutionaries.

PRICE CONTROLS

Government-imposed price controls, enforced by the authority of civil governors in each province, had a long history in twentieth-century Spain. The ineffectiveness of price controls to help growers during the Republic explains why wheat farmers welcomed the price support that the SNT implemented during the civil war. The flexible tasas of the Nationalists allowed farmers larger profits by assuring them that the state would purchase their wheat crop at a reasonable price and gratified peasants, especially in Castile. As we have seen, Nationalist organizations—most importantly, the military quartermaster—frequently ignored their own price controls to purchase food at prices the campesinos demanded and with money peasants welcomed. In contrast, the price controls of the Republic promised affordable food to the urban masses that had defended it when the military rebelled and remained its firmest basis of support. Peasants in the Republican zone were less cooperative with their state. They rejected its currency and failed to deliver sufficient supplies to nourish the army and the civilian population. Nationalists reported that the Republican zone could harvest only 5,395,000 quintals of wheat, when it needed 16,200,000 to feed its people.[1]

A number of historians have argued that the regulatory measures taken by military authorities were responsible for the efficient functioning of agriculture and industry in their zone. Certainly, authorities—including civil governors and provincial officials—enforced the tasas and the *guías* (travel permits) by fining thousands of violators and even jailing some of them. They followed the authoritarian tradition of the "iron surgeon" who would make Spain into a functioning autarky.[2] However, the centrifugal tendencies and forms of egotism were much stronger than the historiography—almost always dominated by political history from above—indicates. Although military leaders commanded, many disobeyed. Tensions between local and national authorities were considerable. Perhaps the Nationalists won the war not because of their centralized military command but rather despite it. Looking on the wartime economy in the Nationalist zone from the perspective of the victory of 1939 exaggerates its efficiency and coherence. It operated more like what the French call "le système D" or what the British characterize as "muddling through."

As in many other domains, Queipo was a pioneer of Nationalist price controls and may have planned for a long war at the very beginning of his Seville reign, whereas it is often said that Franco did so only after his failure to capture Madrid in November 1936. Queipo created the Junta de Abastos de Sevilla, which controlled the olive oil price and its transport and which provided a model for the rest of the Nationalist zone. In early August 1936 the civil governor of Huelva threatened to shoot repeated violators of price controls. Municipal and provincial authorities in Andalusia demanded a full accounting of stored foodstuffs and continually urged consumers to report any infringements. Constant warnings concerning the penalties for disobedience and the fining of thousands indicated that price controls in Andalusia were frequently ineffective. Sellers continued to ignore local and national authorities. So did official buyers, such as the quartermaster, who intelligently reserved the right to purchase supplies at any price. In fact, in Galicia traders would roam the countryside to purchase female calves, which they would resell to the army at a profit greater than 50 percent. Abundant stocks of wheat in Zamora led millers to ignore the tasa and underpay sellers.[3]

Both producers and traders found many ways to avoid controls. Merchants would trade and retrade goods—particularly textiles and clothes whose life span was extended by extensive use of dyes—among themselves in order to generate bills that would justify price increases, a practice civil governors tried to eliminate. Factories and workshops hoarded their products in hopes of higher prices. Thousands were fined for profiteering, speculation, and hoarding and their names were listed in newspapers. The last penalty affected violators in urban rather than rural areas, where newspapers were seldom read. Those desiring official documents, for example, a travel pass, were frequently required to confirm not only that they had not been members of Marxist organizations but also that they were not hiding essential commodities.[4]

In response to mounting disobedience, the Nationalists—like their Republican enemies—staffed an array of bureaucracies to control the prices and transport of food and supplies. Juntas de Precios were established in November 1937 for each "liberated" province and were composed of the civil governor and one representative each from the military governor, Hacienda, Junta Provincial de Abastos, Cámara de Comercio, Junta de Regulación de Importación, and the Falange. Civil governors of each province were authorized through the Juntas Provinciales de Precios to fight speculation and hoarding. The food and especially the clothing crises of early 1938 encouraged the creation in February of the Servicio Nacional de Abastecimiento y Transportes (SNAT). SNAT had the authority to fine those who violated price controls or who ignored transportation permits up to 100,000 pesetas, and it could also confiscate needed commodities. A military mentality and personnel dominated its staff. A ten-member board, only one member of which was appointed by the Falange, directed its operations. In the case of the olive tasa, SNAT was seconded at the local level by the Juntas de Abastos, whose head was the local mayor, assisted by representatives from industry and the official union.[5]

In early February 1938 the minister of the interior, Serrano Súñer, reported "chronic complaints about unjustified price hikes throughout Nationalist territory" and ordered all civil governors to strictly enforce price controls and severely sanction those who violated them. Serrano proposed letting military courts handle cases against recidivists. The minister reacted to a situation where merchants and shopkeepers willfully ignored and rejected tasas. Responding to his superior's order, the civil governor of Seville called on mayors to report those in violation of pricing laws. ABC (Seville) lauded the severity and the rapidity of the governor's warning, since Seville, it claimed, "is today the most expensive city of liberated Spain," a situation that it blamed on greedy "merchants and industrialists." As during the Paris Commune of 1871, cats disappeared from the streets of the city. In March, meat shortages, especially beef, continued to plague the Andalusian capital. In response, fish and eggs rose rapidly in price. For many workers, the "fascist" regime in Seville meant hard work and long hours at low pay with no union representation. Wage earners experienced hunger and rationing of bread, sugar, oil, rice, tobacco, and coal. Two men were fined 50,000 pesetas each, an enormous sum, and another 2,000 pesetas for selling chickpeas to the army quartermaster at rates above the tasa. Government ministers ordered police to confiscate stocks from merchants who were allegedly hoarding.[6]

Producers and middlemen resisted the limitations on their profit margins, which the state imposed to protect urban consumers. The Junta de Abastos of Andalusia and Badajoz claimed to have levied over 3 million pesetas in fines, including one fine of 1 million, another of 400,000, and several of 100,000. This Junta was composed of representatives of various interests, including merchant associations. It continued to impose sanctions of hundreds and even thousands of pesetas and to criminally prosecute dozens of merchants who violated price controls, usually on food and clothing. The latter was particularly difficult to regulate since types and quality varied so widely. Sometimes, faced with a tasa that was too low, the Junta raised the official price. In Huelva hundreds of retailers were sanctioned, and fines amounted to 160,000 pesetas in three months. Álava limited profits of wholesalers to 5 percent and of retailers to 10 percent. In Segovia "a large number of unscrupulous shopkeepers" continued their profiteering, despite fines totaling 75,795 pesetas. León authorities sanctioned "a minority" that refused to follow price guidelines. León butchers and bakers specialized in exaggerating the weight of their bread and meat, causing the local Falangist paper to charge that "their safe . . . is their fatherland."[7]

In the Canaries the Junta Provincial de Abastos recognized that most *detallistas* had been "obedient and patriotic" but that "a certain percentage" was "greedy" and had to be severely fined and publicly exposed. The governor undertook what he called a successful campaign against the many smugglers and drug traffickers who operated with the complicity of port employees. By 1938 the Canaries were dependent on irregular shipments that provided one-half kilo of corn per person, which was to be distributed by mayors to the heads of families. Price of corn or wheat meal had more than doubled since July 1936. The provincial government claimed to have made a successful effort to reduce the price during 1938. The cost of living had nonetheless increased 151 percent after the outbreak of the conflict. In Fuerteventura and Lanzarote especially, the authorities admitted that the population suffered from terrible housing, hunger, and even thirst. These islands may have been extreme cases, but they reflected the shortage of shelter and food—especially flour since there were virtually no milling facilities—that afflicted the entire archipelago during the war. In 1939, mayors rationed and distributed 250 grams of potatoes per resident.[8]

In newly liberated Asturias the Junta provincial de Abastos noted "an alarming rise" of prices. However, by mid-1938 the situation seems to have improved. Essential foods were available, and their costs had risen approximately 33 percent. Nevertheless, some unpatriotic opportunists speculated and monopolized certain commodities—such as eggs and potatoes—for their own profit. Among dozens of violators, the governor expelled one of the members of Gijón Junta provincial de Abastos and fined him 700 pesetas for disregarding the regulations on food sales. The situation was similar in Orense, where food supplies were "fully satisfactory." Nevertheless, the province saw many food items jump from 20 to 50 percent in price after 18 July 1936. Clothing and shoe prices doubled or tripled. Most food merchants followed regulations on prices, but shoe and clothing businesses had to be fined between 200 and 10,000 pesetas to enforce obedience. By the end of the war León authorities tried unsuccessfully to enforce a ceiling of a 25 percent increase on cotton fabric, but inflation-fueled black marketing continued. Merchants would interpret any ambiguity in the regulations in their own interest. For example, they took *tejidos* to mean only cotton goods and raised prices on all other fabrics. They also wanted to meet their fiscal obligations to the state by asking the authorities to accept as payment the unpaid bills of their clients.[9]

Inaccurate and dishonest declarations of wheat stocks sustained a long tradition among millers and farmers. Underreporting had led to the disastrous import of foreign wheat into Spain in 1932, thereby alienating from the Second Republic the wheat growers who saw the price and their potential profits fall dramatically. Self-interested reporting continued during the war. The SNT in Navarre distrusted the statistics that millers provided. The SNT of Seville fined one female miller in Utrera 15,000 pesetas for hiding hundreds of quintals of wheat. In Málaga, millers claimed that the scarcity of wheat and storage bags led them to ignore the tasa, but authorities believed they merely wanted to make larger profits. Small mills feared the unfair competition of larger ones, since the latter had greater storage capacity and could sell directly to the public. The Civil Guard of Aspariegos (Zamora) arrested the local chief of the Falange for purchasing wheat below the tasa. Producers, who were reluctant to sell their wheat to the SNT, were obligated to do so in March 1938.[10]

DENUNCIATIONS

As in the Republican zone, all merchants, tradesmen, and hotel owners under Nationalist control were ordered to clearly post their prices. Ministers, big-city mayors, and the Falange called for cooperation from the public to report shopkeepers and peasants who violated the rules. Informers in cities could denounce violators directly to the civil governors, who in the spring of 1938 established special departments to receive reports concerning breaches of price controls. The Pontevedra civil governor ordered the establishment of offices—reminiscent of the Inquisition—whose task was to encourage and receive written or oral denunciations of violators of price controls in every town and village of the province. The mayor of Villagarcia encouraged delation by ordering the reweighing of meat purchases. An even more effective method was found by certain cities that offered municipal employees who uncovered tax fraud a percentage of the fines levied on the recovered amounts. The Las Palmas governor rewarded informers 50 percent of the stash of hoarded coins that they exposed. Serrano Súñer warned that those who did not denounce could be fined or even imprisoned. Provincial authorities also threatened to punish the silent. For example, overcharging hotel owners were menaced with 1,000- to 5,000-peseta fines, and guests who did not denounce them with 25- to 250-peseta penalties.[11]

Under duress or voluntarily, many responded by reporting violations to the civil governor or the local mayor. In Vigo, denunciations investigated by the municipal police force progressed from 1,940 in 1935, 1,587 in 1936, 3,093 in 1937, and peaked at 3,237 in 1938. Many of these were probably motivated by citizen complaints concerning price controls. Nevertheless, perhaps even more important than the denunciations themselves was the frequent failure to denounce. The reluctance of the public to snitch often disappointed authorities. As has been seen, neighbors did not denounce the ineligible who enrolled under false pretenses for the combatant subsidy. Despite dramatic cases of fines and imprisonment, which the press publicized with the goal of shaming the offender and discouraging future violations, consumers—including military officers and soldiers—often refused to name those who sold for more than the tasa.[12]

Denouncing has been studied, but less so the failure to denounce. Both shared a common egotistical motivation. According to authorities, consumers mistakenly gave priority to their own needs: "Outrageous prices would not exist without the complicity of purchasers who unpatriotically buy according to their own personal interest." The lack of cooperation from consumers rendered officials powerless. Buyers—including those of the state—found it easier to purchase at the market price and, if necessary, to pay in installments than to insist on the official price. Burgos complained that "the consumer is not willing to cooperate to uncover and expose these outrages," an attitude that amounted to "passive suicide." Officials labeled their refusals "civic deficiencies." Likewise, authorities in the Asturian town of San Martín del Rey Aurelio were disappointed that despite public encouragement, only two citizens had come forward to testify about the activities of town employees during the "red" period. They attributed the lack of testimonies to "cowardice," but silence merely reflected prudence and perhaps a judicious municipal solidarity. In certain villages solidarity often overcame political rivalries, and the pueblo would protect its own regardless of ideology. Civil wars foster virtuous cycles of cohesion as well as vicious delation.[13]

Serrano Súñer admitted that consumers were reluctant to help authorities and turned a deaf ear to his call to inform on contravening merchants and hotel owners. Queipo complained that shoppers who did not collaborate with authorities in reporting merchants who sold at high prices were not patriots. His disappointment was similar to that of Manuel Azaña, who recounted that in Valencia and Catalonia the promulgation of price controls resulted in the complete disappearance of food from the marketplace. The president of the Republic was disenchanted that the populace refused to denounce speculators and hoarders. Instead, "it was every person for himself." In Orense, consumers often remained silent about "outrages," despite authorities' inducements. The same was true in Álava and León, where delation was rare and the public uncooperative. Huelva officials, who received only four denunciations from consumers, were surprised and baffled by the refusals. Granada officials complained that delation was scarce, despite an intense press campaign encouraging it. In Ceuta, which imported much of its food and suffered a 68 percent rise in the cost of living, very few denounced profiteers.[14]

Although small towns and villages are said to be breeding grounds for the dense social interaction that generates malicious denunciation, the same social networks and individual interests also spawn a reluctance to inform. In rural ayuntamientos hardly anyone reported violations of price controls, and mayors ignored repeated orders to crack down on offenders. Their comparative self-sufficiency made villagers less subject to the whims of the market and less likely to denounce price hikes. Likewise, support for antiregime elements—for example, *guerrilleros* in mountainous or isolated areas—was often prompted not by leftist ideologies but rather through personal ties or threats by fighters to take revenge on those who refused to assist them.[15]

Even urban residents showed little desire to cooperate with the state and instead engaged in bidding wars with their neighbors for food and clothing. Consumers realized that denouncing a vendor who had unduly raised prices would not make their acquisition of the desired commodity easier or cheaper. Indeed, it would alienate the only persons who might furnish the needed item. Locals felt that a cooperative attitude toward traders and merchants would produce better results than confrontation. Most shoppers in both cities and villages had a personal, if complex, relationship with sellers. The latter were both "exploiters" and neighbors who might provide them with credit in times of need. Furthermore, vendors had ways to justify their price hikes by, for example, fabricating phony invoices. Until a cooperative and discreet buyer appeared, they could hide the merchandise that was unprofitable to sell at the controlled price. They could also offer highly inferior commodities at the official rate.[16]

The failure to denounce expressed distrust of the state. While peasants, merchants, and shopkeepers frequently overcharged or refused to sell at regulated prices, workers—as we have seen—often received wages exceeding the regulated norm. Those who purchased items at prices above the tasa could also be punished. In this context of nearly universal illegality, few wanted to initiate what could quickly degenerate into a Hobbesian war of all against all. Both producers and consumers disregarded excessive state regulations—which, for example, on wheat alone surpassed five singled-spaced and dense pages. The rules on the production, declaration, and sales of olive oil and wine were equally complex, and authorities complained periodically and plausibly that they were not being followed. In particular, exporters and salesmen regularly violated the tasa and ignored other regulations. They often dealt on the black market.[17]

The privatization of politics abounded during the Spanish and other civil wars when individuals attempted to use civil conflict for their own particular purposes, which had little to do with the "master cleavages" of left versus right. Civil war pits citizens against each other not only as political rivals but also as individuals motivated by private enmity. In authoritarian settings the politicization of life often personalizes politics. In the Spanish case authorities—like Nazi (and Stalinist) officials—encouraged individuals with their own individual grievances to denounce "reds." Politics served merely as an excuse for rivals to impound competing shops and stores. Business owners with intimate ties to the Falange accused competitors of being leftists or Masons, and authorities might respond by shutting down the rival firm, imprisoning, or even executing the owner. False denunciations against a creditor who was a "Socialist" might relieve the informer of his debt and the "leftist" of his life. Profits, not politics, motivated many of the most serious denunciations. In Cádiz two individuals were jailed for false accusations that they used to seek personal revenge. Informers whose claims were proven bogus were sanctioned substantial amounts, including several 1,000-peseta fines. In one village, Luelmo (Zamora), the municipal judge, the priest, and a teacher were penalized 50 pesetas for issuing incorrect documents. Informants used the divisions between the traditional right and the Falange to denounce their rivals and advance their own interests.[18]

Despite a guarantee of anonymity, Huesca consumers denounced only violating merchants against whom they had a personal grudge. Anonymous denunciations were more common than signed ones. The former were usually made for purposes of "personal revenge," which often involved debts. Authorities and their controlled press condemned unsigned accusations as "cowardly" acts of "sly little tyrants." Burgos "frequently" received anonymous letters concerning unmerited labor exemptions but ignored them unless addressed and signed. Officials became suspicious of unsigned letters that, in their view, revealed the "gutless" nature of the informer. Authorities sometimes handled fines on the wealthy with discretion, keeping them private and therefore protecting the upper classes from public humiliation. Wealthy individuals with good connections to high-ranking officials had opportunities to have their sanctions inconspicuously reduced.[19]

COINS

Like the violation of price controls, the hoarding of precious metals defied the regime. A common occurrence in many civil wars, the amassing of metallic currencies had a long tradition among Spaniards skeptical of the political economies of both left- and right-wing governments. As in the Republican zone, many persons under Nationalist control removed silver coins from circulation to stockpile them. Quickly, change became scarce. For example, in Palencia coins of 0.25, 0.10, and 0.05 pesetas became so rare that normal commerce was hindered. The same was true throughout the entire province of Ávila. The Junta de Defensa Nacional took countermeasures: it forbade the withdrawal of large amounts of cash, prohibited the export of silver, limited the coins that individuals could possess to the amount legitimately needed to make change, and on 29 November menaced those who hoarded with severe punishments. Unlike Republicans, Nationalists threatened to shoot anyone who refused to accept their paper money. A prohibition on the exportation or hoarding of silver accompanied the program of the Falange.[20]

Local authorities issued decrees pursuing the same goal. The military commander of Lugo recognized that his diktats on hoarding had been ineffective. He initiated house-to-house searches and threatened to court-martial any violators. Peasants in this province had the habit of hiding their mound of money in their home. Thus, hoarding continued, and fines were imposed mostly on urban residents—a merchant with 400 pesetas in coins was fined 2,000 pesetas, two others 5,000, and another individual 750. In Lugo and Pontevedra, small bank notes replaced the silver, copper, and bronze coins that disappeared. Yet shop owners distrusted circulating paper money, whether stamped or unstamped. Despite constant threats from authorities who were imprisoning hoarders, cities in Galicia continued to suffer from a shortage of coins. Strict rules were issued concerning the use of change and bills, but they were frequently disregarded. Reacting to "conflicts" concerning coins in markets and fairs, the military governor of Orense ordered all merchants to deposit each Tuesday and Friday half of their change in the local branch of the Bank of Spain. Regulations requiring deposit of change into bank accounts became more demanding the following month when authorities began to circulate bills of 5 and 10 pesetas, many of which were printed in Germany. The integration of newly "liberated" areas aggravated the problem. In March 1937, authorities attempted to ease the shortage by minting copper and aluminum 1- and 2-peseta coins worth 100 million. A year later they produced 20 million copper and nickel coins of 25 céntimos.[21]

Hoarding continued throughout Andalusia. In his nationally broadcasted radio address, Queipo related that 39,000 pesetas worth of silver coins were found in the residence of a wealthy Utrera resident, who was consequently jailed and fined twice that amount. The general announced other sanctions of thousands of pesetas. The Seville governor felt obligated to limit the amount of change that individuals could hold to 100 pesetas, and informers were awarded 50 percent of the stash that they revealed. A Córdoba businessman received a 10,000-peseta fine for hoarding coins, and eight others were dispatched to a military court. Dozens in Córdoba, Cádiz, and Málaga provinces were jailed, fined, and had their piles worth hundreds or thousands of pesetas confiscated. In Algeciras an ice-cream vendor was found with 5,050 pesetas of silver coins in his home and was imprisoned. In parts of Andalusia, silver coins practically disappeared, forcing the government to circulate bills in denominations of 5 and 10 pesetas. The civil governor of Huelva embarked on a campaign against hoarding throughout 1937. It was apparently ineffective since fines of thousands and imprisonment continued to be levied against a dozen or so offenders. In Seville province, five villages minted their own coins.[22]

Hoarding persisted throughout the Nationalist zone. In Béjar (Salamanca) and Zamora, hoarders—including several women—were fined thousands of pesetas. In Las Palmas, change was insufficient to conduct everyday commercial transactions, compelling the governor to order unannounced inspections in homes and businesses throughout the province. Customers often used the excuse of lacking change to avoid paying for public transportation and other services. In response, the governor ordered riders to carry the necessary coins. However, transport collectors—interested in building up their own personal stock of metals—took advantage of the governor's order and demanded exact change. In newly liberated Asturias the shortage became "one of the major economic problems," and merchants sometimes used the lack of coins as a pretext not to sell the article at the legal price. The end of the war settled the issue when the government withdrew all silver coins from circulation in order to remint them with "the symbols of the new state."[23]

The previous understanding that coins never disappeared from circulation in the Nationalist zone has exaggerated franquista numismatic competence and the willingness of individuals to cooperate with the regime. Nevertheless, despite massive egotistical behavior, the Nationalist zone did not suffer shortages as severe as its Republican counterpart. Soldiers usually possessed enough small change to purchase goods from commercial establishments and street vendors, who surrounded arriving trains, offering them a variety of drinks, sandwiches, and sweets.[24]

MAYORS

Like their Republican enemies and failed twentieth-century counterrevolutionaries, Nationalists had to confront powerful centrifugal forces. Mixing metaphors, the civil governor of Pontevedra wishfully termed ayuntamientos and their mayors "the power base of the new State" and "its first gear," but in the hamlets and villages of Spain, local priorities usually dominated national ones.[25]

Mayors exercised considerable power and took charge of many of the most essential duties. They were required to report violations of price controls and had the capacity to fine violators up to 500 pesetas but could request approval from provincial officials to increase sanctions to 10,000 pesetas. *Alcaldes*, including those of provincial capitals, guaranteed the veracity of olive, corn, barley, and wool production with the goal of avoiding hoarding and profiteering. For example, in Zamora they were expected to report wool holdings and blanket production to the quartermaster. Mayors distributed seed to labradores and pledged to insure that the complicated regulations on wheat—depositing the crop in payment for state loans—were obeyed. Their town halls were responsible for providing an accurate census of livestock. Alcaldes initiated bureaucratic steps to cultivate lands abandoned by either the owner or his workers. They settled disputes between landlords and yunteros. In contrast to the Popular Front period, they were also in charge of making sure that machines and laborers were employed during harvest time. They were responsible for enforcement of wage controls and labor laws, including the mandatory three-hour siesta for harvesters. Mayors determined that fiestas should be celebrated. Many looked the other way when their residents did not attend church and worked on Sunday or during holidays. Alcaldes grabbed the unauthorized power to censor or ban movies.[26]

They needed to collect certain taxes and verify that local taxpayers were up-to-date. Unauthorized charities and fund-raisers had to be reported to higher authorities who could take appropriate sanctions. So did shops, bars, and restaurants that violated after-hours rules. Mayors ensured the initial mobilization of conscripts and confirmed that family members of combatants were eligible for a subsidy or a pension. The latter duty ensured them great influence over soldiers, veterans, and their families. They were supposed to verify periodically the physical condition and the nationality of those excused from military service. They had to eliminate "clandestine" and unauthorized workers and physically able male members of soldiers' families who received a subsidy without working. They made certain that the Policía Rural was correctly managed. In larger towns they could urge the municipalization of utility companies or entire branches—such as butchering—if they failed to provide the necessary services to businesses and consumers.[27]

As had occurred frequently under the Republic, mayors, who were often substantial landowners, were particularly reluctant to follow orders from administrative superiors. As did their cacique predecessors, alcaldes defended local, rural, and especially their personal interests against the national state. They supplied only information that accommodated their needs. They made sure that others paid the bulk of taxes. Members of the traditional (*caciquil*) right who wished to become mayors joined the Falange, thereby diluting its revolutionary fervor in the municipalities. Powerful local families, who had been associated with Primo's Unión Patriótica or later with CEDA, often continued to rule in the countryside. In November 1937, Burgos felt compelled to repeat that all municipal and provincial representatives be committed to the movement and once again excluded from office those who had supported a party belonging to the Popular Front. In Cáceres province 20 percent of municipal employees were sanctioned for behavior "against the National Movement." In Oviedo the smaller the municipality, the less pronounced was Falangist influence. Small-town mayors in that province defended their own interests against those of the state or region. Their power sometimes aroused the protests of labradores who claimed to take the reformist rhetoric of the new regime seriously. The multifaceted duties and powers of mayors led to situations where their disaffected constituents denounced them—in some cases falsely—to higher authorities. Mayors who had made inaccurate statements were fined hundreds of pesetas. In one case, a sanction of 1,000 pesetas was imposed on the mayor of Villaralbo (Zamora) for a false denunciation.[28]

The Ministry of Interior complained that certain villages, towns, and provincial delegations did not collect the monthly contributions required by the Suscripción Nacional established in August 1936. Disobedience led to light fines of several mayors. In Rioja, municipalities refused to meet their provincial financial obligations and became corporate debtors. In Asturias the civil governor noted "marked weakness of revenue," which he blamed on a lack of zeal from mayors who were late collecting local taxes. In Galicia, mayors who were accused of being caciques were unconcerned about repayment of their towns' debts. Their influence allowed them to avoid payments by their own municipalities, which by 1939 owed the provincial government over 700,000 pesetas. Alcaldes were sometimes reluctant to verify that local taxpayers were up-to-date but would invent unauthorized levies. The mayor of Corrales (Zamora) disregarded SNT regulations that, to encourage freer trade, prohibited local taxes on wheat, and he imposed an illegal municipal toll on wheat transactions. The civil governor fired a mayor who retained the wages of road workers. On balance, according to provincial officials, the performance of the mayors in Huesca province was "always unfavorable" because they were usually ignorant, incompetent, and overly attentive to local needs.[29]

Mayors did not inform higher authorities of their villages' stocks of various commodities. For example, in Zamora the tardiness of their reporting led to a significant underestimation of the wheat harvest, which in 1936 and 1937 almost matched the crop harvested in 1935. Authorities noted the reluctance to provide information on livestock. In Zamora dozens of municipalities were fined for disobeying health and accounting regulations concerning the slaughter of animals. In the same province, municipalities and their veterinary inspection teams from five villages were sanctioned 500 pesetas each for failing to furnish livestock statistics. Veterinarians were warned of severe punishment if they falsified information. Several dozen villagers were fined 500 pesetas for failure to supply accurate reports. Authorities had to threaten "severe sanctions" to get reluctant mayors to report their supplies of carob beans used principally for animal food. A general suspicion reigned among livestock owners that supplying accurate information would lead to increased taxation and perhaps confiscation. Mayors did not always cooperate with public health officials to inform them about diseased animals or fulfill their legal obligations to report "rural plagues." In Zamora 73 of 300 ayuntamientos, or nearly 25 percent, neglected to convey labor needs to provincial authorities, failures that "merited punishment."

As in the past, mayors had considerable opportunity for graft. The substantial investment by provincial authorities in soup kitchens provided ample prospects for corruption, and several mayors in La Coruña were fined for failing to provide poor children with adequate meals. The government demanded that alcaldes award seeds on the basis of need and not favor the wealthy or friends, who might sell or feed them to their animals. Correct use of the loaned seeds was significant since the state seeds eventually produced 10 percent of wheat grown in Spain. Residents were tempted to bribe their mayors for their silence or for a valuable piece of administrative paper, such as a *guía*, which would allow export to another province. Alcaldes and their assistants were penalized thousands of pesetas for "administrative illegalities and influence peddling." Early in the conflict, authorities in Andalusia prohibited them from leaving their towns and villages without specific permission from the civil governor.[30]

Officials called on both mayors and local military commanders to sanction violators of price controls "with a firm hand," but mayors did not enforce tasas in shops and stores in the "majority" of villages of Seville province. The situation deteriorated so gravely that merchants in the capital could not buy food at the controlled prices, leaving shops barren and the urban public discontented. Huelva, it seems, suffered a similar problem. So did León, where mayors often did not cooperate with provincial authorities who wanted enforcement of price controls. Huesca mayors were disinterested in implementing tasas and many other regulations. One-third of them ignored orders to supply statistics to the provincial government. The mayors of four Seville villages attempted to alleviate the growing bread shortage throughout the province by allowing their millers more flour than regulations permitted. They were fined 100 pesetas each. Assisted by complicit local physicians, alcaldes were reluctant to inform the Fiscalía de Vivienda about unsanitary conditions in their villages.[31]

The civil governor of La Coruña province sanctioned twenty-two mayors for failure to collect funds for the día de plato único. As has been seen, all residents were expected to give according to their means to the young—usually female—collectors who solicited in teams in towns and villages. The señoritas who served as collectors were often crudely insulted by those—including many women—reluctant to give. Donors were required to descend the staircases of their apartment buildings to pay collectors. The aggressive and the miserly, some of whom tried to use the excuse that they believed the collectors to be imposters, refused to contribute. Hundreds of inhabitants of small and large towns throughout Galicia, Zamora, León, and Asturias were either directly fined—sometimes hundreds of pesetas—or warned about their below-average collection of the one-dish meal and other taxes. Major cities—Pontevedra and Vigo—had rates of collection of the plato único that were on average five to ten times higher than smaller towns and villages. In other words, like most other taxes, the plato único fell heavily on the most urbanized areas of the province. In Pontevedra province in 1938, revenues from the plato increased more than one million pesetas from 1937. However, the city of Vigo, which had approximately 10 percent of the province's inhabitants, contributed 37 percent of the plato revenues. In the provincial capital of Zamora approximately 28,000 to 29,000 pesetas were collected per month. This was a considerable sum, which reached approximately the same amount as the total of fines for violation of price controls during the entire war in the province of Lugo.[32]

The Falangist civil governor of Pontevedra, Colonel Mateo Torres Bestard, remained disappointed by "low revenues from the one-dish meal." Authorities in Vigo fined twenty-four mayors 100 pesetas each "for failure to comply with the governor's circular." Torres Bestard warned his mayors, who had repeatedly shown neither zeal nor alacrity in carrying out his orders, that he would levy large fines on them and their assistants. The latter were often at the mercy of caciques, who successfully avoided attempts to professionalize the office. Despite repeated warnings about failure to collect, ayuntamientos in Lugo province refused to pay their allotment. Officials were certain that "favoritism" influenced collections in small towns: "Municipal Juntas enjoy too much freedom to exempt wealthy taxpayers." In Zamora, authorities warned mayors to file receipts from the plato único on time. In Las Palmas the civil governor advised debtors to pay up and to treat the female collectors with respect. Many, who were not at home when the señoritas passed to collect the levy, never paid their contribution. In León the Falange—backed by the civil governor—established a coercive collecting apparatus staffed by teams of señoritas at dozens of posts strategically situated throughout the city.[33]

GYPSIES

Historians of the civil war have ignored Gypsies. Yet, like the small Jewish minority, they played essential symbolic and real roles in the conflict. The historiographical emphasis on politics and diplomacy has neglected the critical

Gypsy contribution as livestock dealers, which was discussed earlier. It has also omitted their continuing defiance of the Spanish state and its various regimes, including the Nationalist one.

At the very beginning of the conflict, Gypsies invented a novel—and perhaps ironic—way to greet Nationalist forces, which a Situationist interpretation might see as *détournement*. Instead of the standard fascist gesture (required nationally as of 26 April 1937 or even earlier in certain provinces) of one raised arm at a forty-five-degree angle with hand outstretched, they raised both hands, correctly calculating that the Insurgents were an extension of the Civil Guard, who had frequently commanded them to put their hands up. In another incident at the war's inception, Falangists called to one Gypsy, "Raise your hands," searched his body, and aggressively asked whether he was a Communist. He replied: "I've never been a Communist, but a bullfighter's assistant since I was 17." Gypsies tried to show a new respect for private property by voluntarily returning stolen mules, acts that greatly surprised partisans of the movement.[34]

However, for Gypsies and many others in the Nationalist zone, the intimidating effects of terror would diminish and normality return as the war endured. As before the conflict, the Roma were soon identified as thieves as well as livestock dealers. In Zamora the Civil Guard arrested two Roma women accused of selling stolen chickens. In Bormujos (Seville), Civil Guards detained a nineteen-year-old Gypsy female for horse stealing. The guards pursued, shot, and wounded her live-in boyfriend. In Zamora three Gypsy brothers were seized for horse rustling. Three others involved in the ring were arrested, and two horses recovered from them.[35]

For many Spaniards, Gypsies epitomized group solidarity, horsemanship, trickery, and petty crime. *El Pueblo Gallego*, a Falangist organ, initiated a column titled "Gitanerías," which chronicled various petty thefts—two hams, several loaves of bread, a mass of wool—by Gypsies and others. Roma women were especially prominent pilferers. It should be pointed out since male thieves of all ethnicities were drafted, women may have dominated the light-fingered profession. Four female Gypsies who possessed stolen goods were detained. Authorities arrested several more Gypsy women for pilfering clothing. Another Roma female used her automobile to transport stolen property. A ring of five female pickpockets operated regularly in the city of Pontevedra. In La Coruña two female Gypsies were arrested for stealing a box of bananas from a pier. In León a woman denounced two young Gypsy girls who, she alleged, stole her sheets. In Zamora two Roma females were detained for the theft of 600 pesetas in cash. Still another was arrested for fortune-telling.[36]

The filmmaker Benito Peroja portrayed Roma as kleptomaniacs in his 1939 picture, *Suspiros de España*. Gypsies who served as soldiers were subjected to relentless stereotyping. At Christmastime, much to the discomfort of several Gypsy comrades, soldiers stationed in Extremadura sang the following carol:

> En el portal de Belén
> Gitanillos han entrado
> Y al Niño que está en la cuna
> Los pañales le han quitado

They were also known for their use of the blade. In Zamora four Gypsy men were injured in a knife fight. The Gijón municipality purged its police force of Republican sympathizers and hired the unemployed son of a policeman who had been wounded in a battle of the blades by a band of Gypsies who had been seeking vengeance for the unjustified shooting of one of their female members.[37]

An alternate image of Gypsies was what may be called Andalusian romantic. The activities of the Hermandad de los Gitanos at Seville received special attention during Holy Week and afterward. Their sincere Christian piety was lauded. The fiery destruction of the San Román Church, which housed a Gypsy brotherhood, left Queipo distraught and full of romantic fury: "Without a doubt by this act, unpatriotic atheists punished those who fought for the fatherland on our side. Never did a single Gypsy join anti-Spain." Their dances and music were appreciated and celebrated, and often performed before an audience of soldiers. Francisco Alonso's "Danza Gitana" was a popular musical piece.[38]

Begging, another activity traditionally associated with Gypsies, defied both the Falangist and Tridentine glorification of labor that were ideologically dominant in the Nationalist zone. Authorities forbade begging in certain provinces, including at the entrance of churches. The municipality of León was particularly strict. "This city has proven that begging is unnecessary. . . . Even after we give beggars ample food, they and their children continued to accost pedestrians." All who donated to these "charity professionals" would be fined 25 pesetas. In the short term, the repressive policy was effective and cleared the streets and the churches of beggars in several days. The mayor of Zamora planned to arrest all freeloaders sixteen years old or younger. In Vigo the civil governor ordered violators detained. In 1938 its municipal police arrested 1,354 offenders.[39]

LOOTING AND CRIME

Looting was rampant on both sides in the Spanish civil war, but counter-revolutionaries controlled it more successfully and avoided the vicious cycle of peasant hatred and hoarding that plagued their Republican enemies and their counterrevolutionary counterparts in Russia and China. The marauding of soldiers of the Whites' Volunteer Army discredited it. Peasants referred to it as the "Looting Army" not the Volunteer Army. Russian White soldiers supplied themselves at the expense of the population and treated the people with great brutality. White leaders could not end raiding since field officers approved this system of pay and rewards. Even when General Denikin's Supreme Council tried to centralize the control of all booty, commanders in the field practiced their own egotistical "self-equipment." The chief of the British military mission warned Denikin of the extent of "the evil," demonstrating that it was the "bribery and corruption of the supply services and the pride of the officers that had caused their failures in the European war, and showing him that the same defects had ruined [Admiral] Koltchak [sic]." High prices and the fall in the value of the ruble made officers' pay insufficient to support their families, and "even the commander-in-chief himself received less than a simple soldier among the Bolsheviks." The White generals Konstantin Mamontov and Andrei Shkuro won national notoriety as looters. Despite Denikin's criticism of Shkuro's raids, he was reluctant to dismiss him since the Kuban Cossacks, avid for booty, so loyally followed him. His cashiering would have meant the loss of "the most daring cavalry force in the army."[40]

Denikin was unable to control his rear, which became a theater of constant banditry: "Practically every train from Odessa to Kiev . . . was held up, looted, and robbed." His forces continually engaged in murderous pogroms against the Jews of Kiev, where "20,000 of 35,000 Jewish families were robbed and pillaged by the Volunteer Army." Whereas Cossack men pillaged to eat, their leaders sacked for personal enrichment. When in August 1919 Mamontov captured Tambov, a chief Bolshevik supply depot that was less than 400 miles from Moscow, his successful raid "degenerated into a looting expedition." His Don and Kuban Cossacks, the most populous of the Cossack hosts, "wore out their horses carrying loot [and] were anxious to get back to their homes with the booty." The cavalrymen were absent or unfit for vigorous action on several occasions just when they were most needed. The Cossacks destroyed government offices and pillaged warehouses and homes. Instead of employing Tambov's resources in a rational manner to aid the overall White effort, Mamontov's Cossacks engaged in an orgy of destruction. Denikin admitted in a speech delivered at the end of January 1920 to the Supreme Council of the Don that his forces had failed because of "the robberies and licentiousness of the troops and those who encourage them in the same." Only in the spring of 1920 when the war was virtually lost did Denikin's successor, General Peter Wrangel, seriously attempt to halt his soldiers' pillaging. The most astute elements of the Russian counterrevolution realized that the deeply embedded Russian tradition of the *pogrom* greatly harmed the White cause but they were powerless to eradicate it.[41]

Likewise, Admiral Kolchak's army in Siberia quickly became hated in the countryside because it forcibly confiscated peasant produce. Requisitioning especially alienated the mass of subsistence farmers who wanted all sides to leave them alone. Kolchak's forces, particularly Cossacks, engaged in "systematic robbery" and murder in advance or in retreat. In February 1919, when the minister of provisions informed Kolchak about "the imminent stoppage of supplies for the army and . . . the lack of small currency to pay the army's wages," the admiral replied that "he will soon see himself compelled to resort to measures of ataman-bolshevik character, i.e., requisitions, confiscations, contributions, and issues of paper currency directly from his office." Surely enough, by the end of the month fighters "with the consent of their commanders, to provide for their own needs . . . [kept] valuables seized as war booty—money, precious metals, and stones. . . . Officers and civilian employees . . . remain[ed] without pay for months on end." Prime Minister Peter Vologodsky "disapproved of the steady advance of the Kolchak troops westward without securing behind themselves the territory gained while our army is dying of epidemic diseases. [Our army] is utterly tired of this civil war anyway." In September 1919 the commander of the American forces in Siberia, General William Graves, reported that Kolchak's soldiers had treated the population worse than the Bolsheviks and "that practically every soldier had a horse and cart that he had taken from the peasants; that soldiers requisitioned whatever they wanted, sometimes giving a receipt but more often not." In the winter of 1919–20, supply transports never reached the troops, and their horses starved to death. "Many" White soldiers "deserted to the Reds, rebellion existed, and famine was undisguised. . . . Officers fled, rear establishments melted away, commissary chiefs deserted, and army physicians did likewise, leaving typhus sufferers and wounded men to their fate."[42]

Like the Spanish Republic, the GMD began the war with the great advantage of control of the Chinese state. Yet despite this initial edge, the GMD lost. Part of the explanation is that during the Chinese civil war (1945–49), GMD soldiers (including high-ranking officers) plundered and looted more than their Communist enemy. French observers were impressed that the CCP would not permit its troops to loot and pillage even when they requisitioned large landowners. The People's Liberation Army had a long tradition, which could be traced back to its founding, of paying peasants for room and board. Although peasants complained about its use of conscript labor, they often regarded it as something other than a bandit force. Staunch anti-Communists admitted that Red troops "behaved well. They did no looting. There was no petty thievery. If one succumbed to temptation, he was promptly punished" in full view of everyone. "The Chinese peasant was astonished. . . . They had had no such experiences with the National [GMD] Army." Communist efficiency also impressed this observer, a priest. The CCP had quickly taken over a local Jesuit press and printed first-rate propaganda.[43]

Contrary to the expectations of a class analysis, many of the traditional rural elite cooperated with the party because of the excellent discipline of CCP troops and their own experience of GMD misrule. A Protestant minister noted that "even here in Kwangtung we get authentic reports of places where [Nationalist] troops are stationed, where they help themselves to anything they want, and I have one apparently authentic report of one village where someone had been openly critical, as 99 percent of the people are but not so vocally, and they went there and shot ten men out of hand. . . . Government troops are an ineffective lot. They were not meant to wage war but to oppress the people." An American, the Reverend J. H. Mellow, confirmed that "food shortages are in main due to [GMD] Marshal Yen Hsi-shan's extraction from the peasantry of practically their entire grain production." Yen had decided to feed the cities by starving the countryside. CCP activists became popular in Yunnan because Nationalist "mismanagement, . . . oppressive taxation, and excessive conscription" caused popular discontent. In contrast, Communist control of nearby Peihai was "not corrupt" and was "efficient."[44]

The fate of the northeast, especially Manchuria, may have determined the outcome of the Chinese civil war. The arable land in the northeast represented 24 percent of China's total cultivation area. The average size of the plots each farmer cultivated was three times larger than in the rest of the country. Mao insisted that this region would be the battleground that would decide the conflict, because it was only here that the party was able to secure enough logistical support to expand its military operations outside its base areas. In the northeast, Communists imposed "harsh demands" on the people for provisions and placed priority on order, not social justice, since they were reluctant to disturb areas on which they depended for supplies. In Manchuria, Communist officials circumscribed black marketeering, theft, and bribe taking. They won a laudable reputation for honesty, which they retained throughout the civil war by sanctioning cadres and party members who had confiscated property for their own use. In contrast, rural and urban GMD officials were famously venal and hedonistic, engaging in prostitution and gambling. In parts of north China, some traders routinely hid their goods in Communist-held areas when Guomindang armies moved through, stating that it was better to pay fees to the CCP than to have half their storage confiscated by GMD officers. On the outskirts of Beijing in December 1948, a left-wing Christian reported that Communist troops "took neither food nor fuel from the villagers, and would not accept any presents or services. They paid, with their 'Great Wall' currency, for all they needed." On 17 December 1948 Rear Admiral Thomas Inglis, chief of U.S. Naval Intelligence, admitted: "One thing that puzzles us is the superiority and the strategic direction of the Chinese Communists and their ability to support themselves logistically and in communications. It just doesn't seem Chinese."[45]

As in CCP-controlled areas, the regular pay and soundness of currency in Franco's zone made looting less necessary for Spanish Nationalist soldiers than Republican ones. Of course, unauthorized looting did occur, but peasants and shopkeepers assumed correctly that Insurgent troops would purchase their commodities and were more than willing to accept Nationalist currency. Leftist militias in Seville and throughout Spain pillaged with less military and political discipline than their rightist counterparts, with the possible exception of Moroccan troops, who composed less than 10 percent of Franco's forces. In Fuenteovejuno during the Nationalists' 1938–39 winter offensive in Andalusia and Extremadura, a Jesuit chaplain was shocked by his discovery of a commissar's written order to his troops that pleaded with his men not to loot, "even if you see many products that you haven't eaten for a long time." Another chaplain constantly contrasted the discipline of his men with the desertions, looting, and pillaging of the enemy. When Republican soldiers entered Faratella during the Battle of the Ebro, they asked the local women how the "fascists" had treated them. The females' answer that the fascists had behaved correctly may have surprised the questioners. In Asturias, rightists invented the verb "uachepear," which suggested that the UHP (Unión de Hijos del Proletariado or Uníos Hermanos Proletarios), the workers' coalition during the Asturias Revolt of 1934, legitimized their expropriations of food and drink by the use of the acronym. When it left Spain in April 1939, the Condor Legion, responsible for the destruction of Guernica and much else, made sure to pay its financial debts.[46]

As has been seen, African troops were awarded a circumscribed right to plunder. On a quiet front near Madrid, which hardly saw fighting for the first half of 1937, moros were allowed to chop down the trees of "reds" who had abandoned their fields but not of rightists who had remained. Legionnaires and Regulares were permitted to loot unoccupied homes—presumably their owners had fled to the "red" zone and were assumed to be "Communists"—for the first few days after a village or town was taken. In March 1938 the Africanos Tiradores de Ifni sacked and looted an SNT warehouse in Zuera (Zaragoza). They broke the door locks, took some 2,000 kilos of grain to feed their mules, used the door and window as firewood, and converted approximately one hundred sacks—which had become increasingly rare in the Nationalist zone—into pillows or personal luggage. The few Canary soldiers among them transformed a portion of the stolen grain into meal (*gofio*). In newly conquered Lérida in April 1938, legionnaires and especially Moorish troops took nearly everything portable from abandoned homes. Only after several days did authorities stop the pillaging. Cooperative truck drivers transported the booty—bedspreads, sheets, typewriters, and silverware. The Lérida "liberators" conned the city's pleasure professionals by paying them with Republican money since the women remained unaware that the only usable banknotes in the Nationalist

zone had to be authorized by the Burgos government. When conquering Republican territory, legionnaires, most of whom were European, were also
likely to raid any establishment they thought might possess legal Nationalist
banknotes. These warriors might even desert home to give their families the
bundle of newly found wealth and then return to their unit. When Yagüe's
Regulares entered Barcelona at the end of January 1939, some were allowed
several days of pillaging to collect their "war tax." Officers again arranged
for the shipment of Regulares' loot back to their families in Morocco.[47]

In Rioja, Falangists were accused of pilfering the few possessions of poor
families. In Aroche (Huelva) requetés completely trashed a pharmacy whose
owner was a "Communist." Starved soldiers of either side felt entitled to
make private livestock into a nutritious meal. When Catalan requetés captured an abandoned town, they assumed the right to consume all the available farm animals. During the Battle of the Ebro they pillaged uninhabited
residences. In their march through Catalonia at the end of the conflict, Nationalist soldiers looted villagers' animals. Nationalist troops could—and
sometimes did, at least in the South—take whatever they wanted. A lucrative
business in stolen parts arose. Mechanics cannibalized vehicles, and all auto
parts dealers were ordered to verify the origins of their inventory. Stolen tires
were valued at 400 to 600 pesetas each. Civil governors fined merchants who
trafficked in stolen goods.[48]

Early in the conflict in the Nationalist zone, property rights commanded
more respect than in Republican areas. For example, the civil governor in
Vitoria arranged a deal with the inhabitants of Landa (Álava, 176 dispersed
inhabitants) and Ullívarri (140 inhabitants) in which the governor would provide them with security against looting and the villages would reciprocally
furnish young men to the requetés. Nationalist officers considered the latter
their most effective militia given their military training and hierarchical organization. Their efficient logistical support enhanced their usefulness. A clash
between the village of Legorreta and one Carlist militia, La Partida, both of
which claimed supplies abandoned by Republican forces, was settled by the
Junta Central de Guerra de Navarra in favor of the requetés. However, the
Junta eventually dissolved the Partida and integrated its members into other
units since it had gained a deserved reputation for living quite well off the
land, including its more exotic products—anis, tobacco, and coffee.[49]

Nationalist troops were sometimes forbidden to loot under penalty of
death. In Andalusia in July 1938, officials reported pillaging in "liberated"
areas, and they threatened to shoot any of their own soldiers who engaged in
"actions typical of the Red Army." Some Nationalist soldiers made it a point
of pride to return looted items to their rightful owners. Their respect for private property fomented amiable relations with local residents. Following the
devastating Belchite and Codo battles, a unit of Catalan requetés began its

process of recuperation and regrouping in Zaragoza. Apparently, the salaries of the soldiers were sufficient to eat in taverns, purchase a slice of watermelon from the Moorish *zoco* in the center of town, and attend the cinema. They were then transferred to a small town, Canfranc, in the High Pyrenees. Supplied by mules, the soldiers settled in and established a good relationship with the villagers, who appreciated that the requetés compensated them for the sheep they consumed. Residents furnished the men with appropriate shoes and coats for winter weather, which they returned when they were transferred to Torres de Berrellén (Zaragoza).[50]

There they regressed to their routine—breakfast, training, large lunch, religious devotion, ample dinner, bedtime. One recruit claimed that he ate better in his unit than he had at home in Barcelona. Religious festivals, such as the Purísima Concepción of 8 December, were accompanied by large meals, which included numerous courses and after-dinner drinks. Christmas Eve was celebrated in the homes of locals, and, as on other occasions, Margaritas provided them with cognac, turrón, mazapán, jam, cookies, chocolate, tobacco, rolling paper, and, of course, a prayer book. In addition, officers received brand-name cognac and cigars. Soldiers in Navarre's hospitals, who numbered nearly 3,000, were given 10 pesetas and wounded officers, 20. Other Carlist units and legionnaires also received a special banquet for lunch and dinner on *Nochebuena*. One unit ate soup, rabbit, lamb, dessert, turrón, and unlimited wine and cognac. Enough food was on hand to improvise feasts spontaneously. Relations between one requeté and his host family became so close that it provided him with a winter coat, often difficult to find in either army. Their commander ordered that villagers be paid for theft or damage committed by his men, whose pay was correspondingly reduced for any infraction.[51]

In January 1938 the Tercio found Mazarete (Guadalajara) much less hospitable with a population "more red than our berets." In this relatively impoverished province, villagers refused to help feed or clothe the requetés. In response, several began to steal sheep and other livestock, "gastronomical errors" that were quickly sanctioned by their commander. This enforced respect for property won over owners in the village. The baker told the commander's chauffeur that he appreciated the unit's prompt payment for his goods. Religious devotion and big banquets helped to break the winter boredom. Some of the poultry they consumed was pilfered—despite strict orders of their superiors—from villagers who had let their chickens run free. Acts of thievery and (drunken) vandalism were, nonetheless, exceptional and were usually punished by the high command. Financial compensation to locals for looted livestock was not unknown. As a rule, military-civilian relations were said to be positive. For example, in Riaza (Segovia), where the Tercio was briefly stationed, attractive young women—dressed in regional folk costumes—served the young men wines and tobacco at the end of the banquet.[52]

In the fall of 1936, franquista authorities banned any confiscation of farm animals that were absolutely necessary for the harvest and other labor. Requisitions of those with "excess" livestock were limited to 25 percent of the flock. According to a military decree of 1 July 1937, only generals—not the Falange or any other organization—could authorize requisitions. When Spanish Nationalists did requisition items, they often provided useful indemnities. Like automobiles, animals were returned at the end of the conflict. The most popular Republican guerrilleros quickly learned the same lesson and always compensated peasants in worthy cash. Franco himself devoted considerable attention to logistics and supply. He ultimately proved more successful than his opponents or his counterrevolutionary counterparts in meshing money with military power.[53]

Certain types of crimes dropped sharply in the Nationalist zone. The military dictatorship quickly eliminated "proletarian shopping trips" or "social crimes" that had disturbed property owners after the electoral victory of the Popular Front. The draft affected nearly all young men, including criminals; thus, many types of common violations declined among civilians. In the army itself theft among soldiers existed but was severely punished. Draconian measures against thieves were considered necessary not only because they had violated property rights but also since they ruptured the solidarity of the unit. Rather than face trial, a Falangist who had stolen a can of condensed milk and sausage from his corporal preferred to risk death and desert his unit.[54]

In Segovia, crimes against both people and property descended dramatically in the civil war years, although suicides remained stable and traffic violations increased. In Álava, Huelva, and Ávila, common crimes—including juvenile delinquency—plummeted more than 50 percent during the war years. Orense experienced a similar plunge. In Granada province, thefts of wheat declined sharply in 1938. However, it should be noted that military tribunals were handling some of the cases that would have been judged by civilian courts before July 1936. Although largely successful from a fiduciary perspective, the stamping operation to regulate Nationalist paper currency provided new opportunities for con men. In the summer of 1937 sixty-nine persons were accused of counterfeiting stamped banknotes worth a billion pesetas. When stuck with false bills, merchants protested profusely.[55] In sum, the drop in common criminality is yet another example of the ability of the Nationalists to secure their rear.

Even so, juvenile delinquency increased throughout much of the Nationalist zone. In Palencia, although common crime fell, adolescent offenses against property climbed. In La Coruña, four young thieves were arrested on one day. Youngsters specialized in petty theft, such as robbing a small haberdashery of merchandise worth 56 pesetas. Coal became such a valuable commodity that juveniles risked severe punishment by pilfering a bag or two from the docks.

According to the La Coruña prosecutor, youthful violations increased daily. He called for the harshest possible sentences for offenders, even though many provinces did not provide special prisons for juveniles. The mayor of Zamora urged urban and rural police to "intensify their vigilance, especially in the fields near the city, to stop the gangs of dissolute kids who trample and steal the produce." In Zamora, two young authors of a petty theft were fined 500 pesetas each. In addition, they were ordered to return the stolen wheat and pay 86 pesetas of damages to the victim. In Segovia, authorities worried about the increase of violent and reckless acts by young people.

Children became recidivists. In Oviedo, "various gangs of minors specialize in robbing apartments in the absence of their owners. They even steal the lightbulbs in the halls." In another case police arrested three young thieves, fifteen to seventeen years old, and their fence. The gang formed part of a larger ring that sold stolen objects to criminals in other provinces. Two merchants from Lugo were held in connection to the thefts, whose total accumulation filled an entire truck. In León, police broke up a ring of three petty thieves of fifteen and sixteen years old, but other bands of the same age continued to operate in the city, engaging, for example, in nocturnal raids on a wine shop. Also in León, a doctor denounced his eighteen-year-old maid, who had lifted various objects from his home. Police investigated another complaint of theft from a seventy-year-old woman and found that her teenage domestic participated in robbery. On the other hand, several young female servants complained to police that their employers would not pay them promised wages.

The police told the parents of "vagabond children" that they were responsible for violations of property rights. Seville authorities jailed hundreds of children for riding on the bumpers of municipal trams until their parents could pay the fines. They also sanctioned fathers for the misbehavior of their children in the municipal pool. The mayor of Las Palmas banned youngsters from begging and ordered them to attend schools, which they had vacated or never frequented. He imposed fines on parents, even impoverished ones, who permitted their offspring from six to fourteen years old to avoid public or private educational institutions.[56]

CONSCRIPTS AND PRISONERS

The Italian failure at Guadalajara increased Franco's skepticism about a quick war and reinforced his commitment to a war of attrition based on greater manpower and logistical superiority. In many ways, his model became the Allied victory in World War I, not the African campaigns of his early career. Showing the new priority given to both training and logistics, after the stalemate around Madrid in March 1937, General Luis Orgaz was appointed head of "mobilization services and the recuperation of personnel, material, cattle, and automobiles," in addition to his duties instructing officers in rearguard academies. His office was named MIR (Mobilization, Instruction, and Recuperation) and expanded the number of training schools to twenty-two, each with a number of German advisors. Nationalists had greater help from foreigners and knew how to use this aid effectively. Germans serving in Spain outnumbered Soviets fivefold, and the number of Italians who fought was much greater than that of foreign volunteers in the International Brigades. Forty thousand International Brigaders joined Republican forces, whereas 70,000 Moroccans, 78,000 Italians, and 15,000 Germans fought for Franco. These were mostly elite troops who bolstered the Nationalist chances of victory.[57]

In contrast, the overwhelming majority of conscripts on both sides were reluctant to serve in the armed forces and tried when drafted, if at all possible, to avoid the front. As a rule, draftees were more likely to desert than volunteers. In March 1937 in the heartland of conservative Castile, Nationalists found a reluctance to enlist. When persistent material shortages were added to their lack of commitment, common responses were evasion, desertion, or demoralization. On both sides, substantial numbers refused their call-up orders. In Galicia the Nationalists had significant problems with conscripts who did not appear for duty. The naval command prosecuted for desertion sixty twenty-six-year-olds from Pontevedra province who had avoided conscription. The Civil Guard, Falangists, and other authorities arrested dozens, if not hundreds, of young men from Pontevedra and surrounding villages who had failed to appear for duty, who had deserted from the military, or who had even joined the "Marxists" in Asturias. Four conscripts tried to cross the border into Portugal but were apprehended. In 1938 the municipal police of Vigo filed 432 reports on soldiers and 1,765 on conscripts. The propensity of *gallegos* to attempt to escape may be explained by the traditions of emigration, of smuggling over the Portuguese border, and the proximity to the Asturian resistance. Authorities accused deserting "reds" of setting fires in the scrublands of Pontevedra.[58]

Some young men rushed to join the Falange as a way—mistakenly or not—to avoid dangerous military service. In Seville province, urban Falangists were more successful in this goal than their rural counterparts, who were less likely to be exempted from frontline duty. The shirkers resembled Chinese Communist soldiers who preferred a cushy and safe existence in Red areas to fighting the enemy. In villages and small towns, young men who were not serving in the military could not fail to be noticed. In a letter published in the *Diario de León* in April 1937, seven mothers of soldiers from Guijuelo (Salamanca) wrote to Franco complaining that in their village, "boys of 20 to 25 years old stroll around satisfying their own personal needs. We believe that they ought to serve the Patria and respectfully request that you administer justice to them. Their names are on the back [of this letter]." The Las

Palmas newspaper advised women to reject healthy young men who were not in uniform. Delation of supposed shirkers was not an exclusively Spanish phenomenon. During World War II, German military authorities received "numerous" letters—both signed and anonymous—from citizens complaining about able-bodied draft dodgers in their midst.[59]

In November 1936, Nationalist authorities prohibited "the national vice" of requests by notables to exempt family members or friends from frontline duty. In October 1937, when Queipo directly asked Franco to spare Seville Falange officials from military duty, the Caudillo refused. He was sometimes more lenient with other Falange formations who remained in the rear if a general vouched for their usefulness. These less exposed soldiers became humorously known as "dry wet nurses" because "they don't expose their breasts." Even more indulgent were Republican officials who allowed parties and unions broad exemptions until the fall of Gijón in October 1937. The franquistas were less likely to exempt younger men from military service and thereby avoided the demoralizing situation that existed in the Popular Army in which older men with children were drafted, but younger ones were able to obtain exemptions when working in war-related industries. The Insurgents ended exemptions for many militarized workers in December 1937, four months before the Republicans. Nationalists reduced the number of young men (eighteen to twenty-one years old) who had inundated employers in militarized factories with job applications. Franquistas also compelled exempted recruits to undergo periodic examinations by military and local physicians to verify the validity of their medical exemptions.[60]

In the first few months of the struggle, approximately 100,000 in the Nationalist zone volunteered compared with 120,000 for the Republic. As the supply of "active citizens" dried up, officials in both zones had to resort to conscription. Although each camp mobilized age groups at approximately the same time in order to avoid the flight of conscripts to the enemy zone, Nationalists did not draft troops as young or as old, both of whom were more likely to desert. The Republic mobilized twenty-seven age groups, ranging from seventeen to forty-four years old and totaling 1,700,000 men. The Nationalist government conscripted only fourteen age groups, ranging from eighteen to thirty-two years old, totaling 1,260,000 men. Nationalist conscription policies more closely resembled Chinese Communists than Spanish Republicans. Keeping the numbers of those in uniform low would allow more supplies for civilians. In spite of all the campaigns that the Communists conducted in the areas they controlled, only a small part of the peasantry actually participated in the main CCP activities—organizing supplies and fighting the war. Like Maoists, franquistas knew how to limit the numbers of soldiers to match their ability to feed them.[61]

The overwhelming majority of the older draftees were "fathers burdened by a number of children" who did not make particularly effective soldiers. In May 1937, Nationalist authorities in Vigo were still restricting their draft to twenty-one-year-olds. This was also the case in Zamora in the spring of 1938, but by the summer twenty-year-olds were being drafted. At the end of 1938 the Popular Army felt compelled to draft both younger and older men. In March 1938 it called up eighteen- and nineteen-year-olds. Their subsequent military training was primitive and completely insufficient to prepare them for battle. Recalcitrant members of the *quinta del biberón* (baby-bottle draft), as they were known, were pursued by police and Assault Guards throughout Catalonia. In contrast, the youngest Nationalist soldiers were often the most enthusiastic: boys from certain Catholic families who were as young as sixteen or even fourteen devotedly followed their older brothers into combat. In October 1938, Republicans mobilized the class of 1939, which, in theory, still had two years before they were eligible for military service.[62]

Nationalists, who were aware of the reluctance of draftees in their mid-thirties to fight, made direct appeals to older Republican soldiers to desert by telling them their age would exempt them from service in the Nationalist zone. In May 1937 they drafted the oldest to date—twenty-nine-year-olds—assigned them to units at some distance from the front, and assured them that they would remain safely in the rear. Even during the Battle of the Ebro, when manpower needs were enormous on both sides, the Insurgents allocated eighteen "bachelor battalions" of twenty-nine- to thirty-one-year-olds to quiet fronts. Conscripts were also posted on tranquil fronts; volunteers were transferred to more active ones. During offensives, volunteer units composed between 50 and 100 percent of the infantry. Italian manpower policies were not as astute as their Nationalist allies, since General Roatta complained to Rome about the numerous unaggressive older married men under his command.[63]

The manpower policies of the franquistas revealed a powerful paternalism by allowing fathers who had three or more draft-eligible sons—a situation not uncommon given the large families of the era—to liberate one of them from service if two were serving. At roughly the same time, in February 1937 the Republic promulgated a similar but socially more sensitive measure that exempted sons of impoverished widows. News of the exemption encouraged a good number of Nationalist soldiers who qualified to desert to the Republican side. The Nationalists made efforts to meet the labor and harvesting needs of growers and peasants by enacting conscription policies that were more flexible and staggered than those of the Republicans.[64]

Forced labor was not unusual in the Nationalist zone. In Queipo's fiefdom all citizens were compelled to work one day per month or pay 12 pesetas to build homes for injured war veterans. Seville's Fábrica de Artillería employed 500 civilians who labored forty-eight hours per week—a workweek later made general throughout the Nationalist zone—and who were under the obligation to execute overtime without a substantial pay increase. In May 1937 Queipo ordered the civil governor of Córdoba to provide him with 100 workers to repair roads used by military vehicles. The governor called for volunteers but insisted that, if the latter were lacking, he would compel workers to engage in roadwork. He found the response "shameful": of 100,000 residents, only 18, including 4 from the middle classes, volunteered. The disgusted governor closed the provincial borders to make sure that men between twenty and forty would not attempt to avoid labor service. Warnings were issued to "frivolous gentlemen" who spent too much time in bars.[65]

The construction of the Vigo airport recalled the *corvée* (medieval labor service). Planning for the airport had begun in 1927, but no construction had occurred until 1936. To level the future air fields, authorities enrolled male residents between twenty and fifty from Vigo, Lavadores, and Mos. All these men—only soldiers and sailors were exempted—were required to work two days per month at the salary of a *bracero*, or 6 pesetas, per day. However, workers who paid 12 pesetas were exempted from a month's labor. The Junta del Aeropuerto de Vigo, which directed the project, justified the corvée by asserting that the facility would benefit the entire community. Many men remained unconvinced, and authorities posted hundreds, if not thousands, of names of individuals who did not appear for work or who had not paid the required fees. No-shows were threatened with double duty and double fines. Medical inspectors regularly reviewed those who claimed sickness or physical incapacity. Some surreptitiously hired substitutes to labor for them, a practice that military authorities would punish "severely."[66]

In March 1938 when the provincial Falange took control of the construction project from the Junta del Aeropuerto, its representatives responded to sentiment that forced labor unfairly burdened the working classes. In the middle of May 1938 the 700 workers on the site were compelled to listen to speeches of local Falangist leaders. One denied in front of this audience of skeptics that the Falange was in the service of capitalism. Instead, the party was "revolutionary," which meant "he who does not work must leave our Fatherland." The Falange promised to reduce airport workers' monetary quotas and to provide the unemployed with work on the building site. By June 1938 a system of "voluntary contributions" tied to income level had replaced the unpopular personal labor service, and wage labor supplanted the corvée. The Falange proudly proclaimed that no national tax revenue—merely the labor of the people of Vigo—had been used to build the facility. In March 1939 when a runway opened, the provincial Falange ended monthly contributions.[67]

The construction of the Santiago airport, which employed a similar system of forced labor, encountered analogous problems of funding and resistance to work. In newly conquered Asturias, the military instituted forced labor, which became compulsory for males older than sixteen and females older than twenty in "liberated" Oviedo. Hundreds were selected according to their identity card numbers. In Teruel a day of labor for the fatherland was instituted once per week. Pontevedra's civil governor, Manuel Gómez Cantos, a Civil Guard commander who had earned a bloody reputation for suppressing the left in Extremadura in the first months of the war, mobilized sixty workers "voluntarily." They labored without pay to repair storm damage in Puentecesures. The "volunteers" thanked the governor profusely for giving them the opportunity to serve Spain. Like Republicans, Nationalists were capable of conscripting locals to dig fortifications and engage in heavy labor.[68]

In July 1936 the Junta de Defensa Nacional issued a decree that allowed municipalities to mobilize local residents to harvest the crops of families who had soldiers at the front. A diktat by the Generalísimo eliminated Republican labor restrictions imposed by the Municipal Boundaries law, which had prohibited the hiring of workers from districts outside the locality of the owners' holdings. The Caudillo claimed that "there is no unit other than the nation" and suspended all nonessential work in favor of the rapid gathering of the harvest. Harvesters were also permitted to work during religious holidays, even though they were compelled to attend Mass. The Spanish army had a long peacetime tradition of granting leave to soldiers whose labor was needed at harvest time. Wartime needs prevented the continuation of this traditional practice, but authorities were willing to use their increasing number of prisoners to replace drafted rural laborers. However, officials worried that disgruntled laborers might sabotage the harvest by engaging in arson, whose potential damage was enormous since the destructive grazing and farming practices of shepherds and tillers had eliminated forests and other vegetation. Large areas of the south became extremely flammable, and fire insurance was made obligatory for farmers.[69]

Prison authorities in both zones shared a similar work ideology. Both offered their captives redemption through labor, a supposed "guarantee of honor." Nationalist prisoners were forced to attend Mass and worship at altars outfitted with pictures of the Caudillo, the Duce, and the Führer. In the fall of 1938 the Nationalists, who gained a much larger pool of captives than Republicans as the war endured, offered to reduce by half the prisoner's sentence in return for labor in a disciplinary battalion. Infiltrated by informers and closely monitored, these units often served on the front lines. Elite Nationalist units accepted prisoners who wished to redeem themselves through participation in battle.[70]

DESERTIONS

Desertions became a grave concern for both sides. Abandonment of the front by Nationalist soldiers seemed fairly common, even if the number of Republican deserters was larger. Fewer Nationalist desertions can be tied to better training, logistics, pay, and the likelihood of victory as the war endured. At the beginning of the conflict, Nationalist officials trusted Africans more than many of their own men. In Morocco, peasants were rewarded 100 pesetas for each Spanish deserter they caught attempting to flee to the French zone in the south or to neutral Tangiers in the northwest. In the Basque country during the first days of fighting, which coincided with the wheat harvest, cases of desertion were not uncommon among Nationalist recruits. Like leftist militiamen, Navarrese requetés believed that their value as volunteers allowed them to take advantage of peaceful interludes at the front to return home. However, in contrast to their CNT or UGT militiamen, who abandoned the front at will, the requetés left their units usually only after major victories, such as the conquest of Bilbao. In fact, the Tercio de Lácar and the Primera Brigada de Navarra did not participate in the Battle of Brunete because so many requetés had given themselves the right to take leave. In Navarre even the most Carlist villages tolerated significant numbers of deserters, especially if they returned to engage in essential agricultural labors. Requeté egotism or hometown (*patria chica*) loyalty demonstrated that the high command could not easily manipulate even committed Nationalist soldiers in elite units. When Carlist deserters eventually returned to their units, they were severely punished, not as individuals but as a group.[71]

Leave was regularly granted to elite units and to meritorious individuals. In Nationalist ranks, *permiso* was accompanied by a very generous bonus, amounting to several months' pay, and was a customary award for outstanding acts of bravery. Pamplona and its Círculo Tradicionalista offered soldiers on leave a profound delicing followed by fine cocktails and exquisite meals topped off by *digestifs* and communal singing.[72]

Authorities realized that conscription had permitted many of the unreliable to join the Nationalist Army in "red" regions such as Andalusia and even in the more conservative north. Leftists who attempted to disguise themselves by wearing the clothes of Carlists and Falangists might be denounced as *chaqueteros* (turncoats). After October 1937 the Nationalist high command ordered that soldiers suspected of ideological nonconformity be sent to disciplinary work battalions. Yet at the beginning of the struggle, Nationalists encouraged many leftists to "redeem themselves" by volunteering. Perhaps in the majority of cases, former leftists showed the shallowness of their previous ideological commitment and became loyal fighters in the Nationalist Army. Like conservative French Republicans in 1848, Insurgent officials seemed to have been surprisingly successful in enlisting or conscripting numerous proletarians into the ranks of the "party of order." An account by a deserter who had served both sides claimed that Nationalist boot camp was more effective in inculcating loyalty and preventing desertions than its Republican counterpart.

In previously leftist Andalusia, 255,000 men were drafted, more than in any other region. Of these, 55,000 served in the Army of the North. Andalusia was also the source for hundreds, if not thousands, of nurses. Those soldiers who remained in the south were often poorly equipped and ineffective in a region where quiet fronts prevailed. Andalusian troops remained unprepared for battle, and in early 1937 Queipo wrote that 30,000 potential draftees could not be furnished "with even one rifle." Nevertheless, its 132 battalions were instrumental in maintaining order.[73]

Those who chose desertion suffered severe consequences. Like Trotsky during the Russian civil war and Mussolini in his desperate Republic of Saló, both Nationalists and Republicans employed policies of physical and economic reprisals against family members of deserters, reflecting a common understanding of the family as the basic unit of Spanish society. It may have been the Generalísimo himself who insisted upon this "Bolshevik" practice throughout his own zone and whose local authorities executed it efficiently and effectively. In the Nationalist zone, relatives of deserters were threatened unless they betrayed their family members. Close relatives of deserters were jailed during the conflict and after the fighting had ended. When two deserters from the province of La Coruña fled with their weapons to the Republican camp, Nationalist officials ordered the arrest of the adult male members of their immediate families "as a just reprisal and an example." The Pontevedra Civil Guard arrested three siblings (including the sister) of a naval deserter. Several months later they detained two brothers of another deserter. A father and his daughter were apprehended because his son had abandoned the army. The flights of five others, who were from Navarre, also resulted in the detention of their adult male relatives. In 1939 and 1940, to obtain information on the whereabouts of fugitive soldiers, many of whom were "apoliticals" who had merely wished to avoid military service, the new regime imprisoned their relatives, leading to suicide attempts by a number of deserters' mothers. Fathers and brothers of deserters were forced to pay fines—sometimes well into the 1940s—equivalent to their net worth. These policies of familial punishment intimidated many other fugitives and draft dodgers into surrender at the end of the war.[74]

While the motives of these runaways were unclear, some Nationalist soldiers resented what they perceived to be iron and arbitrary discipline that their officers imposed. The clothing shortage—the lack of shoes, underwear, and other garments—remained an important reason for desertion to the Republican zone. Others presumed to be "extremists" or "reds" hated the poor treatment and ostracism reserved for their families in the Nationalist rear. To stop these "frequent desertions," Nationalist commanders recommended both the carrot and the stick. They endorsed the establishment of a network of informers within certain militia units, and they also suggested that village authorities pardon "any previous errors" of relatives of all enlisted soldiers. Officers were disturbed that local authorities persevered in penalizing families of volunteers who had a leftist history. Africanistas of the Spanish Foreign Legion, it should be remembered, had experience with wiping the slate clean and insisted that once an individual volunteered for service, his past mistakes were erased. Cases of unfair treatment or persecution of soldiers and their relatives were numerous enough that high-ranking legionarios requested that the Generalísimo issue a directive imposing "forgive and forget" on all local authorities. The Nationalist high command and provincial authorities made efforts to protect loyal soldiers from attempts by "village bosses" to prosecute them and their families as subversives.[75]

Desertions often took place for personal reasons revolving around the desire to reunite with family. Geography was a determining factor, and men with homes near mountainous or inaccessible regions were more likely to free themselves from military service. In these areas they relied either on cooperative family members or, if in sufficient numerical strength, threats to the locals in order to receive needed logistical support. Even at the end of the conflict, when a Franco victory appeared imminent, a few Nationalist soldiers fled to defend relatives in the Republican zone or to accompany them into exile. The act of desertion itself was often accomplished alone or sometimes with a blood relative or longtime friend. Deserters who failed—often because disorientation led them back into their own lines—usually paid with their lives. Not only was this among the worst breaches of discipline, but the weapons and information they brought to the enemy risked severely damaging the side from which they escaped. There is no complete documentary record of the common practice of summary executions of deserters from Nationalist lines, but, as a warning to others, soldiers of nearby units were forced to witness these killings.[76]

Desertions fomented an atmosphere of defeatism that reduced morale. In a few units the number of those shot for desertion surpassed those killed in battle. Nationalists refused to allow soldiers to hunt within thirty kilometers of the French border and used the most tested veterans as their border police. Both sides preferred to station soldiers—especially Catalans and Galicians— outside their regions of origin in order to discourage flight. On 19 November 1937 Franco prohibited any mention of desertions or demoralization in his army. At the end of 1936 Republican Prime Minister Largo Caballero encouraged enemy deserters by granting each of them 50 pesetas in hard coin or 100 if they were armed, 10 days of leave, and a free round-trip ticket to the destination of their choice. The frequency of desertions—even from elite units— demonstrated fluctuating identities during the civil war. Personal reasons and local conditions usually determined if and when a soldier took flight.[77]

Civil wars have their own dynamic in which many individuals seek to join what they believe will be the winning side. In other words, what causes civil wars is not what sustains them. Self-interest, opportunism, and cynicism can help explain why so many small property owners and proletarians did not resist and even supported the Nationalists. Committed leftist militants who had suffered much for their cause were disappointed that so many of their fellow workers lacked "class consciousness" and quickly cooperated with the Insurgents. Thus, firm control of a town or region can generate various forms of compliance and collaboration from the population. In return for security of life and livelihood, many civilians provided information—a key resource in any war—on the whereabouts of draft dodgers and deserters. Terror, too, played its part. Vigo authorities warned Spanish and foreign ship owners and captains that they would be held responsible for stowaways escaping on their vessels and demanded that their ships be surveyed night and day.[78]

POLITICAL DISSIDENCE

Desertion, hoarding, theft, tax cheating, and resistance to labor expressed individuals' defiance of the state. Although rarer than personal opposition, political dissidence articulated identification with the leftist enemy or a blatant lack of commitment to the uprising. Enforcers labeled hundreds "hostile to the glorious military movement" in the provinces of Galicia, Zamora, and Asturias and fined them hundreds or even thousands of pesetas each. As had occurred after the repression of the June Days and Paris Commune, the uniformed, including militiamen, were publicly lionized and insults to them might be punished by death. Usually, though, those who proffered verbal abuse to officials were fined several hundred pesetas. As in the postwar period, many violators—although they often paid the lesser fines—were women. A few ill-chosen words concerning the movement or the Falange cost hundreds of pesetas and/or a jail sentence. An upraised clenched fist could provoke an even more punitive response, leading to capital punishment. One Oviedo resident, who had consumed too much alcohol, insulted a Civil Guard and a Falangist. As they detained him, he raised a clenched fist and shouted, "Greetings, comrades." A similar incident occurred in Las Palmas, and the offender received two months of prison. In El Ferrol a sailor was immediately shot after raising a clenched fist during a "patriotic" address. The same occurred in Badajoz when a legionario saw an unsuspecting youngster offer a Popular Front salute to the remains of a downed Republican airplane. A sailor in La Coruña who made a clenched fist to thank his French colleagues for giving him a cigarette was arrested. So were others throughout Galicia who made the same gesture.[79]

A drunken Regular who insulted Spanish authorities, including Franco, received 500 lashes and five years of prison. In Lugo on 20 June 1937, forty "unpatriotic" individuals were fined 50 to 100 pesetas for failing to attend the celebration of the capture of Bilbao. An odd case occurred in Teis (Pontevedra), where a woman allegedly insulted the Generalísimo and threatened to burn the home of her neighbor who was sewing clothes for the army. In another bizarre incident, six in León were fined 500 pesetas each for "hampering the accommodation of the Condor Legion." At the end of 1937 a public fight erupted between pro- and anti-Franco groups in Porriño, one of Galicia's major poultry and porcine centers. The dissidents were detained. Another man who played the Marseillaise and the "abominable" Himno de Riego on his phonograph in the presence of a group of friends was apprehended.[80]

The process of vouching for a friend or relative was taken very seriously as desertions of Republican soldiers to the Nationalists increased. In Asturias, nine, including seven Falangists, had vouched—evidently falsely—for their friends or colleagues who were discovered to have been "red." Others were fined 500 pesetas for the same offense. Normally, authorities required statements of confidence from two persons who were "politically reliable." If the deserter or prisoner for whom they vouched returned to the Republican zone, the guarantors suffered serious penalties. Thus, most deserters to the Nationalist zone, even those of dubious loyalty, were reluctant to betray their guarantors. A word from a priest could condemn or save an individual.[81]

Many other "extremists" (the Nationalists' name for anyone supporting any party of the Popular Front) were jailed. In Burgos alone, as late as 1938, the number of imprisoned never dropped below 1,400. The principal jails of Oviedo province held 6,000 prisoners, a number so large that provincial authorities admitted that it estranged the population. Imprisonment throughout the Nationalist zone rendered inmates almost totally dependent on their families for survival, since jails increasingly lacked basic necessities, including food, as the war endured. Those who were imprisoned suffered diseases similar to their freer comrades in the Republican zone: scabies, typhus, and malnutrition. As a further slap, families were forced to solicit written permission to visit relatives with letters obliged to have the "stamp dedicated to the Army," which cost 0.5 peseta, a price some could not afford. High clergymen were exempted from purchasing postage, another example of the restoration of their old regime privileges.[82]

Theaters were required to introduce or end screenings with a picture of the Caudillo accompanied by the opening bars of the national anthem. After April 1937 all members of the audience were required to stand with their arm raised in the fascist salute as the anthem played. Many citizens felt it was prudent to greet passing troops with the raised arm—labeled the Roman salute. A few courageous individuals resisted the gesture despite a publicity campaign emphasizing that "we are Latin, and it [the raised arm] is the greeting of our race." Women seemed to have been more prominent in this form of nonviolent protest than men. Oviedo authorities pointed out that females were "less cautious than men when expressing their feelings" and were more willing to challenge the regime verbally and symbolically. One señorita was fined 500 pesetas for refusing to raise her arm during the performance of the national anthem. Another young girl was jailed. For the same offense, other señoritas escaped with a fine of only 50 or 25 pesetas. Others were fined half that amount for failure to salute (or to remove hats) before the flag. A twenty-five-year-old señorita who declined to make the Roman salute despite repeated warnings was sanctioned 500 pesetas. She was fortunate given that a resident of Pradoluengo (Burgos) received six years in jail for refusing to remove his hat and for rolling a cigarette during the playing of the national anthem. In Vigo the military governor felt compelled to remind his subjects that "the raised arm is obligatory."[83]

Many Catholics took the compulsion to repeat the Roman salute too far and identified the Redeemer of Mankind with fascism: "Since the beginning of our glorious National Movement we have observed the custom of the faithful to salute sacred images with the raised arm. We do not condemn this custom, which is becoming a tradition, but it is not appropriate for Jesus. The Eucharist should be taken kneeling." The inappropriate raised arm reflected the tensions between the Falange and the church. It also revealed the latter's struggle with the state. Although the church received close cooperation and many privileges from government authorities, the latter wanted to subordinate clerical institutions to its own needs. For example, Asturian provincial authorities were reluctant to return properties—such as the Colegios of Gijón and of Oviedo—to the Jesuits. The Colegio de Gijón had become the Cuartel de Simancas and "one of the feats of the Movement," during which an outmanned unit held off Republican militias for nearly a month at the beginning of the war. Officials argued that it should stay in their hands as a museum. Likewise, they preferred that the Colegio de Oviedo, which the state had reconstructed after the damage of 1934 and which then suffered the terrible siege of that city in 1936, should remain a government building. Yet the church-state conflict should not be exaggerated, and both worked together smoothly and cooperated fully with the Falange in many provinces.[84]

Nationalists were centralizers who had no tolerance for Basque or Catalan "separatisms." Publicly speaking in Catalan outraged Nationalist ideologues, who found that listening to the "regional dialect" was "an evident impertinence" during the war. The Nationalist "liberation" of Catalonia led to the imprisonment of at least one instructor of the Catalan language. Performances of Catalan folk dances (*sardanas*) were usually banned in the Nationalist zone. Like Jews, Catalans were often referred to as "dogs." Their priests and those of the Basques were treated with disrespect when they arrived in the Nationalist zone, and some tried to desert from the crusade. Nevertheless, despite suspicions about their commitment, Catalan-speaking soldiers in the Nationalist army freely communicated among themselves in their native language. During the occupation of parts of Catalonia in April 1938, Nationalist forces were ordered not to punish rural residents for speaking in their native tongue. In Barcelona, officials permitted Catalan to be spoken in the home.[85]

IMMORALITIES

Neotraditionalists attempted to eliminate a wide spectrum of "immoralities," which were almost always associated with sexual transgressions. Civil governors banned variety and "immoral" cabaret shows, which also had an unsavory reputation in the Republican zone. They outlawed advertisements that displayed pictures or drawings of women that offered any hint of nudity. The owner of a León café, which had retained the Gallic name of Lion d'Or, was fined 500 pesetas for the "frankly immoral" performance of the "artist" Gloria, who herself received a 150-peseta sanction. Other cabaret owners were jailed. Hours of establishments serving alcohol were limited, and those violating the restrictions fined. In Vigo, military authorities banned pedestrian circulation after 12:30 a.m. The repressive civil governor of Vigo, Gómez Cantos, closed taverns at 9:00 p.m, bars and restaurants at 11:00 p.m., and cafés and casinos at 12:30 or 1:00 a.m. He fined three tavern owners 90 pesetas each and each late-drinking customer 15 pesetas. In recently "liberated" Asturias the civil government outlawed female singers and cabarets for violating "our regime of austerity." Female waiters lost their jobs, and streetwalking was prohibited. One hundred peseta fines enforced a curfew. Canary authorities shut establishments of food, drink, or entertainment between 11:00 p.m. and 2:00 a.m. to prevent "immorality" and to promote an alert work force.[86]

However hypocritically, the state tolerated, taxed, and controlled prostitution. In the Republican zone, leftist organizations, such as the CNT, tried to organize pleasure professionals as a group of exploited proletarians who should become productive wage earners or committed milicianas. In contrast, in the Nationalist zone the role of sex workers altered little after 18 July. Publicly proclaimed puritanism by chaplains and other authorities did not prevent officially tolerated private pleasures. Legionarios were notorious for their female companions, wives, girlfriends, *cantineras*, *putas*, and *vivandières*, who courageously followed them to the frontlines. A Jesuit chaplain complained fruitlessly of the irradicable culture of "wine, gambling, and sex" among his men. Despite his relentless opposition and his attempt to draw a sharp distinction between virtuous Christian women and loose "red" ones, his legionarios continued to frequent prostitutes at the Madrid front. To add insult to injury, they tried to convince the chaplain, who was aware that many had left their wives at home, to allow them to marry their frontline female companions. Despite his opposition to vivandières, another chaplain, when seriously wounded in battle on the Madrid front, gratefully accepted the aid of a legionaria. To paraphrase the Americans, "there are no wounded sexists in foxholes." As in the Republican army, Nationalist soldiers received lectures about avoiding venereal disease, often to little effect. Masturbation was discreetly tolerated.[87]

The war separated husbands from wives and eliminated male bread-winners, leaving women and children destitute. Not surprisingly, in the Nationalist zone prostitution grew considerably, despite opposition from pros-elytizing and prudish Catholics. The large number of soldiers who had to be cured of syphilis repulsed a military chaplain who served as a hospital aide. Antivenereal clinics, which examined both female pleasure professionals and their clients, existed in cities throughout the Nationalist zone. Both Oviedo (population 75,000) and Vigo (population 66,000) had at least four private physicians who specialized in the treatment of venereal diseases.[88]

Prosecutors worried as much about underage prostitution as they did about juvenile delinquency. Many pleasure professionals began their careers at thir-teen years old. In Santa Cruz de Tenerife, a port city with a large number of sailors and tourists, the number of "clandestine prostitutes" was double the figure of women officially enrolled. An unknown number of covert minors provided the same services as 130 adult women enrolled in the thirty-three official brothels of the Canary capital. Authorities claimed that the minors were responsible for the spread of venereal diseases. In this city alone, 24,000 persons were treated annually by the Dispensario Antivenéreo, one of the busiest in Spain. Authorities admitted that treatment for "contagious prosti-tutes" was "totally deficient." They blamed the proliferation of streetwalkers on the "amorality" of the "lower class," which viewed the sale of women's bodies as perfectly acceptable. In the countryside, religious instruction, in-cluding baptism, was totally absent, and even civil marriage was rare. The pleasure professionals seemed even more apolitical than other deideologized occupational groups, such as peasants.[89]

Huesca's regulatory system organized regular inspection two times per week for each of its seventy officially recognized prostitutes. Authorities wanted to expand the inspections to include unregistered female sex vendors, who were often employed as waitresses in cabarets. During the war years venereal disease increased, especially among soldiers. Huesca health-care personnel treated 839 cases in 1936 and 1937. Granada's experience was similar. Prostitutes were is-sued identity cards containing a number and a photograph. The women were obligated to appear at the clinic—financed by monthly taxes on the madams of the "tolerated establishments"—twice per week. Yet, as in Santa Cruz de Tenerife, unregistered minors who exercised "underground prostitution" provided another source of uncontrolled infection. In Ávila all women working in bordellos were also subject to regular medical control at the clinic, where women and men—the latter almost always soldiers—had separate consulting hours so that they would not mix. The military adopted a similar system of disease control for the hundreds of Moroccan prostitutes who had been given permission to cross from Africa.[90]

Provincial leaders refused to consider abolishing their regulated system of prostitution while the war lasted. Authorities realized the hypocritical nature of the toleration, which encouraged the expansion of clandestine and juvenile prostitution, but concluded that *reglamentación* was the preferred solution under the circumstances. Whatever its disadvantages, regulation was generally seen as effective in reducing venereal disease, the most important consideration for the undoubtedly sexist health authorities. Nevertheless, one expert objected to the continuation of tolerated prostitution on Christian and practical grounds. He argued that the state should not encourage vice, that abolition would reduce venereal diseases even more than regulation, and that it was unfair to hold only one group of women responsible for the misbehavior of many in both sexes.[91]

Repression centered on clandestine sex workers. Female streetwalkers and male homosexuals were fined or imprisoned. In La Coruña two men were jailed fifteen days, and five women were penalized 75 pesetas each for "immorality." In Las Palmas, police searched for a German pornographer who had also engaged in "white slavery." In Galicia five women were fined 1,000 to 1,500 pesetas for "covert prostitution." Another 50 pesetas was levied for the same offense. Yet another was sanctioned for trying to prevent the closing of a bordello. In León, secretly plying her trade cost a woman 200 pesetas.[92]

Blasphemy also became a serious crime, "an attack on social morality," and an "individual failing." By virtue of the law of 29 August 1882 to protect "public decency," Serrano Súñer ordered his governors to eliminate "blasphemy against God and the Saints." Blasphemers were fined—sometimes hundreds of pesetas if their economic and social position merited it—jailed, or forced to clean public toilets. Bystanders were encouraged to denounce them to rid the streets of the vulgarity that had supposedly proliferated from 1931 to 1936. Parents were held responsible for their children's words and deeds. Despite triumphalist rhetoric, in Vigo repression was ineffective since "blasphemy returned as in the worst periods" and petty urban criminals once again converted the city into "a moral garbage dump." Immediately after the war the governor ordered his police to halt "children climbing on streetcars, playing ball in the street, shoeless, abandoned, and cursing." These children embarrassed "persons of order and, above all, foreigners."[93]

As part of their project to "re-Christianize" Spain, straitlaced army chaplains wanted to clean up the allegedly foul language of the Republican period. Yet they became frustrated by their lonely struggles against the everyday blasphemy of the troops and insisted—with limited success—on the punishment of swearing soldiers. Some chaplains attempted to limit profanity by fining soldiers, but one Jesuit admitted that if the fines had been applied consistently, they could have quickly purchased a battleship. Instead of using the collected fines for patriotic or humanitarian purposes, he wisely decided to employ them to hold "a banquet without precedents." Fines, reprimands, and moral instruction were all imposed with only limited results. Without severe repression, such as denial of leave, prohibitions on blasphemy were seldom effective among soldiers, who continued to use colorful and vulgar language at will. As in all armies, most appreciated off-color jokes. Pragmatic chaplains felt compelled to tolerate the steady flow of curses. During the war, a few fanatics even attempted to get their Republican prisoners to obey the anticursing rules. After the conflict ended, they and their supporters in the Church sponsored concrete measures in the form of propaganda and repressive legislation to extend the campaign to all of "liberated" Spain. Indeed, in his elderly years Franco nursed the illusion that he had eliminated blasphemy from his country. The emphasis on sanitizing popular language took a turn toward xenophobia. Commercial signs with foreign names were sometimes banned and their owners fined.[94]

Popular behavior in the Nationalist zone did not entirely conform to the orders and wishes of its authorities. Military officers, clergymen, and Falangists were forced to combat not only the Republican enemy but also the economic, political, and sexual misbehavior of their own citizens. Their authoritarian state was much less successful in fighting this guerrilla war than it was on the regular battlefield.

Conclusion
Flawed Victory

The conventional political and diplomatic perspective on the Spanish civil war has focused on the supply of arms to the Popular Army following the Battle of the Ebro. Franquistas insist that the Republic had enough military resources to continue the struggle, whereas Republicans blame the failure to fight on the "betrayal" of the democracies. This political and diplomatic orientation neglects the Republican zone's inability to feed itself. Neither its own production nor imports from the USSR, France, Mexico, and other nations were able to prevent hunger, which delegitimized the Republican regime. In the last months of the war Madrid residents were receiving officially only 100 grams of bread daily plus several hundred grams of rice, beans, or lentils every other day. Tinned or frozen meat was limited to 100 grams per month. Hunger prevents both civilians and soldiers from laboring or fighting and forces them to spend their day hunting for food. Starving women scoured parks and fields near the city for anything edible. Only good connections allowed access to horse, donkey, or mule meat.[1]

As has been seen, this consumption of draft animals, which were essential for plowing and harvesting, was disastrous for Republican agriculture. To overcome the lack of meat, cramped balconies and apartments served as hen houses, and their owners could be seen walking their chickens on leashes on city streets. Republican money became worthless, and only through barter were basic commodities acquired. Cats and dogs metamorphosized into delicacies. Desperate men and women formed long queues outside military barracks to receive the scanty remains of soldiers' meals. As in Russia during its civil war, the elderly who were unable to travel to the suburbs or into the countryside were at a great disadvantage during this struggle for survival. With terrible irony, the vulnerability of the old and the extensive queues in Republican Spain prefigured the misery of the years that immediately followed the Nationalist triumph. Republicans committed the same error as Chinese Nationalists who overestimated the importance of the urban sector and of controlling major cities in a largely agrarian nation. In contrast, Nationalist

Spain was able to satisfy its rural base, which generally grew enough food to supply its military and civilian population. In addition to the clergy, its staunchest supporters were rural property owners who felt that Republican reforms threatened their interests. The Nationalist counterrevolution secured their property and provided sufficient incentives for agricultural production.

When Nationalists conquered the major cities—Barcelona, Madrid, and Valencia—in early 1939, nurturing hungry urban populations became their most urgent and largest problem. In 1939 the AS managed 2,487 canteens (comedores), 1,561 soup kitchens (cocinas de hermandad), and 3,000 child-care centers (centros infantiles). Hundreds of train wagons and motorized vehicles from almost every province conveyed tens of thousands of kilos of provisions to Barcelona and Madrid. SNAT hired ships to supply "the entire nation. . . . Prices rose, but we tried to eliminate hoarding and speculating."[2]

On 18 May 1939 SNAT introduced a national system of rationing that placed price controls on the most common foods. The system of enforced price controls has been termed a franquista "agrarian counterrevolution." Instead, it should be seen as a measure that continued the misguided and antiliberal policies of the Nationalists' Republican foes. Economically, the civil war continued, and the dubious model of the Republican zone—where unrealistic price controls provoked the urban hunger they were designed to counter—took root throughout Franco's New Spain. Overly low Nationalist price controls expanded the incipient black market that was developing during the war. Instead of changing their approach, authorities tried to blame shortages on the "reds'" destruction of the economic infrastructure. However, economic damage in Spain was considerable but less than that of the U.S., Russian, or Chinese civil wars.[3]

The unofficial economy exploded in nearly all provinces (see appendix). In León tens of thousands of pesetas in fines were levied on sellers of ham, sugar, and other merchandise. In Oviedo 62 merchants were sanctioned from 100 to 10,000 pesetas for violating price controls and other regulations. A military tribunal sentenced a Catalan who sold olive oil at three times the tasa to fifteen years in prison. Animal feed was snapped up at any price. Two villagers from Villalube had 882 lambs confiscated and were jailed for transporting them outside Zamora province without authorization. Violators were declared "armchair Jews" and, less innovatively, "greedy Jews" and "hunger profiteers." Producers refused to declare their harvests and constantly trafficked in illegal goods.[4]

One of the best provincial examples of the growth of the black market occurred in Pontevedra. In April 1939 its new civil governor, the former Civil Guard commander Manuel Gómez Cantos, claimed to have "stopped the fish price hikes" by ordering the mayors of Vigo, Marín, and Villagarcía to halt any exports not accompanied by the appropriate travel documents. Gómez Cantos demanded "unquestioned obedience to superiors." He visited the markets himself to stop "the total anarchy" or the nonapplication of price controls that had apparently occurred before he had been named governor. Thus, he implicitly accused his more pragmatic successors of tolerating free markets. As mentioned, price controls were a defense of urban interests; conversely, the struggle against the unofficial economy attempted to subordinate producers of commodities to the needs of urban consumers. Gómez Cantos either fined 75 pesetas or jailed for fifteen days approximately forty fishwives who had disobeyed regulations concerning the sale of seafood. Moreover, the new governor prohibited hotel, restaurant, and bar owners from monopolizing large quantities of seafood and raising prices for the rest of the public. He fined a fishing fleet owner 10,000 pesetas for violating rules on sales of fresh seafood, a fish merchant 5,000, and the leather union 5,000 for overcharging for soles. He sanctioned and jailed others. The governor attempted to profit from the populist resentment of many Gallegans against their industrial elite of mostly Catalan origin. The latter may have protested to the Ministry of Commerce and Industry, which often attempted quietly to defend fined businessmen.[5]

The press reported many women—presumably shoppers, not sellers— were enthusiastic about the actions of the governor, who lowered food costs and the price of fish by 25 percent. They awarded him with a "thunderous ovation" when he visited the markets, and "hundreds" of Vigo women demonstrated in his favor on the city's streets. Gómez Cantos also reduced rents to their legal levels from the market prices that landlords had established prior to his appointment. Yet *El Pueblo Gallego* may have been premature in celebrating the governor's triumph, since, predictably enough, "resistance" to price controls continued. For example, Gómez Cantos levied four fines of 1,000 pesetas for violating price controls, thirty of 500 for not posting them, and three others of 300. Eventually, 400 Vigo merchants were fined 500 pesetas for failure to post prices. Merchants maintained their practice of serving—regardless of their place in the queue—customers who would pay more than the tasa. Shopkeepers then claimed to the others who had patiently remained in line that their stocks were exhausted. Alternatively, they would sell at the tasa only to friends and confidants.[6]

The press implausibly asserted that during his first two weeks in office, the governor had succeeded in eliminating hunger. As in other provinces, fines continued to shower on violators of economic controls. Gómez Cantos was ready to levy even more sanctions, but like many other civil governors, he found his mayors rather uncooperative. He would attempt to replace many whom he called "cacique mayors" with "real Spaniards" whose reputation was guaranteed by the parish priest, local Falange boss, and veterans from elite units. To enforce his controls, he engaged in an orgy of sanctions and imposed nearly 17,000 pesetas in fines in several days. The governor was disappointed with fishing fleet owners who had promised to supply free fish to the poor of the province. Instead, they neglected their charitable commitment, and their vessels sailed to other ports where their catch fetched a higher price. In addition, during the war they had pocketed "fantastic profits by exporting fish to the fronts," and he fined them 3,000 each.[7]

Like fleet owners, fabric merchants of Vigo and Pontevedra defied the tasa. Poor quality and underweight bread and meat continued to plague the markets. So did hoarding, whose authors were fined thousands of pesetas and jailed. The authoritarianism of Gómez Cantos struck the powerful. The industrialist Gaspar Massó was sanctioned "1,500 pesetas for speaking inappropriately and irately to his superior about the issue of travel permits." The governor's policies strictly limited travel outside the province and even place of residence. Although the repression was seemingly egalitarian, it was ineffective. The governor was forced to institute bread rationing and limit daily consumption to 280 grams per person. During his trip to Andalusia to deliver funds directly to Queipo de Llano for the martyred Virgen de la Cabeza (whose sanctuary 1,500 Nationalist soldiers and civilians had bravely defended during the first nine months of the war), Gómez Cantos promised to investigate what he suspected to be illicit trafficking of olive oil to his province. The continuing queues and the severe shortages of oil, potatoes, and rice throughout Spain were implausibly blamed on "Marxist" destruction and theft. The governor used the same repressive threats against "bloodsucking" flour traders as he had against olive oil merchants, and the results were equally disappointing: "Because I refused profiteering, our province has no flour or bread, but I promise the public that I shall solve this in the combative style of our Caudillo." Like Stalin or Mao, the Caudillo may have had military successes, but for decades in peacetime he offered an inadequate economic model. In important cities, long queues reminiscent of the Republican period formed to wait fruitlessly for oil and other provisions. Frustrated consumers, it was implied, had sometimes turned violent. In the city of Pontevedra, queues were prohibited. In Gijón, some braved the long lines with the goal of reselling the purchases that they had made at the controlled price.[8]

At the end of the war, many provinces suffered from a lack of affordable fabric and shoes. Neither buyers nor sellers respected price controls on footwear. Catalan textile factories were saddled with tens of thousands of pesetas in fines for overcharging. Textile manufacturers hoarded their production, refusing to sell it at state-regulated prices. SNAT considered this resistance "a serious defiance of authorities." Merchants completely disregarded price controls on clothes. SNAT called on shop owners to denounce manufacturers who overcharged. Like Gómez Cantos, Seville's mayor felt compelled to engage in personal inspections of the markets to ensure that prices conformed to norms and to encourage distrustful citizens to report contraventions. Even so, authorities noted that merchandise was still being hidden and sold clandestinely. Queues in front of stores selling sugar were officially banned, but the prohibition was often ignored. Soap was sold at prices well above the tasa.[9]

The black market—an arena of egotism and survival—consumed almost 28 percent of national production and would reach 38 percent in 1942–43. Agricultural workers participated in it as both consumers and producers. Often paid in kind, rural laborers also took advantage of the immediate postwar conjuncture to demand higher salaries. In Tarragona they received three times the official wage.[10] They and the campesinos could also profit, however modestly, from the unofficial economy, a development that many historians of the regime who insist only on the links between franquismo and big capital have ignored. Autarky, price controls, and the resulting *estraperlo* that many have interpreted as a defense of the rural oligarchy also acted as a form of protectionism for smaller and less efficient peasants. The black market offered them artificially high and tax-free profits that allowed them to survive much longer than they would have in a regime more favorable to the free market.

Furthermore, Marxist historians have not been sufficiently materialist and have ignored the financial reasons for relative worker quiescence in the Nationalist zone both during and immediately after the war. They have attributed tranquility solely to terror, but some provinces were only very lightly policed and needed many more Civil Guards. Agricultural workers, fishermen, and sometimes miners could survive and even profit from a climate of labor shortages and de facto wage creep. The adaptability of the regime—the quality that led it to survive World War II and to adopt new market-oriented policies in the 1950s—reflected the opportunism of many ordinary Spaniards. Paradoxically, corruption was both a form of resistance to the regime and accommodation with it. The successfully corrupt profited or at least ate. Those who did not have opportunities to engage in illegal activities suffered. Starvation—especially of widows, children, and the elderly on public assistance—spread throughout the country, and the period following the conflict became known as "the years of hunger." However, it should not be forgotten that much of rural Spain ate what it grew, as had occurred before, during, and after the civil war.[11]

In contrast to other counterrevolutionary movements, Nationalist Spain experienced a great rise of corruption at the end, rather than at the beginning of its civil war (see appendix). In other words, flexibility morphed into corruption. Remarkably, until the last stages of the war, the army was relatively honest, in contrast to other counterrevolutionary movements. In the first years of the war, price controls functioned relatively effectively, as they had during the French Revolution's Reign of Terror or in Great Britain during World War II. During the final year of conflict, when victory seemed within reach, some soldiers, including those from elite units, felt free to loot liquor

stores or take trains without purchasing a ticket. With the conquest of Barcelona in February 1939, military personnel acquired a sense of entitlement
after winning a war of attrition. Requetés began to "requisition" vehicles not
for military purposes but for joy riding. In response to soldiers' cannibal-
izing requisitioned automobiles, on 16 March 1939 Franco issued an order
aimed at documenting the origins of all parts used by garages and repair
shops. Requetés stole animals or vegetables from gardens and farms in the
proximity of train stations and traded military supplies (boots, blankets, and
articles of clothing) for food and other products. In Córdoba the army seized
large amounts of grain. In that province the 230 Batallón de Oviedo raided a
granary, the Almacenes de Castro del Río, to feed their animals. Immediately
after the conflict ended, the army monopolized and stole humanitarian supplies.[12] Victorious soldiers no longer delayed gratification.

In León provincial officials tried to suppress an incipient black market and
hoarding of animal feed by campesinos who reasoned that the official price
was too low. Dozens of villagers were fined various amounts at the end of the
war for refusal to deliver their assigned share of straw or oats to the military.
Peasant hoarding of wheat became more common at the end of 1938. Wholesalers, too, held onto their wares to profit from inevitably rising prices. Warehousemen and labradores ignored the needs of the state and in the beginning
of 1939 kept a good portion of their grain for themselves.[13] The peasant base
of the Nationalist movement began to initiate its own autarky, which—as in
the Republican zone during the civil war—would starve urban residents. The
latter could subscribe to the morbid German witticism as the end of World
War II approached: "Enjoy the war, the peace will be worse."

When Nationalist victory became inevitable, sacrifice gave way to petty
profiteering. Corrupt railroad employees had to be bribed to allow priority
transport. Individual labradores gave them tips of 10 to 15 pesetas to facilitate shipments, payments that shocked SNT officials, who realized that their
organization would also have to pay bribes to get rapid delivery. Sufficient
wheat supplies existed, but train transportation became a bottleneck, thus
giving railroad workers a powerful bargaining position, similar to the widespread corruption of train personnel in the Russian civil war. Railroad workers allowed forbidden shipments of hundreds of kilos of seafood to Madrid
and other cities. They must have received significant kickbacks, since fresh
seafood was at a premium in urban Spain. One illegal operation involved at
least seven persons. In León and Asturias, where operations against guerrillas continued in the aftermath of the war, railroad workers, including con-
ductors, subtly siphoned small quantities of good wine from barrels. Trains
carrying coal doused the tops of their cars with lime to discourage pilferers.
Thefts increased in the countryside, where the poor continued their venerable
tradition of illegally gleaning from the fields.[14]

Local leaders of the Falange were sometimes the most egregious black marketeers. One in Busdongo (Asturias), who was a rancher and butcher, clandestinely marketed his meat products to certain shops in León. Indifference and apathy toward the Falange spread among its own militants, who neglected both their duties and their dues. The state became less zealous in prosecuting offenders, especially the largest and most powerful of them. The upper and middle classes had accepted taxation to pay for the war; however, once the conflict ended, they refused to tax themselves to improve education, transportation, and public health. In 1948 Spaniards paid 15 percent of the national income as taxes compared with 21 percent in France and Italy and 33 percent in Great Britain. Paradoxically, the failure of the regime's economic policies put the self-proclaimed autarkic Nationalists at the mercy of foreign suppliers. In April 1939, under pressure from the democracies supplying food aid, the highest officials of the regime, including the Caudillo, were obliged to guarantee that food stolen from humanitarian organizations would be returned.[15]

Franco's elite forces—not conscripts—bore the brunt of the fighting in the first two years of the conflict. Not until 1938 did the Generalísimo begin to use his new mass army of over 1 million men, but elite troops still did much of the bloodiest work in every major battle, including the Ebro. Perhaps it was this reliance on a limited number of relatively well-trained and motivated shock troops—Regulares, legionnaires, requetés, and Falangists—and not Franco's own personal desire to monopolize power that lengthened the war. It must be remembered that the Spanish civil war remained a trench war during which the defense had a distinct advantage, and consequently, "decisive breakthroughs" were nearly as rare as in other trench wars, such as the American Civil War or World War I. No historian has argued that the Great War became a war of attrition because a general or a political leader wanted to consolidate his political and military power. In contrast, traditional political, diplomatic, and military historians have posited that the Generalísimo deliberately waged an overly cautious campaign to consolidate his political position.[16] The Caudillo supposedly desired a long war in order to eliminate his political opposition in both zones. Perhaps, though, a quick war would have served this purpose even more.

Traditional history from above with its concentration on leadership has ignored the experiences of the rank-and-file and instead has focused on the activities of political and military elites. Franco is assumed to have planned and managed the operations and pace of the war virtually alone, but, as has been seen, the men who fought for these elites were not easily manipulated. Soldiers demanded that their commanders fulfill an unwritten contract to satisfy their basic needs and appetites, which made logistical organization a top priority. Rather than attributing the length of the war to Franco's supposed plan to subordinate all political opposition to his personal rule, it is equally if not more plausible to claim that the lack of commitment by many soldiers on both sides created a war of attrition during which those who mastered the political economy of warfare emerged victoriously. Although certain historians have engaged in a healthy debunking of the Caudillo after his long reign of enforced hero worship, to label him as "incompetent" seems doubtful. Such a judgment also reveals the lack of a comparative perspective. Franco was the most successful counterrevolutionary of the twentieth century and proved more competent than Chiang, Denikin, Wrangel, or Kolchak.

To these methodological objections, it should be added that a number of Franco's biographers depict him as highly cautious throughout his life. After all, he became known as "Miss Canary Islands" for his refusal to commit himself fully to the military conspiracy until the assassination of Calvo Sotelo.[17] During the war, the Generalísimo came to be a prudent and thoughtful strategist, hostile to any improvisation, an admirer of the French army and its methods, and, therefore, concerned about logistics and territorial control. He believed in amassing his troops at strategic points and securing their rear but was opposed to a lightning or mechanical war, which young European officers pioneered during the 1930s and which the Germans and Italians put into practice at the beginning of World War II. It could be argued that Franco recognized relatively early that the conflict would develop into a war of attrition and that his priorities were to ensure that his troops had the manpower and means to outlast the enemy. This might explain his attention to logistical support and proverbial caution better than his alleged—and incredibly risky—desire to make the war last so that he could consolidate his own political position. In other words, after the failure to take Madrid, his model became the Allied victory in World War I, not the African colonial wars or the future Blitzkrieg. Like Marshal Pétain during World War I, Franco eventually eschewed the "decisive battle," whether the quick capture of Madrid or Barcelona, in favor of wearing down a logistically inferior enemy. In that sense he welcomed the Republican offensives at Brunete, Belchite, Teruel, and the Ebro.

Nationalist competence puts noninterventionist policies in a new light. The Western democracies have been frequently criticized for failing to intervene on the side of the legal and "democratic" Republic. However, as has been seen, foreign aid was no guarantee of victory in the major revolutionary or counterrevolutionary civil wars of the twentieth century. It cannot be assumed that significant aid to the Spanish Republic by one or more great democratic powers would have succeeded in defeating the Nationalists. Furthermore, if Western democratic assistance had failed to defeat the Insurgents, the consequences might have been profound. Elite and popular opinion in the United States or Great Britain could have become more isolationist or appeasement oriented in the face of the reinforced Nazi and Fascist threat. The democracies might have been even more inclined to permit the Axis to dominate the European continent.

The Nationalist victory also has implications for the study of other civil wars. Recent works on the Russian civil war have argued that it was the Whites' political mistakes that cost them victory. In deciding the outcome of the Russian struggle, political failures were allegedly more decisive than military ones. The Bolsheviks supposedly understood far better than their enemies the political aspects of civil war. During the civil war the Communists achieved a "primitive accumulation of legitimacy" that eluded the Whites.[18] Anti-Communist scholars have emphasized the profound unpopularity of both sides and have argued that the Whites' political failures prevented them from winning. Yet the Spanish Nationalist military leadership was as reactionary and nearly as contemptuous of "politics" as Russian counterrevolutionaries. It made virtually no concessions to "moderate" opinion and never tried, as the Whites sporadically did, to win over the Spanish equivalent of Mensheviks. Spanish Nationalists thus had an even narrower political coalition than the Whites, who gained ephemeral support from Russian liberals (Cadets) and even from some Socialists. The Nationalist program of fighting "for Spain" was as vague as the Whites' struggle "for Russia." Like their Russian counterparts, the Spanish generals believed that military should take precedence over civilian authority. They never established a civilian government, a reason often given for the Whites' failure to win over the population.

It is nearly universally argued that the Whites should have made concessions to national minorities (Finns, Ukrainians, Poles, and others) who would then have assisted them in defeating the Bolsheviks. The counterrevolutionaries' "obsession" with "Russian nationalism" purportedly had "disastrous consequences."[19] However, their dependence on good relations with national minorities and secessionist states was, in part, a reflection of their inability to secure their rear. With a solid base in the countryside, which was a prerequisite for a healthy political economy, the Spanish Nationalists were as intransigent and as tactless concerning Basque and Catalan nationalisms as the Whites with regard to Poles, Finns, and Ukrainians. This failure to compromise with national minorities is even more striking, since the separatist regions of Spain were the most industrialized parts of the country. Furthermore, Iberian nationalisms of the periphery were much more hostile to Spanish counterrevolutionaries than the new nations of the defunct Empire were to Russian counterrevolutionaries. Iberian national minorities—Catalans and Basques—mobilized and fought for the Republic, whereas those of the Russian Empire resisted both Whites and Reds. If White inflexibility on the nationalities' question was a decisive factor in the outcome of the Russian conflict, then the victory of Spanish Nationalists was truly extraordinary.

Historians of China acknowledge GMD corruption and incompetence, but they often attribute the Communist victory to the party's land reform program, which supposedly won over the village "masses." Similarly but from another angle, historians have ascribed the failure of Chinese Nationalists to their disinterest in "fundamental [political] reforms" or "social and economic reforms which would have contributed to the people's welfare." The Chinese Nationalist military-authoritarian regime lacked "a base in society." The GMD "failed at creating the alliances that would have been necessary to uphold its rule." Yet the decisiveness of political and social reforms in the Communist victory in the civil war is debatable. Undoubtedly, "the CCP secured the support of a significant number of rural dwellers in Northeast China through its revolutionary program." "But," another historian adds, "its dedication to redressing the gross inequalities in land distribution in rural areas probably did the party as much harm as good in its military and political struggle to defeat the Guomindang. . . . One of the reasons the CCP won was that Mao Zedong was brought to realize early enough—by 1947—that in the new areas the party controlled, the wartime policy of rent reductions and debt settlements was the maximum social program that could be introduced."[20]

Chinese Communists—like Spanish Nationalists—limited the size of their armies and avoided conscripting more soldiers than they could feed. CCP ability to furnish its troops may be as important in explaining Communist success as political indoctrination and social reforms in Communist-controlled areas. During the revolutionary civil war in the northeast, the CCP recruited approximately 1 million men. The party made sure that the noncombatant laborers that it drafted were given adequate supplies and that provisions were made for their dependents. On the other hand, like many Popular Army soldiers, lower-ranking Chinese Nationalist troops often deserted because of inadequate rations. Both Spanish Nationalist and Chinese Communist propaganda effectively exploited the logistic failures of their enemies. The CCP's ability to organize efficiently a wartime economy fostered its victory. A viable currency encouraged the circulation of goods and allowed the collection of taxes. The Chinese Communists limited their looting and corruption. The PLA and Communist officials won a reputation for hard work and honesty.[21]

The failure of counterrevolutionaries in China and Russia helps to highlight the factors that founded the success of the Spanish Nationalists. They were able to establish a solid currency, limit inflation, and collect taxes. Mercenaries, farmers, and industrialists sought their money. Incentives to agriculturists and the food processors generated enough calories for soldiers and civilians. Motor and animal transport moved necessities relatively efficiently. Health and postal services functioned well. In contrast, the Republic suffered from hyperinflation and an inability to tax. Peasants did not want Republican money and frequently returned to self-sufficiency. Thus, civilians and soldiers in the Republican zone experienced more hunger than in the Nationalist zone. Popular Army troops had less respect for private property, were less disciplined, and looted more regularly than Nationalist forces. The latter repeated the successes of the nineteenth-century French counterrevolutionaries who could call upon rural support to crush urban revolutionaries during the June Days of 1848 and the Paris Commune of 1871.

The bourgeoisie has often been seen as the class that fostered individualism and made egotism into social policy, in contrast to the working class, which is identified with doctrines of solidarity. The Russian and Chinese civil wars lend some credibility to this argument. In both cases, the Communists, who purportedly represented the working class, defeated a self-indulgent and centrifugal coalition of defenders of the owners of the means of production. However, if the Spanish civil war is seen as a class war, the bourgeoisie displayed more cohesion than the working class. Its doctrines of nation, property rights, and religion provoked greater loyalties than the competing ones of internationalism, revolution, and collectivism. Many bourgeois contributed decisively to the success of the counterrevolution by reestablishing their businesses and devoting them to the service of the Nationalists. The trauma of civil war—like that of 1848 in France—led many large and small property owners and others who desired order to return to the faith of their mothers. Like their French counterparts, they were happy to enroll in counterrevolutionary forces and fight for a regime that would offer them an authoritarian political economy and a cultural, although hypocritical, neotraditionalism.

The different trajectories of traditional ruling classes in Spain, Russia, and China during their counterrevolutions in the first half of the twentieth century give some indication of the contrasting positions of these nations at its end. In the 1930s, Spanish counterrevolutionaries proved efficient enough to defeat the Republic. By the late 1950s, they abandoned autarkic rigidity and returned to the more flexible policies that had led them to victory during their civil war. Thus, the late Franco regime began to participate in the Western European industrial and consumer revolutions. Spain modernized along capitalist lines and eventually joined the European Community. Of course, the twentieth-century trajectory of Russia was radically distinct. In the aftermath of their defeat, Russian counterrevolutionaries were killed or exiled. The Bolsheviks destroyed the old aristocracy and bourgeoisie. After the 1920s, the Soviet state modernized heavy industry at great cost, but the USSR remained largely outside the global economy. Only with the fall of Communism would it begin to become integrated—primarily as a provider of raw materials. Chinese Communists showed their flexibility during their civil war. Their pragmatism stands out as much as their redistribution of land. After their victory in civil war, they reverted to Stalinist-like collectivization—the Great Leap

Forward—at a terrible price. In the 1960s they invented their own bloody and counterproductive Cultural Revolution. The adaptability that was evidenced during their civil war reemerged only after 1980, when China—like Spain under Franco—became home to massive investments by capitalist multinational corporations.

Spain's industrial revolution during the long 1960s transformed the nation from a rural into an urban society. The rural material and cultural base that had sustained the victorious counterrevolution disappeared. The proletariat and the small owners in the countryside emigrated to Spanish or northern European cities, compelling the latifundistas to become more productive with fewer laborers. Spanish Catholic neotraditionalism had founded a mass political movement in the 1930s, but by the end of the Franco regime, it had lost its constituency. Its sustaining ideologies—anti-Communism, anti-Masonry, anti-Semitism, and anti-Protestantism—either dissolved or took new forms. Hostility to modernity could not survive in a new Spain, which was generally tolerant and overwhelmingly urban.

Appendix

Fines for Price Control Violations

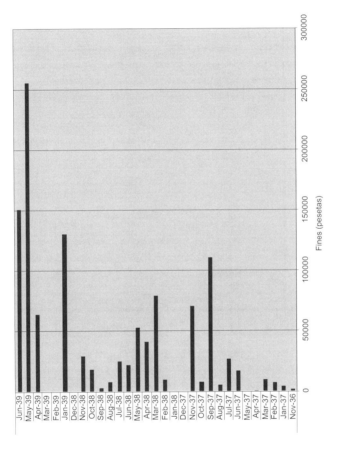

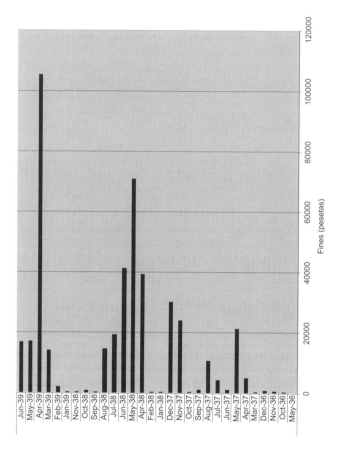

Fines (pesetas)

Source: *El Pueblo Gallego* (Vigo)

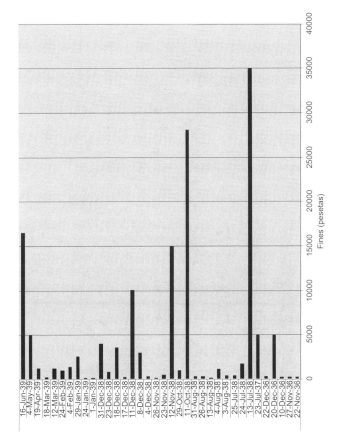

Fines (pesetas)

Source: *Proa* (León)

261

262

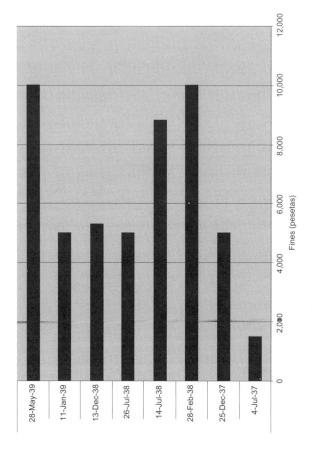

Fines (pesetas)

Source: *La Provincia* (Las Palmas [Gran Canaria])

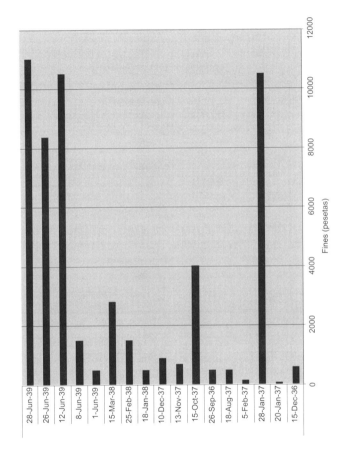

Source: *El Correo de Zamora* (Zamora)

263

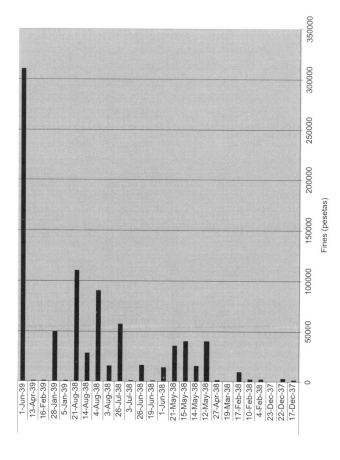

1-Jun-39
13-Apr-39
16-Feb-39
28-Jan-39
5-Jan-39
21-Aug-38
14-Aug-38
4-Aug-38
3-Aug-38
26-Jul-38
3-Jul-38
26-Jun-38
19-Jun-38
1-Jun-38
21-May-38
15-May-38
14-May-38
12-May-38
27-Apr-38
19-Mar-38
17-Feb-38
10-Feb-38
4-Feb-38
23-Dec-37
22-Dec-37
17-Dec-37

0   50000   100000   150000   200000   250000   300000   350000

Fines (pesetas)

Source: *La Nueva España* (Oviedo)

Notes

INTRODUCTION

1. James Simpson, "Economic Development in Spain, 1850–1936," *Economic History Review* 2 (1997): 349; Javier Tébar Hurtado, *Reforma, revolución y contrarrevolución agraria: Conflicto social y lucha política en el campo (1931–1939)* (Barcelona, 2006), 27; Stathis N. Kalyvas, "How Not to Compare Civil Wars: Greece and Spain," in Martin Baumeister and Stefanie Schüler-Springorum, eds., *"If You Tolerate This . . .": The Spanish Civil War in the Age of Total War* (New York, 2008), 259. Cf. Philip B. Minehan, *Civil War and World War in Europe: Spain, Yugoslavia, and Greece, 1936–1939* (New York, 2006), 4, 23.

2. Fernando del Rey, *Paisanos en lucha: Exclusión política y violencia en la Segunda República española* (Madrid, 2008), 186; Antonio Cazorla Sánchez, *Las políticas de la victoria: La consolidación del Nuevo Estado franquista (1938–1953)* (Madrid, 2000), 14; Jesús Palacios and Stanley G. Payne, *Franco, mi padre: Testimonio de Carmen Franco, la hija del Caudillo* (Madrid, 2008), 289; Javier Ugarte Tellería, *La nueva Covadonga insurgente: Orígenes sociales y culturales de la sublevación de 1936 en Navarra y el País Vasco* (Madrid, 1998), 308, 405.

3. Cf. Paul Preston, *The Spanish Civil War: Reaction, Revolution, and Revenge* (New York, 2006), 4.

4. Cf. Julián Casanova, "Pasado y presente de la Guerra civil española," *Historia Social* 60 (2008): 119: "The most important facts of the Civil War have been discovered and the most significant questions answered."

5. Arno Mayer, *The Dynamics of Counter-revolution* (New York, 1971).

6. Preston, *Spanish Civil War*, 128: "Since Non-intervention was to be an empty farce, cynically exploited by Germany and Italy, and later by the Soviet Union, the Spanish Republic was in fact doomed"; Helen Graham, *The Spanish Civil War: A Very Short Introduction* (New York, 2005), iii; Minehan, *Civil War and World War*, 249, 303. For the Communist analysis, see José Martín-Blázquez, *Guerre civile totale* (Paris, 1938), 203.

7. Cf. Antony Beevor, *The Battle for Spain: The Spanish Civil War, 1936–1939* (New York, 2006), 342.

8. Michael Seidman, *Republic of Egos: A Social History of the Spanish Civil War* (Madison, WI, 2002), 43–46; Gabriele Ranzato, *El eclipse de la democracia: La guerra civil española y sus orígenes, 1931–1939*, trans. Fernando Borrajo (Madrid, 2006), 607.

9. Orlando Figes, *A People's Tragedy: A History of the Russian Revolution* (New York, 1996), 665; Peter Kenez, *Civil War in South Russia, 1919–1920: The Defeat of the Whites* (Berkeley, 1977), 24, 108; Vladimir N. Brovkin, *Behind the Front Lines of the Civil War* (Princeton, NJ, 1994); Mark von Hagen, *Soldiers in the Proletarian*

Dictatorship: The Red Army and the Soviet Socialist State, 1917–1930 (Ithaca, NY, 1990), 125.

10. Peter Kenez, *Civil War in South Russia, 1918: The First Year of the Volunteer Army* (Berkeley, 1971), 18; Evan Mawdsley, *The Russian Civil War* (Boston, 1987), 11.

11. José Ángel Sánchez Asiaín, *Economía y Finanzas en la guerra civil española (1936–1939)* (Madrid, 1999), 16; *El Correo de Zamora*, 31 August 1937.

12. Sebastian Balfour, *Deadly Embrace: Morocco and the Road to the Spanish Civil War* (New York, 2002), 303; Salvador Nonell Bru, *El Laureado Tercio de Requetés de Nuestra Señora de Montserrat* (Barcelona, 1992), 136.

13. Miguel Ángel del Arco Blanco, *Las alas del Ave Fénix: La política agraria del primer franquismo (1936–1939)* (Granada, 2005), xvi; Alfonso Lazo, *Retrato de fascismo rural en Sevilla* (Seville, 1998), 40–41; Luis Castro, *Capital de la Cruzada: Burgos durante la Guerra Civil* (Barcelona, 2006), 61; *El Correo de Zamora*, 15 January 1938; Francisco Cobo Romero, *Revolución campesina y contrarrevolución franquista en Andalucía: Conflictividad social, violencia política y represión franquista en el mundo rural andaluz, 1931–1950* (Granada, 2004), 224; Rey, *Paisanos en lucha*, 186, 252.

14. Pedro Corral, *Desertores: La Guerra Civil que nadie quiere contar* (Barcelona, 2006), 139; Giuliana di Febo, *Ritos de guerra y de victoria en la España franquista* (Bilbao, 2002), 118.

15. José Manuel Martínez Bande, *La lucha en torno a Madrid en el invierno de 1936–1937* (Madrid, 1984), 88.

16. *El Correo de Zamora*, 24 April 1938; *ABC*, 3 February 1938, 3 May 1938, 20 August 1938, 25 October 1938; *Proa*, 25 April 1939; Gobierno Civil de León, Memoria, August 1938, 44/2791, Archivo General de Administración (hereafter AGA); *El Correo de Zamora*, 5 and 7 February 1938; *La Provincia*, 28 July 1938.

17. Cf. Chris Ealham and Michael Richards, eds., *The Splintering of Spain: Cultural History and the Spanish Civil War, 1936–1939* (Cambridge, 2005), 15, 19. The authors argue that the heterogeneous nature of the Republican coalition made it less able "to construct meaningful unifying symbols and discourses of mobilization out of history than those who were known as 'the Nationalists.'"

18. James M. McPherson, *Battle Cry of Freedom: The Civil War Era* (New York, 1988), 857.

CHAPTER 1. THE DESTRUCTION OF THE SECOND REPUBLIC

1. Stanley G. Payne, *Spain's First Democracy: The Second Republic, 1931–1936* (Madison, WI, 1993), 34.

2. Tébar Hurtado, *Reforma*, 19–82; Cobo Romero, *Revolución campesina*, 89–121; Lazo, *Retrato de fascismo*, 16; Rey, *Paisanos en lucha*, 124, 188.

3. Rey, *Paisanos en lucha*, 196, 335; Cobo Romero, *Revolución campesina*, 73–90; Lazo, *Retrato de fascismo*, 37, 39.

4. Paolo Farneti, "Social Conflict, Parliamentary Fragmentation, Institutional Shift, and the Rise of Fascism: Italy," in Juan J. Linz and Alfred Stepan, eds., *The*

Breakdown of Democratic Regimes, pt. 2, *Europe* (Baltimore, 1978), 15; Tébar Hurtado, *Reforma*, 82–117; Francisca Rosique Navarro, *La Reforma agraria en Badajoz durante la IIa República* (Badajoz, 1988), 241; Cobo Romero, *Revolución campesina*, 84.

5. Cobo Romero, *Revolución campesina*, 89–121; Rey, *Paisanos en lucha*, 182–204; Nicolás Salas, *Sevilla fue la clave: República, Alzamiento, Guerra Civil (1931–39)* (Seville, 1992), 1:83–90; Fernando Pascual Cevallos, *Luchas agrarias en Sevilla durante la Segunda República* (Seville, 1983), 106; Rafael de Medina [Duque de Medinaceli], *Tiempo pasado* (Seville, 1971), 24–25; *ABC*, 20 July 1936, 17 March 1938.

6. Santiago Casas, "La agenda de la conferencia de Metropolitanos," in Jaume Aurell and Pablo Pérez López, eds., *Católicos entre dos guerras: La historia religiosa de España en los años 20 y 30* (Madrid, 2006), 254; Juan J. Linz and Alfred Stepan, eds., *The Breakdown of Democratic Regimes*, pt. 2, *Europe* (Baltimore, 1978), 56.

7. Michael Seidman, *Workers against Work: Labor in Barcelona and Paris during the Popular Fronts* (Berkeley, 1991), 61; Paul Preston, "The Agrarian War in the South," in Paul Preston, ed., *Revolution and War in Spain, 1931–1939* (New York, 1984), 172; Mercedes Vilanova, *Les majories invisibles* (Barcelona, 1995), 18.

8. Cobo Romero, *Revolución campesina*, 99–116.

9. Payne, *Spain's First Democracy*, 274.

10. Ranzato, *El eclipse de la democracia*, 245; María Cristina Rivero Noval, *Política y sociedad en la Rioja durante el primer franquismo (1936–1945)* (Logroño, 2001), 488; Martín-Blázquez, *Guerre civile totale*, 70; Cobo Romero, *Revolución campesina*, 117–21; José Caballero, *Diario de campaña* (Madrid, 1976), 135; Justo Vila Izquierdo, *Extremadura: La Guerra Civil* (Badajoz, 1984), 18; Rosique Navarro, *La Reforma agraria en Badajoz*, 226.

11. Luis Garrido González, *Colectividades agrarias en Andalucía: Jaén (1931–39)* (Madrid, 1979), 25–29; Cobo Romero, *Revolución campesina*, 118–19; Jacques Maurice, *La reforma agraria en España en el siglo XX (1900–1936)* (Madrid, 1975), 65; Salas, *Sevilla*, 1:143; *El Pueblo Gallego*, 18 June 1936.

12. Tébar Hurtado, *Reforma*, 184; Lazo, *Retrato de fascismo*, 41; Clara Campoamor, *La revolución española vista por una republicana* (Barcelona, 2002), 77; Rey, *Paisanos en lucha*, 128–29, 202, 206–9; Ugarte Tellería, *La nueva Covadonga*, 26, 58–59. Cf. Graham, *Spanish Civil War*, 18: "Culture wars . . . mythologized fears."

13. General Motors, 2 July 1936, Barcelona 1329, Archivo Histórico Nacional-Sección Guerra Civil (hereafter AHN-SGC); Ian Gibson, *The Death of Lorca* (Chicago, 1973), 27–33; Ranzato, *El eclipse de la democracia*, 245; Campoamor, *La revolución española*, 72; Santa Cruz de Tenerife, Memoria, 1938, 44/2792, AGA; Juan Ortiz Villalba, *Sevilla 1936: Del golpe militar a la guerra civil* (Seville, 1998), 261; *La Provincia*, 12 June 1936; José Llordés Badía, *Al dejar el fusil: Memorias de un soldado raso en la Guerra de España* (Barcelona, 1968), 33–35.

14. Payne, *Spain's First Democracy*, 357.

15. José Manuel Martínez Bande, *La invasión de Aragón y el desembarco en Mallorca* (Madrid, 1970), 23; Rafael Quirosa-Cheyrouze y Muñoz, *Política y guerra civil en Almería* (Almeria, 1986), 117–18.

16. Gabriel Cardona, *Historia militar de una guerra civil: Estrategia y tácticas*

de la guerra de España (Barcelona, 2006), 34; Balfour, *Deadly Embrace*, 271. Beevor, *The Battle for Spain*, 79, reports slightly different figures: the Nationalists had 50,000 soldiers, 17 generals, 10,000 officers, but most of the Civil Guard and almost half of the Assault Guard. Ugarte Tellería, *La nueva Covadonga*, 126; Ignacio Martín Jiménez, "La sublevación nacionalista en Valladolid," in Alfonso Bullón de Mendoza and Luis Eugenio Togores, eds., *Revisión de la guerra civil española* (Madrid, 2002), 232.

17. Ugarte Tellería, *La nueva Covadonga*, 119; Corral, *Desertores*, 82–91; Rafael Casas de la Vega, *Las milicias nacionales en la Guerra de España* (Madrid, 1974), 64–170; *El Correo de Zamora*, 24 June 1937; C. Revilla Cebrecos, *Tercio de Lácar* (Madrid, 1975), 330; *ABC*, 23 October 1936; Julio Aróstegui, *Los combatientes carlistas en la Guerra civil española, 1936–1939* (Madrid, 1991), 1:58; Javier Nagore Yárnoz, *En la primera de Navarra (1936–1939): Memorias de un voluntario navarro del Tercio de Radio Requeté de Campaña* (Madrid, 1991), 103.

18. Casas de la Vega, *Las milicias nacionales*, 1:430; Stanley G. Payne, *The Franco Regime, 1936–1975* (Madison, WI, 1987), 132; Ángela Cenarro, "Matar, Vigilar y Delatar: La Quiebra de la sociedad civil durante la guerra y la posguerra en España (1936–1948)," *Historia Social* 22 (2002): 7; Aróstegui, *Los combatientes carlistas*, 2:105; Casas de la Vega, *Las milicias nacionales*, 39; Juan Satrústegui, *Memorias de un anarquista entre las tropas de Franco* (Pamplona, 1994), 163; Stathis N. Kalyvas, *The Logic of Violence in Civil War* (New York, 2006), 40.

19. *ABC*, 4 and 7 August 1936, 18 March 1938; Caballero, *Diario de campaña*, 363; Francisco Sánchez Ruano, *Islam y Guerra civil española: Moros con Franco y con la República* (Madrid, 2004), 68, 190; *El Pueblo Gallego*, 6 September 1936, 1 December 1936, 23 December 1937; *Proa*, [10?] December 1936; Nagore Yárnoz, *En la primera de Navarra*, 123; Satrústegui, *Memorias de un anarquista*, 255.

20. Robert Stradling, *The Irish and the Spanish Civil War, 1936–39* (Manchester, 1999), 83; Adro Xavier [Alejandro Rey Stolle], *Caballero Legionario* (Madrid, [1937?]), 29; Caballero, *Diario de campaña*, 100; José María Iribarren, *El General Mola* (Madrid, 1963), 221; Corral, *Desertores*, 451. Beevor, *The Battle for Spain*, 198, claims that 12,000 Portuguese, known as *Viriatos*, joined the Legion. Christopher Othen, *Franco's International Brigades: Foreign Volunteers and Fascist Dictators in the Spanish Civil War* (London, 2008), 79, asserts that 8,000 Portuguese served in Spain. Juan Urra Lusarreta, *En las trincheras del frente de Madrid: Memorias de un capellán de requetés, herido de guerra* (Madrid, 1966), 227; Alistair Hennessy, "Cuba," in Mark Falcoff and Frederick B. Pike, eds., *The Spanish Civil War: American Hemispheric Perspectives* (Lincoln, NE, 1982), 102; Mark Falcoff, "Argentina," in Falcoff and Pike, *The Spanish Civil War*, 291; Oviedo, 1938, 44/2791, AGA; Memoria de las Palmas, 7 September 1938, 44/3123, AGA.

21. Francisco Cayón García and Miguel Muñoz Rubio, "Transportes y Comunicaciones," in Pablo Martín Aceña and Elena Martínez Ruiz, eds., *La economía de la guerra civil* (Madrid, 2006), 247; Miguel Muñoz Rubio, *RENFE (1941–1991): Medio siglo de ferrocarril público* (Madrid, 1995), 66; José Manuel Martínez Bande, *La lucha por la victoria* (Madrid, 1990–91), 29; Guillermo Martínez-Molinos, "El suministro de carburantes," in Octavio Ruiz-Manjón Cabeza and Miguel Gómez Oliver, eds.,

Los nuevos historiadores ante la Guerra Civil española (Granada, 1990), 221, 228; *El Pueblo Gallego*, 29 July 1938.

22. Rafael Abella, *La vida cotidiana durante la Guerra civil: La España nacional* (Barcelona, 1973), 274; Manuel Garzón Pareja, *Historia de la Hacienda de España* (Madrid, 1984), 2:1131; Elena Martínez Ruiz, "El campo en guerra: Organización y producción agraria," in Martín Aceña and Martínez Ruiz, *La economía*, 111, 140; Angel Viñas, "The Financing of the Spanish Civil War," in Paul Preston, ed., *Revolution and War in Spain, 1931–1939* (London, 1984), 267; Burgos, 21 January 1937, ZN, a. 31, l. 9, c. 23, Archivo General Militar (hereafter AGM); James Simpson, *Spanish Agriculture: The Long Siesta, 1765–1965* (New York, 1995), 219; Ministerio de Agricultura, *Estadística* (Valencia, 1936), 4.

23. Angel Viñas et al., *Política comercial exterior en España* (Madrid, 1975), 142; Viñas, "Financing," 276; Kenez, *Civil War in South Russia, 1919–1929*, 100, 157; Scott Smith, "The Socialists-Revolutionaries and the Dilemma of Civil War," in Vladimir N. Brovkin, ed., *The Bolsheviks in Russian Society: The Revolution and Civil Wars* (New Haven, CT, 1997), 88–99; Sergei Pavliuchenkov, "Workers' Protest Movement Against War Communism," in Brovkin, *The Bolsheviks*, 142; Donald J. Raleigh, ed., *A Russian Civil War Diary: Alexis Babine in Saratov, 1917–1922* (Durham, 1988), xix.

24. Aurora Bosch Sánchez, *Ugetistas y Libertarios: Guerra civil y revolución en el país valenciano, 1936–39* (Valencia, 1983), 18–19; Richard Pipes, *Russia under the Bolshevik Regime, 1919–1924* (London, 1994), 11.

25. Hill to Curzon, 7 June 1919, FO 371 4024, Public Record Office, London (hereafter PRO); C. E. Bechhofer, *In Denikin's Russia and the Caucasus, 1919–1920* (New York, 1971), 171–87.

26. N. G. O. Pereira, "Siberian Atamanshchina: Warlordism in the Russian Civil War," in Brovkin, *The Bolsheviks*, 123–26; "Note on the White-Russian Policies in Mongolia," Boris N. Volkov Papers, Hoover Institution, Stanford, CA; Robert Argenbright, "The Soviet Agitational Vehicle: State Power on the Social Frontier," *Political Geography* 17, no. 3 (1998): 253–72.

27. Bandit activity, 10 November 1949, and Political, 11 November 1949, FO 371 75776, PRO.

28. Alfonso Domingo, *Retaguardia: La Guerra Civil tras los frentes* (Madrid, 2004), 348; Stanley G. Payne, *Politics and the Military in Modern Spain* (Stanford, 1967), 413, 420; Francisco Espinosa Maestre, *La justicia de Queipo: Violencia selectiva y terror fascista en la II División en 1936* (Seville, 2000), 283–89.

29. Ortiz Villalba, *Sevilla 1936*, 114, 150; Espinosa Maestre, *La justicia de Queipo*, 53; Beevor, *The Battle for Spain*, 59; Sánchez Ruano, *Islam*, 169; Antonio Olmedo Delgado and José Cuesta Monereo, *General Queipo de Llano: Aventura y audacia* (Barcelona, 1957), 137; Ian Gibson, *Queipo de Llano: Sevilla, verano de 1936 (Con las charlas radiofónicas completas)* (Barcelona, 1986), 152–82. Cf. Gonzalo Queipo de Llano, *Memorias de la Guerra Civil* (Madrid, 2008), 198.

30. Gibson, *Queipo de Llano*; *ABC*, 24 July 1936, 18 August 1936; Olmedo Delgado and Cuesta Monereo, *General Queipo de Llano*, 138; Salas, *Sevilla*, 2:472; Ortiz Villalba, *Sevilla 1936*, 151–72.

31. *ABC*, 1 October 1936.

32. Salas, *Sevilla*, 2:698; Queipo de Llano, *Memorias*, 195; John R. Hubbard, "How Franco Financed His War," *The Journal of Modern History* 25, no. 4. (December 1953): 393; *ABC*, 6 July 1937; Enrique de la Vega Viguera, *La Pirotecnia Militar de Sevilla: Notas para su historia* (Seville, 1981), 87; Cardona, *Historia militar*, 42; Aróstegui, *Los combatientes carlistas*, 1:312; Revilla Cebrecos, *Tercio de Lácar*, 72; Ranzato, *El eclipse de la democracia*, 279; Fernando Díaz-Plaja, *La guerra de España en sus documentos* (Barcelona, 1966), 172.

33. Salas, *Sevilla*, 2:600; Gibson, *Queipo de Llano*, 89; Cobo Romero, *Revolución campesina*, 124; Espinosa Maestre, *La justicia de Queipo*, 295. A pro-Nationalist author, Salas, *Sevilla*, 1:37, 2:643, 2:653–55, puts the number murdered by the left in Seville and its province between 18 July and 11 September at 476, and by the right between July 1936 and December 1941 at 8,000. Domingo, *Retaguardia*, 149; Francisco Vigueras Roldán, *Los paseados con Lorca: El maestro cojo y los banderilleros* (Seville, 2007), 157; Javier Rodrigo, "Our Fatherland Was Full of Weeds: Violence during the Spanish Civil War and the Franco Dictatorship," in Baumeister and Schüler-Springorum, *"If You Tolerate This . . . ,"* 144.

34. Castro, *Capital de la Cruzada*, 218, 230, 285; Tébar Hurtado, *Reforma*, 233; Domingo, *Retaguardia*, 356; Espinosa Maestre, *La justicia de Queipo*, 195, 463. In the Republican zone, at the end of July 1936, authorities ordered that all corpses be photographed before burial. See Rafael Abella, *La vida cotidiana durante la Guerra civil: La España republicana* (Barcelona, 1975), 94. In the Nationalist zone, after 1936, bodies were no longer thrown into ditches. See María Jesús Souto Blanco, *La represión franquista en la provincia de Lugo (1936–1940)* (La Coruña, 1998), 258. Julián Casanova, *República y guerra civil* (Barcelona, 2007), 409; Alfonso Bullón de Mendoza and Álvaro de Diego, *Historias orales de la Guerra civil* (Barcelona, 2000), 153; Antonio Ruiz Vilaplana, *Burgos Justice: A Year's Experience of Nationalist Spain*, trans. W. Horsfall Carter (New York, 1938), 32; Salas, *Sevilla*, 2:464; Hilari Raguer, *La Espada y la Cruz: La Iglesia, 1936–1939* (Barcelona, 1977), 159; Huesca, Memoria, 1938, 44/2791, AGA; Llordés Badía, *Al dejar el fusil*, 92, 125; Bernabé Copado, *Con la columna Redondo: Combates y conquistas, crónica de guerra* (Seville, 1937), 259; Salas, *Sevilla*, 2:472, 599, 600; *ABC*, 23 August 1936; *El Pueblo Gallego*, 26 August 1936; Sánchez Ruano, *Islam*, 175.

35. Hugo García, *Mentiras necesarias: La batalla por la opinión británica durante la Guerra Civil* (Madrid, 2008), 138; Antonio Bahamonde y Sánchez de Castro, *Un Año con Queipo: Memorias de un Nacionalista* (Barcelona, 1938), 12–13; Ruiz Vilaplana, *Burgos Justice*, 27.

36. Gibson, *Queipo de Llano*, 123; Abella, *La vida cotidiana nacional*, 47; Mola quoted in Salas, *Sevilla*, 1:21–210; Vigueras Roldán, *Los paseados con Lorca*, 46; José Manuel González Torga, "El general Queipo de Llano, pionero en la guerra de las ondas: Propaganda personalizada desde el mando," in Bullón de Mendoza and Togores, *Revisión*, 603; *El Correo de Zamora*, 1 September 1936; Rey, *Paisanos en lucha*, 47; *El Pueblo Gallego*, 18 August 1936, 20 January 1939; *Proa*, 3 February 1939; Javier Cervera Gil, *Ya sabes mi paradero: La guerra civil a través de las cartas de los que vivieron* (Barcelona, 2005), 129.

37. Medina, *Tiempo pasado*, 33; Mustapha El Merroun, *Las tropas marroquíes*

en la guerra civil española, 1936–1939 (Madrid, 2003), 41–62; Palacios and Payne, *Franco, mi padre*, 266.

38. *ABC*, 13 August 1936; *El Pueblo Gallego*, 31 July 1936, 2 August 1936.

39. *ABC*, 29 May 1937; Abella, *La vida cotidiana nacional*, 278–391.

40. Gibson, *Queipo de Llano*, 176–383; Salas, *Sevilla*, 1:40; *ABC*, 7 November 1936, 18 March 1937; Lazo, *Retrato de fascismo*, 12, 99; Cenarro, "Matar," 72; Queipo de Llano, *Memorias*, 119.

41. *El Pueblo Gallego*, 16–18 August 1936, 4 August 1937, 17 September 1937, 13 June 1939; Abella, *La vida cotidiana nacional*, 110; Memoria, Pontevedra, 1937, 44/3122, AGA; Orense, September 1938, 44/2791, AGA; *La Nueva España*, 21 May 1938; María Jesús Souto Blanco, *Los apoyos al régimen franquista en la provincia de Lugo (1936–1940): La corrupción y la lucha por el poder* (La Coruña, 1999), 53, 137, 141; Cervera Gil, *Ya sabes mi paradero*, 273.

42. Salas, *Sevilla*, 1:141; Memoria, Pontevedra, 1937, 44/3122, AGA; Orense, September 1938, 44/2791, AGA; *El Pueblo Gallego*, 26 August 1936, 26 October 1937; *La Nueva España*, 16 February 1937; *Proa*, 1 December 1936; Rivero Noval, *Política y sociedad en la Rioja*, 192, 494; Castro, *Capital de la Cruzada*, 201; Santa Cruz de Tenerife, Memoria, 1938, 44/2792, AGA.

43. *El Pueblo Gallego*, 16 June 1936, 20 January 1938, 12 February 1938, 18 June 1938, 27 December 1938; *La Nueva España*, 18 and 28 May 1938, 5 June 1938, 24 August 1938, 12 January 1939; *ABC*, 6 November 1938; *El Correo de Zamora*, 19 June 1937, 5 December 1937, 15 May 1938, 17 June 1939; *Proa*, 16 July 1937, [3?] August 1937, 3 August 1938, 4 April 1939; *La Provincia*, 5 November 1938; Rivero Noval, *Política y sociedad en la Rioja*, 36.

44. Gustau Nerín, *La guerra que vino de África* (Barcelona, 2005), 233; Gibson, *Queipo de Llano*, 429; *Proa*, 31 January 1939. Geoffrey Jensen, *Franco: Soldier, Commander, Dictator* (Washington, D.C., 2005), 40, reports that Moroccan Jews also kept the keys to their former homes in Granada.

45. Isabelle Rohr, *The Spanish Right and the Jews, 1898–1945: Antisemitism and Opportunism* (Eastbourne, Sussex, UK, 2007), 6–12; El Merroun, *Las tropas marroquíes*, 41. Yet the same author claims (p. 203) that illiterate Moroccan troops had female pen pals. María Rosa de Madariaga, *Los moros que trajo Franco: La intervención de tropas coloniales en la Guerra Civil Española* (Barcelona, 2002), 179; Sánchez Ruano, *Islam*, 225; Balfour, *Deadly Embrace*, 13.

46. Nerín, *La guerra*, 177; Sánchez Ruano, *Islam*, 17, 234; Iribarren, *El General Mola*, 220; Raguer, *La Espada*, 64; *El Correo de Zamora*, 5 December 1936; Caballero, *Diario de campaña*, 269; Javier Domínguez Arribas, *El enemigo judeo-masónico en la propaganda franquista* (Madrid, 2009), 185–88.

47. El Merroun, *Las tropas marroquíes*, 180; Rohr, *The Spanish Right*, 87; Madariaga, *Los moros*, 234, 239; *La Provincia*, 10 August 1938.

48. *ABC*, 4 November 1936, 7 April 1937, 26 August 1937; Sánchez Ruano, *Islam*, 304. For background, see Geoffrey Jensen, *Irrational Triumph: Cultural Despair, Military Nationalism, and the Ideological Origins of Franco's Spain* (Reno, NV, 2002).

49. *ABC*, 6 April 1937; *La Provincia*, 4 April 1937, 12 February 1938; *El Correo de Zamora*, 5 December 1936; José-Carlos Mainer, *Años de Vísperas: La vida de la*

cultura en España (1931–1939) (Madrid, 2006), 197; *La Nueva España*, 28 August 1937; Nagore Yárnoz, *En la primera de Navarra*, 140, 148; Llordés Badía, *Al dejar el fusil*, 288; Bullón de Mendoza and Diego, *Historias orales*, 227.

   50. Sánchez Ruano, *Islam*, 88–89, 156–300; Madariaga, *Los moros*, 12–160. Cf. El Merroun, *Las tropas marroquíes*, 11–49. Cf. also Othen, *Franco's International Brigades*, 34; Nerín, *La guerra*, 28.

   51. Balfour, *Deadly Embrace*, 254–76; Madariaga, *Los moros*, 166–338; El Merroun, *Las tropas marroquíes*, 42–224; Corral, *Desertores*, 432–33; Bullón de Mendoza and Diego, *Historias orales*, 142; Nerín, *La guerra*, 189–287; Sánchez Ruano, *Islam*, 166–246.

   52. Nerín, *La guerra*, 173; Madariaga, *Los moros*, 327; El Merroun, *Las tropas marroquíes*, 44, 198; Sánchez Ruano, *Islam*, 123–336.

   53. Balfour, *Deadly Embrace*, 271; Nerín, *La guerra*, 172, 178; Sánchez Ruano, *Islam*, 436; Madariaga, *Los moros*, 168.

   54. Balfour, *Deadly Embrace*, 278–313. Other estimates place the number who crossed the Mediterranean at 60,000 to 70,000. See Madariaga, *Los moros*, 171–326; Nerín, *La guerra*, 172; El Merroun, *Las tropas marroquíes*, 193, 217; Sánchez Ruano, *Islam*, 251; Jorge Martínez Reverte, *La Batalla del Ebro* (Barcelona, 2003), 35–53; Urra Lusarreta, *En las trincheras*, 275; Abella, *La vida cotidiana nacional*, 214.

   55. María Dolores Algora Wever, "El reflejo de la guerra civil en el protectorado de Marruecos," in Bullón de Mendoza and Togores, *Revisión*, 1031; Madariaga, *Los moros*, 44–46, 87; Salas, *Sevilla*, 2:426; Nerín, *La guerra*, 187; Sánchez Ruano, *Islam*, 196; Abella, *La vida cotidiana nacional*, 133; Satrústegui, *Memorias de un anarquista*, 197; Caballero, *Diario de campaña*, 183; Stradling, *The Irish*, 82; Llordés Badía, *Al dejar el fusil*, 50–125; Copado, *Con la columna Redondo*, 188; *ABC*, 30 July 1936; José Ángel Delgado Iribarren, *Jesuitas en Campaña: Cuatro siglos al servicio de la Historia* (Madrid, 1956), 245; Corral, *Desertores*, 431; Enrique Líster, *Nuestra Guerra: Aportaciones para una historia de la Guerra Nacional Revolucionaria del pueblo español, 1936–1939* (Paris, 1966), 149.

   56. Bullón de Mendoza and Diego, *Historias orales*, 181; Madariaga, *Los moros*, 268–307; Othen, *Franco's International Brigades*, 196; Sánchez Ruano, *Islam*, 184–396; Gabriel Cardona and Juan Carlos Losada, *Aunque me tires el puente: Memoria oral de la batalla del Ebro* (Madrid, 2004), 224; Aróstegui, *Los combatientes carlistas*, 1:139; Revilla Cebrecos, *Tercio de Lácar*, 108.

   57. Llordés Badía, *Al dejar el fusil*, 72; Luis Bastida Pellicer, *Historias de un quinto de 1935* (Seville, 2005), 230; Nerín, *La guerra*, 173–82; Cardona and Losada, *Aunque me tires el puente*, 109; Balfour, *Deadly Embrace*, 314; Sánchez Ruano, *Islam*, 230–306; Madariaga, *Los moros*, 270–328.

   58. Madariaga, *Los moros*, 198–316. On the honesty of a Moroccan who returned two silver candelabras to a local church, see *La Nueva España*, 3 April 1937. Ricardo de la Cierva, *Historia ilustrada de la Guerra civil española* (Barcelona, 1977), 2:379; Corral, *Desertores*, 437; Balfour, *Deadly Embrace*, 254; Satrústegui, *Memorias de un anarquista*, 249; Caballero, *Diario de campaña*, 214–87; Urra Lusarreta, *En las trincheras*, 158; Nerín, *La guerra*, 285; Martínez Reverte, *La Batalla del Ebro*, 144; Cardona and Losada, *Aunque me tires el puente*, 188, 238; Sánchez Ruano, *Islam*, 172; El Mer-

roun, *Las tropas marroquíes*, 199; Stradling, *The Irish*, 68; Llordés Badía, *Al dejar el fusil*, 95, 180; Caballero, *Diario de campaña*, 196; *El Pueblo Gallego*, 4 April 1937.

59. Madariaga, *Los moros*, 282–86; Bastida Pellicer, *Historias de un quinto*, 190; Abella, *La vida cotidiana nacional*, 346; Francis McCullagh, *In Franco's Spain* (London, 1937), 183; Nerín, *La guerra*, 181; Corral, *Desertores*, 435; Ortiz Villalba, *Sevilla 1936*, 220; Bullón de Mendoza and Diego, *Historias orales*, 51.

60. *La Nueva España*, 3 April 1937; McCullagh, *In Franco's Spain*, 183; Sánchez Ruano, *Islam*, 167. El Merroun, *Las tropas marroquíes*, 195, calls "kifi" "traditional Moroccan tobacco." *ABC*, 7 November 1937; Balfour, *Deadly Embrace*, 313; *El Correo de Zamora*, 5 December 1936; Nerín, *La guerra*, 181, 337.

61. Madariaga, *Los moros*, 180, 204. On Moors as shock troops, see Caballero, *Diario de campaña*, 191. Bullón de Mendoza and Diego, *Historias orales*, 50.

62. Madariaga, *Los moros*, 184–398; Sánchez Ruano, *Islam*, 238–41; Aróstegui, *Los combatientes carlistas*, 2:60; El Merroun, *Las tropas marroquíes*, 204; Gobierno, Ceuta, Memoria, August 1938, 44/2790, AGA; Abella, *La vida cotidiana nacional*, 217.

63. Cervera Gil, *Ya sabes mi paradero*, 225; *La Provincia*, 18 January 1939; El Merroun, *Las tropas marroquíes*, 192; Sánchez Ruano, *Islam*, 157; *ABC*, 10 May 1938.

64. Madariaga, *Los moros*, 175–380; Grupo, January 1939, ZN, a. 43, l. 1, c. 32, AGM; *ABC*, 21 March 1939.

65. Madariaga, *Los moros*, 205–356; *ABC*, 29 July 1938, 11 and 20 August 1938, 3 February 1939; Sánchez Ruano, *Islam*, 296–310; Gobierno, Ceuta, Memoria, August 1938, 44/2790, AGA; Cierva, *Historia ilustrada*, 1:258; Martínez Reverte, *La Batalla del Ebro*, 18; Otto Schempp, *Das Autoritäre Spanien* (Leipzig, 1939), 128; Algora, "El reflejo," 1033; *El Pueblo Gallego*, 12 March 1939; *El Correo de Zamora*, 4 January 1939.

66. Balfour, *Deadly Embrace*, 314. Tensions did sometimes exist between moros and other Nationalist soldiers. After the Insurgents had cut the Republican zone in two at Vinaroz, a requeté urinated on a Moroccan attempting to climb aboard his truck. See Nagore Yárnoz, *En la primera de Navarra*, 129. *El Correo de Zamora*, 9 December 1936; Cervera Gil, *Ya sabes mi paradero*, 317; El Merroun, *Las tropas marroquíes*, 80, 195; Madariaga, *Los moros*, 278–96. Cf. Caballero, *Diario de campaña*, 225, when the author prepared a wounded Moroccan for baptism.

67. Madariaga, *Los moros*, 200–81; Balfour, *Deadly Embrace*, 314; Cervera Gil, *Ya sabes mi paradero*, 336; *La Nueva España*, 27 May 1937; Caballero, *Diario de campaña*, 96, 270; *ABC*, 25 July 1937, 26 August 1937; *El Pueblo Gallego*, 11 September 1937, 7 December 1937; Sánchez Ruano, *Islam*, 237.

68. Policarpo Cía Navascués, *Memorias del Tercio de Montejurra* (Pamplona, 1941), 185–235; Martínez Reverte, *La Batalla del Ebro*, 171; Cervera Gil, *Ya sabes mi paradero*, 301. Cf. Hugh Thomas, *Spanish Civil War* (New York, 1963), 247, who doubts reports of the "massacre." Vila Izquierdo, *Extremadura*, 58, relates 4,000 executions. John F. Coverdale, *Italian Intervention in the Spanish Civil War* (Princeton, NJ, 1975), 192, claims that Italian government sources confirmed massive bloodletting. Madariaga, *Los moros*, 299, states that 2,000, not the 4,000 that journalist Jay Allen claimed, were massacred in the Badajoz bullring. Rodrigo, "Our Fatherland Was

Full of Weeds," 145, puts the figure at 6,000. Espinosa Maestre, *La justicia de Queipo*, 166–203; Balfour, *Deadly Embrace*, 296; Othen, *Franco's International Brigades*, 74; Vila Izquierdo, *Extremadura*, 89; Sánchez Ruano, *Islam*, 166–244; *El Correo de Zamora*, 27 January 1938; Bullón de Mendoza and Diego, *Historias orales*, 51, 90.

69. Vila Izquierdo, *Extremadura*, 44–46; Sánchez Ruano, *Islam*, 167–80; Domingo, *Retaguardia*, 184; Balfour, *Deadly Embrace*, 292–93; Abella, *La vida cotidiana nacional*, 294; Madariaga, *Los moros*, 313.

70. Eduardo Pons Prades, *Guerrillas españolas, 1936–1950* (Barcelona, 1977), 322–41. Population and voting information is found in Rosique Navarro, *La Reforma agraria en Badajoz*, 37–304. Gabriel Jackson, *The Spanish Republic and Civil War, 1931–1939* (Princeton, NJ, 1965), 268. See also Burnett Bolloten, *The Spanish Civil War: Revolution and Counter-revolution* (Chapel Hill, NC, 1991), 5. Declaración(es), September 1936, CGG, AGM.

71. Cardona, *Historia militar*, 220; Beevor, *The Battle for Spain*, 121; Caballero, *Diario de campaña*, 59–60; Stanley G. Payne, *Franco: El perfil de la historia* (Madrid, 1992), 55.

72. Aróstegui, *Los combatientes carlistas*, 1:40–309; Cía Navascués, *Memorias*, 24, 120; Ugarte Tellería, *La nueva Covadonga*, 143–388; Nonell Bru, *El Laureado Tercio*, 137; Medina, *Tiempo pasado*, 110; *El Correo de Zamora*, 23 December 1936; Nagore Yárnoz, *En la primera de Navarra*, 91.

73. Nagore Yárnoz, *En la primera de Navarra*, 37; Ugarte Tellería, *La nueva Covadonga*, 208; Sánchez Ruano, *Islam*, 408; Xuan Cándano, *El Pacto de Santoña (1937): La rendición del nacionalismo vasco al fascismo* (Madrid, 2006), 51.

74. Nonell Bru, *El Laureado Tercio*, 151; Casas de la Vega, *Las milicias nacionales*, 80; Caballero quoted in Martínez Bande, *La invasión de Aragón*, 273; George Orwell, *Homage to Catalonia* (New York, 1980); quoted in Bolloten, *The Spanish Civil War*, 258; 5 C.E., February–August 1937, ZN, a. 31, l. 1, c. 1, AGM.

75. Nonell Bru, *El Laureado Tercio*, 135–68. Transfers to more active units were not uncommon among requetés. See Aróstegui, *Los combatientes carlistas*, 1:326, 2:444. On the mobile column, see José María Resa, *Memorias de un requeté* (Barcelona, 1968), 51. Frank Thomas, *Brother against Brother: Experiences of a British Volunteer in the Spanish Civil War*, ed. Robert Stradling (Phoenix Mill, UK, 1998), 119; Casas de la Vega, *Las milicias nacionales*, 1:494.

76. Nonell Bru, *El Laureado Tercio*, 146–77. Soldiers on both sides in the Huesca front cooperated in harvesting grapes. See Abella, *La vida cotidiana nacional*, 352.

77. Coverdale, *Italian Intervention*, 127; José Manuel Martínez Bande, *Nueve meses de guerra en el Norte* (Madrid, 1980), 139, 148; Ronald Fraser, *Blood of Spain: An Oral History of the Spanish Civil War* (New York, 1986), 249; Ramón Salas Larrazábal, *Historia del ejército popular de la Republica* (Madrid, 1973), 358.

78. Robert H. Whealey, *Hitler and Spain: The Nazi Role in the Spanish Civil War, 1936–1939* (Lexington, KY, 1989), 22; Gerald Howson, *Arms for Spain: The Untold Story of the Spanish Civil War* (New York, 1999), 138; Martínez Bande, *La lucha en torno a Madrid*, 36; Gustavo Durán, *Una enseñanza de la guerra española* (Madrid, 1979), 66; Coverdale, *Italian Intervention*, 109; Balfour, *Deadly Embrace*, 302–6; Thomas, *Brother against Brother*, 74–75; Abella, *La vida cotidiana nacional*, 224.

79. Coverdale, *Italian Intervention*, 168–207; Martínez Bande, *La lucha en torno a Madrid*, 297.

80. José Manuel Martínez Bande, *La campaña de Andalucía* (Madrid, 1969), 168–72; Coverdale, *Italian Intervention*, 192; Pons Prades, *Guerrillas españolas*, 117. On executions, see Rodrigo, "Our Fatherland Was Full of Weeds," 145.

81. Informe, 25 February 1937, ZR, a. 59, l. 669, c. 6, AGM; Valencia, 10 February 1937, ZR, AGM; Martínez Bande, *La lucha en torno a Madrid*, 277.

82. William Herrick, *Jumping the Line: The Adventures and Misadventures of an American Radical* (Madison, WI, 1998); Martínez Bande, *La lucha en torno a Madrid*, 149. Cf. Thomas, *Spanish Civil War*, 380, who claims that the Republican forces suffered 25,000 casualties and the Nationalists 20,000. See Coverdale, *Italian Intervention*, 219. Alfredo Kindelán, *Mis cuadernos de guerra* (Madrid, 1945), 66; Líster, *Nuestra Guerra*, 106.

83. Jackson, *Spanish Republic*, 349; Thomas, *Spanish Civil War*, 383; Abella, *La vida cotidiana nacional*, 289–92; Corral, *Desertores*, 396; Aróstegui, *Los combatientes carlistas*, 1:320, 383; Nagore Yárnoz, *En la primera de Navarra*, 141; Domingo, *Retaguardia*, 229.

84. Martínez Bande, *La lucha en torno a Madrid*, 214–96; Coverdale, *Italian Intervention*, 233.

85. Roatta quoted in Coverdale, *Italian Intervention*, 256.

86. Rojo cited in Coverdale, *Italian Intervention*, 252–63; Mussolini quoted in Martínez Bande, *La lucha en torno a Madrid*, 168.

87. Peter Edwards, "Logistics and Supply," in John Kenyon and Jane Ohlmeyer, eds., *The Civil Wars: A Military History of England, Scotland, and Ireland, 1638–1660* (New York, 1998), 262.

88. Juan Pablo Fusi, *Franco: Autoritarismo y poder personal* (Madrid, 2001), 71; Casas de la Vega, *Las milicias nacionales* (Madrid, 1977), 1:329–336; Jensen, *Franco*, 51; Pablo Martín Aceña, "La economía de la guerra civil: Perspectiva general y comparada," in Martín Aceña and Martínez Ruiz, *La economía*, 18–19; Jordi Catalan, "Guerra e industria en las dos Españas, 1936–1939," in Martín Aceña and Martínez Ruiz, *La economía*, 210; Othen, *Franco's International Brigades*, 67; Cía Navascués, *Memorias*, 21; Llordés Badía, *Al dejar el fusil*, 280; Revilla Cebrecos, *Tercio de Lácar*, 124; Nagore Yárnoz, *En la primera de Navarra*, 82.

89. Jackson, *Spanish Republic*, 375–88; Thomas, *Spanish Civil War*, 399–423; Martínez Bande, *Nueve meses de guerra en el Norte*, 174–83; Martín Blázquez, *Guerre*, 267.

90. Pipes, *Russia under the Bolshevik Regime*, 9; Geoffrey Best, *War and Society in Revolutionary Europe, 1770–1870* (New York, 1986), 45; Cuartel, 22 January 1937, CGG, a. 2, l. 145, c. 74, AGM; Antonio Carreras Panchón, "Los psiquiatras españoles y la guerra civil," *Medicina & historia* 13 (1986): 10; Emilio Mira, *Psychiatry in War* (New York, 1943), 73, 114; Gobernador, 10 November 1936, ZN, a. 15, l. 1, c. 88, AGM; Sexta, 23 December 1936, ZN, a. 32, l. 9, c. 4, AGM; Copia, 21 December 1936, ZN, a. 15, l. 1, c. 88, AGM.

91. Héctor Colmegna, *Diario de un médico argentino en la guerra de España, 1936–1939* (Buenos Aires, 1941), 78, 141; Lt.-Col. Buzón, Información, 21 November

1937, ZR, a. 63, 1. 853, c. 7, AGM; Vicente Rojo, *Alerta los pueblos* (Barcelona, 1974), 32; Augustín Souchy Bauer, *With the Peasants of Aragon: Libertarian Communism in the Liberated Areas*, trans. Abe Bluestein (Minneapolis, 1982), 56.

92. See Robert Stradling, *Your Children Will Be Next: Bombing and Propaganda in the Spanish Civil War, 1936−1939* (Cardiff, 2008), 215−29, for a discussion of death and injury figures. Manuel González Portilla and José Maria Garmendia, *La guerra civil en el país vasco: Política y economía* (Madrid, 1988), 83; Ramón Salas Larrazábal and Jesús María Salas Larrazábal, *Historia general de la guerra de España* (Madrid, 1986), 275; Cía Navascués, *Memorias*, 49−78.

93. E. Allison Peers, *Spain in Eclipse* (London, 1943), 6; Bartolomé Aragón Gómez, *Con Intendencia militar de las gloriosas Brigadas Navarras* (Madrid, 1940), 241; *La Nueva España*, 7 February 1937; Colmegna, *Diario*, 247; Schempp, *Das Autoritäre Spanien*, 3; Aróstegui, *Los combatientes carlistas*, 1:136, 161; Casas de la Vega, *Las milicias nacionales*, 1:495; Nagore Yárnoz, *En la primera de Navarra*, 46, 113; Cía Navascués, *Memorias*, 129; Monica Orduña Prada, *El Auxilio Social (1936−1940): La etapa fundacional y los primeros años* (Madrid, 1996), 37.

94. Aragón Gómez, *Con Intendencia militar*, 245; Verónica Sierra, *Palabras huérfanas: Los niños y la Guerra Civil* (Madrid, 2009), 182, 213.

95. Sánchez Asiaín, *Economía*, 48; Santiago Carro, *Observaciones médicas sobre el hambre en la España roja* (Santander, 1938), 2; *El Pueblo Gallego*, 29 July 1938.

96. Colonel Rudolf von Cilander, "La primera batalla sobre Brunete," ZR, a. 69, 1. 1035, c. 13, AGM; Informes, 13 July 1937, ZR, a. 75, 1. 1197, c. 6, AGM; Durán, *Una enseñanza*, 49.

97. "A counterattack by fresh troops can have an effect completely out of proportion to the number of troops attacking. It is basically for this reason that the maintenance of fresh reserves has always been essential in combat, with battles often revolving around which side can hold out and deploy their reserves last." Dave Grossman, *On Killing: The Psychological Cost of Learning to Kill in War and Society* (Boston and New York, 1996), 71.

98. José Manuel Martínez Bande, *La gran ofensiva sobre Zaragoza* (Madrid, 1973), 16−79; Payne, *Politics and Military*, 397.

99. Nonell Bru, *El Laureado Tercio*, 186, 399; Jorge Martínez Reverte, *El arte de matar: Cómo se hizo la Guerra civil española* (Barcelona, 2009), 301.

100. Nonell Bru, *El Laureado Tercio*, 187−262; John A. Lynn, *The Bayonets of the Republic: Motivation and Tactics in the Army of Revolutionary France, 1791−94* (Urbana, IL, 1984), 34; Richard Holmes, *Acts of War: The Behaviour of Men in Battle* (New York, 1985), 91; Grossman, *On Killing*, 149.

101. Acta, 9 October 1937, Aragon R 1, AHN-SGC; Lt.-Col. Buzón, Información, 21 November 1937, ZR, a. 63, 1. 853, c. 7, AGM; Análisis, n.d., ZR, a. 63, 1. 853, c. 18, AGM; Nagore Yárnoz, *En la primera de Navarra*, 72−76; Fraser, *Blood of Spain*, 425; Jackson, *Spanish Republic*, 390.

102. Análisis, n.d., ZR, a. 63, 1. 853, c. 18, AGM; José Manuel Martínez Bande, *La Batalla de Teruel* (Madrid, 1974), 16; Michael Richards, *A Time of Silence: Civil War and the Culture of Repression in Franco's Spain* (Cambridge, 1998), 111−12; Salas Larrazábal, *Historia del ejército*, 1496−97.

103. Nagore Yárnoz, *En la primera de Navarra*, 32–182; Nonell Bru, *El Laureado Tercio*, 169, 553; Thomas, *Brother against Brother*, 79; Revilla Cebrecos, *Tercio de Lácar*, 119; Caballero, *Diario de campaña*, 66; Cía Navascués, *Memorias*, 179–301; Urra Lusarreta, *En las trincheras*, 32–182; *Proa*, 7 July 1937; Cervera Gil, *Ya sabes mi paradero*, 139; Ugarte Tellería, *La nueva Covadonga*, 281.

104. Jackson, *Spanish Republic*, 398–400; Thomas, *Spanish Civil War*, 504–16; Pedro Corral, *Si me quieres escribir: La batalla de Teruel* (Barcelona, 2004), 44; Martínez Bande, *La Batalla de Teruel*, 53.

105. Martínez Bande, *La Batalla de Teruel*, 43–293; Informe, 20 December 1937, ZR, reel 93, AGM, 85–86.

106. Revilla Cebrecos, *Tercio de Lácar*, 130–32; Luis Antonio Bolín, *España: Los años vitales* (Madrid, 1967), 309; Cía Navascués, *Memorias*, 261–83; Nagore Yárnoz, *En la primera de Navarra*, 93–98; Urra Lusarreta, *En las trincheras*, 194–96; Copado, *Con la columna Redondo*, 190; Angel Viñas, *El oro de Moscú: Alfa y omega de un mito franquista* (Barcelona, 1979), 349; Corral, *Desertores*, 185.

107. Nagore Yárnoz, *En la primera de Navarra*, 104–22; Thomas, *Spanish Civil War*, 515; Martínez Bande, *La Batalla de Teruel*, 227.

108. Jackson, *Spanish Republic*, 407; Ejército, 3 March 1938, ZN, a. 15, 1. 13, c. 59, AGM; Thomas, *Spanish Civil War*, 519; Salas Larrazábal, *Historia del ejército*, 1763; Bolloten, *The Spanish Civil War*, 570; Conclusiones, March 1938, ZR, a. 64, 1. 796, c. 16, AGM; Cía Navascués, *Memorias*, 298.

109. Ejército, 29 March 1938, ZN, a. 16, 1. 34, c. 44, AGM; Colmegna, *Diario*, 157; María Rosa de Madariaga, "The Intervention of Moroccan Troops in the Spanish Civil War: A Reconsideration," *European History Quarterly* 4 (1992): 87; Jacinta Gallardo Moreno, *La guerra civil en La Serena* (Badajoz, 1994), 116; Martínez Reverte, *El arte de matar*, 231, 294; Thomas, *Spanish Civil War*, 530.

110. Casas de la Vega, *Las milicias nacionales*, 1:337, 340; Revilla Cebrecos, *Tercio de Lácar*, 155–57; Nagore Yárnoz, *En la primera de Navarra*, 124–27; *ABC*, 30 September 1937, 22 October 1938; *La Provincia*, 2 November 1938; Cardona and Losada, *Aunque me tires el puente*, 33.

111. José Manuel Martínez Bande, *La ofensiva sobre Valencia* (Madrid, 1977), 15–24; Salas and Salas, *Historia general*, 330; Howson, *Arms for Spain*, 234–35; Coverdale, *Italian Intervention*, 351; Viñas, *El oro*, 414.

112. Payne, *Politics and Military*, 401; Cía Navascués, *Memorias*, 354–66.

113. Martínez Reverte, *La Batalla del Ebro*, 62.

114. Cardona and Losada, *Aunque me tires el puente*, 55–87; Cía Navascués, *Memorias*, 372.

115. Nonell Bru, *El Laureado Tercio*, 434; Nagore Yárnoz, *En la primera de Navarra*, 154; Cía Navascués, *Memorias*, 376; Howson, *Arms for Spain*, 241; Roja, *Alerta*, 85.

116. Nonell Bru, *El Laureado Tercio*, 389; Jesús González Bueno, *Paz en guerra* (Cádiz, 1943), 86; Pons Prades, *Guerrillas españolas*, 318.

117. Cardona and Losada, *Aunque me tires el puente*, 96–180; Martínez Reverte, *La Batalla del Ebro*, 63, 530; Nagore Yárnoz, *En la primera de Navarra*, 68; Abella, *La vida cotidiana republicana*, 233, 274.

118. Martínez Reverte, *La Batalla del Ebro*, 25–92. Even many of the elite International Brigaders lacked shoes. See Stradling, *The Irish*, 186; Cardona and Losada, *Aunque me tires el puente*, 17–74; Balfour, *Deadly Embrace*, 256; Aróstegui, *Los combatientes carlistas*, 2:414; Bullón de Mendoza and Diego, *Historias orales*, 39; McCullagh, *In Franco's Spain*, 277.

119. Martínez Reverte, *La Batalla del Ebro*, 83–221; Cardona and Losada, *Aunque me tires el puente*, 123–290.

120. Cardona and Losada, *Aunque me tires el puente*, 97–270; Domingo, *Retaguardia*, 132–33; Nonell Bru, *El Laureado Tercio*, 448–505; Nagore Yárnoz, *En la primera de Navarra*, 153–54; Casas de la Vega, *Las milicias nacionales*, 1:347.

121. Cf. the arguments of Graham, *Spanish Civil War*, 73–74; Paul Preston, *Franco: A Biography* (New York, 1994), 175, 277; and Carlos Blanco Escolá, *La incompetencia militar de Franco* (Madrid, 2000).

122. Cía Navascués, *Memorias*, 290; Sánchez Ruano, *Islam*, 197; Payne, *Politics and Military*, 389; Madariaga, *Los moros*, 273–74; Martínez Reverte, *La Batalla del Ebro*, 165; Corral, *Desertores*, 155–57; Casas de la Vega, *Las milicias nacionales*, 155, 182; Aróstegui, *Los combatientes carlistas*, 2:107–444; *ABC*, 24 April 1937, 23 June 1937, 4 July 1937, 1 September 1937; *El Pueblo Gallego*, 16 February 1938.

123. Martínez Reverte, *La Batalla del Ebro*, 140–508. Casas de la Vega, *Las milicias nacionales*, 1:347, claims that Nationalists had 708 battalions with 500,000 men, of whom 100,000 were volunteers. Cardona and Losada, *Aunque me tires el puente*, 101–255; Cervera Gil, *Ya sabes mi paradero*, 344; Satrústegui, *Memorias de un anarquista*, 280; Coverdale, *Italian Intervention*, 374; Jackson, *Spanish Republic*, 463; Viñas, *El oro*, 420; Howson, *Arms for Spain*, 242–43.

124. Nonell Bru, *El Laureado Tercio*, 410–540; Martínez Reverte, *La Batalla del Ebro*, 111–43; Cardona and Losada, *Aunque me tires el puente*, 132–267; Nagore Yárnoz, *En la primera de Navarra*, 156–69; Bullón de Mendoza and Diego, *Historias orales*, 32; *El Pueblo Gallego*, 13 April 1937; *El Correo de Zamora*, 24 and 25 June 1937, 29 June 1938, 8 December 1938, 11 and 26 March 1939, 8 May 1939, 18 June 1939; Satrústegui, *Memorias de un anarquista*, 296.

125. Cardona, *Historia militar*, 255; Nonell Bru, *El Laureado Tercio*, 417; Martínez Reverte, *La Batalla del Ebro*, 331–492.

126. Nagore Yárnoz, *En la primera de Navarra*, 58; Nonell Bru, *El Laureado Tercio*, 341, 436, 564; Martínez Reverte, *La Batalla del Ebro*, 258.

127. Cardona and Losada, *Aunque me tires el puente*, 214; Domingo, *Retaguardia*, 104; Nagore Yárnoz, *En la primera de Navarra*, 172–90; *ABC*, 17 November 1938; Castro, *Capital de la Cruzada*, 239; Nonell Bru, *El Laureado Tercio*, 397, 637; Revilla Cebrecos, *Tercio de Lácar*, 311, 315.

CHAPTER 2. AUTHORITARIAN POLITICAL ECONOMY

1. Thomas, *Brother against Brother*, 43–44; Joshua A. Sanborn, *Drafting the Russian Nation: Military Conscription, Total War, and Mass Politics, 1905–1925* (Dekalb, IL, 2003), 53, 108; Taisia Osipova, "Peasant Rebellions: Origin, Scope, Dynamics, and Consequences," in Brovkin, *The Bolsheviks*, 168.

2. Keyes to Curzon, 26 April 1920, FO 371 5448, PRO; Iurii Vladimirovich Got'e, *Time of Troubles: The Diary of Iurii Vladimirovich Got'e*, trans. Terence Emmons (Princeton, NJ, 1988), 220; Raleigh, *A Russian Civil War Diary*, xx, 166.

3. Cf. Figes, *A People's Tragedy*, 280; Evan Mawdsley, *The Russian Civil War* (Boston, 1987); George A. Brinkley, *The Volunteer Army and Allied Intervention in South Russia* (Notre Dame, IN, 1966), 280–87. Pipes, *Russian under the Bolshevik Regime*, 25, is one of the few that takes exception to this analysis. See also Brovkin, *Behind the Front Lines*, 6. Both Pipes and Brovkin argue that it was unrestrained Red terror, not Socialist reform, that resulted in the Bolshevik victory.

4. Stephen I. Levine, *Anvil of Victory: The Communist Revolution in Manchuria, 1945–1948* (New York, 1987), 192; Tony Saich, ed., *The Rise to Power of the Chinese Communist Party: Documents and Analysis* (Armonk, NY, 1996), 1198, 1281; Intentions, 9 November 1945, NA M1221, Intelligence Reports, 3292, U.S. Department of State, National Archives (hereafter NA), College Park, MD; Secret, 25 June 1947, NA M1221, Intelligence Reports, 3292, U.S. Department of State, NA; Suzanne Pepper, *Civil War in China: The Political Struggle, 1945–49* (Lanham, MD, 1999), 295, 311.

5. Levine, *Anvil*, 126–216; Saich, *The Rise to Power*, liii, 1201, 1314; Odd Arne Westad, *Decisive Encounters: The Chinese Civil War, 1946–1950* (Stanford, 2003), 136; Wou, *Mobilizing*, 345–83; Pepper, *Civil War in China*, 245.

6. Han-K'eou, 15 September 1947, Asie-Océanie Chine, 134, Archives Diplomatiques (Paris); Moukden, A. Dhoui (consul de France), 8 October 1947, Asie-Océanie Chine, 134, Archives Diplomatiques; C. Thomas Thorne and David S. Patterson, eds., *Foreign Relations of the United States, 1945–1950: Emergence of the Intelligence Establishment* (Washington, 1996), 896; Westad, *Decisive Encounters*, 205; Odoric Y. K. Wou, *Mobilizing the Masses: Building Revolution in Henan* (Stanford, 1994), 348.

7. Kalyvas, *The Logic of Violence*, 10; Corral, *Desertores*, 177–483; Llordés Badía, *Al dejar el fusil*, 308; Bastida Pellicer, *Historias de un quinto*, 204; Abella, *La vida cotidiana nacional*, 316; Ministerio de Agricultura, Servicio Nacional del Trigo, *Veinte años de actuación* (Madrid, 1958), 255; *Proa*, 31 December 1938; SNT Jefatura provincial Zaragoza, 6 December 1938, Interior, 61/13509, AGA; SNT, Burgos, 23 November 1938, 61/13501, AGA; SNT, Jefatura Provincial, Lugo, 28 June 1938, Interior, 61/13500, AGA.

8. *One Year of War, 1936–1937* (Paulist Press, 1937), in George R. Esenwein, *The Spanish Civil War: A Modern Tragedy* (New York, 2005), 115; Schempp, *Das Autoritäre Spanien*, 120; *British Documents on Foreign Affairs*, Series F, Europe, vol. 27, Document no. 92, 126, quoted in Esenwein, *The Spanish Civil War*, 115–16; *ABC*, 20 October 1937.

9. Schempp, *Das Autoritäre Spanien*, 119; José Sorní Mañés, "Aproximación a un estudio de la contrarreforma agraria en España," *Agricultura y Sociedad* 6 (1978): 186; *El Correo de Zamora*, 22 September 1938; *ABC*, 29 November 1936, 13 and 23 January 1937, 5 February 1937, 12 and 21 March 1937; *El Pueblo Gallego*, 27 November 1936.

10. Martínez Ruiz, "El campo en guerra," 136, 143; Sergio Riesco Roche, *La Reforma agraria y los orígenes de la guerra civil: Cuestión yuntera y radicalización patronal en la provincia de Cáceres (1931–1940)* (Madrid, 2006), 330–48; M. I. López

Ortiz and J. Melgarejo Moreno, "El Sector Agrario durante la Guerra Civil," paper presented to the Congreso de la Asociación Española de Historia Económica, Santiago de Compostela, September 2005, 16; Tébar Hurtado, *Reforma*, 236–37; *ABC*, 21 May 1937.

11. *ABC*, 21 May 1937; López Ortiz and Melgarejo Moreno, "El Sector Agrario durante la Guerra Civil," 16; text of the decree in *El Correo de Zamora*, 30 July 1936; *Proa*, 18 July 1937; Tébar Hurtado, *Reforma*, 236–38; Riesco Roche, *La Reforma*, 355, 361; Arco Blanco, *Las alas del Ave Fénix*, 206–7; Sorní Mañés, "Aproximación," 209.

12. Servicio Nacional del Trigo, *Veinte años*, 39. Figures are approximations. José Larraz, *El ordenamiento del Mercado triguero en España* (Madrid, 1935), 32–35.

13. Tébar Hurtado, *Reforma*, 118. On Aznar, see Mercedes Montero, "Los propagandistas católicos y la opinión pública," in Jaume Aurell and Pablo Pérez López, eds., *Católicos entre dos guerras: La historia religiosa de España en los años 20 y 30* (Madrid, 2006), 72. Salas, *Sevilla*, 1:50; Memoria, Ávila, August 1938, 44/2790, AGA; *El Correo de Zamora*, 1 December 1937; Memoria, Álava, 1938, 44/2790, AGA; Gobierno Civil de Segovia, Memoria, 25 August 1938, 44/2792, AGA; Diputación Provincial de Segovia, 11 July 1940, 44/3123, AGA; Informe, Lugo, 13 August 1938, 44/2791, AGA.

14. Martínez Ruiz, "El campo en guerra," 145; *El Correo de Zamora*, 9 September 1936, 10 October 1936. In July 1931 the wheat *tasa* was set between 46 and 53 pesetas and in 1935, between 53 and 58 pesetas. See Castro, *Capital de la Cruzada*, 53–62, and Rey, *Paisanos en lucha*, 449. Diputación Provincial de Salamanca, 1937, 44/31223, AGA; *ABC*, 24 September 1936, 4 November 1936, 17 March 1937, 2 September 1937; Cobo Romero, *Revolución campesina*, 288.

15. *El Correo de Zamora*, 10 October 1936; *ABC*, 5 and 7 November 1936, 1 September 1937, 23 December 1937; *El Pueblo Gallego*, 26 January 1938, 3 April 1938.

16. Servicio Nacional del Trigo, *Veinte años*, 13; Stanley G. Payne, *Falange: A History of Spanish Fascism* (Stanford, 1961), 189; Fernández Cuesta quoted in *ABC*, 4 February 1938; José Luis Orella, "Los técnicos del bando nacional," in Bullón de Mendoza and Togores, *Revisión*, 399, Juan Velarde Fuertes, "Algunos aspectos económicos de la guerra civil," in Bullón de Mendoza and Togores, *Revisión*, 947. On antimarket Falangist policies, see Cazorla Sánchez, *Las políticas de la victoria*, 71.

17. Sánchez Asiaín, *Economía*, 36–39; *El Correo de Zamora*, 30 July 1936, 7 October 1938; Servicio Nacional del Trigo, *Veinte años*, 15.

18. Franco quoted in Servicio Nacional del Trigo, *Veinte años*, 15; *ABC*, 25 August 1937; *El Correo de Zamora*, 20 August 1936; Burgos, Memoria, 1937, 44/3116, AGA; Diputación provincial de Burgos, n.d., 44/2790, AGA.

19. *El Pueblo Gallego*, 1 December 1937; Falange, Jefatura Local, El Carpio, 13 November 1937, 61/13503, AGA; *El Correo de Zamora*, 2 and 28 August 1937, 6, 7, and 10 September 1937, 16 October 1937, 16 November 1937, 5 January 1938, 25 February 1938, 2 March 1938; SNT, Jefatura Provincial de Huesca, 31 October 1937, Interior, 61/13499, AGA.

20. Sánchez Asiaín, *Economía*, 81, 338–39, 343; *ABC*, 7 September 1937, 3 and 5 November 1938, 1 December 1938; *El Correo de Zamora*, 25 August 1938, 28 October 1938; Gabriel Tortella and José Luis García Ruiz, "Banca y política durante el

primer franquismo," in Glicerio Sánchez Recio and Julio Tascón Fernández, eds., *Los empresarios de Franco: Política y economía en España, 1936–1957* (Barcelona, 2003), 68; *El Pueblo Gallego*, 14 February 1939; *Proa*, 31 December 1938.

21. Servicio Nacional del Trigo, *Veinte años*, 16, 19; *El Correo de Zamora*, 6 and 27 October 1936, 18 December 1937, 6 August 1938; Barciela López, "Producción," 668; SNT, Jefatura Provincial Ávila, 25 April 1938, Interior, 61/13493, AGA; Los nuevos precios del trigo, 6 July 1938, Interior, 61/13493, AGA; SNT, 3 November 1938, Interior, 61/13493, AGA; SNT Jefatura provincial Zaragoza, 7 November 1938, Interior, 61/13509, AGA; Jefe Provincial del SNT, Toledo, 20 January 1939, 61/13506, AGA; SNT, Jefatura Provincial Teruel, 16 December 1937, 61/13506, AGA; SNT, Dictamen, 30 September 1938, Interior, 61/13509, AGA; Gracia Clark, *Traders versus the State: Anthropological Approaches to Unofficial Economies* (Boulder, CO, 1988), 5; SNT, Jefatura Provincial de Zamora, 13 May 1938, Interior, 61/13508, AGA; SNT, Jefatura Provincial, Lugo, 28 June 1938, Interior, 61/13500, AGA.

22. Queda informada, 21 February 1939, Interior, 61/13505, AGA; SNT, Jefatura Provincial, Soria, 17 February 1939, Interior, 61/13505, AGA; *ABC*, 25 January 1938; Sr. Alcalde, 18 November 1938, Interior, 61/13507, AGA; SNT, Jefatura Provincial Teruel, 16 December 1937 and 7 February 1939, 61/13506, AGA.

23. *ABC*, 3 December 1937, 14 August 1938; SNT Jefatura provincial Zaragoza, 21 September 1938, Interior, 61/13509, AGA; Excelentísimo Señor, 5 June 1938, Interior, 61/13500, AGA; Jesús María Palomares Ibáñez, *La Guerra Civil en Palencia: La eliminación de los contrarios* (Palencia, 2002), 61; *La Nueva España*, 10 December 1937; SNT, Seville, 12 May 1938, Interior, 61/13505, AGA; Excmo. Sr., Seville, 20 September 1938, Interior, 61/13505, AGA; Eugenio Torres Villanueva, "Los empresarios: Entre la revolución y colaboración," in Martín Aceña and Martínez Ruiz, *La economía*, 459; Miguel Martorell and Francisco Comín Comín, "La Hacienda de guerra franquista," in Enrique Fuentes Quintana and Francisco Comín Comín, eds., *Economía y economistas españoles en la guerra civil* (Barcelona, 2008), 1:905.

24. Servicio Nacional del Trigo, *Veinte años*, 118; *ABC*, 4 December 1937, 1 January 1938, 1 February 1938; *El Correo de Zamora*, 15 January 1938; Los nuevos precios del trigo, 6 July 1938, Interior, 61/13493, AGA; Declaración, 28 June 1938, 26 October 1938, Interior, 61/13500, AGA; SNT, Jefatura Provincial, Lugo, 3 February 1938, 27 June 1938, 14 December 1938, Interior, 61/13500, AGA; SNT, Jefatura Provincial de Zamora, 12 March 1938, Interior, 61/13508, AGA; Reg. Sal., 18 February 1938, Interior, 61/13500, AGA; SNT, Palencia, 27 October 1938, 61/13502, AGA.

25. SNT, Palencia, 7 and 9 December 1937, 21 January 1938, 61/13502, AGA; Diputación Foral y Provincial de Navarra, 19 February 1938, 61/13502, AGA; Sr. Presidente, Palencia, SNT, Burgos, 11 December 1937, 23 November 1938, 61/13501, AGA; SNT, Málaga, 12 November 1938, 61/13501, AGA.

26. Martínez Ruiz, "El campo en guerra," 115; *El Correo de Zamora*, 20 June 1937, 10 January 1938; Carlos Barciela López, "Producción y política cerealista durante la Guerra civil española (1936–1939)," in Gonzalo Anes, Luis Ángel Rojo, and Pedro Tedde, eds., *Historia económica y pensamiento social: Estudios en homenaje a Diego Mateo del Peral* (Madrid, 1983), 670; *ABC*, 16 April 1938, 16 June 1938, 1 November 1938.

27. SNT Jefatura provincial de Cádiz, 14 January 1939, Interior, 61/13496, AGA; Ilmo. Sr., 7 November 1938, Interior, 61/13509, AGA; *La Provincia*, 11 September 1936; *El Correo de Zamora*, 15 October 1936, 16 March 1937; *Proa*, 31 May 1939; Memoria, Granada, 1938, 44/2791, AGA; *ABC*, 9 June 1937; Memoria, Ávila, August 1938, 44/2790, AGA; SNT Jefatura provincial Zaragoza, 7 November 1938, Interior, 61/13509, AGA.

28. *El Correo de Zamora*, 19 and 22 June 1938, 12 and 16 August 1938; 29 November 1938, 8 December 1938; *Proa*, 9, 19, and 30 November 1938, 31 December 1938; Central Nacional-Sindicalista, 29 July 1938, Interior, 61/13507, AGA.

29. Gobierno, Ceuta, Memoria, August 1938, 44/2790, AGA.

30. *ABC*, 18 March 1937, 18 April 1937, 1 September 1937, 21 October 1937, 26 November 1937, 4 and 9 March 1938, 12 May 1938, 15 October 1938. On tobacco, see *La Nueva España*, 27 August 1938. *El Pueblo Gallego*, 27 August 1937; *Proa*, 28 August 1937, 23 November 1938; *El Correo de Zamora*, 4 October 1936, 15 March 1938, 24 April 1938; Ana Quevedo y Queipo de Llano, *Queipo de Llano: Gloria e infortunio de un general* (Barcelona, 2001), 429. Provincial controls occurred earlier than national ones. See *ABC*, 27 January 1938.

31. Gobierno Civil de Segovia, Memoria, 25 August 1938, 44/2792, AGA; Gobierno Civil de León, Memoria, August 1938, 44/2791, AGA; Memoria, Álava, 1938, 44/2790, AGA; *El Correo de Zamora*, 5 November 1937; Gobierno Civil, Huelva, August 1938, 44/2791, AGA.

32. *ABC*, 27 October 1938; *La Nueva España*, 30 March 1937; Castro, *Capital de la Cruzada*, 134; Abella, *La vida cotidiana nacional*, 394.

33. Comité Sindical del Jabón, 26 May 1938, 34/10856, AGA; SNT Jefatura provincial Zaragoza, 14 February 1939, Interior, 61/13509, AGA; Dionisio Martín, *El problema triguero y el nacional sindicalismo* (Valladolid, 1937), 36; Ilmo. Sr., 7 November 1938, Interior, 61/13509, AGA.

34. *El Pueblo Gallego*, 7 and 11 May 1937, 11 September 1938; Memoria, Ávila, August 1938, 44/2790, AGA; *El Correo de Zamora*, 5 December 1938.

35. *El Pueblo Gallego*, 1 December 1936, 22 September 1937, 6 April 1938; *ABC*, 12 and 16 January 1937, 7 September 1937; Memoria, Granada, 1938, 44/2791, AGA; SNT, Jefatura Provincial, Seville, 29 September 1938, Interior, 61/13505, AGA; *Proa*, 10 December 1938; *La Provincia*, 2 September 1938.

36. Kenez, *Civil War in South Russia, 1918*, 99; Sukacev Papers, Hoover Institution.

37. Peter Townsend, *China Phoenix: The Revolution in China* (London, 1995), 397; Wou, *Mobilizing*, 278; Samuel B. Griffith, *The Chinese People's Liberation Army* (New York, 1967), 5; Ralph A. Thaxton, *Salt of the Earth: The Political Origins of Peasant Protest and Communist Revolution in China* (Berkeley, 1997), 309.

38. Yang Pei-sin, "The Speeding Up of Food Requisition," *The Modern Critique*, 1 September 1947, *Chinese Press Review*, Shanghai, article located at New York Public Library (hereafter cited as NYPL); "An Example of Compulsory Contributions in the North," Ta Kung Pao, 11 August 1947, *Chinese Press Review*, Shanghai, NYPL; "Large Areas of Land Left Uncultivated in Central Hupeh," Ho Ping Jih Pao, Shang-

hai, 18 April 1946, *Chinese Press Review*, Shanghai, NYPL; Ting Wei-Tung, "The Livelihood of the People in the Pacification Areas of Shantung," *Shun Pao* (GMD-supervised), 26 March 1948, *Chinese Press Review*, Shanghai, NYPL.

39. Alberte Martínez López, "La ganadería gallega durante el primer franquismo: Crónica de un tiempo perdido, 1936–1960," *Historia Agraria* 20 (2000): 198; Alberte Martínez López, *Cooperativismo y transformaciones agrarias en Galicia, 1886–1943* (Madrid, 1995), 172–73; Lourenzo Fernández Prieto, "Represión franquista y desarticulación social en Galicia: La destrucción de la organización societaria campesina, 1936–1942," *Historia Social* 15 (1993): 57; *El Pueblo Gallego*, 26 September 1937; Castro, *Capital de la Cruzada*, 171; Rivero Noval, *Política y sociedad en la Rioja*, 378; *ABC*, 25 February 1937; *La Nueva España*, 11 March 1939; Llordés Badía, *Al dejar el fusil*, 305; Urra Lusarreta, *En las trincheras*, 150; Torres Villanueva, "Los empresarios," 459; Nagore Yárnoz, *En la primera de Navarra*, 29; Resa, *Memorias de un requeté*, 84.

40. Quoted in Souto Blanco, *La represión franquista*, 193.

41. *El Pueblo Gallego*, 1 December 1936, 14 March 1937, 22 August 1937, 3 and 26 September 1937, 3 October 1937; *El Correo de Zamora*, 5 January 1938; See also Wayne H. Bowen, *Spain during World War II* (Columbia, MO, 2006), 101. *ABC*, 27 January 1938.

42. Memoria, Pontevedra, 1937, 44/3122, AGA; Gobierno Civil, Lugo, 1938, 44/2791, AGA; Orense, September 1938, 44/2791, AGA.

43. *ABC*, 27 January 1938; Memoria, Granada, 1938, 44/2791, AGA; Oviedo, 1938, 44/2791, AGA; Gobierno Civil, Huelva, August 1938, 44/2791, AGA.

44. *Proa*, 31 August 1938, 20 September 1938; *El Correo de Zamora*, 11 November 1938; *La Nueva España*, 18 and 27 February 1938, 3 August 1938; Oviedo, 1938, 44/2791, AGA; *ABC*, 5 February 1938, 12 March 1938, 24 June 1938; Memoria, Granada, 1938, 44/2791, AGA; Castro, *Capital de la Cruzada*, 172; Diputación Provincial de Salamanca, 1937, 44/3123, AGA; Gobierno Civil de Segovia, Memoria, 25 August 1938, 44/2792, AGA.

45. *El Pueblo Gallego*, 20 October 1937, 16–25 November 1937, 1 and 5 December 1937, 11 February 1938; *La Nueva España*, 4 August 1938, 1 November 1938; Memoria, Pontevedra, 1937, 44/3122, AGA; *Proa*, 17 and 21 August 1938, 5 November 1938, 10 December 1938; Memoria, Álava, 1938, 44/2790, AGA; *El Correo de Zamora*, 30 July 1937.

46. Nonell Bru, *El Laureado Tercio*, 289, 417; Aróstegui, *Los combatientes carlistas*, 1:149; McCullagh, *In Franco's Spain*, 266; Nagore Yárnoz, *En la primera de Navarra*, 80; Llordés Badía, *Al dejar el fusil*, 134; *La Provincia*, 2 November 1937; Revilla Cebrecos, *Tercio de Lácar*, 222; *El Correo de Zamora*, 23 March 1938; *Proa*, 10 November 1938; Caballero, *Diario de campaña*, 103; González Bueno, *Paz en guerra*, 208; Bastida Pellicer, *Historias de un quinto*, 217; Francisco X. Peiró, *Fernando de Huidobro: Jesuita y legionario* (Madrid, 1951), 211.

47. Revilla Cebrecos, *Tercio de Lácar*, 72–329; Llordés Badía, *Al dejar el fusil*, 265; *Proa*, 10 November 1938; *La Nueva España*, 23 June 1938; Nagore Yárnoz, *En la primera de Navarra*, 59–179; Peter Kemp, *Mine Were of Trouble* (London, 1957), 126;

El Correo de Zamora, 29 September 1937; Urra Lusarreta, *En las trincheras*, 170, 279; *La Provincia*, 8 April 1937; Caballero, *Diario de campaña*, 106–229; El Merroun, *Las tropas marroquíes*, 196.

48. Medina, *Tiempo pasado*, 81; Aróstegui, *Los combatientes carlistas*, 1:349, 2:499; Casas de la Vega, *Las milicias nacionales*, 1:382; Copado, *Con la columna Redondo*, 48–197; Revilla Cebrecos, *Tercio de Lácar*, 308; *ABC*, 10 September 1936, 1 September 1937; Cervera Gil, *Ya sabes mi paradero*, 284, 399; Cardona and Losada, *Aunque me tires el puente*, 82; Cía Navascués, *Memorias*, 284; Casas de la Vega, *Las milicias nacionales*, 1:367; Nagore Yárnoz, *En la primera de Navarra*, 58–224.

49. Cierva, *Historia ilustrada*, 1:311; *La Nueva España*, 26 June 1938, 12 July 1938, 13 September 1938; Nerín, *La guerra*, 234; Palacios and Payne, *Franco, mi padre*, 88.

50. Martínez Reverte, *La Batalla del Ebro*, 199; Revilla Cebrecos, *Tercio de Lácar*, 89, 242; Caballero, *Diario de campaña*, 141; Llordés Badía, *Al dejar el fusil*, 246; Urra Lusarreta, *En las trincheras*, 150, 279; González Bueno, *Paz en guerra*, 109; Delgado Iribarren, *Jesuitas en Campaña*, 242; Resa, *Memorias de un requeté*, 67; Aróstegui, *Los combatientes carlistas*, 1:149.

51. Cía Navascués, *Memorias*, 98, 228; Nagore Yárnoz, *En la primera de Navarra*, 93–139; Bullón de Mendoza and Diego, *Historias orales de la Guerra civil*, 46; Satrústegui, *Memorias de un anarquista*, 210; Revilla Cebrecos, *Tercio de Lácar*, 230.

52. Revilla Cebrecos, *Tercio de Lácar*, 104, 147; Ugarte Tellería, *La nueva Covadonga*, 155; Nagore Yárnoz, *En la primera de Navarra*, 43–61; Cervera Gil, *Ya sabes mi paradero*, 114.

53. Iribarren, *El General Mola*, 270; *ABC*, 10 October 1936, 30 June 1937; Caballero, *Diario de campaña*, 423; Corral, *Desertores*, 72–74.

54. Cardona and Losada, *Aunque me tires el puente*, 102–80; Nonell Bru, *El Laureado Tercio*, 417; Martínez Reverte, *La Batalla del Ebro*, 183; *ABC*, 10 and 15 September 1937, 3 August 1938; *El Correo de Zamora*, 21 August 1936, 19 November 1936, 15 December 1936; *La Nueva España*, 12 August 1938; Queipo de Llano, *Memorias*, 87; *Proa*, 27 November 1936.

55. *ABC*, 31 October 1936, 5 November 1936, 16 January 1937, 23 May 1937, 13 June 1937, 24 November 1938; *La Nueva España*, 12 December 1937, 30 January 1938, 8 February 1938.

56. *ABC*, 5 November 1936, 7 February 1937, 25 March 1937, 15 April 1937, 10 September 1937, 11 November 1937, 23 December 1937, 24 and 29 March 1938, 14 May 1938; *El Correo de Zamora*, 4 November 1936, 15 December 1936, 21 August 1938, 4 January 1939; *La Nueva España*, 18 February 1938; Burgos, Memoria, 1937, 44/3116, AGA; Zamora, Memoria [1940?], 44/3125, AGA; Memoria, Pontevedra, 1937, 44/3122, AGA; Memoria, Granada, 1938, 44/2791, AGA.

57. *ABC*, 6 January 1939; *El Pueblo Gallego*, 14 April 1937, 13 June 1937, 17 October 1937, 25 May 1938, 2 March 1939; *El Correo de Zamora*, 17 May 1938, 4 and 20 August 1938, 1 September 1938, 11 and 22 October 1938, 5 December 1938, 16 February 1939, 4 May 1939, 19 June 1939; *La Nueva España*, 27 and 30 April 1938, 24 August 1938, 22 November 1938, 12 March 1939, 13 April 1939; *La Provincia*, 4 September 1938, 31 January 1939; *Proa*, 20 August 1937, 17 December 1938, 28 February 1939, 17 March 1939.

58. *La Nueva España*, 22 December 1937, 18 February 1939, 16 and 19 April 1939; *El Correo de Zamora*, 17 October 1937, 5 November 1937, 17 May 1938, 21 and 25 August 1938, 22 October 1938, 1 June 1939; *Proa*, 12 November 1938, 2 February 1939; Burgos, Memoria, 1937, 44/3116, AGA; *ABC*, 7 and 11 May 1939.

59. *El Pueblo Gallego*, 14 October 1938; *El Correo de Zamora*, 16 July 1938, 11 August 1938, 28 September 1938; Comité Sindical del Jabón, 26 September 1938, 34/10856, AGA.

60. *ABC*, 1 May 1937, 15 September 1937, 29 March 1938, 19 May 1938, 2 June 1938; *La Nueva España*, 25 May 1938; Rey, *Paisanos en lucha*, 204.

61. *ABC*, 19–22 April 1938, 29 September 1938; *La Nueva España*, 19 May 1939, 14 June 1939.

62. *La Nueva España*, 1 and 28–31 July 1938, 12 and 26–28 August 1938, 22 and 23 September 1938, 6 October 1938; Zaragoza, Memoria, 1940, 44/3125, AGA; *El Correo de Zamora*, 20 January 1937.

63. *La Nueva España*, 29 December 1937, 8 April 1938, 5, 19, and 27 May 1939, 12 July 1938, 3 and 28 August 1938; David Martín, "Gitanos en la Guerra Civil Española," paper delivered to Congreso Internacional, 1936–39 La Guerra Civil Española, Madrid, 27–29 November 2006, 6, 10; Seidman, *Republic of Egos*, 231; *La Provincia*, 14 January 1938; *El Correo de Zamora*, 11 August 1938, 7 March 1939.

64. *El Pueblo Gallego*, 17 September 1937, 3, 17, and 23 November 1937, 23 December 1937, 8 and 16 January 1938, 27 December 1938; *Proa*, 3 November 1938; *El Correo de Zamora*, 18 January 1938, 25 February 1938, 1 and 24 August 1938, 17 November 1938, 25 January 1939, 6 February 1939, 5 March 1939, 18 and 26 March 1939.

65. *El Correo de Zamora*, 12 and 15 November 1937; *La Provincia*, 18 May 1938; Cervera Gil, *Ya sabes mi paradero*, 122–23; *ABC*, 16 January 1937, 3 September 1937, 21 December 1938; *La Nueva España*, 29 April 1937, 12 July 1938; Copado, *Con la columna Redondo*, 90; Excelentísimo Señor, 5 June 1938, Interior, 61/13500, AGA; Gobierno Civil de León, Memoria, August 1938, 44/2791, AGA; Huesca, Memoria, 1938, 44/2791, AGA; Toledo, Memoria, n.d., 44/3123, AGA.

66. Gobierno Civil de Castellón, 6 September 1938, Interior, 61/13497, AGA; Abella, *La vida cotidiana republicana*, 271; Provincia de Teruel [1940?], 44/3123, AGA. Figures differ somewhat in Teruel, Memoria, 1939, 44/3123, AGA, although the order of magnitude is similar. Tarragona, Cálculo aproximado de daños sufridos, n.d., 44/3123, AGA; Huesca, Memoria, 1938, 44/2791, AGA; *ABC*, 15 February 1939. See also Seidman, *Republic of Egos*, 69, 97–98, 125, 131–33, 170–71.

67. Cardona and Losada, *Aunque me tires el puente*, 63; *ABC*, 29 March 1938; *El Pueblo Gallego*, 11 October 1938; Servicio Nacional del Trigo, *Veinte años*, 279–80; Tarragona, Memoria, 11 March 1940, 44/3123, AGA; *La Provincia*, 14 July 1938.

68. *El Correo de Zamora*, 20 August 1936, 17 August 1938; Gobierno Civil, Lugo, 1938, 44/2791, AGA; *ABC*, 17 November 1937, 27 July 1938; *La Nueva España*, 4 August 1938; Orense, September 1938, 44/2791, AGA; Huesca, Memoria, 1938, 44/2791, AGA.

69. *ABC*, 25 September 1937; *El Pueblo Gallego*, 1 and 8 September 1937, 22 December 1937, 12 April 1938, 8 and 15 September 1938; *El Correo de Zamora*, 11 January

1937, 15 August 1938, 17 and 19 June 1939; Burgos, Memoria, 1937, 44/3116, AGA; Memoria, Palencia, 1938, 44/3123, AGA; *Proa*, 26 August 1938, 13 September 1938; *La Provincia*, 31 July 1938; Huesca, Memoria, 1938, 44/2791, AGA; Llordés Badía, *Al dejar el fusil*, 351.

70. Pascual Díez de Rivera y Casares, *La Riqueza pesquera en España y las cofradías de pescadores* (Madrid, 1940), 53; Nagore Yárnoz, *En la primera de Navarra*, 11–191; Cía Navascués, *Memorias*, 133; Medina, *Tiempo pasado*, 104; Peiró, *Fernando de Huidobro*, 207; Caballero, *Diario de campaña*, 29.

71. *El Pueblo Gallego*, 17 and 29 May 1936, 2, 11, and 18 June 1936, 12 August 1936, 20 December 1937, 3 August 1938; Díez de Rivera, *La Riqueza pesquera*, 26, 33; Gobierno Civil, Huelva, August 1938, 44/2791, AGA.

72. *El Pueblo Gallego*, 9 and 28 August 1936, 5 September 1936, 20 December 1937; Díez de Rivera, *La Riqueza pesquera*, 34–36; Beevor, *The Battle for Spain*, 104; Cayón García and Muñoz Rubio, "Transportes y Comunicaciones," 233; Memoria, Pontevedra, 1937, 44/3122, AGA; Gobierno Civil, Huelva, August 1938, 44/2791, AGA.

73. *El Pueblo Gallego*, 6 September 1936, 3 and 11 June 1937, 5 August 1937, 20 December 1937, 4 March 1938, 28 April 1938, 3 May 1938, 16 June 1938, 22 July 1938, 5 August 1938, 25 September 1938, 25 April 1939; *ABC*, 6 January 1937, 8 April 1938; *La Nueva España*, 23 September 1938; Díez de Rivera, *La Riqueza pesquera*, 10–22.

74. Díez de Rivera, *La Riqueza pesquera*, 11–24; Catalan, "Guerra e industria," 213; *El Pueblo Gallego*, 20 December 1937, 11 August 1938, 21 February 1939; Memoria, Pontevedra, 1937, 44/3122, AGA.

75. Catalan, "Guerra e industria," 212; *El Pueblo Gallego*, 21 November 1937, 20 December 1937, 20 February 1938, 5 and 11 August 1938, 1 November 1938, 21 February 1939; *ABC*, 1 April 1938; Bastida Pellicer, *Historias de un quinto*, 190.

76. *El Pueblo Gallego*, 27 November 1937, 20 December 1937, 16 February 1938, 12 April 1938, 4 August 1938; *La Nueva España*, 23 November 1937, 22 December 1937.

77. Corral, *Desertores*, 447; Nagore Yárnoz, *En la primera de Navarra*, 34; *El Pueblo Gallego*, 17 July 1937, 14 and 28 November 1937, 11 February 1938, 7 and 12 March 1939; Díez de Rivera, *La Riqueza pesquera*, 23; Memoria, Pontevedra, 1937, 44/3122, AGA.

78. *ABC*, 10 October 1937; Memoria, Pontevedra, 1937, 44/3122, AGA; Gobierno Civil de Segovia, Memoria, 25 August 1938, 44/2792, AGA; *El Pueblo Gallego*, 16 June 1938; Gobierno Civil, Huelva, August 1938, 44/2791, AGA; Diez de Rivera, *La Riqueza pesquera*, 48–120; *La Nueva España*, 18 June 1938; Luis Díaz Viana, *Cancionero popular de la Guerra civil española: Textos y melodías de los dos bandos* (Madrid, 2007), 181.

79. Velarde Fuertes, "Algunos aspectos económicos," 949; Thomas, *Spanish Civil War*, 273; Sánchez Asiaín, *Economía*, 256; Torres Villanueva, "Los empresarios," 440.

80. Memoria, Ávila, August 1938, 44/2790, AGA; Viñas, *El oro*, 218–27.

81. Guy Hermet, *La guerre d'Espagne* (Paris, 1989), 184; Hubbard, "How Franco Financed His War," 404; Gianfranco Poggi, *Money and the Modern Mind: George Simmel's Philosophy of Money* (Berkeley, 1993), 152; Viñas, "Financing," 280; How-

son, *Arms for Spain*, 56; Fernando Eguidazu, *Intervención monetaria y control de cambios en España, 1900–1977* (Madrid, 1978), 157.

82. Corral, *Desertores*, 86–90. Cf. El Merroun, *Las tropas marroquíes*, 186, who argues that Moroccan soldiers were not mercenaries because they did not join the supposedly more highly paid Republican troops. Llordés Badía, *Al dejar el fusil*, 182–302.

83. Sánchez Asiaín, *Economía*, 17–292; *ABC*, 18 November 1936; Manuel Garzón Pareja, *Historia de la Hacienda de España* (Madrid, 1984), 2:1155–56; *El Pueblo Gallego*, 22 September 1936, 15 May 1937; *El Correo de Zamora*, 17 September 1936; *La Provincia*, 31 July 1936; McCullagh, *In Franco's Spain*, 140, 251; Pablo Martín Aceña, "La Quiebra del sistema financiero," in Martín Aceña and Martínez Ruiz, *La economía*, 411.

84. Miguel Martorell Linares, "Una Guerra, Dos Pesetas," in Martín Aceña and Martínez Ruiz, *La economía*, 334; Hill, 7 June 1918, in Kenneth Bourne and D. Cameron Watt, eds., *British Documents on Foreign Affairs: The Soviet Union, 1917–1939*, 1:373; Bechhofer, *In Denikin's Russia*, 23; Hill to Curzon, 7 June 1919, FO 371 4024, PRO; Vladimir N. Brovkin, "Introduction," in Brovkin, *The Bolsheviks*, 17; George Young, n.d., FO 371 3960, PRO; Mawdsley, *Russian Civil War*, 137; Kenez, *Civil War in South Russia, 1919–1920*, 63–95; Figes, *A People's Tragedy*, 654.

85. Pepper, *Civil War in China*, 95; E. R. Lapwood and Nancy Lapwood, *Through the Chinese Revolution* (Westport, CT, 1973), 39; Emily Honig, *Sisters and Strangers: Women in the Shanghai Cotton Mills, 1919–1949* (Stanford, 1986), 38; Lloyd E. Eastman, *Seeds of Destruction: Nationalist China in War and Revolution, 1937–1949* (Stanford, 1984), 221; Prof. Chao Lan-ping, "Economic Prospects," *Economic Review*, Shanghai, vol. 3, no. 17, 7 August 1948, *Chinese Magazine Review*, NYPL; Yang Peisin, "The Speeding Up of Food Requisition," *The Modern Critique*, 1 September 1947, *Chinese Press Review*, Shanghai, NYPL; "Commodity Prices," Yi Shih Pao, 11 January 1946, *Peking-Peiping-Tientsin Press Review*, NYPL; Ying Ling, "A Poignant Word About Calamities," Ta Kung Pao, 28 July 1947, *Chinese Press Review*, Shanghai, NYPL; "Defenses in Szechuan against Possible Communist Incursion," *Observer Weekly* (Independent, Liberal), Shanghai, vol. 3, no. 18, 27 November 1947, *Chinese Press Review*, Shanghai, NYPL.

86. "Shanghai's Rice Problem," Ta Kung Pao, 10 December 1948, *Chinese Press Review*, Shanghai, NYPL; "Let Us Barter Gold for Rice," Shang Pao (Commercial Organ), *Chinese Press Review*, Shanghai, NYPL; "Thoughts," Ta Kung Pao, 31 December 1948, *Chinese Press Review*, Shanghai, NYPL.

87. Levine, *Anvil*, 196; Wou, *Mobilizing*, 184; South Hopei, 21 March 1947, in Paul Preston and Michael Partridge, eds., *British Documents on Foreign Affairs: Reports and Papers from the Foreign Office Confidential Print*, pt. 4, series E, *Asia 1946*, 3:111.

88. Nonell Bru, *El Laureado Tercio*, 106; the *Times* quoted in Tortella and García Ruiz, "Banca y política," in Sánchez Recio and Tascón Fernández, *Los empresarios de Franco*, 68; Sánchez Asiaín, *Economía*, 90, 146, 175. Figures differ somewhat in Juan Velarde Fuertes, "Algunos aspectos económicos de la guerra civil," in Bullón de Mendoza and Togores, *Revisión*, 963. Kenez, *Civil War in South Russia, 1919–1920*, 63; Bechhofer, *In Denikin's Russia*, 98.

89. Sánchez Asiaín, *Economía*, 158–288; Informe colectivo, la banca privada

y cajas de ahorro, Burgos, August 1938, 44/2790, AGA; Cierva, *Historia ilustrada*, 2:10; Olmedo Delgado and Cuesta Monereo, *General Queipo de Llano*, 138; Gibson, *Queipo de Llano*, 378; Memoria, Pontevedra, 1939, 44/3122, AGA; Memoria, Álava, 1938, 44/2790, AGA; *El Pueblo Gallego*, 8 November 1936, 2 April 1939; Catalan, "Guerra e industria," 191; *ABC*, 26 March 1938, 24 June 1938.

90. *ABC*, 10 and 18 May 1938, [20?] and 24 June 1938, 24 August 1938; SNT, Palencia, 27 October 1938, 61/13502, AGA; SNT, Jefatura Provincial, León, 28 October 1938, Interior, 61/13500, AGA; *El Pueblo Gallego*, 30 August 1938.

91. Elena Martínez Ruiz, "Las relaciones económicas internacionales: Guerra, política y negocios," in Martín Aceña and Martínez Ruiz, *La economía*, 297–300; Sánchez Asiaín, *Economía*, 87–256; Gibson, *Queipo de Llano*, 334–62; Hubbard, "How Franco Financed His War," 394; Borja de Riquer i Permanyer, *l'últim Cambó (1936–1947): La dreta catalanista davant la guerra civil i el primer franquisme* (Vic, 1996), 182; Garzón Pareja, *Historia de la Hacienda*, 2:1152. The foreign currencies were sometimes returned to their original owners at the end of the war. For Republican gold in 1936, see Ángel Viñas, *La Soledad de la República: El abandono de las democracias y el viraje hacia la Unión Soviética* (Barcelona, 2006), 306–7. *La Provincia*, 10 April 1937; Velarde Fuertes, "Algunos aspectos económicos," 951; Llordés Badía, *Al dejar el fusil*, 190; Olmedo Delgado and Cuesta Monereo, *General Queipo de Llano*, 230; López Ortiz and Melgarejo Moreno, "El Sector Agrario durante la Guerra Civil," 23; *ABC*, 25 August 1936, 25 March 1937, 9 October 1937, 13 January 1938. On olive oil, see Memoria, Granada, 1938, 44/2791, AGA, 148.

92. Sánchez Asiaín, *Economía*, 95; Martínez Ruiz, "Las relaciones económicas internacionales," 279–303; Hubbard, "How Franco Financed His War," 398; *ABC*, 21 March 1937, 27 October 1938; García, *Mentiras necesarias*, 14; Martínez Ruiz, "El campo en guerra," 155–56; *La Provincia*, 4 June 1937; *El Pueblo Gallego*, 6 March 1936; German trade figures in *ABC*, 12 October 1937.

93. Nonell Bru, *El Laureado Tercio*, 539; Ángela Cenarro, *La sonrisa de Falange: Auxilio Social en la guerra y la posguerra* (Barcelona, 2006), 15–16, reports confiscations for the benefit of Auxilio Social. Sánchez Asiaín, *Economía*, 136–67; Sánchez Ruano, *Islam*, 366; Llordés Badía, *Al dejar el fusil*, 295.

94. Hubbard, "How Franco Financed His War," 394; Pablo Martín Aceña, "La Quiebra del sistema financiero," 402; Torres Villanueva, "Los empresarios," 436–47; Abella, *La vida cotidiana nacional*, 99; Salas, *Sevilla*, 2:729; Marqués de San Juan de Piedras Albas, *Héroes y mártires de la aristocracia española, Julio 1936–Marzo 1939* (Madrid, 1945), 193–467; Pablo Díaz Morlán, *Los Ybarra: Una dinastía de empresarios (1801–2001)* (Madrid, 2002), 260; *ABC*, 30 November 1937.

95. Sánchez Asiaín, *Economía*, 89; Hubbard, "How Franco Financed His War," 393; Gibson, *Queipo de Llano*, 153, 247; Figes, *A People's Tragedy*, 655; Kenez, *Civil War in South Russia, 1918*, 72–177; Brovkin, *Behind the Front*, 233; Secret, 25 June 1947, NA M1221, Intelligence Reports, 3292, U.S. Department of State, NA. The other third of China was ruled by local warlords. The Present Position, July 1947, F0371 63326, PRO; Pepper, *Civil War in China*, 172; Lapwood and Lapwood, *Through the Chinese Revolution*, 25.

96. Ortiz Villalba, *Sevilla 1936*, 174; *El Correo de Zamora*, 13 August 1936,

1 February 1937; Abella, *La vida cotidiana nacional*, 53; *ABC*, 4 and 25 August 1936; Garzón Pareja, *Historia de la Hacienda*, 2:1161–64; Sánchez Asiaín, *Economía*, 150, 254; *La Provincia*, 8 November 1937; Cierva, *Historia ilustrada*, 1:379; *El Pueblo Gallego*, 31 July 1936, 9 August 1936; *La Nueva España*, 1 February 1937, 26 August 1937; Iribarren, *El General Mola*, 211.

97. Gibson, *Queipo de Llano*, 159–400; Domingo, *Retaguardia*, 239, 274; *El Pueblo Gallego*, 7 August 1936; Manuel Barrios, *El Último Virrey: Queipo de Llano* (Seville, 1990), 188. On bullfights during the civil war, see Adrian Shubert, *Death and Money in the Afternoon: A History of the Spanish Bullfight* (New York, 1999), 45–213. *ABC*, 8, 15, and 27 September 1936, 17 and 21 October 1936; Informe colectivo, la banca privada y cajas de ahorro, Burgos, August 1938, 44/2790, AGA; Abella, *La vida cotidiana nacional*, 54.

98. Medina, *Tiempo pasado*, 61; Riesco Roche, *La Reforma*, 352; Gibson, *Queipo de Llano*, 260; Barrios, *El Último Virrey*, 188; Quevedo, *Queipo de Llano*, 393.

99. Abella, *La vida cotidiana nacional*, 53; *ABC*, 14 August 1936, 5 November 1936, 9 March 1938; *El Pueblo Gallego*, 27 December 1936; Gibson, *Queipo de Llano*, 260; Memoria, Ávila, August 1938, 44/2790, AGA; Gobierno Civil de Segovia, Memoria, 25 August 1938, 44/2792, AGA; Gobierno Civil de León, Memoria, August 1938, 44/2791, AGA; Orense, September 1938, 44/2791, AGA; Oviedo, 1938, 44/2791, AGA; Huesca, Memoria, 1938, 44/2791, AGA; Memoria, Álava, 1938, 44/2790, AGA; Castro, *Capital de la Cruzada*, 273; Ángela Cenarro, "El poder local durante la guerra civil," in Fuentes Quintana and Comín Comín, *Economía*, 1:257.

100. *ABC*, 30 July 1936, 19 August 1936; Martorell Linares, "Una Guerra, Dos Pesetas," 380; Viñas, *La Soledad de la República*, 132; Lazo, *Retrato de fascismo*, 60, 88; Castro, *Capital de la Cruzada*, 166.

101. Souto Blanco, *La represión franquista*, 37, 148; Rey, *Paisanos en lucha*, 428; Casanova, *República y guerra civil*, 57; *El Pueblo Gallego*, 21 and 22 May 1936; *La Provincia*, 24 July 1936; *ABC*, 7 August 1936, 17 September 1936, 28 March 1937, 29 May 1937, 16 November 1937; Gibson, *Queipo de Llano*, 176, 355.

102. Riquer i Permanyer, *l'últim Cambó*, 61–174; Torres Villanueva, "Los empresarios," 437.

103. Riquer i Permanyer, *l'últim Cambó*, 160–79; Catalan, "Guerra e industria," 191; *ABC*, 13 January 1938; Sánchez Asiaín, *Economía*, 65.

104. Bahamonde y Sánchez de Castro, *Un Año con Queipo*, 46; Nonell Bru, *El Laureado Tercio*, 100; Souto Blanco, *La represión franquista*, 327–30; *El Correo de Zamora*, 18, 23, and 29 December 1936, 9 June 1937; *El Pueblo Gallego*, 17 September 1937, 2 December 1937, 30 April 1938, 4 August 1938; *Proa*, 2 and 28 August 1937, 25 September 1937; *La Provincia*, 15 June 1937, 7 July 1937, 8 November 1937, 19 January 1939; Cenarro, *La sonrisa de Falange*, 22, 46.

105. Bahamonde y Sánchez de Castro, *Un Año con Queipo*, 95; Ortiz Villalba, *Sevilla 1936*, 174; *ABC*, 21 April 1938, 26 April 1939; Gibson, *Queipo de Llano*, 247–448; Cenarro, *La sonrisa de Falange*, 50.

106. Ortiz Villalba, *Sevilla 1936*, 174; *La Provincia*, 19 April 1938; Domingo, *Retaguardia*, 53; Abella, *La vida cotidiana nacional*, 193; *La Nueva España*, 19 November 1937; *ABC*, 27 April 1937.

107. Sánchez Asiaín, *Economía*, 117–318. Nationalists claimed that stock and bond certificates stored in banks located in the Republican zone had been destroyed. See *ABC*, 30 November 1937. Martín Aceña, "La Quiebra del sistema financiero," 413; Payne, *The Franco Regime, 1936–1975* (Madison, WI, 1987), 184.

108. Garzón Pareja, *Historia de la Hacienda*, 2:1148–53; Hubbard, "How Franco Financed His War," 393; Martorell Linares, "Una Guerra, Dos Pesetas," 378; Velarde Fuertes, "Algunos aspectos económicos," 956–59.

109. Martínez Ruiz, "Las relaciones económicas internacionales," 274; Cardona and Losada, *Aunque me tires el puente*, 332; Martorell Linares, "Una Guerra, Dos Pesetas," 382; Viñas, *La Soledad de la República*, 135–37; Garzón Pareja, *Historia de la Hacienda*, 2:1159–63; Torres Villanueva, "Los empresarios," 440; *ABC*, 15 December 1936; Velarde Fuertes, "Algunos aspectos económicos," 961–63; Juan Sardá, "El Banco de España (1931–1962)," in Alfonso Moreno Redondo, ed., *El Banco de España: Una historia económica* (Madrid, 1970), 445; Francisco Comín Comín, "Las economías y los economistas españoles durante la guerra civil española y la posguerra: Una introducción," in Fuentes Quintana and Comín Comín, *Economía*, 1:99–114.

110. War Cabinet, 23 July 1919, FO 371 4029, PRO; William S. Graves, *America's Siberian Adventure* (New York, 1941), 201, 227; Odessa, 22 March 1919, Department of State, Internal Affairs of Russia, roll 20, NA.

111. Quoted in Westad, *Decisive Encounters*, 112–61; Chi Ming, "The Military Situation in North China," *Observer Weekly* (Independent Liberal), vol. 5, no. 12, 4 December 1948, *Chinese Press Review*, Shanghai, NYPL; Levine, *Anvil*, 176; Political Summary for July 1946, in Preston and Partridge, eds., *British Documents on Foreign Affairs*, Pt, 4, Series E, *Asia 1946*, 2:101; "Communist Supply Stations in Shanghai, Soochow and Fenghsien Smashed," Shun Pao (GMD-supervised), Shanghai, *Chinese Press Review*, Shanghai, NYPL; Wou, *Mobilizing*, 332; "Competent Authorities," Chin Yung Jih Pao (Connected with S.Y. Liu and Political Science Group), *Chinese Press Review*, Shanghai, NYPL.

112. Anthony Oberschall and Michael Seidman, "Food Coercion in Revolution and Civil War: Who Wins and How They Do It," *Comparative Studies in Society and History* 47, no. 2 (April 2005): 372–402; "Communist Victories Due to a Strategy of Exhausting Enemies," New China News Agency, Peiping, 29 October 1946, *Chinese Press Review*, NYPL; Cheng Yua-chung, "Three Stages in the Land Problem in Northern Kiangsu," *The Economic Weekly*, Shanghai, 31 October 1946, *Chinese Press Review*, Shanghai, NYPL; "A Bird's-eye View of the Military Situation," Ta Kung Pao (Political Science Group), Shanghai, 14 February 1947, *Chinese Press Review*, Shanghai, NYPL; Intentions, 9 November 1945, NA M1221, Intelligence Reports, 3292, U.S. Department of State, NA; *Mukden Mail*, New Road, Peiping, no. 16, vol. 1, 28 August 1948, *Chinese Magazine Review*, NYPL; A. Dahoui, 30 June 1948, Asie-Océanie Chine, 134, Archives Diplomatiques; "On the Food Administration Problems," Ta Kung Pao, 13 October 1948, *Chinese Press Review*, Shanghai, NYPL; "On the Defense of Changchun," Chung Yan Jih Pao (GMD Organ), *Chinese Press Review*, Shanghai, NYPL.

113. Food requirements, 17 January 1946, China Internal Affairs, U.S. Department of State, LM 184, roll 50, NA; Secstate, 22 May 1946, China Internal Affairs, U.S. Department of State, LM 184, roll 50, NA; Seymour Topping, *Journey between Two*

Chinas (New York, 1972), 16; Raymond J. De Jaegher and Irene Kuhn, *The Enemy Within: An Eyewitness Account of the Communist Conquest of China* (Garden City, NY, 1952), 298.

114. *ABC*, 3, 5, and 11 August 1936, 8 September 1936, 29 March 1938; Huesca, Memoria, 1938, 44/2791, AGA; Gibson, *Queipo de Llano*, 259, 413; Memoria, Granada, 1938, 44/2791, AGA; Ortiz Villalba, *Sevilla 1936*, 173, 264.

115. Ortiz Villalba, *Sevilla 1936*, 153; Casas de la Vega, *Las milicias nacionales*, 1:432; *ABC*, 15 December 1936, 8 December 1938, 9 June 1939; *El Correo de Zamora*, 27 July 1937; *El Pueblo Gallego*, 31 May 1936, 20 May 1937; Vizcaya, Diputación Provincia, n.d., 44/3124, AGA; Souto Blanco, *La represión franquista*, 69.

116. Abella, *La vida cotidiana nacional*, 270; *ABC*, 27 August 1936, 11 October 1936, 29 December 1936, 18 March 1937, 4 April 1937; Olmedo Delgado and Cuesta Monereo, *General Queipo de Llano*, 233; Gibson, *Queipo de Llano*, 260; Schempp, *Das Autoritäre Spanien*, 114; Salas, *Sevilla*, 2:730; *La Provincia*, 23 February 1938; Queipo de Llano, *Memorias*, 194; Martorell Linares and Comín Comín, "La Hacienda," 1:923.

117. *ABC*, 19 August 1936, 1 November 1936, 10 December 1937, 3 December 1938; *El Correo de Zamora*, 5 March 1939; Cenarro, *La sonrisa de Falange*, 10–53; Monica Orduña Prada, "Donativos nacionales e internacionales a Auxilio Social," in Bullón de Mendoza and Togores, *Revisión*, 1088; Bahamonde y Sánchez de Castro, *Un Año con Queipo*, 93–94. *El Correo de Zamora*, 11 August 1938, corroborates Bahamonde's charge. Gobierno Civil de Segovia, Memoria, 25 August 1938, 44/2792, AGA; Gobierno Civil de León, Memoria, August 1938, 44/2791, AGA.

118. *ABC*, 13 July 1937; Bahamonde y Sánchez de Castro, *Un Año con Queipo*, 59–90.

119. *ABC*, 10 April 1937, 12 June 1937, 16 December 1937; *El Pueblo Gallego*, 15 March 1938, 5 August 1938; Lazo, *Retrato de fascismo*, 120; Campoamor, *La revolución española*, 77; Bahamonde y Sánchez de Castro, *Un Año con Queipo*, 90–91; Orduña Prada, *El Auxilio Social*, 214–15.

120. *El Pueblo Gallego*, 4, 13, 14, 20, and 24 July 1937, 1 and 31 December 1937, 19 May 1938; Gobierno Civil, Cáceres, August 1938, 44/2790, AGA; *ABC*, 15 April 1939, 27 May 1939.

121. Simpson, "Economic Development in Spain," 355; *ABC*, 14, 18, and 19 August 1936, 18 December 1936, 10 January 1937; *Proa*, 8 January 1939; SNT Jefatura provincial Zaragoza, 26 September 1938, Interior, 61/13509, AGA.

122. Castro, *Capital de la Cruzada*, 151–80; *La Nueva España*, 16 June 1937; *El Pueblo Gallego*, 6 September 1936, 25 December 1936.

123. *ABC*, 13 and 29 August 1936, 18 and 25 November 1936, 1 September 1937, 4 January 1938, 15 February 1938, 19 May 1938; *La Nueva España*, 12 March 1939; *El Pueblo Gallego*, 9 May 1936, 2 August 1936, 29 October 1937; Gobierno Civil, Cáceres, August 1938, 44/2790, AGA; Memoria, Pontevedra, 1937, 44/3122, AGA; *La Provincia*, 20 January 1937.

124. *La Provincia*, 2 February 1937, 2 August 1938; Provincia de Santa Cruz de Tenerife, 26 August 1940, 44/3123, AGA; Memoria de las Palmas, 7 September 1938, 44/3123, AGA; Santa Cruz de Tenerife, Memoria, 1938, 44/2792, AGA.

125. *El Pueblo Gallego*, 3 September 1937, 3 March 1938, 5 July 1938, 1, 6, 10, and 12 January 1939, 13 April 1939, 2 June 1939; Memoria, Pontevedra, 1937, 44/3122, AGA; *Proa*, 27 December 1938; *La Provincia*, 5 March 1938; Oviedo, 1938, 44/2791, AGA.

126. *ABC*, 19 August 1936, 8 September 1936; Hubbard, "How Franco Financed His War," 394.

127. Memoria, Álava, 1938, 44/2790, AGA; Diputación Provincial de Segovia, 11 July 1940, 44/3123, AGA. Cf. Gobierno Civil de Segovia, Memoria, 25 August 1938, 44/2792, AGA. Memoria, Ávila, August 1938, 44/2790, AGA; Zaragoza, Memoria, 1940, 44/3125, AGA; Sevilla, Memoria, 1938–39, 44/3123, AGA; Miguel Martorell Linares, "La extirpación a fondo de nuestros enemigos: Represión económica y financiación de la guerra en la España franquista (1936–1940)," paper presented to the III Encontro Luso-Espanhol de História Política, University of Évora, Portugal, 4–5 June 2007, 17.

128. Memoria, Palencia, 1938, 44/3123, AGA; *ABC*, 24 March 1937, 4 January 1938, 29 March 1938, 4 January 1939; 9 February 1939; *El Correo de Zamora*, 21 January 1938, 1 February 1938, 21 February 1939; *Proa*, 5 January 1939; *La Provincia*, 7 February 1937, 13 May 1938; *El Pueblo Gallego*, 29 May 1936, 18 January 1939, 1 April 1939, 9 and 10 June 1939; Abella, *La vida cotidiana nacional*, 397; Velarde Fuertes, "Algunos aspectos económicos," 957; Jurado de Utilidades, 2.3, Legajo 19945, AGA; Souto Blanco, *La represión franquista*, 330.

129. *ABC*, 10 January 1937, 18 March 1937, 30 December 1937; *El Pueblo Gallego*, 22 and 26 August 1936; *El Correo de Zamora*, 4 December 1936, 15 January 1937, 27 February 1937, 13 and 23 March 1937; Zaragoza, Memoria, 1940, 44/3125, AGA; Diputación Provincial de Segovia, 11 July 1940, 44/3123, AGA; Gobierno Civil de León, Memoria, August 1938, 44/2791, AGA; Memoria, Pontevedra, 1937, 44/3122, AGA; *La Nueva España*, 19 March 1938; Sevilla, Memoria, 1938–39, 44/3123, AGA.

130. *ABC*, 1 October 1936, 11 February 1937, 25 March 1937, 8 January 1938, 18 March 1938, 24 February 1939; *El Pueblo Gallego*, 16 and 26 August 1936; *Proa*, 14 July 1938; *La Provincia*, 28 February 1937; *La Nueva España*, 16 November 1937, 30 November 1937, 22 December 1937, 20 January 1938.

131. Barrios, *El Último Virrey*, 182–83; Abella, *La vida cotidiana nacional*, 113; Castro, *Capital de la Cruzada*, 111; Velarde Fuertes, "Algunos aspectos económicos," 958; *ABC*, 11 August 1937; *La Provincia*, 31 July 1937; Bahamonde y Sánchez de Castro, *Un Año con Queipo*, 47; Gobierno Civil de Segovia, Memoria, 25 August 1938, 44/2792, AGA; *El Pueblo Gallego*, 12 November 1936.

132. Cenarro, *La sonrisa de Falange*, 182; Javier Martínez de Bedoya, *Memorias desde mi aldea* (Valladolid, 1996), 105; Velarde Fuertes, "Algunos aspectos económicos," 958; Gobierno Civil de Segovia, Memoria, 25 August 1938, 44/2792, AGA; Gobierno Civil de León, Memoria, August 1938, 44/2791, AGA; Junta Provincial de Beneficencia, [1938?], 44/2791, AGA; Gobierno Civil, Huelva, August 1938, 44/2791, AGA; Orense, September 1938, 44/2791, AGA; Huesca, Memoria, 1938, 44/2791, AGA; *ABC*, 25 October 1936, 28 August 1938; *El Correo de Zamora*, 30 October 1936; Raguer, *La Espada*, 69.

133. *ABC*, 7 April 1937, 17 and 29 November 1938; Memoria, Lugo, 30 July 1938, 44/2791, AGA; *La Provincia*, 5 December 1938.

134. Cazorla Sánchez, *Las políticas de la victoria*, 72; Thomas, *Brother against Brother*, 104; Corral, *Desertores*, 91; Souto Blanco, *La represión franquista*, 186; Garzón Pareja, *Historia de la Hacienda*, 2:1151; Velarde Fuertes, "Algunos aspectos económicos," 957; *El Pueblo Gallego*, 11 April 1937; *ABC*, 10 July 1937, 26 June 1938; Gobierno Civil de Segovia, Memoria, 25 August 1938, 44/2792, AGA; Junta Provincial de Beneficencia, [1938?], 44/2791, AGA; Gobierno Civil de León, Memoria, August 1938, 44/2791, AGA; Huesca, Memoria, 1938, 44/2791, AGA; Gobierno Civil, Huelva, August 1938, 44/2791, AGA; Informe, Lugo, 13 August 1938, 44/2791, AGA.

135. *El Correo de Zamora*, 19 and 20 May 1937, 28 April 1938, 22 May 1939; *El Pueblo Gallego*, 6 June 1939; Corral, *Desertores*, 92; *ABC*, 6 December 1936; *La Nueva España*, 14 November 1937.

136. Edwards, "Logistics and Supply," 265; *El Correo de Zamora*, 25 August 1937; *ABC*, 13 March 1937, 9 and 11 April 1937, 29 May 1937, 22 and 31 July 1937, 16 October 1937; *Proa*, 1 and 16 July 1937, 20 August 1937; *El Pueblo Gallego*, 20 June 1937, 23 June 1938, 30 July 1938; *La Nueva España*, 11 and 19 February 1938, 3 and 17 March 1938, 12 May 1938, 21 June 1938, 3 July 1938; *La Provincia*, 15, 20, and 21 May 1937, 4 June 1937, 8 July 1937, 23 December 1937, 12 and 24 February 1938, 15 March 1938, 26 April 1938, 23 August 1938.

137. *ABC*, 14 August 1937, 10 March 1938, 10 May 1938, 5 November 1938, 2–24 February 1939, 5, 7, and 19 May 1939; *La Provincia*, 31 July 1938; Memoria, Ávila, August 1938, 44/2790, AGA; *La Nueva España*, 12 January 1937, 5 June 1938.

138. *El Pueblo Gallego*, 19 May 1937, 12 and 26 June 1937, 18 July 1937, 11 November 1937, 28 April 1938; Memoria, Pontevedra, 1937, 44/3122, AGA. *El Correo de Zamora*, *La Nueva España*, and especially *El Pueblo Gallego* regularly reported the fines.

139. Gobierno Civil de León, Memoria, August 1938, 44/2791, AGA; Memoria, Ávila, August 1938, 44/2790, AGA; Memoria, Granada, 1938, 44/2791, AGA; *ABC*, 1 September 1937; Gobierno, Ceuta, Memoria, August 1938, 44/2790, AGA; *El Correo de Zamora*, 5 March 1939; *El Pueblo Gallego*, 10 and 11 August 1938, 21 June 1938.

140. Gobierno Civil de León, Memoria, August 1938, 44/2791, AGA; *ABC*, 18 June 1937, 11 July 1937, 28 August 1937; Memoria de las Palmas, 7 September 1938, 44/3123, AGA; *El Pueblo Gallego*, 12 August 1937, 28 April 1938, 17 May 1938; *La Provincia*, 31 July 1938.

141. Santa Cruz de Tenerife, Memoria, 1938, 44/2792, AGA; *La Provincia*, 24 December 1937; Informe, Lugo, 13 August 1938, 44/2791, AGA; *La Nueva España*, 11 December 1937.

142. Gobierno Civil de León, Memoria, August 1938, 44/2791, AGA; Memoria, Granada, 1938, 44/2791, AGA; Gobierno Civil, Cáceres, August 1938, 44/2790, AGA; Memoria, Ávila, August 1938, 44/2790, AGA; Gobierno, Ceuta, Memoria, August 1938, 44/2790, AGA; El Merroun, *Las tropas marroquíes*, 192; Corral, *Desertores*, 461.

143. Abella, *La vida cotidiana nacional*, 199. On lack of connection between subsidy and income, see *El Correo de Zamora*, 29 November 1938. On the official subsidy

scale, see *La Nueva España*, 1 November 1938. *Proa*, 31 December 1938; *La Provincia*, 2 December 1938; *ABC*, 4 December 1938; Gobierno Civil de León, Memoria, August 1938, 44/2791, AGA.

144. *El Pueblo Gallego*, 2 March 1939, 2 April 1939; *El Correo de Zamora*, 29 February 1939, 18 June 1939; *La Provincia*, 7 March 1939; *La Nueva España*, 30 November 1937, 16 December 1937, 11 December 1938.

145. Martorell Linares, "Una Guerra, Dos Pesetas," 358–61; Cervera Gil, *Ya sabes mi paradero*, 305; Memoria, Granada, 1938, 44/2791, AGA; Garzón Pareja, *Historia de la Hacienda*, 2:1133; *ABC*, 15 February 1939.

146. Bahamonde y Sánchez de Castro, *Un Año con Queipo*, 53–269; Ortiz Villalba, *Sevilla 1936*, 143–74; Domingo, *Retaguardia*, 105–356; Espinosa Maestre, *La justicia de Queipo*, 175; Souto Blanco, *La represión franquista*, 274; *La Nueva España*, 25 August 1937; Ruiz Vilaplana, *Burgos Justice*, 89–173; Salas, *Sevilla*, 1:143; *El Pueblo Gallego*, 2 October 1936; Souto Blanco, *La represión franquista*, 161–264.

147. José Luis Orella, "Los técnicos del bando nacional," 279; Olmedo Delgado and Cuesta Monereo, *General Queipo de Llano*, 148.

148. Rivero Noval, *Política y sociedad en la Rioja*, 248–49; Ruiz Vilaplana, *Burgos Justice*, 166; Gobierno Civil de Segovia, Memoria, 25 August 1938, 44/2792, AGA; Memoria, Ávila, August 1938, 44/2790, AGA; Memoria, Granada, 1938, 44/2791, AGA.

149. Espinosa Maestre, *La justicia de Queipo*, 175–81; Memoria de las Palmas, 7 September 1938, 44/3123, AGA; Memoria, Granada, 1938, 44/2791, AGA; Reservado, Política Interior, 1938, 44/2790, AGA; Gobierno Civil de Segovia, Memoria, 25 August 1938, 44/2792, AGA; Gobierno Civil, Huelva, August 1938, 44/2791, AGA; Oviedo, 1938, 44/2791, AGA; *La Nueva España*, 19 and 23 September 1937, 25 May 1938; Ruiz Vilaplana, *Burgos Justice*, 169; *ABC*, 8 June 1938; *El Pueblo Gallego*, 3 September 1937.

150. Comandante Militar, 21 November 1938, Talavera, 61/13506, AGA; Quevedo, *Queipo de Llano*, 462; Barrios, *El Último Virrey*, 187; Luis de Armiñan, *Excmo. Sr. General D. Gonzalo Queipo de Llano: Jefe del Ejército del Sur* (Ávila, 1937); Abella, *La vida cotidiana nacional*, 56, 132, 330; Catalan, "Guerra e industria," 197–206; Torres Villanueva, "Los empresarios," 448–52; *ABC*, 27 July 1938, 10 January 1939.

151. Catalan, "Guerra e industria," 195–209; Eugenio Torres Villanueva, "Comportamientos empresariales en una economía intervenida: España, 1936–1957," in Sánchez Recio and Tascón Fernández, *Los empresarios de Franco*, 441. On the anti-Catalanism of Queipo, see Raguer, *La Espada*, 331. Núria Puig, *Bayer, CEPSA, REPSOL, Puig, Schering y La Seda: Constructores de la química española* (Madrid, 2003), 12–225; Memoria, Granada, 1938, 44/2791, AGA, 158; *ABC*, 18 July 1937.

152. Torres Villanueva, "Los empresarios," 458; Catalan, "Guerra e industria," 213–16; *ABC*, 24 June 1938; *La Nueva España*, 29 April 1937; Zaragoza, Memoria, 1940, 44/3125, AGA; *El Pueblo Gallego*, 10 October 1937, 11 November 1937, 17 May 1938, 9 July 1938, 14 September 1938, 5 October 1938, 1 June 1939; Caballero, *Diario de campaña*, 281; *La Provincia*, 10 July 1938; *Proa*, 11 October 1938.

153. *El Correo de Zamora*, 6 October 1937; Peiró, *Fernando de Huidobro*, 209; El Merroun, *Las tropas marroquíes*, 207; Memoria, Palencia, 1938, 44/3123, AGA.

154. *La Provincia*, 1 November 1938; Kemp, *Mine Were of Trouble*, 196. Cf. Car-

los Engel, *Historia de la divisiones del Ejército nacional* (Madrid, 2000), 150. Cierva, *Historia ilustrada*, 1:491; Abella, *La vida cotidiana nacional*, 48; Cía Navascués, *Memorias*, 244; Kalyvas, *The Logic of Violence*, 230.

155. Gobierno Civil de Segovia, Memoria, 25 August 1938, 44/2792, AGA; Memoria, Granada, 1938, 44/2791, AGA; Huesca, Memoria, 1938, 44/2791, AGA; Gobierno, Ceuta, Memoria, August 1938, 44/2790, AGA; *El Pueblo Gallego*, 13 September 1938; *Proa*, 13 September 1938, 9 May 1939; *El Correo de Zamora*, 9 July 1938, 10 April 1939, 7 and 31 May 1939, 7 June 1939; *La Nueva España*, 7 and 18 May 1939, 1, 6, and 13 June 1939.

156. *ABC*, 12 and 14 August 1936; Lina Gálvez Muñoz, "Produciendo para la revolución y produciendo para la reacción: Trabajo y guerra civil," in Martín Aceña and Martínez Ruiz, *La economía*, 475. On Hytasa, see Torres Villanueva, "Comportamientos empresariales," 217.

157. *La Provincia*, 15 October 1937, 9 March 1938. Cf. Helen Graham, "Sexual Politics," in Helen Graham and J. Labanyi, *Spanish Cultural Studies: An Introduction; The Struggle for Modernity* (Oxford, 1995), 110: "Axis aid meant the Nationalists never faced the dilemma of material war needs clashing overtly with ideology." Juan Rey, *Por qué luchó un millón de muertos: Documentos inéditos* (Santander, 1961), 65; *ABC*, 11 September 1937, 3 December 1937, 1 January 1938, 17 November 1938; *Proa*, 18 September 1937; Copado, *Con la columna Redondo*, 263; *Asistencia a Frentes y Hospitales de Navarra: Memoria* (1939), 14; Urra Lusarreta, *En las trincheras*, 186. Cf. Graham, *The Spanish Civil War*, 76: "Women in the Francoist zone were not recruited to industrial war work; German and Italian aid made this unnecessary." Memoria, Álava, 1938, 44/2790, AGA; *El Correo de Zamora*, 18 March 1939; Roger Chickering, "The American Civil War and the German Wars of Unification: Some Parting Shots," in Stig Förster and Jörg Nagler, eds., *On the Road to Total War: The American Civil War and the German Wars of Unification* (Cambridge, 1997), 688.

158. *ABC*, 11 September 1937, 7 and 31 October 1937, 4 and 14 December 1937, 3 November 1938; Caballero, *Diario de campaña*, 184–290; *El Pueblo Gallego*, 26 November 1937; Peiró, *Fernando de Huidobro*, 11.

159. Cierva, *Historia ilustrada*, 1:487; Cardona and Losada, *Aunque me tires el puente*, 84; Thomas, *Brother against Brother*, 106; Nagore Yárnoz, *En la primera de Navarra*, 52; Holmes, *Acts of War*, 249.

160. Catalan, "Guerra e industria," 203; *ABC*, 9 December 1937, 8 December 1938; *La Nueva España*, 1 April 1938; Caballero, *Diario de campaña*, 198–292; Corral, *Desertores*, 266; Martínez Reverte, *La Batalla del Ebro*, 150.

161. Resumen del Señor Juez, November 1936, CGG, reel 159, AGM; Informe, 8 June 1938, reel 45, AGM; Villa de Olleria, 10 October 1936, Madrid, 524, AHN-SGC; Informe, 1 February 1937, ZN, a. 44, l. 4, c. 2, AGM.

162. Martín Aceña, "La economía de la guerra civil," 25–26; Lazo, *Retrato de fascismo*, 54; *El Correo de Zamora*, 8 September 1936, 10 and 28 November 1936, 26 May 1937, 18 May 1938; Rey, *Paisanos en lucha*, 182.

163. *ABC*, 15 and 20 January 1937, 29 May 1937, 9, 11, and 13 June 1937, 28 August 1937, 16 October 1937, 20 and 30 November 1937, 14 December 1937; *La Provincia*, 4 November 1937; *El Pueblo Gallego*, 28 November 1937, 19 December 1937.

164. *ABC*, 30 November 1937, 3 December 1937.

165. *ABC*, 10 March 1938, 14 January 1939; Arco Blanco, *Las alas del Ave Fénix*, 51.

166. *El Pueblo Gallego*, 10 June 1937, 1 and 31 October 1937, 19 May 1938; Toledo, Memoria, n.d., 44/3123, AGA; *La Provincia*, 5 February 1938; *El Correo de Zamora*, 5 and 19 June 1937, 7 July 1937, 12 June 1938; *Proa*, [8?] August 1937; Gobierno Civil de León, Memoria, August 1938, 44/2791, AGA; Gobierno Civil, Lugo, 1938, 44/2791, AGA; Gobierno Civil, Huelva, August 1938, 44/2791, AGA; Huesca, Memoria, 1938, 44/2791, AGA.

167. SNT, Jefe Provincial, Palencia, 19 October 1937, 61/13502, AGA; *El Correo de Zamora*, 12 November 1937, 18 May 1938, 12 and 19 June 1938, 19, 27, and 28 June 1939; *Proa*, 31 December 1938; Toledo, Memoria, n.d., 44/3123, AGA.

168. *El Correo de Zamora*, 19 June 1937, 26 November 1937, 19 June 1938; *ABC*, 19 December 1937, 15 January 1938, 1, 22, 24, and 29 June 1938, 23 September 1938, 27 October 1938; *La Provincia*, 4 November 1937, 7 July 1938.

169. *ABC*, 8 November 1938; *Proa*, 9 and 26 November 1938; *El Pueblo Gallego*, 1 and 11 April 1939.

170. On postwar hunger, see Óscar J. Rodríguez Barreira, *Migas con miedo: Practicas de resistencia al primer franquismo, Almería, 1939–1953* (Almería, 2008), 203, and Rivero Noval, *Política y sociedad en la Rioja*, 380. For France during World War II, see Paul Sanders, *Histoire du Marché noir, 1940–1946* (Paris, 2001), 129. *La Provincia*, 20 October 1938.

171. Sánchez Asiaín, *Economía*, 77; Catalan, "Guerra e industria," 198–99; Velarde Fuertes, "Algunos aspectos económicos," 957; *ABC*, 21 and 29 December 1938; Oviedo, 1938, 44/2791, AGA; Beevor, *The Battle for Spain*, 238.

172. *ABC*, 25 August 1936, 19 December 1937, 14 January 1938, 23 June 1938, 24 August 1938, 19 January 1939; Sánchez Asiaín, *Economía*, 83–85; *La Nueva España*, 28 October 1937; Catalan, "Guerra e industria," 200; Salas, *Sevilla*, 2:697; Gobierno Civil de León, Memoria, August 1938, 44/2791, AGA; Adam Tooze, *The Wages of Destruction: The Making and Breaking of the Nazi Economy* (New York, 2006), 418; Jordi Catalan, "Fabricar para la Guerra, padecer por el frente," in Fuentes Quintana and Comín Comín, *Economía*, 1:564–68.

173. *ABC*, 28 August 1937, 4 December 1938; *La Nueva España*, 23 March 1938, 3 August 1938; *La Provincia*, 10 April 1937, 17 December 1937; *El Pueblo Gallego*, 22 August 1936.

174. Copado, *Con la columna Redondo*, 89; Gibson, *Queipo de Llano*, 423; *ABC*, 10 November 1936, 15 December 1936, 19 September 1937; Gobierno Civil, Huelva, August 1938, 44/2791, AGA.

175. *La Nueva España*, 14, 17–19, and 24 November 1937, 22 December 1937, 29 January 1938.

176. Catalan, "Guerra e industria," 200–210; *ABC*, 11 October 1938; *Proa*, 31 May 1939; Cardona, *Historia militar*, 246; Sánchez Asiaín, *Economía*, 85.

177. *El Correo de Zamora*, 15 October 1937, 15 May 1938; *ABC*, 18 March 1938, 17 September 1938, 21 October 1938, 19 November 1938, 3 February 1939; *La Nueva España*, 19 November 1938; *El Pueblo Gallego*, 3 July 1937, 29 and 31 October

1937, 18 November 1937, 23 and 30 December 1937; *La Provincia*, 27 November 1938; *Proa*, 25 October 1938.

178. Rivero Noval, *Política y sociedad en la Rioja*, 502; *La Nueva España*, 5 and 7 October 1938, 1, 8, and 22 November 1938, 14 January 1939, 5 May 1939; *El Pueblo Gallego*, 24 May 1938.

179. Vladimirovich Got'e, *Time of Troubles*, 309, entry of 4 October 1919. On railroads, see Cayón García and Muñoz Rubio, "Transportes y Comunicaciones," 229–50. *El Pueblo Gallego*, 14 February 1939; Miguel Muñoz Rubio, *RENFE*, 66–72; *El Pueblo Gallego*, 10 June 1936.

180. McCullagh, *In Franco's Spain*, 48, 91, 220. A pro-Franco author, McCullagh called Spanish trains "the worst in Europe." He also contributed articles to the Nationalist press. *La Nueva España*, 1 October 1937; SNT, Jefatura Provincial de Huelva, 31 October 1937, Interior, 61/13499, AGA; Revilla Cebrecos, *Tercio de Lácar*, 319; Nagore Yárnoz, *En la primera de Navarra*, 86; Llordés Badía, *Al dejar el fusil*, 273; *El Correo de Zamora*, 7 May 1939; Gobierno Civil de León, Memoria, August 1938, 44/2791, AGA; *El Pueblo Gallego*, 4 December 1937, 13 May 1938; *Proa*, 23 September 1938, 9 November 1938.

181. Gobierno Civil, Huelva, August 1938, 44/2791, AGA; Memoria, Granada, 1938, 44/2791, AGA; Gobierno, Ceuta, Memoria, August 1938, 44/2790, AGA; Urra Lusarreta, *En las trincheras*, 177; Nagore Yárnoz, *En la primera de Navarra*, 114; Díez de Rivera, *La Riqueza pesquera*, 78; Llordés Badía, *Al dejar el fusil*, 65–272; El Merroun, *Las tropas marroquíes*, 198; Copado, *Con la columna Redondo*, 168; Campoamor, *La revolución española*, 47; González Bueno, *Paz en guerra*, 165; Aróstegui, *Los combatientes carlistas*, 1:180, 212–374; Revilla Cebrecos, *Tercio de Lácar*, 84–162; *El Pueblo Gallego*, 30 March 1939.

182. Llordés Badía, *Al dejar el fusil*, 86; Velarde Fuertes, "Algunos aspectos económicos," 956; Hubbard, "How Franco Financed His War," 404; Paul Preston, *Doves of War: Four Women of Spain* (London, 2002), 24. Cf. Preston, *Spanish Civil War*, 192, which claims that Nazis had "a virtual monopoly of Nationalist commerce with the outside world." *La Nueva España*, 1 April 1938; Cervera Gil, *Ya sabes mi paradero*, 343. See Queipo de Llano, *Memorias*, 130, for his estimate of 18,000 trucks in the Nationalist zone. Nagore Yárnoz, *En la primera de Navarra*, 54, 234; García, *Mentiras necesarias*, 68; *ABC*, 19 April 1938. In October 1936 the Republicans purchased 1,000 trucks and accompanying spare parts from the Soviet Union. See Viñas, *La Soledad de la República*, 234–35. Revilla Cebrecos, *Tercio de Lácar*, 140.

183. Medina, *Tiempo pasado*, 22; Vigueras Roldán, *Los paseados con Lorca*, 144; Bahamonde y Sánchez de Castro, *Un Año con Queipo*, 46–94; Domingo, *Retaguardia*, 80; Garzón Pareja, *Historia de la Hacienda*, 2:1152. The creation of the Junta de Defensa Nacional had been Mola's idea. See Casanova, *República y guerra civil*, 341. *El Pueblo Gallego*, 11 July 1936, 8 and 23 August 1936; *ABC*, 31 July 1936; Cayón García and Muñoz Rubio, "Transportes y Comunicaciones," 231, 241; Salas, *Sevilla*, 2:428; Gibson, *Queipo de Llano*, 213, 219; Ortiz Villalba, *Sevilla 1936*, 151; Souto Blanco, *La represión franquista*, 276; Abella, *La vida cotidiana nacional*, 51; Copado, *Con la columna Redondo*, 147; *Proa*, 31 August 1938; Nagore Yárnoz, *En la primera de Navarra*, 88.

184. Casas de la Vega, *Las milicias nacionales*, 47–48; Revilla Cebrecos, *Tercio de Lácar*, 46, 66, 336; Madariaga, *Los moros*, 264; Espinosa Maestre, *La justicia de Queipo*, 202; Cía Navascués, *Memorias*, 71.

185. Ruiz Vilaplana, *Burgos Justice*, 163; Nagore Yárnoz, *En la primera de Navarra*, 32. Civilian chauffeurs working for the military received special subsidies to purchase food. *ABC*, 5 January 1937, 1 June 1938, 21 and 22 October 1938, 11 May 1939; *El Pueblo Gallego*, 27 November 1937.

186. *ABC*, 14 November 1936, 27 February 1937; *El Pueblo Gallego*, 3 and 29 June 1938, 28 April 1939; *El Correo de Zamora*, 24 December 1936, 26 September 1937, 17 May 1939, 15 June 1939; *La Nueva España*, 14 May 1937, 8 October 1937, 17 December 1937, 27 January 1938, 22 March 1938, 25 May 1938, 30 July 1938; Oviedo, 1938, 44/2791, AGA; Gobierno Civil de León, Memoria, August 1938, 44/2791, AGA.

187. SNT, Jefatura Provincial Zaragoza, 25 March 1938, Interior, 61/13509, AGA; SNT, Jefatura Provincial de Granada, 20 September 1938, Interior, 61/13498, AGA; Delegado Nacional del SNT, Rute, 1 December 1937, Interior, 61/13497, AGA; *ABC*, 13 December 1936; Llordés Badía, *Al dejar el fusil*, 139.

188. Huesca, Memoria, 1938, 44/2791, AGA; Gobierno Civil, Lugo, 1938, 44/2791, AGA; Orense, September 1938, 44/2791, AGA; Memoria, Ávila, August 1938, 44/2790, AGA; Gobierno Civil, Cáceres, August 1938, 44/2790, AGA.

189. Vladimirovich Got'e, *Time of Troubles*, 117, entry of 13 March 1918; Alan Knight, *The Mexican Revolution: Counter-revolution and Reconstruction* (New York, 1986), 1:182. Cf. Chris Ealham, "The Myth of the Maddened Crowd," in Chris Ealham and Michael Richards, eds., *The Splintering of Spain: Cultural History and the Spanish Civil War, 1936–1939* (Cambridge, 2005), 111–32, who posits that joy riding was a revolutionary proletarian and "anti-bourgeois" phenomenon. Cf. also Chris Ealham, *Class, Culture and Conflict in Barcelona, 1898–1937* (New York, 2005), 184. *ABC*, 5 August 1936, 4 November 1936, 10 December 1937; Copado, *Con la columna Redondo*, 34; *El Pueblo Gallego*, 27 September 1936, 11 November 1936; Gobierno Civil de Segovia, Memoria, 25 August 1938, 44/2792, AGA; *La Provincia*, 25 August 1936; *El Correo de Zamora*, 17 August 1938, 1 September 1938; *Proa*, 23 September 1938.

190. *ABC*, 15 June 1938, 20 August 1938, 3 November 1938, 10 January 1939; *La Nueva España*, 27 November 1937, 20 October 1938; *El Pueblo Gallego*, 29 September 1937; Cardona, *Historia militar*, 122; Llordés Badía, *Al dejar el fusil*, 60.

191. *ABC*, 13, 21–27 August 1936, 9 September 1936, 11 October 1936, 1 November 1936, 6 February 1938, 28 August 1938, 28 and 29 April 1939, 2 and 5 May 1939, 18 and 29 June 1939.

192. Velarde Fuertes, "Algunos aspectos económicos," 955; *La Nueva España*, 1 June 1939; *El Pueblo Gallego*, 13 March 1937; Junta de Transportes Civiles de Álava, 31 October 1937, 44/2790, AGA; *ABC*, 21 December 1937; *Proa*, 20 December 1938.

193. Cardona and Losada, *Aunque me tires el puente*, 256–57; Bullón de Mendoza and Diego, *Historias orales*, 62; Nagore Yárnoz, *En la primera de Navarra*, 34; Castro, *Capital de la Cruzada*, 168; Sierra, *Palabras huérfanas*, 135–94. On disorder, see *Claridad*, 15 March 1937, and Pedro Corral, *Si me quieres escribir*, 101–2. Orense, September 1938, 44/2791, AGA; "Minister of Food," *Ta Kung Pao*, 4 October 1947,

Chinese Press Review, Shanghai, NYPL; Acta, Comités de control de *El Liberal* y *Heraldo de Madrid*, 16 August 1937, Madrid 834, AHN-SGC; CNT carteros, 29 April 1938, Madrid 2321, AHN-SGC.

194. Llordés Badía, *Al dejar el fusil*, 220; Caballero, *Diario de campaña*, 78; Peiró, *Fernando de Huidobro*, 213.

195. Cervera Gil, *Ya sabes mi paradero*, 135; Llordés Badía, *Al dejar el fusil*, 74–209; Satrústegui, *Memorias de un anarquista*, 233; Nagore Yárnoz, *En la primera de Navarra*, 51; *ABC*, 19 August 1936, 25 December 1937, 13 November 1938; Caballero, *Diario de campaña*, 240; *La Nueva España*, 19 November 1938; Nerín, *La guerra*, 180; Bullón de Mendoza and Diego, *Historias orales*, 143.

196. *ABC*, 27 December 1936, 4 February 1937, 3 and 9 April 1937, 13 August 1937, 9 and 12 March 1938, 5 May 1938, 24 June 1938, 23 February 1939; *El Pueblo Gallego*, 28 July 1937, 3 and 9 September 1937. *La Nueva España*, 4 November 1937, mentions "a large number of abandoned dogs." Santa Cruz de Tenerife, Memoria, 1938, 44/2792, AGA; Gobierno Civil de Segovia, Memoria, 25 August 1938, 44/2792, AGA; Gobierno Civil, Huelva, August 1938, 44/2791, AGA.

197. *El Pueblo Gallego*, 7 August 1938; Gobierno Civil, Huelva, August 1938, 44/2791, AGA; Gobierno Civil, Cáceres, August 1938, 44/2790, AGA; Gobierno Civil, Lugo, 1938, 44/2791, AGA; Santa Cruz de Tenerife, Memoria, 1938, 44/2792, AGA; Memoria, Ávila, August 1938, 44/2790, AGA; Rey, *Por qué luchó*, 231; Huesca, Memoria, 1938, 44/2791, AGA; Nonell Bru, *El Laureado Tercio*, 385–87; Memoria, Palencia, 1938, 44/3123, AGA; Memoria de las Palmas, 7 September 1938, 44/3123, AGA; Orense, September 1938, 44/2791, AGA; *ABC*, 13 July 1938; Memoria, Álava, 1938, 44/2790, AGA.

198. Abella, *La vida cotidiana nacional*, 221; Mawdsley, *Russian Civil War*, 220; Beevor, *The Battle for Spain*, 308; Cervera Gil, *Ya sabes mi paradero*, 324; Nonell Bru, *El Laureado Tercio*, 15; *La Nueva España*, 8 October 1937, 4 November 1937; Bastida Pellicer, *Historias de un quinto*, 218; *ABC*, 1 September 1937, 5 November 1937, 16 and 25 December 1937, 12 March 1938, 1 June 1938; Iribarren, *El General Mola*, 251; Nagore Yárnoz, *En la primera de Navarra*, 151; Llordés Badía, *Al dejar el fusil*, 125; *El Pueblo Gallego*, 3 June 1936, 12 March 1937, 10 June 1937, 31 May 1938; *Proa*, 18 November 1936, 24 January 1939, 15 April 1939; Caballero, *Diario de campaña*, 74; *La Provincia*, 25 March 1939.

199. Memoria, Ávila, August 1938, 44/2790, AGA; *El Pueblo Gallego*, 30 March 1939; Santa Cruz de Tenerife, Memoria, 1938, 44/2792, AGA; Huesca, Memoria, 1938, 44/2791, AGA; Soviet Russia, 21 February 1920, Internal Affairs of Russia, U.S. Department of State, NA; Memoria, Álava, 1938, 44/2790, AGA; Ilmo. Señor, 15 November 1938, Interior, 61/13493, AGA; Sierra, *Palabras huérfanas*, 27; Palacios and Payne, *Franco, mi padre*, 717.

200. *El Correo de Zamora*, 20 May 1937; Abella, *La vida cotidiana nacional*, 219; Manuel de Ramón Carrión and Carmen Ortiz, *Madrina de guerra: Cartas desde el frente* (Madrid, 2003), 128, 188; Cervera Gil, *Ya sabes mi paradero*, 237; Llordés Badía, *Al dejar el fusil*, 105–254; Rey, *Por qué luchó*, 227; González Bueno, *Paz en guerra*, 120; Medina, *Tiempo pasado*, 116; Satrústegui, *Memorias de un anarquista*, 188; Urra Lusarreta, *En las trincheras*, 299; Nagore Yárnoz, *En la primera de Navarra*, 91; *ABC*,

21 April 1937, 1 August 1937; *La Nueva España*, 27 May 1937, 3 August 1938; *La Provincia*, 24 January 1937; Corral, *Desertores*, 189.

CHAPTER 3. CATHOLIC NEOTRADITIONALISM

1. Medina, *Tiempo pasado*, 65; Riquer i Permanyer, *l'últim Cambó*, 51; Gibson, *Queipo de Llano*, 321; Rey, *Paisanos en lucha*, 173, 330; Bullón de Mendoza and Diego, *Historias orales*, 131.

2. Cardona and Losada, *Aunque me tires el puente*, 141; SNT, Palencia, 9 August 1938, 61/13502, AGA; Gibson, *Queipo de Llano*, 209; *ABC*, 13 August 1936, 10 September 1936; Queipo de Llano, *Memorias*, 79; Caballero, *Diario de campaña*, 51; Copado, *Con la columna Redondo*, 106; *El Pueblo Gallego*, 9 August 1936.

3. Ranzato, *El eclipse de la democracia*, 83, 90; Cenarro, *La sonrisa de Falange*, xv–30; Preston, *Doves of War*, 271; *El Correo de Zamora*, 10 October 1937; *La Nueva España*, 10 February 1938.

4. Cenarro, *La sonrisa de Falange*, 13; Casas de la Vega, *Las milicias nacionales*, 1:332; Schempp, *Das Autoritäre Spanien*, 106; Bahamonde y Sánchez de Castro, *Un Año con Queipo*, 22–85; Farah Mendlesohn, *Quaker Relief Work in the Spanish Civil War* (Lewiston, MA, 2002), 150; Cierva, *Historia ilustrada*, 2:140; Domingo, *Retaguardia*, 163–66.

5. Schempp, *Das Autoritäre Spanien*, 107; *Proa*, 27 November 1936; Cenarro, *La sonrisa de Falange*, 13–14; Revilla Cebrecos, *Tercio de Lácar*, 126; Cervera Gil, *Ya sabes mi paradero*, 284; Bullón de Mendoza and Diego, *Historias orales*, 27.

6. Cenarro, *La sonrisa de Falange*, 31, 36; Howard E. Kershner, *Quaker Service in Modern War: Spain and France, 1939–1940* (New York, 1950); Monica Orduña Prada, "Donativos nacionales e internacionales a Auxilio Social," in Bullón de Mendoza and Togores, *Revisión*, 1083–93; Preston, *Doves of War*, 260; Mendlesohn, *Quaker Relief Work*, 72–77.

7. *Proa*, 11 October 1938; *La Provincia*, 19 May 1937; George D. Sussman, *Selling Mothers' Milk: The Wet-Nursing Business in France, 1715–1914* (Urbana, IL, 1982), 10–11, 164; *El Pueblo Gallego*, 13 March 1938, 22 July 1938.

8. *ABC*, 9 June 1937, 19 and 31 October 1937, 21 March 1938, 21 May 1938; *El Pueblo Gallego*, 22 September 1936, 4 November 1936, 21 October 1937, 25 May 1938; *El Correo de Zamora*, 29 August 1936, 4 November 1937, 17 May 1938; *La Provincia*, 24 September 1937; Bullón de Mendoza and Diego, *Historias orales*, 94.

9. Nonell Bru, *El Laureado Tercio*, 316–32; Caballero, *Diario de campaña*, 281; Bullón de Mendoza and Diego, *Historias orales*, 95; Mary Vincent, "The Spanish Civil War as a War of Religion," in Baumeister and Schüler-Springorum, *"If You Tolerate This . . . ,"* 85; Revilla Cebrecos, *Tercio de Lácar*, 142–299; Nagore Yárnoz, *En la primera de Navarra*, 68.

10. Resa, *Memorias de un requeté*, 55; Llordés Badía, *Al dejar el fusil*, 173–301; Ramón Carrión and Ortiz, *Madrina de guerra*, 53, 61.

11. Ramón Carrión and Ortiz, *Madrina de guerra*, 72, 103, 168; Jaime Tovar Patrón, *Los curas de la última Cruzada* (Madrid, 2001), 194; Peiró, *Fernando de Huidobro*, 211; *ABC*, 5 May 1939; Nonell Bru, *El Laureado Tercio*, 613.

12. Gálvez Muñoz, "Produciendo para la revolución," 474; Carmen Domingo, *Con voz y voto: Las mujeres y la política en España (1931–45)* (Barcelona, 2004), 231; Cervera Gil, *Ya sabes mi paradero*, 368; Bullón de Mendoza and Diego, *Historias orales*, 94.

13. *La Provincia*, 12 January 1937, 24 December 1937; *ABC*, 14 January 1938, 3, 23, and 27 December 1938; *La Nueva España*, 16 February 1938; Llordés Badía, *Al dejar el fusil*, 81; *El Correo de Zamora*, 15 January 1938; Urra Lusarreta, *En las trincheras*, 200; Castro, *Capital de la Cruzada*, 169.

14. *La Provincia*, 29 November 1938; *El Correo de Zamora*, 11 and 20 January 1937; *Proa*, 11 December 1938.

15. *Proa*, 4 December 1938; Ugarte Tellería, *La nueva Covadonga*, 401; *ABC*, 1 September 1937, 13 May 1938, 3 December 1938; *El Pueblo Gallego*, 16 September 1937, 17 October 1937; Tovar Patrón, *Los curas*, 167; Nagore Yárnoz, *En la primera de Navarra*, 111–219; Caballero, *Diario de campaña*, 65; Peiró, *Fernando de Huidobro*, 211, 433; Rafael Valdés, *Un Capellán, héroe de la Legión: P. Fernando Huidobro, S.I.* (Santander, 1938), 116; González Bueno, *Paz en guerra*, 46; Thomas, *Brother against Brother*, 88; Iribarren, *El General Mola*, 238; "Hispánico," *La Defensa del Alcázar* (Logroño, n.d.), 15; Urra Lusarreta, *En las trincheras*, 150, 179.

16. *ABC*, 23 December 1938, 7 January 1939; Revilla Cebrecos, *Tercio de Lácar*, 304–24; Nagore Yárnoz, *En la primera de Navarra*, 181; Llordés Badía, *Al dejar el fusil*, 172; Urra Lusarreta, *En las trincheras*, 209, 290.

17. *Asistencia a Frentes y Hospitales de Navarra: Memoria* (1939), 15; Nagore Yárnoz, *En la primera de Navarra*, 90.

18. Resa, *Memorias de un requeté*, 46; *Asistencia a Frentes*, 17–186; Cardona and Losada, *Aunque me tires el puente*, 194; Cervera Gil, *Ya sabes mi paradero*, 374; Hipólito Escolar Sobrino, *La cultura durante la guerra civil* (Madrid, 1987), 225; Nagore Yárnoz, *En la primera de Navarra*, 137.

19. Resa, *Memorias de un requeté*, 64; *Asistencia a Frentes*, 55; Revilla Cebrecos, *Tercio de Lácar*, 284; Rivero Noval, *Política y sociedad en la Rioja*, 201; Bahamonde y Sánchez de Castro, *Un Año con Queipo*, 23; Aróstegui, *Los combatientes carlistas*, 1:349; Casas de la Vega, *Las milicias nacionales*, 1:312.

20. Domingo, *Retaguardia*, 200–392; Espinosa Maestre, *La justicia de Queipo*, 249, 253; Madariaga, *Los moros*, 318; Abella, *La vida cotidiana nacional*, 76; Lazo, *Retrato de fascismo*, 89; Ortiz Villalba, *Sevilla 1936*, 257–58; Sánchez Ruano, *Islam*, 337–81; Caballero, *Diario de campaña*, 191; Nerín, *La guerra*, 186–235; Bullón de Mendoza and Diego, *Historias orales*, 84.

21. *El Pueblo Gallego*, 1 December 1936, 12 and 26 June 1937, 11 September 1937; Rivero Noval, *Política y sociedad en la Rioja*, 469; Francisco Javier Caspistegui, "Religión, tradicionalismo y espectáculos de masas," in Jaume Aurell and Pablo Pérez López, eds., *Católicos entre dos guerras: La historia religiosa de España en los años 20 y 30* (Madrid, 2006), 336; Sasha Pack, *Tourism and Dictatorship: Europe's Peaceful Invasion of Franco's Spain* (New York, 2006), 32, 79; *La Nueva España*, 25 May 1937; *Proa*, [8?] August 1937; *El Correo de Zamora*, 13 June 1938; Rosa Álvarez Berciano and Ramón Sala Noguer, *El Cine en la zona nacional, 1936–1939* (Bilbao, 2000), 38.

22. Abella, *La vida cotidiana nacional*, 120–322; *El Correo de Zamora*, 10 June 1937.

23. Casanova, *República y guerra civil*, 41; Jackson, *Spanish Republic*, 62; Caballero, *Diario de campaña*, 112–14; Tovar Patrón, *Los curas*, 212.

24. Castro, *Capital de la Cruzada*, 79; Prieto quoted in Medina, *Tiempo pasado*, 101; Iribarren, *El General Mola*, 252; Cía Navascués, *Memorias;* Nonell Bru, *El Laureado Tercio*. On Cía's and Nonell's books, see Aróstegui, *Los combatientes carlistas*, 1:160, 2:316–37. Nagore Yárnoz, *En la primera de Navarra*, 29–30; Tovar Patrón, *Los curas*, 228.

25. González Bueno, *Paz en guerra*, 19, 45; Aróstegui, *Los combatientes carlistas*, 2:25–368; Resa, *Memorias de un requeté*, 52; Tovar Patrón, *Los curas*, 126–59; Delgado Iribarren, *Jesuitas en Campaña*, 188; Caballero, *Diario de campaña*, 152; José Luis González Gullón, "El clero de Madrid: Demografía y distribución," in Aurell and Pérez Lopez, eds., *Católicos entre dos guerras*, 260; Nagore Yárnoz, *En la primera de Navarra*, 52.

26. Cervera Gil, *Ya sabes mi paradero*, 228, 350; Caballero, *Diario de campaña*, 305, 429; Adro Xavier, *Laureada de Sangre: Esbozos históricos de la Cruzada* (Valladolid, 1939), 73; González Bueno, *Paz en guerra*, 19, 153; Sierra, *Palabras huérfanas*, 37; Gobierno Civil de Segovia, Memoria, 25 August 1938, 44/2792, AGA; Memoria, Ávila, August 1938, 44/2790, AGA; Zaragoza, Memoria, 1940, 44/3125, AGA; Gobierno Civil, Lugo, 1938, 44/2791, AGA.

27. *ABC*, 4 January 1939; Rey, *Paisanos en lucha*, 48; Toledo, Memoria, n.d., 44/3123, AGA; Gobierno Civil de León, Memoria, August 1938, 44/2791, AGA; Memoria, Ávila, August 1938, 44/2790, AGA; Xavier, *Laureada de Sangre*, 76; González Bueno, *Paz en guerra*, 21–76.

28. Tovar Patrón, *Los curas*, 197–99; Copado, *Con la columna Redondo*, 119; *ABC*, 12 May 1937; *El Correo de Zamora*, 17 September 1936, 6 September 1938; Mary Vincent, "The Politicization of Catholic Women in Salamanca, 1931–1936," in Frances Lannon and Paul Preston, eds., *Elites and Power in Twentieth-Century Spain: Essays in Honor of Sir Raymond Carr* (Oxford, 1990), 119; *El Pueblo Gallego*, 17 September 1937; *La Provincia*, 11 May 1939; Oviedo, 1938, 44/2791, AGA; Orduña Prada, *El Auxilio Social*, 261.

29. Tovar Patrón, *Los curas*, 194; Rey, *Por qué luchó*, 59–128; Caballero, *Diario de campaña*, 60–221; Xavier, *Laureada de Sangre*, 114; Stéphane Audoin-Rouzeau and Annette Becker, *14–18: Understanding the Great War*, trans. Catherine Temerson (New York, 2002), 130; Raguer, *La Espada*, 64; *ABC*, 4 December 1937; *El Correo de Zamora*, 22 January 1938; Abella, *La vida cotidiana nacional*, 352; Llordés Badía, *Al dejar el fusil*, 320; Copado, *Con la columna Redondo*, 86–221; Delgado Iribarren, *Jesuitas en Campaña*, 196; Iribarren, *El General Mola*, 277; Peiró, *Fernando de Huidobro*, 213–69; González Bueno, *Paz en guerra*, 114.

30. Holmes, *Acts of War*, 239. I wish to thank Rabbi James Apple, former chaplain and captain in the United States Marines, for his insight into this issue. Caballero, *Diario de campaña*, 100–336; Bullón de Mendoza and Diego, *Historias orales*, 206; Urra Lusarreta, *En las trincheras*, 262, 265; Rey, *Por qué luchó*, 151.

31. Martín Aceña and Martínez Ruiz, *La economía*, 9; José Antonio Ortega and Javier Silvestre, "Las consecuencias demográficas," in Martín Aceña and Martínez Ruiz, *La economía*, 96. Casanova, *República y guerra civil*, 407, puts the figure at

600,000 dead. José Semprún Bullón, "Bajas en la contienda: Una reevaluación," in Bullón de Mendoza and Togores, *Revisión*, 331–41, lowers the figures considerably. Population figures in *La Provincia*, 20 May 1939. Corral, *Desertores*, 209; Palacios and Payne, *Franco, mi padre*, 340; Ranzato, *El eclipse de la democracia*, 378–80; Domingo, *Retaguardia*, 11; Vigueras Roldán, *Los paseados con Lorca*, 176; Julius Ruiz, *Franco's Justice: Repression in Madrid after the Spanish Civil War* (Oxford, 2005), 13; Llordés Badía, *Al dejar el fusil*, 79; Stradling, *Your Children Will Be Next*, 30, 225.

    32. Xavier Boniface, *l'aumônerie militaire française (1914–1962)* (Paris, 2001), 144; Urra Lusarreta, *En las trincheras*, 288–301; Valdés, *Un Capellán*, 85; Rey, *Por qué luchó*, 200, 279; Peiró, *Fernando de Huidobro*, 264; Copado, *Con la columna Redondo*, 8–86; Caballero, *Diario de campaña*, 109–358; González Bueno, *Paz en guerra*, 215; Satrústegui, *Memorias de un anarquista*, 234.

    33. *ABC*, 25 August 1936; *El Pueblo Gallego*, 1 October 1936, 12 November 1936; Caballero, *Diario de campaña*, 10, 362; Copado, *Con la columna Redondo*, 119; Cervera Gil, *Ya sabes mi paradero*, 16, 63; Raguer, *La Espada*, 161; Ruiz Vilaplana, *Burgos Justice*, 87, 180; Tovar Patrón, *Los curas*, 216; González Gullón, "El clero de Madrid," 274; Rey, *Por qué luchó*, 232.

    34. Cervera Gil, *Ya sabes mi paradero*, 284; Peiró, *Fernando de Huidobro*, 225; *ABC*, 31 July 1937, 18 February 1938; Llordés Badía, *Al dejar el fusil*, 125–311; Abella, *La vida cotidiana nacional*, 352; Nagore Yárnoz, *En la primera de Navarra*, 137; Rey, *Paisanos en lucha*, 170; Xavier, *Caballero Legionario*, 67; Caballero, *Diario de campaña*, 38, 293, 314; Urra Lusarreta, *En las trincheras*, 15, 28; Satrústegui, *Memorias de un anarquista*, 230; Bullón de Mendoza and Diego, *Historias orales*, 183.

    35. Bastida Pellicer, *Historias de un quinto*, 270; Domingo, *Retaguardia*, 178–295; Martínez Reverte, *La Batalla del Ebro*, 355; Thomas, *Brother against Brother*, 60; Corral, *Desertores*, 442; Cervera Gil, *Ya sabes mi paradero*, 223–24; Souto Blanco, *La represión franquista*, 245; Ruiz Vilaplana, *Burgos Justice*, 33, 34, 59; Revilla Cebrecos, *Tercio de Lácar*, 108; Nagore Yárnoz, *En la primera de Navarra*, 66; Oviedo, 1938, 44/2791, AGA; Castro, *Capital de la Cruzada*, 246; *Proa*, 23 July 1937.

    36. Revilla Cebrecos, *Tercio de Lácar*, 86, 174; Cía Navascués, *Memorias*, 36–305; Medina, *Tiempo pasado*, 70, 86; Satrústegui, *Memorias de un anarquista*, 284; Elizabeth Roberts, "Freedom, Faction, Fame, and Blood: British 'Soldiers of Conscience' in Three European Wars" (PhD diss., University of Sydney, 2007), 127; Llordés Badía, *Al dejar el fusil*, 219–311; Martínez Reverte, *La Batalla del Ebro*, 130–503; Cardona and Losada, *Aunque me tires el puente*, 175–216; Abella, *La vida cotidiana nacional*, 227; Caballero, *Diario de campaña*, 183, 245; Nagore Yárnoz, *En la primera de Navarra*, 126; Stradling, *The Irish*, 62; Thomas, *Brother against Brother*, 104.

    37. Rey, *Por qué luchó*, 132; Caballero, *Diario de campaña*, 339–78; González Bueno, *Paz en guerra*, 146.

    38. Ugarte Tellería, *La nueva Covadonga*, 382; Bullón de Mendoza and Diego, *Historias orales*, 77.

    39. Martínez Reverte, *La Batalla del Ebro*, 118, 258; Aróstegui, *Los combatientes carlistas*, 1:217; Resa, *Memorias de un requeté*, 52; Revilla Cebrecos, *Tercio de Lácar*, 91; Nagore Yárnoz, *En la primera de Navarra*, 119; Ugarte Tellería, *La nueva Covadonga*, 404; Nonell Bru, *El Laureado Tercio*, 338–484; Abella, *La vida cotidiana nacional*, 55.

40. Nagore Yárnoz, *En la primera de Navarra*, 119, 129; Rey, *Por qué luchó*, 171; Urra Lusarreta, *En las trincheras*, 230–31; Ugarte Tellería, *La nueva Covadonga*, 135, 385; Raguer, *La Espada*, 162–67; Ranzato, *El eclipse de la democracia*, 401. Cf. the hagiographical treatment in Xavier, *Caballero Legionario*.

41. Abella, *La vida cotidiana nacional*, 82; Preston, *Doves of War*, 231; Fraser, *Blood of Spain*, 166; Luciano González Egido, *Agonizar en Salamanca: Unamuno (julio–diciembre 1936)* (Madrid, 1986), 108; Andrés Trapiello, *Las armas y las letras: Literatura y guerra civil (1936–1939)* (Barcelona, 1994), 204; Beevor, *The Battle for Spain*, 93; Espinosa Maestre, *La justicia de Queipo*, 137, 177; Javier Rodrigo, *Hasta la raíz: Violencia durante la guerra civil y la dictadura franquista* (Madrid, 2008), 68; Sánchez Ruano, *Islam*, 193; *ABC*, 25 August 1936.

42. Gobierno Civil de Segovia, Memoria, 25 August 1938, 44/2792, AGA; Memoria, Ávila, August 1938, 44/2790, AGA; Thomas A. Kselman, *Death and the Afterlife in Modern France* (Princeton, NJ, 1993), 65, 95; Ruiz Vilaplana, *Burgos Justice*, 203; Caballero, *Diario de campaña*, 112, 190; Cervera Gil, *Ya sabes mi paradero*, 230.

43. *ABC*, 5, 12, 13, and 16 January 1937, 10 and 16 April 1937; Stradling, *The Irish*, 86; McCullagh, *In Franco's Spain*, 230; Caballero, *Diario de campaña*, 166, 323; Revilla Cebrecos, *Tercio de Lácar*, 160; Nagore Yárnoz, *En la primera de Navarra*, 109; Cervera Gil, *Ya sabes mi paradero*, 230.

44. *El Pueblo Gallego*, 10 June 1936; *El Correo de Zamora*, 20 July 1938; Nagore Yárnoz, *En la primera de Navarra*, 42; Caballero, *Diario de campaña*, 178–316; Cía Navascués, *Memorias*, 292.

45. *El Correo de Zamora*, 28 October 1938; *Proa*, 13 July 1938, 11 December 1938; *ABC*, 21 December 1938; *La Provincia*, 21 December 1938; *La Nueva España*, 24 November 1937, 15 March 1938, 30 October 1938.

46. Nerín, *La guerra*, 181; Sánchez Ruano, *Islam*, 238; El Merroun, *Las tropas marroquíes*, 191; Madariaga, *Los moros*, 280–84; Urra Lusarreta, *En las trincheras*, 136, 300; Nagore Yárnoz, *En la primera de Navarra*, 67; Cervera Gil, *Ya sabes mi paradero*, 365; Gonzalo Álvarez Chillida, "Zaragoza en la Guerra Civil: La memoria de un judío aragonés," *Raíces: Revista judía de cultura* 54 (Spring 2003): 47; Caballero, *Diario de campaña*, 105–40; Annette Becker, *War and Faith: The Religious Imagination in France, 1914–1930*, trans. Helen McPhail (New York, 1998), 116–17.

47. Cf. Mainer, *Años de Vísperas*, 84; *ABC*, 7 November 1937; Memoria, Granada, 1938, 44/2791, AGA; Pío Baroja, *Comunistas Judíos y demás ralea* (Valladolid, 1939), 68; Eva Touboul Tardieu, *Séphardisme et Hispanité: l'Espagne à la recherche de son passé* (Paris, 2009), 278.

48. *El Pueblo Gallego*, 3 November 1937; Caballero, *Diario de campaña*, 116; *El Correo de Zamora*, 1 June 1937; Urra Lusarreta, *En las trincheras*, 80; Luis Cano, "Acerca de Cristo Rey," in Aurell and Pérez López, *Católicos entre dos guerras*, 188–89.

49. *ABC*, 29 December 1936, 11 August 1937; Rivero Noval, *Política y sociedad en la Rioja*, 132–33; Palomares Ibáñez, *La Guerra Civil en Palencia*, 25; Escolar Sobrino, *La cultura*, 224; *La Nueva España*, 23 December 1937; Rey, *Por qué luchó*, 177; *El Correo de Zamora*, 30 October 1937, 13 September 1938; Alicia Alted Vigil, *Política del nuevo estado sobre el patrimonio cultural y la educación durante la guerra civil*

española (Madrid, 1984), 74–90; *El Pueblo Gallego*, 21, 23, and 28 June 1938; García, *Mentiras necesarias*, 172.

50. *ABC*, 4 April 1937, 29 May 1937, 24 November 1938, 19 February 1939; *El Pueblo Gallego*, 23 April 1937, 14 September 1937, 17 October 1937, 9 and 11 November 1937, 1 December 1937, 9 June 1939; *El Correo de Zamora*, 15 October 1937.

51. *El Pueblo Gallego*, 29 April 1939; *El Correo de Zamora*, 26 June 1937, 10 January 1939; *Proa*, 28 August 1937, 25 April 1939; Rey, *Por qué luchó*, 113; Tovar Patrón, *Los curas*, 134.

52. *ABC*, 12 and 16 October 1937; Tovar Patrón, *Los curas*, 210; Caballero, *Diario de campaña*, 216, 372; González Bueno, *Paz en guerra*, 146; Febo, *Ritos de guerra*, 38; Beevor, *The Battle for Spain*, 249.

53. *El Correo de Zamora*, 2, 11, and 18 May 1938; Escolar Sobrino, *La cultura*, 220; Alted Vigil, *Política del nuevo estado*, 127; Raguer, *La Espada*, 65; Dawn Ades, Tim Benton, David Elliott, Iain Boyd White, *Art and Power: Europe under the Dictators, 1930–45* (London, 1995), 102–3; Robin Adèle Greeley, *Surrealism and the Spanish Civil War* (New Haven, CT, 2006), 91–115; *Laureados de España* (Madrid, 1940).

54. *ABC*, 18 May 1939; *El Pueblo Gallego*, 21 and 22 February 1939, 16 March 1939; *El Correo de Zamora*, 5 May 1938, 17 May 1939; Alted Vigil, *Política del nuevo estado*, 129; *Proa*, 9 November 1938; *La Provincia*, 10 July 1938.

55. *El Pueblo Gallego*, 22 July 1938; Álvarez Berciano and Sala Moguer, *El Cine en la zona nacional*, 150.

56. *ABC*, 17 April 1938, 26 May 1938, 23 June 1938; Raguer, *La Espada*, 71; *El Correo de Zamora*, 8 April 1937, 16 July 1938, 28 October 1938, 17 November 1938, 24 and 26 May 1939; Zira Box, *España, Año Cero: La construcción simbólica del franquismo* (Madrid, 2010), 198–205; Cervera Gil, *Ya sabes mi paradero*, 207; *Proa*, 19 April 1939; *El Pueblo Gallego*, 20 July 1937, 30 September 1937, 1 October 1937, 29 September 1938; Castro, *Capital de la Cruzada*, 153.

57. *ABC*, 1 September 1937, 17 April 1938; *El Correo de Zamora*, 26 May 1937, 2 August 1937, 6 September 1937; Box, *España*, 73; *El Pueblo Gallego*, 25 May 1937, 3 and 20 June 1937, 3 and 13 July 1937, 6, 25, and 29 September 1938; *La Nueva España*, 27 April 1938, 15 May 1938, 1 June 1938, 31 July 1938, 2 and 3 August 1938; *Proa*, 7 August 1938, 11 September 1938.

58. Cervera Gil, *Ya sabes mi paradero*, 411; Bullón de Mendoza and Diego, *Historias orales*, 226; Caballero, *Diario de campaña*, 349; Zaragoza, Memoria, 1940, 44/3125, AGA; *El Correo de Zamora*, 2 August 1937, 7 September 1937, 18 December 1937; *ABC*, 19 December 1937, 22 March 1938, 29 April 1938, 28 June 1938, 24 August 1938; Llordés Badía, *Al dejar el fusil*, 166.

59. *ABC*, 7 October 1937, 14 November 1937, 18 March 1938; Álvarez Berciano and Sala Moguer, *El Cine en la zona nacional*, 176; *El Pueblo Gallego*, 6 January 1939, 3 March 1939; *El Correo de Zamora*, 15 December 1937; *La Nueva España*, 18 June 1937, 30 April 1938, 25 May 1938; *La Provincia*, 27 August 1936, 15 March 1938, 1 and 23 April 1938, 2 May 1939; Llordés Badía, *Al dejar el fusil*, 64, 152; Tovar Patrón, *Los curas*, 207; Millán Astray cited in Caballero, *Diario de campaña*, 192.

60. Escolar Sobrino, *La cultura*, 212, 284; *Arriba* cited in Vigueras Roldán, *Los paseados con Lorca*, 127; *El Pueblo Gallego*, 18 August 1936; *Proa*, [29?] December

1936; Nagore Yárnoz, *En la primera de Navarra*, 58; Trapiello, *Las armas y las letras*, 181; *ABC*, 12 and 25 August 1936, 9 September 1936, 29 December 1936; Souto Blanco, *La represión franquista*, 278; Cía Navascués, *Memorias*, 279; Abella, *La vida cotidiana nacional*, 114; Matthew Fishburn, *Burning Books* (New York, 2008), 32–33, 62.

61. Vigueras Roldán, *Los paseados con Lorca*, 54; Millán Astray quoted in Souto Blanco, *La represión franquista*, 304; Ortiz Villalba, *Sevilla 1936*, 173, 273; Urra Lusarreta, *En las trincheras*, 298; *El Correo de Zamora*, 18 February 1938.

62. *El Correo de Zamora*, 28 September 1937, 11 August 1938; *ABC*, 9 September 1936, 5 and 9 December 1937; Alted Vigil, *Política del nuevo estado*, 58; McCullagh, *In Franco's Spain*, 269.

63. Díaz Viana, *Cancionero popular*, 156; H. G. Cardozo quoted in Esenwein, *The Spanish Civil War*, 33; *ABC*, 3 and 4 December 1937; *El Pueblo Gallego*, 14 July 1937, 10 October 1937, 19 March 1938, 17 May 1938; *El Correo de Zamora*, 27 September 1937, 4 and 20 November 1937, 23 January 1938; *Proa*, 4 December 1938.

64. Ugarte Tellería, *La nueva Covadonga*, 124–299; Cía Navascués, *Memorias*, 127–307; Abella, *La vida cotidiana nacional*, 29; Nagore Yárnoz, *En la primera de Navarra*, 47–134; Urra Lusarreta, *En las trincheras*, 44–325; Rivero Noval, *Política y sociedad en la Rioja*, 459; Aróstegui, *Los combatientes carlistas*, 2:491; Resa, *Memorias de un requeté*, 44, 51; Casas de la Vega, *Las milicias nacionales*, 1:368; Revilla Cebrecos, *Tercio de Lácar*, 78–212; González Bueno, *Paz en guerra*, 77, 197; Copado, *Con la columna Redondo*, 278; *Proa*, 27 December 1936; Satrústegui, *Memorias de un anarquista*, 236; Caballero, *Diario de campaña*, 92; *ABC*, 22 October 1936, 3 December 1936; *El Correo de Zamora*, 8 January 1937; *La Nueva España*, 7 September 1937. Cf. Preston, *Spanish Civil War*, 226: "Music [was] virtually non-existent" in the Nationalist zone.

65. Martínez Reverte, *La Batalla del Ebro*, 161; Cardona and Losada, *Aunque me tires el puente*, 163; Nonell Bru, *El Laureado Tercio*, 339–447.

66. Llordés Badía, *Al dejar el fusil*, 286; Caballero, *Diario de campaña*, 252; Thomas, *Brother against Brother*, 61; Abella, *La vida cotidiana nacional*, 45, 211; Iribarren, *El General Mola*, 194, 223; *El Correo de Zamora*, 30 March 1939; *ABC*, 30 June 1937; Box, *España*, 303; El Merroun, *Las tropas marroquíes*, 76; Nagore Yárnoz, *En la primera de Navarra*, 92, 114; Caballero, *Diario de campaña*, 96–145.

67. Abella, *La vida cotidiana nacional*, 286.

68. Martínez Reverte, *La Batalla del Ebro*, 489; Nonell Bru, *El Laureado Tercio*, 339, 639; Nagore Yárnoz, *En la primera de Navarra*, 97, 191; Díaz Viana, *Cancionero popular*, 51–94; Bullón de Mendoza and Diego, *Historias orales*, 45; Abella, *La vida cotidiana republicana*, 262–86; *El Correo de Zamora*, 16 October 1936; Cardona and Losada, *Aunque me tires el puente*, 15; Thomas, *Brother against Brother*, 15; *Proa*, 22 July 1938; Brecht cited in Beevor, *The Battle for Spain*, 275.

69. Ugarte Tellería, *La nueva Covadonga*, 183–201; Bastida Pellicer, *Historias de un quinto*, 219.

70. *Proa*, 23 August 1938; Álvarez Berciano and Sala Moguer, *El Cine en la zona nacional*, 43–207.

71. Álvarez Berciano and Sala Moguer, *El Cine en la zona nacional*, 46–53; *ABC*, 29 September 1938; *El Correo de Zamora*, 20 December 1938.

72. *El Correo de Zamora*, 24 December 1936, 5 February 1937, 5 May 1938; Álvarez Berciano and Sala Moguer, *El Cine en la zona nacional*, 34; Barón de Santa Clara, *El Judaísmo* (Burgos, 1938), 41; Castro, *Capital de la Cruzada*, 140; *La Provincia*, 17 October 1937, 2 November 1938; *La Nueva España*, 19 November 1938, 4 and 22 March 1939; *Proa*, 16 September 1938, 14 and 29 January 1939, 1 February 1939, 3 March 1939, 25 June 1939.

73. José Cabeza San Deogracias, *El Descanso del Guerrero: Cine en Madrid durante la Guerra Civil española (1936–1939)* (Madrid, 2005), 13–129; Cervera Gil, *Ya sabes mi paradero*, 142; *El Pueblo Gallego*, 6 September 1936, 7 and 13 November 1936, 22 September 1937, 15 and 17 October 1937, 17 May 1938, 4 November 1938, 29 January 1939; *Proa*, 16 July 1937, 6 and 31 December 1938, 29 January 1939; *La Provincia*, 31 July 1938; *ABC*, 5 June 1937; *La Nueva España*, 23 March 1938.

74. Tony Judt, *Past Imperfect: French Intellectuals, 1944–1956* (Berkeley, 1992), 201; *El Pueblo Gallego*, 31 July 1936, 5 August 1936, 2 October 1936, 12 November 1936, 11 June 1937, 29 October 1937; *Proa*, 25 September 1937; *ABC*, 29 December 1936, 4 December 1937, 29 May 1938; *El Correo de Zamora*, 5 December 1938.

75. *La Provincia*, 18 March 1937, 5 June 1937, 27 August 1938; *Proa*, 6 August 1938; *El Correo de Zamora*, 24 June 1939; Till Kössler, "Children in the Spanish Civil War," in Baumeister and Schüler-Springorum, *"If You Tolerate This . . . ,"* 105; *El Pueblo Gallego*, 11 October 1936, 15 November 1936, 11 April 1937, 2 May 1937, 3 March 1939; Stradling, *Your Children Will Be Next*, 19; Álvarez Berciano and Sala Moguer, *El Cine en la zona nacional*, 59.

76. *El Pueblo Gallego*, 25 August 1936, 27 November 1937, 19 April 1938, 23 September 1938; Álvarez Berciano and Sala Moguer, *El Cine en la zona nacional*, 167, 245; José Luis Borau, *Diccionario del cine español* (Madrid, 1998), 434; Rohr, *The Spanish Right*, 38; *El Correo de Zamora*, 26 September 1936; Xavier, *Laureada de Sangre*, 15; Copado, *Con la columna Redondo*, 292; *ABC*, 16 November 1937.

77. Stanley G. Payne, *Franco and Hitler: Spain, Germany, and World War II* (New Haven, CT, 2008), 215; Rohr, *The Spanish Right*, 38; Domínguez Arribas, *El enemigo*, 33.

78. *El Correo de Zamora*, 26 September 1936, 26 April 1938; Xavier, *Laureada de Sangre*, 15; Copado, *Con la columna Redondo*, 292; *ABC*, 16 November 1937; Díaz-Plaja, *La guerra de España*, 533; Santa Clara, *El Judaísmo*, 39; *La Provincia*, 13 April 1937.

79. *ABC*, 17 February 1937, 1 May 1937, 11 September 1937; *El Pueblo Gallego*, 22 December 1937, 16 February 1938; Rohr, *The Spanish Right*, 41–44; *El Correo de Zamora*, 31 October 1937; *La Nueva España*, 24 December 1937; *Proa*, 12 July 1938, 31 January 1939; Caballero, *Diario de campaña*, 268; Valdés, *Un Capellán*, 24, 172.

80. Santa Clara, *El Judaísmo*, 55, 65; Domínguez Arribas, *El enemigo*, 269–70; *La Nueva España*, 23 November 1937, 18 January 1938, 15 September 1938; Gonzalo Álvarez Chillida, *José María Pemán: Pensamiento y trayectoria de un monárquico (1897–1941)* (Cádiz, 1996), 349; *El Pueblo Gallego*, 22 December 1937, 16 February 1938; *ABC*, 7 November 1937. Rohr, *The Spanish Right*, 73, estimates that at least 12.5 percent of the volunteers were Jewish, a larger proportion than any ethnicity.

81. See Gonzalo Álvarez Chillida, *El Antisemitismo en España: La imagen del*

judío (1812–2002) (Madrid, 2002), 23; Rohr, *The Spanish Right*, 5; Vigueras Roldán, *Los paseados con Lorca*, 105. Pemán was not known for his personal courage, and requetés poked fun at his refusal to witness battle even from a protected position. See Nagore Yárnoz, *En la primera de Navarra*, 64. Madariaga, *Los moros*, 361; *El Correo de Zamora*, 2 September 1937; Cervera Gil, *Ya sabes mi paradero*, 126; *ABC*, 24 July 1936, 27 July 1938, 4 December 1938; Bayle quoted in Casanova, *República y guerra civil*, 360; *La Nueva España*, 5 December 1937; *Proa*, 30 November 1936.

82. Rohr, *The Spanish Right*, 57; Castro, *Capital de la Cruzada*, x, 102; *ABC*, 16 January 1937, 21 March 1937, 17 October 1937, 5, 12, and 18 May 1938, 21 June 1938; Santa Clara, *El Judaísmo*, 39; *La Nueva España*, 26 June 1938, 20 October 1938; *El Correo de Zamora*, 15 January 1938, 5 May 1938; *Proa*, 5 and 12 July 1938.

83. Santa Clara, *El Judaísmo*, 26; *El Pueblo Gallego*, 12 January 1939; *El Correo de Zamora*, 21 August 1936, 15 April 1938, 5 September 1938; *La Nueva España*, 29 April 1937; Rohr, *The Spanish Right*, 75.

84. *ABC*, 29 April 1937, 18 February 1938; Santa Clara, *El Judaísmo*, 63; Rohr, *The Spanish Right and the Jews*, 82; *Proa*, 5 August 1937.

85. *ABC*, 24 July 1936; *El Correo de Zamora*, 10 December 1937, 3 March 1938, 15 May 1938, 25 August 1938, 30 October 1938, 15 June 1939; *La Nueva España*, 20 January 1938; Ruiz Vilaplana, *Burgos Justice*, 178; Rey, *Por qué luchó*, 137; Abella, *La vida cotidiana nacional*, 177; Copado, *Con la columna Redondo*, 113; *El Pueblo Gallego*, 10 September 1938, 12 March 1939; Beevor, *The Battle for Spain*, 339; *Proa*, 10 September 1938; Díez de Rivera, *La Riqueza pesquera*, 44.

86. *El Correo de Zamora*, 11 January 1937, 18 December 1937, 25 August 1938. Pujol had been on the German payroll as early as World War I and throughout the Second Republic. See García, *Mentiras necesarias*, 25, 31. Rivero Noval, *Política y sociedad en la Rioja*, 163; *La Provincia*, 4 April 1937.

87. *El Pueblo Gallego*, 18 November 1936; *Proa*, 20 September 1937; *La Nueva España*, 4 and 12 February 1937, 23 June 1938; *ABC*, 17 and 20 December 1936, 14 April 1937, 21 May 1937, 10 September 1937, 21 July 1938, 7 December 1938; Queipo cited in Álvarez Chillida, *El Antisemitismo en España*, 364; Nerín, *La guerra*, 83; *La Provincia*, 11 September 1938; Baroja, *Comunistas*, 66, 70.

88. Santa Clara, *El Judaísmo*, 7–25; *Proa*, 16 August 1938, 3 November 1938; Álvarez Chillida, "Zaragoza en la Guerra Civil," 45.

89. *La Nueva España*, 18 and 22 January 1938, 7 January 1939; *ABC*, 16 November 1937, 13 September 1938, 9 October 1938, 16 December 1938; *Proa*, 1 February 1939; *El Correo de Zamora*, 25 June 1937; Baroja, *Comunistas*, 70–92; Pío Baroja, *Ayer y Hoy* (Santiago de Chile, 1939), 109–216.

90. *ABC*, 16 November 1937, 24 March 1938, 14 October 1938; *El Pueblo Gallego*, 22 December 1937, 31 July 1938; Díez de Rivera, *La Riqueza pesquera*, 102; *El Correo de Zamora*, 5 September 1938; *La Provincia*, 1 and 23 August 1938; Memoria de las Palmas, 7 September 1938, 44/3123, AGA.

91. *ABC*, 15 April 1937, 7, 20, and 27 April 1938, 13 September 1938, 20 December 1938; *El Pueblo Gallego*, 9 March 1937, 6 January 1938, 11 August 1938; *La Nueva España*, 18 January 1938, 6 September 1938; *Proa*, 11 November 1938; Rohr, *The Spanish Right*, 57.

92. Abella, *La vida cotidiana nacional*, 66; *La Nueva España*, 7 April 1938; *ABC*, 5 and 26 January 1938; *El Pueblo Gallego*, [11?] February 1938.

93. *ABC*, 18, 26, and 30 November 1938; *La Provincia*, 8 January 1939.

94. *El Correo de Zamora*, 4 May 1938; *El Pueblo Gallego*, 16 and 22 November 1938, 1 December 1938; *La Nueva España*, 19 November 1938; *Proa*, 11 and 12 November 1938; *La Provincia*, 12 January 1939.

95. Abella, *La vida cotidiana nacional*, 54; *El Pueblo Gallego*, 3 June 1936, 3 May 1938; *La Nueva España*, 20 January 1937, 6 February 1937; Martínez Reverte, *La Batalla del Ebro*, 455; *ABC*, 22 July 1937, 8 August 1937, 27 December 1938; *Proa*, 2 August 1937, 14 July 1938; Nagore Yárnoz, *En la primera de Navarra*, 253.

96. *La Provincia*, 12 January 1939; *La Nueva España*, 19 November 1938; Rohr, *The Spanish Right*, 46.

97. *ABC*, 9 September 1937, 14 October 1938; *Proa*, 4 December 1938, 2 February 1939; *La Provincia*, 20 September 1938; Wenceslao González-Oliveros in Juan Luis Vives, *Humanismo frente a Comunismo: La primera monografía anticomunista publicada en el mundo, obra de un pensador español*, trans. Wenceslao González-Oliveros (Valladolid, 1937), 82; *La Nueva España*, 28 February 1939; *El Pueblo Gallego*, 24 October 1936, 2 May 1937. Cf. El Merroun, *Las tropas marroquíes*, 180, who accepts the charge of a Zionist-Communist conspiracy at face value: "The international Zionist organization efficiently aided the Communists by organizing throughout the world recruitment offices managed by Jews." Joaquín Pérez Madrigal, *Disparos a cero* (Madrid, 1939), 217–20; Domínguez Arribas, *El enemigo*, 86, 191; Revilla Cebrecos, *Tercio de Lácar*, 223; Álvarez Chillida, *El Antisemitismo en España*, 455–56; Touboul Tardieu, *Séphardisme et Hispanité*, 323.

98. *El Pueblo Gallego*, 16 December 1937; Mainer, *Años de Vísperas*, 87; Álvarez Chillida, *José María Pemán*, 347; *La Nueva España*, 10 September 1937; Santa Clara, *El Judaísmo*, 31; Baroja, *Comunistas*, 67; *ABC*, 20 December 1936; *El Correo de Zamora*, 24 February 1939; *La Provincia*, 11 May 1939.

99. *El Pueblo Gallego*, 2 May 1937; Rohr, *The Spanish Right*, 76; *La Nueva España*, 28 April 1937.

100. Falcoff, "Argentina," 325; Abella, *La vida cotidiana nacional*, 207; *ABC*, 21 June 1938, 13 September 1938, 21 January 1939; Raguer, *La Espada*, 127; Rohr, *The Spanish Right*, 80; *La Nueva España*, 5 July 1938; Mauriac quoted in Beevor, *The Battle for Spain*, 241.

101. *Proa*, 8 September 1938, 1 February 1939; *ABC*, 20 December 1936; *La Nueva España*, 23 April 1937, 3 and 4 July 1938, 19 November 1938; *La Provincia*, 7 July 1938, 11 September 1938; *El Pueblo Gallego*, 27 December 1936; Álvarez Berciano and Sala Moguer, *El Cine en la zona nacional*, 146; *El Correo de Zamora*, 27 August 1938, 5 September 1938; Álvarez Chillida, *José María Pemán*, 336.

102. *ABC*, 6 July 1937, 26 February 1938, 26 March 1938; Álvarez Chillida, *El Antisemitismo en España*, 361–62; *El Pueblo Gallego*, 3 September 1936; Rohr, *The Spanish Right*, 79; *La Nueva España*, 6 March 1938; Xavier, *Caballero Legionario*, 37; Iribarren, *El General Mola*, 216; *Proa*, 11 and 25 March 1939.

103. *ABC*, 3 August 1938, 15 January 1939; *La Nueva España*, 20 August 1938, 4 November 1938, 27 December 1938; *Proa*, 10 January 1939, 1 February 1939; *La*

Provincia, 5 February 1937; Álvarez Chillida, *El Antisemitismo en España*, 335; Rohr, *The Spanish Right*, 83; Baroja, *Ayer y Hoy*, 78–141.

104. *ABC*, 11 July 1937; Abella, *La vida cotidiana nacional*, 324. France became so unpopular that in Zamora the Café Paris was renamed Café Lisboa. See *El Correo de Zamora*, 1 September 1936. *El Correo de Zamora*, 20 and 30 December 1938; Santa Clara, *El Judaísmo*, 45; *Proa*, 4 August 1938.

105. *El Correo de Zamora*, 24 June 1937, 23 and 30 July 1937, 4 August 1938; *Proa*, 23 July 1938; Palomares Ibáñez, *La Guerra Civil en Palencia*, 65; Ruiz Vilaplana, *Burgos Justice*, 183; Castro, *Capital de la Cruzada*, 157; González Bueno, *Paz en guerra*, 128; Caspistegui, "Religión," 332; Cervera Gil, *Ya sabes mi paradero*, 265; *ABC*, 9 October 1938; *La Provincia*, 20 September 1938.

106. Rohr, *The Spanish Right*, 7, 84; Gobierno, Ceuta, Memoria, August 1938, 44/2790, AGA; Álvarez Chillida, *El Antisemitismo en España*, 367–492; Gonzalo Álvarez Chillida, "La eclosión del antisemitismo español: De la II República al Holocausto," in Gonzalo Álvarez Chillida and Ricardo Izquierdo Benito, eds., *El Antisemitismo en España* (Cuenca, 2007), 184–92; El Merroun, *Las tropas marroquíes*, 18, 79; Llordés Badía, *Al dejar el fusil*, 29–30.

107. Yuri Slezkine, *The Jewish Century* (Princeton, NJ, 2004), 42–43; Benoît Pellistrandi, "La realidad social y antropológica del catolicismo y los orígenes religiosos de la Guerra Civil," in Aurell and López, *Católicos entre dos guerras*, 133; Casas, "La agenda de la conferencia de Metropolitanos," 240; José-Vidal Pelaz López, "Los católicos españoles y el cine: De los orígenes al Nacionalcatolicismo," in José-Leonardo Ruiz Sánchez, ed., *Catolicismo y comunicación en la historia contemporánea* (Seville, 2005), 82; González-Oliveros, *Humanismo frente a Comunismo*, 72–82.

108. Ortiz Villalba, *Sevilla 1936*, 287–88; Beevor, *The Battle for Spain*, 83; Copado, *Con la columna Redondo*, 139; García, *Mentiras necesarias*, 59; *ABC*, 1 October 1936, 21 June 1938; Raguer, *La Espada*, 127; Xavier, *Laureada de Sangre*, 211; *La Nueva España*, 8 October 1937; Caballero, *Diario de campaña*, 66; *El Correo de Zamora*, 27 February 1937.

109. *ABC*, 29 March 1938; González Bueno, *Paz en guerra*, 5; Díez de Rivera, *La Riqueza pesquera*, 105; Kemp, *Mine Were of Trouble*, 113; *Pueblo Gallego*, 20 January 1939; *El Correo de Zamora*, 26 January 1939.

110. Vives, *Humanismo frente a Comunismo*, 179.

111. Juan Bautista Vilar, "La persecución religiosa en la zona nacionalista: El caso de los protestantes españoles," in Octavio Ruiz-Manjón Cabeza and Miguel Gómez Oliver, eds., *Los nuevos historiadores ante la Guerra Civil española* (Granada, 1990), 2:171, 176, claims that Nationalists killed proportionally more Protestant clergy than Republicans eliminated Catholic priests. Rodrigo, *Hasta la raíz*, 72; *El Pueblo Gallego*, 13 March 1937; *La Provincia*, 4 and 13 April 1937; Pons Prades, *Guerrillas españolas*, 233–36; Fraser, *Blood of Spain*, 206–7; González Egido, *Agonizar en Salamanca*, 141–48.

112. *El Correo de Zamora*, 5 and 6 May 1938; Cervera Gil, *Ya sabes mi paradero*, 198; Souto Blanco, *La represión franquista*, 187; Bullón de Mendoza and Diego, *Historias orales*, 229; *La Nueva España*, 9 October 1937; *El Pueblo Gallego*, 11 June 1939; Domínguez Arribas, *El enemigo*, 93.

113. Iribarren, *El General Mola*, 218; Memoria de las Palmas, 7 September 1938, 44/3123, AGA; Queipo de Llano, *Memorias*, 343; Álvarez Chillida, *José María Pemán*, 337, 359; Domínguez Arribas, *El enemigo*, 115–255.

CHAPTER 4. DEFIANCE OF THE STATE

1. Larraz, *El ordenamiento*, 16–17; *El Correo de Zamora*, 13 September 1937.

2. Enrique Moradiellos, *1936: Los mitos de la guerra civil* (Barcelona, 2005), 115–16; Carmen Benito del Pozo, *La clase obrera asturiana bajo el franquismo: Empleo, condiciones de trabajo y conflicto (1940–1975)* (Madrid, 1993), 8, also emphasizes centralization of industrial control. Martínez Ruiz, "El campo en guerra," 143; Souto Blanco, *La represión franquista*, 132; *El Correo de Zamora*, 10 March 1939; Arco Blanco, *Las alas del Ave Fénix*, 104; *ABC*, 1 June 1938.

3. *ABC*, 7, 18, and 21 August 1936, 13 September 1936, 29 October 1936, 30 March 1937, 1 April 1937; *El Pueblo Gallego*, 27 December 1936, 15 May 1937, 7 May 1938; *El Correo de Zamora*, 1 June 1937.

4. Abella, *La vida cotidiana nacional*, 111–361; *ABC*, 27 February 1937; *El Pueblo Gallego*, 30 July 1938; Escolar Sobrino, *La cultura*, 274; López Ortiz and Melgarejo Moreno, "El Sector Agrario," 17.

5. *La Nueva España*, 28 October 1937; Martínez Ruiz, "El campo en guerra," 152; Martínez Ruiz, "Las relaciones económicas internacionales," 297, 322; Catalan, "Guerra e industria," 193; Salas, *Sevilla*, 2:666–730; Arco Blanco, *Las alas del Ave Fénix*, 59–99, and personal communication of author; *ABC*, 19 and 23 February 1938, 15 November 1938.

6. *ABC*, 9–15 February 1938, 12 and 23–24 March 1938, 3 September 1938; Domingo, *Retaguardia*, 81–82; Barrios, *El Último Virrey*, 187; *El Correo de Zamora*, 18 May 1938.

7. Gobierno Civil, Huelva, August 1938, 44/2791, AGA; Comité Sindical del Jabón, 15 June 1938, 34/10856, AGA; *ABC*, 13 and 23 March 1938, 24 and 29 April 1938, 23 June 1938; *El Correo de Zamora*, 7 June 1939; Gobierno Civil de Segovia, Memoria, 25 August 1938, 44/2792, AGA; Gobierno Civil de León, Memoria, August 1938, 44/2791, AGA; *Proa*, 3 August 1938.

8. Santa Cruz de Tenerife, Memoria, 1938, 44/2792, AGA; *La Provincia*, 4 and 10 April 1937, 15 July 1937, 3 December 1938, 12 January 1939; Memoria de las Palmas, 7 September 1938, 44/3123.

9. *La Nueva España*, 10 December 1937, 1 June 1939; Oviedo, 1938, 44/2791, AGA; Orense, September 1938, 44/2791, AGA; *Proa*, 25 April 1939, 26 May 1939; Rivero Noval, *Política y sociedad en la Rioja*, 415.

10. *El Correo de Zamora*, 19 June 1939; Jackson, *Spanish Republic*, 86–87; SNT, Navarra, 19 October 1937, 61/13502, AGA; *ABC*, 1 March 1938; SNT, Jefatura Provincial, Salamanca, 5 May 1938, 61/13503, AGA; Señor Delegado, Palencia, 18 November 1938, 61/13502, AGA; *El Correo de Zamora*, 19 September 1937.

11. *ABC*, 29 December 1936, 28 October 1937, 14 January 1938, 17 March 1938, 12 May 1938; *El Pueblo Gallego*, 10, 13, and 26 May 1938, 3 and 7 July 1938; Castro, *Capital de la Cruzada*, 108; *La Provincia*, 8 April 1937.

312 NOTES TO PAGES 213–216

12. *El Correo de Zamora*, 5 and 11 May 1938; *Proa*, [?] December 1936, 17 September 1938; *La Provincia*, 12 May 1938, 10 and 30 May 1939; Ruiz Vilaplana, *Burgos Justice*, 213; *El Pueblo Gallego*, 1 January 1939; *La Nueva España*, 8 January 1937; Gobierno Civil de León, Memoria, August 1938, 44/2791, AGA.

13. *El Pueblo Gallego*, 21 November 1937, 5 May 1938; *La Nueva España*, 28 October 1937, 19 February 1938, 3 August 1938; *El Correo de Zamora*, 24 May 1939; *Proa*, 16 November 1936; Gobierno Civil de León, Memoria, August 1938, 44/2791, AGA; Ugarte Tellería, *La nueva Covadonga*, 378; Kalyvas, *The Logic of Violence*, 307.

14. *ABC*, 8 January 1937, 5 May 1938; *El Correo de Zamora*, 29 November 1938; Azaña cited in Martínez Bande, *La ofensiva sobre Zaragoza*, 28–29; Manuel Azaña, *Obras completas* (Madrid, 1990), 3:520; Orense, September 1938, 44/2791, AGA; Gobierno Civil de León, Memoria, August 1938, 44/2791, AGA; Memoria, Álava, 1938, 44/2790, AGA; Gobierno Civil, Huelva, August 1938, 44/2791, AGA; Memoria, Granada, 1938, 44/2791, AGA; Gobierno, Ceuta, Memoria, August 1938, 44/2790, AGA.

15. Memoria, Granada, 1938, 44/2791, AGA; Souto Blanco, *La represión franquista*, 194, 200.

16. Memoria, Ávila, August 1938, 44/2790, AGA; Sanders, *Histoire du Marché noir*, 83; *ABC*, 18 May 1939; *El Pueblo Gallego*, 30 December 1937.

17. *ABC*, 29 May 1937, 19 and 24–25 June 1937, 31 August 1937, 4 September 1937, 4, 7, 10, and 24 November 1937, 21 April 1938, 27 November 1938, 5 January 1939; *El Pueblo Gallego*, 14 September 1938; *El Correo de Zamora*, 6 January 1938.

18. Kalyvas, *The Logic of Violence*, 14–360; Souto Blanco, *La represión franquista*, 78, 180; Cenarro, "Matar," 67; Kershner, *Quaker Service*, 104; Ortiz Villalba, *Sevilla 1936*, 232; Cazorla Sánchez, *Las políticas de la victoria*, 102. For a broad view, see Sheila Fitzpatrick and Robert Gellately, eds., *Accusatory Practices: Denunciation in Modern European History, 1789–1989* (Chicago, 1997). Domingo, *Retaguardia*, 344; Bahamonde y Sánchez de Castro, *Un Año con Queipo*, 89; Madariaga, *Los moros*, 317; Ruiz Vilaplana, *Burgos Justice*, 163; *ABC*, 31 July 1937, 27 November 1937; *El Pueblo Gallego*, 22 August 1936, 25 May 1937; *El Correo de Zamora*, 22 and 23 June 1937, 15 December 1937, Souto Blanco, *Los apoyos*, 15.

19. Huesca, Memoria, 1938, 44/2791, AGA; *El Correo de Zamora*, 12 November 1936; Satrústegui, *Memorias de un anarquista*, 151; *La Nueva España*, 18 December 1937, 3 August 1938; Souto Blanco, *La represión franquista*, 330, 342; Ruiz Vilaplana, *Burgos Justice*, 166.

20. *Proa*, 13 November 1936; Abella, *La vida cotidiana nacional*, 110–11, 125, 225; Memoria, Palencia, 1938, 44/3123, AGA; Memoria, Ávila, August 1938, 44/2790, AGA; Sánchez Asiaín, *Economía*, 144, 148; *ABC*, 20 and 24 November 1936.

21. *ABC*, 18 November 1936, 17 March 1937, 17 April 1938; *El Pueblo Gallego*, 12, 21, and 24 November 1936, 6, 18, and 23 March 1937, 9, 14, and 27 April 1937, 15, 28, and 30 May 1937, 12, 13, and 15 June 1937, 10 and 14 October 1937, 6 November 1937; *Proa*, 15 November 1936; Gobierno Civil, Lugo, 1938, 44/2791, AGA; Memoria, Pontevedra, 1937, 44/3122, AGA; Castro, *Capital de la Cruzada*, 111; Informe colectivo, la banca privada y cajas de ahorro, Burgos, August 1938, 44/2790, AGA; Velarde Fuertes, "Algunos aspectos económicos," 959; Sánchez Asiaín, *Economía*, 119; *El Correo de Zamora*, 14 April 1938.

22. *La Provincia*, 25 and 28 March 1937; *ABC*, 18 and 28 March 1937, 6 April 1937, 1 May 1937, 8 August 1937, 15 June 1937, 15 September 1937, 13, 16, and 27 November 1937, 2 and 30 December 1937; Luis Barrera Coronado, *1936–1939, La moneda de necesidad en la provincia de Sevilla* (Madrid, 1989), 8.

23. *El Pueblo Gallego*, 3 July 1937, 1 and 4 September 1937, 23 October 1937, 23 and 31 December 1937, 30 August 1938, 12 February 1939; *La Nueva España*, 14 December 1937, 14 May 1937, 3 July 1938, 18 September 1938; *Proa*, [1?] September 1937; *El Correo de Zamora*, 30 March 1937, 5 and 14 April 1937, 5 June 1937; *La Provincia*, 12 December 1937; 31 May 1938; 16 and 21 June 1938; *ABC*, 24 January 1939.

24. Martorell Linares, "Una Guerra, Dos Pesetas," 348, 355; Abella, *La vida cotidiana nacional*, 338; Revilla Cebrecos, *Tercio de Lácar*, 320.

25. *El Pueblo Gallego*, 31 October 1937; Miguel Ángel Del Arco Blanco, *Hambre de siglos: Mundo rural y apoyos sociales del franquismo en Andalucía Oriental (1936–1951)* (Granada, 2007), 101.

26. Oviedo, 1938, 44/2791, AGA; *ABC*, 21 October 1936, 29 November 1936, 30 March 1937, 12 and 21 May 1937, 11 and 29 June 1937, 5, 10, and 11 September 1937, 16 and 30 January 1938, 12 February 1938, 20 March 1938, 12 May 1938, 1 and 23 June 1938, 5 and 15 November 1938, 4 January 1939; *El Pueblo Gallego*, 3 and 18 November 1937, 3 March 1938, 10 and 12 May 1938, 3 June 1939; *El Correo de Zamora*, 13 August 1936, 25 September 1936, 10 October 1936, 22 and 23 July 1937, 10 September 1937, 24 February 1939, 25 May 1939; *La Nueva España*, 31 May 1938; *Proa*, [?] December 1936; Álvarez Berciano and Sala Noguer, *El Cine en la zona nacional*, 42.

27. *ABC*, 24 April 1937, 18 June 1937, 1 September 1937, 15 October 1937, 9 March 1938, 3 November 1938, 10 May 1939; *La Provincia*, 28 February 1937, 20 October 1938, 12 January 1939; *El Pueblo Gallego*, 10 June 1937, 18 April 1939; *El Correo de Zamora*, 19 July 1937, 30 October 1937, 27 January 1938, 18 February 1938, 23 March 1938; *Proa*, 9 and 10 November 1938, 14 and 24 January 1939; Bastida Pellicer, *Historias de un quinto*, 216.

28. *El Pueblo Gallego*, 19 June 1936; Memoria, Ávila, August 1938, 44/2790, AGA; Rivero Noval, *Política y sociedad en la Rioja*, 330–43; *El Correo de Zamora*, 18 December 1936, 5 June 1937, 7 July 1937, 2 August 1937, 4 November 1937; Gobierno Civil, Cáceres, August 1938, 44/2790, AGA; Oviedo, 1938, 44/2791, AGA; Sr. Ingeniero, 6 December 1937, Interior, 61/13505, AGA.

29. *El Pueblo Gallego*, 19 March 1938, 12 April 1938; Rivero Noval, *Política y sociedad en la Rioja*, 284; *La Nueva España*, 27 January 1938, 16 February 1938; Memoria, Pontevedra, 1937, 44/3122, AGA; Memoria, Pontevedra, 1939, 44/3122, AGA; *ABC*, 24 April 1937, 15 October 1937, 3 November 1938; SNT, 12 March 1938, Interior, 61/13508, AGA; *El Correo de Zamora*, 7 February 1938; Huesca, Memoria, 1938, 44/2791, AGA.

30. *El Pueblo Gallego*, 22 August 1937, 28 April 1938; *El Correo de Zamora*, 5 June 1937, 13 September 1937, 20 November 1937, 2 February 1938, 13, 18, 20, and 21 September 1938, 25 February 1939, 30 March 1939; *ABC*, 17 August 1938.

31. *ABC*, 30 January 1938, 12, 13, and 18 March 1938; Gobierno Civil, Huelva, August 1938, 44/2791, AGA; Gobierno Civil de León, Memoria, August 1938, 44/

2791, AGA; Huesca, Memoria, 1938, 44/2791, AGA; *El Pueblo Gallego*, 27 December 1936.

32. *ABC*, 30 January 1938, 12, 13, and 18 March 1938; Gobierno Civil, Huelva, August 1938, 44/2791, AGA; Gobierno Civil de León, Memoria, August 1938, 44/2791, AGA; Huesca, Memoria, 1938, 44/2791, AGA; *El Pueblo Gallego*, 27 December 1936.

33. *El Pueblo Gallego*, 5 December 1937, 9 January 1938, 28 April 1938; Diputación Provincial de Salamanca, 1937, 44/3123, AGA; Memoria, Lugo, 30 July 1938, 44/2791, AGA; *El Correo de Zamora*, 25 July 1937; *La Provincia*, 4 June 1938, 10 August 1938; *Proa*, 5 August 1937.

34. *ABC*, 28 April 1937; *El Pueblo Gallego*, 11 September 1936; Medina, *Tiempo pasado*, 52; Iribarren, *El General Mola*, 220.

35. *El Pueblo Gallego*, 6 and 8 May 1936; Baroja, *Ayer y Hoy*, 181; *El Correo de Zamora*, 26 December 1938, 17 June 1939; *ABC*, 3 March 1938.

36. *El Pueblo Gallego*, 28 January 1937, 17 July 1937, 3 September 1937, 31 December 1937, 31 May 1938; *El Correo de Zamora*, 10 January 1939; *Proa*, 9 August 1938, 5 October 1938, 10 and 14 January 1939.

37. Álvarez Berciano and Sala Moguer, *El Cine en la zona nacional*, 235; Cervera Gil, *Ya sabes mi paradero*, 393; Xavier, *Caballero Legionario*, 193; Xavier, *Laureada de Sangre*, 121; *El Correo de Zamora*, 17 September 1938; *La Nueva España*, 6 October 1938.

38. *ABC*, 29 April 1937, 21 and 26 April 1938, 14 May 1939; *El Pueblo Gallego*, 29 September 1937; Martín, "Gitanos en la Guerra Civil Española," 2–11; Queipo de Llano, *Memorias*, 51.

39. *El Pueblo Gallego*, 4 December 1937, 1 January 1939; *La Nueva España*, 20 and 27 June 1939; *La Provincia*, 19 April 1938; *Proa*, [29?] December 1936, 1 January 1937; *El Correo de Zamora*, 13 May 1937.

40. Llordés Badía, *Al dejar el fusil*, 117; González Bueno, *Paz en guerra*, 209; Queipo de Llano, *Memorias*, 217; A. B. Murphy, *The Russian Civil War: Primary Sources* (New York, 2000), 212; Kenez, *Civil War in South Russia, 1918*, 205; Brinkley, *The Volunteer Army*, 288; "The Anti-Bolshevik Movement in South Russia, 1920," in Bourne and Watt, *British Documents on Foreign Affairs*, pt. 2, vol. 3, 78; Bechhofer, *In Denikin's Russia*, 184.

41. Henry G. Alsberg, "In the Wake of Denikin," quoted in Rex A. Wade, ed., *Documents of Soviet History: The Triumph of Bolshevism* (Gulf Breeze, FL, 1991), 1:403–7; Denikin quoted in Final Report, Major-General H.C. Holman, December 1920, FO 371 5448, PRO; Delano Dugarm, "Peasant Wars in Tambov Province," in Brovkin, *The Bolsheviks*, 181; Delano Dugarm, "Local Politics and the Struggle for Grain in Tambov, 1918–21," in Donald J. Raleigh, ed., *Provincial Landscapes: Local Dimensions of Soviet Power, 1917–1953* (Pittsburgh, 2001).

42. Vladimir N. Brovkin, "Introduction," in Brovkin, *The Bolsheviks*, 11; Brovkin, *Behind the Front Lines*, 198–99; Norman Pereira, "The Partisan Movement in Western Siberia, 1918–1920," *Jahrbücher für Geschichte Osteuropas* 38 (1990): 89; Graves, *America's Siberian Adventure*, 148, 237; Diary of P. V. Vologodsky as Prime Minister of Admiral Kolchak's Cabinet, Omsk, 6 February 1919, Hoover Institution.

43. Westad, *Decisive Encounters*, 8: "The civil war is first of all the story of how the GMD leaders, by their decisions, squandered most of the relative advantages they had in 1945." Situation en Chine du Sud, March 1948, Asie-Océanie Chine, 134, Archives Diplomatiques; Wou, *Mobilizing*, 141, 155; Yung-Fa Chen, *Making Revolution: The Communist Movement in Eastern and Central China, 1937–1945* (Berkeley, 1986), 396; De Jaegher and Kuhn, *The Enemy Within*, 39–75.

44. Chen, *Making Revolution*, 431; Canton, 20 December 1947, Ady Papers, Yale Divinity School, New Haven, CT; 22 June 1948, FO 371 69536, PRO.

45. "Agricultural Conditions in the Northeast," Ta Kung Pao, 3 October 1947, *Chinese Press Review*, Shanghai, NYPL; Westad, *Decisive Encounters*, 109–83; Levine, *Anvil*, 170; Dorothy Jacobs-Larkcom, *As China Fell: The Experiences of a British Consul's Wife, 1946–1953* (Devon, 1976); Pepper, *Civil War in China*, 314; Lapwood and Lapwood, *Through the Chinese Revolution*, 45. French reports, "Coup de main communiste sur Tunghsien," Asie-Océanie Chine, 102, Archives Diplomatiques, confirm the absence of looting. Thorne and Patterson, *Foreign Relations of the United States*, 896.

46. Nagore Yárnoz, *En la primera de Navarra*, 136; Thomas, *Brother against Brother*, 72–105; Llordés Badía, *Al dejar el fusil*, 159; Salas, *Sevilla*, 1:34, 322; Cervera Gil, *Ya sabes mi paradero*, 98; González Bueno, *Paz en guerra*, 209; Cía Navascués, *Memorias*, 39–247. During the Battle of the Ebro, Líster shot looters. See Cardona and Losada, *Aunque me tires el puente*, 53–112. *La Nueva España*, 14 November 1937; *El Pueblo Gallego*, 20 April 1939.

47. Llordés Badía, *Al dejar el fusil*, 131, 151; Thomas, *Brother against Brother*, 58; Stradling, *The Irish*, 68; Espinosa Maestre, *La justicia de Queipo*, 208; Satrústegui, *Memorias de un anarquista*, 118–261; González Bueno, *Paz en guerra*, 29; Informes, 11 and 19 May 1938, Interior, 61/13509, AGA; Bullón de Mendoza and Diego, *Historias orales*, 136; Beevor, *The Battle for Spain*, 120, 378; Sánchez Ruano, *Islam*, 367.

48. Bullón de Mendoza and Diego, *Historias orales*, 119–21; Copado, *Con la columna Redondo*, 93; Nagore Yárnoz, *En la primera de Navarra*, 57; Xavier, *Laureada de Sangre*, 76; Nonell Bru, *El Laureado Tercio*, 539; Cardona and Losada, *Aunque me tires el puente*, 340; Llordés Badía, *Al dejar el fusil*, 295–97; T.P., n.d., 32 División, ZN, a. 41, 1. 3, c. 43, AGM; *ABC*, 20 March 1937; *El Pueblo Gallego*, 15 January 1939, 28 March 1939; *La Nueva España*, 23 April 1937.

49. Ugarte Tellería, *La nueva Covadonga*, 133, 404; Casanova, *República y guerra civil*, 171.

50. Thomas, *Brother against Brother*, 58; Telegrama, 25 July 1938, ZN, 112 División, a. 37, 1. 1, c. 10, AGM; Medina, *Tiempo pasado*, 103; Nonell Bru, *El Laureado Tercio*, 286–92; Ramón Carrión and Ortiz, *Madrina de guerra*, 255.

51. Nonell Bru, *El Laureado Tercio*, 295–304; Revilla Cebrecos, *Tercio de Lácar*, 314; *Asistencia a Frentes y Hospitales*, 42–44; Thomas, *Brother against Brother*, 82; Aróstegui, *Los combatientes carlistas*, 2:256, 490; Nagore Yárnoz, *En la primera de Navarra*, 86; Resa, *Memorias de un requeté*, 114.

52. Nonell Bru, *El Laureado Tercio*, 304–610; Abella, *La vida cotidiana nacional*, 349–52; Llordés Badía, *Al dejar el fusil*, 319; González Bueno, *Paz en guerra*, 51.

53. *ABC*, 6 November 1936; Castro, *Capital de la Cruzada*, 167; *El Correo de*

Zamora, 1 August 1937; Kemp, *Mine Were of Trouble*, 142; Angel Viñas et al., *Política comercial exterior*, 1:145; *El Pueblo Gallego*, 3 June 1939; Pons Prades, *Guerrillas españolas*, 354; Payne, *The Franco Regime*, 152; William H. McNeill, *The Pursuit of Power: Technology, Armed Force, and Society since A.D. 1000* (Chicago, 1982), 25.

54. Santa Cruz de Tenerife, Memoria, 1938, 44/2792, AGA; Memoria, Ávila, August 1938, 44/2790, AGA; Corral, *Desertores*, 173; *El Pueblo Gallego*, 11 May 1938; Cervera Gil, *Ya sabes mi paradero*, 237; Caballero, *Diario de campaña*, 251.

55. Gobierno Civil de Segovia, Memoria, 25 August 1938, 44/2792, AGA; Gobierno Civil, Huelva, August 1938, 44/2791, AGA; Memoria, Ávila, August 1938, 44/2790, AGA; Memoria, Álava, 1938, 44/2790, AGA; Orense, September 1938, 44/2791, AGA; SNT, Jefatura Provincial de Granada, 26 September 1938, Interior, 61/13498, AGA; *ABC*, 22 July 1937; Abella, *La vida cotidiana nacional*, 257; *El Pueblo Gallego*, 16 May 1937.

56. Memoria, Palencia, 1938, 44/3123, AGA; *El Pueblo Gallego*, 27 April 1937, 3 June 1937, 3 July 1938, 7 August 1938; *Proa*, 22 July 1938, 7 and 21 August 1938, 9 November 1938, 18 February 1939, 20 April 1939, 4 June 1939; *El Correo de Zamora*, 4 June 1937, 16 January 1938; *La Provincia*, 25 June 1938; Gobierno Civil de Segovia, Memoria, 25 August 1938, 44/2792, AGA; *La Nueva España*, 15 and 17 March 1938; *ABC*, 16 and 17 November 1937, 13 July 1938, 14 May 1939.

57. Payne, *Politics and Military*, 388–89; Palacios and Payne, *Franco, mi padre*, 339; *ABC*, 13 August 1937.

58. Corral, *Desertores*, 531; Caballero, *Diario de campaña*, 363; Urra Lusarreta, *En las trincheras*, 275; Aróstegui, *Los combatientes carlistas*, 2:285; *El Pueblo Gallego*, 14 and 30 May 1937, 3, 20, 24, 28, and 29 July 1937, 4, 7, 14, and 16 September 1937, 10 and 17 October 1937, 11, 13, 16, and 26 November 1937, 30 December 1937, 19 January 1938, 26 February 1938, 9 and 30 August 1938, 8 September 1938, 5 October 1938, 1 January 1939, 28 March 1939, 6 and 22 June 1939.

59. Corral, *Desertores*, 108–11; Lazo, *Retrato de fascismo*, 30; Kalyvas, *The Logic of Violence*, 385; Llordés Badía, *Al dejar el fusil*, 143; *La Provincia*, 15 January 1937; Robert Gellately, "Denunciations in Twentieth-Century Germany: Aspects of Self-Policing in the Third Reich and the German Democratic Republic," in Fitzpatrick and Gellately, *Accusatory Practices*, 205.

60. Corral, *Desertores*, 121–534; Castro, *Capital de la Cruzada*, 229; *ABC*, 4 December 1937, 10 September 1938, 10 January 1939; *El Pueblo Gallego*, 21 September 1937, 20 and 23 October 1938.

61. Salas and Salas, *Historia general*, 120–24; Michael Alpert, *El ejército republicano en la guerra civil* (Madrid, 1989), 63; Julián Casanova, *Anarquismo y revolución en la sociedad rural aragonesa, 1936–1938* (Madrid, 1985), 85; Hermet, *La guerre d'Espagne*, 155, 181; Corral, *Desertores*, 151–534; Gálvez Muñoz, "Produciendo para la revolución," 469. Michael Alpert, "Soldiers, Politics, and War," in Paul Preston, ed., *Revolution and War in Spain, 1931–1939* (New York, 1984), 218, gives a figure of 1,025,500 soldiers for the Nationalists. Using Soviet sources, Stanley G. Payne, *The Spanish Revolution* (New York, 1970), 343, offers figures of a similar magnitude. Westad, *Decisive Encounters*, 108.

62. Cervera Gil, *Ya sabes mi paradero*, 398; *El Pueblo Gallego*, 20 May 1937,

10 August 1938; *El Correo de Zamora*, 13 April 1938, 2 August 1938; Cardona and Losada, *Aunque me tires el puente*, 50–52; González Bueno, *Paz en guerra*, 110, 122.

63. Corral, *Desertores*, 152–533; Casas de la Vega, *Las milicias nacionales*, 1:348.

64. Corral, *Desertores*, 103–5; *ABC*, 19 March 1938; *La Provincia*, 19 November 1938; Ugarte Tellería, *La nueva Covadonga*, 31; López Ortiz and Melgarejo Moreno, "El Sector Agrario," 22.

65. Bahamonde y Sánchez de Castro, *Un Año con Queipo*, 53; Gálvez Muñoz, "Produciendo para la revolución," 486; *La Nueva España*, 28 October 1937; *ABC*, 5 and 12 May 1937.

66. *El Pueblo Gallego*, 18 and 29 September 1936, 18, 20, and 22 October 1936, 7 and 25 November 1936, 25 May 1937, 15 June 1937, 24 August 1937, 31 October 1937, 15 January 1938, 10 November 1938; *El Correo de Zamora*, 7 August 1936.

67. *El Pueblo Gallego*, 29 March 1938, 17 May 1938, 5 and 12 June 1938, 11 December 1938, 28 March 1939.

68. *El Pueblo Gallego*, 26 January 1938, 9 July 1938, 11, 13, and 22 June 1939; *La Nueva España*, 7 and 12 January 1937, 12, 14, 17, and 20 February 1937; Domingo, *Retaguardia*, 392, 395; Cardona and Losada, *Aunque me tires el puente*, 159.

69. Corral, *Desertores*, 68–84; *El Pueblo Gallego*, 4 June 1937; *La Nueva España*, 8 June 1937, 10 April 1938; Gálvez Muñoz, "Produciendo para la revolución," 465; *El Correo de Zamora*, 13 June 1938; Salas, *Sevilla*, 2:659; *ABC*, 12 May 1937.

70. *ABC*, 19 October 1938, 24 February 1939; Caballero, *Diario de campaña*, 295; Castro, *Capital de la Cruzada*, 234; Domingo, *Retaguardia*, 249; Corral, *Desertores*, 281, 513; Aróstegui, *Los combatientes carlistas*, 2:312.

71. Caballero, *Diario de campaña*, 197–290; Nerín, *La guerra*, 184; Ugarte Tellería, *La nueva Covadonga*, 128–386; Revilla Cebrecos, *Tercio de Lácar*, 102–214; Nagore Yárnoz, *En la primera de Navarra*, 24–48; Aróstegui, *Los combatientes carlistas*, 1:176.

72. Llordés Badía, *Al dejar el fusil*, 158, 226; Revilla Cebrecos, *Tercio de Lácar*, 115; Nagore Yárnoz, *En la primera de Navarra*, 71.

73. Cenarro, "Matar," 75; Ortiz Villalba, *Sevilla 1936*, 175; Corral, *Desertores*, 229–68; Lazo, *Retrato de fascismo*, 35; Aróstegui, *Los combatientes*, 2:88, 128; Salas, *Sevilla*, 2:663–96; Casas de la Vega, *Las milicias nacionales*, 1:382.

74. Exco., 1 June 1937, ZN, a. 19, 1. 4, c. 17, AGM; Corral, *Desertores*, 242–320; *La Nueva España*, 12 April 1938; Souto Blanco, *La represión franquista*, 91–178; *El Pueblo Gallego*, 17 July 1937, 4 September 1937.

75. Nagore Yárnoz, *En la primera de Navarra*, 78; Corral, *Desertores*, 183–246. On lack of clothing for elite units, see Revilla Cebrecos, *Tercio de Lácar*, 161. V. Cuerpo, 9–10 June 1937, ZN, a. 41, 1. 1, c. 4, AGM; Cuerpo, 3 June 1937, CGG, a. 2, 1. 145, c. 76, AGM; Lazo, *Retrato de fascismo*, 35; Cervera Gil, *Ya sabes mi paradero*, 458–60; James Matthews, "'Our Red Soldiers': The Nationalist Army's Management of its Left-Wing Conscripts in the Spanish Civil War, 1936–39," *Journal of Contemporary History* 45, no. 2. (April 2010): 353–62.

76. Corral, *Desertores*, 34–205; Llordés Badía, *Al dejar el fusil*, 121; Satrústegui, *Memorias de un anarquista*, 245; Souto Blanco, *La represión franquista*, 192–95; Caballero, *Diario de campaña*, 186, 293.

77. Corral, *Desertores*, 54–141; Kalyvas, *The Logic of Violence*, 47; Aróstegui, *Los combatientes carlistas*, 1:148; Llordés Badía, *Al dejar el fusil*, 133.

78. Kalyvas, *The Logic of Violence*, 75–132; Lazo, *Retrato de fascismo*, 109; Glicerio Sánchez Recio, "El franquismo como red de intereses," in Glicerio Sánchez Recio and Julio Tascón Fernández, eds., *Los empresarios de Franco: Política y economía en España, 1936–1957* (Barcelona, 2003), 21; Ortiz Villalba, *Sevilla 1936*, 258; Corral, *Desertores*, 288, 289; *El Pueblo Gallego*, 20 August 1936.

79. See *El Pueblo Gallego*, *El Correo de Zamora*, *La Nueva España*, and *Proa* from the autumn of 1936 to the spring of 1939. Ortiz Villalba, *Sevilla 1936*, 153, 174; Rodríguez Barreira, *Migas con miedo*, 182; Castro, *Capital de la Cruzada*, 247; Sánchez Ruano, *Islam*, 193.

80. Nerín, *La guerra*, 190; *El Pueblo Gallego*, 8 July 1937, 21 December 1937, 4 and 16 August 1938, 25 September 1938, 5 October 1938; *Proa*, 7 May 1939; *La Nueva España*, 14 November 1937. When Franco's troops entered Madrid, Radio España destroyed its recording of the "shameful" Himno de Riego. See *El Correo de Zamora*, 30 March 1939.

81. Llordés Badía, *Al dejar el fusil*, 158; *La Nueva España*, 24 December 1937, 6 February 1938; Bastida Pellicer, *Historias de un quinto*, 204–5; Palomares Ibáñez, *La Guerra Civil en Palencia*, 75; Raguer, *La Espada*, 174–75: "There were many more Popular Front supporters who saved priests than priests who saved Popular Front supporters."

82. Reservado, Política Interior, 1938, 44/2790, AGA; Souto Blanco, *La represión franquista*, 213; *ABC*, 10 November 1936; Cervera Gil, *Ya sabes mi paradero*, 466; Raguer, *La Espada*, 89.

83. *El Pueblo Gallego*, 1 October 1936, 29 July 1937, 10 August 1937, 15 and 17 September 1937, 29 March 1938, 20 May 1938, 20 January 1939; Abella, *La vida cotidiana nacional*, 63; *La Nueva España*, 23 April 1937, 20 January 1938; Oviedo, 1938, 44/2791, AGA; *ABC*, 24 March 1938; *Proa*, 21 July 1938; *El Correo de Zamora*, 5 and 18 June 1937; Olmedo Delgado and Cuesta Monereo, *General Queipo de Llano*, 149–50; Gibson, *Queipo de Llano*, 96–350; Castro, *Capital de la Cruzada*, 150.

84. *El Correo de Zamora*, 7 June 1939; Oviedo, 1938, 44/2791, AGA; Gobierno Civil, Lugo, 1938, 44/2791, AGA.

85. *ABC Sevilla*, 21 October 1937; Bullón de Mendoza and Diego, *Historias orales*, 51–181; Llordés Badía, *Al dejar el fusil*, 79–374; Raguer, *La Espada*, 59; Caballero, *Diario de campaña*, 376–78; Sánchez Ruano, *Islam*, 339, 366.

86. *El Pueblo Gallego*, 25 and 26 August 1936, 27 December 1936, 3, 22, and 23 October 1937, 24 July 1938, 15, 18, and 22 April 1939; Cabeza San Deogracias, *El Descanso del Guerrero*, 181; *Proa*, 11 April 1939; Bullón de Mendoza and Diego, *Historias orales*, 180; *La Nueva España*, 8 January 1937, 6 February 1938; *La Provincia*, 17 December 1937, 14 January 1938.

87. Satrústegui, *Memorias de un anarquista*, 169–87; Caballero, *Diario de campaña*, 123–402; Iribarren, *El General Mola*, 221; Thomas, *Brother against Brother*, 81; Urra Lusarreta, *En las trincheras*, 312, 326; Castro, *Capital de la Cruzada*, 158.

88. Abella, *La vida cotidiana nacional*, 129, 325; Aróstegui, *Los combatientes carlistas*, 1:326; Cervera Gil, *Ya sabes mi paradero*, 372; Rivero Noval, *Política y sociedad*

en la Rioja, 482; *El Pueblo Gallego*, 21 November 1936; *La Nueva España*, 5 June 1938.

89. *El Pueblo Gallego*, 9 August 1938, 3 March 1939; Santa Cruz de Tenerife, Memoria, 1938, 44/2792, AGA; Souto Blanco, *La represión franquista*, 200.

90. Memoria, Huesca, 1938, 44/2791, AGA; Memoria, Granada, 1938, 44/2791, AGA; Memoria, Ávila, August 1938, 44/2790, AGA; Nerín, *La guerra*, 181.

91. Memoria, Huesca, 1938, 44/2791, AGA; Memoria, Granada, 1938, 44/2791, AGA; Memoria, Álava, 1938, 44/2790, AGA.

92. *El Pueblo Gallego*, 24 July 1937, 17 September 1937, 22 December 1937, 16 February 1938, 31 May 1938, 3 July 1938; *La Provincia*, 19 August 1936, 21 June 1938; *Proa*, 5 August 1938.

93. See *La Nueva España*, *El Correo de Zamora*, *Proa*, and especially *El Pueblo Gallego* from 1937 to 1939.

94. Rey, *Por qué luchó*, 166; Caballero, *Diario de campaña*, 35–397. Cf. the pious accounts in Delgado Iribarren, *Jesuitas en Campaña*, 197; Valdés, *Un Capellán*, 78; and Copado, *Con la columna Redondo*, 86. Tovar Patrón, *Los curas*, 203; González Bueno, *Paz en guerra*, 79–275; Cervera Gil, *Ya sabes mi paradero*, 204–360; Nagore Yárnoz, *En la primera de Navarra*, 71; Peiró, *Fernando de Huidobro*, 254; Bastida Pellicer, *Historias de un quinto*, 214; Palacios and Payne, *Franco, mi padre*, 539; *La Nueva España*, 18 February 1938.

CONCLUSION

1. Cierva, *Historia ilustrada*, 2:423; Caballero, *Diario de campaña*, 393; Schempp, *Das Autoritäre Spanien*, 108–9. For an important contribution to the debate on hunger and the end of the war, see Francisco Alía Miranda, "La agonía de la República: El golpe de Casado en la Mancha," *Historia Social* 65 (2009): 65–84.

2. Schempp, *Das Autoritäre Spanien*, 107; Sierra, *Palabras huérfanas*, 89; *ABC*, 8 March 1938, 27 January 1939, 2 February 1939.

3. *ABC*, 18 May 1939; Arco Blanco, *Las alas del Ave Fénix*, 137. Provincial controls occurred earlier than national ones. See *ABC*, 27 January 1938. On corn, see *El Pueblo Gallego*, 24 May 1936. Martín Aceña, "La economía de la guerra civil," 49.

4. *Proa*, 31 May 1939, 16, 23, and 25 June 1939; *La Nueva España*, 1 June 1939; *El Correo de Zamora*, 7 May 1939, 8 June 1939.

5. *El Pueblo Gallego*, 15, 16, 18, 21, and 25 April 1939; Memoria, Pontevedra, 1937, 44/3122, AGA.

6. *El Pueblo Gallego*, 18, 21, 23, and 25–28 April 1939; *Proa*, 23 August 1938, 3 January 1939.

7. *El Pueblo Gallego*, 29 and 30 April 1939, 2 May 1939, 2 and 20 June 1939; Rodríguez Barreira, *Migas con miedo*, 29.

8. *El Pueblo Gallego*, 2, 11, 14, 17, and 21–27 June 1939; *El Correo de Zamora*, 27 May 1939; *La Nueva España*, 26 and 30 April 1939, 5 May 1939, 14 and 27 June 1939; *Proa*, 5 July 1938.

9. *El Pueblo Gallego*, 30 April 1939; *ABC*, 7 February 1939, 25 and 26 April 1939, 10 and 18 May 1939; *Proa*, 29 April 1939, 31 May 1939.

10. Ministerio de Agricultura, Servicio Nacional del Trigo, *Veinte años de actuación*, 72; Tarragona, Cálculo aproximado de daños sufridos, n.d., 44/3123, AGA.

11. Memoria, Ávila, August 1938, 44/2790, AGA. For a similar situation in France during World War II, see Sanders, *Histoire du Marché noir*, 9. Souto Blanco, *La represión franquista*, 248–49; Castro, *Capital de la Cruzada*, 318; Bullón de Mendoza and Diego, *Historias orales*, 111; Arco Blanco, *Hambre de siglos*, 312–14.

12. Souto Blanco, *La represión franquista*, 224; Souto Blanco, *Los apoyos al régimen franquista*, 23–125; John Butterworth, *The Theory of Price Control and Black Markets* (Aldershot, 1994), 16–19; *La Provincia*, 2 September 1938; Satrústegui, *Memorias de un anarquista*, 241, 255; Nagore Yárnoz, *En la primera de Navarra*, 194–96; *ABC*, 26 and 29 March 1938; SNT, Jefatura Provincial, Córdoba, 15 November 1938, Interior, 61/13497, AGA; Copia, Intendencia, 15 November 1938, Interior, 61/13497, AGA; SNT, Jefatura Provincial Córdoba, 29 March 1939, Interior, 61/13497, AGA; Mendlesohn, *Quaker Relief Work*, 121–22.

13. *Proa*, 9 October 1938, 29 January 1939, 4 February 1939, 12 March 1939, 31 May 1939; Sr. Jefe Provincial del SNT Córdoba, 8 November 1938, Interior, 61/13497, AGA; SNT Jefatura Provincial, 5 November 1938, 61/13497, AGA; SNT Jefatura Provincial Zaragoza, 4 November 1938, Interior, 61/13509, AGA; SNT, Jefatura Provincial Ávila, 16 January 1939, Interior, 61/13493, AGA.

14. SNT Jefatura Provincial Zaragoza, 7 November 1938, Interior, 61/13509, AGA; *El Pueblo Gallego*, 19 March 1938, 4 June 1939; Llordés Badía, *Al dejar el fusil*, 339–44; Lazo, *Retrato de fascismo rural*, 62–63.

15. Llordés Badía, *Al dejar el fusil*, 359; Lazo, *Retrato de fascismo rural*, 116; Palacios and Payne, *Franco, mi padre*, 717; Kershner, *Quaker Service*, 94.

16. Payne, *Politics and Military*, 389; Madariaga, *Los moros*, 273–74; Casas de la Vega, *Las milicias nacionales*, 160. Cf. the arguments of Graham, *Spanish Civil War*, 73–74, Preston, *Franco*, 175, 277, and Blanco Escolá, *La incompetencia militar*.

17. Jensen, *Franco*, 69; Payne, *Franco: El perfil de la historia*, 32; Fusi, *Franco*, 58.

18. Kenez, *Civil War in South Russia, 1919–1920*, xiv–311; von Hagen, *Soldiers in the Proletarian Dictatorship*, 125–26.

19. Kenez, *Civil War in South Russia, 1919–1920*, 141.

20. Pepper, *Civil War in China*, 400; Griffith, *The Chinese People's Liberation Army*, 95; Eastman, *Seeds*, 171–225; Westad, *Decisive Encounters*, 10–11, 329; Steven I. Levine, "Mobilizing for War: Rural Revolution in Manchuria as an Instrument for War," in Kathleen Hartford and Steven M. Goldstein, eds., *Single Sparks: China's Rural Revolutions* (Armonk, NY, 1989), 154.

21. Levine, *Anvil*, 150; Levine, "Mobilizing," 168; Eastman, *Seeds*, 165; Shanghai, 15 July 1949, China Internal Affairs, U.S. Department of State, LM 184, roll 62, NA. See Feng Chongyi and David S. G. Goodman, eds., *North China at War: The Social Ecology of Revolution, 1937–1945* (Lanham, MD, 2000), 10.

Bibliography

ARCHIVAL SOURCES

Ady Papers, Yale Divinity School, New Haven, Connecticut
Archives Diplomatiques, Paris
Archivo General de Administración (AGA), Madrid
Archivo General Militar (AGM), Ávila
Archivo Histórico Nacional-Sección Guerra Civil (AHN-SGC), Salamanca
Hoover Institution, Stanford, California
National Archives (NA), College Park, Maryland
Public Record Office (PRO), London

PERIODICALS

ABC (Seville)
Claridad (Madrid)
El Correo de Zamora (Zamora)
La Nueva España (Oviedo)
La Provincia (Las Palmas [Gran Canaria])
El Pueblo Gallego (Vigo)
Proa (León)
Chinese Press Review, New York Public Library (NYPL)

BOOKS

Abella, Rafael. *La vida cotidiana durante la Guerra civil: La España nacional*. Barcelona, 1973.
———. *La vida cotidiana durante la Guerra civil: La España republicana*. Barcelona, 1975.
Ades, Dawn, Tim Benton, David Elliott, and Iain Boyd White. *Art and Power: Europe under the Dictators, 1930–45*. London, 1995.
Algora Wever, María Dolores. "El reflejo de la guerra civil en el protectorado de Marruecos." In *Revisión de la guerra civil española*, edited by Alfonso Bullón de Mendoza and Luis Eugenio Togores, 1021–34. Madrid, 2002.
Alía Miranda, Francisco. "La agonía de la República: El golpe de Casado en la Mancha." *Historia Social* 65 (2009): 65–84.
Alpert, Michael. *El ejército republicano en la guerra civil*. Madrid, 1989.
———. "Soldiers, Politics, and War." In *Revolution and War in Spain, 1931–1939*, edited by Paul Preston, 202–24. New York, 1984.

Alted Vigil, Alicia. *Política del nuevo estado sobre el patrimonio cultural y la educación durante la guerra civil española.* Madrid, 1984.

Álvarez Berciano, Rosa, and Ramón Sala Moguer. *El Cine en la zona nacional, 1936–1939.* Bilbao, 2000.

Álvarez Chillida, Gonzalo. *El Antisemitismo en España: La imagen del judío (1812–2002).* Madrid, 2002.

———. "La eclosión del antisemitismo español: De la II República al Holocausto." In *El Antisemitismo en España,* edited by Gonzalo Álvarez Chillida and Ricardo Izquierdo Benito, 181–206. Cuenca, 2007.

———. *José María Pemán: Pensamiento y trayectoria de un monárquico (1897–1941).* Cádiz, 1996.

———. "Zaragoza en la Guerra Civil: La memoria de un judío aragonés." *Raíces: Revista judía de cultura* 54 (Spring 2003): 43–47.

Aragón Gómez, Bartolomé. *Con Intendencia militar de las gloriosas Brigadas Navarras.* Madrid, 1940.

Arco Blanco, Miguel Ángel del. *Las alas del Ave Fénix: La política agraria del primer franquismo (1936–1939).* Granada, 2005.

———. *Hambre de siglos: Mundo rural y apoyos sociales del franquismo en Andalucía Oriental (1936–1951).* Granada, 2007.

Argenbright, Robert. "The Soviet Agitational Vehicle: State Power on the Social Frontier." *Political Geography* 17, no. 3 (1998): 253–72.

Armiñan, Luis de. *Excmo. Sr. General D. Gonzalo Queipo de Llano: Jefe del Ejército del Sur.* Ávila, 1937.

Aróstegui, Julio. *Los combatientes carlistas en la Guerra civil española, 1936–1939.* 2 vols. Madrid, 1991.

Asistencia a frentes y hospitales de Navarra: Memoria. Spain, 1939.

Audoin-Rouzeau, Stéphane, and Annette Becker. *14–18: Understanding the Great War.* Translated by Catherine Temerson. New York, 2002.

Azaña, Manuel. *Obras completas.* 4 vols. Madrid, 1990.

Bahamonde y Sánchez de Castro, Antonio. *Un Año con Queipo: Memorias de un Nacionalista.* Barcelona, 1938.

Balfour, Sebastian. *Deadly Embrace: Morocco and the Road to the Spanish Civil War.* New York, 2002.

Barciela López, Carlos. "Producción y política cerealista durante la Guerra civil española (1936–1939)." In *Historia económica y pensamiento social: Estudios en homenaje a Diego Mateo del Peral,* edited by Gonzalo Anes, Luis Ángel Rojo, and Pedro Tedde, 649–75. Madrid, 1983.

Baroja, Pío. *Ayer y Hoy.* Santiago de Chile, 1939.

———. *Comunistas Judíos y demás ralea.* Valladolid, 1939.

Barrera Coronado, Luis. *1936–1939, La moneda de necesidad en la provincia de Sevilla.* Madrid, 1989.

Barrios, Manuel. *El Último Virrey: Queipo de Llano.* Seville, 1990.

Bastida Pellicer, Luis. *Historias de un quinto de 1935.* Seville, 2005.

Bechhofer, C. E. *In Denikin's Russia and the Caucasus, 1919–1920.* New York, 1971.

Becker, Annette. *War and Faith: The Religious Imagination in France, 1914–1930.* Translated by Helen McPhail. New York, 1998.

Beevor, Antony. *The Battle for Spain: The Spanish Civil War, 1936–1939.* New York, 2006.

Benito del Pozo, Carmen. *La clase obrera asturiana bajo el franquismo: Empleo, condiciones de trabajo y conflicto (1940–1975).* Madrid, 1993.

Best, Geoffrey. *War and Society in Revolutionary Europe, 1770–1870.* New York, 1986.

Blanco Escolá, Carlos. *La incompetencia militar de Franco.* Madrid, 2000.

Bolín, Luis Antonio. *España: Los años vitales.* Madrid, 1967.

Bolloten, Burnett. *The Spanish Civil War: Revolution and Counter-revolution.* Chapel Hill, 1991.

Boniface, Xavier. *L'aumônerie militaire française (1914–1962).* Paris, 2001.

Borau, José Luis. *Diccionario del cine español.* Madrid, 1998.

Bosch Sánchez, Aurora. *Ugetistas y Libertarios: Guerra civil y revolución en el país valenciano, 1936–39.* Valencia, 1983.

Bourne, Kenneth, and D. Cameron Watt, eds. *British Documents on Foreign Affairs: Reports and Papers from the Foreign Office Confidential Print.* Part 2, Series A, *From the First to the Second World War: The Soviet Union, 1917–1939.* 15 vols. Frederick, MD, 1984.

Bowen, Wayne H. *Spain during World War II.* Columbia, MO, 2006.

Box, Zira. *España, Año Cero: La construcción simbólica del franquismo.* Madrid, 2010.

Brinkley, George A. *The Volunteer Army and Allied Intervention in South Russia.* Notre Dame, IN, 1966.

Brovkin, Vladimir N. *Behind the Front Lines of the Civil War.* Princeton, NJ, 1994.

———, ed. *The Bolsheviks in Russian Society: The Revolution and Civil Wars.* New Haven, CT, 1997.

Bullón de Mendoza, Alfonso, and Álvaro de Diego. *Historias orales de la Guerra civil.* Barcelona, 2000.

Bullón de Mendoza, Alfonso, and Luis Eugenio Togores, eds. *Revisión de la guerra civil española.* Madrid, 2002.

Butterworth, John. *The Theory of Price Control and Black Markets.* Aldershot, 1994.

Caballero, José. *Diario de campaña.* Madrid, 1976.

Cabeza San Deogracias, José. *El Descanso del Guerrero: Cine en Madrid durante la Guerra Civil española (1936–1939).* Madrid, 2005.

Campoamor, Clara. *La revolución española vista por una republicana.* Barcelona, 2002.

Cándano, Xuan. *El Pacto de Santoña (1937): La rendición del nacionalismo vasco al fascismo.* Madrid, 2006.

Cano, Luis. "Acerca de Cristo Rey." In *Católicos entre dos guerras: La historia religiosa de España en los años 20 y 30,* edited by Jaume Aurell and Pablo Pérez López, 173–201. Madrid, 2006.

Cardona, Gabriel. *Historia militar de una guerra civil: Estrategia y tácticas de la guerra de España.* Barcelona, 2006.

Cardona, Gabriel, and Juan Carlos Losada, *Aunque me tires el puente: Memoria oral de la batalla del Ebro*. Madrid, 2004.

Carreras Panchón, Antonio. "Los psiquiatras españoles y la guerra civil." *Medicina & historia* 13 (1986): 1–16.

Carro, Santiago. *Observaciones médicas sobre el hambre en la España roja*. Santander, 1938.

Casanova, Julián. *Anarquismo y revolución en la sociedad rural aragonesa, 1936–1938*. Madrid, 1985.

———. "Pasado y presente de la Guerra civil española." *Historia Social* 60 (2008): 113–28.

———. *República y guerra civil*. Barcelona, 2007.

Casas, Santiago. "La agenda de la conferencia de Metropolitanos." In *Católicos entre dos guerras: La historia religiosa de España en los años 20 y 30*, edited by Jaume Aurell and Pablo Pérez López, 231–54. Madrid, 2006.

Casas de la Vega, Rafael. *Las milicias nacionales en la Guerra de España*. Madrid, 1974.

Caspistegui, Francisco Javier. "Religión, tradicionalismo y espectáculos de masas." In *Católicos entre dos guerras: La historia religiosa de España en los años 20 y 30*, edited by Jaume Aurell and Pablo Pérez López, 327–49. Madrid, 2006.

Castro, Luis. *Capital de la Cruzada: Burgos durante la Guerra Civil*. Barcelona, 2006.

Catalan, Jordi. "Fabricar para la guerra, padecer por el frente." In *Economía y economistas españoles en la guerra civil*, edited by Enrique Fuentes Quintana and Francisco Comín Comín, 1:557–99. Barcelona, 2008.

———. "Guerra e industria en las dos Españas, 1936–1939." In *La economía de la guerra civil*, edited by Pablo Martín Aceña and Elena Martínez Ruiz, 161–228. Madrid, 2006.

Cayón García, Francisco, and Miguel Muñoz Rubio. "Transportes y Comunicaciones." In *La economía de la guerra civil*, edited by Pablo Martín Aceña and Elena Martínez Ruiz, 229–72. Madrid, 2006.

Cazorla Sánchez, Antonio. *Las políticas de la victoria: La consolidación del Nuevo Estado franquista (1938–1953)*. Madrid, 2000.

Cenarro, Ángela. "Matar, Vigilar y Delatar: La Quiebra de la sociedad civil durante la guerra y la posguerra en España (1936–1948)." *Historia Social* 22 (2002): 65–86.

———. "El poder local durante la guerra civil." In *Economía y economistas españoles en la guerra civil*, edited by Enrique Fuentes Quintana and Francisco Comín Comín, 1:249–78. Barcelona, 2008.

———. *La sonrisa de Falange: Auxilio Social en la guerra y la posguerra*. Barcelona, 2006.

Cervera Gil, Javier. *Ya sabes mi paradero: La guerra civil a través de las cartas de los que vivieron*. Barcelona, 2005.

Chen, Yung-fa. *Making Revolution: The Communist Movement in Eastern and Central China, 1937–1945*. Berkeley, 1986.

Chickering, Roger. "The American Civil War and the German Wars of Unification: Some Parting Shots." In *On the Road to Total War: The American Civil War and the German Wars of Unification*, edited by Stig Förster and Jörg Nagler, 683–91. Cambridge, 1997.

Chongyi, Feng, and David S. G. Goodman, eds. *North China at War: The Social Ecology of Revolution, 1937–1945*. Lanham, MD, 2000.

Cía Navascués, Policarpo. *Memorias del Tercio de Montejurra*. Pamplona, 1941.

Cierva, Ricardo de la. *Historia ilustrada de la Guerra civil española*. Barcelona, 1977.

Clark, Gracia. *Traders versus the State: Anthropological Approaches to Unofficial Economies*. Boulder, CO, 1988.

Cobo Romero, Francisco. *Revolución campesina y contrarrevolución franquista en Andalucía: Conflictividad social, violencia política y represión franquista en el mundo rural andaluz, 1931–1950*. Granada, 2004.

Colmegna, Héctor. *Diario de un médico argentino en la guerra de España, 1936–1939*. Buenos Aires, 1941.

Comín Comín, Francisco. "Las economías y los economistas españoles durante la guerra civil española y la posguerra: Una introducción." In *Economía y economistas españoles en la guerra civil*, edited by Enrique Fuentes Quintana and Francisco Comín Comín, 1:7–168. Barcelona, 2008.

Copado, Bernabé. *Con la columna Redondo: Combates y conquistas, crónica de Guerra*. Seville, 1937.

Corral, Pedro. *Desertores: La Guerra Civil que nadie quiere contar*. Barcelona, 2006.

———. *Si me quieres escribir: La batalla de Teruel*. Barcelona, 2004.

Coverdale, John F. *Italian Intervention in the Spanish Civil War*. Princeton, NJ, 1975.

De Jaegher, Raymond J., and Irene Kuhn. *The Enemy Within: An Eyewitness Account of the Communist Conquest of China*. Garden City, NY, 1952.

Delgado Iribarren, José Ángel. *Jesuitas en Campaña: Cuatro siglos al servicio de la Historia*. Madrid, 1956.

Díaz Morlán, Pablo. *Los Ybarra: Una dinastía de empresarios (1801–2001)*. Madrid, 2002.

Díaz-Plaja, Fernando. *La guerra de España en sus documentos*. Barcelona, 1966.

Díaz Viana, Luis. *Cancionero popular de la Guerra civil española: Textos y melodías de los dos bandos*. Madrid, 2007.

Díez de Rivera y Casares, Pascual. *La Riqueza pesquera en España y las cofradías de pescadores*. Madrid, 1940.

Domingo, Alfonso. *Retaguardia: La Guerra Civil tras los frentes*. Madrid, 2004.

Domingo, Carmen. *Con voz y voto: Las mujeres y la política en España (1931–45)*. Barcelona, 2004.

Domínguez Arribas, Javier. *El enemigo judeo-masónico en la propaganda franquista*. Madrid, 2009.

Dugarm, Delano. "Local Politics and the Struggle for Grain in Tambov, 1918–21." In *Provincial Landscapes: Local Dimensions of Soviet Power, 1917–1953*, edited by Donald J. Raleigh, 59–81. Pittsburgh, 2001.

———. "Peasant Wars in Tambov Province." In *The Bolsheviks in Russian Society: The Revolution and Civil Wars*, edited by Vladimir N. Brovkin, 177–200. New Haven, CT, 1997.

Durán, Gustavo. *Una enseñanza de la guerra española*. Madrid, 1979.

Ealham, Chris. "The Myth of the Maddened Crowd." In *The Splintering of Spain: Cultural History and the Spanish Civil War, 1936–1939*, edited by Chris Ealham and Michael Richards, 111–32. Cambridge, 2005.

———. *Class, Culture and Conflict in Barcelona, 1898–1937*. New York, 2005.

Ealham, Chris, and Michael Richards, eds. *The Splintering of Spain: Cultural History and the Spanish Civil War, 1936–1939*. Cambridge, 2005.

Eastman, Lloyd E. *Seeds of Destruction: Nationalist China in War and Revolution, 1937–1949*. Stanford, 1984.

Edwards, Peter. "Logistics and Supply." In *The Civil Wars: A Military History of England, Scotland, and Ireland 1638–1660*, edited by John Kenyon and Jane Ohlmeyer, 234–71. New York, 1998.

Eguidazu, Fernando. *Intervención monetaria y control de cambios en España, 1900–1977*. Madrid, 1978.

Engel, Carlos. *Historia de las divisiones del Ejército nacional*. Madrid, 2000.

Escolar Sobrino, Hipólito. *La cultura durante la guerra civil*. Madrid, 1987.

Esenwein, George R. *The Spanish Civil War: A Modern Tragedy*. New York, 2005.

Espinosa Maestre, Francisco. *La justicia de Queipo: Violencia selectiva y terror fascista en la II División en 1936*. Seville, 2000.

Falcoff, Mark. "Argentina." In *The Spanish Civil War: American Hemispheric Perspectives*, edited by Mark Falcoff and Frederick B. Pike, 291–348. Lincoln, NE, 1982.

Falcoff, Mark, and Frederick B. Pike, eds. *The Spanish Civil War: American Hemispheric Perspectives*. Lincoln, NE, 1982.

Farneti, Paolo. "Social Conflict, Parliamentary Fragmentation, Institutional Shift, and the Rise of Fascism: Italy." In *The Breakdown of Democratic Regimes*, pt. 2, *Europe*, edited by Juan J. Linz and Alfred Stepan, 3–33. Baltimore, 1978.

Febo, Giuliana di. *Ritos de guerra y de victoria en la España franquista*. Bilbao, 2002.

Fernández Prieto, Lourenzo. "Represión franquista y desarticulación social en Galicia: La destrucción de la organización societaria campesina, 1936–1942." *Historia Social* 15 (1993): 49–65.

Figes, Orlando. *A People's Tragedy: A History of the Russian Revolution*. New York, 1996.

Fishburn, Matthew. *Burning Books*. New York, 2008.

Fitzpatrick, Sheila, and Robert Gellately, eds. *Accusatory Practices: Denunciation in Modern European History, 1789–1989*. Chicago, 1997.

Fraser, Ronald. *Blood of Spain: An Oral History of the Spanish Civil War*. New York, 1986.

Fuentes Quintana, Enrique, and Francisco Comín Comín, eds. *Economía y economistas españoles en la guerra civil*. 2 vols. Barcelona, 2008.

Fusi, Juan Pablo. *Franco: Autoritarismo y poder personal*. Madrid, 2001.

Gallardo Moreno, Jacinta. *La guerra civil en La Serena*. Badajoz, 1994.

Gálvez Muñoz, Lina. "Produciendo para la revolución y produciendo para la reacción: Trabajo y guerra civil." In *La economía de la guerra civil*, edited by Pablo Martín Aceña and Elena Martínez Ruiz, 461–89. Madrid, 2006.

García, Hugo. *Mentiras necesarias: La batalla por la opinión británica durante la Guerra Civil.* Madrid, 2008.

Garrido González, Luis. *Colectividades agrarias en Andalucía: Jaén (1931–39).* Madrid, 1979.

Garzón Pareja, Manuel. *Historia de la Hacienda de España.* 2 vols. Madrid, 1984.

Gellately, Robert. "Denunciations in Twentieth-Century Germany: Aspects of Self-Policing in the Third Reich and the German Democratic Republic." In *Accusatory Practices: Denunciation in Modern European History, 1789–1989,* edited by Sheila Fitzpatrick and Robert Gellately, 185–221. Chicago, 1997.

Gibson, Ian. *The Death of Lorca.* Chicago, 1973.

———. *Queipo de Llano: Sevilla, verano de 1936 (Con las charlas radiofónicas completas).* Barcelona, 1986.

González Bueno, Jesús. *Paz en guerra.* Cádiz, 1943.

González Egido, Luciano. *Agonizar en Salamanca: Unamuno (julio–diciembre 1936).* Madrid, 1986.

González Gullón, José Luis. "El clero de Madrid: Demografía y distribución." In *Católicos entre dos guerras: La historia religiosa de España en los años 20 y 30,* edited by Jaume Aurell and Pablo Pérez López, 255–82. Madrid, 2006.

González Portilla, Manuel, and José Maria Garmendia. *La guerra civil en el país vasco: Política y economía.* Madrid, 1988.

González Torga, José Manuel. "El general Queipo de Llano, pionero en la guerra de las ondas: Propaganda personalizada desde el mando." In *Revisión de la guerra civil española,* edited by Alfonso Bullón de Mendoza and Luis Eugenio Togores, 595–606. Madrid, 2002.

Got'e, Iurii Vladimirovich. *Time of Troubles: The Diary of Iurii Vladimirovich Got'e.* Translated by Terence Emmons. Princeton, NJ, 1988.

Graham, Helen. *The Spanish Civil War: A Very Short Introduction.* New York, 2005.

———. "Sexual Politics." In *Spanish Cultural Studies: An Introduction; The Struggle for Modernity,* edited by Helen Graham and J. Labanyi, 99–116. Oxford, 1995.

Graves, William S. *America's Siberian Adventure.* New York, 1941.

Greeley, Robin Adèle. *Surrealism and the Spanish Civil War.* New Haven, CT, 2006.

Griffith, Samuel B. *The Chinese People's Liberation Army.* New York, 1967.

Grossman, Dave. *On Killing: The Psychological Cost of Learning to Kill in War and Society.* Boston, 1996.

Hagen, Mark von. *Soldiers in the Proletarian Dictatorship: The Red Army and the Soviet Socialist State, 1917–1930.* Ithaca, NY, 1990.

Hennessy, Alistair. "Cuba." In *The Spanish Civil War: American Hemispheric Perspectives,* edited by Mark Falcoff and Frederick B. Pike, 101–58. Lincoln, NE, 1982.

Hermet, Guy. *La guerre d'Espagne.* Paris, 1989.

Herrick, William. *Jumping the Line: The Adventures and Misadventures of an American Radical.* Madison, WI, 1998.

Hispánico. *La Defensa del Alcázar.* Logroño, n.d.

Holmes, Richard. *Acts of War: The Behaviour of Men in Battle.* New York, 1985.

Honig, Emily. *Sisters and Strangers: Women in the Shanghai Cotton Mills, 1919–1949.* Stanford, 1986.

Howson, Gerald. *Arms for Spain: The Untold Story of the Spanish Civil War.* New York, 1999.

Hubbard, John R. "How Franco Financed His War." *The Journal of Modern History* 25, no. 4 (December 1953): 390–406.

Iribarren, José María. *El General Mola.* Madrid, 1963.

Jackson, Gabriel. *The Spanish Republic and Civil War, 1931–1939.* Princeton, NJ, 1965.

Jacobs-Larkcom, Dorothy. *As China Fell: The Experiences of a British Consul's Wife, 1946–1953.* Devon, 1976.

Jensen, Geoffrey. *Franco: Soldier, Commander, Dictator.* Washington, DC, 2005.

———. *Irrational Triumph: Cultural Despair, Military Nationalism, and the Ideological Origins of Franco's Spain.* Reno, NV, 2002.

Judt, Tony. *Past Imperfect: French Intellectuals, 1944–1956.* Berkeley, 1992.

Kalyvas, Stathis N. "How Not to Compare Civil Wars: Greece and Spain." In *"If You Tolerate This . . .": The Spanish Civil War in the Age of Total War,* edited by Martin Baumeister and Stefanie Schüler-Springorum, 247–66. New York, 2008.

———. *The Logic of Violence in Civil War.* New York, 2006.

Kemp, Peter. *Mine Were of Trouble.* London, 1957.

Kenez, Peter. *Civil War in South Russia, 1918: The First Year of the Volunteer Army.* Berkeley, 1971.

———. *Civil War in South Russia, 1919–1920: The Defeat of the Whites.* Berkeley, 1977.

Kershner, Howard E. *Quaker Service in Modern War: Spain and France, 1939–1940.* New York, 1950.

Kindelán, Alfredo. *Mis cuadernos de guerra.* Madrid, 1945.

Knight, Alan. *The Mexican Revolution: Counter-revolution and Reconstruction.* 2 vols. New York, 1986.

Kössler, Till. "Children in the Spanish Civil War." In *"If You Tolerate This . . .": The Spanish Civil War in the Age of Total War,* edited by Martin Baumeister and Stefanie Schüler-Springorum, 101–32. New York, 2008.

Kselman, Thomas A. *Death and the Afterlife in Modern France.* Princeton, NJ, 1993.

Lapwood, E. R., and Nancy Lapwood. *Through the Chinese Revolution.* Westport, CT, 1973.

Larraz, José. *El ordenamiento del Mercado triguero en España.* Madrid, 1935.

Laureados de España. Madrid, 1940.

Lazo, Alfonso. *Retrato de fascismo rural en Sevilla.* Seville, 1998.

Levine, Stephen I. *Anvil of Victory: The Communist Revolution in Manchuria, 1945–1948.* New York, 1987.

———. "Mobilizing for War: Rural Revolution in Manchuria as an Instrument for War." In *Single Sparks: China's Rural Revolutions,* edited by Kathleen Hartford and Steven M. Goldstein, 151–75. Armonk, NY, 1989.

Linz, Juan J., and Alfred Stepan, eds. *The Breakdown of Democratic Regimes.* Part 2, *Europe.* Baltimore, 1978.

Líster, Enrique. *Nuestra Guerra: Aportaciones para una historia de la Guerra Nacional Revolucionaria del pueblo español, 1936–1939.* Paris, 1966.

Llordés Badía, José. *Al dejar el fusil: Memorias de un soldado raso en la Guerra de España.* Barcelona, 1968.

López Ortiz, M. I., and J. Melgarejo Moreno. "El Sector Agrario durante la Guerra Civil." Paper presented to the Congreso de la Asociación Española de Historia Económica, Santiago de Compostela, September 2005.

Lynn, John A. *The Bayonets of the Republic: Motivation and Tactics in the Army of Revolutionary France, 1791–94.* Urbana, IL, 1984.

Madariaga, María Rosa de. "The Intervention of Moroccan Troops in the Spanish Civil War: A Reconsideration." *European History Quarterly* 4, no. 3 (January 1992): 67–97.

———. *Los moros que trajo Franco: La intervención de tropas coloniales en la Guerra Civil Española.* Barcelona, 2002.

Mainer, José-Carlos. *Años de Vísperas: La vida de la cultura en España (1931–1939).* Madrid, 2006.

Martín, David. "Gitanos en la Guerra Civil Española." Paper delivered to Congreso Internacional, 1936–39 La Guerra Civil Española, Madrid, 27–29 November 2006.

Martín, Dionisio. *El problema triguero y el nacional sindicalismo.* Valladolid, 1937.

Martín Aceña, Pablo. "La economía de la guerra civil: Perspectiva general y comparada." In *La economía de la guerra civil,* edited by Pablo Martín Aceña and Elena Martínez Ruiz, 13–52. Madrid, 2006.

———. "La Quiebra del sistema financiero." In *La economía de la guerra civil,* edited by Pablo Martín Aceña and Elena Martínez Ruiz, 393–429. Madrid, 2006.

Martín Aceña, Pablo, and Elena Martínez Ruiz, eds. *La economía de la guerra civil.* Madrid, 2006.

Martínez Bande, José Manuel. *La Batalla de Teruel.* Madrid, 1974.

———. *La campaña de Andalucía.* Madrid, 1969.

———. *La gran ofensiva sobre Zaragoza.* Madrid, 1973.

———. *La invasión de Aragón y el desembarco en Mallorca.* Madrid, 1970.

———. *La lucha en torno a Madrid en el invierno de 1936–1937.* Madrid, 1984.

———. *La lucha por la victoria.* Madrid, 1990–91.

———. *Nueve meses de guerra en el Norte.* Madrid, 1980.

———. *La ofensiva sobre Valencia.* Madrid, 1977.

Martín-Blázquez, José. *Guerre civile totale.* Paris, 1938.

Martínez de Bedoya, Javier. *Memorias desde mi aldea.* Valladolid, 1996.

Martínez López, Alberte. *Cooperativismo y transformaciones agrarias en Galicia, 1886–1943.* Madrid, 1995.

———. "La ganadería gallega durante el primer franquismo: Crónica de un tiempo perdido, 1936–1960." *Historia Agraria* 20 (2000): 197–224.

Martínez-Molinos, Guillermo. "El suministro de carburantes." In *Los nuevos historiadores ante la Guerra Civil española,* edited by Octavio Ruiz-Manjón Cabeza and Miguel Gómez Oliver, 2:215–33. Granada, 1990.

Martínez Reverte, Jorge. *La Batalla del Ebro.* Barcelona, 2003.

————. *El arte de matar: Cómo se hizo la Guerra civil española.* Barcelona, 2009.
Martínez Ruiz, Elena. "El campo en guerra: Organización y producción agraria." In *La economía de la guerra civil,* edited by Pablo Martín Aceña and Elena Martínez Ruiz, 107–59. Madrid, 2006.
————. "Las relaciones económicas internacionales: Guerra, política y negocios." In *La economía de la guerra civil,* edited by Pablo Martín Aceña and Elena Martínez Ruiz, 273–327. Madrid, 2006.
Martín Jiménez, Ignacio. "La sublevación nacionalista en Valladolid." In *Revisión de la guerra civil española,* edited by Alfonso Bullón de Mendoza and Luis Eugenio Togores, 227–44. Madrid, 2002.
Martorell Linares, Miguel. "La extirpación a fondo de nuestros enemigos: Represión económica y financiación de la guerra en la España franquista (1936–1940)." Paper presented to the III Encontro Luso-Espanhol de História Política, Evora, 4–5 June 2007.
————. "Una Guerra, Dos Pesetas." In *La economía de la guerra civil,* edited by Pablo Martín Aceña and Elena Martínez Ruiz, 329–56. Madrid, 2006.
Martorell Linares, Miguel, and Francisco Comín Comín. "La Hacienda de guerra franquista." In *Economía y economistas españoles en la guerra civil,* edited by Enrique Fuentes Quintana and Francisco Comín Comín, 1:901–37. Barcelona, 2008.
Matthews, James. "'Our Red Soldiers': The Nationalist Army's Management of its Left-Wing Conscripts in the Spanish Civil War, 1936–39." *Journal of Contemporary History* 45, no. 2 (April 2010): 344–63.
Maurice, Jacques. *La reforma agraria en España en el siglo XX (1900–1936).* Madrid, 1975.
Mawdsley, Evan. *The Russian Civil War.* Boston, 1987.
Mayer, Arno. *The Dynamics of Counter-revolution.* New York, 1971.
McCullagh, Francis. *In Franco's Spain.* London, 1937.
McNeill, William H. *The Pursuit of Power: Technology, Armed Force, and Society since A.D. 1000.* Chicago, 1982.
McPherson, James M. *Battle Cry of Freedom: The Civil War Era.* New York, 1988.
Medina, Rafael de [Duque de Medinaceli]. *Tiempo pasado.* Seville, 1971.
Mendlesohn, Farah. *Quaker Relief Work in the Spanish Civil War.* Lewiston, MA, 2002.
Merroun, Mustapha El. *Las tropas marroquíes en la guerra civil española, 1936–1939.* Madrid, 2003.
Minehan, Philip B. *Civil War and World War in Europe: Spain, Yugoslavia, and Greece, 1936–1939.* New York, 2006.
Ministerio de Agricultura. *Estadística.* Valencia, 1936.
Ministerio de Agricultura, Servicio Nacional del Trigo. *Veinte años de actuación.* Madrid, 1958.
Mira, Emilio. *Psychiatry in War.* New York, 1943.
Montero, Mercedes. "Los propagandistas católicos y la opinión pública." In *Católicos entre dos guerras: La historia religiosa de España en los años 20 y 30,* edited by Jaume Aurell and Pablo Pérez López, 61–87. Madrid, 2006.
Moradiellos, Enrique. *1936: Los mitos de la guerra civil.* Barcelona, 2005.

Murphy, A. B. *The Russian Civil War: Primary Sources.* New York, 2000.

Muñoz Rubio, Miguel. *RENFE (1941–1991): Medio siglo de ferrocarril público.* Madrid, 1995.

Nagore Yárnoz, Javier. *En la primera de Navarra (1936–1939): Memorias de un voluntario navarro del Tercio de Radio Requeté de Campaña.* Madrid, 1991.

Nerín, Gustau. *La guerra que vino de África.* Barcelona, 2005.

Nonell Bru, Salvador. *El Laureado Tercio de Requetés de Nuestra Señora de Montserrat.* Barcelona, 1992.

Núñez Seixas, Xosé Manoel. *¡Fuera el Invasor! Nacionalismos y movilización bélica durante la Guerra civil española (1936–1939).* Madrid, 2006.

Oberschall, Anthony, and Michael Seidman. "Food Coercion in Revolution and Civil War: Who Wins and How They Do It." *Comparative Studies in Society and History* 47, no. 2 (2005): 372–402.

Olmedo Delgado, Antonio, and José Cuesta Monereo. *General Queipo de Llano: Aventura y audacia.* Barcelona, 1957.

Orduña Prada, Monica. *El Auxilio Social (1936–1940): La etapa fundacional y los primeros años.* Madrid, 1996.

———. "Donativos nacionales e internacionales a Auxilio Social." In *Revisión de la guerra civil española,* edited by Alfonso Bullón de Mendoza and Luis Eugenio Togores, 1083–93. Madrid, 2002.

Orella, José Luis. "Los técnicos del bando nacional." In *Revisión de la guerra civil española,* edited by Alfonso Bullón de Mendoza and Luis Eugenio Togores, 397–406. Madrid, 2002.

Ortega, José Antonio, and Javier Silvestre. "Las consecuencias demográficas." In *La economía de la guerra civil,* edited by Pablo Martín Aceña and Elena Martínez Ruiz, 53–106. Madrid, 2006.

Ortiz Villalba, Juan. *Sevilla 1936: Del golpe militar a la guerra civil.* Seville, 1998.

Orwell, George. *Homage to Catalonia.* New York, 1980.

Osipova, Taisia. "Peasant Rebellions: Origin, Scope, Dynamics, and Consequences." In *The Bolsheviks in Russian Society: The Revolution and Civil Wars,* edited by Vladimir N. Brovkin, 154–76. New Haven, CT, 1997.

Othen, Christopher. *Franco's International Brigades: Foreign Volunteers and Fascist Dictators in the Spanish Civil War.* London, 2008.

Pack, Sasha. *Tourism and Dictatorship: Europe's Peaceful Invasion of Franco's Spain.* New York, 2006.

Palacios, Jesús, and Stanley G. Payne. *Franco, Mi padre: Testimonio de Carmen Franco, la hija del Caudillo.* Madrid, 2008.

Palomares Ibáñez, Jesús María. *La Guerra Civil en Palencia: La eliminación de los contrarios.* Palencia, 2002.

Pascual Cevallos, Fernando. *Luchas agrarias en Sevilla durante la Segunda República.* Seville, 1983.

Pavliuchenkov, Sergei. "Workers' Protest Movement against War Communism." In *The Bolsheviks in Russian Society: The Revolution and Civil Wars,* edited by Vladimir N. Brovkin, 141–53. New Haven, CT, 1997.

Payne, Stanley G. *Falange: A History of Spanish Fascism.* Stanford, 1961.

————. *Franco: El perfil de la historia.* Translated by Carlos Caranci. Madrid, 1992.

————. *Franco and Hitler: Spain, Germany, and World War II.* New Haven, CT, 2008.

————. *The Franco Regime, 1936–1975.* Madison, WI, 1987.

————. *Politics and the Military in Modern Spain.* Stanford, 1967.

————. *Spain's First Democracy: The Second Republic, 1931–1936.* Madison, WI, 1993.

————. *The Spanish Revolution.* New York, 1970.

Peers, E. Allison. *Spain in Eclipse.* London, 1943.

Peiró, Francisco X. *Fernando de Huidobro: Jesuita y legionario.* Madrid, 1951.

Pelaz López, José-Vidal. "Los católicos españoles y el cine: De los orígenes al Nacional-catolicismo." In *Catolicismo y comunicación en la historia contemporánea,* edited by José-Leonardo Ruiz Sánchez, 77–91. Seville, 2005.

Pellistrandi, Benoît. "La realidad social y antropológica del catolicismo y los orígenes religiosos de la Guerra Civil." In *Católicos entre dos guerras: La historia religiosa de España en los años 20 y 30,* edited by Jaume Aurell and Pablo Pérez López, 125–40. Madrid, 2006.

Pepper, Suzanne. *Civil War in China: The Political Struggle, 1945–49.* Lanham, MD, 1999.

Pereira, Norman G. O. "The Partisan Movement in Western Siberia, 1918–1920." *Jahrbücher für Geschichte Osteuropas* 38 (1990): 88–97.

————. "Siberian Atamanshchina: Warlordism in the Russian Civil War." In *The Bolsheviks in Russian Society: The Revolution and Civil Wars,* edited by Vladimir N. Brovkin, 122–38. New Haven, CT, 1997.

Pérez Madrigal, Joaquín. *Disparos a cero.* Madrid, 1939.

Pipes, Richard. *Russia under the Bolshevik Regime, 1919–1924.* London, 1994.

Poggi, Gianfranco. *Money and the Modern Mind: George Simmel's Philosophy of Money.* Berkeley, 1993.

Pons Prades, Eduardo. *Guerrillas españolas, 1936–1950.* Barcelona, 1977.

Preston, Paul. "The Agrarian War in the South." In *Revolution and War in Spain, 1931–1939,* edited by Paul Preston, 159–81. New York, 1984.

————. *Doves of War: Four Women of Spain.* London, 2002.

————. *Franco: A Biography.* New York, 1994.

————. *The Spanish Civil War: Reaction, Revolution, and Revenge.* New York, 2006.

Preston, Paul, and Michael Partridge, eds. *British Documents on Foreign Affairs: Reports and Papers from the Foreign Office Confidential Print.* Part 4, Series E, *From 1946 through 1950, Asia 1946.* 9 vols. Bethesda, MD, 1999.

Puig, Núria. *Bayer, CEPSA, REPSOL, Puig, Schering y La Seda: Constructores de la química española.* Madrid, 2003.

Queipo de Llano, Gonzalo. *Memorias de la Guerra Civil.* Madrid, 2008.

Quevedo y Queipo de Llano, Ana. *Queipo de Llano: Gloria e infortunio de un general.* Barcelona, 2001.

Quirosa-Cheyrouze y Muñoz, Rafael. *Política y guerra civil en Almería.* Almería, 1986.

Raguer, Hilari. *La Espada y la Cruz: La Iglesia, 1936–1939*. Barcelona, 1977.

Raleigh, Donald J., ed. *A Russian Civil War Diary: Alexis Babine in Saratov, 1917–1922*. Durham, NC, 1988.

Ramón Carrión, Manuel de, and Carmen Ortiz. *Madrina de guerra: Cartas desde el frente*. Madrid, 2003.

Ranzato, Gabriele. *El eclipse de la democracia: La guerra civil española y sus orígenes, 1931–1939*. Translated by Fernando Borrajo. Madrid, 2006.

Resa, José María. *Memorias de un requeté*. Barcelona, 1968.

Revilla Cebrecos, C. *Tercio de Lácar*. Madrid, 1975.

Rey, Fernando del. *Paisanos en lucha: Exclusión política y violencia en la Segunda República española*. Madrid, 2008.

Rey, Juan. *Por qué luchó un millón de muertos: Documentos inéditos*. Santander, 1961.

Richards, Michael. *A Time of Silence: Civil War and the Culture of Repression in Franco's Spain*. Cambridge, 1998.

Riesco Roche, Sergio. *La Reforma agraria y los orígenes de la guerra civil: Cuestión yuntera y radicalización patronal en la provincia de Cáceres (1931–1940)*. Madrid, 2006.

Riquer i Permanyer, Borja de. *L'últim Cambó (1936–1947): La dreta catalanista davant la guerra civil i el primer franquisme*. Vic, 1996.

Rivero Noval, María Cristina. *Política y sociedad en la Rioja durante el primer franquismo (1936–1945)*. Logroño, 2001.

Roberts, Elizabeth. "Freedom, Faction, Fame, and Blood: British 'Soldiers of Conscience' in Three European Wars." PhD diss., University of Sydney, 2007.

Rodrigo, Javier. *Hasta la raíz: Violencia durante la guerra civil y la dictadura franquista*. Madrid, 2008.

———. "Our Fatherland Was Full of Weeds: Violence during the Spanish Civil War and the Franco Dictatorship." In *"If You Tolerate This . . .": The Spanish Civil War in the Age of Total War*, edited by Martin Baumeister and Stefanie Schüler-Springorum, 135–53. New York, 2008.

Rodríguez Barreira, Óscar J. *Migas con miedo: Practicas de resistencia al primer franquismo, Almería, 1939–1953*. Almería, 2008.

Rohr, Isabelle. *The Spanish Right and the Jews, 1898–1945: Antisemitism and Opportunism*. Eastbourne, Sussex, UK, 2007.

Rojo, Vicente. *Alerta los pueblos*. Barcelona, 1974.

Rosique Navarro, Francisca. *La Reforma agraria en Badajoz durante la IIa República*. Badajoz, 1988.

Ruiz, Julius. *Franco's Justice: Repression in Madrid after the Spanish Civil War*. Oxford, 2005.

Ruiz Vilaplana, Antonio. *Burgos Justice: A Year's Experience of Nationalist Spain*. Translated by W. Horsfall Carter. New York, 1938.

Saich, Tony, ed. *The Rise to Power of the Chinese Communist Party: Documents and Analysis*. Armonk, NY, 1996.

Salas, Nicolás. *Sevilla fue la clave: República, Alzamiento, Guerra Civil (1931–39)*. 2 vols. Seville, 1992.

Salas Larrazábal, Ramón. *Historia del ejército popular de la Republica.* Madrid, 1973.

Salas Larrazábal, Ramón, and Jesús María Salas Larrazábal. *Historia general de la guerra de España.* Madrid, 1986.

Sanborn, Joshua A. *Drafting the Russian Nation: Military Conscription, Total War, and Mass Politics, 1905–1925.* Dekalb, IL, 2003.

Sánchez Asiaín, José Ángel. *Economía y Finanzas en la guerra civil española (1936–1939).* Madrid, 1999.

Sánchez Recio, Glicerio. "El franquismo como red de intereses." In *Los empresarios de Franco: Política y economía en España, 1936–1957,* edited by Glicerio Sánchez Recio and Julio Tascón Fernández, 13–22. Barcelona, 2003.

Sánchez Ruano, Francisco. *Islam y Guerra civil española: Moros con Franco y con la República.* Madrid, 2004.

Sanders, Paul. *Histoire du Marché noir, 1940–1946.* Paris, 2001.

San Juan de Piedras Albas, Marqués de. *Héroes y mártires de la aristocracia española, Julio 1936–Marzo 1939.* Madrid, 1945.

Santa Clara, Barón de. *El Judaísmo.* Burgos, 1938.

Sardá, Juan. "El Banco de España (1931–1962)." In *El Banco de España: Una historia económica,* edited by Alfonso Moreno Redondo, 419–79. Madrid, 1970.

Satrústegui, Juan. *Memorias de un anarquista entre las tropas de Franco.* Pamplona, 1994.

Schempp, Otto. *Das Autoritäre Spanien.* Leipzig, 1939.

Seidman, Michael. *Republic of Egos: A Social History of the Spanish Civil War.* Madison, WI, 2002.

———. *Workers against Work: Labor in Barcelona and Paris during the Popular Fronts.* Berkeley, 1991.

Semprún Bullón, José. "Bajas en la contienda: Una reevaluación." In *Revisión de la guerra civil española,* edited by Alfonso Bullón de Mendoza and Luis Eugenio Togores, 331–41. Madrid, 2002.

Shubert, Adrian. *Death and Money in the Afternoon: A History of the Spanish Bullfight.* New York, 1999.

Sierra, Verónica. *Palabras huérfanas: Los niños y la Guerra Civil.* Madrid, 2009.

Simpson, James. "Economic Development in Spain, 1850–1936." *Economic History Review* 2 (1997): 348–59.

———. *Spanish Agriculture: The Long Siesta, 1765–1965.* New York, 1995.

Slezkine, Yuri. *The Jewish Century.* Princeton, NJ, 2004.

Smith, Scott. "The Socialists-Revolutionaries and the Dilemma of Civil War." In *The Bolsheviks in Russian Society: The Revolution and Civil Wars,* edited by Vladimir N. Brovkin, 83–104. New Haven, CT, 1997.

Sorní Mañés, José. "Aproximación a un estudio de la contrarreforma agraria en España." *Agricultura y Sociedad* 6 (1978): 181–211.

Souchy Bauer, Augustin. *With the Peasants of Aragon: Libertarian Communism in the Liberated Areas.* Translated by Abe Bluestein. Minneapolis, 1982.

Souto Blanco, María Jesús. *La represión franquista en la provincia de Lugo (1936–1940).* La Coruña, 1998.

———. *Los apoyos al régimen franquista en la provincia de Lugo (1936–1940): La corrupción y la lucha por el poder*. La Coruña, 1999.

Sussman, George D. *Selling Mothers' Milk: The Wet-Nursing Business in France, 1715–1914*. Urbana, IL, 1982.

Stradling, Robert. *The Irish and the Spanish Civil War, 1936–39*. Manchester, 1999.

———. *Your Children Will Be Next: Bombing and Propaganda in the Spanish Civil War, 1936–1939*. Cardiff, 2008.

Tébar Hurtado, Javier. *Reforma, revolución y contrarrevolución agraria: Conflicto social y lucha política en el campo (1931–1939)*. Barcelona, 2006.

Thaxton, Ralph A. *Salt of the Earth: The Political Origins of Peasant Protest and Communist Revolution in China*. Berkeley, 1997.

Thomas, Frank. *Brother against Brother: Experiences of a British Volunteer in the Spanish Civil War*. Edited by Robert Stradling. Phoenix Mill, UK, 1998.

Thomas, Hugh. *Spanish Civil War*. New York, 1963.

Thorne, C. Thomas, and David S. Patterson, eds. *Foreign Relations of the United States, 1945–1950: Emergence of the Intelligence Establishment*. Washington, DC, 1996.

Tooze, Adam. *The Wages of Destruction: The Making and Breaking of the Nazi Economy*. New York, 2006.

Topping, Seymour. *Journey between Two Chinas*. New York, 1972.

Torres Villanueva, Eugenio. "Comportamientos empresariales en una economía intervenida: España, 1936–1957." In *Los empresarios de Franco: Política y economía en España, 1936–1957*, edited by Glicerio Sánchez Recio and Julio Tascón Fernández, 199–224. Barcelona, 2003.

———. "Los empresarios: Entre la revolución y colaboración." In *La economía de la guerra civil*, edited by Pablo Martín Aceña and Elena Martínez Ruiz, 431–60. Madrid, 2006.

Tortella, Gabriel, and José Luis García Ruiz. "Banca y política durante el primer franquismo." In *Los empresarios de Franco: Política y economía en España, 1936–1957*, edited by Glicerio Sánchez Recio and Julio Tascón Fernández, 67–100. Barcelona, 2003.

Touboul Tardieu, Eva. *Séphardisme et Hispanité: L'Espagne à la recherche de son passé*. Paris, 2009.

Tovar Patrón, Jaime. *Los curas de la última Cruzada*. Madrid, 2001.

Townsend, Peter. *China Phoenix: The Revolution in China*. London, 1995.

Trapiello, Andrés. *Las armas y las letras: Literatura y guerra civil (1936–1939)*. Barcelona, 1994.

Ugarte Tellería, Javier. *La nueva Covadonga insurgente: Orígenes sociales y culturales de la sublevación de 1936 en Navarra y el País Vasco*. Madrid, 1998.

Urra Lusarreta, Juan. *En las trincheras del frente de Madrid: Memorias de un capellán de requetés, herido de guerra*. Madrid, 1966.

Valdés, Rafael. *Un Capellán, héroe de la Legión: P. Fernando Huidobro, S.I.* Santander, 1938.

Vega Viguera, Enrique de la. *La Pirotecnia Militar de Sevilla: Notas para su historia*. Seville, 1981.

Velarde Fuertes, Juan. "Algunos aspectos económicos de la guerra civil." In *Revisión de la guerra civil española*, edited by Alfonso Bullón de Mendoza and Luis Eugenio Togores, 945–66. Madrid, 2002.

Vigueras Roldán, Francisco. *Los paseados con Lorca: El maestro cojo y los banderilleros.* Seville, 2007.

Vila Izquierdo, Justo. *Extremadura: La Guerra Civil.* Badajoz, 1984.

Vilanova, Mercedes. *Les majories invisibles.* Barcelona, 1995.

Vilar, Juan Bautista. "La persecución religiosa en la zona nacionalista: El caso de los protestantes españoles." In *Los nuevos historiadores ante la Guerra Civil española*, edited by Octavio Ruiz-Manjón Cabeza and Miguel Gómez Oliver, 2:169–85. Granada, 1990.

Viñas, Angel. "The Financing of the Spanish Civil War." In *Revolution and War in Spain, 1931–1939*, edited by Paul Preston, 266–83. London, 1984.

———. *El oro de Moscú: Alfa y omega de un mito franquista.* Barcelona, 1979.

———. *La Soledad de la República: El abandono de las democracias y el viraje hacia la Unión Soviética.* Barcelona, 2006.

Viñas, Angel, Julio Viñuela, Fernando Eguidazu, Carlos Fernández-Pulgar, and Senén Florensa. *Política comercial exterior en España.* Madrid, 1975.

Vincent, Mary. "The Politicization of Catholic Women in Salamanca, 1931–1936." In *Elites and Power in Twentieth-Century Spain: Essays in Honor of Sir Raymond Carr*, edited by Frances Lannon and Paul Preston, 107–26. Oxford, 1990.

———. "The Spanish Civil War as a War of Religion." In *"If You Tolerate This . . .": The Spanish Civil War in the Age of Total War*, edited by Martin Baumeister and Stefanie Schüler-Springorum, 74–89. New York, 2008.

Vives, Juan Luis. *Humanismo frente a Comunismo: La primera monografía anticomunista publicada en el mundo, obra de un pensador español.* Translated by Wenceslao González-Oliveros. Valladolid, 1937.

Wade, Rex A., ed. *Documents of Soviet History: The Triumph of Bolshevism.* 2 vols. Gulf Breeze, FL, 1991.

Westad, Odd Arne. *Decisive Encounters: The Chinese Civil War, 1946–1950.* Stanford, 2003.

Whealey, Robert H. *Hitler and Spain: The Nazi Role in the Spanish Civil War.* Lexington, KY, 1989.

Wou, Odoric Y. K. *Mobilizing the Masses: Building Revolution in Henan.* Stanford, 1994.

Xavier, Adro [Alejandro Rey Stolle]. *Caballero Legionario.* Madrid, [1937?].

———. *Laureada de Sangre: Esbozos históricos de la Cruzada.* Valladolid, 1939.

Index

desertions of, 52–53, 237, 253; funerals of, 166, 178; hacked to death, 42; logistical support of, 50, 67, 71, 109, 142, 158, 163; looting of, 228–29, 252; in Málaga, 54; militias, 27; and mules, 98–100; in Pamplona, 140, 150, 152; singing of, 187–88. *See also* Carlists; Margaritas; Navarre

requisitioning: of animals, 99–102, 146, 230; in Chinese civil war, 93, 112; of foodstuffs, 92, 153; of housing, 128; in Russian civil war, 225; of vehicles, 56, 90, 131, 151–54, 252

revenues. *See* taxes

Ridruejo, Dionisio, 185

Ridruejo, Epifanio, 111

"Riego Hymn" (song), 188, 241, 318n80

Rioja: looting in, 228; meat in, 93; taxes in, 219; volunteering in, 26

Ríos, Fernando de los, 193

Río Tinto, 148, 171

Rivière, Francisco Luis, 116

Roatta, Mario, 54, 57, 234

Rodezno, Conde de, 182

Rojo, Vicente, 57, 73, 76

Roosevelt, Franklin, 199

Rosenberg, Marcel, 193

Ruiz Vilaplana, Antonio, 34

Rumania, 199

Russia. *See* Soviet Union

Russian civil war, xi, 3–5, 8, 58, 238; corruption in, 117, 155, 223–24; counterrevolutionaries in, 7–8, 27, 255; currency in, 111–13, 136, 256; desertions in, 78; foreign aid in, 6–7, 78, 122–24; hunger in, 29, 152, 247; logistics in, 11–12, 29, 70, 78–79, 81, 92, 149, 256; and national minorities, 255; officers in, 79; public health in, 157; railroads in, 150, 152, 252; rear in, 29–31; as war of attrition, 10

Russian Orthodox Church, 7

Sáenz de Tejada, Carlos, 182

Sagrado Corazón de Jesús, 180

Sahagún, 87

Saint Teresa, 172, 182, 206

Sainz Rodríguez, Pedro, 182

Salamanca, 177; as headquarters, 128, 139; hoarding in, 217; meat in, 95, 102; shirking in, 232; University of, 205, 207; wheat in, 84

Sallent, 18

Sanabria, 86

Sanjurjo, José, 14, 25–26

Santa Clara, Baron de, 193, 197

Santa Cruz de Tenerife. *See* Tenerife

Santander, 35, 94, 180; campaign for, 59, 64, 66; hunger in, 161; Popular Front in, 58

Santa Teresa, 172, 182, 206

Santiago de Compostela, 35, 140, 157, 181, 184–85, 235

Santo Cristo de Ochandiano, 180

Sanz Bachiller, Mercedes, 127, 161–62

sardines, 100; canning of, 10, 107–9; as staple, 41, 53, 62, 72–73, 75, 77 *See also* fishing; Galicia; Vigo

Sartaguda, 31

Scarlet Pimpernel (film), 192

Second Republic (Spanish), 10, 36, 151; and Catholics, 184; and chaplains, 168–71; comparisons to, 3–4, 13; economy of, 149, 212; and Jews, 193, 200; and land reform, 15; productivity during, 17, 143; taxes during, 128, 130

Sedó, Luis Alfonso, 139

seeds, 40, 46, 80, 84, 86, 220

Segovia, 229; animals in, 95; Catholicism in, 177; crime in, 153, 230–31; defiance of price controls in, 211; donations of, 118, 126; food in, 90; illiteracy in, 170; inflation in, 140; land tenure in, 83; repression in, 49; taxes in, 129–32, wheat in, 84

Serrano Súñer, Ramón, 9, 46, 96, 140–41, 184, 195–96, 202, 205, 210, 212–13, 245

Sert, José María, 182

Sert, Josep Luis, 181

Servicio de Inspección del Trabajo, 149

Servicio de Trabajo de la Falange, 182

Seville, 164, 179–81, 184, 191, 196, 232–33; animals in, 103–4; coins in, 216–17, 220; conquest of, 31–34; crimes in, 17, 137, 227; donations in, 164–65; fines in, 127, 134–35, 205, 259; food in, 50, 81, 118, 150; illiteracy in, 170; industries in, 97, 138–41, 149, 234; inflation in, 95, 145, 147; Moroccans in, 38–39, 44, 47; price controls in, 209–12, 250; public health in, 46, 83, 156–57; repression in, 33–34, 231; requisitioning in, 35, 154; taxes in, 24, 106, 125–26, 128–33; unions in, 16; volunteering in, 27, 36–37. *See also* art; Gypsies